THE EUROPEAN UNION BEYOND BREXIT

Seventh Edition

Ralph H. Folsom
Professor of Law
University of San Diego
A.B. Princeton University, J.D. Yale Law School
LLM London School of Economics

CONCISE HORNBOOK SERIES™

WEST ACADEMIC

860 Blue Gentian Road, Suite 350
Eagan, MN 55121
1-877-888-1330

Published in the United States of America

ISBN: 979-8-89209-878-6

Preface to the Seventh Edition

The European Union Beyond BREXIT is part of West Academic Publishing's Concise Hornbook series. It presents an advanced analysis for students and professionals seeking to understand the law of the world's largest common market.

Chapter 1 presents the history, growth and future of the European Union. Chapters 2 and 3 focus on critical EU processes, law-making and litigation. Without an understanding of them, it is nearly impossible to function as a lawyer working with European Union Law.

Chapter 4 covers the bedrock "Four Freedoms:" Free movement of goods, services, capital and people. Chapter 5 contains a broad selection of internal EU policies, ranging from taxation to agriculture. The European Union's complex external trade and foreign investment law (of special interest to North Americans) is analyzed in Chapter 6.

Chapter 7 presents extended coverage of European Union "business competition" (antitrust) law, typically the area of "first contact" for non-EU traders and investors. Chapter 8 explores BREXIT and Beyond issues, including divorce terms and future relations under the UK-EU Trade and Cooperation Agreement of 2021.

The Treaty Establishing the European (Economic) Community, aka the Treaty of Rome 1957 (as amended), was the founding legal document of European integration. The Lisbon Reform Treaty of 2009 amended, retitled and re-numbered the Treaty of Rome as the "Treaty on the Functioning of the European Union (TFEU)." Under the Reform Treaty, all references to the European Community were changed to European Union. The Maastricht Treaty on European Union of 1993 (TEU) remains in force as amended by the Reform Treaty.

The TFEU and TEU treaties appear in Appendices 1 and 2. The EU Charter of Fundamental Rights (binding since 2009) is reproduced in Appendix 3. Appendix 4 provides a summary of the post-BREXIT EU-UK Trade and Cooperation Agreement (2021).

The European Union Beyond BREXIT is the seventh edition of this Concise Hornbook. With embedded documents, it can be used as a free course book under West's Study Aids Program. Your comments and suggestions for the next edition are welcomed.

PROF. RALPH H. FOLSOM
rfolsom@sandiego.edu

San Diego
August 2024

Acknowledgments

Many colleagues and students have contributed over the years to my learning and understanding of European Union law. For me, it really all began in Britain from 1972–75 when I was an LLM student at the London School of Economics followed by two years as a Lecturer in Law at the University of Warwick. Those were formative times, not only for me, but also for Britain as it joined the European Economic Community in 1973.

Since 1975 I have benefited from teaching and professional contacts at the University of San Diego's summer legal studies programs in Europe founded by Professor Herbert Lazerow. These programs are organized each year through the USD Institute on International and Comparative Law. I am also indebted to French law faculties, especially at Paris I, Brest, Aix-Marseille, Toulouse, Montpellier, and Sciences-Po in Aix, for repeated Visiting Professor opportunities.

Special thanks to West Academic Publishing for their support over many years.

A Timeline of European Integration

1949—COMECON Treaty (Eastern Europe, Soviet Union)

1950—European Convention on Human Rights

1951—European Coal and Steel Community (ECSC) ("Treaty of Paris")

1957—European Economic Community Treaty (EEC) ("Treaty of Rome"), European Atomic Energy Community Treaty (EURATOM)

1959—European Free Trade Area Treaty (EFTA)

1968—EEC Customs Union fully operative

1973—Britain and Denmark switch from EFTA to EEC; Ireland joins EEC; Norway rejects membership; remaining EFTA states sign industrial free trade treaties with EEC

1979—Direct elections to European Parliament

1981—Greece joins EEC

1983—Greenland "withdraws" from EEC

1986—Spain and Portugal join EEC; Portugal leaves EFTA

1987—Single European Act amends EEC Treaty to initiate campaign for a Community without internal frontiers by 1993; qualified majority legislative votes commence

1990—East Germany merged into Community via reunification process

1991—COMECON defunct; trade relations with Central Europe develop rapidly

1993—Maastricht Treaty on European Union (TEU); EEC Treaty renamed EC Treaty

1995—Austria, Finland, and Sweden join EU; Norway votes no again

1999—Amsterdam Treaty

1999—Common currency (EURO) managed by European Central Bank commences with 11 members

2002—ECSC Treaty expires; coverage added to EC Treaty

2003—Treaty of Nice; EU Charter of Fundamental Rights "declared"; draft Constitution for Europe released

2004—Cyprus, Estonia, Slovenia, Poland, Hungary, the Czech Republic, Slovakia, Latvia, Lithuania, Malta join EU

2005—Constitution for Europe overwhelmingly defeated in France and Netherlands

2007—Accession of Bulgaria and Romania; Reform Treaty of Lisbon proposed

2008—Irish voters reject Reform Treaty

2009—Reform Treaty approved in Ireland . . . takes effect Dec. 1; EU Charter of Fundamental Rights becomes binding law; EC Treaty renamed Treaty on the Functioning of the European Union (TFEU)

2010—Greece and Ireland bailed out; 1 trillion EURO financial crisis safety net created

2011—Portugal bailed out; EURO in crisis

2012—Spanish and Italian banks bailed out, Greece bailed out again; EURO in extreme crisis; Treaty on Stability, Coordination and Governance (TSCG) adopted by 25 member states creating a permanent European Stability Mechanism crisis loan fund and a Fiscal Compact with balanced budget rules; ECB agrees to buy unlimited short-term national bonds

2013—Croatia joins EU, Cyprus bailed out

2014—Scotland votes to remain in the UK

2015—Greece bailed out for third time; mass migration to Europe; terrorism inside EU increases

2016—UK votes to leave EU (BREXIT); migrant and terrorist waves escalate

2017—BREXIT negotiations commence

2020—BREXIT effective Jan. 31, 2020, COVID-19 virus arrives

2021—EU-UK Trade and Cooperation Agreement governs future relations

2022—Russia invades Ukraine

Major EEC Treaty (1957) Amendments

1987—Single European Act

1993—Maastricht Treaty

1999—Amsterdam Treaty

2002—ECSC Treaty folded into EC Treaty

2003—Treaty of Nice

2005—Defeat of Treaty establishing Constitution for Europe

2009—Reform Treaty of Lisbon

Chronology of European Union Membership

1957—France, Germany, Italy, Belgium, Netherlands, and Luxembourg create EEC (6)

1973—United Kingdom, Eire and Denmark (9)

1981—Greece (10)

1986—Spain and Portugal (12)

1995—Austria, Finland, and Sweden (15)

2005—Cyprus, Estonia, Slovenia, Poland, Hungary, Czech Republic, Slovakia, Latvia, Lithuania, and Malta (25)

2007—Bulgaria and Romania (27)

2013—Croatia (28)

2020—BREXIT (27)

EURO Zone Participants (19)

1999—Germany, France, Ireland, Spain, Portugal, Austria, Italy, Netherlands, Luxembourg, Belgium, Finland

2001—Greece

2007—Slovenia

2008—Cyprus, Malta

2009—Slovakia

2011—Estonia

2014—Latvia

2015—Lithuania

About the Author

Ralph H. Folsom has been a Professor at the University of San Diego School of Law since 1975. A graduate of Princeton University, Yale Law School and the London School of Economics (LLM), Professor Folsom teaches, writes and consults extensively in the field of international business law.

Folsom has been a Senior Fulbright resident scholar in Singapore and a Visiting Professor at the University of Hong Kong, University of Aix-Marseille, University of Brest, University of Paris, University of Toulouse, University of Puerto Rico, Monash University in Australia and Tecnológico de Monterrey in México.

Professor Folsom's has co-authored a popular problem-oriented course book with West Academic Publishing: *International Business Transactions,* now in its 14th edition.

Professor Folsom has also written in the West Concise Hornbook Series:

International Litigation and Arbitration

International Trade Law

The USMCA and Free Trade Agreements and

International Business Transactions (co-authored).

Web Resources

The official European Union website (*www.europa.eu*) is so complete that it is tempting to list only it under EU Law Web Resources. Treaties, legislation, case law, studies, reports and proposals . . . they are all there and much more. For direct access to EU legal materials, use *www.eur-lex.europa.eu*. For complete, easy to access coverage of Court of Justice opinions, use *www.curia.europa.eu*.

For national law of the member states, see:

www.n-lex.europa.eu

Research Guides:

www.eurounion.org

Summary of Contents

Table of Contents

THE EUROPEAN UNION BEYOND BREXIT

Seventh Edition

Chapter 1

THE HISTORY OF THE EUROPEAN UNION

Table of Sections

PART A. OLD EUROPE

War, today in Ukraine, twice in the Twentieth Century and for ages previously, has plagued the European continent. The desire for peace and avoidance of human rights' horrors after World War II helps explain the beginnings of European integration.

§ 1.0 European Convention on Human Rights (1950)

Over 40 nations adhere to the Council of Europe's post-war European Convention for the Protection of Human Rights and Fundamental Freedoms (1950). Derived from the Universal Declaration on Human Rights, this Convention has been ratified by every EU member state and by other European nations, *e.g.*, Turkey and Russia. Long ago, the Commission proposed that the European Union accede to the Human Rights Convention. This was finally authorized under the Reform Treaty of 2009, but accession has been delayed in part because there are two "supreme" courts involved.

There is a catalogue of human rights enumerated in the Convention, which are recognized as general principles of EU law. These rights include freedom of expression, liberty, personal security, family, life, property, privacy, fair trial, effective remedies, equal treatment, religious, marital, associational and trade or professional rights, along with prohibitions against torture, slavery, forced labor, punishment without law and discrimination. All members of the Council of Europe have abolished the death penalty, and the Council monitors torture and prison conditions throughout its nations.

The ECHR is comprised of one judge from each Council of Europe member state. Panels of seven judges from the Human Rights Court, which has a huge backlog, decide such complaints and can award "just satisfaction" (damages and legal expenses). Notable cases have held the UK in violation of the Convention for hooding and beating prisoners in Northern Ireland, denied the right of a fetus to sue its mother, upheld Spain's illegalization of the Basque Party in pursuit of terrorism, declared Islamic sharia law incompatible with democracy, prevented detention of the mentally ill in Germany, supported the status of women in a case upholding Turkish dissolution of The Welfare Party, and held Russia repeatedly in breach of the Convention for torture and executions in Chechnya.

Other notable cases have declined to extend free speech rights to UK shopping malls (rejecting landmark U.S. law), awarded damages for unlawful UK detention of suspected terrorists, recognized a right of silence for accused persons, condemned Greek asylum-seeker conditions, and upheld Turkish, French and Swiss bans on ostentatious religious clothing (headscarves, turbans) while overturning Italy's placement of crucifixes in public schools. The ECHR found British Army dismissals for homosexuality contrary to the right of privacy and has broadly supported LGBT rights, though not marriage rights.

Americans should particularly note that the Human Rights Court has ruled that extradition of alleged criminals (think Julian Assange) who face a possible death sentence and the "death row phenomenon" in the United States amounts to torture or an inhuman or degrading treatment or punishment in breach of the Convention. Likewise, CIA "renditions" of terrorist suspects have formed the basis for damages awards under the Convention.

The European Court of Justice has been influenced by the Human Rights Court's extensive jurisprudence in developing a growing body of European Union human rights principles. See Section 2.12. Allegations of violations of the ECHR by Russia and Ukraine are pending.

§ 1.1 ECSC Treaty (1951)

As Allied control of West Germany declined in the late 1940s, the return of Germany's basic war industries became a prominent issue. Coal and steel were seen as essential to war-making potential on the Continent. Many feared that if these basic industries were left in national hands, future wars between traditional enemies might emerge. Winston Churchill, in his famous Zurich speech of 1946, urged the establishment of a United States of Europe. He meant that there should be a partnership between France and Germany. The United Kingdom would simply act as a friend and sponsor of this partnership but would not participate. France, especially, was concerned about what it often called "the German problem." The solution that emerged in 1951 was the creation of the European Coal and Steel Community (ECSC).

The Coal and Steel Community was the first of Western Europe's major treaties of integration. The basic theory behind this development was that war would be more difficult to pursue if European institutions empowered with substantial regulatory authority controlled the coal and steel industries. Known as the Schuman Plan after Robert Schuman, the Foreign Minister of France, the ECSC was opened for membership in 1950. Although addressed to much of Europe, only France, West Germany, Italy and the three Benelux countries (Belgium, Luxembourg and The Netherlands) joined by signing the Treaty of Paris in April of 1951. West Germany and Italy, of course, were still politically weak from the aftermath of World War II. The Benelux countries, though often united in perspective, were not significantly influential to the development of the European Coal and Steel Community. Thus, the Community essentially represented French ideas, and these ideas permeated its founding treaty.

The ECSC Treaty of Paris was a complicated document of 50 years duration, now incorporated into the EEC Treaty of Rome (below). It is very detailed and legalistic, what the French call a "traité-loi." Its regulatory approaches to the coal and steel industries are diverse. On the one hand, there were provisions which permitted substantial European control over prices, the level of subsidies, investment incentives, production levels, transportation rates, discriminatory and restrictive trade practices, employment and industrial structure. These controls represented a regime of French "dirigisme." At the same time, other provisions of the ECSC Treaty contemplated freer trade and more competitive coal and steel markets with only occasional governmental intervention. Over the years, regulation of the coal and steel industries in the ECSC has gone through different cycles but predominantly followed the French regime.

The ECSC Treaty of Paris remains the legal basis for European Union law governing these two industries. However, the ECSC Treaty expired near the end of the year 2002. At that time the coal and steel industries were subsumed under the much broader and more economically significant EEC Treaty of Rome of 1957 which established the European Economic Community (EEC) for an "unlimited period" of time.[1]

Lasting Regional Institutions

The most critical features of the ECSC Treaty of Paris were those establishing regional institutions for the governance of coal and steel. Here the French perspective that new institutions were required, to which substantial power would be conveyed by national governments, prevailed. The willingness to transfer control over coal and steel to European institutions seems even more remarkable when the prevalence of government ownership of companies in those industries. In contrast, the British at that time were of the view that governance of coal and steel in the pursuit of peace did not require the establishment of numerous powerful European institutions.

It is in the ECSC Treaty that the four fundamental institutions of the European Union originate: The Council of Ministers, the Commission, the Court of Justice, and the European Parliament.

These institutions are sometimes referred to as *supranational* in character although this term is no longer in fashion. They are neither national nor international (*i.e.*, intergovernmental). Within the limits of the treaties empowering them, they exercise sovereignty. It is to the ECSC institutions that responsibility for the establishment and operation of a free trade area and regulation of coal and steel was

---

[1] Article 356, TFEU.

given. Indeed, some powers granted the Commission (initially called the High Authority) by the ECSC Treaty of Paris are not to be found in the subsequent EEC Treaty of Rome. For example, the Commission is given the power to levy taxes directly on coal and steel enterprises. This is a power that is generally absent from the EEC Treaty.

Each of the four major institutions of the European Union will be reviewed subsequently. For now, it is worth noting that their origins strongly reflected the French view that only European institutions could solve "the German problem."

§ 1.2 The EEC and EURATOM Treaties (1957)

As the post-war economies of Europe revitalized, it became increasingly evident that France and Britain were vying for leadership of Western Europe. Each had its own vision of how to proceed beyond the limited European Coal and Steel Community with which Britain became loosely "associated" in the 1950s. The British maintained that a free trade area, as distinct from more advanced forms of integration such as a customs union, a common market, an economic community or an economic union, was all that was required for economic integration in Western Europe.

The major difference between a free trade area and a customs union is the presence of a common external tariff in the latter. Common market treaties additionally provide for the free movement of what economists call the "factors of production": capital, labor, enterprise and technology. Economic communities seek to coordinate or harmonize economic policies important to the functioning of the common market, *e.g.*, transport, taxation, monetary matters and government subsidies. Economic unions embrace substantially more harmonization or coordination of national policies related to the economy of the union. The difference between a treaty establishing an economic community and one creating an economic union is in the number and importance of integrated national policies.

Britain continued to believe regional integration could be achieved with a minimum of European governance and a maximum of retention of national sovereignty, themes that returned under BREXIT. See Chapter 8. France, on the other hand, generally envisioned a broader economic community modeled and implemented on the basic design provided by the ECSC Treaty, although even it had begun to express reservations about the degree of power vested in the ECSC. France had the support and could point to the successful integration of the Benelux countries.

Belgium, Luxembourg and The Netherlands had signed a Customs Union Treaty in January of 1948. By the middle of the 1950s, the Benelux Nations were close to agreement on a comprehensive economic union. Benelux integration was already providing substantial economic growth to its member nations. Though not as heavily structured with European institutions as the Coal and Steel Community, the Benelux union served as a pacesetter for wider European economic integration. The EEC Treaty of Rome (1957) expressly permits the existence and completion of the Benelux Union to the extent that its objectives are not attained through the European Union.[2]

In June of 1955 a conference of the foreign ministers of the European Coal and Steel Community held in Messina, Italy and responding to a Benelux memorandum authorized an intergovernmental committee to study and report on the prospects for a Western European common market and peaceful use of atomic energy. This committee, still heavily influenced by French perspectives but increasingly subject to a resurgent West Germany under the skilled leadership of Konrad Adenaurer, laid the foundations for the EEC Treaty of Rome establishing the European Economic Community in 1957.

The Committee was led by a dynamic Belgian, Paul-Henri Spaak. Its report is sometimes referred to as the Spaak Plan and focuses on the fusion of markets. Adoption of the Committee's report and its embodiment in the Treaty of Rome was influenced by another dynamic Frenchman long an advocate of European integration. Jean Monnet organized a pressure group known as the Action Committee for the United States of Europe.

EEC Treaty of Rome (1957)

The EEC Treaty of Rome established the European Economic Community in 1957. As amended and renamed, it remains the penultimate source of European Union law.

In November 1993, the EEC Treaty was officially renamed the Treaty establishing the European Community. Dropping the word "Economic" from its title was symbolic of the expanded political, social and other non-economic roles of the Community in European affairs. At the same time, the Maastricht Treaty on European Union (TEU) was superimposed over the EEC Treaty (thereby adding certain common provisions as well as coverage of foreign and security policy and justice and home affairs). The resulting document was

---

2 Article 350, TFEU.

titled the "Treaty on European Union together with the Treaty establishing the European Community (EC)."

In 2009, the Reform Treaty of Lisbon amended, retitled and renumbered the EC Treaty as the Treaty on the Functioning of the European Union (TFEU). The Maastricht TEU Treaty was retained, but notably amended by the Reform Treaty. Together, the TFEU and TEU have the "same legal value" as founding treaties of the Union.

Some have analogized the EEC Treaty of Rome (now TFEU) to a constitution. Certainly, it is the founding document of the European Community, which is the principal pillar of The European Union. The European Court of Justice has referred to the Treaty as the "constitutional charter of a Community based on the rule of law[3]." Under this charter, the member states have limited their sovereignty in ever widening fields of law. Unlike the Coal and Steel Treaty, the TFEU is open-ended in much of its language, a "traité-cadre" or "traité de procédure" in French terms. It provides the framework and process upon which to build Regional Europe. When compared with the narrowness of the Treaty of Paris establishing the European Coal and Steel Community in 1951, the original EEC Treaty is breathtaking in scope.

EURATOM (1957)

At the same time, by separate treaty in 1957, a third European community was created. This is the European Atomic Energy Community (EURATOM). EURATOM is a very specialized community focused on joint research and peaceful development of atomic energy. Its Supply Agency owns all fissionable materials located within member states not intended for defense requirements. Substantial electricity continues to be supplied by nuclear plants, notably in France.

EURATOM has joined the Treaty on the Non-Proliferation of Nuclear Weapons. In the Chernobyl aftermath, renewed attention has been paid to EURATOM safety standards and the Court of Justice has held that the Commission's advisory opinion must be obtained prior to approval of the final plans for radioactive effluent disposal.[4] Nevertheless, EURATOM is the least significant of the three European communities.

The EEC Treaty and the EURATOM Treaty followed the institutional pattern of the ECSC Treaty. Each of these three treaties empowers a Council of Ministers, a Commission (called High Authority in the ECSC Treaty), an Assembly (Parliament) and a

3 Re Draft Treaty on European Economic Area (1991) ECJ Opinion 1/91.

4 Saarland v. Minister for Industry, Posts, Telecommunications and Tourism, (1988) Eur.Comm.Rep. 5013.

Court of Justice. This led to an unnecessary and confusing institutional structure which was remedied in part by merging the Court and Parliament in 1957 and later by the so-called "Merger Treaty" of 1967.

Since then, there has been one Council, one Commission, one Parliament and one Court, all staffed by the same people. Each of these European Union institutions, however, derives its power and authority from the terms and conditions of whatever treaty it is acting under.

In other words, the treaties were not merged, only their institutions. Thus prior to 2002, when the Commission acted on coal and steel matters, the legality of its actions was measured by the ECSC Treaty. The EURATOM treaty controls When the Council legislates on atomic energy.

§ 1.3 COMECON and EFTA (1959)

Early United States support for European integration came through the Marshall Plan which was distributed through the Organization for European Economic Cooperation. This organization had no real political power, but successfully mediated some differences in national economic policies prevalent during the late 1940s. By 1957, the cold war between the United States and the Soviet Union was evident. This caused the United States to be generally supportive of the EEC initiative under the theory that a united Europe would present a stronger defense to Soviet aggression.

The Soviets, in turn, increasingly emphasized Eastern European integration through the Council for Mutual Economic Assistance (COMECON). This effort, commenced in 1949, was basically seen as a counterweight to the developments in Western European integration. Locked behind the Iron Curtain, the countries of Eastern Europe found themselves producing whatever the Soviet economic plans required. In exchange, they mostly received subsidized oil and other basic resources.

European Free Trade Area (EFTA)

The EEC Treaty as drafted in 1957 was much less "dirigiste" than the Coal and Steel Treaty. Nevertheless, Britain once again abstained from membership because of the nature and extent of the European control over the economy. Britain, too, was still preoccupied with its empire-based trade relations. Europe was important, but it had not yet become critical to British trading interests.

The fragmentation of Europe's economy during the 1950s became even more accentuated by the emergence of another competing organization. Led by Britain, many of the fringe or traditionally neutral nations of Western Europe organized themselves into the European Free Trade Association (EFTA) in 1959. Austria, Denmark, Iceland, Norway, Portugal, Sweden and Switzerland joined this undertaking. With eight nations, essentially surrounding the core six nations who created the EEC in 1957, Britain felt that it had contained French influence and ideas in the economic sphere.

True to British perspectives, the EFTA Treaty was very limited in scope. It applied only to free trade in industrial goods, omitting coverage of agriculture, transport, labor, capital, technology and services to mention only a few areas fully incorporated into the EEC Treaty. Moreover, the British view on the nature of the governmental institutions required to achieve industrial free trade prevailed. A single institution, the EFTA Council, was created. Since it normally followed a unanimous voting principle, each of the member states retained a veto over new policy developments within the EFTA group. The surrender of national sovereignties to EFTA was minimized.

By 1960 Europe was economically divided into three major trade groups. France and an increasingly powerful West Germany led Italy and the Benelux states in the European Coal and Steel and Economic Communities. Britain and its partners were loosely integrated through the European Free Trade Association. And the whole of Eastern Europe came under the sway of Soviet dominance through COMECON. In addition, Finland became associated with EFTA and Greece and Turkey were associated with the EEC. Only Spain under Franco remained an economic outcast. More than a decade passed before major shifts in these alliances occurred.

§ 1.4 The EEC Treaty, the GATT and the Customs Union Dilemma

The General Agreement on Tariffs and Trade (GATT), adopted in 1947 and much amended and interpreted since then, governs many features of the world trading system. See my Concise Hornbook on *International Trade Law.* Over 165 nations, including those of the European Union, now adhere to the GATT and a host of "Uruguay Round" agreements administered by the World Trade Organization. In 1957, when the EEC Treaty was signed, the United States, Britain and other GATT members protested that the Treaty was not in accord with the terms of Article 24 of the GATT.

GATT Article 24

Article 24 permits contracting parties to enter free trade and customs union agreements of a fixed or evolutionary character. The premise here is that regional economic groups can be viewed as gradual steps (second-best alternatives) along the road to freer, less discriminatory *world* trade. All regional forms of economic integration are inherently discriminatory in their trade impact. As non-universalized trade preferences, they tend to simultaneously *create* trade among member states and *divert* trade between member states and the rest of the world. Thus, while trade creation may represent an improvement in the allocation of scarce world resources, trade diversion may generate an opposite result.

With free trade areas, diversionary trade effects are usually not distinct because of the absence of a common trade wall against outsiders. Trade diversion nonetheless occurs. "Rules of origin" in free trade area treaties keep third-party imports from seeking the lowest tariff or highest quota state and then exploiting the trade advantages within a free trade area. Under rules of origin, free trade areas are "free" only for goods substantially originating therein. This causes member state goods to be preferred over goods from other states. Rules of origin within a free trade area can be as trade diversionary as a common trade policy in other forms of regional economic integration.

With customs unions, common markets, economic communities and economic unions, trade diversion is more obvious given a common trade policy for third-party states. In these circumstances the resulting "trade creation" and "trade diversion" effects are known generally in economic literature as the "customs union dilemma."[5] In light of the discussion of rules of origin in free trade areas, it might be better to call this the "dilemma of regional economic integration."

Article 24 attempts to manage the internal trade-creating and external trade-diverting effects of regional economic groups. Free trade area and custom union proposals should run the gauntlet of a formal GATT (now WTO) approval procedure during which "binding" recommendations are possible to bring the proposals into conformity with Article 24. Such recommendations might deal with Article 24 requirements for the elimination of internal tariffs and other restrictive regulations of commerce on "substantially all" products originating in a customs union or free trade area. Or they might deal with Article 24 requirements that common external tariffs not be "on the whole higher or more restrictive" in effect than the general incidence of prior existing national tariffs. The broad purpose of

---

[5] *See* J. Viner, *The Customs Union Issue* (1950).

Article 24, acknowledged therein, is to facilitate trade among the GATT contracting parties and not to raise trade barriers.

Article 24 and European Integration

It is through this GATT approval mechanism that most regional economic treaties, including those of Western Europe, have passed *without* substantial modification. Only the EFTA Treaty seems to have come genuinely close to meeting the terms of Article 24. The GATT, not the regional economic treaties, most often has given way. With the European Coal and Steel Community only two products were involved. Clearly no case could be made for its compliance with the requirement of elimination of internal trade barriers on "substantially all" products. Hence, the GATT members, passing over Article 24's own waiver proviso for proposals leading to a customs union or a free trade area "in the sense of Article 24," reverted to Article 25. That article allows a two-thirds vote by the contracting parties to waive any GATT obligation.

During passage through the GATT of the EEC Treaty, many "violations" of the letter and spirit of Article 24 were cited by nonmembers. The derivation of the common external tariff by arithmetically averaging existing national tariffs was challenged as more restrictive of trade than previous arrangements. Such averaging for a given product fails to take account of differing national import volumes. If a product was faced originally with a lower-than-average national tariff and a larger than average national demand, the new average tariff is clearly more "restrictive" of imports than before. Averaging in high tariffs of countries of low demand quite plausibly created more restrictions on third-party trade. If so, the letter and spirit of Article 24 were breached.

The economic association of Overseas Territories (mainly former French, Dutch, and Belgian colonies) with the EEC also raised considerable difficulty under Article 24. The Community argued that these "association" agreements were free trade areas in the long run, while the GATT officials viewed them as rather open efforts at purely preferential tariff status. Similar problems arose later in the GATT review of the multitude of "evolving" free trade area treaties with Mediterranean nations.

In 1975, the openly preferential and discriminatory Lomé Convention negotiated between the European Community and forty-six African, Pacific and Caribbean nations (including many former colonies) challenged the evolutionary character of Community "free trade areas" with developing states. Once again it was GATT and not the European Community that gave way. In fairness, since 2000 the

Cotonou Agreement at least pledges the EU and its Lomé partners to reciprocal free trade principles.

Despite these and other arguments, the EEC Treaty passed through the GATT study and review committees without final resolution of its legal status under Article 24. Postponement of these issues became permanent. GATT attempts—through the lawyer-like conditions of Article 24 to maximize trade creation and minimize trade diversion—must be seen in the European context as generally inadequate. Treaty terms became negotiable demands that were not accepted.

For more on free trade areas and customs unions around the globe, see my Concise Hornbook on *The USMCA and Free Trade Agreements*.

§ 1.5 EFTA and the EEC Reconciled (1973)

During the 1960s, Britain began to come to grips with the loss of its empire. Although special trading relations were often preserved with former colonies through the Commonwealth network, it became increasingly apparent that Britain's economic future lay more in Europe than Africa, Asia or the Caribbean. Moreover, the EEC had helped to spur a phenomenal economic recovery on the Continent at a time when many were questioning the competitiveness of British industry. For these reasons, and others, Britain began to seek membership as early as 1961 (only two years after the formation of EFTA). France under the leadership of Charles De Gaulle would have none of it. Since the Treaty of Rome provided (as the Treaty on European Union still does) that all new memberships require a unanimous Council vote, France was effectively able to veto the British application. It was not until the resignation of De Gaulle in 1969 that the British were able in due course to secure membership in the EEC.

New Members (1973)

Agreement on the terms of British accession (including withdrawal from EFTA and the elimination of trade preferences with major Commonwealth nations) was reached in 1971, with an effective date of January 1973. The switch from EFTA to the EEC by Britain under Conservative Party leadership was undertaken with an ambivalence that continues to be evident. It was only with reluctance that the British accepted the surrenders of sovereignty inherent in the EEC Treaty. From 1973 onwards, more and more of the economic life of the United Kingdom would be governed by the four institutions of the European Community (now Union). British reluctance to join the Common Market was replayed in a 1975 national referendum under a Labor Party government. Approximately 60 percent of the populace voted to remain a member of the Community.

Denmark also switched sides in 1973. Norway was scheduled to become a member of the EEC at that time, and the terms of its membership had been negotiated, but the people of Norway rejected the Community in a national referendum. The rejection had a lot to do with the requirements of the Common Fisheries Policy which would have unacceptably opened Norwegian waters to fishermen from the Continent, Britain and Ireland (which followed the British lead into the Community in 1973). This Policy also regulates the type and number of fish that can be caught in EU waters, significantly subsidizes the fishing industry, and protects it from foreign competition.

In addition to the expansion of the EEC to nine members, 1973 brought an even greater degree of European economic integration. Although EFTA remained intact, each of the remaining EFTA nations signed bilateral trade treaties with the expanded Community. These treaties governed trade relations between all EFTA nations and the Community until 1994. They essentially provided industrial free trade. Thus the 1973 enlargement of the European Economic Community was the catalyst for the most wide-scale and comprehensive effort at Western European integration yet to take place, the reconciliation of the EFTA and EEC trading alliances. This was an historic watershed in European economic integration.

New Members (1980s)

During the 1980s there was a strong trend toward increased membership in and expansion of the European Economic Community (now European Union). The only exception to this trend was the "withdrawal" of Greenland in 1983. Greenland had been admitted with Denmark in 1973 but voted to withdraw in a home rule referendum essentially rejecting the Common Fisheries Policy. It is now associated with the EU as an overseas territory of Denmark.

Greece joined in 1981, and Portugal and Spain became members in 1986. Portugal left the EFTA group, and Spain finally overcame the yoke of General Franco.

§ 1.6 The European Economic Area (1991), EU-Swiss Agreements, Membership Criteria

Expanded relations between the European Community (now Union) and the seven remaining EFTA states have been under negotiation since the 1980s. These negotiations envisioned closer economic relations short of membership. Late in 1991, a linkage of the two groups in what is called a European Economic Area (EEA) was agreed.

The EEA generally embraces Union law on free movement of goods, services, persons (subject to "emergency brake" exceptions), and capital. But integration on agricultural, fisheries and tax policy is excluded and the EFTA nations retain their own border controls, tariffs, currencies and external trade policies. Antidumping measures, countervailing duties and illicit commercial practices law will not be applied to EEA trade. Political and defense union is also excluded from the EEA agreement.

The EEA agreement reached in October of 1991 envisioned the creation of several inter-regional organizations vested with law-making and dispute settlement powers. These included an EEA Council, an EEA Joint Committee (EU parallel is the Committee of Permanent Representatives), an EEA Court of Justice and Court of First Instance, an EEA Joint Parliamentary Committee, an EEA Consultative Committee (EU parallel is Economic and Social Committee), and an EFTA Surveillance Authority (EU parallel is the Commission). The latter will focus on EFTA application of EU competition law.

Judicial Authority

In December of 1991, the European Court of Justice (ECJ) issued an opinion that the EEA Courts were not compatible with the EEC Treaty of Rome.[6] The Court was particularly concerned with its own supremacy as the final arbiter of Community law. This sent the negotiators back to the drawing board on dispute settlement. A revised EEA agreement was concluded early in 1992 with a scheduled effective date of January 1, 1993. The ECJ found this agreement compatible with the EEC Treaty.[7]

As revised, the European Economic Area agreement provides for a new EFTA Court of Justice. In all cases of disparate jurisprudence, the EEA creates a "Joint Committee" consisting of EU and EFTA political representatives. This Committee will not have judicial powers. It will review conflict on the EEA between the ECJ and the EFTA Court but exercise no control over them. If the case law diverges and the Joint Committee fails to reach a solution, correction procedures may be invoked.

Under these procedures, the European Court of Justice upon request issues an Opinion on the matter. This Opinion presumably would be followed by the EFTA party to the dispute. Courts in EFTA

---

[6] 1 Opinion 1/91 (Dec. 14, 1991).

[7] Opinion 1/92 (April 10, 1992).

nations may request an advisory decision by the ECJ when EFTA law is identical to Union law. Presumably, again, this decision would be binding. If the dispute is not referred to the ECJ, either party may take "safeguard measures." If these measures do not resolve the matter, then either party may ultimately refer the dispute to binding arbitration.

Swiss Rejection of EEA, EU-Swiss Agreements

The revised 1991 EEA agreement had to be ratified by the European Parliament as well as all EU and EFTA nations. Perhaps not surprisingly, the Swiss rejected the EEA in a national referendum held in December 1992. This rejection casts doubt upon possible Swiss membership, but it did not cause the EEA to falter. Subsequent negotiations in 1993 produced a still further revised agreement minus Switzerland. This version of the EEA then made the required rounds of ratification and came into force January 1, 1994. Today it applies only to Iceland, Lichtenstein and Norway.

A series of bilateral 1999 EU agreements with Switzerland cover free movement of persons, transport, agriculture, procurement and mutual recognition. In 2004, additional EU-Swiss agreements were reached on taxation of savings, fighting fraud, Swiss participation in the Schengen and Dublin Accords, trade in processed agricultural goods, environmental cooperation, media programs and avoidance of double taxation on pensioners.

The EU-Swiss bilateral agreements are "static", meaning they do not evolve unless mutually agreed, but are subject to EFTA Court interpretations. Moreover, each side may withdraw from the package of agreements. Although the Swiss people have approved by referendum withdrawal from the free movement of persons agreement, the Swiss government has delayed implementation out of fear of upsetting the other EU-Swiss bilateral agreements.

EU-Swiss continual negotiations and diverse individual agreements represent a pattern that may follow UK-EU relations post BREXIT. See Chapter 8.

New Members (1990s)

One reason for the Union's advancement of the EEA and reluctance to accept new members was its intensive internal focus on the 1992 campaign for a fully integrated common market. Other reasons involve the practical problems associated with governance of a regional organization with substantial numbers of nations. With 12 member states in the early 1990s, the EU found it difficult to arrive at a consensus and move forward towards further integration without substantially overriding national interests. A community with more members would presumably be all that more difficult to run. Nevertheless, membership in the European Union for all EFTA states that want it is a foregone conclusion.

There has been an incorporation of what was East Germany into the Union through the reunification process. The accession of East Germany renewed concerns over the role of Germany in Europe. Instead of large member states (France, West Germany, Italy and formerly the United Kingdom) of roughly equal populations, united Germany has substantially more people and potentially much more economic clout than any other member. This caused anxieties about keeping that country well anchored by European institutions.

The Maastricht Summit accords (December 1991) opened the door to new membership, and negotiations with Austria, Sweden, Finland and Norway began in earnest in 1993. Accession agreements for these countries were concluded early in 1994 and ratification by the European Parliament was obtained in May of that year. Each of these countries scheduled a national referendum on membership in the EU. The Austrians voted by a 2 to 1 margin to join. The Finns and Swedes also ratified accession, but Norway once again voted no.

Norwegian farmers and fisherman led the opposition, assisted by the economic independence provided by North Sea oil and gas. Norway (an EAA member) now finds itself in the curious position of replicating much Common market law and contributing to the EU budget, all without representation in European Union institutions.

Membership Criteria

It has always been a rule, at times unwritten, that EU members and applicants must support democratic governments. This principle was applied to Greece during the coup by the colonels in the late 1960s and early 1970s. The Community suspended trade relations during this period and the coup certainly delayed admission of that country. The commitment of the Community (now Union) to governance by representative democracy, the rule of law, social justice and respect for human rights was formalized in 1977 under a Declaration on Democracy by the heads of all the member state governments. At the same time, the Council, Commission and Parliament issued a Joint Declaration on Fundamental Rights to much the same effect.

New applicants must embrace the ever-expanding body of regional legislation and case law, the EU "acquis communautaire." Short of exceptions or postponements negotiated through "accession treaties," this is a monumental undertaking.

With 15 member states, the European Union in 1995 became a powerful and lucrative economic market. Its aggregate population and gross domestic product exceeded that of the United States and Canada, which implemented a Free Trade Agreement in 1989. The addition of Mexico and the emergence of a North American Free Trade Area in 1994 were just some of the continuing repercussions of the need to compete with the European Union in the global marketplace.[8]

At the Copenhagen Summit in June of 1993, the European Council set the following formal membership criteria for applicant countries:

(1) Stable democracies based upon a rule of law, human rights and protection of minorities;

(2) Market economies able to compete with the EU; and

(3) The ability to make full commitments to EU political, monetary and economic union ("acquis communautaire").

PART B. NEW EUROPE

§ 1.7 Europe at the Turn of the Century

New Members (2004–2007)

The turn of the century once again found Europe looking outward, though not without reservations. Starting in 1997, following the Commission's recommendations and a series of association agreements (Europe agreements), the European Union commenced negotiations for membership with Cyprus, Estonia, Slovenia, Poland, Hungary, the Czech Republic, Malta, Romania, Bulgaria, Lithuania, Latvia and Slovakia. Long in the making, accession agreements were finalized in 2002/2003 with entry for ten new member states definitively scheduled for May 1, 2004. Particularly sensitive issues such as full participation in agricultural subsidies and free movement of workers were finessed with extended transition periods.

Nine of the 2004 member states ratified accession in national referendums, with only Greek Cyprus not holding a plebiscite. Romania and Bulgaria subsequently joined in 2007, creating a Union with over 500 million citizens and the world's largest common market. But what exactly were these new member states joining?

---

8 *See* my Concise Hornbook on *The USMCA and Free Trade Agreements.*

"Old Europe" melded with "New Europe" under a vastly complex legal regime. To understand this complexity, one must reach back to the seminal campaign for a "Europe without Internal Frontiers."

§ 1.8 Europe Without Internal Frontiers (1992)

The campaign for a European Community without internal frontiers by the end of 1992 was the product of Commission studies in the 1980s which concluded that a hardening of the trade arteries of Europe had occurred. The Community was perceived to be stagnating relative to the advancing economies of North America and East Asia. Various projections of the wealth that could be generated from a truly common market for Western Europe suggested the need to revitalize the region. A "white paper" drafted under the leadership of Lord Cockfield of Britain and issued by the Commission in 1985 became the blueprint for the 1992 campaign.

The Commission's white paper identified three types of barriers to a Europe without internal frontiers—physical, technical and fiscal. Physical barriers occur at the borders. For goods, they included national trade quotas, health checks, agricultural monetary compensation amount charges, statistical collections and transport controls. For people, physical barriers concern clearing immigrations, security checks and customs. Technical barriers mostly involve national standards and rules for goods, services, capital and labor which operate to inhibit free movement among the member states. Medical and surgical equipment and pharmaceuticals provide traditional examples of markets restrained by technical trade barriers. Fiscal barriers identified in the Commission's 1985 white paper centered on different value-added and excise taxation levels and the corresponding need for tax collections at borders. There were, for example, wide value-added tax (VAT) differences on auto sales within the Common Market.

The Commission estimated that removal of these barriers could save the Community upwards of 100 billion ECUs (European Currency Units) in direct costs. In addition, another roughly 100 billion ECUs could be gained as price reductions and increased efficiency and competition took hold. Overall, the Commission projected an increase in the Community's gross domestic product of between 4.5 to 7 percent, a reduction in consumer prices of between 6 to 4.5 percent, 1.75 to 5 million new jobs, and enhanced public sector and external trade balances. These figures were thus said to represent "the costs of non-Europe".

Single European Act, Schengen Accord

Major amendments to the EEC Treaty were undertaken in the Single European Act (SEA) which became effective in 1987. Amendments to the Treaty can occur by Commission or member state proposal to the Council which calls an intergovernmental conference to unanimously determine their content. The amendments are not effective until ratified by all the member states in accordance with their respective constitutional requirements.[9] Proposals originating in the Commission's 1985 white paper on a Europe without internal frontiers were embodied in the Single European Act. The SEA amendments not only expanded the competence of the European Community institutions, but also sought to accelerate the speed of integration by relying more heavily on qualified majority (not unanimous) voting principles in Council decision-making. See § 2.7.

The Single European Act envisioned the adoption of 282 new legislative measures designed to fully integrate the goods, services and capital markets by the end of 1992. Nearly all these measures and others were adopted by the Council.[10] Implementation at the national level proceeded more slowly, especially regarding insurance, investment advisors and procurement. By 1996, the Commission reported that the single market program had increased internal trade by 20–30%, added 1% in GDP growth annually, and generated over 900,000 jobs.

Realization of the goal of a Europe without internal frontiers *for people* proved harder to achieve. Most members agreed to remove their internal frontier controls on people under the 1990 "Schengen Accord." This accord was the product of intergovernmental agreement, not EU legislation. Ireland and the United Kingdom do not participate, but non-members Norway and Iceland do. The Schengen Accord covers such sensitive issues as visas, asylum, immigration, gun controls, extradition and police rights of "hot pursuit." The main points of contention were cross-border traffic of immigrants and criminals, especially terrorists and drug dealers. These issues were resolved largely by promises of greater intergovernmental cooperation, notably through computer linkages.

Much of the substance of the Schengen Accord was incorporated into the EC Treaty by the Amsterdam Treaty of 1999 (below). Nine of the ten 2004 member states plus Switzerland participate in Schengen since 2008, dramatically altering the eastern perimeter of the European Union. Bulgaria and Romania are not Schengen members.

---

9 Article 48, Treaty on European Union.

10 *See* Section 2.14.

The absence of customs and immigration controls at nearly all borders within the European Union was a direct result of the campaign for a Europe without internal frontiers. In recent years, this remarkable achievement has been seriously undermined by cross-border controls targeting the flood of migrants that have been arriving in Europe since 2014.

§ 1.9 The Maastricht Treaty on European Union (1993), Opt-Out Rights

Well before the realization of a Europe without internal frontiers under the Single European Act, Community and national leaders were forging another momentous round of European integration. These efforts bore fruit in the December 1991 summit meeting of the European Council in Maastricht, The Netherlands, where the "Treaty on European Union" (TEU) was signed. The Maastricht agreement, like the Single European Act, significantly amended the EEC Treaty (re-named the EC Treaty). Furthermore, it added what amount to side agreements on a common foreign and security policy[11] and cooperation regarding justice and home affairs. Like the Single European Act's provisions on foreign policy, these side agreements did not amend the EC Treaty and stand on their own as separate international agreements or "pillars". As such, they were not subject to judicial review of the Court of Justice.

The most important Maastricht amendments to the EC Treaty concerned the ambiguous principle of "subsidiarity"[12] and economic and monetary integration, *notably a detailed timetable for the convergence of national economies and creation of a common currency.*[13] Other significant amendments included the conveyance to Parliament of a limited legislative and international agreements' veto, a power to conduct inquiries into maladministration of the EU, and a right to reject Commission appointments and new member state applicants.[14]

The TEU also added new Articles on cooperation regarding education, health and culture, the development of European Union citizenship rights and a formal commitment to respect the rights protected by the European Human Rights Convention,[15] expanded economic aid to the least developed members (the "cohesion fund"),[16] authorization of the Court of Justice to sanction delinquent member

---

[11] *See* Section 1.13.

[12] *See* Section 2.0.

[13] *See* Section 4.16.

[14] *See* Section 2.2.

[15] *See* Section 2.12.

[16] *See* Section 5.12.

state governments by fines and penalties,[17] and a Social Protocol (Britain excepted).[18] The TEU formally authorized Union legislation on consumer protection, industrial policy, energy, tourism, visas and coordinated police action, largely by qualified majority voting which was also extended to transportation and most environmental law.[19]

Ratification and Opt-Out Rights

The ink was no sooner dry on the Treaty on European Union when Denmark's voters by a slim margin rejected ratification in June 1992. Ireland and France (by an equally slim margin) ratified the TEU in national referenda and by year's end the Maastricht agreement had been ratified in all but Denmark and the United Kingdom. After concessions to Denmark were made at the December 1992 Edinburgh summit of the European Council, a new referendum was scheduled for May 1993. Denmark obtained confirmation of its right to opt out of a common currency and new rights to opt out of the TEU provisions on common defense, European citizenship and home and justice affairs.

Europe a la carte carried the day, a harbinger for the ongoing membership negotiations with Austria, Sweden, Finland and Norway. The Danes ultimately approved Maastricht, and a bitter Parliamentary battle in Britain brought similar results in August of 1993. After a constitutional challenge to ratification failed in Germany, the Treaty on European Union became effective November 1, 1993.

The following chart presents "multi-speed Europe" and the major "opt-out" rights under Maastricht of various member states:

United Kingdom	—	Social Protocol
		Common Currency
		Schengen Accord (internal border controls over people)
Ireland	—	Schengen Accord
Denmark	—	Schengen Accord
		Common Currency
		Defense
		Justice and Home Affairs
		European Citizenship

---

17 *See* Section 3.9.

18 *See* Section 5.19.

19 *See* Section 2.7.

It should be noted that the United Kingdom under the Labour Party administration of Prime Minister Blair opted into the region's Social Policy and the Social Protocol was repealed. Additional opt-outs were created by the Reform Treaty of 2009:

Czech Republic	—	Fundamental Rights Charter
Ireland	—	Justice and Home Affairs
Poland	—	Fundamental Rights Charter
United Kingdom	—	Justice and Home Affairs, Fundamental Rights Charter

§ 1.10 The Amsterdam Treaty (1999)

The Maastricht Treaty on European Union of 1993 called for another round of intergovernmental negotiations to revise both the TEU and the EC Treaty. Late in 1997, these negotiations bore fruit in the Amsterdam Treaty, which then faced national referenda and court challenges during the ratification process.

The Amsterdam Treaty is in many respects best known for what it did *not* accomplish, namely major institutional and agricultural policy reforms in anticipation of European Union membership expansions. The Treaty did significantly extend Parliament's co-decision legislative powers, and institutionalized procedures (suspension of voting rights) to deal with "serious and persistent" member state violations of democracy, human rights and the rule of law. It authorized legislative action to secure "freedom, security and justice" (an effective transfer of much of the TEU justice and home affairs power), including asylum, extradition and the essentials of the Schengen Accord, all subject to Court of Justice review but also British, Danish and Irish opt outs. Additional legislative powers covered employment incentives, public health, fraud prevention, customs cooperation, transparency principles and social policy (formerly the Social Protocol).

A complex provision on "flexibility" sought to allow, subject to detailed controls but generally not (after Nice) vetoes, a minimum of nine member states to establish "closer cooperation" than others. This provision appears to reflect the realities of less than comprehensive participation in existing policies and programs such as defense, the common currency, the Schengen Accord and the like. By 2014, "enhanced cooperation" was in effect for divorce and legal separation law, and the Unitary Patent.

Lastly, the Amsterdam Treaty added a special protocol on the principles of subsidiarity and proportionality and attempted to secure greater support for common foreign and security policies.

§ 1.11 The Treaty of Nice (2003)

With the Amsterdam Treaty in place, and new memberships looming, yet another round of intergovernmental negotiations swiftly commenced. By 2001, the Treaty of Nice was signed and sent on its way for national ratifications. Like the Amsterdam Treaty and its predecessors, Nice amended the EC Treaty, notably extending qualified majority legislative voting in the Council, authorizing the creation of specialized "judicial panels" attached to the Court of First Instance, and increasing the possibility of closer cooperation ("flexibility") by less than the Union's full membership. This provision led in 2013 to the adoption of the European Unitary Patent regime, Italy and Spain not participating.

More significantly, the Enlargement Protocol to the Treaty of Nice established the rules of governance once the ten new members acceded in 2004 (twelve in 2007). These byzantine institutional changes for the European Council, Commission, Parliament and Courts are covered in Chapters 2 and 3. Finally, a Charter of Fundamental Rights was "proclaimed" at Nice, but not made binding as a matter of law, and therefore not subject to ratification. See Chapter 3.

Ratification of the Treaty of Nice and its Enlargement Protocol ran into unexpected opposition in Ireland. Often cited as a model of how the European Union can benefit small countries, Irish law mandates a national referendum on EU ratifications. In the first vote, admittedly a low turnout, the Irish people soundly rejected the Treaty of Nice. Fear of loss of regional benefits to the economically struggling new members may have been critical to this surprising result. A year later, in 2002, after a major persuasion campaign by the Irish government and no provision for "opt-outs," the people voted "yes" on Nice by a wide margin. Shortly thereafter, the accession of the new member states to the European Union was finalized.

§ 1.12 Political Union

Economic integration has outstripped the Union's political growth. Many suggest that the European Union suffers from a "democratic deficit." How long can governance of the Union postpone its rendezvous with democracy? The predominance of the Council has become increasingly embarrassing and intolerable. Incremental changes have prevailed. But what might be the result? One vision of the future has the Council of Ministers becoming an "upper house" like the United States Senate to the House of Representatives, though most probably with more power. In this scenario, the Commission becomes the Executive Branch of the EU government. It could have a directly elected President who then appoints a Cabinet with Parliamentary or Council approval. The variations on these themes are endless, as the Convention on the Future of Europe (below) found out.

Another vision of the future was adopted, way before its time, in 1984 by Parliament. In its "Draft Treaty establishing European Union" (Spinelli Report), the Parliament showed strong federalist proclivities. This Treaty would have totally replaced the Treaty of Rome. The law-making powers of the Council would be shifted to the Parliament and Commission with limited member state ability to block new policy initiatives. There would also be serious sanctions on member states who persistently breach their EU duties. The Court of Justice would get the power to appeal decisions of national courts. A common monetary system, common citizenship and effective protection of fundamental human rights were also part of Parliament's vision of the European Union. In contrast, the defeated Constitution for Europe and 2009 Reform Treaty (below) look timid.

§ 1.13 Foreign and Security Policy

The Foreign Ministers of the member states regularly meet and seek to coordinate EU foreign policy and security matters. These ministers have their own secretariat in Brussels to monitor and implement common foreign policy positions. Junior staff members supervise much of this work through what is called the European Political Committee. The Commission is represented at all meetings of this Committee and the Foreign Ministers. The Parliament, however, is merely briefed after the fact about these meetings and is for the most part limited to asking questions of the Foreign Ministers.

The heads of state and government also meet twice a year in what is called "the European Council," as distinct from the Council of Ministers. The President of the Commission participates in meetings of the European Council. These meetings have increased the degree of foreign policy cooperation (known as "political cooperation") within the Union, but not without criticism. The European Council and the Foreign Ministers' meetings function outside the EC Treaty (now TFEU) and its various policy making mandates and voting procedures, including consultation, cooperation or co-decision with Parliament. Hence, foreign policy coordination is purely intergovernmental in nature, and does not involve supranational EU mandates. It is said that "*une forme originale de diplomatie concertée*" now exists. The Reform Treaty clearly states that the Court of Justice does not have jurisdiction over foreign and security policy and related acts of the Union. However, member states can submit to such jurisdiction if they wish.

Foreign policy cooperation has been a part of Union affairs since 1970 and was formally recognized in Article 30 of the Single European Act of 1987. Under the Maastricht and Amsterdam Treaties, the Union's national foreign ministers decide which areas of foreign and security policy merit "joint action," a "common position," or a "common strategy." The details of such activities are now generally set by those ministers acting by qualified majority voting or with the "constructive abstention" of some members. This type of political cooperation remains outside the framework of the TFEU and is considered a separate "pillar" of the Union.

The Reform Treaty provides for the election by the member states of a High Representative of the Union for Foreign Affairs and Security Policy, whose term of office is not limited in time. The High Representative can initiate policy proposals, which the European Council may or may not adopt. The High Representative administers the EU "diplomatic service" (European External Action Service), a notable power. He or she also presides over the Foreign Affairs Council of Ministers and serves as a Vice-President of the Commission, an amalgam of hats intended to reduce institutional rivalry.

Henry Kissinger once lamented: "Who do I call when I want to talk to the EU?" While the President of European Council, another new post created under the Lisbon Reform Treaty, might object, that call could be placed to the High Representative. Alas, the TEU as amended by Lisbon, is less than clear. The President is specifically charged with externally representing the EU concerning Common Foreign and Security Policy.

Given leadership confusion, the European Union erratically speaks with a single voice on foreign affairs. This has been evident regarding developments in Central Europe and the Middle East, notably regarding the battle between Hamas and Israel with Spain, Norway and Ireland recognizing an independent Palestinian state, Erratic foreign policy also emerged regarding Cyprus, South Africa, Rwanda, Angola, Iran, Myanmar, Cambodia, Afghanistan and sanctioning Russia over Crimea and Ukraine. Furthermore, the remarkable disunity and dithering displayed by EU nations over the break-up and ethnic cleansing in Yugoslavia casts a long shadow over the political cooperation goals of the Union. In many respects, the Balkans represent a critical test of the Union's foreign and security policy apparatus. The EU did better on Kosovo than Bosnia, but can the EU secure peace and freedom in its own backyard?

The increasing involvement of the European Union in world politics also makes it more difficult for traditionally neutral nations like Austria, Sweden and Ireland. Already there are arguments over whether it is possible to segregate the Union's economic and political spheres for membership purposes.

§ 1.14 Defense

In the early years of the Coal and Steel Community, a European Defense Community (EDC) treaty was drafted and nearly adopted. It failed when the French National Assembly refused to ratify it in 1954. Under this proposal, a European army would have been placed under the control of a European Ministry of Defense functioning within the North Atlantic Treaty Organization (NATO) alliance. The institutional structure of the EDC would have been like that employed in the Coal and Steel Community. The rejection by the French National Assembly was led by the Gaullists and the French Communist Party who quite simply did not want to surrender sovereignty over the French army, even if this meant that the West Germans could re-arm on their own.

Following a British initiative, however, a looser confederation for military purposes was established in 1954 through the Western European Union (WEU). It was under this Union that West Germany and Italy re-armed and were integrated into the NATO alliance. In 2000, the WEU transferred its principal activities to the European Union even though not all EU members belong to the WEU. In 2010, the WEU expired.

The vision of a common defense policy has started to become a reality. At the 1991 Maastricht Summit, agreement was reached on language explicitly stating that defense cooperation is expected of member states. Moreover, the Western European Union is to serve as the bridge between the Union and NATO. The Maastricht Treaty on European Union referred to the "eventual framing" of a common defense policy to be implemented through the WEU as another separate "pillar" of the Union. The Amsterdam Treaty altered this language to "progressive framing," a subtle change in Euro-speak meant to convey progress.

In 1992, the WEU defense and foreign ministers issued the "Petersburg Declaration." This Declaration affirms the ongoing efforts to develop a new Franco-German military brigade. By 2003, EU-led forces of 50,000–60,000 persons were ready for deployment in peace and rescue operations. Their presence in the Balkans has made a difference. The Reform Treaty of 2009 authorizes EU engagement in disarmament, conflict prevention and post-conflict stabilization operations.

A new "solidarity clause" in the TFEU commits member states to joint action after terrorist attacks or other disasters, including military forces as needed. The integration of Europe's defense may be the ultimate in politically sensitive issues. Neutrality, the NATO alliance (even after Sweden and Finland joined NATO following Russia's invasion of Ukraine), and a host of national interests stand in the way of a common defense policy for the European Union. In 2017, with BREXIT on the horizon, EU leaders backed a new defense cooperation plan (Pesco) potentially allowing joint purchase of critical equipment, and joint overseas missions. Some of these goals have been achieved in support of Ukraine's defense against Russia's invasion.

Transfers of sovereignty over war, peace, military forces, military weapons, and military command are momentous issues not only for the EU member states, but the world.

§ 1.15 The Convention on the Future of Europe and Defeat of Its Constitution (2005)

The growth in membership in the European Union raised fundamental issues of governance. The Nice Enlargement Protocol offered patchwork solutions, but would they measure up to the task? Less than a year after signing on to the Nice Treaty, the heads of state meeting at the Laeken Summit of the European Council established the 105-member Convention on the Future of Europe. Popularly referred to as a "constitutional convention," this body's very existence recognized that the traditional means of governance as revised by the Enlargement Protocol may not be up to the task.

Members of the Convention were drawn from national governments and parliaments, the European Parliament, and Commission. The 12 future member states had nonvoting observer status at the Convention. Chaired by former French President Valery Giscard d'Estaing and driven by an inner 12-member presidium, the Convention became a focal point for change. Lobbying on all fronts was intense, running from strong federalists to states rights' advocates. In June of 2003, the Convention released its draft Treaty establishing a Constitution for Europe, some 260 pages of complex text merging the EC, Maastricht TEU and EURATOM treaties. The draft went under review by the EU member states, which unanimously signed off on a final version in June of 2004.

The Constitution for Europe

The proposed Constitution was the subject of conflicting sometimes bizarre interpretations. The Union's Charter of Fundamental Rights ("declared" at Nice) was to become binding EU law, but apply only to EU institutions, personnel and law. The supremacy of EU law (Chapter 4) was openly acknowledged, the Union's "legal personality" secured, and the principle of "subsidiarity" (Chapter 3) retained but subordinated to broad Union objectives. Most policy areas were to be "shared" with the member states, which nevertheless appeared to retain vetoes over foreign policy, social security, taxation and defense. An EU "Foreign Minister," President of the European Council, and EU Armaments Agency were proposed.

Qualified majority voting was to disappear as the triple legislative majority system (Chapter 3) adopted under the Nice Treaty reduced to a double majority in the Council of Ministers to enact law: 55 percent of the member states representing at least 65 percent of the Union's population, but not until 2009. By 2014, the Commission was to be "shrunk" to two-thirds the number of member states. Member states for the first time could withdraw from the Union, but they could also be "suspended" by their fellow members.

The Constitution needed individual ratification in all 25 member states, some of which held national referendums. Optimists suggested that the Constitution would take effect by 2006. Pessimists believed it would (and should) end up in a waste bin. The pessimists were right. In 2005, roughly 55% of the French people, and 62% of the Dutch voted NO loud and clear.

Many variables seem to have been at work: Dislike of national leaders (especially President Chirac of France), visions of Turkish membership in the EU, use of the provocative "C" word (Constitution), job competition from the new member states, and resentment of the Brussels elite. These NO votes were so definitive that virtually all suggestions for "reworking" the Constitution failed to gain traction. With its 50th Anniversary looming, European Union integration was at a standstill.

§ 1.16 The Reform Treaty of Lisbon (2009)

By 2007, with the defeat of the European Constitution fading, EU leaders went back to work on advancement of the Union. Presidents Sarkozy of France and Merkel of Germany, in particular, pushed for a "mini-treaty" during the summer of 2007. Gone was all reference to the "C" word. Promoted as technical amendments to the TEU and Rome Treaty, a proposed "Reform Treaty" (Treaty of Lisbon), emerged late in that year from an Intergovernmental Conference. All references to the European Community would be expunged in favor of European Union, and the EC Treaty renamed the "Treaty on the Functioning of the Union."

All member states save Ireland were ready to proceed with ratification *without* calling for national referendums. The target date for implementation of the Reform Treaty was 2009, prior to elections for the European Parliament. But in July of 2008, Irish voters rejected the Reform Treaty in a low turnout stalked by the same fears that generated a no vote in Ireland on the Treaty of Nice in 2002. By October of 2009, however, the Irish (during a massive economic meltdown) returned a YES vote at the polls. On Dec. 1, 2009, the Reform Treaty of Lisbon took effect.

The TFEU of 2009 significantly alters the opening tenor of what was the Treaty establishing the European Community. It commences with a key principle: The TFEU organizes the functioning of the Union and determines the areas, limitations and arrangements for exercising the Union's competences (powers) (Article 1). Articles 2–6 define the categories and areas of exclusive, shared and supportive Union competences. See Chapter 3. Some anticipated in these provisions another expansion of regional powers over national sovereignty. Others hoped they would preserve national prerogatives against invasive supranational jurisdiction. Both sides of this debate acknowledge that "federal/state" relations had become the fulcrum of internal EU affairs.

The Reform Treaty notably created a Presidency elected by the European Council, established an EU diplomatic service under a foreign policy chief, eliminated national vetoes on justice and home affairs (migration, criminal and civil justice, judicial and police cooperation) (the UK and Eire can opt out), and rendered the Charter of Fundamental Rights binding law (subject to a Polish and a second UK opt out). The Union also acceded to the 1950 European Convention on Human Rights. See Section 1.0. Legislative voting rules in the Council were simplified to a double majority representing 55% of the states and 65% of the EU population, starting in 2014. With few exceptions, future EU legislation is co-decided under "normal legislative procedures" (see Section 2.2) by the Council and the Parliament, which also gets to approve the full EU budget.

In addition, under Lisbon, the European Central Bank was officially designated an EU institution, despite its fear that this could jeopardize independence. At French insistence, "undistorted competition" as a basic goal was removed from Treaty-status to a protocol and a "social market economy" standard is set. National parliaments get enhanced watchdog rights on subsidiarity. There is a solidarity clause against terrorism, express recognition of EU humanitarian aid programs and expanded provisions on mandatory democratic principles. The President of the Commission will be nominated the Council and elected by the Parliament. For the first time, a right of member state withdrawal by agreement from the Union was established.

Unlike all prior treaties, the TFEU does *not* anticipate a future round of EU negotiations and TFEU/TEU amendments. This leads some commentators to wonder if the European Union has reached its apex. The rise of openly EU-hostile political parties in almost every member state adds to the perspective that the EU may have become more of a problem than a solution.

§ 1.17 Future Members of the European Union

The late President Mitterrand of France once said that European history is accelerating. Former Chancellor Kohl of Germany said that the deepening and simultaneous expansion of the European Union are decisive for securing peace and freedom . . . European integration has remained a question of war and peace in the new millennium. European Union law reflects these truths.

Turkey has been associated with the EU as a trade ally since 1963. Relations were suspended during the military takeover of Turkey from 1981 to 1986. Turkey formally applied for membership in 1987 but was kept under study for many years, although a customs union was achieved in 1995. Turkey has been a strategic NATO ally for decades and serves as buffer state between the EU and the volatile Middle East. This helps explain why the United States has always been a strong supporter of Turkey's EU application. Late in 2004, the EU finally agreed to open membership negotiations with Turkey.

Apart from concerns about the stability of democracy, human rights and rule of law in Turkey, waning interest in the EU by the Turks, Greek membership in the Union and the unresolved divide of Cyprus would seem to make admission unlikely. That said, the linchpin role of Turkey against radical Islam and Middle East migrants has made its relations with the EU ever more critical. In exchange for limited visa-free travel, large sums of money and revival of membership talks, Turkey agreed in 2016 to take back migrants stranded in Greece and tighten the flow of people into the EU. More recently, an attempted coup and repressions by President Erdogan have made the prospect of EU membership for Turkey even more difficult.

Membership is limited by the Treaty on European Union to "European states". Morocco's informal application was rejected because it is not a European nation. Turkey's application presents difficult questions about its status in Europe and the meaning of the Treaty. Does "European" only have geographic implications or is there an expectation that members must also be culturally or religiously European?

Formal membership negotiations are also underway with Iceland (now on hold), Albania, Northern Macedonia, Bosnia Montenegro and Serbia/Kosovo. As the costs of economic isolation and nonparticipation mount, another wave could conceivably bring in more countries of the former Soviet Union, notably Moldova and Ukraine.

The European Union over the decades has functioned like a magnet. The larger its size, the greater its force. In 2013, Croatia became the 28th member state. With the campaign for a single market mostly realized, the attraction of the EU increased. With the creation of the EURO, and increase in the EU membership and market, the magnetic force of the Union remains powerful even after BREXIT.

§ 1.18 The European Union as a Trade Policy Model

The European Union has served as a model for economic integration elsewhere in the world. For example, the Andean Community (ANCOM) modeled itself on the EEC (as the EU was then called), as did the Southern African Customs Union (SACU), and the Central American Common Market (CACM). These regional economic groups have suffered internal discord, economic stress and limited success.[20] Yet, for the most part, they still aspire to become as comprehensive and effective as the European Union. MERCOSUR, established in 1991 by Brazil, Argentina, Paraguay and Uruguay, probably comes closest to reproducing the EU model.

The EU trade policy model contrasts with the ASEAN (Association of Southeast Asian Nations) and LAFTA (now ALADI, the Latin American Integration Association) groups.[21] These groups have targeted more limited goals as free trade areas. Neither rises to the significance or depth of NAFTA 1994 or its 2020 sequel, the USMCA.[22] Hundreds of bilateral free trade agreements have been negotiated since NAFTA, including some by the European Union, notably with Canada (CETA), Japan, Mexico (updated 2019), and MERCOSUR. See Chapter 6.

At this writing, the European Union and NAFTA/USMCA present competing trade policy models that have each drawn

---

[20] *See* D. Gantz, *Regional Trade Agreements: Law, Policy and Practice* (2009), Chapters 12, 13 and 15.

[21] *Id.*, Chapters 12 and 14.

[22] *See* my Concise Hornbook on *The USMCA and Free Trade Agreements.*

adherents in the developing world. Apart from their core economic differences (customs union v. free trade area), the EU model embraces a remarkable legal superstructure to achieve economic integration. Chapters 2 and 3 of this book detail the regional legislative and litigation systems of the Union. In contrast, the NAFTA/USMCA model is minimalist, legally speaking. Multiple varieties of arbitration are used to resolve disputes, and there are no regional legislative or litigation systems.[23]

Which model offers the best way forward? With BREXIT, the collapse of enforcement of the World Trade Organization (WTO)agreements, along with U.S. withdrawal by President Trump from the Obama Administration's hard won Trans-Pacific Partnership (TPP), analysis of this question has taken on added meaning. The EU has more recently has pursued a free trade model "with European characteristics" in its agreements with Canada (CETA), Japan, Mexico, MERCOSUR and others. See Chapter 6.

---

[23] *Id.*

Chapter 2

LAW-MAKING IN THE EUROPEAN UNION

Table of Sections

§ 2.0 The Principle of Subsidiarity and the Power to Legislate

The European Union has been creating law at a dazzling speed. It is almost impossible to function on EU matters without an understanding of the region's law-making institutions and procedures, a remarkable capacity almost completely absent under NAFTA/USMCA. Attorneys, executives and others actively seek to influence the development of European law in ways which reflect their interests.

Primary, Secondary and "Soft" Law

The two founding treaties of the European Union, the Treaty on the Functioning of the European Union (TFEU) and the Maastricht Treaty on European Union (TEU), are the "primary" sources of regional law. They are, in this author's opinion "quasi-constitutional." The treaties have had a common set of institutions since 1967. These are the Council of Ministers, the Commission, the Parliament and the Court of Justice (to which the Court of First Instance, now renamed the General Court, was attached in 1989). These institutions, supplemented by national legislatures, courts and tribunals, have been busy generating a remarkably vast and complex body of "secondary" law.

Some legislative acts are adopted directly at the EU level, but much of it is enacted by national governments under the "direction" of the Union. Similarly, some (and the most important) of the case law of the EU is created by decisions of the European Court of Justice or and its companion General Court, but much development of law also occurs in the national courts acting in many instances with "advisory rulings" from the Court of Justice. European Union secondary law also includes international obligations, often undertaken through "mixed" EU and national negotiations and ratifications.

There are two primary types of legislative acts, directives and regulations (see below). These acts should be distinguished from declarations, resolutions, guidelines, notices, policy statements, recommendations, opinions and individual decisions, all of which rarely involve legislative acts and are sometimes referred to as "soft law." For example, the 1981 European Council resolution on the adoption of EU passports with uniform characteristics fits this mold. This symbolic resolution has been fully implemented, adding to the consciousness of the European Union among its citizens. Another example is the Council's Declaration on Democracy (1977) which "codifies" the longstanding tradition that no European state can join or remain associated with the EU without a pluralistic democratic form of government. A third example is the formulation of foreign policy resolutions by the European Council.

Legislative Powers

The starting point for a basic understanding of law-making is, as always, the founding treaties. The TFEU is premised upon the idea of a regional government of limited or derived powers ("compétences d'attribution"). That is to say, the TFEU does not convey a general power to create law. European Union law-making is either specifically authorized or dependent upon the terms of Article 352. That article permits action if "necessary to attain, in the course of the operation of the common market, one of the objectives of the Union and this Treaty has not provided the necessary powers."

Article 352 has been used repeatedly, and in ways which suggest that there are relatively few limits upon what the Union can legislate, or negotiate by way of international agreements, once a political consensus has been reached to move forward. For example, Article 352 was widely used as the legal basis for environmental programs well prior to the Single European Act amendments that specifically authorize action in this field. In the early years, the Court of Justice had slowly been fashioning a doctrine of *implied* powers under the EEC Treaty, most notably concerning external relations' powers.[1] However, the Court of Justice has more recently been retreating from the doctrine of implied powers, though it did approve of criminal sanctions for environmental offenses as an implied power.[2]

The Reform Treaty of 2009, in new TFEU provisions, enumerates categories and areas of exclusive, shared and supportive EU competences or powers. These enumerations determine when and to what degree the EU and/or the member states may legislate. Exclusive EU competences (Article 3 TFEU) include the customs union, internal market competition rules, EURO zone monetary policy, marine conservation, and the Common Commercial Policy (external trade relations), including foreign investment. The Union also has exclusive competence over international agreements provided for in EU legislative acts, necessary to enable the exercise of its internal powers, or those agreements whose conclusion may affect common rules or alter their scope. In all these areas, member states may legislate only if empowered by the Union to do so, or to implement EU acts.

When the TFEU enumerates a shared competence (Article 4), the Union may legislate. Member states may legislate only to the extent the EU has not done so or ceased to exercise a shared competence. Shared competences include the internal market, social policy, cohesion, agriculture and fisheries, the environment, consumer protection, transport, trans-European networks, energy, the area of freedom, security and justice, and common public health safety concerns. Special more permissive rules allow member states greater latitude in the areas of research, technology development, space, third world development and humanitarian aid.

---

[1] *See* Fédération Charbonnìee de Belgique v. High Authority, (1955–56) Eur.Comm.Rep. 245; Germany v. Commission, (1987) Eur.Comm.Rep. 3203 (Immigration of External Workers); Commission v. Council, (1971) Eur.Comm.Rep. 263 (*ERTA*).

[2] *Compare* Opinion 1/94 (1994) Eur.Comm.Rep. I 5267 (WTO) (rejection of implied powers) with Spain v. Council, (1995) Eur.Comm.Rep. I–1985 (medicinal product certificates upheld as implied internal market power) and Commission v. Council, (2005) Eur.Comm.Rep. I–7879 (criminal sanctions for environmental offenses implied).

Lastly, the Union is authorized to legislate in support of, to coordinate with, or to supplement (but not supersede) member state competence in areas designated in Article 6 TFEU. These include human health, industry, culture, tourism, education and training, youth, sport, civil protection and administrative cooperation. EU acts in these areas may not entail harmonization of member state laws or regulations.

Subsidiarity

The Treaty on European Union (Maastricht) and to a lesser extent the Single European Act (1987) formalized a "subsidiarity" principle. The Amsterdam Treaty of 1999 added a Protocol on the application of the principles of subsidiarity and proportionality. These much-debated principle holds that the Union can act in areas where it does not *exclusively* have power only if the member states cannot sufficiently achieve the objectives, *i.e.*, "by reason of scale or effects [the] proposed action [can] be better achieved by the Union." In all cases, European Union action must not go beyond what is necessary to achieve the objectives of the TFEU (proportionality principle).[3]

Subsidiarity is seemingly a kind of "states' rights" amendment intended to limit the growth of regional government in Europe, though Euro-federalists construe it expansively. An inter-institutional agreement by the Council, Commission and European Parliament on the application of subsidiarity principles by all EU institutions has been negotiated. Subsidiarity guidelines were adopted by the European Council in December of 1992[4] and a Protocol on the Application of the Principles of Subsidiarity and Proportionality was adopted in conjunction with the 1999 Amsterdam Treaty. The Commission regularly reviews proposed and existing legislation under the subsidiarity principle. This has caused legislative proposals and acts to be withdrawn or amended.

Under the Subsidiarity Protocol, moreover, if a third or more of the *national* Parliaments give reasoned opinions that a proposal breaches the subsidiarity principle, the Commission must undertake reconsideration. Since the Reform Treaty of 2009, national parliaments get notice early in the EU legislative process and can force the Commission and even the Council and Parliament to review proposed laws in terms of subsidiarity. National parliaments may also file suits before the European Court of Justice to seek annulment

---

3 Article 5, TEU.

4 *Guidelines on Subsidiarity* (Conclusions of the Presidency—Edinburgh, December 12, 1992).

of EU legislative acts on subsidiarity grounds. The Committee of the Regions can do likewise.

The European Council takes the position that EU subsidiarity principles do not have direct effect in the member state legal systems.[5] If this is correct, subsidiarity issues cannot be raised in litigation before member state courts and tribunals.[6] However, interpretation of these principles and review of compliance by European Union institutions are subject to judicial review before the Court of Justice through challenges initiated by a member state or another EU institution.[7] It is the Court, therefore, that will ultimately determine whether and to what degree subsidiarity will limit governance by the European Union, a task it has undertaken gingerly.[8] Should subsidiarity preclude Union action, member states are still required to ensure fulfillment of their Treaty obligations and abstain from measures that could jeopardize their objectives.[9]

Although variations do occur from treaty to treaty, the Union's legislative, administrative and judicial processes are generally similar. Unless otherwise indicated, the analysis in this chapter is drawn from the Treaty on the Functioning of the European Union. A review of the diagram in Section 2.8 may assist the reader in understanding the text that follows, particularly the law-making institutions.

§ 2.1 Legislation—Directives and Regulations

Legislative and Non-Legislative Acts

Article 288 of the TFEU clarifies the powers of the Council of Ministers and the Commission, in accordance with the Treaty, to make regulations and issue directives. EC regulations are similar in form to administrative regulations commonly found in North America. EC directives, on the other hand, have no obvious parallel. The Court of Justice has repeatedly affirmed that both regulations and directives must state the "reasons" on which they are based.[10]

---

5 *See* Conclusions of the Presidency, Edinburgh Summit, Dec. 12, 1992, Annex 1 to Part A.

6 *See* Section 3.1.

7 *See* Sections 3.8, 3.9 and 3.10.

8 For decisions deferential to EU legislative powers and recitals of need, *see* Germany v. Parliament and Council, (1997) Eur.Comm.Rep. I–2405 (deposit-guarantee schemes), United Kingdom v. Council, (1995) Eur.Comm.Rep. I–5755 (working time), Netherlands v. Parliament and Council, (2001) Eur.Comm.Rep. I–07079 (Oct. 9, 2001) (bio-tech) and The Queen v. Secretary for Health, (2002) Eur.Comm.Rep. I–11453 (tobacco).

9 Article 4(3), TEU.

10 Germany v. Commission, (1963) Eur.Comm.Rep. 63.

A directive establishes Union policy. It is then left to the member states to implement the directive in whatever way is appropriate to their national legal system. This may require a new statute, a Presidential decree, an administrative act or even a constitutional amendment. Sometimes it may require no action at all. As Article 288 indicates, a directive is "binding as to the result to be achieved" but "leave[s] to the national authorities the choice of form and methods." Most of the legislative acts of the single market campaign are directives. All directives contain time limits for national implementation: The more controversial the policy, the longer the likely allotment of time.

The Reform Treaty of 2009 makes it clear member states must adopt all measures necessary to implement legally binding Union acts. But if, at the end of the deadline, the directive is not transposed into national law, some of its dispositions may under the doctrine of "direct effect" be binding, nevertheless. This doctrine is discussed in Section 3.1.

Legislative Procedures

The Commission's civil servants initiate the process of legislation by drafting proposals which the Council of Ministers (from the governments of the member states) has the power to adopt into law. Although the Council may request the Commission to submit legislative proposals,[11] it cannot force the Commission to do so except by way of litigation before the Court of Justice nor draft legislative proposals itself. This makes the Commission the focal point of lobbying activities. The Commission's legislative proposals are always influenced by what it believes the Council will accept. The Council, however, has the right to amend legislative proposals by unanimous vote. Readers will immediately note that the European Parliament does not have the power to propose legislation, nor the power to enact it!

Parliament's role was traditionally consultative. Over time it became and remains the source of proposed amendments. These absences of Parliamentary power are so fundamental that many observers decry a "democratic deficit" in the European Union. This deficit has been partially remedied by conveying limited "co-decision" powers to Parliament, a right to veto or reach a common position with the Council on selected legislative proposals. Parliament's role in law-making is detailed in Section 2.2.

The Treaty on European Union created an advisory Committee of the Regions.[12] This Committee is composed of representatives of

---

11 Article 241, TFEU.

12 *See* Articles 305–309, TFEU.

regional and local bodies throughout the Union. Like the Economic and Social Committee, it must be consulted on certain types of Union action. Moreover, it is free to render an opinion without prior request. The Committee of the Regions appears chiefly to be an attempt at bringing local officials into the regional legislative and decision-making processes.

§ 2.2 The Parliament—Consultation, Cooperation and Co-Decision

The European Parliament (first called the Assembly in the treaties) was originally composed of representatives appointed by member state governments. In other words, the people's representation was indirect, although the Members of the European Parliament (MEPs) had to be serving in their national parliaments. Since 1979, universal suffrage has been employed to directly elect the representatives of the citizens of the Union to their Parliament. Voter turnout has typically been low.

Under the TFEU, there is a cap of 720 MEPs plus its President. Representation in the Parliament is degressively proportional by population, with a minimum of 6 and a maximum of 96 MEPs per state. MEPs serve 5-year terms and are divided into transnational political groups. The European Parliament is a kaleidoscope of European politics. For example, there are groupings of Socialists, Greens, Liberals, Nationalists, the European People's Party (center-right), the Progressive Alliance of Socialists and democrats (center-left), and unaffiliated MEPs. Even these groupings fail to capture the full picture of diversity as the groups often realize once they start talking to each other in 23 languages with over 1000 translators.

Since it takes a majority of votes to pass a measure in Parliament, alliances are essential. There are numerous standing Parliamentary Committees. Each is responsible for reviewing and reporting on legislative proposals within its expertise, such as agriculture, external relations, etc. In addition, unofficially allied groups of MEPs with special interests in particular areas of Union development (*e.g.*, the EURO and the internal market) have been formed. These groups are quite influential in proposing legislative amendments under the cooperation and co-decision procedures discussed below.

The member states fulfilled their obligations under the EEC Treaty for direct elections. In 1998 they enacted "uniform procedures" for these elections. European Union MEPs these days cannot also be representatives in their national parliaments. Some commentators have suggested that this leads to an estrangement between European Union and national politicians. The member states have failed to decide where the Parliament is located. Presently, Parliament's plenary sessions are held in Strasbourg, its committee meetings in Brussels and its secretariat is in Luxembourg.[13] Each nation has vied for a permanent assignment of the European Parliament to it. And the member states have sued to protect their existing allocations.[14] One suspects that this litigation reflects the economic more than the political value associated with Parliament and its expense-account-spending members.

Legislative Powers

With direct elections, the impetus toward greater Parliamentary input into the legislative process has magnified. Traditionally, the Parliament has a right to be consulted and to give an "opinion" as part of the Union's legislative process. That opinion is not binding upon the Commission or Council, but it can prove increasingly awkward if it is disregarded. For example, in 1980 the Court of Justice held that the Council acts illegally if it legislates without waiting for the Parliament's opinion.[15] Left unanswered is how long Parliament may delay giving an opinion when merely consulted on legislation. If the Council amends the Commission's legislative proposal substantively, the Parliament has the right to be consulted and to issue a second opinion.[16] Since 1977, a "conciliation procedure" is used whenever the Council departs from an opinion of the Parliament on proposed legislation of importance to the Union's income or expenses. This procedure was instituted by a Joint Declaration of the Parliament, Council and Commission.[17]

The Single European Act of 1987 created a "cooperation procedure." This gave Parliament more of a voice on selected legislation. Basically, when the Treaty required adherence to this procedure, the Parliament could reject or seek to amend the Council's "common position" on a legislative proposal from the Commission. One early study indicated that Parliament introduced nearly 1,000 amendments after the cooperation procedure was adopted in 1987. Of these, 72 percent were accepted by the Commission and 42 percent ultimately adopted by the Council. The "cooperation procedure"

---

13 The European Council affirmed these allocations in a formal decision taken at the 1992 Edinburgh Summit.

14 *See* Luxembourg v. Parliament, (1983) Eur.Comm.Rep. 255 (Parliament may hold all plenary sessions in Strasbourg); France v. Parliament, (1988) Eur.Comm.Rep. 4821 (Parliament may hold exceptional plenary sessions in Brussels); Luxembourg v. Parliament, (1984) Eur.Comm.Rep. 1945 (Parliament could not transfer secretariat from Luxembourg); Luxembourg v. European Parliament, (1991) Eur.Comm.Rep. I–5643 (refusal to annul increased Parliamentary staffing in Brussels).

15 Roquette Frères SA v. Council, (1980) Eur.Comm.Rep. 3333.

16 ACF Chemiefarma v. Commission, (1970) Eur.Comm.Rep. 661; European Parliament v. Council, (1992) Eur.Comm.Rep. I–4193 Case C–295/90.

17 Official Journal C98/1 (1975).

applied selectively. Most significantly, it applied to nearly all internal market measures following the Single European Act of 1987. With the development of the cooperation procedure, and success in persuading the Commission and Council to adopt its amendments, Parliament became a second center of legislative lobbying. The TFEU repealed the cooperation procedure in favor of "co-decision" (below).

The European Parliament also acquired significant powers under the 1993 Maastricht Treaty on European Union. On legislation, under what is called the "co-decision" procedure of TFEU Article 294, it has what amounts to a legislative veto over selected matters if conciliation through direct negotiations with the Council cannot be achieved. Co-decision after Maastricht applied to single market, education, culture, health, consumer protection, environmental, transportation and research affairs. Parliament in fact first exercised its veto rights over a biotechnology directive, out of concern about potential human cloning and against a corporate takeover directive which did not allow for "poison pill" defenses.

Three distinct European legislative processes resulted in 1993, each defined in terms of the role Parliament plays: Consultative, Cooperative and Co-decisional.

The Amsterdam Treaty of 1999, the Nice Treaty of 2003 and the Reform Treaty of 2009 mandated co-decision in many additional legislative areas, including international trade and the Common Agricultural Policy. Today, co-decision dominates the EU legislative process and is referred to as "normal legislative procedure." Parliament still cannot draft or initiate legislation, but its veto power ensures influence and a sparingly used negative power over legislative outcomes.

Most conciliation committees formed under the co-decision procedure have reached legislative compromises satisfactory to the Council and Parliament. Such committees are often comprised of representatives of the Council Presidency, Chairs of the relevant European Parliament committees, and Commission officials in charge of the legislative dossier. Such compromises reduce the power of the Commission in Europe's law-making process. Even so, the European Parliament as a legislative institution is still waiting to come of age.

Ancillary Powers

Other powers of the European Parliament should be noted. First, it can put written and oral questions to the Council and the Commission on virtually any Union matter, legislative or otherwise. This prerogative mostly has a nuisance and information gathering value. Absent forceful persuasion, it is not terribly influential.

Second, Article 234 of the TFEU gives the Parliament the power to "censure" the Commission by a two-thirds vote. A motion of censure would require all Commissioners to resign, but the member states acting in common accord (not the Parliament) get to choose the new Commissioners, although Parliament may veto the nominees, and it now elects the President of the Commission. These could conceivably be the very people just censured. Parliament cannot selectively censure one Commissioner, nor can it censure the Council of Ministers at all.

A motion of censure has at times been threatened by Parliament, but never adopted. In 1999, Parliament came very close to censuring the commission for its inadequacies on corruption and mismanagement in regional programs. After an embarrassing report by a committee of experts, the Commission resigned en masse rather than face formal censure.

Further, the Parliament can initiate a lawsuit against the Council or Commission under Article 265 of the TFEU for failure to act. Parliament did exactly this when it sued the Council over the failure to implement a Common Transport Policy as required by the Treaty. The Court of Justice ruled that the Council had failed to act but denied the Parliament a remedy given the imprecise nature of the Council's obligation to act.[18] Nevertheless, the Council has since undertaken a number of reforms in the transport sector.[19]

The Parliament has selected other litigation alternatives. It can intervene as an interested party in cases pending before the Court, which it did quite successfully when challenging a regulation enacted by the Council without its consultation and opinion.[20] But it does not appear to have a right to file briefs in Article 267 litigation.[21] Since the Nice Treaty (2003), it can litigate the legality of acts of the Commission or Council under Article 263 even if its own prerogatives are not at stake.

Parliament's powers were expanded in 1993 by The Maastricht Treaty on European Union. If an international agreement touches upon a co-decisional area, or has institutional or budgetary implications, Parliament must approve.[22] The Parliament also has a veto over the nomination of the Commissioners and their President and may create committees to inquiry into alleged "contraventions or

---

[18] European Parliament v. Council, (1985) Eur.Comm.Rep. 1513.

[19] *See* Chapter 4.

[20] Roquette Frères SA v. Council, (1980) Eur.Comm.Rep. 3333.

[21] *See* Chapter 3.

[22] *See* Article 218, TFEU.

maladministration" of Union law.[23] One-fourth of the members of the Parliament must request the creation of such committee. Issues of this kind may come to Parliament's attention from citizens through a petitioning procedure to the Parliament or to its Ombudsman.[24] Since the Parliament must further assent to new member states, yet another veto power was established by the Treaty on European Union. The Reform Treaty of 2009 gives Parliament the power to submit proposals for revision of the founding treaties. In 2013, Parliament rejected the proposed budget as excessively austere.

§ 2.3 Budgetary Legislation, Wealth Transfers

The Coal and Steel Community was financed exclusively by taxes levied against producers. The European Economic Community was originally financed by contributions from the member states. This created a fiscally dependent relationship. Since 1971, the Union is funded through its "own resources," but still dependent upon the member states for their collection and transfer. The Union's income is now principally derived from the common external tariff, agricultural levies on imports, a small but growing portion of the value-added tax (VAT) collected in every state, and an assessment based upon the gross domestic product (GDP) of the member states.

Some countries (like Germany) are habitually net payors to the Union budget. Others (like Greece and Portugal) have been net payees receiving funds under the Union's various common policies. Britain, initially a large net payor, negotiated a special rebate agreement in 1984 which returned substantial sums to it from EU revenues. The UK remained a net payor into the EU budget, a reality that caused financial concerns in Brussels after BREXIT. France, Sweden, Italy, Belgium, Denmark, Austria and the Netherlands are also net contributors, with the twelve new Central European member states eager net recipients.

Article 310 of the TFEU requires a balanced Union budget. This requirement has been met by increasing the level of regional revenues and, occasionally, reducing (agricultural) expenditure. Revenue-raising decisions are undertaken by the heads of state and government acting through the European Council. In other words, Parliament lacks the power to tax. Control over the spending of these resources, however, is another area where Parliament has sought to acquire power.

---

[23] *See* Article 226, TFEU.

[24] *See* Article 228, TFEU.

Budgetary Procedures

The budgetary process is outlined in Article 314 of the TFEU. The Commission creates a preliminary draft budget which it forwards to the Council of Ministers. The Council revises it and then sends a draft budget to Parliament. Parliament can reject the draft budget in its entirety, something it did in 1979 and 1984. Until recently, Parliament only had the power to propose changes in the budget regarding matters "necessarily resulting from this Treaty or from acts adopted in accordance therewith." This increased Parliamentary influence over "compulsory expenditures" (mostly agricultural subsidies), but the Council had the final word.

Since 1975, Parliament has had ultimate control by way of amendment over "non-compulsory" EU expenditures, about one-third of the budget. As a practical matter, this gives Parliament influence over expenditures in many of the new and important policy areas. The Reform Treaty of 2009 eliminates the distinction between compulsory and non-compulsory expenditures, vesting full power over the budget in Parliament. In 2013, Parliament exercised this power in rejecting the proposed budget as too austere. An EU "Court" of Auditors serves as a watchdog over financial affairs in the Union.

§ 2.4 Which Council?

Council of Ministers

The foregoing analysis of the legislative process illustrates the dominant role given to "the Council" in EU affairs. The Council, also known since 1993 as the Council of the European Union, is a bit of a moving target. The Council consists of representatives of the governments of the member states. There are presently 27 Council Members since the accession of Bulgaria and Romania minus the UK after BREXIT. However, the people who comprise the Council change according to the topic at hand. The national ministers of foreign affairs, agriculture, economy and finance (Ecofin), social affairs, environment, etc. are sent to Brussels to confer and vote on EU matters within their competence.

Several different Council meetings can take place at once. Some refer to the Ecofin Council, the Environment Council, the Agriculture Council and so forth to differentiate the various Councils. The Presidency of these Councils rotates among the member states every six months and a certain amount of competition has emerged to see who can achieve the most under their Presidency. It is from all these meetings that the legislation of the European Union pours forth.

The Council is greatly assisted in their work by a Committee of Permanent Representatives known as COREPER. The Committee is comprised of high-ranking national civil servants and based in Brussels. COREPER in turn consults extensively with many "working groups" composed of other national civil servants with expertise in areas of Union concern. Thus, by the time a legislative proposal from the Commission reaches the Council for a vote, the proposal has been thoroughly reviewed by COREPER and the appropriate working groups. If there is no controversy, the proposal is scheduled as an "A point" on the Council's agenda and virtually certain to be adopted If no agreement is reached within COREPER, the proposal becomes a "B point" on the agenda which means that the Council of Ministers will discuss and debate its merits. All formal votes of the Council of Ministers are made public. Since the Reform Treaty of 2009, Council proceedings have been publicly held. These changes are part of a broader program aimed at greater institutional "transparency" and less bureaucratic secrecy.

European Council

Then there is the "European Council." With growth, legislative and other decisions have inevitably become more political and thus more difficult. A new institution has emerged to keep the EU moving, mostly forward but arguably (at times) backward. The European Council consists of the heads of the state or government of the member nations, a kind of ultimate Council of Ministers. The heads of state have met twice a year since 1974 to formulate broad policy guidelines or initiatives for the Union. For example, the European Council has shown leadership on direct elections to Parliament, the European Monetary System, new memberships and innovative legislative agendas.

Its meetings are sometimes called "summits," and Article 2 of the Single European Act of 1987 formally recognizes their existence. The Reform Treaty of 2009 established an elected President of the European Council, a post that lasts 2.5 years. Despite this development, the traditional 6-month Rotating Council Presidency was retained. It remains uncertain exactly how these two Presidencies are intended to interact.

European Council summits (though sometimes fractious) have generally proved to be quite successful. They have greatly facilitated the development of common foreign and security policy positions, and on justice and internal affairs. Although these meetings are undertaken in close consultation with the Commission and Parliament, they are not subject to the procedural rules of the TFEU or TEU. For example, whereas the Council of Ministers must seek an opinion, cooperate or co-decide with Parliament on legislative acts, the European Council need not do so. Whether the European Council can be subjected to judicial review by the Court of Justice is most unclear. This is the case even though European Council pronouncements (*e.g.*, the Social Charter in 1989,[25]) may have important legal implications for the Union. Some fear that the European Council's ability to operate outside the treaties may exacerbate the "democratic deficit."

§ 2.5 Voting Procedures of the Council of Ministers

The voting procedures of the Council of Ministers and the European Council are critical to an understanding of law-making. The TFEU provides for "qualified majority voting" unless otherwise specified. The point of contention is always whether unanimous or "qualified majority" voting is required.

Demise of the Luxembourg Accord and Unanimous Voting

Ignoring EEC Treaty terms, the "Luxembourg Accord" in the past favored unanimous voting. In 1965, France under General De Gaulle walked out of a Council meeting in a dispute over revenue and budgetary policy. Many believe that the real reason for the dispute was the fact that qualified majority voting was due to come into force in 1966. This was the major crisis of the early years of the Community of six. A compromise agreement was reached which when "very important interests" are at stake committed the Council to reaching solutions by consensus if possible. This "Luxembourg Accord" then proceeds to express disagreement over what is to be done if a consensus cannot be reached. The French delegation took the view that discussions must continue until unanimity is achieved. The five other delegations took the position that the Treaty rules apply and a decision by qualified majority vote must follow.

For many years the Luxembourg Accord was followed under the French perspective. Qualified majority voting was almost non-existent. Surprisingly, there was no challenge by the Commission before the Court of Justice to this breach of the Treaty's terms. Arguably, the Council was not acting in accordance with an essential procedural requirement of the Treaty. As the Community grew in member states, it became more and more difficult for the Council to arrive at a consensus. New legislation and new policy initiatives floundered as institutional and trade arteries hardened.

Unanimous voting had the practical effect of giving each member state a veto over legislation and policy developments. Fortunately, at this stage only a limited number of such treaty mandates remain, notably regarding tax and discrimination legislation. Unanimous voting also prevails over family law, police

[25] *See* Chapter 5.

co-operation and administrative co-operation. The significance of unanimous voting requirements was driven home in 1997 by British "non-cooperation" in regional affairs as a protest blockage of its beef and cattle exports in the wake of the outbreak of "Mad Cow disease." British non-cooperation lasted about a month before a gradual removal of the ban on British beef was agreed. During that month, regional matters requiring a unanimous vote were held in suspended animation pending resolution of the dispute.

The Commission recognized the economic costs, especially Europe's competitive position with North America and Japan. The Commission proposed in its "white paper" of 1985 a return and indeed expansion of qualified majority voting. These proposals bore fruit in the Single European Act of 1987. This Act amended the EEC Treaty extensively. It was the authority for the legislation associated with the campaign to achieve a Europe without internal frontiers by the end of 1992, and much of that legislation was adopted by qualified majority vote. Moreover, the Act amended the Treaty in a few instances to change unanimous voting requirements to a qualified majority.

The Maastricht Treaty on European Union of 1993, the Amsterdam Treaty of 1999, the Nice Treaty of 2003 and the Reform Treaty of 2009 made similar changes. The net result, operationally speaking, has been the demise of the French perspective to the Luxembourg accord. Unanimity is still sought, sometimes at great lengths, but qualified majority voting generally prevails.

Qualified Majority Voting

Much of the voting in the Council of Ministers takes place on a "qualified majority" basis. See § 1.16. The rules that define this procedure are given in Article 238 TFEU. Prior to Nov. 1, 2014, and thereafter upon request by a member state until March 31, 2017, for 28 member states there were a total of 345 votes, with Germany, France, Italy and Britain having 29 qualified majority votes each. Spain and Poland have 27 votes, Romania 14 votes, the Netherlands 13 votes, and Belgium, Greece, Portugal, the Czech Republic and Hungary 12 votes. Austria, Sweden and Bulgaria 10 votes, Denmark, Ireland, Finland, Slovakia and Lithuania 7 votes, Luxembourg, Latvia, Slovenia, Estonia and Cyprus 4 votes, and Malta 3 qualified majority votes.

To adopt legislation by qualified majority under this system 255 votes had to be cast in favor by a majority of the member states (for measures requiring a proposal from the Commission) *or* two-thirds of the members (for all other measures). In addition, the qualified majority had when challenged by a member state to constitute 62 percent of the total EU population. Thus, compared with the law prior to the 2003 Treaty of Nice Enlargement Protocol, two demanding rules were added: (1) The majority or two-thirds member state requirement; and (2) the percentage of population challenge requirement. The third requirement, the qualified majority vote count, was tightened by slightly raising the percentage of votes needed to pass legislation. Byzantine hardly seems adequate to describe these "triple majority" rules on qualified majority voting.

Since March of 2017, in all cases including post BREXIT, a qualified majority is defined as at least 55% of the members of the Council (with a minimum number of 15) who represent member states comprising 65% of the population of the Union. Any blocking minority must include at least 4 Council members. Thus, a simplified "double majority" voting system was established by the 2009 Reform Treaty.

Note that under these formulas for voting in the EU Council, the "Big" nations cannot ordinarily prevail without some support from smaller nations. Put conversely, if the little nations stick together, they can block almost any legislation. Over the years, as the Union grew from 6 to 9 to 10 to 12 to 15 to 25 to 28, now post BREXIT 27 members, these political dynamics have generally been preserved in the qualified majority voting rules. Other "blocking minorities" can emerge on North-South and East-West EU lines.

§ 2.6 [Reserved]

§ 2.7 [Reserved]

§ 2.8 Diagram of the EU Legislative Process

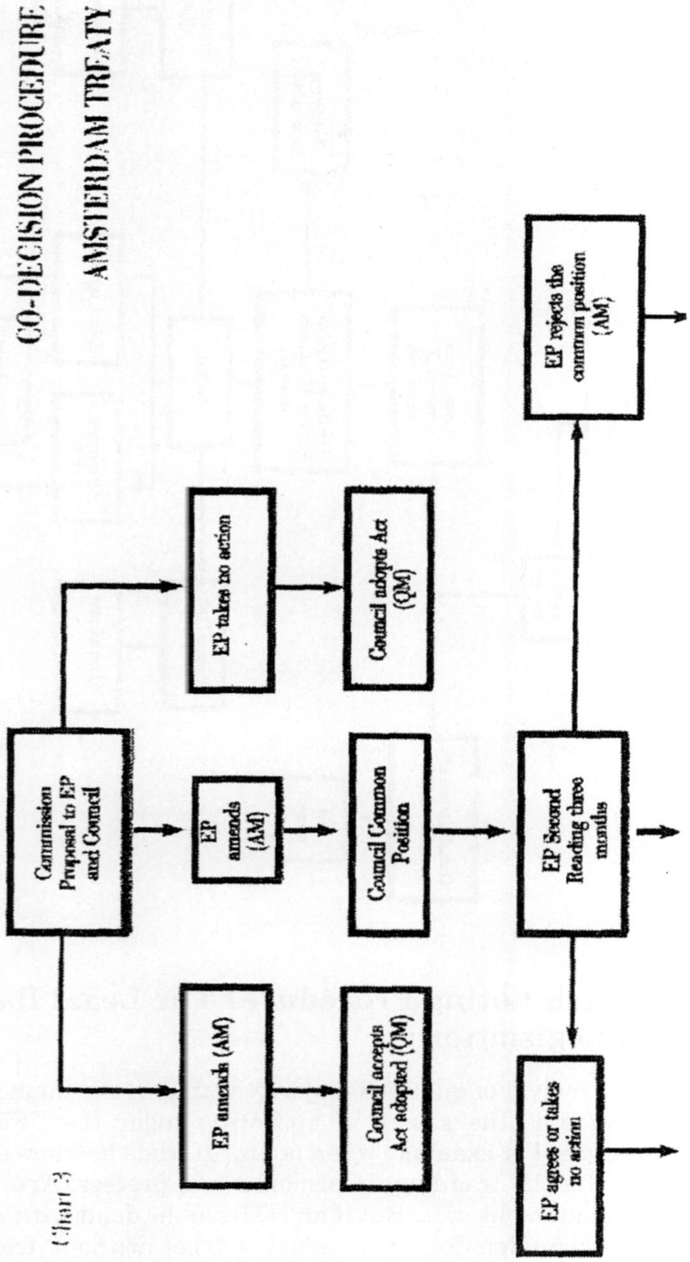

Chart 3

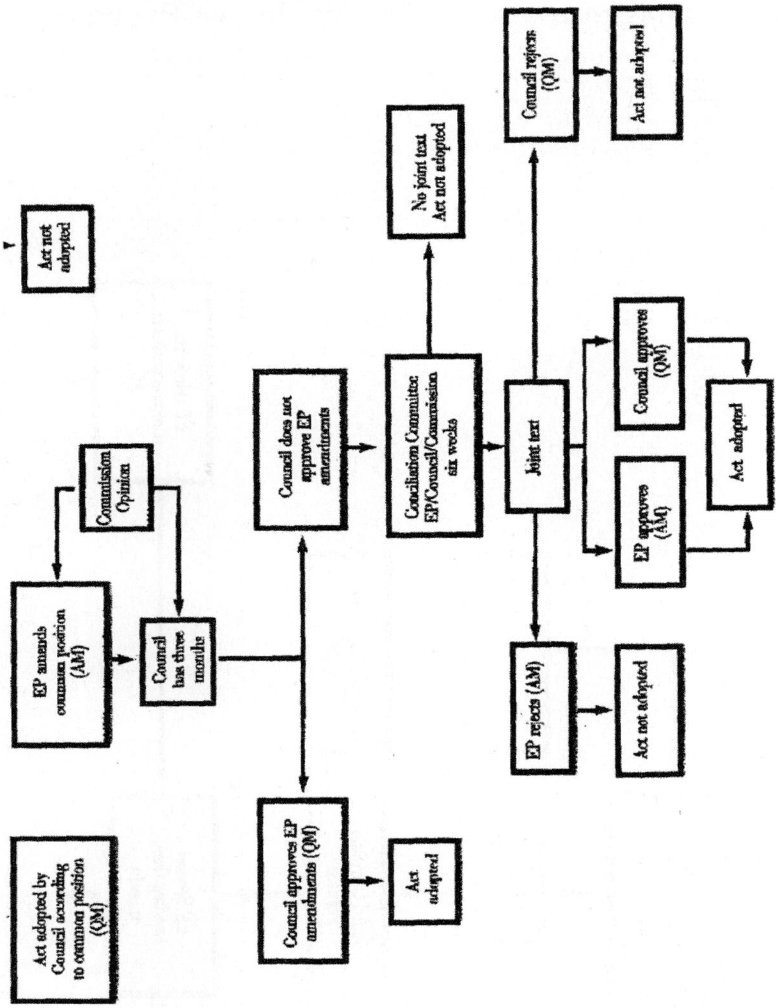

§ 2.9 Which Voting Procedure? The Legal Basis of Legislation

With the revival of qualified majority voting in the Council, one critical question is the source of authority under the TFEU for legislative action. For example, when nontariff trade barriers (NTBs) are removed via the traditional harmonization process, Article 115 mandates a unanimous vote. But if an NTB can be dealt with as part of the 1992 campaign for an internal market without frontiers, Article 114 stipulates a qualified majority in most cases. Naturally, the Council (composed of government representatives) and the member states favor interpretations that result in unanimous voting and greater retention of national sovereignty.[26] Naturally, the Parliament favors interpretations that require use of the cooperation and co-decision legislative procedures. Most of the latter areas correspond with qualified majority voting rules. Naturally, countries with "opt outs" favor interpretations which preserve those rights.

The Commission, as the independent "guardian of the treaties," favors interpretations that promote integration and particularly the internal market campaign. It thus tends to side with Parliament in disputes over the source of power for EU legislative enactments. But it did not do this when proposing post-Chernobyl safety legislation under EURATOM instead of Article 114 TFEU. This had the effect of avoiding Parliamentary cooperation procedures. The Parliament subsequently sued the Council before the European Court, which ruled its challenge to the EURATOM safety legislation admissible but denied relief on the merits. Germany, on the other hand, successfully persuaded the ECJ to annul the first Tobacco Advertising Directive as impermissible under Article 114.[27]

Article 352, "Necessary" Legislative Powers

Legal basis issues frequently reach the Court of Justice. Legislative authority issues came to a head in a Commission prosecution against the Council initiated on the very day that the Single European Act was signed.[28] In this case, the Court of Justice ruled that the Council violated Article 296 TFEU by failing to clearly state the legal basis for regulations implementing the generalized system of tariff preferences (GSP) for goods originating in the developing world. More importantly, the Court held that the Council enacted the regulations on the wrong legal basis. Both violations, which were longstanding Council practices, amounted to unlawful failures to act in accordance with the Treaty.

The Commission had proposed adoption of the GSP regulations under the common external commercial policy provisions, specifically Article 207 TFEU which employs qualified majority voting. The

---

26 *See* United Kingdom v. Council, (1988) Eur.Comm.Rep. 855 (beef hormones directive validly adopted by qualified majority vote, unanimous vote not required). For other decisions favoring qualified majority voting in disputes over the legal basis of Union legislation, *see* United Kingdom v. Council, (1988) Eur.Comm.Rep. 855, Commission v. Council, (1989) Eur.Comm.Rep. 3743, Greece v. Council, (1990) Eur.Comm.Rep. 1527, Commission v. Council, (1989) Eur.Comm.Rep. 1425.

27 Compare European Parliament v. Council, (1991) Eur.Comm.Rep. 4529 (Case 70/88) with Germany v. Parliament and Council, (2000) Eur.Comm.Rep. I–8419.

28 Commission v. Council, (1987) Eur.Comm.Rep. 1493. For other major cases on determining the legal basis of legislation, *see* Commission v. Council, (1991) Eur.Comm.Rep. I–2867 (titanium dioxide), Commission v. Council, (1993) Eur.Comm.Rep. I–939 (waste disposal), United Kingdom v. Council, (1996) Eur.Comm.Rep. I–5755 (working time), and Spain v. Council, (2001) Eur.Comm.Rep. I–779 (Danube Convention).

Council replaced this proposal with vague language simply referring to "the Treaty" as the legal basis for its acts. In court, the Council explained that this reference was really to Article 207 *and* Article 352.

Article 352 authorizes legislation necessary to achieve objectives for which specific enabling powers are otherwise not found in the TFEU. Article 352 had been previously used by the Council as the legal basis for several innovative programs and laws, including the Monetary Cooperation Fund, the Center for Development of Vocational Training, the Foundation for the Improvement of Living and Working Conditions, and environmental, research and development and energy legislation. It had also been used in areas where the Treaty contains other provisions, including agriculture, the customs union, services, the right of establishment and (as in the GSP case) external commercial policy.

Article 352 legislation must be enacted by a unanimous Council vote and does not require cooperation with Parliament. By ruling that Article 207 alone was the proper legal basis for GSP regulations, the Court nullified the Council's unanimous decision and reaffirmed its power to subject Council actions to judicial review. The Commission now has more leeway when proposing legislation for which the Treaty stipulates qualified majority voting under what has become known as the "center of gravity" test.[29] And the Council is clearly limited in its use of Article 352 to situations where no other authority to act is found in the Treaty on the Functioning of the European Union. This doctrine has even been held to require the Council to adopt legislation under the general principle of equal treatment rather than Article 352.[30]

§ 2.10 The Commission as an Institution and Law Maker

The pivotal role of the Commission in the law-making process of the European Union should be evident. It alone drafts legislative proposals. As the GSP litigation makes clear, the Commission can also prosecute when proper legislative procedures are not followed. Furthermore, in certain areas (notably agriculture and competition law), the Commission has been delegated by the Council the authority to issue implementing regulations and decisions that establish law. These acts detail administrative rules rather than

[29] *See* Commission v. Council, (1993) Eur.Comm.Rep. I–939 (Case C–155/91) (waste disposal directive properly based on Article 175 not 95); Germany v. Parliament and Council, (2000) Eur.Comm.Rep. I–8419 (tobacco advertising directive could not be based on Article 95).

[30] *See* Parliament v. Council, (1992) Eur.Comm.Rep. I–04193 (Case C–295/90) (student residence rights).

create new or broad policies. Thus, the Council establishes the "target prices" for agriculture, but the Commission issues thousands of regulations aimed at realizing these goals.

The Commission has also promulgated an important series of "group exemption" regulations under competition law.[31] These cover franchising, patent licensing, exclusive dealing and a variety of other business agreements. Lastly, the Commission is authorized by Article 106 TFEU to issue (on its own initiative) directives addressed to member states regarding public enterprises.[32] This authority avoids the usual Union legislative process. The Reform Treaty of 2009 added a citizen's initiative procedure. One million EU citizens from a significant number of member states may "invite" the Commission to submit proposals in areas of regional concern.

When exercising law-making powers conferred upon it by the Council, the Commission must first consult various committees. These requirements are known as the "comitology" rules of the Council.[33] These rules, in essence, allow the Council to actively monitor the Commission as a law maker. In most cases, they vest a power of reversal or modification in the Council.

The Commissioners and Their Tasks

Who and what is the European Commission? Under the Nice Treaty Enlargement Protocol, there were 27 Commissioners, one from each member state. The Reform Treaty reduced the number of Commissioners to two-thirds the number of member states starting in 2019. Commissioners are appointed by a qualified majority of the EU Council subject to Parliament's approval for five-year renewable terms. The President of the Commission is similarly appointed by the European Council and Parliament.

Great efforts taken to ensure the independence of Commissioners from their home governments. Article 245 stipulates that Commissioners must be chosen based on competence and their independence must be "beyond doubt." Any breach of this trust by Commissioners could lead to compulsory retirement, or since the Nice Treaty, dismissal by the President of the Commission.

Unlike the Ministers of the Council, Commissioners are not supposed to function as representatives of their nations. Over the years, in large measure, this has been true. Indeed, Prime Minister Thatcher once failed to renew a British Commissioner's appointment because he had "gone native." Sent over to Brussels in a stormy

---

31 *See* Chapter 7.

32 *See* Chapter 7.

33 Council Decision No. 87/373, Official Journal L197/33 (1987).

period when the Prime Minister was quite hostile to Union developments, this Commissioner proceeded to act independently, too independently as it turned out. His non-renewal, however, broke with a longstanding tradition of regular reappointments for competent Commissioners. Renewal decisions have thus become more politicized in recent years and Commissioners no doubt look over their shoulders towards home as their four-year terms begin to expire.

Policy Portfolios

Each Commissioner supervises one or more "Directorate-Generals" or departments of the Commission. These "portfolios" are determined by the President of the Commission. Each Directorate-General (DG) has a Director-General of a nationality different than that of its supervising Commissioner. Each DG has a specific allocation of administrative, legislative drafting and law enforcement duties. Each DG has a staff of highly paid Eurocrats selected in part to ensure national diversity. The staff regulations officially refer to a "geographical distribution" (quotas) of employees based upon the populations of the various member states. Acts performed by Commissioners and their staff in official capacity are immune from legal proceedings in national courts.[34] Union employees are also exempt from national income taxation, although they pay a nominal tax.[35]

The DGs correspond roughly to the main divisions of the treaties. Many consider that there are an excessive and inefficient number of governmental departments. And some DGs, like environment and external relations, are seriously understaffed while others (especially personnel and information) seem grossly overstaffed. The number of Directorates-General changes periodically as do their assignments. Ordinarily, these include Directorates for:

- External Relations
- Economic and Financial Affairs
- Industry
- Competition
- Employment and Social Affairs
- Agriculture

[34] Sayag v. Leduc, (1968) Eur.Comm.Rep. 395.

[35] Hamblet v. Belgium, (1960) Eur.Comm.Rep. 559 (official's salary cannot be used when calculating income of spouse).

- Transport
- Development
- Trade
- Information, Communication, Culture, Audiovisual
- Environment, Nuclear Safety and Civil Protection
- Science, Research and Development
- Telecommunications, Information Market and Exploitation of Research
- Fisheries
- Internal Market
- Regional Policies and Cohesion
- Energy
- Credit and Investment
- Budgets
- Financial Control
- Customs Union and Indirect Taxation
- Education Training and Youth
- Enterprise Policy, Distributive Trades, Tourism and Cooperatives
- Consumer Policy and Consumer Health

Each Commissioner also supervises a personal staff, known as a cabinet. Critics maintain that there has been excessive growth in the size and power of cabinets. These staff members have been known to override the advice of the various Directors-General and generally isolate their Commissioners from professional civil servant input. Defenders of these trends maintain that some of the DGs have been less than competent, and that the Commissioners need another, less bureaucratic perspective. The truth no doubt lies somewhere in between. Just as there are energetic and effective Commissioners, Directors-General and cabinets, none of these offices is immune from the deadwood syndrome.

Voting Procedures

The TFEU also establishes voting rules for the Commission. Simple majority votes prevail. As a matter of custom, considerable deference is usually given to the Commissioner in charge of a DG when legislative or other proposals are being reviewed by the Commission as a whole. This is sometimes achieved by circulating files with proposed actions which are implemented unless objections are shortly received. Individual Commissioners can be delegated authority to act for the body on routine matters. For example, when the Commissioner on Agriculture adopts new regulations, these are likely to involve such delegation.

Other Commission Tasks

The Commission performs numerous functions in addition to those concerning Community law-making. The most important of these include its prosecutorial powers against individuals and enterprises for breach of EU law, and against member states for failure to adhere to their treaty obligations.[36] The Commission also administers the EU budget and publishes a general and a series of specific annual reports (*e.g.*, on competition policy), all of which are a good way to survey Union affairs. The Commission negotiates the Union's international trade and other agreements.[37] However, the Commission's representative power in this field can be contested. In a judgment rendered in 1994, the Court of Justice determined that the antitrust agreement signed between the Commission and the United States government should have been concluded by the Council of Ministers.[38]

The agreement was challenged under Article 260 TFEU by France (with the support of Spain and The Netherlands). Article 260 gives the Council the competence to conclude international agreements. Following the Court's decision, the agreement needed to be approved by the Council which presented no difficulty since the substance of the agreement was never questioned. This case has emphasized the necessity to settle questions related to responsibilities within the EU, particularly considering concerns over the Commission's competence in GATT/WTO negotiations.[39]

§ 2.11 The Court of Justice as a Law Maker

United States students of law and attorneys are familiar (if not always comfortable) with the law-making role of American courts. This perspective is a product of the common-law tradition inherited from England made explicit by the teachings of American realists. Such awareness is less present in European legal communities for a variety of reasons. One important factor is the pre-dominance of the civil law tradition on the Continent. This tradition, with its heavy reliance upon abstract inductive (not deductive) reasoning, tends to

---

36 *See* Chapters 2 and 7.

37 *See* Chapter 6.

38 France v. Commission, (1994) Eur.Comm.Rep. I–03641 (Case C–327/91).

39 Opinion 1/94 (1994) Eur.Comm.Rep. I–5267 (WTO).

obscure rather than illuminate the way in which judges on the Continent do in fact make law.

Like their common-law counterparts, European judges must often fill in legislative gaps and arrive at conclusions based upon broadly worded legal language. Anyone who has ever read a civil law "Code" knows that it invites, indeed often requires, law-making by judges. Nevertheless the mystique that judges only apply the law, not create it, weighs heavily in the minds of many Europeans.

It is against this background that the law-making achievements of the European Court of Justice take on a truly remarkable significance. There are presently 27 justices on the Court, one from each member nation plus (traditionally when an odd number was required) a rotating justice. Thus, only two or perhaps three are trained in common law. All are prominent jurists who serve six-year terms by appointment of the member states acting in common accord. The Court was created by the Treaty of Paris in 1951 establishing the Coal and Steel Community. At that time neither Britain nor Ireland was a member. Its procedures and methods (but not its mentality) remain solidly based upon civil law, especially French law, traditions.[40]

The Court of Justice emerged in its earliest years as a powerful law maker. In part, this role was thrust upon it by the open-ended, constitutional language of the EEC Treaty. This is noticeably less true of the ECSC and EURATOM treaties. In part, also, the Court simply embraced the role, drawing power and influence to itself while constantly pushing Europe forward through its "integrationist jurisprudence." The supremacy doctrine[41] and the "doctrine of direct effect"[42] have been called the twin pillars of this jurisprudence. No less potentially significant are the rules of interpretation requiring national courts to construe their laws to facilitate Union policies and the general principles of law articulated by the Court. Escaping the jurisdiction of the Court of Justice played a role in Brexit.

§ 2.12 General Principles of Law—Fundamental Rights, EU Charter of Rights and Freedoms, European Human Rights Convention

The law-making role of the Court of Justice is evident when it recognizes general principles of law, a kind of common law of the Common Market. This is like what occurs when the Court finds the

---

40 *See* Chapter 3.

41 *See* § 2.13.

42 *See* Chapter 3.

general principles of tort liability common to the member states as required by Article 340 TFEU.[43] However, there is no other express Treaty authorization for the development by the Court of general principles of EU law. Article 19 TEU does oblige the ECJ and the Court of First Instance (renamed the General Court under the TFEU) to ensure that "the law" is observed when interpreting and applying the Treaty.

In different contexts, as part of "the law," the Court of Justice has recognized a right of legitimate expectation,[44] a right to be heard,[45] the duty to respect fundamental human rights,[46] a right to equality of treatment,[47] a duty to employ means that are proportional (not excessive) to the end sought (proportionality principle),[48] and a right against age discrimination.[49] It is important to note that the Court can and has declared legislation invalid if it fails to adhere to general principles of law. These principles, as articulated by the Court of Justice, are a *higher* source of law capable of overriding legal acts of the European Union.[50]

Other general principles of European Union law recognized by the Court of Justice include contractual certainty,[51] legal certainty,[52] effective judicial protection,[53] bans on double jeopardy and age discrimination,[54] property rights,[55] the right to engage in trade union activities,[56] and protection against arbitrary or disproportionate governmental intervention in private activities.[57] A limited attorney-

---

[43] *See* Chapter 3.

[44] Töpfer v. Commission, (1978) Eur.Comm.Rep. 1019.

[45] Transocean Marine Paint Association v. Commission, (1974) Eur.Comm.Rep. 1063.

[46] Rutuli v. Minister for the Interior, (1975) Eur.Comm.Rep. 1219.

[47] Louwage v. Commission, (1974) Eur.Comm.Rep. 81.

[48] Internationale Handelsgesellschaft mbH v. Einfuhr-und Vorratsstelle für Getreide und Futtermittel, (1970) Eur.Comm.Rep. 1125; Buitoni SA v. FORMA, (1979) Eur.Comm.Rep. 677; United Kingdom v. Council, (1996) Eur.Comm.Rep. I–5755.

[49] Werner Mangold v. Rüdiger Helm, (2005) Eur.Comm.Rep. I–9981 (Case C–144/04).

[50] *See* Regina v. Intervention Board, (1985) Eur.Comm.Rep. 2889 (principle of proportionality invalidates Community regulation).

[51] Brasserie de Haecht v. Wilkin-Janssen, (1973) Eur.Comm.Rep. 77.

[52] Openbaar Ministerie v. Bout, (1982) Eur.Comm.Rep. 381.

[53] Johnston v. Chief Constable, (1986) Eur.Comm.Rep. I–1651.

[54] Gözütok and Brügge, (2003) Eur.Comm.Rep. I–1345 (double jeopardy); Mangold v. Helm, (2005) Eur.Comm.Rep. I–9981 (age discrimination).

[55] Nold v. Commission, (1974) Eur.Comm.Rep. 491; Hauer v. Land Rheinland-Pfalz, (1979) Eur.Comm.Rep. 3727; Kadi v. Council and Commission, (2008) Eur.Comm.Rep. I–6351.

[56] Union Syndicale, Massa and Kortner v. Council, (1974) Eur.Comm.Rep. 917.

[57] *See* Roquette Frères SA and Directeur général de la concurrence, (2002) Eur.Comm.Rep. I–9011.

client privilege of confidentiality has been recognized by the Court of Justice as a general principle of law applicable to Union proceedings. This right, however, only applies to external EU-licensed counsel.[58] A limited doctor-patient right of confidentiality has also been acknowledged by the Court.[59]

Legal Certainty

A good example of the way in which ECJ-recognized general principles of law can permeate Union affairs is presented by the principle of legal certainty. This principle means that Union acts must be clear, precise and predictable to those subject to them.[60] Legal certainty has been invoked in connection with Union competition, agricultural, customs, and social security law to protect individuals and their rights. For example, social security notices to workers in other member states must be in a language the worker can understand.[61] In general, legal certainty bars the adoption of retroactive legislation.[62] And the Court's decisions can, in the name of legal certainty, apply only prospectively.[63] ECJ decisions otherwise are taken to represent what was always the correct law and thus retroactively date back to the creation of the law under consideration.[64]

Fundamental Rights Doctrine

The Court's decisions in the field of fundamental rights also draw upon the different constitutional traditions of the member states.[65] The Court, in this respect, does not see itself as merely replicating human rights found in common at the national levels. It is instead "inspired" by these traditions and the 1950 European Human Rights Convention (see § 1.01) to create of its own accord a European Union law of fundamental human rights and freedoms.[66] Such human rights are not absolute and public interest exceptions

---

58 AM & S v. Commission, (1982) Eur.Comm.Rep. 1575.

59 M v. Commission, (1980) Eur.Comm.Rep. 1797.

60 Ireland v. Commission, (1987) Eur.Comm.Rep. 5041; Administration des Douanes v. SA Gondrand Frères, (1981) Eur.Comm.Rep. 1931.

61 Re Farrauto, (1975) Eur.Comm.Rep. 157.

62 Re Racke, (1979) Eur.Comm.Rep. 69; Amylum v. Council, (1982) Eur.Comm.Rep. 3107.

63 Defrenne v. Sabena, (1976) Eur.Comm.Rep. 455; Blaizot v. University of Liege, (1988) Eur.Comm.Rep. 379.

64 Amministrazione delle Finanze v. Denkavit Italiana, (1980) Eur.Comm.Rep. 1205; Procureur de la République v. Waterkeyn, (1982) Eur.Comm.Rep. 4337.

65 Stauder v. City of Ulm, (1969) Eur.Comm.Rep. 419. This approach was codified in Article 6 of the Treaty on European Union.

66 Internationale Handelsgesellschaft mbH v. Einfuhr-und Vorratsstelle für Getreide und Futtermittel, (1970) Eur.Comm.Rep. 1125.

not disturbing "the substance" of those rights may be allowed.[67] The Reform Treaty of 2009 recognizes the constitutional traditions common to the member states and the European Convention on Human Rights as part of the general principles of EU law.

The TFEU is not completely devoid of human rights protections. Article 18 TFEU, for example, establishes the fundamental principle of non-discrimination on grounds of nationality, including corporate nationality. This principle has been frequently invoked in litigation, very often to set aside national rules embodying such discrimination.[68] Discrimination on grounds of nationality by private parties acting within the scope of the Treaty is also prohibited.[69] Furthermore, Article 18 applies to the Union and its institutions.[70] The principle of non-discrimination on grounds of nationality applies to covert activities.[71] Speaking generally, the Court of Justice has ruled that Article 18 requires comparable situations not to be treated differently and different situations not to be treated in the same way, unless such treatment is objectively justified (permissible differentiation).[72]

Other provisions of the TFEU also touch upon fundamental human rights. These include the right to challenge Council or Commission action taken in breach of essential procedural requirements[73] and equal pay for equal work.[74] In addition, Article 345 provides that the Treaty shall not prejudice the rules of the member states governing property ownership. However, this has not stopped the Commission and Council from extensively regulating agricultural land.[75] And the Court of Justice has significantly limited the exercise of intellectual property rights when they inhibit internal trade.[76]

The Lisbon Reform Treaty of 2009 added fundamental rights provisions to the TFEU that track some of the Court's jurisprudence. Article 10, for example, mandates combating discrimination based on

---

67 Nold v. Commission, (1974) Eur.Comm.Rep. 491.

68 *See* Patrick v. Ministre des Affaires Culturelles, (1977) Eur.Comm.Rep. 1199; Knoors v. Secretary of State for Economic Affairs, (1979) Eur.Comm.Rep. 399; Cowan v. Le Trésor Public, (1989) Eur.Comm.Rep. 195.

69 Walrave and Koch v. Association Union Cycliste Internationale, (1974) Eur.Comm.Rep. 1405.

70 Italy v. Commission, (1963) Eur.Comm.Rep. 165.

71 Sotgiu v. Deutsche Bundespost, (1974) Eur.Comm.Rep. 153.

72 Sermide v. Cassa Conguaglio Zucchero, (1984) Eur.Comm.Rep. 4209.

73 *See* Chapter 3.

74 *See* Chapter 5.

75 Hauer v. Land Rheinland-Pfalz, (1979) Eur.Comm.Rep. 3727 (planting of new wine grapes barred).

76 *See* Chapter 4.

sex, racial or ethnic origin, religion or belief, disability, age or sexual orientation. Animal rights are recognized in Article 13 as are rights under national law of churches and religions associations or communities (Article 17).

European Human Rights Convention

The Court of Justice has recognized the relevance and drawn upon the European Convention for the Protection of Human Rights and Fundamental Freedoms (1950). For example, the Court of Justice drew upon Article 10 of the European Convention as support for freedom of expression within Union broadcasting law,[77] and Article 6 for the right to a fair hearing.[78] This Convention has been ratified by every EU member state, along with others, such as Russia and Turkey. It is summarized in Section 1.0 of this book.

The Commission repeatedly proposed that the European Union accede to the Human Rights Convention, which finally was authorized under the Reform Treaty of 2009, but has yet to happen not the least because there are two "supreme" courts involved. Upon accession, the Union will be bound by the catalogue of human rights enumerated in the Convention. These include property, privacy, fair trial, equal treatment, religious, associational and trade or professional rights.[79] The European Court of Human Rights in Strasbourg normally decides such complaints.[80]

EU Charter of Fundamental Rights

In 2000, a Charter of Fundamental Rights was "proclaimed" (but not made legally binding) by the European Council. The Charter focuses on dignity, freedoms, equality, solidarity, citizens' rights and justice as its fundamental values. Its scope is far ranging: the death penalty is forbidden, as is "the reproductive cloning of human beings." Privacy rights, freedom of expression, "human dignity," the rights to work, health care and education, broad antidiscrimination rights (including against sexual orientation), the rights of children and the elderly, and the right to "cultural diversity" and "academic freedom" are recognized. Access to documents,[81] petitioning rights, personal data protection, legal aid,[82] a fair trial and criminal

---

77 Elliniki Radiophona Tiléorassi (ERT) AE v. Dimotiki Etairia Pliroforissis (DEP) + Anor, (1991) Eur.Comm.Rep. I–2925 Case (C–260/89).

78 Pecastaing, (1980) Eur.Comm.Rep. 691.

79 *See* Connolly v. Commission, (2001) Eur.Comm.Rep. I–1611 (freedom of expression recognized).

80 *See* Matthews v. United Kingdom, 28 Eur.Human Rights Rep. 361 (Feb. 18, 1999) (absence of elections to European Parliament in Gibraltar violates Convention).

81 *See* Article 15, TFEU and Regulation 1049/2001, O.J. L 145/43 (May 31, 2001).

82 *See* DEB Deutsche Energiehandels, (2010) Eur.Comm.Rep. (Case 279/09) (legal aid for companies).

procedure rights, and a general ban against "abuse of rights," are also enshrined.

The Charter's relationship to the European Human Rights Convention is intended to be consistent, allowing for the possibility of higher levels of protection.[83] Prior to 2009, many critics cited the inability of the ECJ to enforce the Charter as its principal flaw, although the Court of Justice did draw upon it in developing its general principles of human rights, significantly so in family reunification and property rights cases. The Reform Treaty renders the Charter binding EU law, indeed indicating it has "the same legal value" as the TFEU and TEU.

Poland, the UK and the Czech Republic obtained "opt-outs" from the Charter, which otherwise binds member states only when implementing EU law. The Commission has developed a Fundamental Rights checklist for evaluating legislative proposals. Unlike the Convention, however, the EU Charter does not create individual remedies for damages. See Section 1.0.

In 2011, the European Court of Justice broadly invalidated the widespread practice of charging men and women different rates for life, auto and health insurance.[84] The ECJ found such practices discriminatory in violation of the EU Charter of Fundamental Rights. The Charter prohibits sex discrimination and additionally states that "equality between men and women must be ensured in all areas." Member states had until Dec. 21, 2012, to conform their laws to this ruling. Premiums for men rose, for women they fell.

§ 2.13 Supremacy Doctrine

None of the European Union treaties addresses the question of what to do when national and Union laws are in conflict. There is no supremacy clause analogous to that found in the United States constitution and NAFTA/USMCA. The issue is critical to the success or failure of European Union law in all its manifestations; the founding treaties, directives, regulations, ECJ and GC decisions, international obligations, the general principles of Union law, etc. Its omission from the treaties was perhaps necessary to secure their passage through various national parliaments. But the issue did not disappear, it was merely left to the European Court to resolve.

---

[83] *See* Tietosoujavaltuutettu v. Satakunnan, (2010) Eur.Comm.Rep. (Case C–73/07) (balancing personal data privacy rights with free expression by media rights).

[84] Re Assn Belge des Consommateurs Test-Achats, (2011) Eur.Comm.Rep. (Case C–236/09).

In a very famous 1964 decision, the Court ruled that it simply had to be the case that Union law is supreme.[85] The Court reasoned that the whole of the Common Market edifice would be at risk if national laws at variance with regional law could be retained or enacted:

> The transfer by the states from their domestic legal systems to the Community [Union] legal system of the rights and obligations arising under the Treaty carries with it a permanent limitation of their sovereign rights, against which a subsequent unilateral act incompatible with the concept of the Community cannot prevail.

The Reform Treaty of 2009, via Declaration No. 17, confirms the supremacy of EU law when undertaken within its conferred powers.

Invalidity of National Laws

Under its supremacy doctrine, the European Court of Justice has (effectively speaking) invalidated countless national laws as in conflict with EU law. It is conceivable that such laws could retain validity in cases not involving a conflict, although this would be a rare event. Supremacy notwithstanding, one of the Declarations to the 1993 Maastricht Accord indicates that European Union does not prevent member states from maintaining or introducing more stringent law on working conditions, social policy, consumer protection and the environment, provided those laws are compatible with the TFEU. This Declaration is consistent with the relevant provisions of the Treaty on these subjects.

Repeal or amendment of conflicting national law is a duty of the member states that can be reviewed by the Court of Justice in further legal proceedings.[86] An alternative growing in use and encouraged by the European Court is creative judicial interpretation by national courts so as to incorporate Union law requirements and avoid conflicts.[87] For quite some time after *Costa v. ENEL,* and even somewhat today, national courts, legislatures and executive branches have resented the supremacy doctrine. They adhere, in the end, to this judge-made law because of their mutual interest in the success of the Union enterprise and their respect for the rule of law by its prestigious Court.

National Constitutional Rights and Supremacy

One especially sensitive point has been the conflict of national constitutional rights and EU law. Many Continental states have written constitutions, and some have specialized courts or tribunals

---

85 Costa v. ENEL, (1964) Eur.Comm.Rep. 585.

86 Commission v. France, (1981) Eur.Comm.Rep. 2299.

87 Von Colson and Kamann v. Land Nordrhein-Westfalen, (1984) Eur.Comm.Rep. 1891.

vested with exclusive powers of constitutional interpretation. Both Germany and Italy, for example, have such "constitutional courts." The Court of Justice has explicitly ruled that *every* national court or tribunal must apply EU law in its entirety so to set aside *any* conflicting provisions of national law. This duty arises out of European Union law.[88]

In France, implementation of this duty by its highest courts has been mixed. The Conseil d'Etat (but not the Cour de Cassation) initially refused to invalidate French law when in conflict with EU law because it (under French law) was not empowered to review the constitutionality of administrative acts. The Conseil d'Etat did not acknowledge EU law as a source of review power and duty.[89] But there are signs that the Conseil d'Etat has come in from the cold on supremacy and the direct effect of EU law.[90]

The German and Italian constitutional courts also initially refused to strike down inconsistent national law.[91] Indeed, the Bundesverfassungsgericht went so far as to review and find EU law deficient as against German constitutional protections for human rights. Both courts have retreated from their initial positions. Practically speaking, they have accepted the supremacy doctrine of the European Court and their duty to set aside contrary national law.[92]

In the human rights area, however, neither has fully given up its review powers as the controversial German Constitutional Court rulings regarding the Maastricht Treaty on European Union, the European Arrest Warrant, the Reform Treaty, EURO bailouts and Europe's regulation of trade in bananas (yes, bananas) make all too

---

[88] Nold v. Commission, (1974) Eur.Comm.Rep. 491; Amministrazione delle Finanze v. Simmenthal Spa, (1978) Eur.Comm.Rep. 629.

[89] Re Syndicat Général des Fabricants de Semoules de France, (1970) Common Mkt.L.Rep. 395 (Conseil d'Etat); Compare Administration de Douanes v. Société Café Jacques Vabre, (1975) Common Mkt.L.Rep. 367 (Cour de Cassation adheres to EU law supremacy).

[90] *See* Re Application of R. Nicolo, (1990) 1 Common Mkt.L.Rep. 173 (supremacy of EU law acknowledged when Conseil d'Etat functions as an electoral court); Re Maurice Boisdet, (1991) 1 Common Mkt.L.Rep. 3; Dame Perreux, No. 298348 (Oct. 30, 2009) (direct effect of EU directives recognized) (discussed by Mehdi in 48 Common Mkt. L. Rev. 439 (2011).

[91] *See* Frontini et al v. Ministero delle Finanze, (1974) 2 Common Mkt.L.Rep. 386; Solange I, (1974) 2 Common Mkt.L.Rep. 551.

[92] *See* Solange II, (1988) 25 Common Mkt.L.Rep. 201; Granital Spa v. Administrazione delle Finanze (1984) translated in 21 Common Mkt.L.Rev. 756. *But see* Wunsche Handelsgellschaft, (1987) 3 Common Mkt.L.Rep. 225 (suggesting German constitutional court will not review EU legislation against German human rights standards because of Community law developments in ECJ cases).

clear.[93] ECB bond buying ("quantitative easing") was ultimately challenged before the German Constitutional Court. In 2020, that court ruled against the ECB, asserting that its monetary rescue policies had failed to be "proportional". This ruling threatens to undermine the principle of supremacy of EU over national law.

In a case where Irish constitutional restraints on the advertising of the availability of abortion services in Britain were challenged as incompatible with the Treaty, there were signs within the Irish Supreme Court that supremacy might not prevail.[94] In Denmark any use of implied powers under Article 352 TFEU as the legal basis for regional acts is constitutionally suspect.

The collision and reconciliation of the European Court's supremacy doctrine with national constitutions illustrates an essential feature of the Union's legal system. The efficacy of the system depends heavily upon the willingness of national judges to acknowledge and adhere to EU law, to adhere to the European Court's interpretation of that law. This dependency has meant that the outer limits of the Court's authority and credibility are really to be found amongst the national judiciaries. On supremacy, the European Court has largely prevailed. Indeed, even in Britain where issues of supremacy are hypersensitive, the House of Lords has indicated:

> If the supremacy. . . of Community [Union] law over the national law of Member States was not always inherent in the EEC Treaty it was certainly well established in the jurisprudence of the European Court of Justice long before the United Kingdom joined the Community. . . . Under the terms of the [European Communities] Act of 1972 it has always been clear that it was the duty of a United Kingdom court, when delivering final judgment, to override any rule of national law found to be in conflict with any directly enforceable rule of Community law. . . . Thus there is nothing in any way novel in according supremacy to rules of Community law in those areas to which they apply. . .[95]

In other areas, notably the question of giving "direct effect" to EU directives,[96] the process of education and persuasion continues.

---

93 *See, e.g.,* Solange II, supra; Fragd Spa v. Amministrazione delle Finanze (1989) reported in Caja, 27 Common Mkt.L.Rev. 83.

94 *See* Society for the Protection of Unborn Children (Ireland) Ltd. v. Grogan, (1990) Common Mkt.L.Rep 689.

95 Regina v. Secretary of State for Transport (Factortame), (1991) 1 All Eng.Rep. 70 (Lord Bridge).

96 *See* Chapter 3.

§ 2.14 Single Market Legislation: 1992-Plus at a Glance

Article 115 TFEU empowers the Council of Ministers, acting on Commission proposals, to issue directives for the "approximation" (better known as "harmonization" or "coordination") of national laws directly affecting the establishment or operation of the Common Market. Such directives must be adopted unanimously within the Council. Since a vast number of national laws affect the Common Market, the potential scope of Article 94 is very broad.

This scope, over the years since 1957, was not fully exploited principally because of the unanimous Council voting requirement. Indeed, by 1986 with a Union of twelve nations, innovative legislation under Article 115 became quite difficult to obtain. That is why one major thrust of the 1987 Single European Act was the inclusion of Article 114 TFEU. It specified qualified majority voting (see Section 2.5) in the Council of Ministers for much of the single market legislative agenda. Qualified majority voting procedures also apply to directives used to harmonize national laws (*e.g.*, subsidies) distorting the conditions of competition in the Common Market.

Harmonization of national laws of concern to the Common Market is critical to advancing European Union integration. Harmonization can, for example, remove many of the barriers to free movement, including those expressly permitted by Article 36 and the *Cassis* and *Keck* line of cases. See Chapter 4. It can do the same for the public security exceptions to the free movement of workers and the self-employed, as well as to the freedom to provide services across borders, discussed in Chapter 4 as well. Harmonization is critical to removal of the tax and NTB frontiers within the Union which were a central focus of the campaign for a Europe without internal frontiers. See Chapter 5. In addition, harmonization can reach out to areas not specifically treated in the Treaty, but which are of consequence to the functioning of the Common Market. A good example is government procurement law covered in Section 5.4.

By 1992, the European Union had implemented 282 regulations and directives to create a Single Internal Market. Many of these laws address nontariff trade barriers. In addition, during the remainder of the decade, the EU adopted several hundred additional laws related to market integration that were not formally part of the 1992 program. The listing below is a representative sampling of the scope of European Union legislation undertaken to create a common market.

Simple pressure vessels

Toys

Construction products

Machine safety

Agricultural & forestry tractors

Cosmetics

Quick frozen foods

Flavorings

Food emulsifiers

Food preservatives

Jams

Fruit juices

Food inspection

Definition of spirited beverages & aromatized wines

Coffee extracts & chicory extracts

Food additives

Materials & articles in contact with food

Tower cranes (noise)

Household appliances (noise)

Tire pressure gauges

Hydraulic diggers (noise)

Detergents

Lawn mowers (noise)

Radio interferences

Automobiles, trucks, and motorcycles and their emissions

Liquid fertilizers & secondary fertilizers

Weighing instruments

Gas appliances

Personal protection equipment

Global Approach to Testing & Certification

Infant formula

Mutual Recognition of Tests

New rules for harmonizing packing, labeling and processing requirements

Ingredients for food & beverages

Irradiation

Nutritional labeling

Classification, packaging, & labeling of dangerous preparations

Extraction solvents

Harmonization of regulations for the health industry (including marketing)

Medical specialties

High technology medicines

Veterinary medicinal products

Active implantable medical devices

Pharmaceuticals

Medical devices

In-vitro diagnostics

Changes in government procurement regulations

Coordination of procedures on the award of public works & supply contracts

Extension of E.C. law to telecommunications, utilities, transport; services

Harmonization of regulation of services

Mutual funds

Broadcasting

Tourism

Air transport

Electronic payment cards

Information services

Life & nonlife insurance

Banking

Securities

Maritime transport

Road passenger transport

- Road haulage
- Railways

Liberalization of capital movements

- Long-term capital, stocks
- Short-term capital

Consumer protection regulations

- Misleading definitions of products
- Indication of prices
- Liability of defective products
- Consumer Protection Policy
- Consumers Consultative Council
- General product safety

Harmonization of taxation

- Value added taxes
- Excise taxes on alcohol, tobacco, and other

Harmonization of laws regulating company behavior

- Trademarks
- Accounting operations across borders
- Protection of computer programs
- Transaction taxes
- Company law
- Mergers & acquisitions
- Copyrights
- Cross border mergers
- Bankruptcy

Harmonization of veterinary & phytosanitary controls

- Antibiotic residues
- Bovine animals and meat
- Porcine animals and meat
- Plant health
- Fish & fish products
- Live poultry, poultry meat and hatching eggs

Pesticide residues in fruit & vegetables

Pesticide residues in animal origin products

Elimination and simplification of national transit documents and procedures for intra-EU trade

Introduction of the Single Administrative Document (SAD)

Abolition of customs presentation charges

Elimination of customs formalities & the introduction of common border posts

Harmonization of rules pertaining to the free movement of labor and the professions within the EU

Mutual recognition of higher educational diplomas

Comparability of vocational training qualifications

Specific training in general medical practice

Training of engineers

Activities in the field of pharmacy

Activities related to commercial agents

Income taxation provisions

Elimination of burdensome requirements related to residence permits

Autos

Speed limitation devices

External projections of rear panel

Masses and dimensions

Field of vision of motor vehicles

Rear view mirrors of motor vehicles

Braking devices

Engine power of motor vehicles

Roadworthiness

Side guards

Indicator lamps

Light and light signaling

Type approval for sound levels

Headlamps

Marker lamps

Rear fog lamps

Safety belts and restraint systems

Tires

Spray suppression devices

Safety glazing of autos

Health and Safety/Social Charter

Banning of certain chemical agents from workers

Safety and health of workers

Minimum safety & health at the workplace: physical plant design

Work equipment used at the workplace

Right of residence

Worker protection from risks to exposure of carcinogens

Handling heavy loads/risk of back injury

Worker protection from risks to exposure to biological agents

Worker protection from risks to exposure to asbestos

Employer obligation to inform employees of conditions for contracts or employment relationship

Social Security Schemes

Workers with fixed-duration or temporary employment relationship

Safety signs at work

Exposure to noise at work

Right of residence for EC workers not yet or no longer employed

Charter of Fundamental Social Rights

Organization of working time

Protection at work of pregnant women who have given birth

Operational protection of outside workers

Safety and health at temporary or mobile work sites

Mobility improvement of workers

Safety and health workers in extraction industries

Protection of workers from radioactive waste

Freedom of movement of workers

European Agency for Safety and Health at Work

Employee participation and enterprise

Energy

Transit of electricity through grids

Natural gas through grids

Promotion of energy efficiency (SAVE Program)

Efficiency of hot-water boilers with liquid or gaseous fuels

Sulfur content of gasoil

Environment

PCB's

Asbestos

Shipments of hazardous waste

Pollution caused by waste from titanium oxide

Limitation of sulfur dioxide and particulates

Genetically modified organisms

Freedom of information on the environment

Waste

Lead content of petrol

Urban waste-water treatment

Substances that deplete the ozone layer

Civil liability for damage caused by waste

Substances discharged into the aquatic environment

European Environment Monitoring and Information Network

Control of the environmental risks of existing substances

Eco-labeling

Pollution caused by nitrates in the waters

Waste landfills

Packaging and packaging waste

Telecommunications

Legal protection of micro circuits

Type approval of terminal equipment

Introduction of ISDN

Standardization on information technology and telecommunications

Competition in telecom terminal equipment

Information Services Market

Information technology and telecom in health care

Telecom services with open network provisions

Visual display units

Competition for telecommunications services

Trans-European Networks

Radio paging equipment/frequency bands

Computer programs

Digital European cordless telecommunications

Development of a common market on telecom services

Green paper for telecom services and equipment

Development of an audiovisual industry

Personal data and information security

Public digital telecommunications networks

Open network provision to leased lines

Frequency bands of digital short-range

Satellite broadcasting and cable transmission

International telephone access codes in the EC

Computer reservation services

Chapter 3

LITIGATING EUROPEAN UNION LAW

Table of Sections

§ 3.0 Introduction

There has been an explosive growth in litigation of European Union law. The bulk of this growth has taken place in private litigation before national courts and tribunals. For example, contracts disputes can raise a host of Union law questions. Is an exclusive dealing distribution contract enforceable as a matter of competition law? Can goods to which a sales contract applies be freely traded inside the Common Market? Is payment for sales across borders protected by EU law? Does an employment contract fail to provide equal pay for equal work? Can employees be terminated because of their nationality? May patent licensing agreements contain grant-back clauses? Can franchisees be limited to certain geographic markets? What joint ventures can be established for research and development purposes?

Administrative decisions present another fertile field of European law litigation. When can customs officers seize goods in transit between member states? When can they collect money in such situations? When can immigration authorities keep workers from other member states out? When can they deport them? When can professional licensing boards deny the applications of citizens of Union nations? Can national authorities deny EU nationals the right to establish a restaurant? Can they require residency or work permits? What about the families of all these persons? What about pensions, social security, health insurance and other job-related benefits for resident EU workers? These listings only scratch the surface of EU law administrative litigation in national courts and tribunals.

National courts and tribunals are vested with wide (but not final) authority to resolve EU legal issues. That authority rests with the European Court of Justice and its associated General Court, supreme arbiters of the vast body of EU law, hearing upwards of 600 cases a year. The British, in their BREXIT negotiations, made it clear that escaping the jurisdiction of the EU Courts was a primary goal. See Chapter 8.

The explosion in EU law litigation must be qualified. Not all areas of European Union law fall within the jurisdiction of the European Court of Justice (ECJ) and its judicial doctrine. For example, to the extent that the nations involved rely upon intergovernmental conventions to reach their goals, these agreements do not follow the typical litigation patterns described below. Such conventions will have their own dispute settlement mechanisms unless they specifically convey jurisdiction to the ECJ. The "Brussels Convention" on jurisdiction and enforcement of civil and commercial judgments (see Section 3.12) made such a conveyance.

Moreover, commencing with the 1987 Single European Act amendments, certain areas of European Union activity have been deliberately undertaken outside the normal legislative and litigation frameworks of the Union. At this point, only EU foreign and security policy matters, including defense, fall outside the litigation system analyzed in this chapter.

§ 3.1 Direct Effects Doctrine

The right to commence litigation in national forums must be given to the plaintiff by national law. In other words, European Union law has not (as yet) been interpreted to create national causes of action.[1] What it does do, according to the "direct effects doctrine," is give litigants the right to raise many issues ("Euro-defenses" and "Euro-offenses") in national courts and tribunals. In doing so, individuals often function as guardians of the founding treaties. When challenging member state governments, private parties rely on the "vertical direct effect" of EU law. When asserting rights against other private parties, the "horizontal direct effect" of EU law applies. Americans might analogize this role to that of "private attorneys general," a law enforcement technique adopted in several United States statutes. The Court of Justice has noted that the vigilance of private litigants enforcing their rights is an important element in the Union's legal system.[2]

The direct effects ("l'effet utile") doctrine is, to a very large degree, a product of the jurisprudence of the European Court of Justice. It can apply to EU treaties, directives, regulations, decisions and international agreements. When any of these measures are of direct effect, this impact generally commences from the date of its entry into force.[3] But the direct effects doctrine is not automatically applied. For example, although the General Agreement on Tariffs and Trade (GATT) is binding upon the Union and its member states, it has typically been construed by the Court not to have direct legal effects.[4] Likewise, WTO agreements are unlikely to have direct effect.[5] Both the Council of Ministers and the European Council tend to issue resolutions or declarations when there is a political consensus but no desire to adopt legislation. For the most part, the Court of Justice has held such acts incapable of creating direct legal effects in the member states.[6]

Regulations

The legal effects of regulations are the easiest to understand. Article 288 TFEU provides that regulations are "directly applicable

---

1 *See* Wöhrmann v. Commission, (1962) Eur.Comm.Rep. 501 (Plea of illegality does not amount to an independent cause of action).

2 Van Gend en Loos v. Nederlandse Administratie der Belastingen, (1963) Eur.Comm.Rep. 1.

3 Amministrazione delle Finanze v. Salumi, (1980) Eur.Comm.Rep. 1237.

4 *See* International Fruit Company v. Produktschap voor Groenten en Fruit, (1972) Eur.Comm.Rep. 1219; FEDIOL v. Commission, (1989) Eur.Comm.Rep. 1781 (Case 70/87); Germany v. Council, (1994) Eur.Comm.Rep. I–4973 (bananas). *Compare* Bresciani v. Amministrazione della Finanze, (1976) Eur.Comm.Rep. 129 (Yaoundé Convention trade agreements directly effective and thus override conflicting national law); Hauptzollamt Mainz v. Kupferberg, (1982) Eur.Comm.Rep. 3641 (EC-Portugal Free Trade Agreement has direct effect).

5 Portuguese Republic v. Council, (1998) Eur.Comm.Rep. I–7379. *See* Schieving-Nijstad Vof v. Groeneveld, (2001) Eur.Comm.Rep. I–5851.

6 Pubblico Ministero v. Manghera, (1976) Eur.Comm.Rep. 91; Schülter v. Hauptzollamt Lörrach, (1973) Eur.Comm.Rep. 1135.

in all member states." In other words, regulations have immediate, unconditional legal effect without any need for national implementation. They are law in the member states from the moment of issuance, binding upon all individuals, business organizations and governments.[7] For litigants, when regulations are applicable, they control the outcome. This is true under the supremacy doctrine even in the face of contrary national law.[8]

Directives

Directives are more difficult to understand. Article 288 does *not* specify that they shall have "direct applicability." In part, their design prohibits this. Directives are addressed to member states, instructing them to implement (in whatever way is required) certain Union policies within a fixed timetable. These policies do not become law in the member states until implemented or, if timely implementation does not follow, until the European Court rules that the directive is of "direct effect." Some national courts, notably in France, have opposed this judge-made doctrine.[9]

Not all directives have direct effect. The Court of Justice has selectively ruled that only those directives that establish clear and unconditional legal norms and do not leave normative discretion to the member states are of direct effect.[10] Most "framework" (action plan) directives will not meet these criteria. Once the ECJ has decided that a European Union directive has direct effect, litigants can rely on it to the full extent of its application to member states, public service entities,[11] and local governments.[12] Litigants can challenge contrary national law, including defective implementing measures if required, and can challenge criminal laws.[13]

---

[7] *See, e.g.,* Politi SAS v. Ministry of Finance of the Italian Republic, (1971) Eur.Comm.Rep. 1039; Fratelli Zerbone SNC v. Amministrazione delle Finanze, (1978) Eur.Comm.Rep. 99.

[8] *See* Chapter 2. *See especially* Variola v. Amministrazione delle Finanze dello Stato, (1973) Eur.Comm.Rep. 981 (no member state legislation necessary or permissible after EU regulation).

[9] *See especially* In re Cohn-Bendit, (1978) 1979 Common Mkt.L.Rep. 702 (French Conseil d'Etat); German Federal Tax Court (Bundesfinanzhof) V.B. 51/80 (July 16, 1980), *reversed on appeal* In re Application of Frau Kloppenburg, (1988) 3 Comm.Mkt.L.Rep. 1 (Fed.Constit.Ct.1987).

[10] Van Duyn v. Home Office, (1974) Eur.Comm.Rep. 1337; Becker v. Finanzamt Münster-Innenstadt, (1982) Eur.Comm.Rep. 53.

[11] Foster v. British Gas, (1990) 1 Eur.Comm.Rep. 3313.

[12] Fratelli Costanzo v. Milano, (1989) Eur.Comm.Rep. 1839.

[13] Pubblico Ministero v. Ratti, (1979) Eur.Comm.Rep. 1629; Criminal Proceedings against Bordessa, (1995) Eur.Comm.Rep. I–361.

Interpretative Duties

Unlike regulations, directives cannot be used to challenge private activities. Thus it is said that directives do not have "horizontal" direct effects.[14] Even so, the Court of Justice has held that in applying national law the national courts and tribunals are required by Article 4(3) TEU to interpret their law in light of the wording and purposes of all EU directives.[15] National law must be interpreted in the light of regional directives even if the directive has not yet been implemented.[16] Some commentators have characterized these duties as involving the "indirect effect" of directives.

The obligation to interpret national law in view of EU directives "is limited by the general principles of law which form part of Union law and in particular the principles of legal certainty and non-retroactivity."[17] Even so, in considerable private litigation before the tribunals and courts of member states, directives will be given effect through judicial interpretations of national law. This is likely to have the same practical impact as would adoption of a "horizontal" direct effects doctrine at the regional level.

Moreover, it has been argued that Article 4(3) TEU mandates that *all* provisions of national law (not just those touched by Union directives) must be interpreted in conformity with all European Union law (not just directives).[18] If this argument becomes binding law, the doctrine of direct effects will reach a zenith which few would have ever dreamed.

§ 3.2 Directly Effective Treaty Provisions

The third major category of directly effective law originates in the founding treaties. The Court of Justice has ruled that parts of these treaties can have immediate, binding legal effect in the member states. Here again the Court has been selective, sorting out which

---

14 Marshall v. Southampton and South West Hampshire Area Health Authority (teaching), (1993) Eur.Comm.Rep. I–4367 (Case C–271/91). Faccini Dori v. RECREB SRL, (1994) Eur.Comm.Rep. I–3325 (consumer contract rights denied because of state failure to timely implement directive).

15 *See* Von Colson and Kamann v. Land Nordrhein-Westfalen, (1984) Eur.Comm.Rep. 1891; Oberkreisdirektor des Kreises Borken v. Moormann, (1988) Eur.Comm.Rep. 4869; Lister v. Forth Dry Dock Engineering Co., 1 All Eng.Rep. 1194 (House of Lords, 1989) (*Von Colson* principles followed in employee rights case).

16 Marleasing SA v. La Comercial Internacional de Alimentación SA, (1990) 1 Eur.Comm.Rep. 4135 (*Compare* Duke v. GEC Reliance, 1 All Eng.Rep. 626 (House of Lords, 1988) (*Von Colson* principles not followed in equal treatment case)).

17 Case 80/86, Officier van Justitie v. Kolpinghuis Nijmegen, (1987) Eur.Comm.Rep. 3969.

18 *See* Barber v. Guardian Royal Exchange Assurance Group, (1990) 1 Eur.Comm.Rep. 1889 (Advocate General's Opinion). *See also* Grimaldi v. Fonds des Maladies Professionnelles, (1990) Eur.Comm.Rep. I–04407 (Case 322/88) (EU Recommendations have indirect effect).

treaty provisions establish clear, unconditional and nondiscretionary legal norms. Those many articles of the treaties that are largely aspirational, procedural or written as guidelines for the exercise of member state discretion are unlikely to have direct effect.[19]

The Court of Justice has consistently refused to view the treaties as merely creating obligations among the contracting states. Citing Article 267 TFEU, the Court finds acknowledgment that the TFEU was intended to have effect in national legal regimes:

> The conclusion to be drawn . . . is that the Community [Union] constitutes a new legal order of international law for the benefit of which the States have limited their sovereign rights, albeit within limited fields, and the subjects of which comprise not only Member States but also their nationals. Independently of the legislation of Member States, Community law therefore not only imposes obligations on individuals but is also intended to confer upon them rights which become part of their legal heritage. These rights arise not only where they are expressly granted by the Treaty, but also by reason of obligations which the Treaty imposes in a clearly defined way upon individuals as well as upon the Member States and the institutions of the Community.[20]

Once the Court has held a TFEU term directly effective in the member states, litigants before national courts and tribunals can rely fully upon it. They can, under the supremacy doctrine, use it to set aside contradictory national law. Like regulations, directly effective Treaty provisions can apply horizontally to private parties.[21] This follows, in the court's view, because national courts are an arm of the states that signed the Treaty and therefore bound to apply the law in all cases. The same logic has not been carried over to directives.[22]

Directly Effective Treaty Provisions

The following is a partial list of the articles of the TFEU that have been held directly effective by the European Court of Justice. Many of these decisions are qualified.

Article 18	—	no discrimination on grounds of nationality
Articles 28–29	—	customs union free trade rules

[19] *See* Spa Salgoil v. Italian Ministry for Foreign Trade, (1968) Eur.Comm.Rep. 453 (Articles 33(1) and (2) discretionary and not directly effective).

[20] Van Gend en Loos v. Nederlandse Administratie der Belastingen, (1963) Eur.Comm.Rep. 1.

[21] Defrenne v. Sabena, (1976) Eur.Comm.Rep. 455.

[22] Marshall v. Southampton and South West Hampshire Area Health Authority (teaching), (1993) Eur.Comm.Rep. I–4367 (Case C–271/91).

Article 30	—	no internal customs duties or measures of equivalent effect
Article 34	—	no internal trade quotas or measures of equivalent effect
Article 36	—	no disguised restraints on internal trade
Article 37	—	state trading monopolies cannot discriminate between nationals
Article 45	—	free movement and employment of workers without nationality discriminations
Article 49	—	right of establishment for self-employed
Article 55	—	no discrimination on capital participation in companies
Article 56(1)	—	freedom to provide services across borders
Article 57(3)	—	national treatment of cross-border service providers
Articles 63–65	—	current payments and capital transfers
Articles 92, 95, 96	—	transport discriminations prohibited
Articles 101, 106	—	competition law prohibitions
Articles 107(1), 108(3)	—	state subsidies cannot distort competition without Commission approval
Article 110	—	national treatment on taxation of goods
Article 111	—	no excessive tax rebates upon exports
Article 157	—	equal pay for equal work, equal treatment

The following treaty provisions have generally been held *not* to have direct legal effect. Again, many of these ECJ decisions are qualified.

Article 4(3), TEU	—	member state obligations to facilitate and not jeopardize Treaty
Article 108	—	state subsidies
Article 117	—	harmonization of laws
Article 130	—	balance of payments

§ 3.3 National Legal Remedies for Directly Effective Law

Directly effective European Union law creates national legal rights and obligations. What remedies can be secured in national courts and tribunals when European law has these effects? The TFEU does not provide a ready answer. In general, the Court of Justice has held that directly effective rights must be enforceable in the national courts by means of remedies that are real, effective and non-discriminatory.[23] Interim or preliminary judicial and administrative remedies may be required to protect directly effective rights when national *or* Union law is challenged.[24]

The precise determination of those remedies is a matter for the national courts to decide. For example, one British court issued a notable interim order requiring public authorities to promise to pay damages if that country's Sunday trading bans ultimately were found invalid under Union law as the "price" for interlocutory injunctions sought by the authorities against Sunday traders.[25] In another British case, the House of Lords referred equal treatment remedial issues concerning a ceiling on recovery of damages and denial of interest to the Court of Justice. The Court ruled against both limitations as inadequate to restore equality of treatment.

In Britain, the Court of Appeal ruled that a failure on the part of the government to adhere to TFEU obligations does *not* give rise to an action for damages even when directly effective rights are involved.[26] This litigation was commenced by French turkey producers who lost sales when Britain imposed import restraints, allegedly for animal health reasons. The Court of Justice had

[23] Rewe Zentralfinanz v. Landwirtschaftskammer Saarland, (1976) Eur.Comm.Rep. 1989; Amministrazione delle Finanze v. San Giorgio, (1983) Eur.Comm.Rep. 3595; Marshall v. Southampton and South West Hampshire Area Health Authority (teaching), (1993) Eur.Comm.Rep. I–4367 (Case C–271/91).

[24] Regina v. Secretary of State for Transport, (1990) Eur.Comm.Rep. I–02433 (Case C–213/89); Zuckerfabrik Süderdithmarschen v. Hauptzollamt Itzehoe, (1991) Eur.Comm.Rep. I–415 (Cases 143/88 and C–92/89).

[25] Kirklees BC v. Wickes Building Supplies, 4 All Eng.Rep. 240 (Court of Appeal, 1991). *See* Torfaen Borough Council v. B & Q PLC Ltd., (1989) Eur.Comm.Rep. 3851.

[26] Bourgoin SA v. Ministry of Agriculture, Fisheries and Food, (1985) 3 All Eng.Rep. 585, (1986) 1 Common Mkt.L.Rep. 267.

previously ruled that the restraints were unlawful under Article 31 as measures of equivalent effect to quotas. The British restraints were not subject to the animal health exception created by Article 30 because they were economically motivated, *i.e.*, they were disguised restraints on internal free trade. The plaintiffs in *Bourgoin* apparently could have obtained injunctive relief had Britain continued to impose its restrictions after the European Court's decision.[27]

There was some question whether *Bourgoin* meets the general criteria of the Court of Justice for real, effective and nondiscriminatory national legal remedies when directly effective EU rights are at stake. The case was settled before reaching the House of Lords by payment to Bourgoin of 3.5 million Pounds Sterling for damages, costs and interest by the UK government. Similar remedial issues have been litigated in Britain concerning directly effective European Union competition law.[28] In contrast, the French Conseil d'Etat has awarded damages against the French government for harm caused by a breach of Union law.[29] Dutch law also permits such recoveries,[30] as does Spanish law.[31]

Member State Liability for Damages

In a major decision, *Francovich*, the Court of Justice has ruled that member state liability for damages to individuals caused by the state's infringement of Union law is inherent in the scheme of the TFEU.[32] This obligation follows from member state duties under Article 4(3) TEU to ensure fulfillment of EU law. The case involved an Italian failure to implement a directly effective EU directive on employee benefits in the event of insolvency. Whether or not the unimplemented directive is of direct effect does not matter, and faulty implementation or retention of contrary domestic law also gives rise to state liability whenever three conditions are met: (1) the law infringed is intended to confer individual rights; (2) the infringement is sufficiently serious; and (3) there is a direct causal link between the breach and damages sustained.[33]

---

27 Commission v. United Kingdom, (1982) Eur.Comm.Rep. 2793. *Accord,* Regina v. Secretary of State for Transport, (1990) 3 Common Mkt.L.Rep. 375 (House of Lords).

28 Articles 101 and 102., *See* Chapter 7.

29 Ministre du Commerce Extérieur v. Alivar (March 23, 1984).

30 Roussel Laboratories (Hague District Court, July 18, 1984).

31 *See* Canal Satélite Digital, Case 1/46/1999 (Spanish Tribunal Supremo, June 12, 2003).

32 Francovich + Ors v. Italian Republic, (1991) Eur.Comm.Rep. I–5357 (Cases C–6 and C–9/90).

33 Brasserie du Pecheur SA v. Germany, joined Cases C–46, 48/93 (1996) Eur.Comm.Rep. I–1029.

Member state liability for damages generally tracks Community tort liability under Article 340[34] and extends to administrative as well as legislative acts and omissions.[35] In a second major decision, *Kobler*, the Court of Justice has indicated that it is possible for individuals to sue member states for damages when *national courts* exceptionally breach EU law.[36] The Commission has also challenged member state judicial interpretations that run contrary to EU law.[37]

In the absence of precise European Union rules on remedies for directly effective legal rights, the results vary from country to country and context to context. Many cases involve the question of repayment of custom duties, customs charges and taxes paid to governments under national laws that are invalidated by Union law. Others concern national laws implementing EU law which is subsequently invalidated by the Court of Justice.[38] The Court has reiterated in these decisions that the means of recovery for monies unlawfully paid to governments are controlled by national law. Thus, statutes of limitations,[39] the forum, interest on the amounts paid and related issues are national legal questions.

The Court has also reiterated that procedural hurdles which discriminate against recoveries based upon EU rights when measured against procedures for similar domestic recoveries do not satisfy the requirements of the TFEU.[40] And, in general, national rules on recovery of unlawful payments to governments cannot have the practical result of making it impossible to recover such sums.[41]

§ 3.4 Article 267—Referrals by National Courts and Preliminary Rulings

The European Court of Justice derived its doctrine of directly effective law partly from Article 267 TFEU. This article is the

---

34 *See* Section 3.10.

35 R. v. Ministry of Agriculture, Fisheries and Food (Hedley Lomas), (1996) Eur.Comm.Rep. I–2553.

36 Köbler v. Austrian Republic, (2003) Eur.Comm.Rep. I–00000 (Case C–224/01).

37 Commission v. Italy, (2003) Eur.Comm.Rep. I–8003.

38 Deville v. Administration des Impôts, (1988) Eur.Comm.Rep. 3513. *See* Marshall v. Southhampton and South West Hampshire Area Health Authority (teaching), (1993) Eur.Comm.Rep. I–4367 (Case C–271/91) (equal treatment remedies).

39 *But see* Emmott v. Minister for Social Welfare, (1991) Eur.Comm.Rep. 4269 (national statutes of limitations do not run until member state has fulfilled Directive duties).

40 Express Dairy Foods Ltd. v. Intervention Board for Agricultural Produce, (1980) Eur.Comm.Rep. 1887.

41 *Compare* Re Jules Borker, (1980) Eur.Comm.Rep. 1975 (Bar Council of Cour de Paris not a tribunal preliminary ruling request rejected); with Broekmeulen v. Huisgarts Registratie Commissie, (1981) Eur.Comm.Rep. 2311 (Dutch Appeals Committee for General Medicine is a tribunal of the state; request accepted).

linchpin that joins the national legal systems of the member states to the European Court.

Article 267 vests jurisdiction in the European Court to give "preliminary rulings" (sometimes called "advisory rulings") on the interpretation of the Treaty, the validity and interpretation of acts by the Union's institutions and other matters. These rulings occur when national courts or tribunals (faced with an issue of Union law) request them. Professional bodies may or may not constitute "tribunals of a member state" for these purposes.[42] Since the Treaty of Nice (2003), the ECJ has the power to allow some Article 267 cases to go to the General Court (formerly Court of First Instance). Article 267 proceedings commonly last about 18 months. However, since 2008, highly expedited proceedings are possible regarding police and judicial cooperation in criminal matters, and freedom, security and justice cases.[43]

Discretionary References

Article 267 requests or "references" are discretionary with the judges of the lower-level courts and tribunals of the member states. They cannot be initiated as a matter of right by litigants, nor by arbitrators designated by contract to resolve a dispute when those arbitrators are not functioning as a court or tribunal of a member state.[44] This is a particularly notable decision because ever increasing numbers of business disputes are being taken to binding arbitration. The only recourse for review of an arbitrator's interpretation of Union law is through ancillary or enforcement proceedings in the national courts.

Whenever a national court considers a reference necessary to enable judgment, it may seek the advice of the European Court by posing questions to it. It may do so even when the European Court or a higher national court has already ruled on the question of EU law at hand. In other words, the common law doctrine of binding precedent does not remove the discretion of lower courts to invoke Article 267.[45] Similarly, the fact that appeals are mandatory under

---

42 Nordsee v. Reederei Mond, (1982) Eur.Comm.Rep. 1095 (German arbitration court reference rejected). *See* Corbiau v. Administration des Contributions, (1993) Eur.Comm.Rep. I–1277 (Case C–24/92) (Luxembourg Director of Taxes cannot refer questions under Article 234).

43 Decision 2008/79, OJ L24/42.

44 Nordsee v. Reederei Mond, (1982) Eur.Comm.Rep. 1095 (German arbitration court reference rejected). *See* Corbiau v. Administration des Contributions, (1993) Eur.Comm.Rep. I–1277 (Case C–24/92) (Luxembourg Director of Taxes cannot refer questions under Article 234).

45 Rheinmühlen-Düsseldorf v. Einfuhr-und Vorratsstelle für Getreide und Futtermittel, (1974) Eur.Comm.Rep. 33. *But see* to the contrary Duke v. GEC Reliance Systems Ltd., (1987) 2 Common Mkt.L.Rep. 24 (English Court of Appeal).

national law does not block utilization of Article 267 references to the ECJ if the lower court believes such a reference is necessary to enable it to give judgment.[46]

In practice, lower courts refer EU law issues to the ECJ quite regularly. However, these referral decisions may be subject to an interlocutory appeal within the national legal system.[47] Such an appeal will not ordinarily require the ECJ to suspend its review of and decision on the reference.[48] But if the appeal of the referral has the effect under national law of suspending the referral decision, then the Court of Justice will suspend its Article 267 proceeding.[49] Thus, in most cases, the national interlocutory appeal of the referral decision, and the ECJ's Article 267 proceeding, will move forward simultaneously. Should the decision to refer be reversed on appeal, the Court of Justice will terminate its proceeding and not rule under Article 267.[50]

Assuming the request comes from a proper national court or tribunal, the European Court of Justice cannot refuse the reference, even when it has already ruled on the EU legal issue.[51] Once underway, the Commission almost always files a written brief expressing its opinion in Article 267 proceedings. The government of the member state whose court or tribunal is the source of the reference typically does so as well. Private parties "interested" in the questions being referred may not intervene.[52] After a preliminary ruling of the European Court is secured, the national court is obliged to implement that ruling in its final judgment.[53] The ruling is also binding on appeal of that judgment, and (at a minimum) persuasive in courts of other nations.[54]

---

[46] Mecanarte-Metalurgica da Lagoa Lda v. Chefe do Servico da Conferencia final da Alfandega do Porto, (1991) Eur.Comm.Rep. I–3277 (Case C–348/89).

[47] Rheinmühlen-Düsseldorf v. Einfuhr-und Vorratsstelle für Getreide und Futtermittel, (1974) Eur.Comm.Rep. 33. *But see* Campus Oil Ltd. v. Minister for Industry and Energy, (1984) Eur.Comm.Rep. 2727(Article 234 references not subject to interlocutory appeal under Irish law).

[48] *Id.*

[49] SA Chanel v. Cepeha Handels Maatschappij NV, (1970) Eur.Comm.Rep. 404.

[50] Rheinmühlen, supra.

[51] Re Da Costa en Schaake, (1963) Eur.Comm.Rep. 11.

[52] Biogen Inc. v. Smithkline Beecham Biological S.A., (1996) Eur.Comm.Rep. I–717.

[53] Rewe Zentralfinanz v. Landwirtschaftskammer Saarland, (1976) Eur.Comm.Rep. 1989.

[54] International Chemical Corp. v. Amministrazione delle Finanze, (1983) Eur.Comm.Rep. 119; SpA Int'l Chemical Corp. v. Amministrazione delle Finanze dello Stato, (1981) Eur.Comm.Rep. 1191.

Validity of EU and National Laws

The discretion of national courts to refer EU law questions to the European Court is largely removed whenever the question is one of the *invalidity* (not interpretation) of Union law. Such invalidity is ordinarily retrospective, nullifying EU law *ab initio.*[55] The Court of Justice has ruled that only it and not the national courts can determine the invalidity of an EU legal measure. The Court reasoned that divergent invalidity determinations could place the unity of the Union's legal order in jeopardy and detract from the general principle of legal certainty. However, national courts can declare EU legislation valid and proceed accordingly.[56]

There is a dispute as to whether the European Court can pronounce without request upon the effects of an invalid Union measure, *e.g.*, whether monies paid previously can be recovered. The Court asserts the power to spell out the consequences of its invalidity rulings under Article 267 TFEU.[57] It draws upon the analogy to Article 264 which conveys to the ECJ the power to determine the effects of decisions made in the context of Article 263 challenges to Council, Commission, Parliamentary or other EU action.[58]

The highest French courts are split as to the duty to follow the Court's Article 267 rulings on the consequences of invalid Union law. The Cour de Cassation adheres, while the Conseil d'Etat rejects. The Conseil d'Etat limits adherence to ECJ rulings to the scope of the questions posed by the national courts. The Court's rulings on repayment in *Roquette* were treated as gratuitous and not controlling since not requested.[59] This dispute illustrates, more generally, the distinct tendency on the part of the European Court not to see itself confined by the limits of the questions posed by national forums under Article 267. Rarely, however, has such a hostile national response been received upon delivery of the ruling.

On questions of the validity of *national* laws under the EU legal regime, the lower courts retain complete discretion to use the Article 267 reference procedure, or to immediately set aside national laws under the supremacy doctrine.[60] Genuine disputes as to the compatibility of the national law of another member state may be referred to the European Court under Article 267. The Court will

[55] Roquette Frères SA v. Hauptzollamt Geldern, (1994) Eur.Comm.Rep. I–01445 (Case C–228/92). *See* Firma Foto-Frost v. Hauptzollamt Lübeck-Ost, (1987) Eur.Comm.Rep. 4199.

[56] *Id.*

[57] Roquette v. French Customs, (1980) Eur.Comm.Rep. 2917.

[58] *See* § 3.7.

[59] Conseil d'Etat (1985) Rec. des Décisions 233.

[60] *See* § 2.12.

provide criteria for interpreting Union law to enable the referring court to solve the legal problem it faces. For example, in one decision on reference from a German court, by implication the European Court suggested that an Italian law conflicted with Directive 76/768 on cosmetics.[61]

Nevertheless, the Court's preliminary ruling jurisdiction cannot be invoked through "sham litigation" where there is no genuine dispute before the national court, only a desire to challenge the validity of national law.[62] Purely hypothetical questions, and questions the ECJ believes are not connected to the underlying dispute, will not be answered by Court when responding under Article 267.[63] The Court of Justice has also begun to reject Article 267 references that fail to provide adequate factual and legal information to enable it to respond.

Mandatory References

In the early years, lower courts and tribunals in the member states hesitated to invoke the preliminary ruling procedure of Article 267. In some cases, this was a matter of ignorance, in others a matter of national pride. Over the years, Article 267 references of EU law issues have risen dramatically. Today, they amount to about half of the Court's caseload. Article 267 references are undertaken not only out of need for advice, but also because of a growing sense of judicial cooperation in the Union. Absent such cooperation, there is a great risk that different interpretations of European law would proliferate among member state forums.

For the lower courts, Article 267 references are discretionary. For courts of last resort (no appeal as a matter of right), Article 267 *requires* a reference to the European Court except in interlocutory proceedings.[64] This requirement ensures that the European Court will have the last and supreme word on EU legal issues. Thus, if a litigant is willing to exhaust his or her national judicial remedies, access to the European Court is supposed to be guaranteed. In many instances, this is exactly what happens. In others, the doctrine of "*acte clair*" has been invoked so as to avoid mandatory Article 267 references.

---

[61] Kommanditgesellschaft Eau de Cologne et al. v. Provide SRI, (1989) Eur.Comm.Rep. 3891.

[62] Foglia v. Novello, (1980) Eur.Comm.Rep. 745; (1981) Eur.Comm.Rep. 3045.

[63] *See* Wienand Meilicke v. ADV/ORGA F.A. Meyer AG, (1992) Eur.Comm.Rep. I–04871 (Case C–83/91); Manuel José Lourenço Dıaz v. Director da Alfânndega do Porto, (1992) Eur.Comm.Rep. I–04673 (Case C–343/90); Re der Weduwe, (2002) Eur.Comm.Rep. I–11319 (Case C–153/00).

[64] Hoffmann-La Roche v. Centrafarm, (1977) Eur.Comm.Rep. 957.

§ 3.5 *Acte Clair*

"*Acte clair*" originates in the French law. It posits that appeals need not be taken whenever the law and result in the case at hand are clear. Appeals in such circumstances are wasteful of judicial and litigant time and energy. The problem in the European Union context, of course, is that differences of opinion as to the clarity of EU law will often exist. Indeed, since the Court of Justice has on occasion reversed itself,[65] one could argue that absolute clarity in EU Law never exists. If abused by national courts of last resort, *acte clair* could break rather than occasionally remove the linchpin of Article 267.

Entreprises Garoche Case

The *Entreprises Garoche* case provides a good example of French invocation of *acte clair* so as to totally avoid an Article 267 reference. A Dutch boat builder entered into a three-year exclusive dealing agreement with a French agent concerning France, Belgium, Switzerland, Monaco, and Corsica. The Dutch builder undertook to refrain from selling in these territories directly or indirectly through agents. Shortly thereafter he sold two boats through an Italian dealer to two customers domiciled in Monaco. The French agent sued for breach of the exclusive dealing contract. The Tribunal de Commerce de Paris awarded him damages.

The Cour d'Appel de Paris and then the Cour de Cassation held that the contract was void under Article 101 TFEU and not subject (for lack of notification to the Commission) to individual exemption under Article 101(3). Furthermore, the contract was outside the protection afforded by group exemption Regulation 67/67 because the isolation of national markets from other distributors resulted in high prices being charged by the French agent and hence did not allow consumers "a fair share of the resulting benefit." The principle of the illegality under Article 101(1) of absolute territorial protection clauses prevailed.[66] Moreover, the direct effect of EU competition law in the French courts was not in doubt. The Dutch builder could rely on it as a matter of right.

None of these three French courts found it necessary to refer any of the issues in *Entreprises Garoche* to the European Court of Justice. Both the Tribunal de Commerce and the Cour d'Appel invoked the *acte clair* doctrine while noting that their decisions were subject to appeal and hence not mandatorily referable. The Cour de Cassation,

[65] *See* In re Keck and Mithouard, Joined Cases C–267, 268/91, 1993 Eur.Comm.Rep. I–6097 and Metock v. Minister for Justice, Equality Law Reform, (2008) Eur.Comm.Rep. I–6241 (Case C–127/08).

[66] *See* Chapter 7.

from which no appeal lies under the French legal system, agreed that the dispute was fundamentally centered on an interpretation of Article 3 of Regulation 67/67. That Regulation was clear to the highest French court considering a 1971 European Court of Justice opinion. Consequently a "fresh interpretation" by way of reference in 1973 to the European Court was not required.[67] Although it is difficult to criticize the actual results of the *Garoche* case in the French courts, their application of *acte clair* illustrates how dependent European Union law is on national courts and national legal principles.

CILFIT Case

Despite an initial annoyance at French invocations of *acte clair*,[68] courts in other member states soon became converts. By 1982, when the European Court ruled definitively on the validity of this practice, it was faced with widespread but not particularly abusive utilization of *acte clair*. In *CILFIT,* the Italian Corte Suprema di Cassazione made a mandatory referral of the *acte clair* issue to the European Court. That is to say, the question it posed to the European Court was whether it was absolutely obliged to refer all issues of interpretation of EU law to the Court. The European Court deferentially incorporated *acte clair* into Union law as a gloss on the otherwise straightforward language of Article 267. In doing so, however, it was able to spell out the terms and conditions for its invocation:

> The correct application of Community [Union] law may be so obvious as to leave no scope for any reasonable doubt as to the manner in which the question raised is to be resolved. Before it comes to the conclusion that such is the case, the national court or tribunal must be convinced that the matter is equally obvious to the courts of the other Member States and to the Court of Justice. Only if those conditions are satisfied may the national court or tribunal refrain from submitting the question to the Court of Justice and take upon itself the responsibility for resolving it. . . .
>
> It must be borne in mind that Community legislation is drafted in several languages and that the different language versions are all equally authentic. An interpretation of a provision of Community law thus involves a comparison of the different language versions. . . . Even where the different language versions are entirely in accord with one another, Community law uses terminology which is peculiar to it. Furthermore, it must be emphasized that legal concepts do not necessarily have the same

[67] Entreprises Garoche v. Société Striker Boats, (1973) 1974 Common Mkt.L.Rep. 469.

[68] *See especially* Re Société des Pétroles Shell-Barre, (1964) Common Mkt.L.Rep. 462 (Conseil d'Etat).

meaning in Community law and in the law of the various Member States.[69]

§ 3.6 Multiple Official Languages

In *CILFIT*, the European Court issues a reminder of the problems of language in interpreting European Union law. The Coal and Steel Treaty sought to avoid these problems by making French the only official language of that treaty.[70] There are over 20 official EU languages. Each working language can be consulted on questions of interpretation. However, with Treaty terms (such as Article 267) it is important to remember that English was *not* an official language prior to 1973 when the British and Irish joined. Thus, with reference to older legal documents *and* the EEC Treaty of Rome (now TFEU), French, German, Dutch or Italian versions are arguably more authoritative. The French version is considered the most authoritative of all because the Treaty of Rome was originally drafted in French.

At a minimum, reference to different versions will promote greater understanding of European law. Attorneys practicing EU law routinely consult different language versions of European regulations, directives, decisions and treaties. North American attorneys should note that British and Irish legal English does not always correspond to American or Canadian legal language. Even when the words are the same, the concepts and doctrine may differ.

The European Court of Justice, when confronted with linguistic difficulties, has stressed the need to reconcile different official texts without giving preference to any one language.[71] Difficulties of this kind are minimized in the foreign policy arena (which operates outside the TFEU)[72] by using only English and French in the European Council. To the same effect, in Court of Justice or General Court proceedings, the plaintiff generally gets to choose the official *language of the case* unless the defendant is from or is a member state (in which case the language of that member state prevails). When Article 267 proceedings are involved, the language of the nation whose court or tribunal is making the reference is official. The official language of the case is used in pleadings, documents and oral hearings.

The Court's decision will be published in all working Union languages but only the language of the case is authentic. By custom, French is the internal working language of the Court of Justice. This

---

69 CILFIT v. Ministro della Santa, (1982) Eur.Comm.Rep. 3415.

70 Article 100 of the Treaty of Paris.

71 Regina v. Bouchereau, (1977) Eur.Comm.Rep. 425.

72 *See* Chapter 1.

means that judgments are debated and drafted in French. All other versions are translations, even when French is not the language of the case. Parliament, the Commission and the Court in public session, on the other hand, are a veritable babble of languages with simultaneous translations occurring. There are over 200 different possible pairs of official languages.

§ 3.7 Articles 263 and 265—Challenging Regional Institutions

In *CILFIT,* the Court of Justice also warned against the transferability of legal concepts within the Union. Article 263 TFEU provides a good example of these kinds of problems.

Article 263 gives the Court the power to review the legality of acts of the Council of Ministers, Commission, European Central Bank, acts jointly undertaken by the Parliament and Council, and acts of Parliament intended to produce legal effects on third parties. In unusual circumstances, individual acts of Parliament may also be challenged.[73] Acts which are merely preparatory, such as the commencement of a competition law investigation by the Commission, cannot be challenged.[74] To be challengeable, the "legal interests" of those under investigation must have been affected.[75] Member states, the Commission or Council, and directly concerned individuals may challenge regulations, directives or enforcement decisions on specified grounds.

Prior to the Maastricht Treaty on European Union, Parliament had no express authority to challenge Council or Commission action under Article 263. Now it and the European Central Bank may make such challenges for the purpose of protecting their prerogatives. No challenges may be brought against Council or Commission recommendations or opinions, but "soft" legal instruments (communications, instructions) that impose legal burdens or obligations can be challenged.

Challenging Acts

There are four grounds for challenging (often called "appealing") acts of Union institutions. These are specified in Article 263 and originate in French administrative law governing "action en recours pour excès de pouvoir." The same grounds apply to challenges under Article 265 TFEU, which concern failures to act as required by the Treaty ("action en carence"). The four grounds are:

---

73 Les Verts v. Parliament, (1986) Eur.Comm.Rep. 1339.

74 IBM Corp. v. Commission, (1981) Eur.Comm.Rep. 2639.

75 *Id.*

(1) Lack of competence (*i.e., ultra vires,* or lack of jurisdiction or authority to act);[76]

(2) Infringement of an essential procedure ("administrative due process");[77]

(3) Infringement of the TFEU or any related rule of law (including general principles of EU law[78] and international law); and

(4) Misuse of powers.

Each of these grounds for challenging acts or failures to act has been extensively and uniquely developed in the jurisprudence of the European Court. For example, the term "misuse of powers" in Article 263 originated in the French administrative law concept of *détournement de pouvoir.* Research on and an understanding of French administrative law thus becomes important to Article 263.[79]

Misuse of powers is a term of art in British administrative law which is narrower than the U.S. concept of abuse of administrative discretion. The original French concept is generally limited to situations of "subjective wrong" as when public institutions or personnel use their powers for personal benefit, such as to favor a relative or for financial gain. The concept of *détournement de pouvoir* does not transfer easily from French into British or United States law and language. Moreover, as *CILFIT* suggests, the Court of Justice is entirely free to develop its own doctrine in this area independent of its French origins.[80]

Article 263 TFEU litigation must be brought within two months of the publication of the act that is being challenged or its notification to the appellant (in the absence of notice, two months from the day when that person had knowledge of it), as the case may be. Article 264 authorizes the Court to declare acts of Union institutions null and void if the appeal is well founded. This explains why Article 263 litigation is sometimes referred to as "actions for annulment." Regulations may be partially or fully annulled, or retain validity

---

76 *See* the discussion of "legal bases" for legislative acts in Section 2.9.

77 Article 296. *See, e.g.,* Transocean Marine Paint Assn. v. Commission, (1974) Eur.Comm.Rep. 1063; Germany v. Commission, (1963) Eur.Comm.Rep. 63.

78 *See, e.g.,* Bela-Mühle Josef Bergmann v. Grows-Farm GmbH, (1977) Eur.Comm.Rep. 1211 (principle of equal treatment voids agricultural regulation). The general principles of Community law are discussed in Section 2.12.

79 *See* ASSIDER v. High Authority, (1954–56) Eur.Comm.Rep. 63 (Advocate-General's opinion).

80 *See* Guiffrida v. Council, (1976) Eur.Comm.Rep. 1395 (sham competition for EC job is misuse of power).

until replaced, at the Court's discretion.[81] Article 263 cannot be used to challenge the validity of national legislation.[82]

Challenging Failures to Act

Challenges for failure to act under Article 265 TFEU can only be brought if the relevant EU institution has first been called upon to act, and only if it fails to "define its position" within two months thereafter. This definition is not necessarily an act that can itself be challenged under Article 263.[83] The challenge for failure to act may then be brought in two additional months provided the institution's duty to act was owed to the plaintiff.[84] If an Article 265 challenge is well founded, Article 266 in essence authorizes the Court to order action by the institution. In both Article 263 and 265 litigation, Article 264 imposes a duty on the EU institution, as appropriate, to "take the necessary measures to comply with the judgment of the Court of Justice."

§ 3.8 Articles 263 and 265—Challenging EU Institutions, Pleas of Illegality

Standing Issues

One limitation on Article 263 actions before the Court concerns the appeal rights of natural and legal persons. Such persons may only challenge decisions addressed to them, or regulations or decisions addressed to others which are of "direct and individual concern" to them. The Court for the most part narrowly construed the concept of "directly concerned individuals" so as to effectively limit the number of private challenges capable of being raised under Articles 263.[85] However, in the competition law area where private interests are at stake when individual exemptions are issued by the Commission,[86] the Court was more liberal in its allowance of challenges by concerned third parties.[87] Jurisdiction to hear competition law

---

81 Article 264(2); Commission v. Council, (1989) Eur.Comm.Rep. 259.

82 Oleificio Borelli v. Commission, (1992) Eur.Comm.Rep. I–06313 (Case C–97/91).

83 GEMA v. Commission, (1979) Eur.Comm.Rep. 3173.

84 Lord Bethell v. Commission, (1982) Eur.Comm.Rep. 2277.

85 *See, e.g.,* Commission v. Jégo-Quéré & Cie SA, (2004) Eur.Comm.Rep. I–2365; Union de Pequenos Agricultores v. Council, (2002) Eur.Comm.Rep. I–06677 (Case C–50/00); France v. Comafrica SpA and Dole, (1999) Eur.Comm.Rep. I–185; Confédération Nationale des Producteurs de Fruits et Legumes, (1962) Eur.Comm.Rep. 471; Calpak SpA v. Commission, (1980) Eur.Comm.Rep. 1949; Union Deutsche Lebensmittelwerke v. Commission, (1987) Eur.Comm.Rep. 2265. *But see* Les Verts v. Parliament, (1986) Eur.Comm.Rep. 1339 (political group has standing to challenge electoral budget decision).

86 *See* Chapter 7.

87 Metro SB-Grossmärkte GmbH & Co. KG v. Commission, (1977) Eur.Comm.Rep. 1875 (complainant allowed to challenge).

challenges by private parties to Commission actions in the competition field has been transferred since 1989 to the European General Court.

The selectively liberal approach to Article 263 standing was also followed regarding Commission decisions on antidumping duties, internal state aids, countervailable subsidies applicable to Union imports, and illicit commercial practices of non-member nations.[88] The Reform Treaty of 2009 eased the conditions for individuals to obtain Article 263 relief. The requirement of "individual concern" is dropped. It is sufficient that individuals are directly affected by EU decisions or acts, and no implementing measures are involved.

The four grounds for appeal found in Article 263 are repeated in Article 265 which governs the failure of an EU institution to undertake actions required by the TFEU or other Union law. Actions by individuals and enterprises challenge the failure to address an act to the appellant. They cannot be used to compel discretionary Commission acts, such as Article 258 prosecutions of member states or competition law prosecutions of anticompetitive practices.[89]

Pleas of Illegality

The expiration of the two-month period for challenges to acts under Article 263 is not a firm statute of limitations. Article 277 allows any party to a proceeding where a regulation is in issue to plead the grounds for challenge specified in Article 263 to claim its inapplicability before the Court of Justice. This means, as a practical matter, that European Union regulations can be challenged at any time by what is called a "plea of illegality." Moreover, the European Court has extended this plea to directives, decisions and other acts of the Union institutions.[90] Private parties may thus wait until the implementation of Union law is of immediate concern to them without losing an ability to test the legality of that law.

Pleas of illegality are frequently made in EU torts and contracts litigation, and can be made before national courts and tribunals

---

[88] Philip Morris Holland BV v. Commission, (1980) Eur.Comm.Rep. 2671 (prospective recipient of state aid may challenge denial of authorization by Commission); COFAZ SA v. Commission, (1986) Eur.Comm.Rep. 391 (complainant allowed to challenge aid authorization by Commission); Allied Corp. v. Commission, (1984) Eur.Comm.Rep. 1005 (named exporters may challenge imposition of dumping duties); Timex Corp. v. Council and Commission, (1985) Eur.Comm.Rep. 849 (complainant may challenge antidumping decisions); FEDIOL v. Commission, (1983) Eur.Comm.Rep. 2913 (complainant may challenge countervailing duties decision); FEDIOL v. Commission, (1989) Eur.Comm.Rep. 1781 (Case 70/87) (complainant may challenge illicit commercial practices decision).

[89] Alfons Lütticke GmbH v. Commission, (1966) Eur.Comm.Rep. 19; Lord Bethell v. Commission, (1982) Eur.Comm.Rep. 2277.

[90] Simmenthal v. Commission, (1977) Eur.Comm.Rep. 777.

which must refer such issues to the Court of Justice or General Court.[91] Pleas of illegality are not allowed if the complainant had standing to challenge the act of the Union under Article 263 but failed to do so in a timely manner.[92] Under this approach, it is unclear whether member states can plea illegality since they always have Article 263 standing.[93]

Institutional Litigation

Articles 263 and 265 have spawned an interesting series of institutional litigations. In these cases, the Council, Commission and Parliament end up suing each before the European Court of Justice. These suits reflect the struggle for power and influence among these institutions. One major limitation upon them had been the absence of a general authority for Parliamentary suits under Article 263 against Council or Commission acts.[94] Prior to the Treaty of Nice of 2003, such suits could only be filed only when Parliamentary legislative prerogatives were at stake.[95] The Nice Treaty removed that limitation.

The Parliament is authorized by the TFEU to file Article 265 suits when the Council or Commission has failed to act. The Parliament successfully sued the Council over its failure to act in accordance with Treaty obligations to implement a Common Transport Policy.[96] The Council in turn has successfully sued Parliament for excessive budgetary allocations.[97] The Commission has challenged the Council frequently before the European Court. Sometimes several institutions gang up on one. For example, the Commission (with Council and Parliamentary support) successfully challenged the European Central Bank's creation of an independent anti-fraud unit.[98] Some of its most important victories concern the proper "legal basis" for Union legislation and international agreements.[99]

Articles 263 and 265 also provide the member states with the means to challenge the Commission. This is the reverse of the type of

---

[91] Universität Hamburg v. HZA Hamburg-Kehrwieder, (1983) Eur.Comm.Rep. 2771; Foto Frost v. HZA Lubeck Ost, (1987) Eur.Comm.Rep. 4199.

[92] Simmenthal v. Commission, (1977) Eur.Comm.Rep. 777.

[93] *See* Italy v. Commission, (1966) Eur.Comm.Rep. 389; Commission v. Belgium, (1978) Eur.Comm.Rep. 1881.

[94] European Parliament v. Council, (1988) Eur.Comm.Rep. 5615 (Comitology).

[95] European Parliament v. Council, (1990) Eur.Comm.Rep. 2041 (Chernobyl). Article 173, Treaty of Rome as amended by TEU.

[96] European Parliament v. Council, (1985) Eur.Comm.Rep. 1513.

[97] Council v. European Parliament, (1986) Eur.Comm.Rep. 288.

[98] Commission v. European Central Bank, (2003) Eur.Comm.Rep. I–1651.

[99] Commission v. Council, (1989) Eur.Comm.Rep. 1493 (GSP preferences); (1971) Eur.Comm.Rep. 263 (the *ERTA* decision).

litigation that flows from Article 258 prosecutions of member states by the Commission.[100] Member state challenges of legislative acts by the Council seem likely to rise as more qualified majority voting occurs, and the minority seeks legal redress.[101] Article 269 TFEU allows member states to challenge the legality on serious infringement of human rights grounds of European Council and Council of Ministers acts.

§ 3.9 Article 258—Commission Prosecutions of Member States

Article 258 authorizes the Commission (alone) to bring an action before the Court of Justice against member states that have failed to fulfill their obligations under the TFEU. This authority is reinforced by some basic normative rules. In Article 4(3) TEU, the member states undertake to adopt "all appropriate measures" to ensure the fulfillment of obligations arising out of the founding treaties or resulting from action taken by the institutions of the Union. They "shall facilitate" achievement of its tasks and "shall abstain" from jeopardizing its objectives. These fundamental principles have frequently been the subject of litigation as the Commission seeks to enforce member state duties under European law.

Although it has not yet done so, it appears that the Commission could prosecute a member state *court* for failure to fulfill its treaty obligations (*e.g.,* mandatory Article 267 references). Government passivity in the face of private conduct (angry French farmer blockades) creating obstacles to internal trade has been successfully prosecuted.[102] Informal promises to comply with EU regulations can be prosecuted, in this case repeatedly over decades against France.[103]

The Commission's prosecutorial powers under Article 258 must be distinguished from its ability in selected other circumstances to "directly" file actions against member states before the Court of Justice. Such direct actions do not involve the lengthy procedures described below in connection with Article 258 prosecutions. The Commission is authorized to sue the member states "directly" when

---

100 *See, e.g.,* Germany v. Commission, (1987) Eur.Comm.Rep. 3203 (lack of competence to act); Ireland v. Commission, (1987) Eur.Comm.Rep. 5041 (violation of EU law); Netherlands v. Commission, (1971) Eur.Comm.Rep. 639 (failure to act). The Council can likewise be challenged by the member states under Articles 230 and 232. *See* United Kingdom v. Council, (1988) Eur.Comm.Rep. 855 (infringement of essential procedural requirement).

101 *See* Chapter 2.

102 *See* Commission v France, (1997) Eur.Comm.Rep. I–6959. *See* Regulation 2679/98.

103 Commission v. France, (1974) Eur.Comm.Rep. 359; Commission v. France, (1996) Eur.Comm.Rep. I–1307 (French merchant seaman).

they infringe Union rules on government subsidies to enterprises.[104] This can also be done when the member states "improperly" invoke Article 36 exceptions to single market legislation adopted by qualified majority voting in the Council of Ministers.[105]

Procedures and Penalties

Prior to commencing any Article 258 prosecutions before the Court of Justice, the Commission first delivers notice, and the member state may submit a reply. Hundreds of such infringement notices are issued annually. The next stage involves issuance by the Commission of a reasoned opinion setting time limits for compliance. These time limits must be reasonable.[106] The member state can submit a reply if it wishes. The burden of proof shifts to the Commission when a member state claims to have conformed to the opinion within the stipulated time limits.[107] Negotiations may ensue at any time, and settlements frequently result. Almost 80 percent of all formal proceedings under Article 258 are settled.

If no settlement is reached, the Commission commences suit before the Court of Justice. Compliance after this point does not moot or remove the suit.[108] The most common type of Article 258 enforcement action filed with the Court of Justice concerns member state failures to implement directives. Constitutional, political or legal problems are unacceptable excuses for such failures.[109] Nor is the failure of other member states to implement the directive.[110] All Article 258 prosecutions are discretionary with the Commission and cannot be forced by individual complaints.[111]

Article 258 specifically requires member states to take the measures necessary to remedy failures identified by the Court in Article 258 proceedings. Prior to 1993, there were no obvious means by which the Court could enforce its judgments under Article 258 against member states. This contrasted with the power of the Court and the Commission in some areas of Union law to levy fines and penalties against individuals and corporations. Such fines and penalties can be collected in judgments enforced in the national

---

[104] *See* Chapter 5.

[105] *See* Chapter 4.

[106] Commission v. Belgium, (1988) Eur.Comm.Rep. 305.

[107] Commission v. Italy, (1973) Eur.Comm.Rep. 101; Commission v. Italy, (1987) 3 Common Mkt.L.Rep. 483.

[108] Commission v. Italy, (1988) 2 Common Mkt.L.Rep. 951.

[109] Commission v. Italy, (1979) Eur.Comm.Rep. 771; Commission v. Belgium, (1980) Eur.Comm.Rep. 1473 (Type approval directives).

[110] Commission v. France, (1979) Eur.Comm.Rep. 2729; Commission v. Blanguernon, (1990) Eur.Comm.Rep. I–00083 (Case C–38/89).

[111] Alfons Lütticke GmbH v. Commission, (1966) Eur.Comm.Rep. 19.

courts.[112] To compel a member state to follow Union law, the Commission had little alternative but to bring yet another enforcement proceeding for determination before the Court. It has actually done this on occasion.[113]

However, the Maastricht Treaty on European Union authorized the ECJ to levy fines and daily penalties against member states that do not take the measures necessary to remedy their Treaty failures.[114] Private litigants may also remedy member state failures, functioning in effect as attorneys general of Union law.[115]

The unwillingness of member states to carry out Court rulings under Article 258 is a problem. It could test the very fabric of the TFEU. The Commission has commenced thousands of infringement proceedings against member states and won over 90% of the time. An additional enforcement option would be to allow the Court to authorize the withholding of EU subsidies and benefits from nonconforming states. Sanctions of this kind were possible under the Coal and Steel Treaty by joint Commission and Council action.[116]

Article 273 allows member states to submit (by special agreement) disputes concerning the TFEU to the European Court. In Article 344, the member states have agreed not to submit such disputes to any method of settlement other than those of the Treaty. Article 259 authorizes member states to prosecute each other before the European Court for failure to fulfill Treaty obligations. For diplomatic and institutional reasons, these options are almost never pursued.[117] The preferred approach is to persuasively complain to the Commission and then allow it to commence an Article 258 prosecution. Article 259 supports this approach by mandating a cooling-off period of three months during which the Commission considers the arguments of both member states and issues a reasoned opinion.

---

112 Article 299, TFEU.

113 Commission v. Italy, (1972) Eur.Comm.Rep. 527; Commission v. France, (1979) Eur.Comm.Rep. 2729; Commission v. Italy, (1993) Eur.Comm.Rep. I–00191 (Case C–101/91).

114 *See* Commission v. Greece, (2000) Eur.Comm.Rep. I–5047 (rubbish tip II); Commission v. France, (1991) Eur.Comm.Rep. I–2727 (daily penalties, fisheries) confirmed case C–304/02 (July 12, 2005). In 2009, France was ordered by the ECJ to pay a 10 million EURO fine for failure to timely implement GMO directive 2001/118. Commission v. France, (2008) Eur.Comm.Rep. I–9159.

115 *See* Minister for Fisheries v. Schoenenberg, (1978) Eur.Comm.Rep. 473 (Irish law invalid); Meijer v. Department of Trade, (1979) Eur.Comm.Rep. 1387 (British law invalid).

116 *See* Article 88 of ECSC Treaty of Paris.

117 *But see* Ireland v. France (1977) Case 58/77 (withdrawn); France v. United Kingdom, (1979) Eur.Comm.Rep. 2923 (fisheries dispute).

§ 3.10 Contract and Tort Litigation—General Court (Formerly Court of First Instance)

Article 47 TEU provides that the European Union is a legal person. As such, it can sue and be sued like most corporations or governments. These disputes can involve employees of the Union, parties with whom it has contracted and those who are victims of its negligence or other tortious behavior.

The TFEU conveys exclusive jurisdiction to the Court of Justice over employment and non-contractual liability disputes.[118] It also can function as an arbitrator pursuant to dispute settlement clauses of contracts.[119] Contract disputes involving the Union may otherwise be entertained in the national courts.[120] The contractual liability is governed by the law applicable to the contract in question.[121]

General Court (Formerly Court of First Instance)

Much of the work of the Court of Justice in employment and non-contractual liability litigation is now handled by the European Court of First Instance (CFI), renamed the General Court (GC) under the Reform Treaty of 2009. This court was authorized by 1987 Single European Act amendments. The CFI/GC has been "attached" to the European Court of Justice. Its general jurisdiction now extends to most EU litigation, including since the Treaty of Nice, preliminary rulings as authorized. However, the Court cannot hear Article 258 prosecutions of member states by the Commission, nor Article 263 or 265 challenges to EU institutional acts or failures to act when these are initiated by member states or Union institutions. It can hear such challenges and related "pleas of illegality" when they are privately initiated, for example, in the business competition law area.[122]

In 1993, the Council extended the jurisdiction of the GC to all direct actions brought by natural or legal persons except antidumping cases.[123] In 1994, antidumping and countervailing duty cases were also brought within the scope of its jurisdiction. The GC has additionally been granted jurisdiction over Union trademark disputes arising out of the Office for Harmonization in the Internal Market (OHIM). For example, Wrigley was denied registration of its Doublemint trademark because it described one of the product's common characteristics, a ruling upheld by the Court. It is widely

---

[118] Articles 268–270, TFEU.

[119] Article 272, TFEU.

[120] Articles 274–276, TFEU.

[121] Article 340, TFEU.

[122] *See* Chapter 7.

[123] Council Decision 93/350, O.J. 1993 L144/21.

perceived that the General Court is now overloaded, even with staff cases heard before the Civil Service Tribunal. The TFEU anticipates offloading other areas to "specialized courts," for which the GC would function as an appeals court.

The purpose, in general, behind the creation of the CFI/GC was to relieve the Court of Justice of some of its caseload. It commenced doing this in November of 1989. However, there is a right of appeal on points of law from the GC to the Court of Justice. Article 51 of the Council Decision establishing the General Court indicates that such appeals lie on the grounds of lack of competence, procedural failures that adversely affect the appellants' interests, and infringement of Union law by the GC. In addition, the Treaty of Nice amendments to Article 256 specify that GC preliminary rulings posing a serious risk to the unity or consistency of Union law may be reviewed by the ECJ. Any failure by the GC to follow prior ECJ decisions could amount to such an infringement

Non-Contractual Liability

The General Court is partially heir to an interesting body of law on non-contractual (tort) liability created by the Court of Justice. In this area, the Court's role as a law maker was fully anticipated by the treaties. Article 340 provides that the non-contractual liability of the European Union is governed by the "general principles common to the laws of the member states." Under these principles, the Union is obliged to "make good any damage caused by its institutions or servants in the performance of their duties." For example, the negligent disclosure by the Commission of the identity of an informant who was a former employee of a company subject to EU competition law sanctions was an actionable tort.[124] In this case, a Swiss informant was arrested, held in solitary confinement, interrogated, and convicted under Swiss law for economic espionage. While in prison, his wife was interrogated by Swiss police officers and then committed suicide.

The European Court of Justice, and now the General Court, when damages are sought in litigation properly before it, has had to determine just what general principles of non-contractual liability are common to the laws of the member states. At first, of course, there were only six civil law states to consider. Now there are 27 member states, including only one common law jurisdiction (Ireland). The Court of Justice has ruled that Article 340 does not require adherence to the highest common denominator of liability law in the member states. Rather, the Court's duty is to track down in the national laws

---

[124] Adams v. Commission, (1985) Eur.Comm.Rep. 3539. *See* Article 214 of the Treaty of Rome creating an EU duty of confidentiality.

the elements or measures necessary to create liability principles which are fair and viable.[125] Such principles can include no-fault under the founding treaties.[126]

It is now generally recognized that the Union is liable in non-contractual cases whenever its tortious conduct causes actual damages.[127] Such conduct includes faults of its officers and agents committed within the scope of their duties, including negligence, bad faith, and intentional misconduct. Drawing from French administrative law, the Court has also recognized torts resembling "faute de service." These liabilities occur when the Union fails to function in the reasonably efficient manner expected of a well-run government even if such a fault cannot be traced to negligence or misconduct by specific officials.[128]

Tortious conduct giving rise to liability also includes unlawful legal measures, *e.g.,* EU regulations and directives, and unlawful failures to adopt such measures. The "plea of illegality" is used to challenge such activities. At first, the Court of Justice held that damages actions on these bases could only be pursued if successful challenges had been previously undertaken under Articles 263 or 265.[129] In a good demonstration of its willingness to reverse itself, the Court has since held the opposite.[130] Similarly, private parties need not challenge the validity of EU acts in national litigation prior to seeking damages relief before the Court. Here again the Court of Justice reversed its initial ruling to the contrary in the interest of the "proper administration of justice. . . and procedural efficiency."[131]

Nevertheless, the chances of obtaining individual damages relief for legislative acts of the European Union are not great. The Court has limited this possibility to manifest and grave disregard by EU institutions of the limits of their powers amounting to a breach of superior rules of law protecting individuals.[132] This is known as the "*Schöppenstedt* formula." And when directives are implemented at the national level in ways which cause damage, national remedies (if

---

[125] Plaumann & Co. v. Commission, (1963) Eur.Comm.Rep. 95.

[126] *See* Article 40 of the Treaty of Paris mandating a finding of fault in coal and steel cases.

[127] Alfons Lütticke GmbH v. Commission, (1971) Eur.Comm.Rep. 325.

[128] *See* Compagnie Continentale France v. Council, (1975) Eur.Comm.Rep. 117.

[129] Plaumann & Co. v. Commission, (1963) Eur.Comm.Rep. 95.

[130] Alfons Lütticke, supra; Aktien-Zuckerfabrik Schöppenstedt v. Council, (1971) Eur.Comm.Rep. 975.

[131] Merkur-Aussenhandels GmbH v. Commission, (1973) Eur.Comm.Rep. 1055.

[132] Bayerische HNL Vermehrungsbetriebe GmbH & Co. KG v. Council and Commission, (1978) Eur.Comm.Rep. 1209; Amylum NV v. Council and Commission, (1979) Eur.Comm.Rep. 3497.

available and effective) must first be pursued.[133] Directives that partly harmonize an area of law intended for total harmonization are not actionable even if discriminatory.[134]

§ 3.11 Judicial Practice and Procedure

The structure and procedures of the European Court of Justice (ECJ) and the General Court (GC) are quite similar. Each presently has, for example, 27 judges who serve six-year renewable terms upon appointment by the member states acting in common accord. There is one judge from each member state, plus (traditionally when an odd number was required) an additional judge who rotates from the five largest member states. The GC sits in chambers of three to five judges. The Court of Justice is also divided into chambers but may sit *en banc* or as a "grand chamber" of 14 judges when cases are brought before it by member states or Union institutions, and in many Article 267 preliminary rulings. Some case reporters now identify the Court's opinions by chamber number.

To an American, the Court's most distinguishing features are its emphasis on written (versus oral) procedures, the dominance of the Court (not the parties) over development of the evidence, and the absence of dissenting opinions.

Proceedings

The Protocol on the Statute of the Court of Justice and the Courts' Rules of Procedure (approved by the Council) establishes a two-part proceeding. The written part commences with an application to the Court's registrar and designation of an agent or legal representative. This designation must occur. In other words, litigants may not represent themselves before the Court. Any lawyer entitled to practice before a national court of a member state may act before the Court of Justice or General Court. The application serves as a "complaint" for notice purposes and thereby limits (in most cases) the issues and evidence that can be raised in the proceeding. Its filing also triggers the assignment of a reporting judge ("juge rapporteur") and an Advocate-General to the case. The fact of the application and a summary of the issues presented is published in the Official Journal.

The application is also sent to the respondent who has one month to file a written "defense." Plaintiff may then reply, to which the defendant may submit a rejoinder. All these written submissions

---

133 Krohn & Co. Import-Export GmbH v. Commission, (1986) Eur.Comm.Rep. 753; Asteris AE + Ors v. Hellenic Republic, (1990) Eur.Comm.Rep. 5515.

134 Les Assurances du Crédit S.A. v. Council and Commission, (1991) Eur.Comm.Rep. I–01799 (Case C–63/89).

to the court resemble full evidentiary and legal briefs more than pleadings. When Article 267 preliminary ruling procedure is being used, the parties, member states, the Commission and (where appropriate) the Council may submit written briefs to the Court. The Parliament does not appear to have this right of submission, but the member states and the EU institutions (including Parliament) always have a right to intervene in cases before the Court. Individuals and enterprises with an interest in the litigation have the same right. Trade and professional associations, consumer groups and unions have been particularly active as intervenors.

At the discretion of the Court, a preliminary inquiry may be held. The Court (typically acting through the reporting judge) can pose questions to the litigants. The role of a court in posing questions is part of the civil law tradition which predominates on the Court. It is a procedure that most common law students familiar with a more adversarial system will find a bit unusual. The Court also has the power to examine witnesses, call experts and generally develop the evidence before it. Limited rights of cross-examination are allowed to counsel when this occurs.

The second part of the proceeding before the Court is oral. The Court first hears the views of the reporting judge in charge of the case and then counsel for both sides. At the end of the oral procedure, the Court hears the *Advocate-General,* a special lawyer employed by the Union to analyze and evaluate all cases before the Court and give public opinions on the proper result under EU law. Americans are typically unfamiliar with the role of an Advocate-General since there is no parallel in United States procedure. The closest parallel is the French Commissaire du Gouvernement at the Conseil d'Etat. The Advocate-General does not represent anyone and is a kind of permanent *amicus curiae* on behalf of justice.

Advocates-General (AG) are appointed for six-year terms to the Court of Justice and General Court by the member states acting in common accord. Their opinions are often much more informative than those of the Court in any given case. Whereas the Advocate-General is willing to spin out various hypotheticals and consider the broader ramifications of the legal principles at issue, the Court tends to write its opinions in a terse and summary fashion. It should be stressed that lawyers working with EU law commonly use the opinions of the Advocate-General in their practice to forecast future developments and to better understand the judgments issued by the Court. Some of the most controversial cases in European Union law have involved instances where the Court has declined to agree with the opinions of the Advocate-General.[135]

Judgments

The Court's judgment is drafted in French by the reporting judge. This draft is then discussed by the full court or chamber. The Court's decision is rendered *without dissent* in the language of the case. The absence of dissenting opinions shelters the judges from nationalistic pressures and critics. But it also makes analysis of opinions and projection of trends in the case law more difficult.

Costs are normally borne by the losing party. Costs, for these purposes, generally include the Court's expenses, witnesses and experts, travel and subsistence of the parties to the Court's proceedings, and reasonable legal fees.[136] The Court's assessment powers on costs are wide, and substantial litigation over costs has ensued. However, most litigation results in a settlement agreement as between the parties on payment of costs. The loser must also pay the costs of intervenors supporting the successful litigant.[137] The Court may make cash legal aid awards in appropriate cases and in the absence of national legal aid.[138]

Litigation brought before the Court does not automatically suspend the act being challenged. It continues to operate pending the Court's decision. The Court (*i.e.*, the President of the Court) may order suspension when it considers this necessary, along with any "interim measures." This is done only in exceptional circumstances of harm to the applicant.[139] Pecuniary judgments of the Court against persons (not member states) are enforceable under the terms of Article 299 TFEU. Once authenticated, the Court's judgment is enforced according to the ordinary judgment-creditor procedures of the member state where it is executed.

The Rules of Procedure permit revisions of Court judgments.[140] No revision can occur more than ten years after judgment, and requests for revisions must be submitted within three months of the

---

135 *See* Van Gend en Loos v. Nederlandse Administratie der Belastingen, (1963) Eur.Comm.Rep. 1; Consten and Grundig v. Commission, (1966) Eur.Comm.Rep. 299; Defrenne v. Sabena, (1976) Eur.Comm.Rep. 455; Commission v. Council, (1971) Eur.Comm.Rep. 263 (*ERTA*).

136 *See* Article 72 of the ECJ Rules of Procedure.

137 Hoogovens v. High Authority, (1962) Eur.Comm.Rep. 253.

138 Lee v. Minister for Agriculture, (1980) Eur.Comm.Rep. 1495 (Article 234 reference in a civil case from Ireland). *See* DEB Deutsche Energiehandels v. Germany, (2010) Eur.Comm.Rep. (Case 279/09) (legal aid for companies).

139 United Kingdom v Commission, (1996) Eur.Comm.Rep. I–3903 (interim ban on British beef upheld in "mad cow" crisis); NTN Toyo Bearing Co. Ltd. v. Council, (1977) Eur.Comm.Rep. 1721; Commission v. Ireland, (1977) Eur.Comm.Rep. 1411.

140 Articles 92–94.

knowledge of new facts of decisive importance justifying revision. Such facts must have originally been unknown to both the Court and the litigant.[141] Moreover, if the information could have been easily obtained during litigation, no revision of judgment will be allowed.[142]

Article 102 of the Rules of Procedure permits requests for interpretation of Court judgments when there are "difficulties" as to its meaning or scope. Such requests can be made by the parties or any Union institution with an interest in the judgment. They are granted when the effect of the judgment on the parties is uncertain, not when the consequences for others are at issue.[143] Finally, third parties may seek reconsideration of Court judgments which will cause them damage. Requests for reconsideration must be made within two months of judgment, and the applicant must demonstrate no prior notice of the litigation.[144]

§ 3.12 Jurisdiction and Enforcement of Civil and Commercial Judgments

The 1968 Jurisdiction and Enforcement of Judgments Convention (Brussels Convention) regulates jurisdiction among the member states and facilitates enforcement of civil and commercial judgments of the courts of the member states in each other's courts. In other words, the Brussels Convention introduces "full faith and credit" principles to the European Union. Much of its substance is reproduced in the Lugano Convention on Jurisdiction and Enforcement of Judgments in Civil and Commercial Matters (1988). The Lugano Convention extends these principles to all ratifying EFTA countries, such as Switzerland.

The Brussels Convention was converted for all but Denmark from an international agreement into legislation by Council Regulation 44/2001. Several amendments were added at that time. In addition, Regulation 1348/2000 (amended by Regulation 1393/2007) establishes speedy and reliable means for service of civil or commercial legal process. Regulation 1206/2001 facilitates the cross-border taking of evidence in civil and commercial matters. These regulations take the 1965 and 1970 Hague Conventions as their inspirations.

It is important to remember that the Brussels Convention and Regulation 44/2001 govern jurisdiction as well as enforcement of national court judgments. This means, as a practical matter, that it

---

[141] Acciaieria di Roma v. High Authority, (1960) Eur.Comm.Rep. 165.

[142] Fonderie Acciarierie Giovanni Mandelli v. Commission, (1971) Eur.Comm.Rep. 1.

[143] High Authority and European Court v. Collotti, (1965) Eur.Comm.Rep. 275.

[144] Re Breedband, (1962) Eur.Comm.Rep. 145.

applies from the outset of the litigation once a jurisdictional challenge is raised and not just after judgment has been reached. Interpreting the Brussels Convention and the Regulation thus initially is the task of national trial courts. One elementary issue is the scope of applicability of the Convention to "civil and commercial matters."[145] The Convention does not define these terms, except by exclusion.

Most revenue, customs and administrative litigation along with legal status, capacity, matrimonial property, wills, succession, bankruptcy, social security and arbitration matters are not covered by the Brussels Convention. Intellectual property licensing contracts are not covered.[146] In 1998, however, a separate EU Convention on Jurisdiction, Recognition and Enforcement of Judgments in Matrimonial matters was concluded.[147] In 2000, Regulation 1346/2000 established jurisdictional, procedural and recognition rules for insolvency proceedings. In 2007, Regulation 864/2007 detailed conflict-of-law rules applicable to non-contractual obligations (torts) throughout the European Union ("Rome II Regulation"), while Regulation 593/2008 ("Rome I Regulation") did likewise for contractual obligations. Regulation 1393/2007 facilitates reliable service of documents across borders in civil and commercial litigation.

The ECJ has adopted an independent approach to the meaning of civil and commercial matters drawn from the Convention's purposes and the general principles of relevant law found in the member states. Special attention has been given to the original six civil law jurisdictions and their distinction between public and private law. Thus, most exercises of public authority by administrative bodies do not fall within the Convention.[148] Marital dissolution property settlements are not covered by the Convention,[149] but suits against estates by third parties over title to realty are.[150] Employment contracts fall within its scope.[151] The Convention's rules of jurisdiction thus mandate classification of the litigation in terms of the exclusions to civil and commercial matters.

---

[145] Brussels Convention, Article 1.

[146] Falco Privatstiftung & Rabitsch v. Weller-Lindhorst, (2009) Eur.Comm.Rep. (Case C–533/07).

[147] O.J. C221 (July 16, 1998).

[148] *See* Lufttransportunternehmen GmbH & Co. K.G. v. Eurocontrol, (1976) Eur.Comm.Rep. 1541 (recovery of route charges); Netherlands v. Rüffer, (1980) Eur.Comm.Rep. 3807.

[149] de Cavel v. de Cavel, (1979) Eur.Comm.Rep. 1055.

[150] CHW v. GJH, (1982) Eur.Comm.Rep. 1189.

[151] Sanicentral v. Collin, (1979) Eur.Comm.Rep. 3423.

It is not clear whether Britain post BREXIT will follow the EU Judgments Convention/Regulations. See Chapter 8.

Jurisdiction

The Brussels Convention and Regulation 44/2001 apply to all persons who are domiciled in a member state even if they are not citizens thereof. Thus, a United States-owned subsidiary incorporated in an EU state benefits from the Convention, whereas its parent would not. This coverage is important regarding the application of so-called "exorbitant jurisdiction" (below) and enforcement of judgments derived therefrom which will *not* apply to the subsidiary but will apply to the parent. Defendants are to be sued where they are domiciled. The concept of "domicile" is thus critical. As the Convention does not define it, this is left to national law. National courts must be satisfied that jurisdiction is taken in accordance with the Convention.[152] Co-defendants may be sued in non-domiciliary jurisdictions so closely connected that expediency requires suit to avoid the risk of irreconcilable judgments.[153]

Persons may be sued in forums outside their state of domicile only if the Convention/Regulation so provides. It is unclear whether this approach effectively negates the British tradition of *forum non conveniens*. The Convention provides for special jurisdictions as alternatives to domicile. Contract disputes can ordinarily be litigated where the "place" of performance of the obligation occurs as determined by the law controlling the contract.[154] This includes disputes as to the existence of contracts.[155] Regulation 44/2001 replacing the Brussels Convention renders the place of performance of the obligation as that agreed, or in the case of sale of goods, the place of delivery of the goods, or in the case of provision of services, the place of provision. Special new rules govern employment contracts and favor employees.[156] Torts may be litigated at the place where the event or damage occurred.[157] This has been construed to

---

[152] Group Josi Reinsurance Company SA v. Universal General Insurance Co, (2000) Eur.Comm.Rep. I–5925; Duijnstee v. Goderbauer, (1983) Eur.Comm.Rep. 3663. *See* Brussels Convention, Article 19.

[153] Regulation 44/2001, Article 6.

[154] Industrie Tessili Italiana Como v. Dunlop A.G., (1976) Eur.Comm.Rep. 1473. *See also* Ivenel v. Schwab, (1982) Eur.Comm.Rep. 1891 (commercial agency contracts also where work performed) and Leathertex v. Bodetex, (1999) Eur.Comm.Rep. I–6747 (commercial agency).

[155] Effer v. Kantner, (1982) Eur.Comm.Rep. 825.

[156] Regulaton 44/2001, Articles 18–21; *See* Mulrox IBC Ltd. v. Hendrick Geels, (1993) Eur.Comm.Rep. I–4075 (employment contract place of performance is where employee works).

[157] Dumez France SA and Tacoba SARL v. Hessische Landesbank, (1990) Eur.Comm.Rep. I–49; Handelskerij G.J. Bier B.V. v. Mines de Potasse d'Alsace, (1976)

mean either the place where the defendant acted (*e.g.*, manufactured a product) or where the injury was suffered.

The contract rules of the Brussels Convention do not apply to damages' actions between manufacturers and purchasers of their products with whom they have no privity of contract, even when the chain of sale is through wholly owned subsidiaries.[158] Such actions are ordinarily governed by the rules applicable to non-contractual (tortious) liability.

If there are several contractual obligations in question, the national court must distinguish between principal and secondary obligations. In one case, a German architect sued a Dutch client over fees for plans for construction of buildings located in Germany. The principal obligation at issue was payment, not the plans or construction, which could be pursued in the courts of the Netherlands where the fees were to be paid. However, employment and consumer contracts come under special provisions designed to protect the weaker party. For example, the focus may be upon the place of work and not the place of the payment obligation when that would favor employees.

Civil damages or restitution flowing from criminal acts are to be litigated in the forum of the crime. Cases involving branches, agencies or other establishments may be pursued where the branch, agency or other establishment is located or in the domicile of the principal. The mere appointment of a commercial agent does not appear to trigger this rule.[159] Suits for recovery of family and other support obligations ("maintenance") may be brought where the creditor is domiciled or "habitually resident," another undefined term.[160]

Additional Convention/Regulation rules for jurisdiction which operate as alternatives to the general rule of suit where the defendant is domiciled have been created for trusts, admiralty, insurance (policyholder, insured and beneficiary domicile options)[161] and consumer contracts (consumer domicile). The rules on jurisdiction favor only ordinary consumers, not business consumers.[162] Consumers, for these purposes, are economically weaker and less experienced private persons not engaged in

---

Eur.Comm.Rep. 1735; Bier B.V. v. Mines de Potasse d'Alsace SA, (1976) Eur.Comm.Rep. 1735.

158 Jakob Handte & Co. GmbH v. Traitements Mécano-chimiques des Surfaces, (1992) Eur.Comm.Rep. I–03967 (Case C–26/91).

159 Blanckaert & Willems v. Trost, (1981) Eur.Comm.Rep. 819.

160 *See* Delvaux v. Commission, (1976) Eur.Comm.Rep. 167.

161 Regulation 44/2001, Article 9(1).

162 Société Bertrand v. Paul Ott KG, (1978) Eur.Comm.Rep. 1431.

commercial or professional activities. A German company trading currency futures could not, therefore, benefit from the consumer domicile option of the Brussels Convention in its suit against a New York broker.[163]

In a few areas, the Brussels Convention and Regulation 44/2001 convey exclusive jurisdiction to specified courts regardless of domicile or party agreement on choice of forum.[164] These concern real property, company validity, public register, intellectual property validity, and enforcement of judgment litigations. As exceptions to the general rule, they have been narrowly construed. For example, although disputes between landlords and tenants (including unpaid rent)[165] are treated as subject to exclusive jurisdictional rules under the Convention, disputes between tenants and sub-tenants are not.[166]

The Brussels Convention and Regulation 44/2001 deny enforcement by EU domiciliaries against EU domiciliaries of certain judgments deemed to be based on "exorbitant jurisdiction" (*e.g.*, jurisdiction based solely on citizenship or asset-based *in personam* jurisdiction). But, in a discriminatory measure of importance, it permits EU domiciliaries to enforce judgments based upon exorbitant jurisdiction against non-EU domiciliaries.[167] Thus, a North American trader with assets somewhere in the Union could find itself at the wrong end of such discrimination. Other grounds for denial of enforcement of a judgment that is subject to the Brussels Convention include public policy, violation of defendant's procedural rights (service, notice), and the existence of an irreconcilable judgment of the enforcement court or another court (even one of a nation not party to the Brussels Convention).

Article 21 of the Brussels Convention provides that when the same cause of action is being litigated before the courts of two member states, the second court to be seized with litigation must stay or dismiss the proceeding pending resolution of the jurisdiction of the first court seized. This is the case even if the defendant is not domiciled in a member state, such as when the defendant is a U.S. insurance carrier.[168] *The first seized rule* has generated defensive

[163] Shearson Lehmann Hutton Inc. v. TVB Treuhandgesellschaft für Vermögensverwaltung und Beteiligungen mbH, (1993) Eur.Comm.Rep. I–139 (Case C–89/91).

[164] Brussels Convention Article 16; Regulation 44/2001, Article 22.

[165] Rösler v. Rottwinkel, (1985) Eur.Comm.Rep. 99 (Case 241/83).

[166] Sanders v. van der Putte, (1977) Eur.Comm.Rep. 2383. *See* Dansommer A/S v. Götz, (2000) Eur.Comm.Rep. I–393 (tour operator and tenancy).

[167] *See* Article 28(1), Brussels Convention.

[168] Overseas Union Insurance v. New Hampshire Insurance, (1991) Eur.Comm.Rep. I–03317 (Case C–351/89).

suits by debtors, sometimes referred to as "Italian torpedoes", in EU jurisdictions known to have very slow procedures. Likewise, even a court designated by the parties must await resolution of the first court's jurisdiction.[169]

It is in this sense that the doctrine of *forum non conveniens* is said to be precluded by the Brussels Convention, an analysis similarly confirmed by the ECJ in 2005 as regards courts *outside* Brussels Convention states.[170] Likewise, anti-suit injunctions cannot interfere with the jurisdictional rules of the Convention.[171]

Party Autonomy

Article 17 of the Brussels Convention affirms party autonomy to choose in writing a dispute settlement forum. This freedom does not apply regarding insurance, consumer contract and exclusive jurisdiction areas. The Convention's affirmation of party autonomy will override national rules contrary to such autonomy, even in the employment area. Article 17 has been construed rather narrowly and party awareness and appreciation of the significance of choice of forum clauses must be proved. There must be, in other words, informed written consent. Company statute clauses adopted by shareholders designating jurisdiction can meet these criteria.[172]

However, when international trade contracts are involved, compliance with custom and practice is sufficient to enforce the choice of forum.[173] The parties may avoid the stringency of Article 17 by designating determinative issues (*e.g.,* place of performance of contracts) in their contract. The chosen place of performance will have jurisdiction.[174] Such choices notwithstanding, if a party appears in another forum other than to contest jurisdiction, acquiescence to that forum will allow the litigation to proceed.[175]

Article 17 permits parties from outside the Union to join in the selection of a member state court without fear of an exercise of

---

169 Erich Gasser GmbH v. MISAT, (2003) Eur.Comm.Rep. I–00000 (Case C–116/02).

170 Omusu v. Jackson (Case C–281/02) (March 1, 2005).

171 Allianz SpA v. West Tankers Inc, (2009) Eur.Comm.Rep. I–663; Turner v. Grovit, (2004) Eur.Comm.Rep. I–3565.

172 Powell Duffryn v. Wolfgang Peteriet, (1992) Eur.Comm.Rep. I–01745 (Case 214/89).

173 *See, e.g.,* Estasis Salotti v. RuWa, (1976) Eur.Comm.Rep. 1831 (placement of choice of court clause on reverse side of offer insufficient); Galeries Segoura SPRL v. Rahim Bonakdarian, (1976) Eur.Comm.Rep. 1851; MS Tilly Russ, (1984) Eur.Comm.Rep. 02417 (Case 71/83); Berghoefer GmbH v. ASA SA, (1986) Eur.Comm.Rep. 02699 (Case 221/84).

174 Zelger v. Salinitri, (1980) Eur.Comm.Rep. 89.

175 Elefanten Schuh v. Jacqmain, (1981) Eur.Comm.Rep. 1671; Spitzley v. Sommer, (1985) Eur.Comm Rep. 00787 (Case 48/84).

jurisdiction elsewhere (*e.g.*, the place of performance) in the EU. Article 17 also provides that if any judicial forum selection was concluded for the benefit of only one party, *that* party may sue elsewhere. The idea of permitting the sole beneficiary of what some might see as an adhesion clause to escape from its forum selection obligations has not been found compelling.[176]

Recognition and Enforcement

The regulatory regime governing jurisdiction established in the Brussels Convention and Regulation 44/2001 makes recognition and enforcement of subsequent civil and commercial judgments in the EU nearly automatic. This is true for money and non-money judgments, settlements and authentications. Moreover, recognition and enforcement of national court judgments falling within the jurisdictional scope of the Convention occurs regardless of the nationality or domicile of the parties. To facilitate use of the Convention, *full* legal aid in the enforcing state must be given to anyone who obtained full *or* partial legal aid in the source state. Recognition (but not enforcement)[177] of the judgment is possible as soon as it is enforceable in its state of origin, even if appeals or further review are pending or available.

The *ex parte* enforcement procedures of the Brussels Convention and Regulation 44/2001 are exclusive and must be undertaken "without delay."[178] This means that no collateral attack by the parties to the judgment may occur in another EU state and that the successful plaintiff must adhere to Convention procedures even if there are alternative means at less cost of obtaining enforcement.[179] National courts are prohibited from charging a sliding scale of fees.

To obtain enforcement, the applicant needs only provide supporting documentation on the original judgment and its enforceability under the law of the state of origin and, if required, translations. At this stage, the defendant is not summoned to appear. The decision on grant or denial of recognition and enforcement must be notified to the defendant and can be appealed by the losing party. The defendant may also appeal on points of law. But there is a presumption of recognition for judgments falling within the Convention which can only be rebutted on the grounds set out in Articles 27 and 28. The enforcing court may issue whatever interim protective relief measures it deems necessary to secure assets while

---

176 *See* Anterist v. Crédit Lyonnais, (1986) Eur.Comm.Rep. 1951 (selection of bank's domicile court insufficient proof of intent to benefit bank exclusively).

177 *See* Industrial Diamond Supplies v. Riva, (1977) Eur.Comm.Rep. 2175.

178 Brussels Convention, Article 34.

179 DeWolf v. Cox, (1976) Eur.Comm.Rep. 1759.

appeals are pending even if such protection is not generally available under national law.[180]

There are five grounds under Articles 27 and 28 (as modified by Regulation 44/2001) for refusing full or partial recognition and enforcement of judgments under the Brussels Convention. These are reviewed *ex parte* by the enforcing court, subject to appeal, and include:

- Public policy (but not as applied to Convention's jurisdictional rules).[181]
- Protection of defendants' rights (*e.g.*, service, opportunity to be heard, and adequate time to prepare a defense).[182]
- Irreconcilable conflict with an existing judgment in the enforcing state.
- Conflict with an earlier judgment between the same parties and on the same cause of action in a state not party to the Convention.
- An agreement with a third-party nation not to enforce judgments based upon exorbitant jurisdiction.

Since recognition and enforcement will be granted absent an *existing* judgment to the contrary in the enforcing state, the Convention essentially gives *res judicata* effect to civil and commercial judgments throughout the European Union. But this does not mean that third party creditors interested in the enforcement because it might affect their own claims may not seek independent legal redress rescinding execution of an enforcement order under the Convention.[183] Proper service of process under the law of the country of the defendant is a prerequisite to enforcement of a default commercial judgment even when the defendant becomes aware by other means of the lawsuit and could have taken advantage of procedural rights in the courts of the judgment country.[184]

---

[180] Capeloni and Anor v. Pelkmans, (1985) Eur.Comm.Rep. 3147 (Case 119/84).

[181] Rohr v. Ossberger, (1981) Eur.Comm.Rep. 2431. *See* Krombach v. Bambersk, (2000) Eur.Comm.Rep. I–1935 (denial of fair hearing violates public policy).

[182] *See* Klomps v. Michel, (1981) Eur.Comm.Rep. 1593; Pendy Plastic Products B.V. v. Pluspunkt Handelsgesellschaft mbH, (1982) Eur.Comm.Rep. 2723; Debaecker and Plouvier v. Bouwman, (1986) Eur.Comm.Rep. 01779 (Case 49/84).

[183] *See* Deutsche Genossenschaftsbank v. Brasserie du Pcheur, (1985) Eur.Comm.Rep. 1981 (Case 148/84).

[184] Minalmet GmbH v. Brandeis Ltd., (1992) Eur.Comm.Rep. I–5661 (Case C–123/91).

Chapter 4

FREE MOVEMENT OF GOODS, SERVICES, CAPITAL AND PEOPLE

Table of Sections

§ 4.0 The Four Freedoms

This chapter concerns the free movement of goods, persons, services and capital. The implementation since 1957 of these "Four Freedoms" has been a slow and not entirely successful process. Indeed, as the campaign for a fully integrated market illustrated, considerable amendment and rejuvenation of the Treaty of Rome (now TFEU) has been required. The Single European Act of 1987 established the goal of creating a Europe genuinely "without internal frontiers," leaving customs, immigration and other controls solely to points of entry. The target for the completion of this task was the end of December 1992. Hundreds of new legislative acts and a host of EU agencies were adopted in its pursuit, with substantial progress on all fronts until the wave of mass migration began to hit Europe in 2014.

We commence with free movement of people, an almost nonexistent right under NAFTA/USMCA.[1]

§ 4.1 Free Movement of People

The Union has increasingly focused its attention on the creation of what it calls a "People's Europe." This focus is multidimensional. It includes traditional free movement rights of workers and the self-employed, and their families,[2] and of professionals and others operating in the services sector.[3] The "People's Europe" has been expanded to include general rights to reside anywhere in the EU for non-workers, such as students, the retired and persons who are independently wealthy.[4]

The Maastricht Treaty on European Union formally introduced the idea of European citizenship into EU law and brought with it a selected bundle of civil rights. These include the right to run for office and vote wherever resident in local and European Parliament elections, and the right to be represented abroad diplomatically by other member state consular or embassy services.[5]

European Union passports have replaced national passports and driving licenses have been standardized. In 2004, EU health insurance cards were introduced to facilitate access to "necessary" care when traveling in other member states. The ECJ has repeatedly ruled that citizens exercising their free movement and residence rights cannot suffer discrimination under home country programs, for example pension and unemployment benefits.[6]

Schengen and Dublin Accords

Dismantling border controls over the free movement of people within the European Union, a goal of the 1992 campaign for a Europe without internal frontiers, has not proven to be an easy task. It has been undermined by mass migration to the EU and the COVID-19 restraints. The Benelux states, Germany, Italy, Spain, Greece, Portugal and France agreed to remove their internal frontier controls on people under the 1990 "Schengen Accord". This accord was the

---

[1] NAFTA/USMCA creates several "white collar" visas for traders, investors, company transferees and professionals. *See* my Concise Hornbook on *The USMCA and Free Trade Agreements.*

[2] *See* Section 4.10.

[3] *See* Sections 4.11, 4.12, 4.13, 4.14.

[4] *See* Section 4.9.

[5] *Id. See* Directive 2004/38 (the citizenship directive).

[6] Turpeine Case C–520/04 (Nov. 9, 2006); DeCuyper v. Office National de l' Emploi, Case C–406/4 (July 18, 2006).

product of intergovernmental agreement, not EU legislation. As such, the Schengen Accord was an early harbinger of what is often called a "two-speed" Union or "Europe la carte". At this writing, Ireland and the United Kingdom do not participate, but nonmembers Iceland and Norway do. Nine of the ten member states (Cyprus excluded) that entered in 2004, along with Switzerland, participate in Schengen since 2008, but Croatia, Romania and Bulgaria do not.

The Schengen Accord covers such sensitive issues as visas, asylum, immigration, gun controls,[7] extradition and police rights of "hot pursuit." The main points of contention were cross-border traffic of immigrants and criminals, especially terrorists and drug dealers.[8] These issues were resolved largely by promises of greater intergovernmental cooperation, notably via the European Arrest Warrant which removes the need for deportation proceedings.[9]

Substantial ratification of the Dublin Asylum Convention and Directive 2005/85 on refugee status by Union states brought greater uniformity in that area, enhanced in 2008 by a "Pact" on immigration and asylum policy that stops "mass amnesties" (Spain, 2005) and establishes a "blue card" for skilled immigrants. In 2009, the Court of Justice ruled that asylum seekers need not demonstrate that they are specifically targeted for harm if there is widespread and indiscriminate violence in their home countries (in this case, Iraq).

Grants of asylum confer residence permits and the right to work legally. The Reform Treaty of 2009 confirmed common approaches to "asylum shopping", resulting in a general rule that asylum determinations should be made by the applicant's first EU country of entry. Other member countries can send asylum seekers to that first entry state. But German courts have refused to deport applicants to Greece and Italy for want of adequate and humane living conditions.

Mass Migration

Mass migration may well be the most divisive and difficult of all EU problems.

Relatively few persons denied asylum are deported from the EU, though this is changing in the face of mass migration from the Middle East, Africa and Afghanistan. German Chancellor Merkel's initial welcome of roughly 1 million migrants and Sweden's significantly open-door policy encouraged more mass migration waves, principally via Greece and up through the Balkans. Nevertheless, in 2023 the

---

7 *See* Council Directive 91/477.

8 *See* Council Regulation 900/92.

9 Framework Decision 2002/584/JHA, O.J. L190/1.

EU tightened its asylum and migration rules favoring faster resolution of claims in entry countries.

Public and governmental resistance grew in Hungary, Bulgaria, Austria, Germany, and throughout the EU, particularly as many of the migrants were Muslims. The EU, with substantial German support, agreed to pay Turkey large sums to restrain and house refugees seeking to reach Greek islands not far off the Turkish coast. This agreement effectively channeled Middle Eastern and Afghani migrants to Libya, where smugglers arranged boats (often unseaworthy) to take them along with African migrants primarily to Italy, overwhelming that country's capacities. EU reinforcement of war-torn Libya's coastal patrols has to some degree limited the flow of refugees from that country.

Other points of migrant entry to the EU include Spain, notably via its two North African coastal enclaves, and air flights to anywhere in the EU. It is estimated that there are roughly 10 million illegal migrants in the European Union, and no doubt more on the way. Securing the exterior borders of the EU, assuming that can be achieved, will likely take decades. But is that soon enough? Already, mass migration has fueled the growth of nativist European perspectives and political parties.

Justice and Home Affairs

One focus of the Maastricht Treaty on European Union, established as a separate "pillar," was cooperation on justice and home affairs. The member states have committed their interior ministries to coordinate their laws on asylum, immigration, frontier controls, crime, customs, terrorism and drugs. Under the Amsterdam Treaty of 1999, much of the Schengen Accord and other European policies on visas, asylum,[10] immigration and free movement of persons were brought under the TFEU, subject to opt out rights for Denmark, Britain and Ireland. This transfer had the notable effect of conveying jurisdiction in these areas to the European Court of Justice.

The separate TEU pillar on justice and home affairs was essentially reduced to police and judicial cooperation in criminal matters (*e.g.*, EUROPOL, Eurojust and EURO warrant), but opened to the possibility of ECJ judicial review in 2014. The Reform Treaty eliminated justice and home affairs as a separate TEU pillar, moving all such matters to the Treaty on the Functioning of the European Union. However, the Court of Justice does not have jurisdiction to

[10] *See* Directives 2003/9 and 2004/83 creating minimum standards for receiving asylum seekers and Regulation 343/2003 ("Dublin II" asylum review rules).

review police, law and order and internal security operations inside the member states.

§ 4.2 Free Movement of Goods

The free movement of goods within the European Union is based upon the creation of a customs union. Under this union, the member states have eliminated customs duties among themselves.[11] They have established a common customs tariff for their trade with the rest of the world,[12] a feature completely absent from NAFTA/ USMCA, with Canada, Mexico and the United States retaining different tariffs. Quantitative restrictions (quotas) on trade between member states are also prohibited, except in emergencies and other limited situations.[13] The right of free movement applies to goods that originate in the Common Market and to those that have lawfully entered it and are said to be in "free circulation."[14]

Measures of Equivalent Effect

The establishment of the customs union has been a major accomplishment, though not without difficulties. The member states not only committed themselves to the elimination of tariffs and quotas on internal trade, but also to the elimination of "measures of equivalent effect."[15] The elastic legal concept of measures of equivalent effect has been interpreted broadly by the European Court of Justice and the Commission to prohibit a wide range of trade restraints, such as administrative fees charged at borders which are the equivalent of import or export tariffs.[16] Charges of equivalent effect to a tariff must be distinguished from internal taxes that are applicable to imported and domestic goods. The latter must be levied in a nondiscriminatory and non-protective manner (Article 110, TFEU), while the former are prohibited entirely (Articles 28, 30). There has been a considerable amount of litigation over this distinction.[17]

---

11 Article 30, TFEU.

12 *See* Chapter 6.

13 Articles 34–37, TFEU.

14 Articles 28 and 29, TFEU.

15 *See* especially Articles 30, 34, 35, TFEU.

16 Sociaal Fonds v. SA Ch. Brachfield, (1969) Eur.Comm.Rep. 211; Rewe Zentralfinanz v. Landwirtschaftskammer Westfalen-Lippe, (1973) Eur.Comm.Rep. 1039; Commission v. Italy, (1969) Eur.Comm.Rep. 193. *But see* Commission v. Germany, (1988) Eur.Comm.Rep. 5427 (border fees to cover costs of inspections required by EU law may be lawful).

17 *See* Chapter 5. *See e.g.*, Industria Gomma, Articoli Vari v. Ente Nazionale *ENCC*, (1975) Eur.Comm.Rep. 699; Humblot v. Directeur des Services Fiscaux, (1985) Eur.Comm.Rep. 1367 (tax on goods not domestically produced invalid).

The elasticity of the concept of measures of an equivalent effect is even more pronounced in the Court's judgments relating to quotas. This jurisprudence draws upon an early Commission directive (no longer applicable) of extraordinary scope.[18] In this directive, the Commission undertook a lengthy listing of practices that it considered illegal measures of equivalent effect to quotas. It is still occasionally referenced in Commission and Court of Justice decisions. The directive's focus was on national rules that discriminate against imports or simply restrain internal trade.

Cassis Formula

This "effects test" soon found support from the ECJ. In a famous case, the Court of Justice ruled that Belgium could not block the importation of Scotch whiskey via France because of the absence of a British certificate of origin as required by Belgian customs law.[19] The Court of Justice held that any national rule directly or indirectly, actually or potentially capable of hindering internal trade is generally forbidden as a measure of equivalent effect to a quota. However, *if* European Union law has not developed appropriate rules in the area concerned (here designations of origin), the member states may enact "reasonable" and "proportional" (no broader than necessary) regulations to ensure that the public is not harmed.[20] This is commonly called the "*Cassis* formula." Products meeting reasonable national criteria, the *Cassis* opinion continues, may be freely traded elsewhere in the Union.[21] This is the origin of the innovative "mutual reciprocity" principle used in significant parts of the legislative campaign for a Europe without internal frontiers.

The *Cassis* decision suggests the use of a Rule of Reason analysis for national fiscal regulations, public health measures, laws governing the fairness of commercial transactions and consumer protection. Environmental protection and occupational safety laws of the member states have been similarly treated. Under this approach, for example, a Danish "bottle bill" requiring use of approved soft drink and beer containers was held disproportionately restrictive of internal trade. The use of only approved containers was therefore unreasonable.[22] However, the Danes' argument that a deposit and

---

[18] Commission Directive 70/50 on the Abolition of Measures which have an Effect Equivalent to Quantitative Restrictions, 1970 O.J. L13/29 (Special Edition) (I), p. 17.

[19] Procureur du Roi v. Dassonville, (1974) Eur.Comm.Rep. 837.

[20] *See* the "Cassis de Dijon" case, Rewe Zentral AG v. Bundesmonopolverwaltung für Branntwein, (1979) Eur.Comm.Rep. 649 (German *minimum* alcoholic beverage rule not reasonable). *See also* Commission Communication, O.J. C256/2 (March 10, 1980).

[21] *See* the Commission Communication Concerning the *Cassis* Case, O.J. C256/2 (March 10, 1980).

[22] Commission v. Denmark, (1988) Eur.Comm.Rep. 4607.

return system was environmentally necessary prevailed. This was (absent the approved container rules) a reasonable restraint on internal trade recognized by the Court under the *Cassis* formula for analyzing compelling state interests. Likewise, a Belgian law prohibiting the importation of general wastes from neighboring countries was found reasonable and not in breach of EU free trade principles.[23]

There are cases which suggest that "cultural interests" may justify national restrictions on European Union trade. For example, British, French and Belgian bans on Sunday retail trading have survived initial scrutiny under the *Cassis* formula.[24] British prohibitions of sales of sex articles, except by licensed sex shops, were EU compatible[25] and French legislation prohibiting the sale or rental of cassettes within one year of a film's debut also survived such scrutiny under the *Cassis* formula.[26] National laws prohibiting sales below cost, when applied without discrimination as between imports and domestic products, are not considered to affect trade between the member states. In the remarkable *Keck* decision signaling a jurisprudential retreat, the ECJ ruled "contrary to what has previously been decided" that "selling arrangements" may not be challenged the traditional *Cassis* formula.[27] Deceptive trade practices laws ordinarily do not amount to "selling arrangements,"[28] but national laws regulating sales outlets[29] and advertising[30] may.

In recent years, member state regulations capable of being characterized as governing "marketing modalities" or "selling arrangements" have sought shelter under *Keck*. For example, the French prohibition of televised advertising (intended to favor printed media) of the distribution of goods escaped the rule of reason analysis of *Cassis* in this manner, but the Swedish ban on magazine ads for alcoholic beverages did not since it discriminated against market

---

[23] Commission v. Belgium, (1992) Eur.Comm.Rep. I–4431 (Case C–2/90).

[24] Torfaen Borough Council v. B & Q PLC Ltd., (1989) Eur.Comm.Rep. 3851; UDS v. Sidef Conforma & Ors, (1991) Eur.Comm.Rep. 997 (Case C–312/89); Re Marchandise & Ors, (1991) Eur.Comm.Rep. I–1027 (Case C–332/89); Reading Borough Council v. Payless DIY Ltd + Ors, (1992) Eur.Comm.Rep. I–6493 (Case C–304/90).

[25] Quietlynn Ltd. v. Southend Borough Council, (1990) 1 Eur.Comm.Rep. 3051.

[26] Cinéthéque SA v Fédération Nationale des Cinémas Francais, (1985) Eur.Comm.Rep. 2605.

[27] *See* Re Keck and Mithouard, (1993) Eur.Comm.Rep. I–6097 (Cases C–267/91, C–268/91).

[28] Verband Sozialer Wettbewerb v. Clinique Laboratories, (1994) Eur.Comm.Rep. I–317.

[29] Commission v. Greece, (1995) Eur.Comm.Rep. I–1621.

[30] Societe d'Importation Edouard Leclerc-Siplec v. TFI Publicite, (1995) Eur.Comm. I–179. *Compare* Konsumertombusmannen (KO) v. Gourmet International Products ABS, (GIP), (2001) Eur.Comm.Rep. I–6493.

access by imports. Some commentators see in *Keck* and its progeny an unarticulated attempt by the Court to take subsidiarity seriously. Others are just baffled by its newly found tolerance for trade distorting national marketing laws. But the Court of Justice poignantly refused to extend *Keck* to the marketing of services, and some commentators suggest *Keck* may be fading into obscurity.

Under *Cassis,* national rules requiring country of origin or "foreign origin" labels have fallen as measures of effect equivalent to quotas.[31] Likewise, the selective "Quality Produce from Germany" label fell to free trade principles.[32] So have various restrictive national procurement laws, including a "voluntary" campaign to "Buy Irish."[33] Minimum and maximum retail pricing controls can also run afoul of the Court's expansive interpretation of measures of equivalent effect.[34] Compulsory patent licensing can amount to a measure of equivalent effect nullified by operation of Union law. Where demand for the patented product was satisfied by imports from another member state, the U.K. could not compulsorily require manufacturing within its jurisdiction.[35] Member states may not impose linguistic labeling requirements to block trade and competition in foodstuffs. In one case, a Belgian law requiring Dutch labels in Flemish areas was nullified as in conflict with the TFEU.[36] These cases vividly illustrate the extent to which litigants are invoking the Treaty and the *Cassis* formula in attempts at overcoming commercially restrictive national laws.

The Court has made it clear that all the Rule of Reason justifications for national regulatory laws are temporary. Adoption of Common Market legislation in any of these areas would eliminate national authority to regulate trading conditions under *Cassis* and (presumably) *Keck*.[37] These judicial mandates, none of which are specified in the TFEU, vividly illustrate the powers of the Court of

---

[31] Commission v. Ireland, (1981) Eur.Comm.Rep. 1625; Commission v. United Kingdom, (1985) Eur.Comm.Rep. 1202.

[32] Commission v. Germany, (2002) Eur.Comm.Rep. I–9977 (Case C–325/00).

[33] Commission v. Ireland, (1988) Eur.Comm.Rep. 4929 (product standards); Commission v. Ireland, (1982) Eur.Comm.Rep. 4005 (Buy Irish). *But see* The Apple and Pear Development Council v. K.J. Lewis, Ltd., (1983) Eur.Comm.Rep. 4083 (permissible promotion of local agricultural products).

[34] Re Ricardo Tasca, (1976) Eur.Comm.Rep. 291; Openbaar Ministerie v. Van Tiggele, (1978) Eur.Comm.Rep. 25.

[35] Commission v. United Kingdom, (1992) Eur.Comm.Rep. I–0829 (Case C–30/90).

[36] Piageme ASBL v. Peeters BVBA, (1991) Eur.Comm.Rep. I–2971 (Case C–369/89).

[37] Oberkreisdirektor des Kreises Borken v. Moormann B.V., (1988) Eur.Comm.Rep. 4869.

Justice to expansively interpret the Treaty and rule on the validity under EU law of national legislation affecting internal trade in goods.

§ 4.3 Article 36 and the Problem of Nontariff Trade Barriers

The provisions of the EEC Treaty of Rome (now TFEU) dealing with the establishment of the customs union do not adequately address the problem of nontariff trade barriers (NTBs). As in NAFTA and the world community, the major trade barrier within the European Union has become NTBs. To some extent, in the absence of a harmonizing directive completely occupying the field,[38] this is authorized. Article 36 TFEU permits national restraints on imports and exports justified on the grounds of:

(1) Public morality, public policy ("ordre public") or public security;

(2) The protection of health and life of humans, animals or plants;

(3) The protection of national treasures possessing artistic, historical or archeological value;[39] and

(4) The protection of industrial or commercial property.

Article 36 amounts, within certain limits, to an authorization of nontariff trade barriers among the EU nations. This "public interest" authorization exists in addition to, but somewhat overlaps with, the Rule of Reason exception formulated under Article 34 in *Cassis* above. However, in a sentence much construed by the European Court of Justice, Article 36 continues with the following language: "Such prohibitions or restrictions shall not, however, constitute a means of arbitrary discrimination or a disguised restriction on trade between member states."

Case Law

In a wide range of decisions, the Court of Justice has interpreted Article 36 in a manner which generally limits the ability of member states to impose NTB barriers to internal Union trade. Britain, for

---

[38] *See* Firma Eau de Cologne v. Provide, (1989) Eur.Comm.Rep. 3891 and Pubblico Ministero v. Ratti (1979) Eur.Comm.Rep. 1629 (Article 30 preempted by EC directives). *But see* Article 114 TFEU regarding internal market directives where member states retain certain Article 36 prerogatives (discussed in Section 4.4) and cases allowing member states to "supplement" EU directives on the basis of genuine need, including Ministère Public v. Grunert, (1980) Eur.Comm.Rep. 1827, In re Motte, (1985) Eur.Comm.Rep. 3887, Ministère Public v. Muller, (1986) Eur.Comm.Rep. 1511, Ministère Public v. Bellon, (1990) Eur.Comm.Rep. 4683.

[39] *See* Council Directive 93/7 securing the right of return of national cultural treasures removed unlawfully after Dec. 31, 1992.

example, may use its criminal law under the public morality exception to seize pornographic goods made in Holland that it outlaws,[40] but not inflatable sex dolls from Germany which could be lawfully produced in the United Kingdom.[41] Germany cannot stop the importation of beer (*e.g.*, Heineken's from Holland) which fails to meet its purity standards.[42] This case makes wonderful reading as the Germans, seeking to invoke the public health exception of Article 30, argue all manner of ills that may befall their populace if free trade in beer is allowed. Equally interesting are the unsuccessful Italian health protection arguments against free trade in pasta made from common (not durum) wheat,[43] the failure of French standards' arguments against free trade in foie gras[44], and the rejection of Spain's "chocolate substitutes" labeling rule for chocolate containing vegetable fats.[45]

But a state may obtain whatever information it requires from importers to evaluate public health risks associated with food products containing additives that are freely traded elsewhere in the Common Market. This does not mean that an importer of muesli bars to which vitamins have been added must prove the product healthful, rather that the member state seeking to bar the imports must have an objective reason for keeping them out of its market.[46] Assuming such a reason exists, the trade restraint may not be disproportionate to the public health goal.[47] A notable ECJ opinion invalidated a French public health ban on U.K. beef imports maintained after a Commission decision to return to free trade following the "mad cow" outbreak.[48]

Public security measures adopted under Article 36 can include external as well as internal security. In one case, the validity of national CoCom restrictions on the export of strategic goods to the U.S.S.R. was noted.[49] An unusual case under the public security

---

[40] Regina v. Henn and Darby, (1979) Eur.Comm.Rep. 3795.

[41] Conegate Ltd. v. H.M. Customs and Excise, (1986) Eur.Comm.Rep. 1007.

[42] Commission v. Germany, (1987) Eur.Comm.Rep. 1227. *But see* Aragonesa de Publicidad Exterior SA (APESA) + Anor v. Departamento de Sanidad y Seguridad Social, (1991) Eur.Comm.Rep. I–4151 (Cases C–1/90 and C–176/90) (advertising ban applied to strong alcoholic beverages can be justified on public health grounds).

[43] Re Drei Glocken GmbH and Criminal Proceedings against Zoni, (1988) Eur.Comm.Rep. 4233, 4285.

[44] Commission v. France, (1998) Eur.Comm.Rep. I–06197 (Case C–184/96).

[45] Commission v. Spain, (2003) Eur.Comm.Rep. I–459.

[46] Officer van Justitie v. Sandoz BV, (1983) Eur.Comm.Rep. 2245.

[47] Commission v. United Kingdom (UHT Milk), (1983) Eur.Comm.Rep. 203.

[48] National Farmers' Union v. Secrĕtariat Gĕnĕral, (2002) Eur.Comm.Rep. I–9079.

[49] Ministre des Finances v. Richardt, (1991) Eur.Comm.Rep. I–4621 (Case C–367/89).

exception contained in Article 36 involved Irish petroleum products' restraints.[50] The Irish argued that oil is an exceptional product always triggering national security interests. Less expansively, the Court acknowledged that maintaining minimum oil supplies did fall within the ambit of Article 36. The public policy exception under Article 36 has been construed along French lines (ordre public). Only genuine threats to fundamental societal interests are covered.[51] Consumer protection (though a legitimate rationale for trade restraints under *Cassis*), does not fall within the public policy exception of Article 36.[52] Permitting environmental protesters to block the Brenner Pass for 30 hours is acceptable public policy in support of fundamental assembly and expression rights.[53]

§ 4.4 Intellectual Property Rights as Trade Barriers

A truly remarkable body of case law has developed around the authority granted national governments in Article 36 to protect industrial or commercial property ("intellectual property") by restraining imports and exports. These cases run the full gamut from protection of trademarks and copyrights to protection of patents and know-how. There is a close link between this body of case law and that developed under Article 101 concerning restraints on competition.[54]

Trade restraints involving intellectual property arise out of the fact that such rights are nationally granted. Owners of intellectual property rights within the Union are free under most traditional law to block the unauthorized importation of goods into national markets. There is a strong tendency for national infringement lawsuits to serve as vehicles for the division of the Common Market. Considerable energy has been spent by the Commission on developing Common Market rights that would provide an alternative to national intellectual property rights. Late in 1993, the Council reached agreement on a Common Market trademark regime and the Council adopted Directive 89/104, which harmonizes member state laws governing trademarks.[55] As a result, for example, the United Kingdom enacted the Trade Marks Act of 1994.

---

50 *See* Regina v. Thompson, (1978) Eur.Comm.Rep. 2247 (coinage).

51 Campus Oil Ltd. v. Minister for Industry and Energy, (1984) Eur.Comm.Rep. 2727.

52 Kohl KG v. Ringelhan and Rennett SA, (1984) Eur.Comm.Rep. 3651; Silhouette International v. Hartlauer, (1998) Eur.Comm.Rep. I–4799 (Austrian manufacturer's trademark rights block imports of its sunglasses from Bulgaria).

53 Schmidberger v. Austria, (2003) Eur.Comm.Rep. I–5659 (Case C–112/00).

54 *See* Chapter 7.

55 *See* § 5.25.

The Court of Justice has ruled that goods bearing trademarks registered somewhere in the EU may be freely circulated marked with an "R" in a circle after the trademark. National law on unfair competition cannot be used to impede trade in such goods on the grounds that the mark in question is not registered in the country of sale.[56] In the copyright field, several directives have harmonized European law, perhaps most importantly on copyrights for computer software (No. 91/250).

A long-proposed EU Patent Convention finally came into force in 2014 as the EU Unitary Patent (UP) regime. It is applicable in all EU member states save Spain and Italy, miffed by the omission of their languages as "official". The UP regime operates in French, German or English through its headquarters in Paris. It can issue or revoke a Common Market patent valid in any contracting state. Transfers and licenses for part of the Union are possible.

The cost-saving UP is an alternative to (but not a replacement for) national patent and European Patent Convention rights. However, the UP requires its signatories to harmonize national patent laws to conform to Unitary Patent rules on infringement, litigation procedures, exhaustion of rights and other issues. New Unified Patent Courts of First Instance and Appeal have been created in Luxembourg. By 2021 their centralized jurisdiction governs infringement and validity disputes concerning national patents, European patents and Unified patents.

Exhaustion Doctrine

The European Court of Justice has addressed these problems under Article 36 and generally resolved against the exercise of national intellectual property rights in ways which inhibit free trade inside the Union. In many of these decisions, the Court acknowledges the existence of the right to block trade in infringing goods but holds that the *exercise* of that right is subordinate to the TFEU. The Court has also fashioned a doctrine which treats national intellectual property rights as having been *exhausted* once the goods to which they apply are freely sold on the market.[57] One of the few exceptions to this doctrine is broadcast performing rights which the Court considers incapable of exhaustion.[58] Records, CDs and cassettes embodying such rights are, however, subject to the exhaustion doctrine once released into the market.[59] Such goods often end up in

---

56 Pall Corp. v. P.J. Dalhausen, (1990) Eur.Comm.Rep. I–4827 (Case C–238/89).

57 *See,* regarding trademarks, Van Doren + Q. GmbH v. Lifestyle Sports, (2003) Eur.Comm.Rep. I–3051 (Case C–244/00).

58 *See* Coditel v. Ciné Vog Films SA, (1980) Eur.Comm.Rep. 881; (1982) Eur.Comm.Rep. 3381.

59 Musik-Vertrieb membran Gmbh v. GEMA, (1981) Eur.Comm.Rep. 147.

the hands of third parties who then ship them into another member state.

The practical effect of many of the rulings of the Court of Justice is to remove the ability of the owners of the relevant intellectual property rights from successfully pursuing infringement actions in national courts.[60] When intellectual property rights have a single proprietor and have been placed on goods by consent, as when a licensor authorizes their use in other EU countries, then infringement actions to protect against parallel imports of the goods to which the rights apply are usually denied. This may not be the case, however, when voluntary trademark assignments that are not anticompetitive are involved. In such cases, the ECJ has demonstrated some concern for consumer confusion when trade in parallel goods occurs.

It is only when intellectual property rights do not have a single proprietor (thus sharing a "common origin") or the requisite consent is absent that they stand a chance of being upheld to stop trade in infringing products.[61] Compulsory licensing of patents, for example, does not involve consensual marketing of products. Patent rights may therefore be used to block trade in goods produced under such a license.[62] But careful repackaging and resale of goods subject to a common or even different trademark may occur against the objections of the owner of the mark.[63] And compulsory licensing cannot be conditioned upon import bans applicable to the beneficiary licensee. Such bans offend the free movement of goods law of the EU and unfairly create investment incentives.[64]

Centrafarm Case

An excellent example of the application of the judicial doctrine developed by the Court of Justice in the intellectual property field

---

60 *See, e.g.*, Administration des douanes v. Rioglass SA and Transremar SL, (2003) Eur.Comm.Rep. I–3711 (Case C–115/02).

61 *See* CNL-Sucal v HAG, (1990) Eur.Comm.Rep. I–3711 (Case C–10/89) (wartime expropriation of trademark removes common origin). *See also* Terrapin (Overseas) Ltd. v. Terranova Industrie CA Kapferer & Co., (1976) Eur.Comm.Rep. 1039.

62 Pharmon BV. v. Hoechst AG, (1985) Eur.Comm.Rep. 2281.

63 Hoffman-La Roche & Co. AG v. Centrafarm Vertriebsgesellschaft Pharmazeutischer Erzeugnisse mgH, (1978) Eur.Comm.Rep. 1132; Pfizer, Inc. v. Eurim-Pharm GmbH, (1981) Eur.Comm.Rep. 2913; Bristol-Myers Squibb & Orrs v. Paranova, (1996) Eur.Comm.Rep. I–3457; Pharmacia & Upjohn v. Paranova, (1999) Eur.Comm.Rep. I–6927; Boehringer Ingelheim KG v. Swingward Ltd and Douelhurst Ltd, (2002) Eur.Comm.Rep. I–3759 (Case C–143/00); Merck, Sharp + Dohme GmbH v. Paranova Pharmazeutica, (2002) Eur.Comm.Rep. I–3703 (Case C–443/99).

64 Generics (UK) Ltd. v. Smith, Kline & French Laboratories, Ltd., (1992) Eur.Comm.Rep. I–5335 (Case C–191/90).

under Article 36 can be found in the *Centrafarm* case.[65] The United States pharmaceutical company, Sterling Drug, owned the British and Dutch patents and trademarks relating to "Negram." Subsidiaries of Sterling Drug in Britain and Holland had been respectively assigned the British and Dutch trademark rights to Negram. Owing in part to price controls in the UK, a substantial difference in cost for Negram emerged as between the two countries. Centrafarm was an independent Dutch importer of Negram from the UK and Germany. Sterling Drug and its subsidiaries brought infringement actions in the Dutch courts under their national patent and trademark rights seeking an injunction against Centrafarm's importation of Negram into The Netherlands.

The Court of Justice held that the intellectual property rights of Sterling Drug and its subsidiaries could not be exercised in a way which blocked EU trade in "parallel goods." In the Court's view, the exception established in Article 36 for the protection of industrial and commercial property covers only those rights that were specifically intended to be conveyed by the grant of national patents and trademarks. Blocking trade in parallel goods after they have been put on the market with the consent of a common owner, exhausting the IP rights in question, was not intended to be part of the package of IP benefits conveyed. If Sterling Drug succeeded, arbitrary discrimination or disguised restriction on Union trade would be achieved in breach of the language which qualifies Article 36. Thus, the European Court of Justice ruled in favor of the free movement of goods within the Common Market even when that negates clearly existing national legal remedies.[66]

Silhouette Case

While the goal of creation of the Common Market can override national intellectual property rights when internal trade is concerned, these rights apply fully to the importation of goods from outside the European Union.[67] North American exporters of goods allegedly subject to rights owned by Europeans may therefore find entry into the EU challenged by infringement actions in national courts. This is notably true regarding trade in gray market goods.[68] In *Silhouette,* for example, the Austrian owner of designer sunglasses

---

[65] Centrafarm BV v. Sterling Drug Inc., (1974) Eur.Comm.Rep. 1147.

[66] For more on parallel trading in pharmaceuticals, *see especially* GlaxoSmithKline Services Ltd v. Commission, (2006) Eur.Comm.Rep. II–02969 (Case T–168/01).

[67] *See* E.M.I. Records Ltd. v. CBS United Kingdom Ltd., (1976) Eur.Comm.Rep. 811.

[68] Silhouette International v. Hartlauer, (1998) Eur.Comm.Rep. I–4799 (Case C–355/96); Zino Davidoff SA v. A + G Imports Ltd., (2001) Eur.Comm.Rep. I–8691 (Cases C–414/99 to 416/99).

was able to block their importation into the EU from Bulgaria (prior to its EU membership). In a bit of clever lawyering, Levi Strauss successfully cited *Silhouette* to keep low-price (made in the USA) Levi's out of the EU, thus preserving higher revenues in their EU market. Monsanto, on the other hand, was unable to invoke its European GMO patent rights to block importation of Argentinian bioengineered soybeans.[69]

§ 4.5 NTBs and the Single Market

Nontariff trade barrier problems were the principal focus of the campaign for a fully integrated Common Market. It is estimated that the retention of customs frontiers, even in the absence of tariffs and quotas, costs the Union approximately 11 billion dollars a year. Many new legislative acts have been adopted, or are in progress, which target NTB trade problems inside the EU.[70] There are basically two different methodologies being employed. When possible, a common European Union standard is adopted. For example, legislation on auto pollution requirements adopts this methodology. Products meeting these standards may be freely traded inside the Common Market. Traditionally, this approach (called "harmonization") has required the formation of a consensus within the Union as to the appropriate level of protection. Once adopted, harmonized standards must be followed.[71]

This approach can be deceptive, however. Some harmonization directives contain a list of options from which member states may choose when implementing those directives.[72] In practice, this leads to differentiated national laws on the same so-called harmonized subject. Furthermore, in certain areas (notably the environment and occupational health and safety), the TFEU and certain directives[73] expressly indicate that member states may adopt laws that are more demanding than the Union's legislation. The result is, again, less than complete harmonization, but a far cry from NAFTA's explicit reservation of "NTB rights" for Canada, Mexico and the United States.

Under Article 114, added by the Single European Act of 1987, most single market legislation was adopted by qualified majority

---

69 Monsanto v. Toepfer Int'l and Cefe tra BU, (2010) Eur.Comm.Rep.

70 *See* "1992-Plus at a Glance" in § 2.14.

71 Pubblico Ministero v. Ratti, (1979) Eur.Comm.Rep. 1629 (dangerous solvents); Commission v. United Kingdom, (1988) Eur.Comm.Rep. 3921 (dim-dip lighting); Kemilkaieinspektionen v. Toolex Alpha, (2000) Eur.Comm.Rep. I–5681 (dangerous substances).

72 *See* the discussion of products liability in Chapter 5.

73 *See* Buet v. Ministere Public, (1989) Eur.Comm.Rep. 1235; Queen v. Secretary of State for Health, (1993) Eur.Comm.Rep. I–3545.

voting in the Council of Ministers. Notable exceptions requiring a unanimous vote included new laws on taxation, employment and free movement of persons. However, if a 1992 measure was adopted by a qualified majority, the public interest exceptions to free internal trade specified in Article 36 apply.[74] This may provide an escape clause for member states that were outvoted in the Council on single market legislation. Indeed, Article 114 extends the scope of Article 36 to include "major needs" relating to national protection of the working or natural environments. The Commission must be notified of any member state use of such an exception, which it or another member state can then challenge directly before the European Court as an "improper use." In doing so, the Commission need not adhere to the lengthy procedures used with Article 258 prosecutions of member states.[75]

Harmonization Principles

Many efforts at the harmonization of European environmental, health and safety, standards and certification, and related law have been undertaken. Nearly all of these are supposed to be based upon "high levels of protection."[76] Some have criticized what they see as the "least common denominator" results of harmonization of national laws under the campaign for a Europe without internal frontiers.

One example involves the safety of toys. Directive 88/378 permits toys to be sold throughout the Common Market if they satisfy "essential requirements." These requirements are broadly worded in terms of flammability, toxicity, etc. There are two ways to meet these requirements: (1) produce a toy in accordance with CEN standards (drawn up by experts); or (2) produce a toy that otherwise meets the essential safety requirements. Local language labeling requirements necessary for purchaser comprehension have generally, though not always, been upheld.[77]

The least common denominator criticism may be even more appropriate to the second legislative methodology utilized in the internal market campaign. The second approach is based on the *Cassis* principle of mutual reciprocity.[78] Under this "new" minimalist approach, EU legislation requires member states to recognize the laws of other member states and deem them acceptable for purposes

---

74 *See* § 4.3.

75 *See* Chapter 3.

76 Article 114, TFEU.

77 *See* Piageme & Orrs v. Peeters, (1995) Eur.Comm.Rep. I–2955; Colim v. Bigg's Continent Noord, (1999) Eur.Comm.Rep. I–3175.

78 *See* § 4.2.

of the operation of the Common Market.[79] For example, major legislation has been adopted in the area of professional services.[80] By mutual recognition of higher education diplomas based upon at least three years of courses, virtually all professionals have now obtained legal rights to move freely within the Union in pursuit of their careers. This is a remarkable achievement.

§ 4.6 Product Standards and Testing

An important part of the battle against nontariff trade barriers (NTBs) in the European Union involves product testing and standards. More than half of the legislation involved in the single market campaign concerned such issues. Since 1969, there has been a standstill agreement among the EU states to avoid the introduction of new technical barriers to trade. A 1983 directive (No. 83/89) requires member states to notify the Commission of proposed new technical regulations and product standards. The Commission can enjoin the introduction of such national rules for up to one year if it believes that a Union standard should be developed,[81] and failures to notify can invalidate national rules.[82]

The goal is to move from different sets of regulatory approvals to one unified Union system embodying essential requirements on health, safety, and environmental and consumer protection. Goods that meet these essential requirements will bear a "CE mark" and can be freely traded. Manufacturers will self-certify their compliance with relevant EU standards. Design and production process standards generally follow the ISO 9000 series on quality management and assurance. Firms must maintain a technical file documenting compliance and produce the file upon request by national authorities.

Standards Bodies

Private regional standards bodies have been playing a critical role in the development of this system. These include the European Committee for Standardization (CEN), the European Committee for Electrotechnical Standardization (CENELEC), and the European Telecommunications Standards Institute (ETSI). Groups like these have been officially delegated the responsibility for creating thousands of technical product standards. They are subject to EU law

---

79 *See, e.g.,* Council Resolution on a New Approach to Technical Harmonization and Standards, 1985 O.J. C136/1.

80 *See* Council Directive 89/48. Council Directive 92/51 expanded the mutual recognition of diplomas to cover post-secondary and secondary education and training.

81 Council Directive 83/169. *See* Directives 98/34, 98/48 (extension to on-line services).

82 CIA Security International v. Signalson, (1996) Eur.Comm.Rep. I–2201.

on the free movement of goods lest they create market barriers.[83] These EU private bodies have been turning out some 150 common standards each year. North American producers have frequently complained that their ability to be heard by European standards' bodies is limited. They have had little influence on EU product standards to which they must conform to sell freely in the Common Market.

Directives on the safety of toys, construction products and electromagnetic compatibility have been issued.[84] These directives adopt the so-called "new approach" of setting broad, exclusive standards at the Union level which if voluntarily met guarantee access to every member state market. Under the "old approach", which still applies to most standards for processed foods, motor vehicles, chemicals and pharmaceuticals, EU legislation on standards is binding law. The technical specifications and testing protocols of these directives must be followed and (unlike the new approach) the member states may add requirements to them. Under either approach, goods meeting Union standards will bear a CE mark.[85]

Testing and Certification

Testing and certification of products is another part of the EU campaign. The main concern of North American companies is that recognition of U.S., Canadian and Mexican tests be granted by the European Union. Many North American exporters have had to have their goods retested for Union purposes. The EU is generally committed to a resolution of such issues under what it calls a "global approach" to product standards and testing. This involves creation of a regional system for authorizing certification and testing under common rules and procedures.[86] In negotiations undertaken as part of the Uruguay Round on revising the Standards Code of the GATT, the EU gave its commitment to giving recognition to "equivalent technical regulations" of other nations, and to avoidance of unnecessary obstacles to trade.

In 1991, the United States and the European Union issued a nonbinding joint communiqué on product standards and certification procedures. Each side states its commitment to using international consensus standards in their legal régimes. This commitment extends to private sector product standard bodies. Regarding certification, the EU indicates that testing facilities located outside

---

83 Fra.bo SpA DVGW, (2012) Eur.Comm.Rep. (Case C–171/11).

84 *See* Council Directives 88/378, 89/106 and 89/336.

85 *See* Council Directive 93/68.

86 Council Resolution Dec. 21, 1989, O.J. C10 (Jan. 16, 1990).

its borders will be able to obtain "Notified Body" (official) status for the purpose of applying the many new EU product standards. Such facilities may include subcontractors of official Notified Bodies. Nevertheless, a Department of Commercial official has concluded:

While it may not be the least cost route, the most straightforward means to certify compliance with EU legal health and safety requirements is to follow European standards and testing procedures. Incompatibility between North American and European standards, testing procedures, quality assessment systems, and certifications can mean additional testing costs for U.S. exporters who want to qualify their products for sale in the EU market.[87] More recently, private European food standards set by Global Gap have spread to North American farmers and retailers, including Wal-Mart and McDonald's.

Product Standards Legislation

The following is a sampling of EC product standard laws. Occupational health and safety laws are covered in Chapter 5.

Transport

- Directives 70/156, 87/358, 92/53 (approval of motor vehicles)
- Directives 70/311, 92/62 (steering equipment)
- Directives 71/127, 88/321 (rear view mirrors)
- Directives 71/320, 88/194 92/54 (motor vehicle braking)
- Directives 77/143, 92/55 (motor vehicle exhaust)
- Directives 80/1269, 88/195 (motor vehicle engine power)
- Directives 85/3, 88/214 (truck weights and dimensions)
- Directive 86/217 (tire pressure gauges)
- Directives 88/366, 90/360 (motor vehicle field of vision)
- Directives 83/449, 91/225 (roadworthiness tests for motor vehicles)
- Directive 89/173 (tractor weights and dimensions)
- Directives 89/277, 89/278, 89/516, 89/517, 89/518 (motor vehicle lamps and signals)
- Directive 89/297 (motor vehicle side guards)

Duesterberg, "Federal Government Response to the EC 1992 Challenge in Standards, Testing and Certification," *Business America* (Feb. 24, 1992). *See* Hagigh, "Obtaining EC Product Approvals after 1992," *Id.* at p. 30.

- Directives 89/459, 92/23 (motor vehicle tires)
- Directives 90/638, 90/629 (motor vehicle safety belts)
- Directive 91/226 (motor vehicle spray suppression)
- Directive 92/22 (motor vehicle safety glass)
- Directive 92/24 (motor vehicle speed limitation devices)
- Directives 93/29–93/34 (wheel vehicles)

Consumer Goods

- Directive 73/23 (low voltage electrical appliances)
- Directive 87/404 (simple pressure vessels)
- Directive 88/378 (toy safety)
- Directives 89/336, 92/31 (radio electromagnetic incompatibility)
- Directive 92/42 (hot water heaters)
- Directive 92/75 (energy consumption appliance labels)

Industrial Goods

- Directive 86/663 (self-propelled industrial trucks)
- Directives 87/402, 89/681, 88/465, 89/173, 89/682, 89/680 (tractors)
- Directive 87/405 (tower cranes-sound)
- Directives 88/571, 90/487 (dangerous electrical equipment)
- Directive 89/106 (construction products)
- Directive 89/240 (test methods for industrial trucks)
- Directive 89/392 (machine safety)
- Directive 2004/22 (measuring instruments)
- Regulation 1907/2006 (REACH, chemicals)

Miscellaneous

- Directives 84/529, 90/486 (electrically operated lifts)
- Directive 90/384 (non-automatic weighing instruments)
- Directive 90/396 (gas appliances)
- Directive 92/38 (satellite broadcasting of television signals)

§ 4.7 Pharmaceutical and Medical Products

A surprising number of European Union directives and other legislative acts focus on harmonization and mutual recognition of the law governing pharmaceuticals and other medical products. These acts focus primarily on product registration, research, manufacturing, pricing and advertising.

Legislative Digest

The following is a sampling of EU legislation in the pharmaceuticals and medicinal products area:

- Directive 65/65 (proprietary medicinal products) as particularly amended by Directives 75/319, 91/356, 92/73
- Directive 75/318 (medicinal standards and protocols)
- Directive 78/25 (coloring)
- Directives 81/851, 92/18 (veterinary medicinal products)
- Directive 81/852, 92/74 (veterinary standards and protocols)
- Directive 84/539 (electro-medical equipment)
- Directive 86/609 (protection of animals)
- Directives 87/18, 88/320 (good laboratory practices)
- Directive 89/105 (transparency of pricing measures)
- Directive 89/342 (immunologicals)
- Directive 89/343 (radiopharmaceuticals)
- Directive 89/381 (blood products)
- Directive 89/341 (generics)
- Directive 90/385 (medical implants)
- Directive 92/27 (labeling and information)
- Directive 92/28 (advertising)
- Directive 92/26 (prescriptions)
- Directive 92/25 (wholesale practices)
- Directive 93/39 (medicinal product standards and testing)
- Regulation 2309/93 (biotechnology products)
- Directive 98/8 (biocidal products)

- Directive 2001/83 (medicinal products)
- Directive 2002/98 (blood products)
- Regulation 726/2004 (medicinal products authorization)

Directive 92/28 restricts pharmaceutical advertising. There is a ban on advertising prescription drugs to the public. The advertising of over-the-counter medicines must be clear and not misleading. The gift of free samples to medical doctors is also restrained, as is the sponsorship of conferences by pharmaceutical companies. Directive 92/27 requires the listing of pharmaceutical ingredients and proper usage on a label. Detailed information on precautions and possible side effects is also mandatory.

The Court of Justice has clarified the dividing line between cosmetic and medicinal products.[88] Products which by presentation or by function are used with a view towards restoring, correcting or modifying physiological functions are medicinal and must be authorized by state authorities. Cosmetic products are subject to a separate series of EU directives[89] which do not generally require authorization.

New cosmetics tested on animals have been completely banned since 2013. In the *Upjohn* litigation, the Court was concerned with a hair growth product that was treated as a medicinal by one company and a cosmetic by another. The Court took a broad view of the definition of "medicinals" found in Directive 65/65, emphasizing that mere representation of the product for physiological functions suffices to bring the product under state authorization requirements. Likewise, herbal teas advertised as having therapeutic qualities even though there is no scientific basis for such claims were "medicinal products" falling under Directive 65/65 and subject to national regulation.[90] Germany's classification of *all* vitamins as medicinals was ruled an invalid trade barrier,[91] whereas Denmark's regulation of the marketing of foods to which vitamins or minerals are added was a legitimate public health control.[92]

Trade Issues

Free trade in medicinal products has been a contentious area. One leading Court of Justice opinion struck down a German law

88 The Upjohn Co. + Anor v. Farzoo Inc. + Anor, (1991) Eur.Comm.Rep. I–1703 (Case C–112/89); Re Monteil + Anor, (1991) Eur.Comm.Rep. I–1547 (Case C–60/89). *See* Council Directive 65/65.

89 *See* Council Directives 76/768, 92/7, 93/35.

90 Re Ter Vaart, (1992) Eur.Comm.Rep. I–5485 (Case C–219/91).

91 Commission v. Germany, (2004) Eur.Comm.Rep. I–00000 (Case 387/99).

92 Commission v. Denmark, (2003) Eur.Comm.Rep. 9693 (Case C–192/01).

requiring import certificates for medicinal products that were repackaged.[93] The importer has a duty to see that medicinals are packaged and marketed in accordance with national law. Repackaging of pharmaceuticals traded across state borders is both legal and common.[94] At present, national monopolies granted to pharmacists over the sale of medicinal products have survived scrutiny as trade barriers under TFEU examinations by the Court of Justice. National export controls over medical goods related to the COVID-19 pandemic raised prominent EU free trade issues.

National courts must decide whether such monopolies are necessary consumer protection laws and whether their goals might not be achieved by less restrictive means.[95] Mail ordering of medicinals is protected by free trade principles and Directive 2001/83.[96] That said, the ECJ has allowed pharmaceutical companies to limit supplies to wholesalers in member states with low price caps who resell drugs in high cap countries, an inroad on "parallel trading" rights.[97]

Evaluation Agency

Council Regulation 2309/93 created the European Agency for the Evaluation of Medicinal Products to evaluate and authorize technologically advanced medicinal products, notably those derived from biotechnology, intended for use in humans or food-producing animals. Prescription drug companies can seek EU-wide "centralized" marketing approval from this agency,[98] or individually obtain "decentralized" national approvals. If Union authorization is not required, all national authorizations for the marketing of medicinal products must be mutually recognized and such products may be freely traded in the EU. Support for such mutual recognition is derived from the harmonization of standards for medicinal products and their testing.[99] Centralized marketing technique approvals bind parallel importers.[100] Similar treatment and free

---

[93] Freistaat Bayern v. Eurim-Pharm GmbH, (1991) Eur.Comm.Rep. I–1747 (Case C–347/89).

[94] *See* Section 4.4.

[95] Re Delattre, (1991) Eur.Comm.Rep. I–1487 (Case 369/88).

[96] Deutscher Apothekerverband eV v. DocMorris NV, (2003) Eur.Comm.Rep. I–I–14887 (Case C–322/01).

[97] *See* Section 4.4.

[98] *See* Regulations 1084/2003 and 1085/2003, Council Directive 2003/63.

[99] *See especially* Council Directive 93/39.

[100] *See* Aventis Pharma Deutschland GmbH v. Kohlpharma GmbH, (2002) Eur.Comm.Rep. I–7761 (Case C–433/00).

trade in authorized veterinary products has also been accomplished.[101]

§ 4.8 Food Products

Another area where the European Union has been especially active legislatively is food products. These laws focus on labeling, product contents, additives and packaging. In 2002, the European Food Safety Authority was created in response to "mad cow" and other food crises. It has been very influential on food safety legislation.[102] Private European food guidelines have also been influential in U.S. markets. . . Global Gap for example is now followed by Wal-Mart and McDonald's.

Legislative Digest

The following is a sampling of EU legislation in the foodstuffs area:

- Directives 64/54, 85/585 (preservatives)
- Directives 74/329, 86/102, and 89/393 (emulsifiers, etc.)
- Directive 79/112 (labeling and advertising)
- Directives 79/581, 88/315 (pricing of foodstuffs)
- Directive 80/777 (natural mineral waters)
- Directive 85/373 (coffee extracts)
- Directive 86/197 (alcoholic strength labels)
- Directive 88/314 (pricing of non-foodstuffs)
- Directive 88/344 (extraction solvents)
- Directives 88/388, 91/71 (flavorings)
- Directive 88/593 (fruit jams)
- Directives 89/107, 90/612 (food additives)
- Directive 89/108 (quick-frozen food)
- Directive 89/109 (materials coming into contact with food)
- Directive 89/394 (fruit juices)
- Directive 89/396 (lot identification)
- Directive 89/397 (official control of food)

---

101 Council Directive 93/40.

102 *See* Pfizer Animal Health v. Council, (2002) Eur.Comm.Rep. II–3305 (Case T–13/99).

- Directive 89/398 (particular nutritional uses)
- Directive 89/347 (egg products)
- Regulation 1576/89 (spirit drinks)
- Directives 90/128, 93/9 (plastic materials in contact with food)
- Directive 90/220 (GMOs)
- Directive 90/496 (nutritional labeling)
- Directive 90/642 (pesticide residues)
- Directive 91/321 (infant formulae)
- Directives 91/325, 91/326, 91/410, 91/442 (classification, packaging and labeling of dangerous substances)
- Directives 91/492, 91/493 (fish products)
- Directives 91/494, 91/495, 91/497 (poultry and meat products)
- Regulation 2092/91 (organic foods)
- Regulation 315/93 (food contaminants)
- Directive 93/43 (food hygiene)
- Directive 96/5 (cereals and baby foods)
- Directive 97/41 (maximum food pesticides)
- Directive 2000/13 (food labels)
- Directive 2000/36 (chocolate)
- Directive 2001/01 (preserved meats)
- Regulation 466/2001 (contaminants)
- Directive 2002/16 (food packaging)
- Regulation 2092/91 (organic foods)
- Directive 2003/60 (pesticides)
- Regulations 852/2004, 853/2004, 854/2004 (Hygiene Package)

Labels

Directive 79/112 requires the following information to be listed on all food packaging labels: (1) the name under which the product is sold; (2) the list of ingredients; (3) the net quantity; (4) the "use by" date of minimum durability; (5) any special storage conditions or conditions of use; (6) the name or business name and address of the manufacturer or the packager, or of the seller established within the Union; (7) the place of origin, especially where labels might mislead the consumer; and (8) instructions for use when it would be impossible to make appropriate use of the foodstuff in the absence of such instructions. Manufacturers have the responsibility to identify and label all "health risks."

The nutritional value of a product must be designated on the package. Nutrition labeling refers to statements regarding energy value, or any of the following nutrients: protein, carbohydrates, fat, fiber, sodium, and assorted vitamins and minerals. Statements that include phrases such as "provides, provides at a reduced rate, or does not provide" refer to health risk in a foodstuff. The manufacturer has the responsibility to ensure that products are worthy of energy value claims. The indication of minimum durability is not required on fresh fruits, vegetables, wines, beverages containing greater than ten percent alcohol, baked goods and pastries consumed within a 24-hour period, vinegar, cooking salt, solid sugar, and confectionery products consisting of flavored sugars.

Ingredients which are present in packages must be listed in a clear, concise manner in languages expected to be easily understood by national customers. Food and beverage products must be labeled with a list of ingredients and alcohol content percentages. Directive 89/396 requires lot marks on all packaged foods distributed throughout the EU. Lot marks are designated by the placement of the letter "L" on the package. It is said that the new lot marking directive will have a major impact on the U.S. food sector, where food does not generally bear this type of marking. The directive also mandates a special format in which foods are dated. This format differs from the one currently used in the United States.

In 1992, the Council adopted two additional regulations on food labeling and food quality. The first concerns the use of protected geographical indications (PGIs) and protected designations of origin (PDOs) on foodstuffs, excepting wine and spirits. This regulation seeks to keep generic names from being registered. The second regulation deals with certificates of specific character for foodstuffs meeting EU criteria and specifications. Registration and Union inspection requirements for such certificates focus on the use of traditional raw materials or processing techniques.

Trade Issues

The Court of Justice has vigorously promoted free internal trade in foodstuffs. Member state food standards may not generally impede the flow of food products across borders in the absence of identifiable health and safety risks. The Court has repeatedly decided that consumer protection goals are adequately met by use of informative labeling regarding food ingredients,[103] characteristics and origin. Such labeling may be required by national law, but free movement of foodstuffs may not otherwise be impeded. This line of reasoning originated in the famous *Cassis de Dijon* case[104] involving German *minimum* alcoholic content controls as applied to French liquors. Thus, absent bona fide health and safety concerns,[105] each member state must ordinarily recognize the food product standards of other member states. Principles of mutual recognition also underlie much of the EU foodstuffs legislation outlined above.

§ 4.9 General Rights of Residence

A general right is accorded EU nationals to move freely for purposes of residence throughout the Union and benefits students, retirees and the populace at large.[106] This right should be distinguished from the free movement rights of workers discussed in the next section. The chief concern about a general right of residence is coverage for health and social welfare purposes, and a possible run towards those states with more generous programs. Whether BREXIT might cause EU nationals in the UK and their British counterparts on the continent to lose their residency rights was a major concern. See Chapter 8.

Council Directive 90/364 and 2004/38 extend a general right of residence to all member state nationals of independent means and their families (including co-habitants) provided they do not become a burden on the public finances of the host country. Intergovernmental transfers cover the costs of local health care for EU resident nationals.

Spouses and dependent children (even those who are *not* EU nationals) are entitled to work in the country where the non-working EU spouse has taken up residence. These principles also apply to employees and the self-employed who have retired.[107] Parents of EU children in need of caretaking have residency rights, even if the child was deliberately born in Ireland to obtain citizenship there.[108]

---

103 *See, e.g.,* Commission v. Spain, (2003) Eur.Comm.Rep. I–469 (chocolate).

104 Rewe Zentral AG v. Bundesmonopolverwaltung für Branntwein, (1979) Eur.Comm.Rep. 649. *See,* particularly, Baumbast and R. v. Secretary of State for the Home Department, (2002) Eur.Comm.Rep. I–7091.

105 *See, e.g.,* Gilli and Andres, (1980) Eur.Comm.Rep. 2071; Commission v. Italy, (2003) Eur.Comm.Rep. I–6445 (approval of caffeine-added beverages not justified).

106 *See* Article 18(1), Treaty of Rome and Directive 2004/38.

107 Council Directive 90/365.

108 Zhu and Chen v. Secretary of State for the Home Department, (2004) Eur.Comm.Rep. I–9925.

EU nationals and their families seeking to exercise their right of residence in another member state must ordinarily demonstrate sufficient financial resources and health insurance coverage. "Sufficiency" for these purposes connotes resources in excess of the level which would trigger social assistance in the host state. Retired persons must prove that they receive a disability, retirement or old age pension meeting this criterion.

Directive 2003/109 governs long-term residents who are *not* EU nationals. After five years, most such persons are entitled to long-term residency immigration status.

Students

Students have a general right of residence for educational purposes throughout the Union provided they can show sufficient resources, health insurance and enrollment in the host state. The student's family (but not co-habitant) may accompany him or her and work in that state and obtain social benefits when not working.[109] The student's enrollment must be his or her principal purpose for residing in the host country. All general rights of residence are subject to exceptions based upon public policy, health or safety.[110]

Students seeking vocational training in another member state cannot be subjected to discriminatory tuition fees not charged to nationals.[111] In one decision, the Court of Justice took a broad view of "vocational training" under Article 167 TFEU. Any form of education which prepares someone for a qualification in a particular trade, profession or employment is included. This is the case regardless of age or the level of the training, and even if the study program involves some general education. A French national, for example, was therefore entitled to train in strip cartoon arts without paying special fees at a Belgian city academy.

Students also benefit from an EU initiative known as ERASMUS. This program supports "vocational" student mobility and enrollment rights, even when research is primarily involved.[112] University education is treated as vocational by the Court of Justice. Tens of thousands of students are now exchanged under this program each year. It has been extended to students from EFTA and many

---

109 Council Directive 90/366. *See* Teixeira v. London Borough of Lambeth, (2010) Eur.Comm.Rep. (Feb. 23, 2010).

110 *See* the discussion of these issues in connection with workers' rights in the next section.

111 Gravier v. City of Liège, (1985) Eur.Comm.Rep. 593. *Accord,* Raulin v. Minister of Education and Science, (1992) Eur.Comm.Rep. I–1027 (Case C–357/89).

112 *See* Commission v. Council, (1989) Eur.Comm.Rep. 1425 (ERASMUS).

Central European countries but removed for UK students (save those from Northern Ireland) post BREXIT. See Chapter 8.

The 1993 Maastricht Accord authorized cooperative EU action and "incentive measures" on education, vocational training, youth, cultural, and public health affairs. The Amsterdam Treaty of 1999 added employment incentives to this authority. These provisions explicitly rule out harmonization by Union mandate in these fields and thus reflect the growing trend toward "subsidiarity."[113]

The Bologna Process started in 1998 brought common Bachelor's and Masters degree systems to 46 European Nations, including all from the EU.

§ 4.10 Free Movement of Workers, the Self-Employed and Their Families

The foundations of the Union include the free movement of people, services and capital. These are often referred to in economic literature as the "factors of production." Their inclusion in the TFEU distinguishes it from other trade treaties which merely create customs unions.

In the early years of the European Community, many Italian workers moved north into the factories of West Germany and to a lesser extent France as the rebuilding of the European economy took place. Membership in the EU was eagerly sought in later years by Greece, Portugal and Spain to acquire these rights for their expatriate workers. Prior to membership, Greek, Portuguese and Spanish workers were subject to much less liberal national laws on guest workers. These national laws continue for the most part to govern the rights of the large number of Turkish and Slavic employees in Germany, North Africans in France and Commonwealth citizens in Britain. Special employment rights (but not national treatment) have been given to Turkish workers in the Union under the "Ankara Agreement" which acknowledges Turkey's associate status with the European Union.[114]

Freedom of movement for workers is secured in Article 45, and by an extensive range of legislative acts which have implemented this right. Whereas, for example, North Americans must obtain work permits to undertake employment within the European Union, this is not required of citizens and legally resident aliens of the member

---

113 *See* Section 2.0.

114 For a case exploring the rights of Turkish workers in the EU under that country's association agreement with the Union, *see* Kus v. Landeshauptstadt Wiesbaden, (1992) Eur.Comm.Rep. I–6781 (Case C–237/91).

states,[115] or Iceland, Liechtenstein and Norway under the European Economic Area treaty. They may seek employment on the same basis as nationals of the EU state where the job is located. In other words, workers from Union countries enjoy "national treatment."[116]

Dual Nationals

National treatment rights have caused renewed interest by North Americans and others in becoming "dual nationals." Irish and Italian "laws of return" generally permit emigrants born in Europe *and* their children or grandchildren to obtain Irish and Italian citizenship. British subjects who are patrials may generally do likewise. German law grants nationality to *descendants* of persons who were German citizens or German nationals, with a special preference for refugees of Nazism. Poland and Hungary likewise have special preferences for descendants of victims of Nazism. As a rule, however, Germany allows only German nationality, not dual nationality.

Dual nationals with a member state citizenship may not be denied their Union rights by another member state. For example, an Argentinian/Italian was entitled to reside and enter business in Spain.[117] But British Overseas Citizens may be denied UK residency rights.[118]

The U.S. government permits dual nationality for Americans. The free movement benefits of being a European national make this status quite attractive for lawyers and other professionals. Some U.S. employers routinely search their personnel databases for possible dual national candidates. This is especially true for service providers, for example aircraft maintenance or computer companies, that may wish to fly in staff for emergency repairs in Europe without worrying about visas or work permits.

Social Advantages

The right of expatriate European Union workers to bring their families,[119] obtain social services, housing, education and pensions in

---

115 Vander Elst v. Office des Migrations Internationales, (1994) Eur.Comm.Rep. I–3803.

116 Council Regulation 1612/68; Commission v. France, (1974) Eur.Comm.Rep. 359. (French citizenship quota for crews on ships invalid).

117 Micheleitti & ORS v. Delegación del Gobierno en Cantabria, (1992) Eur.Comm.Rep. I–4239 (Case C–369/90).

118 Queen v. Secretary of State (Kaur), (2001) Eur.Comm.Rep. I–1237.

119 *See especially* Baumbast and R. v. Secretary of State for the Home Department, (2002) Eur.Comm.Rep. I–7091 (spousal and child rights post-divorce/ separation) and Metock v. Minister for Justice, Equality and Law Reform, (2008) Eur.Comm.Rep. I–6241 (Case 127/08) (spouses previously denied asylum have right to live with EU workers). *See also* The Netherlands v. Reed, (1986) Eur.Comm.Rep. 1283

a nondiscriminatory manner is all provided in a wealth of EU law on "social advantages." There is no Union social security system. Rather, the Union assures equal treatment of claims made against national systems covering health care, old age, pensions, taxation, housing, unemployment, family benefits, and workers' compensation.[120] The exercise of the right of free movement by EU workers cannot be subject to the issuance of restrictive residency or entrance permits.[121] They can be required within a reasonable time to report their presence to the host member state.[122] A valid identity card from their home state is all that is required to prove a worker's right to reside elsewhere in the Union.[123]

Part-time and probationary workers (such as teachers seeking licensure) are included, as are the unemployed who actively seek work.[124] However, a six months limitation on the right to enter another member state in search of work is reasonable and not contrary to free movement law.[125] In one decision, the European Court of Justice struck down a longstanding Greek law restricting ownership of land to Greeks as contrary to free movement rights.[126] In another widely known decision, free movement rights were extended to professional athletes.[127]

(companions; Re Humer, (2002) Eur.Comm.Rep. I–1205) (Case C–255/99) (children's rights).

[120] *See, e.g.,* Regina v. Warry, (1977) Eur.Comm.Rep. 2085 (health care); Frilli v. Belgium, (1972) Eur.Comm.Rep. 457 (old age); DiPaolo v. Office National de l'Emploi, (1977) Eur.Comm.Rep. 315 (unemployment); Reina v. Landeskreditbank Baden-Württemberg, (1982) Eur.Comm.Rep. 33 (family benefits); Pennartz v. Caisse Primaire d'Assurance Maladie des Alpes-Maritimes, (1979) Eur.Comm.Rep. 2411 (workers' compensation); Finanzamt Köln-Alstadt v. Schumacker, (1995) Eur.Comm.Rep. I–225 (taxation); Commission v. Italy, (1988) Eur.Comm.Rep. 29 (housing loans); Gonzalez v. INSS, (2013) Eur.Comm.Rep. (Case C–282–11) (pensions).

[121] Rutuli v. Minister for the Interior, (1975) Eur.Comm.Rep. 1219; State v. Royer, (1976) Eur.Comm.Rep. 497; Regina v. Pieck, (1980) Eur.Comm.Rep. 2171; Lawrie Blum v. Land Baden-Württemberg, (1986) Eur.Comm.Rep. 2121; Clean Car Auto Service v. Landeshauptmann Von Wien, (1998) Eur.Comm.Rep. I–2521.

[122] Re Watson and Belman, (1976) Eur.Comm.Rep. 1185.

[123] Giagounidis v. City of Reutlingen, (1991) Eur.Comm.Rep. I–1069 (Case C–376/89).

[124] Lawrie Blum v. Land Baden-Württemberg, (1986) Eur.Comm.Rep.2121; Kempf v. Staatssecretaris van Justitie, (1986) Eur.Comm.Rep. 1741; Lair v. Universitat Hanover, (1988) Eur.Comm.Rep. 3161; Regina v. Antonissen, (1991) Eur.Comm.Rep. I–0745 (Case C–292/89).

[125] Regina v. Antonissen, (1991) Eur.Comm.Rep. I–0745 (Case C–292/89).

[126] Commission v. Greece, (1989) Eur.Comm.Rep. 1461.

[127] Union Royale Belge des Societes de Football v. Bosman, (1995) Eur.Comm.Rep. I–4921.

Free Movement Exceptions

The only blanket exception to the regime of free movement of workers is established in Article 45(4) TFEU. Employment in the "public service" of member states is exempted. The public service, for these purposes, involves jobs with official authority, including the judiciary, the police, defense forces and tax inspectors.[128] Licensed attorneys fall outside the public service, even though they may be required in order to litigate in national courts.[129] Municipal positions are also included when there is participation in the exercise of public power, which was the case for example in Brussels with the city architect but not city hospital nurses.[130] Secondary school teachers are not part of the public service. Such positions are therefore open to Union competition,[131] but may be subject to language requirements.[132]

Member states may restrict the free movement of workers from other Union nations on grounds of public policy (ordre public), public security or public health.[133] These provisions have been litigated extensively. In a long series of decisions, the European Court has evolved rules which limit the power of EU states to expel or deny admission to workers whose past conduct is objectionable. Only when that conduct is effectively combatted if engaged in by its own nationals may restraints on expatriate Union workers be applied.[134]

Public policy reasons for limiting the free movement rights of EU workers must be based on the existence of a genuine and serious threat affecting fundamental societal interests.[135] Past criminal convictions, alone, are insufficient. COVID-19 public health worker restraints raise similar issues.

Reverse Discrimination

The Common Market law prohibiting discrimination against workers from member states does not reach national laws that discriminate against a country's own citizens regarding free

---

[128] Sotgiu v. Deutsche Bundespost, (1974) Eur.Comm.Rep. 153.

[129] Reyners v. Belgium, (1974) Eur.Comm.Rep. 631.

[130] Commission v. Belgium, (1982) Eur.Comm.Rep. 1845.

[131] Bleis v. Ministère de l'Education Nationale, (1992) Eur.Comm.Rep. I–5627 (Case C–4/91). Allue v. Universita di Venezia, (1989) Eur.Comm.Rep. 1591.

[132] Groener v. Minister for Education, (1989) Eur.Comm.Rep. 3967. *Compare* Angonese v. Cassa di Risparmio di Bolzano, (2000) Eur.Comm.Rep. I–4139.

[133] Article 45(3), TFEU; Council Directive 64/221.

[134] *Compare* Van Duyn v. Home Office, (1974) Eur.Comm.Rep. 1337 (denial of right of Church of Scientology secretary from Holland to work in U.K. upheld) with Adoui and Cornuaille v. Belgium, (1982) Eur.Comm.Rep. 1665 (denial of right of French waitresses suspected of prostitution to work in Belgium invalid).

[135] Regina v. Bouchereau, (1977) Eur.Comm.Rep. 425.

movement and employment. In other words, "reverse discrimination" can occur where EU law protects the rights of workers from other states, but national law denies similar rights to workers of that nation.[136] In one reverse discrimination case, the right of Italy to prosecute the Italian biotherapists and planotherapists for unauthorized medical practice was upheld notwithstanding EU right of establishment law on diploma recognition and medical doctors.[137]

Conversely, when a worker has exercised the right to employment elsewhere in the Union, he or she is entitled to pay home country social benefit taxes even if much lower than where the work is performed.[138] Such workers can also be paid the minimum wage in their host country, often less than the prevailing wage where they work. Hence employers bringing in "posted" workers from less expensive countries (Latvia to Sweden, for example) are less expensive to employ than locals. This "social dumping" via "posted workers" is much criticized.

§ 4.11 Right of Establishment—Professionals; Lawyers

The right to go into business as a self-employed person or through agencies, branches or subsidiaries in another member state is secured by Article 59 TFEU. This is known as the "right of establishment." Many Union entrepreneurs, for example, have used this right to open restaurants throughout the EU. The right of self-establishment carries with it nearly the same bundle of national treatment rights and exceptions associated with employed workers.[139] It is also subject to the *Cassis* formula.

Implementation of the right of establishment for professionals is anticipated in Article 64 by the issuance of Union legislation mutually recognizing diplomas and national licenses. Medical doctors, dentists, veterinarians, architects, insurance agents, nurses, midwives, pharmacists and others have benefited from these provisions and the substantial implementing law that now accompanies them. The Council in 1982 adopted directives about freedom to supply services in the case of travel agents, tour operators, air brokers, freight forwarders, ship brokers, air cargo agents, shipping agents, and hairdressers.

---

136 Regina v. Saunders, (1979) Eur.Comm.Rep. 1129; Moser v. Land Baden-Württemberg, (1984) Eur.Comm.Rep. 2539; Scholz v. Opera Universitaria di Cagliari, (1999) Eur.Comm.Rep. I–505.

137 Re Nino, (1990) Eur.Comm.Rep. I–3537 (Cases C–54/88, C–91/88, C–14/89).

138 Knoors v. Secretary of State for Economic Affairs, (1979) Eur.Comm.Rep. 399.

139 *See* The Council's General Program for the Abolition of Restrictions on Freedom of Establishment (1962).

It has been relatively easy to deal with those liberal professions (*e.g.*, medicine and allied professions) in which diplomas and other evidence of formal qualification relate to equivalent competence in the same skill. It did, however, take 17 years to negotiate the directive on free movement of veterinarians. And litigation over the implementation of these directives continues. For example, it took a Commission prosecution to remove the French requirement that doctors and dentists give up their home country professional registrations before being licensed in France.[140] Directive 2005/36 creates a broad legal framework for recognition of professional qualifications.

Diploma Directives

Typically, European Union law on the right of establishment creates minimum professional training standards which, if met, will result in mutual recognition. Substantial variations in training may trigger special admissions requirements, such as time in practice, an adaptation period or an aptitude test.[141] A major single market directive applies this approach to virtually all EU professionals receiving diplomas based upon a minimum of three years of study.[142] A subsequent directive requires mutual recognition of certificates and diplomas awarded for less than three years study,[143] which has been construed to apply to one-year masters degrees (LLMs).[144]

The ECJ has ruled that the diploma directives are of direct effect and can be relied upon by individuals regardless of the state of national implementation.[145] Mutual recognition in this instance means that access is gained to host country professional bodies. This is different from the home country licensing method of mutual recognition used for banking, insurance and investment advisors.[146] Even in the absence of such legislation, professional disqualification on grounds of nationality is prohibited.[147] When an EU directive establishes practical training requirements for mutual recognition purposes, the host state must give credit for home state training

---

140 Commission v. France, (1986) 1 Common Mkt.L.Rep. 57.

141 *See* Commission v. Italy, (2002) Eur.Comm.Rep. I–2235.

142 Council Directive 89/48. *See* Burbaud v. Ministere de l'Emploi et la Solidarite, (2003) Eur.Comm.Rep. I–00000 (Case C–285/01) (hospital administrator's diploma).

143 Council Directive 92/51.

144 Kraus v. Land Baden-Württemberg, (1993) Eur.Comm.Rep. I–1663.

145 Peros v. Tehniko E. Ellados, Case C–141/04 (July 15, 2005).

146 *See* § 4.12.

147 Patrick v. Ministre des Affaires Culturelles, (1977) Eur.Comm.Rep. 1199 (architects).

taken in academic courses. In this case, a German-trained architect received credit and was entitled to practice in Belgium.[148]

EU law on the mutual recognition of professional qualifications and diplomas received a consolidation under Directive 2005/36. Cross-border provision of services and the right of establishment were affirmed, subject to "knowledge of necessary languages." British professionals post BREXIT no longer benefit from the EU diploma recognition regime. See Chapter 8.

Legal Profession

Considerable difficulty has been encountered in lifting restrictions within member states on the freedom to provide legal services. For example, within the legal profession there may be only a small amount of training or required knowledge held in common by a "lawyer" from a civil law jurisdiction (*e.g.*, an avocat from France) and a "lawyer" from a common law jurisdiction (*e.g.*, a solicitor from Ireland). As a result, the initial directive relating to lawyers' services took a delicate approach to the question of freedom to provide legal services and stops short of dealing with a right of establishment.[149]

This 1977 directive allows a lawyer from one member state, under that lawyer's national title (*e.g.*, abogado, rechtsanwalt, barrister), to temporarily provide services in other member states. This includes the right to appear in court without retaining local co-counsel unless representation by counsel is mandatory under national laws.[150] Once retained, a local lawyer need not actually conduct the litigation. It is sufficient that the local attorney is retained to "act in conjunction with" the proceedings.[151] But the EU legal services directive cannot be used to circumvent national rules on professional ethics, particularly where a dual nationality lawyer has been disbarred and then moves to another state.[152]

Right of Establishment for Lawyers

Directive 77/249 gave rise to lawyer identity cards issued under the auspices of *Commission Consultative des Barreaux Européens* (C.C.B.E.), which has been charged to propose a specific directive about a right of establishment for lawyers. However, the mutual recognition of diplomas accomplished in Council Directive 89/48

148 Bauer v. Conseil National de l'Ordre des Architectes, (1992) Eur.Comm.Rep. I–2797 (Case C–166/191). *See* Commission v. Spain, (2000) Eur.Comm.Rep. I–10375 (architects' activities); Josef Corsten, (2000) Eur.Comm.Rep. I–7919 (self-employed architect lays floors, no duty to register as skilled trade).

149 *See* Council Directive 77/249.

150 Commission v. Germany, (1988) Eur.Comm.Rep. 1123.

151 Commission v. France, (1991) Eur.Comm.Rep. I–3591 (Case C–294/89).

152 Gullung v. Conseil de l'Ordre des Avocats (Colmar), (1988) Eur.Comm.Rep. 111.

applies to lawyers.[153] The maximum adaptation or training period allowed under this directive is three years. In 1997, the long-awaited right of establishment directive was adopted.[154] It mirrors much of the prior law but makes it easier (than under the diploma directive) to join the local bar after three years of practice under home country title in the host state. This permits, for example, a German lawyer to bypass diploma and bar exam requirements of other EU countries in less time than most local lawyers spend meeting those criteria. Requiring local bar association membership is permitted under EU law.[155]

The C.C.B.E. adopted a common Code of Conduct for lawyers in 1988. It is hoped that this Code will ultimately become binding in all member states. It seeks to harmonize rules of conduct on confidentiality, conflicts of interest, segregation of client funds and malpractice insurance. In other areas, the Code does not harmonize, but rather provides choice of law rules to resolve conflicting national approaches to advertising, contingent fees and membership on boards of directors. The host country's rules in these areas will apply to lawyers providing services across borders under Directive 77/249. Home country rules apply as to fee arrangements.[156] Some EU jurisdictions (*e.g.*, Germany) allow multi-professional practices, but a Dutch ban on practicing law in full partnership with accountants was upheld primarily because of the absence of strict codes of ethics for accountants.[157] In 2007, the C.C.B.E. agreed upon a common set of post-degree legal training standards focused on outcomes not inputs.

Admission to the practice of law is still governed by the rules of the legal profession of each member state. Several European Court judgments have upheld the right of lawyer applicants to be free from discrimination on grounds of nationality, residence or retention of the right to practice in home jurisdictions.[158] For example, a Greek lawyer who had a doctorate in German law and had worked for some time advising on Greek and EU law in Munich was denied admission

---

[153] *See* Morgenbesser v. Consiglio dell'Ordine degli avvocati di Genova, (2003) Eur.Comm.Rep. I–13467 (Case C–313/01) (French maitrisse en droit degree must be recognized in Italy which has no equivalent).

[154] Council Directive 98/5. Unsuccessfully challenged in Luxembourg v. Parliament and Council, (2000) Eur.Comm.Rep. I–9131.

[155] Ebert v. Budapesti Ügyvédi Kamara, (2011) Eur.Comm.Rep. (Case C–359/09).

[156] Cipolla v. Meloni, (2006) Eur.Comm.Rep. I–I–11241 (Cases C–94/04, 202/04) (Mandatory Italian fee schedules).

[157] Wouters v. The General Council of the Dutch Order of Advocates, (2002) Eur.Comm.Rep. I–1577.

[158] Reyners v. Belgium, (1974) Eur.Comm.Rep. 631; Thieffry v. Conseil de l'Ordre des Avocats de Paris, (1977) Eur.Comm.Rep. 765; Van Binsbergen v. Bestuur van de Bedrijfsvereniging voor de Metaalnijverheid, (1974) Eur.Comm.Rep. 1299; Gebhard v. Consiglio Dell'Ordine Degli Avocati di Milano, (1995) Eur.Comm.Rep. I–4165.

to the German bar. On appeal, the Court of Justice held that Article 59 obligates member states not to impede the movement of lawyers in the Union.

The member state must compare an applicant's specific qualifications with those detailed by national law. Only if the applicant does not meet all the necessary qualifications may the host state require additional courses or training.[159] Moreover, the ECJ has ruled that law graduates who have not trained or qualified in their home states may take aptitude tests to qualify or obtain training in other EU states[160]. . . a kind of "have law degree will travel" outcome. Once qualified as an attorney elsewhere within the EU, individuals may even return to their home state to take aptitude (not bar exam) tests for qualification.[161]

By joining the bar in another EU country, lawyers acquire the right to establish themselves in more than one nation. The multinational law firm, pioneered by Baker and McKenzie in the United States and duplicated in the United Kingdom, has relatively few counterparts on the continent practicing of European Union law. Slowly, however, attorneys from member states are establishing affiliations and sometimes partnerships which reflect and service the economic, political and social integration of Europe. These "European law firms" often compete with existing branches of United States and British multinational firms for the lucrative practice of EU law.

In professional fields, the real barrier to movement of people across borders is language. In some instances, linguistic requirements for jobs are lawful despite their negative impact on free movement rights.[162] As much as the Union may succeed in its campaign for truly establishing an integrated market, the language barriers within the EU will remain. Although younger generations are increasingly multilingual, a professional who cannot speak to his or her clients or students is unlikely to succeed in another member state.

---

159 Vlassopoulou v. Ministerum fuer Justiz, Bundes und Europaangelegenheiten, (1991) Eur.Comm.Rep. I–4087 (Case C–340/89).

160 Morgenbesser v. Consiglio dell'Ordine degli avvocati di Genova, (2003) Eur.Comm.Rep. I–13467 (Case C–313/01).

161 Koller, (2010) Eur.Comm.Rep. (Case C–118/09).

162 *See* Groener v. Minister for Education, (1989) Eur.Comm.Rep. 3967. (Irish required for vocational teaching job); Haim v. Kassenzahrartzliche Vereinigung, (2000) Eur.Comm.Rep. I–5123 (German required to practice dentistry).

§ 4.12 Freedom to Provide and Receive Services Across Borders

The freedom of nonresidents to provide services within other parts of the Union is another part of the foundations of the TFEU.[163] The freedom to provide services (including tourism) implies a right to receive and pay for them by going to the country of their source.[164] Free movement to receive unavailable or just better medical care is protected, along with reimbursement rights.[165] Commercial, craft and professional services are included within this right, which is usually not dependent upon establishment or registration in the country where the service is rendered.[166] In other words, the freedom to provide or receive services across borders entails a limited right of temporary entry into another member state.

The Council has adopted a general program (notably including the Services Directive of 2006/123) for the abolition of national restrictions on the freedom to provide services across Union borders. This freedom is subject to the same public policy, public security and public health exceptions applied to workers and the self-employed. For example, Italian rules requiring that only pharmacists to operate pharmacies were justified as a matter of public health.[167] The Council's program has slowly been implemented by a series of legislative acts applicable to professional and nonprofessional services. As with the right of self-establishment, discrimination based upon the nationality or non-residence of the service provider is generally prohibited even if no implementing EU law has been adopted.[168]

In parallel with law developed in connection with the free movement of goods, the Court of Justice in *van Binsbergen* indicated that EU governments may require providers of services from other states to adhere to professional public interest rules under the *Cassis*

---

[163] Articles 56 and 57, TFEU.

[164] Luisi and Carbone v. Ministero del Tesoro, (1984) Eur.Comm.Rep. 377; Cowan v. Le Trésor Public, (1986) Eur.Comm.Rep. 195 (British tourist entitled to French criminal injury compensation); Society for the Protection of Unborn Children Ireland v. Grogan, (1991) Eur.Comm.Rep. I–a4685 (abortion services).

[165] *See, e.g.,* Muller-Faure v. Onderlinge Waarborg-Maatschappij OZ, (2003) Eur.Comm.Rep. I–4509.

[166] Proceedings against Corsten, (2000) Eur.Comm.Rep. I–7919 (Oct. 3, 2000) (skilled trades); Säger v. Dennemeyer + Co., (1991) Eur.Comm.Rep. I–4221 (patent agents); Commission v. France, (1991) Eur.Comm.Rep. I–659 (tour guides); Commission v. Germany, (1986) Eur.Comm.Rep. 3755; Ministère Public v. van Wasemael, (1979) Eur.Comm.Rep. 35 (employment agencies).

[167] Article 74, TFEU. *See* Commission v. Italy, (2009) Eur.Comm.Rep. I–4103.

[168] Van Binsbergen v. Bestuur van de Bedrijfsvereniging voor de Metaalnijverheid, (1974) Eur.Comm.Rep. 1299 (legal representation); Coenen v. Sociaal Economische Raad, (1975) Eur.Comm.Rep. 1547 (insurance intermediary).

formula. These rules must be applied equally to all professionals operating in the nation, and only if necessary to ensure that the out-of-state professional does not escape them by reason of establishment elsewhere. In other words, if the professional rules (*e.g.*, ethics) of the country in which the service provider is established are equivalent, then application of the rules of the country where the service is provided does not follow.

Following *Cassis*, and notably not *Keck*, the Court of Justice has affirmed member state marketing controls over the sale of lottery tickets (social policy and fraud interests)[169] and over "cold calling" solicitations for commodities futures.[170] Telemarketing in most other areas is forbidden, except with prior consumer consent, under a 1977 directive.

Financial Service Passports, Bankers' Bonuses

Bankers, investment advisors and insurance companies have long awaited the arrival of a truly common market. Their right of establishment in other member states has existed for some time. The right to provide services across borders without establishing local subsidiaries was forcefully reaffirmed by the Court of Justice in 1986.[171] This decision largely rejected a German requirement that all insurers servicing the German market be located and established there. Legislative initiatives undertaken in connection with the single market campaign promise to create genuinely competitive cross-border European markets for banking,[172] investment[173] and insurance[174] services. Licensing of insurance and investment service companies and banks meeting minimum capital, solvency ratio and other EU requirements as implemented in member state laws is done on a "one-stop" home country "passport" basis.

This system no longer automatically applies to British service providers, subject post BREXIT to regulatory "equivalence" determinations by the EU. Movement to the Continent of British-based financial services companies, including U.S. firms based in London, is underway. See Chapter 8.

Under EU licensing rules, banks, for example, cannot maintain individual equity positions in non-financial entities more than 15 percent of their capital funds, and the total value of such holdings

---

169 Her Majesty's Customs and Excise v. Schindler, (1994) Eur.Comm.Rep. I–1039.

170 Alpine Investments v. Minister Van Financien, (1995) Eur.Comm.Rep. I–1141.

171 Commission v. Germany, (1986) Eur.Comm.Rep. 3755.

172 *See* Section 4.13.

173 *See* Section 4.15.

174 *See* Section 4.14.

cannot exceed 50 percent of those funds.[175] They can participate and service securities transactions and issues, financial leasing and trade for their own accounts. The investment services directive requires home country supervision of the "good repute" and "suitability" of managers and controlling shareholders.[176]

Member states must ordinarily recognize home country licenses and the principle of home country control. For example, Council Directive 89/646 ("the Second Banking Directive") employs the home country single license "passport" procedure to liberalize banking services throughout the Union. The validity of British banking, securities and insurance "passports" is in doubt after BREXIT.

Host states retain the right to regulate a bank's liquidity and supervise it through monetary policy and in the name of the "general good." Similarly, no additional insurance permits or requirements may be imposed by host countries when large industrial risks (sophisticated purchasers) are involved. However, when the public at large is concerned (general risk), host country rules still apply.[177] Major auto and life insurance directives employing one-stop licensing principles were adopted late in 1990.[178] The auto insurance directive reproduces the large versus general risk distinctions found in the Second Non-Life Insurance Directive. Host country controls over general risk auto insurance policies are retained until 1995. Host country permits are also required when life insurers from other member states actively solicit business.

In the wake of the global financial crisis that commenced in 2008, the EU has capped bankers' upfront cash bonuses at between 20 to 30%, with the remainder paid in stock or as "contingent capital" that will not be paid if the bank is in trouble. About half of the bonuses must be deferred for at least three years and can be "clawed back" if the bank's stock performs poorly. The base salaries of bankers are not limited and may expand under the bonus rules. Bonuses for hedge-fund managers are not presently governed by EU law.

The limits on bankers' bonuses are part of the ECB Single Rulebook and Single Supervisory Plans adopted in the wake of repeated EURO crises, discussed at the end of this chapter.

---

175 Council Directive 89/646.

176 *See* Commission v. Italy, (1996) Eur.Comm.Rep. I–2691 (incorporation rule for stock brokers breaches freedom of establishment).

177 Council Directive 88/357 ("the Second Non-Life Insurance Directive").

178 Council Directives 90/619 (life insurance) and 90/618 (auto insurance).

Reciprocity and the United States

Unless there is "effective market access" under United States law for European firms, U.S. companies entering the Europe after 1992 may be unable to obtain the benefits of common service markets. This problem is generally referred to as the "reciprocity requirement" of EU legislation. The issue re-emerged in connection with BREXIT, with financial firms wondering if UK law post-BREXIT will give them reciprocity (single passport rights) in the EU. See Chapter 8.

It is this kind of requirement that gave the campaign for a Europe without internal frontiers the stigma of increasing the degree of external trade barriers. Many outsiders, in rhetoric which sometimes seems excessive, refer to the development of a "Fortress Europe" mentality and threat to world trading relations.

There was a rush by non-EU bankers, investment advisors and insurers to get established in the Union before January 1, 1993, to qualify for home country licenses. North Americans and others outside the Union have been particularly concerned about certain features of the new legislation mandating effective access in foreign markets for European companies before non-Union firms may benefit from the liberalization of services within the Common Market. Since state and federal laws governing banking, investment services and insurance are quite restrictive, and in no sense can it be said that one license permits a company to operate throughout the United States, one result of European integration has arguably been reform of U.S. regulatory legislation. Since 1994 the United States has noticeably relaxed its rules on interstate banking and largely repealed the Glass-Steagall Act limitations on universal banking.

§ 4.13 Banking

This section focuses on European Union legislation on banking, capital movements and consumer credit. These include:

- First Banking Directive 77/780.
- Second Banking Directive 89/646.
- Consumer Credit Directives 87/102, 90/88.
- Money Laundering Directive 91/308.
- Large Exposures of Credit Institutions Directive 92/121.
- Own Funds (Capital Requirements) Directive 89/299 as amended by Directive 92/16.
- Solvency Ratios Directive 89/647.

- Capital Movements Directive 88/361.
- Deposit Guarantee Schemes Directive 94/19.

Banking Directives

European Union regulation of banks originated with the First Banking Directive,[179] adopted by the Council of Ministers in 1977. This directive harmonized the conditions for the exercise of the right of establishment by "credit institutions." Such institutions are defined as undertakings "whose business is to receive deposits and other repayable funds from the public and to grant credits for its own account."[180] To exercise the right of establishment under the First Banking Directive two basic conditions were imposed. At least two people of good repute and experience had to run the credit institution which itself had to possess separate and adequate minimum own funds (capital base). These are minimum EU banking standards. Member States can, and frequently do, impose stricter requirements.

The preamble to the First Banking Directive states that "the rules governing branches of credit institutions having their head office outside the Union [*e.g.,* U.S. banks] should be analogous in all Member States." The Directive requires that such branches should not be treated more favorably by the different member states than the branches of EU credit institutions. The Second Banking Directive amended the First.[181] It enables authorized credit institutions relying on a "single license" from home state governments to carry on banking activities throughout the EU via branches or cross-border services. Authorization from the host State is not needed.[182] The provisions of the Second Banking Directive were implemented in all Member States by January 1, 1993.

The combined minimum requirements for a single license as a "credit institution" under the Second and the First Banking Directives are as follows: (1) Capital of at least 5 million EUROs or, in exceptional circumstances, 1 million EUROs; (2) management by two persons of good repute and sufficient experience; (3) submission of a business plan, including an organizational structure; and (4) suitable major shareholders (holders of 10 percent or more of the shares or voting rights or those who may exercise "significant influence"). Higher "Basel" capital requirements for banks are now in place.

---

179 Council Directive 77/780.

180 Council Directive 77/780, Article 1.

181 Council Directive 89/646.

182 *See* Societe Civile Immobiliere Parodi v. Banque H. Albert de Bary, (1997) Eur.Comm.Rep. I–3899.

Member states may impose more demanding requirements on their own credit institutions. Such requirements cannot, however, be imposed on credit institutions authorized in other member states. Some commentators have suggested that this provides an incentive to seek out the home state jurisdiction with the least demanding requirements. A credit institution with a single license is entitled to carry on all the activities listed in the Directives throughout the Union even if the regulations of the host state prohibit domestic credit institutions from doing so.

A credit institution's single license authorization may cover traditional banking activities, such as deposit-taking and lending. It may also permit lease financing, transmission services, payment services, loan guarantees and commitments, money market trading, futures and options, exchange and interest rate services, participation in securities issues, underwriting, corporate finance, merger and acquisition services, portfolio management and advice, credit reference services and custodial services.

If a credit institution wishes to establish a branch elsewhere in the Union, it must notify its home state of its intention and supply the following information: (1) The relevant member state where it intends to establish a branch; (2) a business plan; (3) the address in the host state; and (4) the names of the managers of the branch. In most cases, the home state banking authority must forward within three months this information (together with the amount of the bank's capital base, its solvency ratio and details of any deposit guarantee scheme) to the competent authority of the host state. The host state then has two months in which to "prepare for the supervision of the credit institution." It may impose conditions on the activities of the branch "if necessary" in the interest of the "general good."

When providing cross-border services the credit institution must first notify the authorities of its home state. The home state then has a month within which to send notice to the host state. Host state authorities are entitled to take "appropriate measures" to prevent or punish banking irregularities committed within their territories. For example, restrictions may be placed by host states on the advertising of financial services.

Mergers and acquisitions are also regulated by the Banking Directives. Anyone intending to acquire a "qualifying holding" (a direct or indirect holding representing 10 percent or more of the capital or voting rights) or increase a qualifying holding so that either the proportion of voting rights or capital held reaches thresholds of 20, 33 or 50 percent must inform the home state. These authorities have up to three months to oppose the acquisition if not satisfied as to the acquirer's suitability. "Suitability" is assessed in terms of the ability to provide sound and prudent management of a credit institution. Similar restrictions will cover the disposal or reduction of a qualifying holding. All credit institutions will be required to disclose the details of qualifying holdings to their home states. Sanctions can include the suspension of voting rights.

Credit institutions also have two limits imposed on their shareholdings in other entities. Holdings in businesses that are neither credit institutions nor financial institutions are generally restricted to 10 percent of their own funds. The aggregate value of all such participations is limited to 50 percent of the capital base. The supervision of a credit institution, *e.g.*, on accounting and internal controls, is the responsibility of the home state. The host state authority shares responsibility with the home state for supervising the liquidity of branches within its territory. The host state authority also has complete responsibility for monetary policy measures.

Host state regulation on the grounds of general good is covered in the Second Banking Directive. The preamble states that a host state may "require compliance" with specific provisions of its national laws and regulations where these are for the general good, provided that such provisions are compatible with Union law, intended to protect the general good and do not duplicate equivalent rules under the legislation or regulation of the home member state. This authorization only applies to "unlisted" activities (those activities not covered by the single license) of credit institutions of member states and all activities of noncredit institutions.

Regarding "listed" activities the member states must ensure that there are no obstacles to carrying on activities receiving mutual recognition in the same manner as in the home member state, if the latter do not conflict with legal provisions protecting the general good in the host member state. Thus, pending harmonization of "general good" rules, there will be considerable scope for divergent host state general good laws. For example, though credit institutions are expressly granted the right to advertise their services through all available means of communication in host states, such advertising is subject to rules adopted in the interests of the general good governing the form and the content of such advertising. There is no provision for the "mutual recognition" of advertising rules and consequently host state regulations will apply when necessary to protect unsophisticated customers.

Credit institutions from outside the EU that incorporate and obtain a single license under the provisions of the Second Banking Directive will be free to enjoy its benefits. Branches of non-EU banks cannot obtain those benefits. However, a "reciprocity" test must be satisfied before non-EU financial institutions can take full advantage of the new regime. The original reciprocity provisions of the Second Banking Directive were amended following criticism from outside the Union. The United States especially feared that these provisions would be interpreted to require "mirror-image reciprocity". Since the Glass-Steagall Act prohibits banks in the U.S. from engaging in securities business and as U.S. banking laws have traditionally prohibited cross-border branching, mirror-image reciprocity would not have been possible.

The Second Banking Directive on "reciprocity" stipulates that: (1) Member states notify the Commission when they have authorized or allowed acquisitions by banks owned (directly or indirectly) by outsiders; (2) member states inform the Commission of difficulties encountered by their banks in establishing or carrying on activities in countries outside the Union; (3) the Commission report to the Council whether EU banks are being granted equivalent market access in non-EU countries and receiving national treatment (effective market access and national treatment will be viewed in terms of initial entry as well as subsequent operations and acquisitions); (4) if the Commission considers that a Union bank is not being so treated, it may initiate negotiations with the country concerned.

The Commission can also require member states to limit or suspend both requests for banking authorizations and the acquisition of shares in Union banks. Neither restraint can continue for more than three months unless authorized by the Council. Non-EU banking subsidiaries located in the Community at the time the Commission and Council take retaliatory action are grandfathered such that these limitations and suspensions cannot apply to their creation of subsidiaries or acquisitions.

One practitioner has reached the following conclusions regarding the Banking Directives:

> The implementation of the Second Banking Directive and the concept of a single license should mean that U.S. banks are able to benefit from relatively greater economies of scale through selling a wider array of services in a larger geographic market. Banks will have the opportunity to reduce their operating costs by, for instance, consolidating their management or their back-office operations. The chance to sell cross-border services, or to set up a branch that has standardized reporting and accounting requirements and which does not need to be independently capitalized, should also reduce costs. However, the corollary of creating a greater competitive environment is that it may bring operating and profit margins down. To get the benefit of a single license, a U.S. bank will have to set up a subsidiary in a Member

State which must obtain authorization from that Member State to act as a credit institution. Unfortunately, this may involve higher costs than just operating through a branch network, for example, higher tax and capital costs.[183]

Capital Requirements

The capital requirements directives of the EU are based on the Basel Report on the International Convergence of Capital Measurement and Capital Standards produced by the Committee on Banking Regulations and Supervisory Practices meeting at the Bank for International Settlements in Basle, Switzerland in July 1988 and its successors. Capital requirements addressed to credit risk are set out in the Own Funds Directive and the Solvency Ratio Directive. The Own Funds Directive[184] was adopted by the Council in April 1989 and the Solvency Ratio Directive in December 1989.[185] These two Directives, along with the Second Banking Directive, were brought into force by the Member States January 1, 1993. Directive 92/121 provides for the monitoring and control of large exposures of credit institutions. No exposure to a client or a group of connected clients may exceed 25 percent of the institution's own funds.

The Own Funds Directive seeks to set minimum EU standards. It stipulates the maximum number of items that can be included in a bank's capital base and the maximum level of the qualifying amounts for each of those items. Each member state has discretion over which capital base items they use and whether to adopt a lower ceiling for the qualifying amounts than that specified in the Own Funds Directive. The Directive acknowledges a distinction between types of own funds like the Basle Report's distinction between Tier 1 and Tier 2 capital requirements. This distinction is expressed using the terminology of "original own funds" and "additional own funds". The difference in quality between original and additional own funds is reflected in the respective proportions of these two elements of aggregate own funds. Thus, additional own funds must not exceed original own funds, and certain items of additional own funds must not exceed 50 percent of original own funds.

The Own Funds Directive allows inclusion of the following items as "own funds": (1) Paid up share capital, plus share premium accounts but excluding cumulative preference shares; (2) reserves and profits carried forward from the year-end profit and loss account; (3) revaluation reserves; (4) funds for general banking risks (See

---

183 Travers, "Banking and Capital Movements," in Folsom, Lake and Nanda (eds.), *European Community Law After 1992: A Practical Guide for Lawyers Outside the Common Market* (Kluwer, 1992).

184 Council Directive 89/299.

185 Council Directive 89/647.

Directive 91/633); (5) certain value adjustments; (6) selected other items; (7) securities of indeterminate duration and other selected instruments; (8) the commitments of the members cooperative societies and the joint and several commitments of the borrowers of funds; and (9) fixed term cumulative preference shares and certain subordinated capital. The items set out in paragraphs (1) and (2) constitute original own funds. The funds for general banking risks referred to in paragraph (4) are provisionally included in "own funds" without restriction but subject to review. This means that the items set out in paragraph (3) and paragraphs (5) to (9) constitute additional own funds, the level of which must be limited by reference to the amount of original own funds.

The total of a credit institution's additional own funds must not exceed 100 percent of the amount of the original own funds having first deducted, at book value, any of its own shares, the value of intangible assets such as goodwill and material losses for the current financial year. In addition, the aggregate amount of the items referred to in paragraphs (8) and (9) above must not exceed 50 percent of original own funds after the same deductions. There is a general requirement that the items listed in paragraphs (1) to (4) must be available to a credit institution for unrestricted and immediate use to cover risks and losses as soon as they occur. The amounts being brought into account for the purposes of calculating "own funds" under these headings must be net of any foreseeable tax charge at the time of calculation or be adjusted to consider any such tax charge.

The Solvency Ratio Directive requires banks to maintain capital at levels equal to a certain proportion of assets. The credit institution's own funds, as calculated in accordance with the Own Funds Directive, constitute the numerator, the denominator being total assets and off-balance sheet items which have been risk-adjusted. This is then expressed as a percentage. The target ratio is 8 percent. The provisions of the Solvency Ratio Directive are another attempt to set minimum EU standards. The solvency ratio must be calculated not less than twice a year and the solvency ratio of a credit institution with subsidiaries is generally calculated on a consolidated basis.

Money Laundering

A Money Laundering Directive[186] reinforces the commitments made by member states to the United Nations Convention against the illicit traffic in narcotic drugs and psychotropic substances (Vienna, 1988) and the Council of Europe Convention on laundering,

---

[186] Council Directive 91/308 extended and revised by Directive 2001/97.

tracing, seizure and confiscation of proceeds of crime (Strasbourg November 1990). The Money Laundering Directive focuses on civil, not criminal, law. Member states must ensure that laundering of money derived from criminal activity (not just drug trafficking) is prohibited. They must ensure that banks and other financial institutions (including insurance companies) clearly identify their customers before entering business relations.

Any transaction or series of transactions amounting to 15,000 EUROs or more necessitates an investigation into the customer's identity. Credit and financial institutions must carry out such an investigation even when the amount involved is lower if there is any suspicion of money laundering. The information obtained must be kept for 5 years from the date following the end of the relationship with the customer or, in the case of transactions, 5 years from the date of execution of the transaction.

Credit and financial institutions must provide information about money laundering to the relevant authorities. They must establish appropriate internal monitoring procedures to ensure that the necessary information is obtained. A suspect transaction cannot be carried out until the relevant authorities have been informed. The authorities may order the credit or financial institution not to execute that transaction. There is an exception for those cases where delay in executing a transaction might alert the suspected launderers to the existence of an investigation. In those cases, the transaction can be executed, and the relevant authorities informed afterwards. In any event, the institution concerned must not tell its customer of any of this. The Directive requires the member states to enact legislation entitling employees and directors of banks, insurance companies and other relevant financial institutions to disclose customer information without liability. Member states are not precluded from adopting stricter provisions.

Directive 97/5 on cross-border credit transfers sets minimum information standards, maximum transfer time limits, and identification requirements.

§ 4.14 Insurance

This section focuses on European Union laws on insurance. These laws include:

- First Non-Life Insurance Directive 73/239
- Second Non-Life Insurance Directive 88/357
- Third Non-Life Insurance Directive 92/49
- First Life Insurance Directive 79/267

- Second Life Insurance Directive 90/619
- Third Life Insurance Directive 92/96
- Insurance Agents and Brokers Directive 77/92
- Reinsurance Directives 64/225 and 78/473
- Auto Insurance Directive 90/232

Non-Life Insurance Directives

The First Non-Life Insurance Directive was adopted in 1973. It establishes common rules on admission to the insurance business, requirements for undertaking such business and withdrawal from the offering of insurance. This first directive covers insurance for accidents, sickness, transport, general liability, and credit and suretyship. National export credit insurance operations are excluded from its coverage. Any insurance company that wants to establish itself in another member state must obtain a license from that state. In other words, the First Non-Life Insurance Directive did not establish a single insurance licensing system. It merely established minimum criteria that must be fulfilled to obtain national authorizations in host states.

Under this directive, insurance companies seeking to do business in other member states must provide the national authorities with a variety of information based upon their home country operations. Such information concerns the types of insurance they are authorized to write, solvency and financial resources. The application must also provide a "scheme of operation" which details the financial structure of the company. If the national authorities refuse to permit an insurance company based in another EU country to undertake business in their jurisdiction, that company must be given a right of judicial review. Notably, this right is not extended to insurance companies from outside the Union, *e.g.*, the United States and in the future Britain.

To qualify to do business, non-EU insurance companies must be entitled to undertake insurance under their national laws and be approved by the relevant national authorities. Although the Union may agree with non-Union countries to specific provisions concerning insurance companies, including reciprocity, the First Non-Life Insurance Directive does not mandate reciprocity. This directive was supplemented by Directive 73/240 which facilitates the right of insurance companies to establish themselves anywhere inside the Union under national treatment conditions. Host states may demand proof of good standing and the absence of prior bankruptcies, but such proof can be provided through home country documentation.

The Second Non-Life Insurance Directive was adopted in 1988. This directive builds upon the first and makes an important distinction between large risk and mass risk insurance business. Mass risk business relates largely to private individuals and is not governed by the Second Non-Life Insurance Directive. Large risks are covered, and these are defined to include policy holders with balance sheets of approximately 12 million EUROs, net turnovers of 24 million EUROs and 500 employees. Starting January 1993 these thresholds were lowered by 50 percent. The effect of this reduction will be to expand the scope of the Second Non-Life Insurance Directive. Insurance companies are free to provide their services across borders anywhere inside the European Union as regards large risks. For these purposes, as in the banking area, home country licensing and control principles have been adopted. Host country licensing and controls continue in effect for mass risk insurance.

The Third Non-Life Insurance Directive was implemented in most member states on July 1, 1994. This directive completes the internal market with respect to non-life insurance. Home country licensing and control are extended for all coverages, including individual consumers. This directive, together with others concerning insurance accounts, seeks to ensure a sound financial basis for all European Union insurance companies. It specifically regulates the types of assets that may be used as technical reserves by insurance companies. Member states can require that their contract law continue to apply to mass risk insurance issued for their territory. However, contracts concerning large risks will enjoy complete freedom regarding choice of law.

Various national requirements regarding compulsory insurance are continued throughout the non-life insurance directives and made subject to notification requirements to the national authorities. Special directives are aimed at eliminating particularly restrictive German legal requirements concern credit insurance and suretyship insurance,[187] as well as legal expenses insurance.[188] Directive 2002/13 raises the solvency margin requirements of non-life insurance firms.

Life Insurance Directives

The First Life Insurance Directive was adopted in 1979. This directive focuses on the right to establish insurance subsidiaries in other member states, including rules on admission, doing business and withdrawal. It harmonizes financial guaranties connected with life insurance and the requirements for authorization of the right to

187 Council Directive 87/343.

188 Council Directive 87/344.

sell such insurance. The First Life Insurance Directive prohibits simultaneous operation of life and non-life insurance businesses by one company. However, there is a grandfather clause retaining such rights for companies existing as of 1979. For such companies, certain segregation requirements are established. Minimal rules on technical reserves and solvency margins are also established. Insurance companies from outside the Union are generally permitted in the EU if they meet their home country legal and administrative requirements for life insurance companies. No mandatory reciprocity rule is enacted in the First Life Insurance Directive, although reciprocal agreements with third countries are anticipated by the directive.

The Second Life Insurance Directive was adopted in 1990. This directive generally follows the positions taken in the Second Non-Life Insurance Directive. It focuses on cross frontier provision of insurance services. Companies can sell life insurance across borders subject only to home country licensing controls provided the policyholder has taken the initiative to obtain the policy. This is referred to as a "passive sale." When the company has approached potential policyholders in other member states (active sales), local authorities must be notified, and the host country rules will generally apply except in cases of group coverage.

The passive sales permission contained in the Second Life Insurance Directive does not apply for three years when brokers are employed in the host country (even if the client has approached the broker on his or her own initiative). This means that host country rules will govern such passive sales through brokers until roughly the end of 1993. In all cases where passive sales are made across borders, the insurance company must provide a certificate of solvency and a certificate listing the classes of insurance it is licensed to offer in its home country. These certificates must be presented to the host country authorities. In addition, the home country must certify that it does not object to the provision of cross-frontier insurance by one of its companies.

The Third Life Insurance Directive was implemented in most member states on July 1, 1994. As in the non-life insurance area, this directive allows companies to operate freely throughout the Union based on home country rules that adhere to limited standards of consumer protection established at the European Union level. The conditions for allowing such freedom to provide services are provided for by further harmonization of provisions relating to the prudential supervision of insurers. Each member state must recognize the insurance supervisory systems of others as equally prudential.

The reduced requirement to obtain only a single authorization, sometimes called a "single passport", available following the implementation of the Third Insurance Directives, is not available to the pure re-insurers or small mutual associations excluded by the First Insurance Directive. Non-EU insurers with their head offices outside the Union, yet with branches in member states, will not be able to take advantage of the "single passport" rules, a concern for British companies after BREXIT.

Single passports generally apply to subsidiaries of such insurers set up in a member state. While the financial supervision of a company with a head office in a member state is primarily carried out by the "home" member state under the Third Insurance Directives, the host state authorities retain power to prevent persons entering certain types of contracts and to prohibit advertising where it is considered to accord with the common good. Mergers and acquisitions in the insurance industry are regulated under this directive, and each insurer may be required to notify its premiums and reserves to the member states. Directive 2002/12 increases the solvency margins required of life insurers.

The so-called BCCI directive (No. 92/121), prompted by several cases of fraud (particularly the Bank of Credit and Commerce International case), requires that where a financial undertaking is part of a group sufficient information relating to the group must be provided so as to allow the group to be supervised effectively.

Brokers

Insurance brokers and agents are subject to general European Union rules regarding their licensure. These predominantly concern commercial or professional knowledge. The relevant rules are established in Council Directive 77/92. Reinsurance and coinsurance are the subject of two Council Directives, 64/225 and 78/473. These directives extend the right of establishment and freedom to provide services in the reinsurance and coinsurance fields. Participation in such activities is now exclusively governed by the Union rules as administered by national insurance regulatory authorities. In 1990, the Council adopted Directive 90/618 concerning motor vehicle liability insurance. This directive was the successor to Council Directives 72/166 and 84/5. It coordinates national laws on the level and content of compulsory civil liability insurance for automobiles.

Commission Regulation 3932/92 creates a competition law group exemption for insurance industry agreements, decisions and concerted practices. Cooperation between insurance companies regarding statistical compilations of claims, amounts paid, and risks taken that is intended to facilitate mortality tables and common risk premium tariffs is allowed provided the companies are not identified. The Regulation permits creation and distribution of optional standard policy conditions for direct insurance and common profit realization models. Co-insurance and co-reinsurance groups for specified risk categories are also exempted from Article 101 for up to 10 and 15 percent of the market respectively.

Gender Bias

In 2011, the European Court of Justice broadly invalidated the widespread practice of charging men and women different rates for life, auto and health insurance.[189] The ECJ found such practices discriminatory in violation of the EU Charter of Fundamental Rights. The Charter prohibits sex discrimination and additionally states that "equality between men and women must be ensured in all areas." Member states had until Dec. 21, 2012, to conform their laws to this ruling. Premiums for men rose, for women they fell.

§ 4.15 Investment Services

The European Union has adopted directives intended to integrate investment services under a single home state licensing regime like that adopted for banking. These are the Investment Services Directive and the Capital Adequacy Directive, both effective January 1, 1996.[190] The Investment Services Directive (ISD) creates minimum standards for authorization of investment firms and advisors by member state authorities and stock exchanges. All persons whose regular occupation or business is the provision of investment services to third parties on a professional basis fall within the directive. The ISD divides responsibilities for supervision between the home and host states. The home state will be responsible throughout the Union for authorization and prudential supervision of the firm, with the host state being responsible for applying conduct of business rules and other rules to be made in the "general good"; these rules will apply only to the business which the firm carries on in the host state.

Home state authorization will allow investment firms to obtain membership in the stock and electronic trading exchanges of all other member states subject only to business conduct and "general good" regulation by the host state. There will be no need to become "established" in the host country, but branches may be opened there. Such branches will, however, be subject to the prudential supervision of the firm's home state. This prudential supervision will include fitness and properness, administrative and accounting methods,

---

189 Re Assn Belge des Consommateurs Test-Achats, (2011) Eur.Comm.Rep. (Case C–236/09).

190 Council Directives 93/22, 93/6.

holding and protection of client securities and funds and conflicts of interest. Trade in commodities is not governed by the ISD.

One controversial aspect of Union law on investment services concerns the "transparency" of stock markets. Minimum disclosure duties are established for stock exchanges such that investors will have all commercially useful and accessible information relevant to stock trading, including price movements and share volumes. Only in unusual circumstances may these duties be suspended (*e.g.*, very large transactions, illiquid trades, and very small markets).

The Capital Adequacy Directive (CAD) requires minimum capitalization for investment firms to which CAD applies. A minimum requirement of 125,000 EUROs applies to investment firms which provide investment services and operate from investor instructions, including holding client funds and securities, but which do not deal with their own account or underwrite issues. This requirement is reduced for investment firms which are not permitted to hold client funds and securities, to deal for their own account or to underwrite issues. For all other investment firms, the requirement is 730,000 EUROs. An additional minimum of 25 per cent (thirteen weeks) of the preceding year's fixed overhead costs must be maintained. Furthermore, the CAD directive details minimum capital requirements for market risk exposure. These rules apply to both investment companies *and* banks or other credit institutions trading securities. They cover position, settlement, counterparty, foreign-exchange and other risks undertaken in their "trading books."

The broad thrust of the EU investment services directives is to place banks and investment firms on an equal footing as regards single licensing and capital adequacy controls in securities trading. National restraints upon the direct trading of securities by banks had to be removed by 1999. As under the Union's banking legislation, existing U.S. and other third-party investment advisors are grandfathered in their European operations. New licenses to non-Union advisors are subject to a review of foreign country treatment of EU counterparts, a prospect of concern to British firms after BREXIT.

§ 4.16 A Common Currency and Financial Bailouts

The TFEU is also concerned with the free movement of money. "Current payments" associated with import/export transactions in goods and services, as well as wage remittances, are routinely made and protected. This includes money taken abroad to make payment for tourist, medical, educational or business travel services.[191] But it does not include the unsubstantiated export of banknotes.[192]

Free movement of capital goals of the TFEU was much delayed. In fairness, the Treaty initially just required member states to be "as liberal as possible" in granting exchange control authorizations for investment capital transfers. This provision acknowledged the sensitivity of the member states' concerns about balance of payments and currency values.[193] It was not until the implementation of the single market campaign that new legislative acts of the Union firmly entrenched the right of individuals and companies to move capital across borders without substantial limitation.[194] This approach was strongly reaffirmed by Maastricht amendments prohibiting "all restrictions on the movement of capital" inside the EU *and* as between the EU and third party nations.[195] This blanket right is subject to existing third party restraints regarding investment, real estate, financial services and securities. Also permitted are restraints to prevent "infringements of national law" (taxation especially)[196] and for reasons of public policy or security.[197]

European Monetary System

The capital movements legislation, combined with the various banking and investment services reforms and Maastricht amendments, promises to bring forth a remarkable new financial sector in the European Union. It also supports the EURO replacing national currencies. In moving toward monetary union, the member states created the European Monetary System (EMS). When the EMS was established in 1979, member states deposited 20 percent of their gold and dollar assets with the European Monetary Cooperation Fund in exchange for an equivalent amount of European Currency Units (ECUs). This fund is used as a non-cash means of settlement between central banks undertaking exchange rate support.

---

191 Luisi and Carbone v. Ministero del Tesoro, (1984) Eur.Comm.Rep. 377. *See* Criminal Proceedings against Sanz de Lera, (1995) Eur.Comm.Rep. I–4821 (prior declarations but not prior authorizations permissible).

192 Re Casati, (1981) Eur.Comm.Rep. 2595.

193 Articles 63–66, 75, TFEU.

194 Council Directive 88/361.

195 *See* Svensson v. Ministre du Logement, (1995) Eur.Comm.Rep. I–3955 (denial of interest rate subsidy indirectly restricts free movement of capital); Association Eglise de Scientologie de Paris v. The Prime Minister, (2000) Eur.Comm.Rep. I–1335 (French prior authorization for investments too indefinite, contrary to free movement of capital rights); In re Trummer and Mayer, (1999) Eur.Comm.Rep. I–1661 (Austrian mortgage registration national currency rule invalid).

196 *See* Sandoz v. Finanzlandeskirektion, (1999) Eur.Comm.Rep. 7041 (Austrian tax not justified).

197 *See* Svensson and Scientologie de Paris cited above. *See also* In re Albore, (2000) Eur.Comm.Rep. I–5965 (July 13, 2000) (real estate and security).

The legal basis for the European Monetary System and European Currency Units was substantially advanced by the addition of Article 120 TFEU under the Single European Act of 1987. This article committed the member states to further development of the EMS and ECU, recognized the cooperation of the central banks in management of the system, but specifically required further amendment of the Treaty if "institutional changes" were required. In other words, a common currency managed by a central bank system was *not* part of the campaign for a Europe without internal frontiers. Draft plans for such developments surfaced in the Commission using the U.S. Federal Reserve Board as a model. Britain, always concerned about losses of economic sovereignty (what greater loss is there?), proposed an alternative known as the "hard ECU." This proposal would have retained the national currencies but added the hard ECU as competitor of each, letting the marketplace in most instances decide which currency it preferred.

In December of 1989, the European Council (outvoting Britain) approved a three-stage approach to economic and monetary union (EMU). Stage One began July 1, 1990. Its focus was on expanding the power and influence of the Committee of Central Bank Governors over monetary affairs. This Committee was a kind of EuroFed in embryo. It was primarily engaged in "multilateral surveillance." Stage One also sought greater economic policy coordination and convergence among the member states.

Stage Two anticipated the creation of a European Union central banking system but functioned with the existing national currencies in the context of the EMS and ERM. Stage Two was a learning and transition period. In October of 1990, it was agreed (save Britain) that Stage Two would commence January 1, 1994. This deadline was actually met and the European Monetary Institute was installed in Frankfurt. It was the precursor to the European Central Bank.

Stage Three involved the replacement of the national currencies with a single currency, the EURO, managed by a European Central Bank. In December of 1991, agreement was reached at Maastricht to implement Stage Three no later than Jan. 1, 1999, with a minimum of seven states. Britain and Denmark reserved a right to opt out of Stage Three.

All member states had to meet strict economic convergence criteria on inflation rates, government deficits, long-term interest rates and currency fluctuations. To join the third stage, a country was supposed to have an inflation rate not greater than 1.5 percent of the average of the three lowest member state rates, long-term interest rates no higher than 2 percent above the average of the three lowest, a budget deficit less than 3 percent of gross domestic product (GDP), a total public indebtedness of less than 60 percent of GDP, and no devaluation within the ERM during the prior two years. These criteria likewise govern admission of other member states into the EURO zone. One could argue they have been honored more in the breach than conformity.

EURO Zone

The economic performance of member states in 1997 became the test for admission to the economic and monetary union. Since both France and Germany had trouble meeting the admissions criteria, this opened a window for much more marginal states such as Belgium, Italy and Spain to join immediately. Greece also subsequently qualified for the EURO zone. As expected, Denmark, Britain and Sweden opted out of initial participation in the common currency. The Danes did so by voting No in a year 2000 national referendum. The Swedes voted similarly in 2003. By 2014, Slovenia, Malta, Estonia, Cyprus, Slovakia, Lithuania and Latvia had joined the EURO zone for a total of 19 out of 28 states.

On January 1, 1999, the participating states fixed the exchange rates between the EURO and their national currencies. National notes and coins were removed from the market by July 2002 as the EURO was installed. The EURO has been used for most commercial banking, foreign exchange and public debt purposes since 1999. It has also been adopted (voluntarily) by the world's securities markets, and by Monaco, San Marino, the Vatican, Andorra, Montenegro and Kosovo. Denmark and Bulgaria have pegged their national currencies to the EURO. The EURO zone Council and Parliament, acting under "co-decision," can adopt rules for the use of the EURO as a single currency.

The arrival of the EURO has important implications for the United States and the dollar. For decades, the dollar has been the world's leading currency, although its dominance has been declining since the early 1980s. Use of the Deutsche Mark and Yen in commercial and financial transactions, and in savings and reserves, had been steadily rising. The EURO is likely to continue the dollar's decline in these markets. It is certainly the hope of many Europeans that they have successfully created a rival to the dollar. NAFTA/USMCA, in contrast, does not even hint at a common North American currency.

European Central Bank, Financial Bailouts

It was also agreed at Maastricht that in the third stage the European Central Bank (ECB) and the European System of Central Banks (ESCB) would start operations. The ECB and ESCB are governed by an executive board of six persons appointed by the member states and the governors of the national central banks. The ECB and the ESCB are independent of any other European institution and in theory free from member state influence. Their primary responsibility is to maintain price stability, specifically keeping price inflation below two percent per year. In contrast, the U.S. Federal Reserve has two primary responsibilities: maximum employment and stable prices.

The main functions of the ECB and ESCB are: (1) define and implement regional monetary policy; (2) conduct foreign exchange operations; (3) hold and manage the official foreign reserves of the member states; and (4) supervise the payments systems. The ECB has the exclusive right to authorize the issue of bank notes within the Common Market and must set interest rates to principally achieve price stability. The Court of Justice may review the legality of ECB decisions. The ECB works closely with the Ecofin Council's broad guidelines for economic policy, such as keeping national budget deficits below 3 percent of GDP in all but exceptional circumstances (2 percent decline in annual GDP).

If the Ecofin considered a national government's policy to be inconsistent with that of the region, it could recommend changes including budget cuts. If appropriate national action did not follow such a warning, the Ecofin could require a government to disclose the relevant information with its bond issues, block European Investment Bank credits, mandate punitive interest-free deposits, or levy fines and penalties. Regrettably, the fiscal enforcement system established when the EURO was created did not work. The Commission's attempt to obtain sanctions against Germany and France in 2004 for failure to comply with the 3 percent budget deficit rule was denied by the Court of Justice.[198]

Since 1999, many EURO states have been under threat of sanctions for failure to comply with the 3 percent budget deficit rule, most notably Greece, Portugal, Spain, Italy and Ireland after the global financial meltdown of 2008–09. Yet no EURO Zone member state was ever sanctioned, suggesting this system for controlling national deficits was toothless. It has essentially been replaced by the 2012 Treaty on Stability, Coordination and Governance (TSCG, below). Some commentators suggest that the most effective discipline has come from external financial markets.

Despite a specific Article 125 TFEU prohibition against Union bailouts for member state governments, as the European financial crises have demonstrated, bailouts of debt-ridden EURO zone members may occur. A 110 billion EURO rescue package for Greece

---

[198] European Parliament v. Council, (1985) Eur.Comm.Rep. 1513.

was organized by the IMF, ECB and European Commission (the "Troika") in 2010 over German laments. Fearing a cascade of financial crises in Spain, Portugal, Italy and Ireland, a 1 trillion EURO liquidity safety net was devised using EU-backed bonds, special purpose EU-guaranteed investment loans, and more IMF funds. In addition, the ECB for the first time began buying EURO zone national government bonds in the open market.

All this caused Germany to publicly re-think its traditional role as paymaster and proponent of the European Union and EURO. Clearly the EURO was not as good as the fondly remembered Deutsche Mark. Sure enough, Ireland tapped into this safety net for over 100 billion EUROs late in 2010 followed by Portugal in 2011. In 2012, massive ECB loans to Spanish and Italian banks and their governments staved off bailouts and moderated interest rates, and Greece was bailed out a second time. These actions ran down the safety net and ECB resources. Most private holders of Greek debt have been pushed into a renegotiated deal with roughly a 50% "haircut" in the value of their holdings.

Fearing a meltdown, in July of 2012 the ECB President promised to "do whatever it takes" to save the EURO. This statement brought an immediate and surprisingly enduring calm to currency and financial markets. Nevertheless, in 2013, Cyprus was bailed out by the Troika under plan that for the first time "bailed in" bank bondholders and uninsured depositors (notably Russians) who were obliged to take significant reductions in their assets. Cyprus also promised budget and spending cuts, increased corporate, interest, and gambling taxes, reduced public sector employment, pension overhauls with higher retirement ages, and declines in health care expenditures.

In addition, since 2013, EU bailouts require sovereign bond holders to take losses under "collective action clauses" designed to keep individual investors from blocking restructured debt deals. Mandatory losses can be imposed when Euro-zone nations are deemed insolvent by the European Central Bank, the European Commission and the IMF, acting somewhat like a "bankruptcy court," and the Euro-zone finance ministers unanimously are in accord.

All this bond buying was ultimately challenged before the German Constitutional Court. In 2020, that court ruled against the ECB, asserting that its monetary rescue policies had failed to be "proportional". This ruling threatens to undermine the principle of supremacy of EU over national law. See Chapter 2.

Treaty on Stability, Coordination and Governance (TSCG), ECB Bond Buying and Bank Regulation

In March of 2012, with market pressures and threats of a Greek default or exit from the EURO Zone escalating, 25 of the 27 EU members (minus Britain and the Czech Republic) adopted a Treaty on Stability, Coordination and Governance (TSCG) intended to provide a "permanent" solution to the EURO crisis. Only Ireland allowed its voters a referendum on this Treaty, which was negotiated outside the regular TFEU framework. The Irish, their bailout in progress, voted in favor of ratification by approximately a 60% margin. Importantly, ratification by the German Parliament was upheld by Germany's Constitutional Court under that country's "eternal democracy" clause.

The TSCG has two principal components: The European Stability Mechanism (ESM) and a "Fiscal Compact."

Effective in 2013, the ESM created a permanent 900 billion EURO loan fund, 27% of which is financed by Germany. Any increase in the ESM fund must be approved by the German Parliament. EURO Zone countries may apply for bailout loans conditioned upon fiscal and economic reforms. All EURO Zone national parliaments must approve any ESM rescue package. Finland has indicated its approval may require loan collateral.

The "Fiscal Compact" incorporates a "balanced budget" rule. "Automatic corrective measures" apply if excessive budgets are reached. The EU Commission monitors national budget deficits using numerous economic indicators under its "European Semester" system. Breach of the Compact can result in enforcement actions before the European Court of Justice with penalties payable to the ESM.

In addition, in 2012, the European Central Bank announced its willingness to buy unlimited, short-term national government bonds if an ESM rescue is secured by a EURO Zone member (Outright Monetary Transactions). Germany's revered Bundesbank openly opposed this announcement, which had the support of the Merkel government. Like ESM loans, such purchases will be conditioned upon fiscal and economic austerity commitments with the ECB serving as the regulator of Zone banks.

The extent of the ECB's regulatory powers was much debated, though ECB licensing and penalty powers over large banks represented a regulatory base line under what is known as the Single Supervisory Mechanism. Under what is called the 2012 Single Rulebook plan, more demanding capital requirements were established, as were controversial bankers' bonus limits, and more integrated deposit insurance and failed bank resolution schemes under a Single Resolution Board. Failing Spanish and Italian banks have been "resolved" by the Board, sometimes without taxpayer bailouts, sometimes with. Taken together, these programs form the core of an emerging EU banking union with the ECB at its center.

There is a multi-part attempt at "permanently" solving the EURO crisis: The ESM, Fiscal Compact, ECB bond buying and ECB bank regulatory powers. This attempt once again seeks to come to grips with systemic flaws that have haunted the EURO since its creation. . . .can national spending policies be stabilized, coordinated, and governed in support of a common currency?

Since all EURO Zone countries are jointly liable for ESM and ECB monies, this amounts to a partial mutualization of national debt risk. It is not, however, as some have suggested is needed, EURO bonds backed by the EURO Zone. That said, the TSCG is certainly a step in that direction. Thanks principally to the ECB President's 2012 promise to "do whatever it takes" to save the EURO, no ESM rescues or Outright Monetary Transfers have been undertaken as yet.

The EURO Crisis Continues . . .

The EURO was conceived as a unifier for Europe. It has become instead a divisive wedge among creditors and austerity weary debtor nations. That said, by 2014 Ireland and Portugal had refinanced and exited their bailouts without credit line safety nets, taken to be "success" stories. Cyprus did likewise in 2016. But Greece, Italy and Spain remain troubled, and the EURO Zone crisis is anything but over.

No ESM in sight, but with deflation and economic stagnation apparent, the ECB undertook starting in 2015 a massive, unprecedented, and controversial "quantitative easing (QE)" program buying up national government debt. This program resembled that which the U.S. Federal Reserve had been pursuing for some time. In 2016, the ECB extended its bond buying program to select corporate debt and reduced bank loans to zero interest for up to four years These QE policies have reduced European government borrowing costs, tended to reinforce European equity prices, and weakened the EURO (thus enhancing exports).

Meanwhile, Greece elected a government strongly opposed to the austerity conditions attached to its bailouts, lowering the Grexit threshold. There was cause for opposition to the austerity loan conditions. Over the first six years, Greece received over 240 billion Euros in bailout funds, plus the private sector debt restructuring, yet its economy has shrunk by at least 25%, and its debt to GDP ratio has risen dramatically to over 175%. In short, the bailouts and their conditions have proven self-destructive, making it less (not more) likely that Greece can ever repay its debts.

Greek society paid a very heavy price: Unemployment became widespread, poverty grew, young people and bank deposits fled, property values descended, authoritarian rule raised its ugly head, and disillusionment was pervasive. Corruption and tax evasion remained entrenched.

Amidst another Greek crisis in 2015, the EURO initially plunged in value, but rallied somewhat by mid-2015, just in time for a third bailout of Greece by the Troika. This bailout, like its predecessors and over IMF objections, did not reduce the amount of Greek national debt. One year later in 2016, it was déjà vu all over again. Greece needed more financial support to avoid default, and the IMF, after a somewhat scathing internal review of its participation in the second Greek bailout, pushed hard for debt reductions. Germany and the EU limited their support to extending Greek debt maturities, along with interest rate and debt repayment caps. This support was notably contingent upon pension and tax collection reforms in Greece.

By 2024, little had had changed. The IMF was still unwilling to participate in the third bailout, Germany unwilling to write off Greek debt, and the Greek government and its people continue to suffer. An essential question is whether a Greek default can be absorbed without taking down other EURO Zone states and the EURO itself? In other words, whether a Greek default would prove contagious is the key systemic question. Portugal and Ireland, the bailout "success" stories, remain deeply indebted. Spain and Italy have survived on cash infusions that make the debt of Greece look miniscule, and major Italian banks appear insolvent. Nativist French politician Marine Le Pen ran on a FREXIT platform promising to withdraw from the EURO in the 2017 French elections, and other anti-EURO parties are advancing in local elections.

Years later, the 2012 ESM mechanism has yet to be invoked, and Commission review of Fiscal Compact compliance has been "flexible". Hence the "permanent" solution to the EURO crisis created in 2012 is in doubt. Even some of the world's best financial market wizards say there is no clear-cut answer to the question of what happens in Europe or globally if Greece defaults or a EURO member withdraws from the Zone.

§ 4.17 Common Transport Policy

The Union's common transport policy is another objective that the TFEU outlines. Despite its critical role in the free movement of goods and people within the Common Market, transportation is an area in which the Treaty's aspirations remained unfulfilled for many years. Trade restraints in road, rail and air transportation within the European Union were commonplace. Indeed, the level of frustration with the lack of integration in this field was reflected in a 1985 lawsuit filed by the Parliament against the Council before the European Court of Justice seeking to force the Council to fully implement the Treaty's goals for a more common and integrated transportation market.[199] The Court found that there had been a "failure to act" by the Council which had to be remedied within a reasonable time. There have been important reforms in the transportation field since then.

Road Transport

After much delay, progress has been made in road transportation. Legislation has been issued to abolish discrimination arising from different (but still regulated) rates and from conditions applied to like goods in like circumstances. European Union law also deals with common rules for international road carriage, restrictions upon drivers' hours, and installation of tachygraphs that record such hours. The latter requirement caused a furor in Britain because it stopped drivers from "moonlighting" extra runs.[200] Differences among the Member States about road taxes, safety requirements, noise levels, and truck weights and dimensions have been mostly resolved.

In 1988, a Council directive vastly increased the number of Union authorizations for interstate carriage of goods. Since 1993, such authorizations are unlimited, though subject to qualitative licensing controls.[201] Another Council Regulation removes restraints on motor carriers hauling goods inside other member states (cabotage).[202] At least in this area, the Council has seriously addressed its obligations under the 1985 Court of Justice judgment of inaction.

NAFTA/USMCA fundamentally provides for free trucking and foreign ownership of transport firms within North America.[203] Not

---

199 European Parliament v. Council, (1985) Eur.Comm.Rep. 1513.

200 Commission v. United Kingdom, (1979) Eur.Comm.Rep. 419.

201 Council Directive 1841/88.

202 Council Regulation 2454/92.

203 R. Folsom and W.D. Folsom, *The USMCA, NAFTA, Re-Negotiated and Its Business Implications.*

surprisingly, the Teamsters Union has vehemently opposed these provisions since the inception of NAFTA. Their lobbying and lawsuits effectively blocked Mexican trucks from significantly entering the U.S. market. Mexico took the U.S. failure in this regard to arbitration and won unanimously. A pilot program under President George W. Bush was commenced, but Congress withdrew financial backing in the Obama stimulus bill. Mexico retaliated with over $2.4 billion in tariffs on U.S. goods. A settlement subsequently allowed qualified Mexican trucks to role on U.S. highways, and Mexico removed its retaliatory tariffs. Clearly, road transport is an area where NAFTA/USMCA could learn much from the European Union experience.

Maritime Transport

Council Regulations 4055–58/86 on maritime transport services move in the same direction (especially by removing so-called national flag reservations) but fail to deal with "cabotage" (transport within one EU state). European Union competition law rules apply, as do its antidumping rules.[204] This represents the first application of dumping law in the services sector.

Air Transport, Open Skies Agreement

Air transport has been a tougher nut to crack. Market-sharing, profit pooling and other restrictive cartel practices have long victimized Europe's flying public. Not surprisingly, many of the Union's airlines are governmentally owned. In the so-called *Nouvelles Frontières* case, the Court of Justice struck a blow for greater competition and consumer benefit by legitimizing EU and national law enforcement actions against restrictive airline practices.[205] Price fixing by air carriers and state approvals of rates (including on flights to and from the Union) are unlawful unless specifically exempted by the Commission.[206]

Since these decisions, Commission threats of prosecution combined with new legislation deregulating the market have made some headway at flying friendlier skies in Europe. These laws are known as the First (1987) and Second (1990) Air Transport Liberalization Packages. For example, the old system that allowed any carrier on a route to veto low-fare proposals by other airlines was replaced by the "double disapproval" rule. It now takes disapproval by two civil air authorities to negate low-fare proposals. Moreover, the right of governments to oppose the introduction of new fares and

---

[204] *See* Chapters 6 and 7.

[205] Ministère Public v. Asjes, (1986) Eur.Comm.Rep. 1425. *See* Council Directives 3975/87 and 3976/87.

[206] Ahmed Saeed Flugreisen v. Zentrale zur Bekämpfung unlauteren Wettbewerbs, (1989) Eur.Comm.Rep. 803.

market access was limited.[207] The Commission (after winning a major case before the Court of Justice)[208] has also announced an intention to take over from the member states the responsibility for negotiating international air-traffic agreements. Traditionally, these agreements have been bilaterally undertaken at the national level.

Early in 1992, the Council adopted the Third Package of Liberalization measures on air transport.[209] Under this package, airlines have substantial freedom to set ticket prices, operating throughout the Union under a single license issued by national authorities employing common EU financial and safety criteria (European Common Aviation Area). Each airline can acquire freight and passengers in other EU nations (cabotage rights). National authorities may regulate flights and prices to and from non-member countries, and within their internal markets. National authorities may also intervene if they deem Union fares unreasonably low or high, with the airline retaining a right to appeal such interventions to the Commission.

Late in 1992, the Council issued a series of additional regulations on airline license criteria, market access, consumer protection and competition.[210] Although it employed a four-year transition period, the Third Package of Liberalization had an immediate impact. Sparked by Lufthansa's price-cutting, airline rate competition has improved. Discounter Ryanair for example is successfully adapting the Southwest Airlines formula to the EU market.

After 15 years of negotiation, the European Union and the United States finally reached agreement on "open skies." Starting in 2008, U.S. and EU airlines have been free to determine their number of transatlantic flights, routes and fares. Passenger traffic rose, costs declined, and airline revenues increased. The agreement does not affect foreign ownership or internal flight restrictions in either jurisdiction. A second agreement, negotiated twice, covers transatlantic air passenger records' disclosure.[211]

Acting unilaterally, the EU enacted an airline emissions tax that impacted U.S. and other foreign carriers operating in EU airspace.

---

207 *See* Council Directives 87/601 (tariffs), 87/602 (market access) and Council Regulations 3975/87, 3976/87 on competition law. Taken together, these measures are sometimes referred to as the "First Package of Liberalization." The "Second Package" created more flexibility on fares and market access. *See* Council Regulations 2432/90 (tariffs) and 2343/90 (market access).

208 Commission v. Belgium, (2002) Eur.Comm.Rep. I–9681.

209 *See* Council Directives 2407/92, 2408/92 and 2409/92.

210 Council Regulations 2407–2411/92.

211 Decision 2007/551/CFSP/JHA, OJ L204/16.

American air carriers unsuccessfully challenged British implementation of this system before the European Court of Justice.[212]

Transport Legislation

The Treaty on European Union added provisions to the TFEU intended to foster the growth of trans-European networks, including transportation.[213] Special emphasis is placed on inter-operability and access issues. The following is a sampling of EU transport laws regarding fares and market access. Technical laws covering vehicle and operator safety are omitted.

- Regulation 4055/86 (freedom to provide maritime services)
- Regulation 4056/86 (maritime services and competition law)
- Regulation 4057/86 (unfair maritime pricing)[214]
- Regulation 4058/86 (ocean cargoes)
- Directive 87/601 and Regulation 2342/90 (scheduled airfares)
- Directive 87/602 and Regulation 2343/90 (air passenger sharing and market access)
- Regulations 3975/87, 2344/90 (competition law and airlines)
- Regulation 4060/87 (road and inland waterway border controls)
- Regulation 1841/88 (road transport quotas)
- Regulation 2671/88 (coordination of airline capacity, revenues, tariffs and slot allocations at airports)
- Regulation 4058/89 (road carrier rates)
- Regulations 4059/89, 296/91 (provision of intrastate services by nonresident road carriers)
- Directive 91/224 (combined railroad carriage)
- Regulation 294/91 (air cargo services)

---

[212] Air Transport System of America et al v. Secretary of State for Energy and Climate Change, (2012) Eur.Comm.Rep. (Case C–366/10).

[213] *See* Article 154.

[214] *See* "The Hyundai Case," O.J. 1989 L4/1; Council Regulation 15/89 (unfair maritime services result in special duties).

- Regulation 2454/92 (road transport services by nonresident carriers)
- Directives 96/26, 98/76 (road haulers, licenses)
- Directive 96/48 (high-speed rail)
- Directive 99/62 (road tolls)
- Directive 2002/15 (working time, road transport)
- Regulation 411/2004 (competition rules apply to airlines)
- Decision 2004/96 (U.S. commitments to protect personal data of air travelers)
- Directive 2004/49 (railway safety)
- Directive 2004/54 (road tunnel safety)
- Regulation 549/2004 (air travel/safety framework)

Detailed road, rail, maritime and air transport rules largely maintain EU transportation principles as between Britain and the EU post BREXIT. See Chapter 8 and Appendix 4.

Chapter 5

EUROPEAN UNION BUSINESS LAW

Table of Sections

§ 5.0 Introduction

Article 114 of the TFEU empowers the Council of ministers, acting on Commission proposals, to issue directives for the "approximation" (better known as "harmonization" or "coordination") of national laws directly affecting the establishment or operation of the Common Market. Such directives must be adopted unanimously within the Council. Since a vast number of national laws affect the Common Market, the potential scope of Article 114 is very broad.

This scope, over the years since 1957, was not fully exploited, principally because of a unanimous Council voting requirement. Indeed, by 1986 and a Community of twelve nations, innovative legislation under Article 114 became quite difficult to obtain. That is why one major thrust of the 1987 Single European Act was the inclusion of Article 115. See Section 2.5. It specifies qualified majority voting in the Council of ministers for much of the single market legislative agenda. Qualified majority voting procedures also apply to directives used to harmonize national laws (*e.g.*, subsidies, procurement) distorting the conditions of competition in the Common Market.

Harmonization of national laws of concern to the Common Market is critical to advancing European integration. Harmonization can, for example, remove many of the barriers to free movement previously discussed in Chapter 4, including those expressly permitted by Article 36 and the *Cassis* and *Keck* line of cases. It can do the same for the public security exceptions to the free movement of workers and the self-employed, as well as to the freedom to provide services across borders. Harmonization is critical to removal of the tax and nontariff trade barrier (NTB) frontiers, a central focus of the campaign for a Europe without internal frontiers. In addition, harmonization can reach out to areas not specifically treated in the TFEU, but which are of consequence to the functioning of the Common Market.

Some of the most dramatic surrenders of national sovereignty to EU institutions occur in the business law area, a fact with which Britain under BREXIT is now wrestling. If a common market is to result, many national economic policies must be coordinated or conformed to regional standards. Nothing remotely comparable in scale or depth exists under NAFTA/USMCA. Much of the "*acquis communautaire*" that new member states must implement in their national legal systems is found in EU policy programs.

This chapter provides illustrations of efforts under the Treaty on the Functioning of the European Union (TFEU) to minimize the trade distorting impact of national economic laws. Taxation, one of the very few remaining areas where unanimous Council voting is still required, is an excellent and perhaps the most difficult example.

§ 5.1 VAT and Excise Taxation, Savings Taxation

If each government were to legislate freely and differently on taxation, the operation of the Common Market would clearly be affected. Article 110 TFEU forbids discriminatory or protective taxation based on nationality or the origin of products. The goal of this article is to prohibit the use of tax laws as a trade barrier and ensure that goods which compete are equally taxed. The practical effect of Article 110 is to convey substantial powers of judicial review over national tax law and policy to the European Court. France, for example, has repeatedly found its annual car taxes under such review. France based this tax on a power rating scale the practical effect of which was to tax all French autos at a rate lower than imported cars. This tax system was twice held invalid under Article 110.[1] A Greek tax on imported cars not applied domestically also ran afoul of Article 110.[2] So too did an Italian tax on bananas.[3]

Value-Added Taxes

Sales taxes and what the Europeans refer to as "turnover taxes" can also have a trade distorting impact. Each member state now has a turnover tax generally referred to as the value-added tax (VAT). This was not always the case. Britain, for example, had to switch from a sales tax to a VAT upon joining the EU. VAT is a cumulative multistage tax system encountered in virtually every transaction of goods *or services* throughout the Union. United States attorneys might ponder what their clients' reactions would be if they added service taxes to their fees.

The Sixth VAT Directive[4] adopted in 1977 was particularly notable. It established a uniform basis for VAT assessment within the EU governing territorial application, taxable transactions, the place of taxable transaction, chargeable events and the chargeability of the tax, applicable rates and exemptions, deductions, and persons liable for VAT and their obligations.

Although harmonization has been achieved as to the nature of the required tax system, differing levels of VAT taxation within the Union continue to distort trade relations. Britain, for example,

---

1 Humblot v. Directeur des Services Fiscaux, (1985) Eur.Comm.Rep. 1367; Re Feldain, (1987) Eur.Comm.Rep. 3536. *See*, more recently, De Danske Bilimportorer v. Skatteministeriet, (2003) Eur.Comm.Rep. I–6065.

2 Commission v. Hellenic Republic, (1990) Eur.Comm.Rep. I–1567 (Case C–105/92). *Accord*, Commission v. Greece, (1997) Eur.Comm.Rep. I–5981.

3 Commission v. Italy, (1987) Eur.Comm.Rep. 2013.

4 Council Directive 77/388.

generally charged one uniform VAT rate of 15 to 17.5 percent but zero rated "necessities." Italy, on the other hand, had three levels of VAT with luxuries taxed at times as high as 38 percent. Furthermore, each country established tax collection points at its borders to assure the collection of the proper amount of VAT for products in accordance with national law (the "destination principle"). These "tax frontiers" probably represented the most significant nontariff trade barrier in the Union prior to 1993.

Many considered the ability of the European Union to achieve a consensus as to the proper levels of VAT and excise taxation, or at least to reduce the degree of differences in such taxation among the member states, to be the litmus test of the campaign for a fully integrated market. Late in 1992, the Council formally agreed to closer alignment of most VAT rates. At this point, members must apply a standard VAT rate of no less than 15% (most have rates of 20% or higher), with limited lower rates applicable to food, books and medical equipment. Since 2003, VAT is collected on Internet sales and services, including digital downloads.

The tax frontiers have been eliminated by imposing VAT reporting and collection duties on importers and exporters using the destination principle on VAT rates. Under the destination method, goods are shipped within the Common Market net of tax and incur VAT upon entry into the importing country. Customers must obtain a VAT registration number which must be given to their cross-border suppliers. The suppliers will report these numbers and transactions to the relevant national tax authorities, all of whom are electronically linked.

The harmonization of VAT rules inside the Union has had a wide-ranging impact. Regarding the taxation of boats, for example, it used to be that an importer for personal use could gain VAT exemption by exporting the boat every 6 to 12 months to another country. This was commonly done. However, a 6-month VAT exemption limit for the entire Union has been imposed since 1993. This means that a VAT exemption can be had only by leaving the EU for 6 months, a much more difficult requirement given European geography and most boater preferences. VAT, on the other hand, does not apply to EU-made used boats purchased inside the Union.

Excise Taxes

Excise duties are an obvious example of the potential for trade distortion through taxation. Excise taxes on imported liquor, for example, must be levied at the same rate, on the same basis and by the same methods as domestic competitors. Low alcohol, cheap wines imported into Britain thus could not be taxed more than beer.[5] Nor could France discriminate in taxation of wine versus grain spirits.[6] But the prohibition against discriminatory internal taxation does not apply where there are no similar or competing national products.[7]

The excise tax frontier has been eliminated by moving to a system of interlinked bonded warehouses between which goods can move easily. To help prevent smuggling from low-tax to high-tax member states, the Council agreed to "presumption of fraud" limits on duty-paid imports. These limits are 110 liters of beer, 90 liters of wine, 800 cigarettes, and 10 liters of spirits. An individual must prove, if challenged by a customs official, that imports above these limits are for private consumption rather than for resale. The UK, Denmark and Ireland countries which have high excise tax rates, used the presumption.

As with VAT, excise taxation will continue to follow the destination principle.[8] The Commission hopes to move to taxation on origin principles. An origin-based system would apply VAT to exported goods before they are shipped, thus collecting tax revenues in the country where the value was added.

Tax Enforcement, Savings Taxation

As a supplement to the extensive tax treaty network among members of the Union on tax enforcement, the Council adopted the 1977 Tax Authorities Mutual Assistance Directive. The Directive provides for information exchange between the tax authorities of the Union's member states. It requires information sharing when a reduction of tax in one member state is likely to give rise to an increase in tax in another. The Directive covers VAT, income taxation, capital gains and the sale of property, but does not affect excise duties. All information exchanged is held in confidence. A 1990 directive sought to extend the Mutual Assistance Directive to inheritance and gift taxes. It also sought to remove administrative and legal barriers to cross-border disclosure and enforcement, including a proposed agreement to override secrecy laws in cases of alleged tax fraud.

Luxembourg vetoed the proposal, illustrating the need for unanimous Council votes on tax legislation. Luxembourg was especially concerned with the degree of disclosure required of banks. Council Directive 2003/48 addresses taxation of interest income of

---

[5] Commission v. United Kingdom ("Wine and Beer"), (1983) Eur.Comm.Rep. 2265.

[6] Commission v. France, (1980) Eur.Comm.Rep. 347.

[7] Commission v. Denmark, (1990) Eur.Comm.Rep. 4509 (Case C–47/88).

[8] Council Directive 92/12.

nonresidents by promoting the exchange of tax information and withholding, nonmember Switzerland included. This directive is expected to particularly hit Germans with bank accounts in Luxembourg and Switzerland, but also covers Monaco, Lichtenstein, Andorra and San Marino. Directive 2003/49 eliminates taxes levied in source countries on interest and royalty payments between associated companies.

§ 5.2 Corporate Taxation

There are wide variations on corporate income tax levels among the EU member states, which low-tax countries like Ireland view as essential to attract foreign investment. Ireland successfully fought to retain low corporate taxation under its more recent "bailout" package. Controversial *flat* corporate and personal income tax systems have emerged in several "New Europe" states, *e.g.*, Estonia and Slovakia. "Old Europe" states like France and Germany with high tax rates are objecting strenuously to "fiscal dumping." Harmonization of corporate taxes has been proposed, but the unanimous voting rules for tax legislation make such proposals difficult to enact.

There are directives on taxation of cross-border mergers, taxation of dividends from subsidiaries to parents, and a convention on arbitration of transfer pricing disputes. Some discriminatory corporate tax measures have been struck down by the Court of Justice. In 1997, a voluntary Code of Conduct on Corporate Taxation was adopted. This Code seeks to avoid use of "predatory" tax incentives to attract investment, although Ireland gets to keep its 12 percent income tax rate on manufacturers. By 2003, an agreement on passing along withholdings or reporting payment of bank interest to the recipient's home country was agreed upon, with nonmember Switzerland included. This particularly hit Germans with bank accounts in Luxembourg and Switzerland, but also covers Monaco, Liechtenstein, Andorra and San Marino.

Business tax rules that discriminate on nationality grounds may breach the right of establishment secured by Article 49 TFEU. In one decision, the Court of Justice invalidated French tax rules that denied tax credits to shareholders of branches operated in France by companies from other member states.[9] These credits were generally available to domestic enterprises, including French subsidiaries of foreign firms. The Court found such discrimination to violate Article 49. The principal opposition to the French tax rules came from the insurance sector. Another decision involving banking affirms the right of private parties to challenge national tax laws that are

---

9 Commission v. France, (1986) Eur.Comm.Rep. 273.

discriminatory as applied to deposits obtained by persons from other member states.[10] The right to be free from discrimination on grounds of nationality has also been extended to corporations doing business in other EU jurisdictions, particularly in cases of tax liability discrimination between local and "non-resident" companies. In one notable application, the U.K. was required to make tax refunds to non-resident enterprises on the same basis as to British corporations.[11]

The Council has also been active in the corporate tax area, focusing particularly on double taxation issues. A 1969 Directive abolished stamp duties on securities.[12] It also created a limited tax rate band for capital formation, share issuance, and other asset contributions. However, the transfer of profits between two companies having a common shareholder can be subject to capital taxation[13] and branch offices equipped with equipment and personnel engaging in their own activities can benefit from a reduction in capital taxation.[14] Share transfers between unlimited liability shareholders and limited liability shareholders are not subject to capital duties.[15] Transactions subject to capital duty are taxable only in the member state where the effective center of management is located. For those without a company center in the Union, the member state of the company's registered office is the taxing jurisdiction.

The Council adopted directives in 1990 on the taxation of cross-border mergers,[16] the taxation of dividends paid by subsidiaries to parent companies,[17] and a five-year "trial" convention on arbitration of transfer pricing tax disputes between member states.[18] Additional directives on taxation of interest and royalties as between parent and subsidiary companies, and the allocation of losses as between them have followed.[19] Nevertheless, there are substantial differences

---

10 *See* Van Eycke v. A.S.P.A., (1988) Eur.Comm.Rep. 1469 (Case 267/86).

11 Regina v. Inland Revenue Commissions, (1993) Eur.Comm.Rep. I–04017 (Case 330/91).

12 Council Directive 69/335.

13 Weber Haus v. Finanzamt Freiburg-Land, (1992) Eur.Comm.Rep. (Case C–49/91).

14 Commerz-Credit-Bank v. Finanzamt Saarbrücken, (1992) Eur.Comm.Rep. I–05225 (Case C–50/91).

15 Finanzamt Kassel-Goethestrasse v. Kommanditgesellschaft Viesmann, (1993) Eur.Comm.Rep. I–00971 (Case C–280–91).

16 Council Directive 90/434.

17 Council Directive 90/435.

18 Convention 90/463.

19 Directive 2003/49, 2003 OJ L157/49.

among the member states on corporate taxation. One tax practitioner has summarized these differences as follows:

> The Netherlands, Luxembourg and Spain have wholly un-integrated classical structures. Greece and Portugal have partial integration with respect to dividends at the corporate level, the former through dividend deductions and the latter through a split-rate system. The remaining seven States provide relief for dividend taxation at the shareholder level under some form of imputation or credit system. Rates are also widely divergent, with basic rates on undistributed profits ranging up from zero to 56%, imputation credits up to 56.25%, and withholding tax rates on distributed profits from zero to 50%.
>
> The taxation of dividends, interest and royalties which are paid from one member state to another currently bears no relationship to the underlying corporation tax or to withholding tax paid elsewhere. As a result, the combined corporate taxes borne by particular dividend streams within the EC may vary considerably from one country to another. Imputation credits, moreover, generally are not extended to shareholders in other EC States and the treatment of foreign source income differs markedly from country to country. Further, while some countries tax foreign source income but give a credit for underlying taxes paid elsewhere, others will exempt the income from further taxation under provisions of domestic law or treaty arrangements. Treatment of income arising from branch operations also may differ from that applied to dividends from subsidiaries.[20]

The European Court of Justice has affirmed the right of member states to tax *portfolio* dividends of resident companies.[21] In recent years, highly preferential tax agreements between member state authorities and multinational companies, many of them American (Starbucks, Amazon, Apple, McDonald's), have been challenged by the Commission as unlawful subsidies, the subject of the next section. These Commission prosecutions seek to require member states, against their wishes, to recoup taxes from the multinationals.

Mergers Taxation

The 1990 Mergers Taxation Directive facilitates corporate transfers and reorganizations without immediate tax costs by eliminating tax on any capital gains, allowing cross-border transfer of tax-exempt reserves, and allowing transfer and carry-forward of unutilized tax losses. Depreciation and any future gains or losses on

---

20 Rich and Wilson, "EC Taxation in 1992" in Folsom, Lake and Nanda (eds.), *European Community Law After 1992: A Practical Guide for Lawyers Outside the Common Market* (Kluwer, 1992).

21 Haribo Lakritzen Hans Riegel. . . v. Finanzamt Linz, (2011) Eur.Comm.Rep. (Case C–436/08 and C–437/08).

the transferred assets are calculated by applying the transferor's basis. The member state that has allowed the deferral of tax retains the power to tax any profits on the ultimate disposition of the relevant assets. It also continues to tax the ongoing business operations in that member state after the transfer.

The Mergers Taxation Directive applies only to transactions between companies in the Union. The companies must therefore be residents and subject to tax in a member state. The directive applies to mergers, divisions, share exchanges and asset transfers. These transactions include most stock-for-stock acquisitions, corporate combinations, divisions and liquidations. However, shareholders of the transferor company may only receive stock in most cases. In limited circumstances, an additional cash or property "boot" may be allowed. A member state may deny or withdraw these tax benefits if it determines that a principal objective of the underlying transaction is tax avoidance or evasion. The absence of valid commercial purpose may give rise to a presumption that the transaction was motivated by tax evasion or tax avoidance. Tax relief may also be denied if a company reorganizes to avoid worker participation obligations.

Parent-Subsidiary Taxation

The 1990 Parent-Subsidiary Taxation Directive removes withholding on profits distributed by subsidiaries to parent companies in different member states. Likewise, the member states of parent companies may not tax distributions of profits received from subsidiaries. The directive took effect Jan. 1, 1992, and applies to companies that are resident for tax purposes and subject to corporate tax in a member state. Dividends paid to a parent company, or a stockholder located outside the EU are subject to ordinary tax rules. A parent company exists if it has held 25 percent of the capital or voting rights of a company resident and is subject to tax in another member state for at least two years. A parent's member state will not generally tax distributed profits received from a subsidiary except upon liquidation.

The parent's member state may, alternatively, tax the profits distributed to the parent. But it must allow a credit (the "deemed-paid credit") for the corporation tax paid by the subsidiary. Each member state of a parent company may disallow deductions against the taxable profits of the parent for any costs or losses relating to the holding or disposing of stock in the subsidiary. Moreover, profits distributed by a subsidiary to a parent company are withholding tax exempt provided the parent company holds a minimum of 25 percent of the subsidiary's capital.

Transfer Pricing

The 1990 Transfer Pricing Arbitration Convention adopts an "arm's length" standard to govern dealings between related entities in two states, an enterprise in one state with its permanent establishment in another member state, or an entity of one state with a permanent establishment in a third country of an entity of a second state. If the tax authorities are unable to agree within two years, an *advisory* commission delivers an opinion on the case. This advisory commission is composed of an equal number of representatives of the competent tax authorities and an "uneven number of independent persons of standing" appointed by mutual agreement. The tax authorities must reach a decision within six months of the advisory commission's opinion.

The authorities are bound by the opinion unless they subsequently reach a mutually agreeable alternative. Double taxation is deemed to have been eliminated when either the profits included are only taxed in one state or the taxable charge in one state is reduced by an amount equal to the tax chargeable in the other state. Businesses liable for a "serious penalty" (defined by national rules) because of transfer pricing violations have no recourse to the Arbitration Convention. The Convention does not limit any pre-existing rights under current bilateral double taxation treaties.

§ 5.3 Government Subsidies

The Union's competition policy is a natural consequence of its Common Market. The dismantling of internal tariffs, quotas, and measures of equivalent effect opens traditionally sheltered national markets to competition through trade in goods and services. Having created the playing field, so to speak, the TFEU seeks through its rules on competition to ensure that the field is as level as possible for all who participate. Fear of unfair subsidization after BREXIT was a major concern in the EU-UK negotiations. See Chapter 8.

These rules are of two basic types: Business competition (*i.e.*, antitrust) and government subsidies. This section focuses on internal EU subsidies law; Chapter 6 covers subsidies law applicable to EU exports. The business competition rules of the Union originate in Articles 101–106 TFEU. They are of such enormous importance to all who do business with the Union that Chapter 7 is devoted exclusively to them.

Subsidies by governments are one of the most intractable of world and Common Market trade problems. In the first place, there are subsidies everywhere. For example, most tax laws (including the Internal Revenue Code) are littered with subsidies. Secondly, identification and calculation of the amount of subsidy can be extremely difficult. The EU, like the GATT/WTO, has spent years just cataloging subsidies. As early as 1988 the Commission concluded that the member states spent approximately 100 billion ECUs annually on state subsidies. This amounted to about $2,000 per person engaged in manufacturing. Much of this aid goes to "crisis industries" that are declining, but a reasonable amount is targeted at growth sectors, technology development and general support. COVID-19 pandemic subsidies proliferated in 2020.

Moreover, subsidies are almost endemic where the member states own or are heavily invested in enterprises. Some enterprises have been acquired by governments out of bankruptcy to save jobs. Some have been established for strategic, prestige or capital requirement reasons. Others have simply been nationalized as a matter of social policy. In recent years, there has been a trend (but not a stampede) towards privatization of enterprises owned by EU governments. Neither nationalization nor privatization is mandated or controlled by the TFEU.[22]

The Commission has taken the position that any action by a member state as an owner that is different from a private investor can violate the subsidy or competition law[23] rules of the TFEU. Such actions may include cash payments, debt write-offs, acceptance of rates of return that are below market, implied or express guarantees of loans, cheap financing, new equity capital in circumstances a private investor would avoid and dividend waivers.[24] In adopting this position, the Commission is relying heavily upon Article 107 TFEU.

Treaty Provisions

Article 107(1) declares incompatible with the Common Market every national "aid" (subsidy) that distorts or threatens to distort competition by favoring certain businesses or goods. For example, state aids intended to benefit workers but implemented through a reduction in public charges to textile corporations in Italy were caught within Article 107(1). The impact of the subsidy, not its purposes, determines its character.[25] French textile industry aids financed partly by import levies were similarly prohibited because of

---

22 Costa v. ENEL, (1964) Eur.Comm.Rep. 585 (Italian nationalization of electricity companies).

23 *See* Chapter 7.

24 For example, after 18 years of litigation, the Commission prevailed in *Chronopost II* with its argument that logistical and commercial assistance from La Poste, a state monopoly, violated EU subsidy rules. *See* (2008) Eur.Comm.Rep. (Joined Cases C–341/06, C–342/06).

25 Italy v. Commission, (1974) Eur.Comm.Rep. 709.

their discriminatory impact.[26] Though the money may be private in origin, a state aid exists when that money is distributed through a public body.[27] Provision of subsidies through state-owned enterprises is also caught.[28] Investment subsidies that strengthen the position of a company in the Common Market fall within Article 107(1) as threats to the distortion of competition.[29]

Article 107(2) declares the following subsidies *compatible* with the Treaty: (a) social aid granted to individuals without discrimination as to the origin of goods; (b) natural disaster aid; and (c) economic aid to East Germany (a reservation now mooted by German unification).[30] Furthermore, Article 107(3) lists several aids which *may* be compatible with the Common Market if approved by the Commission. These include regional subsidies to promote development in areas of high unemployment or abnormally low standards of living, subsidies for important projects of common European interest and subsidies to remedy serious disturbances in the economy of a member state. Also included are subsidies to facilitate the development of certain economic activities or areas (*e.g.*, shipbuilding) provided they do not adversely affect trading conditions to an extent contrary to the common interest. Finally, any subsidy may be lawful if approved by the Council acting by qualified majority vote.

Enforcement

The Commission is charged in Article 108 with keeping all state aids under "constant review," which it does mostly by way of a reporting system. The duty of member state governments to report on the provision of subsidies to industry has been repeatedly upheld by the European Court.[31] If a subsidy is not compatible with the Common Market per Article 107 or is being misused, the Commission may render a decision to that effect against the member state unless the Council unanimously approves of the aid. Such Commission decisions terminate the ability to receive further state aid payments.[32] Absent compliance, the Commission can enforce its decision by bringing an action *directly* before the European Court of Justice. The Commission need not follow the more deliberate

---

26 France v. Commission, (1970) Eur.Comm.Rep. 487.

27 Commission v. France, (1985) Eur.Comm.Rep. 439.

28 Italy v. Commission, (1991) Eur.Comm.Rep. I–01433 (Cases C–303/88, C–305/89).

29 Philip Morris Holland BV v. Commission, (1980) Eur.Comm.Rep. 2671.

30 *See* Germany v. Commission, (2000) Eur.Comm.Rep. I–6857 (state aids for small businesses in former East Germany not 87(2) exempt).

31 France v. Commission, (1990) Eur.Comm.Rep. I–00307 (Case 301/87).

32 Capolongo v. Azienda Agricola Maya, (1973) Eur.Comm.Rep. 611.

procedures established in Article 258 for ordinary prosecutions of member states not adhering to their EU obligations.[33]

Enterprises sometimes sue the Commission for failure to act against state subsidies. In one case, a French pasta maker sued the Commission for damages under Article 260 TFEU because of its failure to act against Italian subsidies to domestic pasta manufacturers. Holding that a causal link had not been established between the Commission's failure to act and the French company's damages, the Court of Justice agreed that the case was rightly dismissed.[34] The final assessment of the compatibility of subsidies with the Treaty is the exclusive responsibility of the Commission. National courts involved in subsidies litigation because of the direct effect of Article 108(3) operate in a different capacity. Their job is to protect individual rights, not to determine the legality of state subsidies.[35]

Certain patterns have emerged in the Union's law on state subsidies. Regional development aids are generally supported, especially since the Single European Act of 1987 made elimination of regional economic disparities a priority. The whole of Greece, Portugal and Ireland, for example, have been treated as underdeveloped regions for subsidy law purposes.[36] Indeed, the Union itself engages in the same subsidies under its Regional Policy[37] Industrial aids to ease unemployment and modernize smokestack industries (coal, steel, textiles, shipbuilding) have generally been allowed. Production and marketing subsidies have generally been disallowed. Research and technological development subsidies, especially for energy saving projects, often pass muster. Since environmental protection subsidies violate the polluter must pay principle of EU Environmental Policy, such subsidies are not frequently approved.

The Commission's role relative to national subsidies has gradually changed over the years from prosecutorial watchdog against discriminatory and anticompetitive aids to coordinator of national subsidy policies and levels. In this capacity, the Commission can find itself negotiating specific subsidy amounts or refunds with national governments, *e.g.*, French subsidies to state-owned Renault and Air France. The power of prosecution under Article 107 remains.

---

33 *See, e.g.*, Commission v. United Kingdom, (1977) Eur.Comm.Rep. 921; Commission v. Germany, (1973) Eur.Comm.Rep. 813.

34 Bertrand v. Commission, (1976) Eur.Comm.Rep. 1.

35 Fédération Nationale du Commerce Exterieur des Produits Alimentaires + Ors v. France, (1992) Eur.Comm.Rep. I–05505 (Case C–354/90).

36 *See* Official Journal C 212/2.

37 *See* § 5.12.

No member state, for example, may match another nation's subsidy.[38]

The Court of Justice has affirmed the power of the Commission to order refunds of offending national subsidies.[39] The Commission can order suspensions in national aid payments until prior illegal aid is repaid.[40] In 2019 the Commission ordered Ireland to claw back $14.5 billion from Apple for alleged unlawful tax subsidies. However, in 2020 the ECJ ruled against the Commission's argument that "selective economic advantages" had been granted by Ireland in the *Apple* prosecution.

Many have suggested authorizing the Commission to levy fines and penalties against member states that fail to adhere to European Union law on subsidies. The Commission can order suspensions in national aid payments until prior illegal aid is repaid.

§ 5.4 Procurement

Every government, at whatever level, tends to favor local producers when spending the taxpayers' money. Various "Buy American" laws permeate much of the military and civil procurement of the federal, state and local governments in the United States. The impact of such laws has been diminished by U.S. participation in the optional WTO Procurement Code, and by even more liberal procurement commitments under NAFTA. Since Mexico does not adhere to the WTO Code, its procurement commitments under NAFTA/USMCA are especially notable, as are those of the CAFTA partners. China, which is not a party to the WTO Code, has nevertheless become a notable procurement award winner in the EU.

The governments of the European Union nations are no different. Nevertheless, through a long series of harmonizing directives issued by the Council and aggressive decisions of the European Court, the effects of Buy French, Buy Greek and Buy Greater London Council types of laws are slowly being overcome. For example, the Court's opinion in the *Buy Irish* case struck down a program of public advertisements urging consumers to voluntarily buy only goods marked with a "Guaranteed Irish" symbol. This program combined private and governmental funds and officials. It was declared a measure of equivalent effect to a quota hindering EU trade in breach of Article 34.[41] Public supply contracts that establish

---

[38] Steinike und Weinlig v. Germany, (1977) Eur.Comm.Rep. 595.

[39] Commission v. Germany, (1973) Eur.Comm.Rep. 813; Commission v. Belgium, (1988) 2 Common Mkt.L.Rep. 258 (failure of timely repayment is breach of Treaty obligations).

[40] Deggendorf GmbH, (1997) Eur.Comm.Rep. I–02549 (Case 91/391).

[41] Commission v. Ireland, (1982) Eur.Comm.Rep. 4005.

regional preferences, in this case the Mezzogiorno of Italy, violate Article 34 and the principles of free internal Community trade. Such preferences cannot be justified under Article 36, nor as a state aid under Article 107.[42]

Procurement Directives

The Council has issued a series of directives intended to open government procurement to competitive bids from all Union enterprises. The first focus of this effort was on tendering procedures for public works projects.[43] Discriminations based on nationality which amount to the equivalent of trade quotas are prohibited under an early 1969 directive. Discriminatory procedural rules concerning the award of public works and construction contracts are standardized in a 1971 directive. These public works directives apply to contracts exceeding one million ECUs.

The second focus of the effort to combat discriminatory government procurement patterns is on supply contracts for goods and services to member governments, their regional and local subdivisions, public agencies and the like. A 1977 directive requires most public supply contracts to be announced in advance in the Official Journal.[44] The announcement must also include the criteria for selection of bidders or suppliers, which may not be discriminatory. This directive does not apply to purchases of military supplies but covers purchases of nonmilitary supplies used by military forces. Certain national governmental monopolies, *e.g.,* water, gas and electricity, were excluded from its application. A 1980 directive amended these rules to bring them into conformity with the 1979 GATT Code on Government Procurement, to which the EU was a party. The 1980 directive, nevertheless, maintained a margin of preference for EU enterprises seeking governmental supply contracts within the Union.

The early procurement legislation did not live up to expectations. Purchasing entities and public authorities undertaking construction projects continued to give preference to domestic suppliers and contractors. A survey revealed the most common and serious breaches of Union procurement rules: (1) failure to advertise contracts in the *Official Journal*; (2) abuse of the exceptions permitting single tendering; (3) discriminatory administrative, financial or technical requirements in tenders, especially the

42 DuPont de Nemours Italiana SpA v. Unita Sanitaria Locale No. 2 di Carrara, (1990) Eur.Comm.Rep. I–00884 (Case C–21/88).

43 Council Directive 71/305 amended by Directive 89/440 and consolidated in Directive 93/37.

44 Council Directive 77/62 amended by Directives 80/767, 88/295 and consolidated in Directive 93/36.

insistence on compliance with national standards even when EU law does not allow this; (4) illegal disqualification or elimination of bidders or applicants from other Member States, for example by discriminatory selection criteria; and (5) discrimination at the award stage.

It was reported in late 1986 that approximately 98 percent of all procurement contracts went to national suppliers. Single tendering (unpublicized, noncompetitive contract awards) and selective supplier arrangements (unpublicized, selectively competitive contract awards) continue to hurt Union efforts at overcoming buy-local preferences. Other problems exist with exemptions from EU procurement law for special needs such as "speed of delivery," "security" and "particular specifications." Procedural and substantive reforms of the existing directives were developed by the Commission in 1986. These reforms covered notice requirements, longer bid periods, publication of contract awards (who won), use of European specification standards (not national standards), and reduction of exemption industries (energy, transport, water and telecommunications).

A legislative simplification of EU procurement rules was accomplished in Directives 2004/17 (Utilities) and 2004/18 (Public Sector). For the first time, firms convicted of corruption are excluded from procurement.

Buy EU

Reform of procurement rules was part of the unified internal market campaign. Early in 1988, the Council adopted a directive tightening up the procedural aspects of the Union's procurement rules to reduce single tendering.[45] Under another 1988 directive, public construction bidding was similarly reformed. Council Directives 89/665 and 92/59 coordinated member state remedies for review of the award of public supply and public works contracts. Council Directive 92/50 extends the Union's open procurement rules and procedures to public service contracts more than 200,000 EURO, excepting research and development and property contracts.

In 1990, a directive was adopted which in 1993 opened public contracts to EU firms in the Union's telecommunications, energy, transport and water industries.[46] This directive contains a controversial "Buy EU" clause which allows public authorities to dismiss bids with less than 50 percent Union content and gives EU suppliers a minimum margin of preference of 3 percent. Late in 1991, the United States threatened to retaliate against the Buy EU rules

---

45 *See* Council Directives 89/665, 89/440.

46 *See* Council Directives 90/531, 92/13 consolidated in Directive 93/38.

of this directive by unilaterally imposing trade sanctions on EU goods imported into the U.S. market. This threat was announced under Title VII of the Omnibus Trade and Competitiveness Act of 1988. The EU responded by first pointing out the greater degree of procurement preferences accorded under Buy American law.

Negotiations on this issue outside the Uruguay Round led in 1993 to a compromise Memorandum of Understanding. The EU agreed not to discriminate against U.S. suppliers, goods or services, and to open certain energy contracts.[47] The U.S. agreed to waive certain federal "Buy American" provisions as applied to bids of EU origin and to try to persuade the states to do likewise.

No agreement was reached regarding telecommunications procurement. This led first to U.S. procurement sanctions,[48] followed by EU retaliation.[49] Germany, however, seemingly broke ranks with the Union by negotiating a bilateral telecommunications agreement with the U.S. This resulted in the suspension of the U.S. sanctions as applied to Germany and much consternation within the European Union.

Since 1995, Europe and the United States have participated in the WTO Procurement Agreement. This has helped reduce transatlantic trade and procurement tensions.

§ 5.5 Products Liability

Products liability law is one field where the Union acted before the single market campaign to harmonize national rules. Prior to the EU products liability directive, the rules of law on products liability of the individual member states varied greatly. Traditional negligence liability with plaintiff's burden of proof was the rule in Italy, Portugal, Spain and Greece. A presumption of liability shifting the burden of proof to the defendant which bordered on strict products liability governed in Germany, Denmark, the Netherlands, the United Kingdom and Ireland. Absolute strict liability, creating a presumption liability that could not be overcome, was the rule in France, Belgium and Luxembourg.

Strict Liability

Council Directive 85/374 established, for all member states, a regime of strict (no-fault) defective products liability. The injured person is required to prove damage, the defect and a causal relationship between defect and damage. The term "product" applies to "all movables, with the exception of primary agricultural products

---

47 Council Decision 93/323.

48 Executive Order 12845.

49 Council Regulation 141/93.

and games, even though incorporated into another movable or into an immovable" and specifically includes electricity. Both new and used products are covered. However, the evaluation of whether a product is defective takes place at the time when the "producer" has most recently put the product into circulation. Manufacturers of components are treated as such producers.

Producers also include manufacturers of finished products, suppliers of raw materials or component parts and persons who, by putting names, trademarks or other distinguishing features on products, present themselves as producers. Licensors are not generally treated as producers, but their licensees are. Thus, department stores and commercial chains will be regarded as producers if they sell products manufactured by others under their own names without referring to actual origin. They will be jointly and severally liable with the actual producer. However, if a department store has had a product specially made under the designation "specially manufactured for [or] by," the department store should not be regarded as a "producer."

Any person who imports products into the Union for distribution in business is deemed a producer. This rule only concerns persons who import products into the Union, not persons who import from one member state to another. The importer's intentions at the time of importation are crucial. If the product was originally imported in the course of business, the importer will be regarded as a producer even if the product is later dedicated to personal use. An importer who originally imported the product for personal use, but later decides to use the product commercially, does not become a producer. The burden of proof that the product is not imported in business rests with the importer. Whether the doctrine of strict products liability applies to retailers is decided by each member state.

A product is defective "when it does not provide the safety which a person is entitled to expect." It is not the injured person's expectations that control, but rather the normal expectations of purchasers of such products. The reasonable expected use of the product is determined when evaluating defects of production, design or the lack of adequate warnings or instruction. The gravity of the potential injury, the probability of the occurrence of injury, and the consumer's awareness of the danger are analyzed to determine whether adequate warnings or instructions have been given.

Exceptions and Defenses

The exception for "primary agricultural products" includes fish products but excludes all products that "have undergone initial processing." The line between primary and initially processed products thus becomes quite important and will no doubt be subjected to judicial interpretation. Moreover, member states can elect to include primary agricultural products under their strict liability regime. Luxembourg appears to be the only nation to do so to date. The Products Liability Directive does not apply to services. However, if a defective product is used when rendering services, the producer may be held strictly liable for any damages. The person rendering services will only be liable if he or she has acted with negligence.

Strict liability is tempered by certain defenses, notably the "state-of-the-art" defense which excludes liability if the manufacturer could not have discovered the defect when the product was made. However, the member states have the option of omitting this defense, which (to date) only Luxembourg has done. The British version of this defense, implemented in the 1987 Consumer Protection Act, was unsuccessfully challenged as too broad by the Commission before the European Court of Justice.[50] Strict liability is also tempered in the award of damages by contributory negligence principles.

The calculation and types of damages that may be recovered and damages caps are largely left to national law. The award of "pain and suffering" or punitive damages is under member state control, as is the imposition of total limits on recovery. Germany, Greece and Portugal have set such total limits. A three-year statute of limitations ordinarily applies, and a ten-year absolute bar on liability is established in the Council directive on products' liability.

For some EU nations, such as Ireland and Spain, this directive mandated a fundamental switch away from liability systems grounded entirely in negligence principles. France, on the other hand, considered the directive too generous to manufacturers. All three were pursued by the Commission for their implementation failures.[51] Nevertheless, Americans who have studied the painstaking way strict products liability doctrine was crafted in state courts are often surprised by the sweeping implementation of comparable law in the European Union. One explanation lies in the goal of free movement and a desire to equalize the risks of liability (and the insurance costs) that most often accompany the distribution of goods to the public.

There is, also, greater acceptance in Europe of the need to compensate accident victims regardless of fault. Moreover, the absence of a well-financed plaintiff's bar, contingency legal fees,

---

50 Commission v. United Kingdom, (1997) Eur.Comm.Rep. I–2649.

51 *See, e.g.,* Commission v. French Republic, (2002) Eur.Comm.Rep. I–03827 (Case 52/00).

juries and rules that require each party to pay their own legal costs (*i.e.*, the loser generally pays in Europe) have made products' liability litigation infrequent. These factors facilitated the passage of the products liability directive and its implementation by the member states. The Products Liability Directive has, with certain adaptations, been extended to the EFTA countries (excluding Switzerland and Liechtenstein) by virtue of its inclusion in the Annex to the European Economic Area Agreement which came into force on January 1, 1994.

§ 5.6 Consumer Protection and Credit, the Precautionary Principle

The European Union has had a consumer protection and information policy since 1975. Its consumer protection role was recognized in 1993 amendments to the TFEU.[52] The member states, however, may enact more stringent protective measures provided they are compatible with the Treaty.[53] In addition to products liability (above), EU law covers health and safety product labeling and manufacturing. Foodstuffs, cosmetics, detergents, vehicles, textiles, toys, dangerous substances, medicines, chemicals (the REACH regulations), fertilizers, pesticides and animal feed are some of the areas now governed by Union consumer protection law. There is, for example, a directive which fixes the maximum level of pesticide residues on fruits and vegetables.[54]

The Commission operates an information exchange network on products that present grave and immediate danger to consumers. The source member state notifies the Commission of the hazard, and the Commission forwards this information to the other member states. Opinions of the European Food Safety Authority play a critical role in this regard.[55]

All products dangerous to humans or the environment are subject to the Union's *dangerous substances directives*.[56] This includes explosives, flammable, toxic and carcinogenic substances. No such products are to be allowed on the market until after a review of their "forseeable risks" and "unfavorable effects" by national authorities. Child-resistant packaging is ordinarily required as is labeling using a common "CE" black on orange-yellow symbol. Any

---

[52] *See* Article 169, TFEU. *But see* VTB-VAB NV v. Total Belgium NV, (2009) Eur.Comm.Rep. (Cases C–261/07 and C–299/07) (blanket Belgian law against "combined offers" invalid).

[53] *Id.*

[54] Council Directive 76/895 (amended by Directive 90/642).

[55] *See* Pfizer Animal Health v. Council, (2002) Eur.Comm.Rep. II–3305.

[56] Council Directive 67/548.

special risks associated with the product and safety advice must be spelled out on the label. Dangerous substances meeting the terms and conditions of this directive may be freely traded within the Union, each nation relying on the authorities of all other EU countries to implement the directive as to manufacturers within their borders.

An EU *product safety directive* has also been adopted. Council Directive 92/59 revised by Directive 2001/95 applies to all products not subject to more specific Union law on safety. Suppliers may place only safe products on the market. A safe product does not present any risk, or only risks considered acceptable and consistent with a high standard of protection. In assessing the acceptability of risk, the product's intended or reasonably foreseeable use must be evaluated. The supplier must give the user sufficient information to assess acceptable risks and to monitor the safety of the product. Suppliers will be deemed to meet the general safety requirement if they comply with Union standards or (in their absence) member state safety requirements. The directive requires member states to have the power to impose sanctions for violations, including the power to ban products from the market, but it does not require that consumers be given a damages remedy for unsafe products.

One consistent theme in EU consumer protection law is the *precautionary principle*. Health, safety and environmental risks are often regulated in advance of a thorough scientific analysis of their significance. A "beef hormones" ban, for example, was the subject of longstanding World Trade Organization dispute with the United States, whose beef exports to the EU dropped significantly. Although the U.S. "won" this dispute, the precautionary principle not being recognized in WTO law, the ban continued despite retaliatory U.S. tariff sanctions against EU exports of cheese, ham, sweaters and other products. Finally, in 2009, settlement of the beef hormones dispute was accomplished. The U.S. removed its retaliatory tariffs, and the EU allowed more non-hormone U.S. beef into its market. Hormone treated beef from anywhere remains excluded from the European Union.

In an increasingly globalized world economy, EU product and service regulations frequently prevail as other jurisdictions and multinational firms adopt them. Obedience to precautionary principles is spreading, from International Accounting Standards to personal data privacy (see below).

Consumer Contracts and Credit

Council Directive 93/13 covers *unfair terms in standardized consumer* contracts concluded after Dec. 31, 1994. Such terms do not bind consumers, and the member states are obliged to take effective measures to ensure their discard by suppliers and sellers. Consumer groups must be allowed to proceed before courts or authorities involved with determinations of unfairness in consumer contracts of general use. Standardized contract terms are considered "unfair" if they evidence bad faith and cause a significant imbalance in the parties' rights and obligations under the contract.[57] A non-exhaustive list of examples of unfair terms is annexed to the directive. These examples include liability limits, seller rights to unilaterally alter the contract without good cause and restraints upon consumer legal remedies. Member states remain free to provide for higher levels of consumer protection against unfair terms in standardized contracts.

The Unfair Commercial Practices (UCP) Directive 2005/29[58] bans a range of *aggressive or misleading* schemes, including bait and switch advertising, fake free offers, pyramid sales, "advertorials," and false curative health claims. It also broadly prohibits consumer harassment, coercion and undue influence. National legislation may *not* provide for stricter standards.[59]

The Council has adopted two important *consumer credit directives*. Directive 87/102 seeks to ensure that consumers receive precise information from creditors as to the true costs of credit. "Consumers" for these purposes do not include business customers. "Creditors," on the other hand, must be acting in a trade, business or profession. The directive applies to "credit agreements" involving loans or deferred payment, but not installment contracts. Leasing agreements, charge cards and other selected contracts are exempted. Directive 90/88 establishes an annual percentage rate of charge (APR) disclosure requirement. These directives are discussed in Section 4.12 on banking.

Directive 99/44 concerns the sale of consumer goods and associated guarantees. Basically, the seller must deliver goods conforming to the contract of sale. If nonconformity is discovered within two years, the consumer generally is entitled to free repair or replacement, a price adjustment or contract termination. Final sellers in turn have recourse against producers and intermediate sellers. Directive 98/27 mandates the availability of injunctive relief in connection with eleven consumer rights directives, including for example misleading advertising (see Section 5.7), medicinal products

---

[57] *See* Oceano Grupo Editorial SA v. Murciano Quintero, (2000) Eur.Comm.Rep. I–04941 (June 27, 2000) (encyclopedia sales, choice of distant court forum clause).

[58] 2005 OJ L149/2.

[59] VTB-VAB NV v. Total Belgium NV, (2009) Eur.Comm.Rep. (Case Nos. C–261/07, C–299/07).

advertising, unfair contract terms, time shares, distance sales, package travel, product guarantees and off premise sales.

Under the "rogue traders" regulation, national law enforcement authorities co-ordinate action against cross-border breaches of EU consumer protection law undertaken by email, the Internet, telemarketing or direct mail.[60]

Consumer Protection Legislation

The following is a sampling of major EU consumer protection laws (note that E-commerce and "distance selling" are covered in Sections 5.26–5.30):

- Directive 67/548 (classification, packaging and labeling of dangerous substances) as amended by Directives 88/379, 91/325, 91/326, 93/18, 93/21, 94/410
- Directive 79/112 (labeling, presentation and advertising of foodstuffs)
- Directives 79/530, 92/75 (labeling of energy consumption of household appliances)
- Directive 79/581 (selling price and price per unit of foodstuffs)
- Directive 80/232 (nominal quantities and nominal capacities for pre-packaged products)
- Directive 84/450 (misleading advertising)
- Directive 85/577 (off premise selling)[61]
- Directive 85/510 (use of asbestos)
- Directives 87/102 and 90/88 (consumer credit)
- Directive 87/357 (dangerous imitation products)
- Directive 87/404 (simple pressure vessels)
- Directive 88/314 (selling price and price per unit of non-food products)
- Directive 88/378 (toy safety)
- Directive 89/622 (labeling of tobacco products)
- Directive 90/239 (tar yield limits for cigarettes)
- Directive 90/314 (package holidays)

---

60 Regulation 2006/2004, (2004) O.J. L 364/1.

61 Faccini Dori v. RECREB SRL, (1994) Eur.Comm.Rep. I–3325 (implications of Italian failure to implement directive on time); *See* Re Di Pinto, (1991) Eur.Comm.Rep. I–495 (Case–361/89) (door-to-door solicitation of advertising contracts not covered).

- Directive 91/442 (child resistant fastenings)
- Directive 92/59 (product safety)
- Directive 93/13 (unfair standard contract terms)
- Directive 94/47 (time shares)
- Directive 97/7 (distance selling)
- Directive 98/27 (injunctive relief)
- Directive 99/44 (guarantees)
- Directive 2002/65 (distance selling of consumer financial services)
- Directive 2003/15 (cosmetics)

§ 5.7 Advertising

European Union law has touched upon advertising in a variety of ways. Cigarette advertising, for example, is banned in television broadcasts. Tobacco advertising is broadly banned.[62] The EU Broadcasting directive[63] regulates advertising aimed at children. Directives also exist on the advertising of foodstuffs,[64] medicinal products,[65] dangerous substances,[66] and consumer credit.[67] A general directive on misleading advertising was adopted in 1984.[68]

This directive indicates that advertising is misleading if it deceives or is likely to deceive consumers *and* is likely to affect their economic behavior or injure a competitor. Thus, the directive is intended to protect competitors as well as consumers. Advertising of gray market autos as new, subject to the warranty of the manufacturer, and less expensive than those sold by established dealers was not false or misleading.[69] Cross-border broadcasters are subject to home and host nation rules on misleading ads.[70]

---

[62] Council Directive 2003/33 replacing annulled Directive 98/43.

[63] *See* § 5.14 and Konsumentbudsmannen v. De Agostini (Svenska) Forlag, (1997) Eur.Comm.Rep. I–3843 (Swedish rules on children's ads unenforceable); Germany v. Parliament and Council (Tobacco Advertising I), (2000) Eur.Comm.Rep. I–8419; Germany v. European Parliament and Council (Tobacco Advertising II), (2006) Eur.Comm.Rep. I–11573.

[64] Council Directive 79/112.

[65] Council Directive 92/28.

[66] Council Directive 92/32.

[67] Council Directive 87/102.

[68] Council Directive 84/450.

[69] Procureur de la République v. X, (1992) Eur.Comm.Rep. I–131 (Case C–373/90).

[70] Konsumentbudsmannen v. De Agostini (Svenska) Forlag, (1997) Eur.Comm.Rep. I–3843.

Misleading advertising, including bait and switch, is banned under Directive 2005/29, discussed in Section 5.6.

Each member state is required to establish adequate means for monitoring and controlling misleading advertising. This may involve impartial administrative controls or legal proceedings. Self-regulatory controls by trade associations and the like are permissible but must not replace legal or administrative remedies. Such remedies must include cease and desist orders and the power to require corrective statements All advertisers can be required to provide evidence of the accuracy of any factual claims they make. Comparative advertising is included.[71] National legislation prohibiting conspicuous or eye-catching comparative ads violates the Union's free trade rules. In this decision, the ECJ nullified a German law as applied to advertising by a French cosmetics company.[72] In another decision, the ECJ affirmed the right of Google to continue selling ads linked to searches for brand names. . . in this case Louis Vuitton.[73] The decision effectively reverses the French Cour de Cassation.

§ 5.8 Securities

Article 55 TFEU creates a right of national treatment as regards participation in the capital of profit-making companies. In other words, discrimination based upon nationality cannot be practiced when it comes to corporate capital. In addition, several important EU directives have been adopted in the securities field. These concern admission of securities to stock exchange listings,[74] the issuance of a prospectus,[75] and regular information disclosures by publicly traded companies.[76] Some commentators have suggested that the net result of these directives will be a "Common Market Prospectus." Once approved by a member state, a prospectus conforming to EU rules can be used throughout the Community subject to minimal additional disclosure requirements.[77] In 2007, a shareholder's rights Directive 2007/36 was promulgated.

---

71 Council Directive 97/55 amending Directive 84/450. *See* Pippig Augenoptik GmbH v. Hartlauer Handelsgesellschaft mbH, (2003) Eur.Comm.Rep. I–03095 (Case 44/01) (reviewing lawful comparative advertising).

72 Schutzverband gegen Unwesen in der Wirtschaft v. Yves Rocher GmbH, (1993) Eur.Comm.Rep. 02361 (Case C–126/91).

73 Portakabin Ltd v. PrimaKabin BV (Case 558/08) (July 8, 2010).

74 Council Directives 79/279, 80/390, 87/345, 90/211, 03/34.

75 Council Directive 89/298, 03/34.

76 Council Directives 79/279, 82/121.

77 *See especially* Council Directives 80/390 (as amended May 30, 1994) and 2003/34.

Early Securities Law Directives

The 1989 Prospectus Directive[78] created prospectus requirements for nearly all transferable securities publicly offered within a member state. The directive exempted Euro-securities (equities and bonds) that are not the "subject of a generalized campaign of advertising or canvassing." The directive was inapplicable to offers of securities to a "restricted circle of persons." Government securities, securities offered in connection with a takeover bid or merger and certain debt securities were also exempt. The Prospective Directive contained a mutual recognition clause. When public offerings are made within short intervals in two or more member states, a prospectus prepared and approved in accordance with EU law must be recognized and accepted in all member states. An additional mutual recognition directive adopted in 1990 further integrated the listing and public offering processes.[79] In 2003, a New Prospectus Directive (No. 03/34, discussed below) was adopted, repealing the 1989 Prospectus Directive.

The 1979 Listing Conditions Directive[80] established minimum conditions for the admission of securities to a stock exchange listing in the EU. These conditions concerned the size of the issuer, its history and the distribution of its shares in the market. The directive created reporting obligations for issuers of listed securities. It provided that if shares of a non-EU company are not listed in the issuer's home country or principal market, they could not generally be listed in a Union country. However, if the national authorities are satisfied that the absence of a listing "is not due to the need to protect investors," an EU listing could follow. Non-EU issuers were required to meet the minimum conditions and obligations of the 1979 Listing Conditions Directive.

The 1980 Listing Particulars Directive[81] coordinated member state disclosure requirements. Member states had to ensure that securities listings in their territories were accompanied by the release of a disclosure document ("listing particulars"). This document was akin to an SEC registration statement and had to enable investors to make an "informed assessment" of the financial position and prospects of the issuer. This directive thus imposed a general obligation to disclose material facts in the listing application. The Listing Particulars Directive allowed a member state to create exemptions, such as an exemption for securities for which the issuer released an equivalent disclosure document during the preceding

[78] Council Directive 89/298.

[79] Council Directive 90/211.

[80] Council Directive 79/279.

[81] Council Directive 80/390.

year. The directive detailed debt and equity disclosure requirements. These particulars could not be published until they were approved by the national authorities. They could be published either by insertion in newspapers or as a brochure available to the public. The directive did *not* require disclosure documents to be delivered to investors when securities are purchased.

Directive 94/18 amended the Listing Particulars Directive giving further flexibility regarding secondary listings and transfers from second-tier markets. It provided that, where securities are admitted to listing in one member state and the issuer wishes to list them in another, that member state may grant an exemption from the obligation to produce new listing particulars. The directive also contained a further exemption allowing a waiver of the requirement to produce listing particulars where an issuer wants to transfer from a second-tier market to the official list in the same member state.

A 1987 Directive[82] applied when applications are made to list securities on two or more exchanges located in the European Union. The listing particulars in such cases follow home state rules and are approved by home state authorities. Other member states had to recognize these documents without requiring approval by their authorities and without requiring additional information. This 1987 directive allowed EU countries to restrict mutual recognition to listing particulars of issuers having registered offices in a member state. In 2003, the New Prospectus Directive 03/04 replaced the Listing Particulars Directive.

New Prospectus Directive

The New Prospectus Directive (No. 2003/34) covers all securities offered to the public or admitted to trading on a regulated market. The prospectus must provide all necessary information for investors to make informed assessments in an "easily analyzable and comprehensible form." Either a single or "subdivided" prospectus can be used. A subdivided prospectus consists of three documents: (1) a registration; (2) a securities note; and (3) a summary note. Once a subdivided prospectus is approved, the registration is valid for 12 months. Thus, only the security and summary notes need to be revised in subsequent offerings. The prospectus must be prepared according to International Accounting Standards.

Home country registration by issuers of securities results in sending notices of approval to host state authorities who are bound to honor them. Translation requirements are minimized. Exemptions cover government bonds, small issues and qualified sophisticated buyers. The prior "mutual reciprocity" approach is abandoned. That

---

82 Council Directive 87/345.

said, an EU-wide securities and exchange commission has not been created, and whether the New Prospectus Directive will gain marketplace adherents remains to be seen. It is supplemented by the Transparency Directive's minimum requirements for publicly traded securities regarding periodic financial reports, disclosure of major share holdings and dissemination of information.

Markets in Financial Instruments Directive

Commencing in 2007, a "Little Bang" in European securities trading took place. The Markets in Financial Instruments Directive (MiFID) became effective. Under it, gradually, stock trading within the EU should become more competitive and less costly. Utilizing the "single passport" home country licensing approach, financial companies can now trade freely across borders within a minimum of regulatory red tape. MiFID also attempts to protect securities' buyers, classifying them as professional, eligible or retail, with appropriate standards for each category. National stock exchange monopolies have ended, and electronic exchanges grew. MiFID 2 in 2018 imposed deeper disclosure duties and regulatory controls on EU securities markets.

Mutual, Pension and Alternative Investment (Hedge, Private Equity and Real Estate) Funds

Council Directive 85/611 on open-end investment companies ("unit trusts" or mutual funds) was implemented in 1985. It allows marketing in other member states based upon home country authorization meeting the minimum EU standards of the directive. There is no "reciprocity rule" in the Unit Trust Directive that might hinder North American mutual fund companies wishing to operate in Europe. The Unit Trust Directive controls the structure, obligations, investment policies and disclosure obligations of unit trusts and investment companies. With certain exceptions, such entities may only invest in transferable securities listed on an EU stock exchange, traded on a regulated market in a member state, or traded on an approved exchange or regulated market in a nonmember state. Unit trusts and investment companies must repurchase or redeem units from holders upon request. Directive 2001/107 regulates the prudential management and access to markets of UCITs.

Council Directive 2003/41 concerns pension funds. High levels of protection for members and beneficiaries are required. Cross-border administration of pension schemes is facilitated using mutual recognition principles along with customized investment strategies following the "prudent person principle." Whether to use pay-as-you-go or funded pension schemes is left to member state discretion.

In 2010, the EU adopted an Alternative Investment Fund Managers (AIFM) Directive. It focuses on supervision of hedge, private equity, real estate and other institutional funds. Disclosure duties, leverage regulations, investor protections, pay rules, depository requirements and buy-outs are governed by the AIFM. This directive is a spin-off from the global financial crisis that commenced in 2008. It took effect in 2013.

Market Abuses and Insider Trading

In 1988, the Council adopted an "anti-raider" directive requiring disclosure of the acquisition or disposal of 10 percent or more of a publicly listed company.[83] Securities "market abuses," including stock buy-back programs, are covered in Directive 2003/6. Market manipulations and public disclosure of inside information, along with investment recommendations and disclosure of conflicts of interest, also fall within its scope.

Until 1988, only three of the member states had laws regulating insider trading. Nevertheless, a directive on insider trading was finalized in 1989,[84] and now contained in Directive 2003/6. This directive prohibits trading based on inside information "with full knowledge of the facts" by primary and secondary insiders. Specifically, this prohibition applies to any person who possesses inside information from membership in the structure of the issuer, share ownership, or access to information through employment, professional or other duties. Persons who possess inside information, the source of which "could not be other than" one of the previously enumerated persons, are also covered. Disclosure of inside information to third parties outside the normal course of employment or professional duties, and procurement of securities by others based on such information is prohibited. Inside information is defined as nonpublic information "of a precise nature" which if made public would be "likely to have a significant effect on the price" of securities.

Many perceive that EU insider trading law closely parallels U.S. securities law principles. However, unlike U.S. law, the European Union directive only applies to securities traded on markets regulated by "public bodies" that operate regularly and are accessible directly or indirectly to the public. The directive specifically permits member states to exclude transactions without a professional intermediary undertaken outside a regulated market. One concern with the directive is that it allows member states to choose which types of penalties apply to insider trading violations. These directives were extended with certain adaptations to EFTA countries (except

83 Council Directive 88/627.

84 Council Directive 89/592, replaced by Directive 2003/16.

Switzerland and Liechtenstein) by virtue of their inclusion in the Annex to the European Economic Area Agreement which came into force on January 1, 1994.

In September of 1991, the United States Securities and Exchange Commission (SEC) and the Commission signed a joint communiqué intended to improve bilateral and multilateral cooperation in the securities law field. Information exchange, cooperative approaches to financial integrity of issuers and securities market oversight are covered by this communiqué.

§ 5.9 Company Law and Corporate Governance

Article 49 TFEU obliges member states to enter negotiations with each other about equal protection of citizens, abolition of double taxation, mutual recognition of firms and companies, the possibility of international mergers, and simplification of enforcement of judgments. Article 49 was the backdrop against which member states signed in 1968 a Convention on Mutual Recognition of Companies and Other Bodies Corporate. This Convention sought to ensure that Treaty benefits extend to such legal personae. Unfortunately, it never achieved full ratification by the member states. Article 49 on the right of establishment entitles companies based in one member state to set up agencies, branches or subsidiaries in other member states, even when this avoids paid-in capital requirements.[85] Thousands of U.K. companies have been set up to avoid Continental paid-in capital requirements.

In the absence of an EU convention on legal personalities, nothing in the right of establishment permits a company to freely transfer its place of incorporation (seat) and administrative center to another member state without home state permission where that is required. In this case, the British Daily Mail newspaper sought to change to Dutch citizenship to take advantage of lower taxes.[86] Questions relating to the company's status (liability of limited partners and managing directors, capacity to sue, capital requirements etc.) must be governed by the law of incorporation of the company.[87] The ECJ has also generally upheld on right of establishment grounds corporate or branch tax advantages obtained from states of incorporation.[88]

---

[85] Centros v. Erhvervs-OG Selskabsstyrelsen, (1999) Eur.Comm.Rep. II–1459; Kamer van Koophandel v. Inspire Art, (2003) Eur.Comm.Rep. I–10155. Accord, CARTESIO, Case C–210/06 (ECJ, Dec. 16, 2008).

[86] Re Daily Mail, (1988) Eur.Comm.Rep. 5483.

[87] *E.g.*, Überseering, (2003) Eur.Comm.Rep. I–9919 (capacity to sue).

[88] *Centros*, supra; Marks & Spencer v. Halsey, (2005) Eur.Comm.Rep. I–10837; Cadbury Schweppes v. Inland Revenue, (2006) Eur.Comm.Rep. I–7995.

Company Law Directives

The Council has adopted several non-controversial coordination directives under Article 44 advancing Union company law. These in theory seek to avoid the race to the bottom problems associated with Delaware corporate law in the United States. The first directive sets out requirements for disclosure, validity and nullity of share capital companies. The ECJ has ruled that the listing of grounds for nullifying the formation of a company found in the First Company Law Directive exhausts all such possibilities. Grounds for nullification based upon the Spanish Civil Code requirement of "causa" could not be utilized since that Code must be construed in conformity with that Directive.[89]

The Second deals with the classification, subscription and maintenance of capital of public and large companies. Increases in share capital must be approved by company shareholders with preemptive rights. Companies are generally forbidden from acquiring their own shares. Governmental acts authorizing increases in company capital to ensure survival which prejudice the preemptive rights of shareholders are impermissible.[90] The Second Company Law Directive was amended in late 1992 to close a loophole by prohibiting parent companies from buying through subsidiaries more than 10 percent of their own shares when faced with hostile takeovers.[91]

The Third Company Law Directive concerns the internal merger of public companies. Modern procedures for mergers with related and unrelated companies are established. Asset and liability acquisitions and new company formations are allowed. Shareholder rights are specified. The sixth directive governs sales of assets of public companies, including certain shareholder, creditor and workers' rights. The fourth standardizes the treatment of annual accounts (*e.g.*, in their presentation, content, valuation and publication). It requires public presentation of a "true and fair view" of company assets, liabilities, finances, profits and losses. Small and medium-sized firms can publish abridged accounts. All companies must present comparable figures for the preceding year. The valuation of assets and liabilities must be prudent, consistent and reflect the company as a going concern.

---

89 Marleasing SA v. La Comercial Internacional de Alimentación SA, (1990) 1 Eur.Comm.Rep. 4135. Regarding the first directive, *see also* Daihatsu Handler v. Daihatsu Deutschland, (1997) Eur.Comm.Rep. II–6843; Commission v. Germany, (1998) Eur.Comm.Rep. II–5149.

90 Kerafina-Keramische und Finanz Holding AG & Anor v. Hellenic Republic, (1992) Eur.Comm.Rep. I–5699 (Cases C–234/91, C–135/91).

91 *See* Council Directive 92/101.

The Fourth Directive even details the notes that must accompany annual accounts. In addition, shareholders must be given a report by management annually on the development of the business, future plans, research activities and company purchase of their own shares. There is a permissive provision relating to inflation or current cost accounting. There is some doubt about the degree of relation to similar requirements of the United Kingdom accounting bodies or "generally accepted accounting practices" in the United States. Directive 2001/65 spells out "fair value" accounting rules, notably for derivatives. Regulation 1606/2002 mandated the use of International Accounting Standards by publicly traded companies. In 2006, new rules on the auditing of company accounts were adopted, as well substantial amendments to EU accounting directives.[92]

The Sixth Company Law Directive complements the third directive and addresses the division or "scission" of public limited companies, where they wind up without liquidation. The Seventh concerns requirements for consolidated accounts of groups of companies. Consolidated accounts must follow the rules of the fourth directive as supplemented by the seventh. Consolidated accounts are required if an EU firm has legal or *de facto* control over other companies through majority shareholdings, appointment or removal power over management in a subsidiary, the right to exercise dominant influence, or the possibility of shareholder agreements conveying majority voting rights. Consolidated accounts must treat the group as a single enterprise regarding transactions among the companies. The Eighth Company Law Directive provides certain minimum standards and qualifications for auditors of company accounts. The Ninth Directive facilitates electronic shareholder voting, proxy voting and shareholder questioning rights.

There are other less controversial company law directives. The Tenth Directive 2005/56 deals with cross-border company mergers. The Eleventh (adopted in 1989) involves disclosure by branches operating in other EU states, and the Twelfth (also adopted in 1989) affects single member private limited liability companies.

Hostile takeovers, a sensitive area, are the subject of the Thirteenth Directive 2004/25. This directive to require equal treatment of shareholders and specify permissible defensive measures was denied in 2001 by a tie vote in Parliament.

Works Councils

Several controversial proposals for company law directives are in varying stages of evolution. These include a fifth directive on company structure and administration which has been long delayed

---

92 Directive 2006/46, (2006) O.J. L224/1; Directive 2006/43, (2006) O.J. L157/87.

due to differing views about the functions of single and two-tier boards of directors and officers, and worker representation at these levels. Another controversial topic (the "Vredeling proposal") would have required substantial information sharing between companies and their employees.

The 1994 "works council" Directive 94/45 requires councils in companies with more than 1000 employees and operating with 150 employees in at least two member states. Workers must be given information on and an opportunity to respond to a broad range of topics including the firm's economic and financial situation, employment, work methods and mergers and layoffs. But the information can be withheld when disclosure might "seriously harm" the functioning of the company or be "prejudicial" to it. Thousands of works councils now operate with little controversy. Directive 94/45 applies to parent companies located outside the EU.[93] It was revised and codified in Directive 2009/38.

Status of Company Law Directives

The following directory gives the status of European Union company law directives:

- First Council Directive (Adopted) 68/151
- Second Council Directive (Adopted) 77/91
- Third Council Directive (Adopted) 78/855
- Fourth Council Directive (Adopted) 78/660
- Fifth Council Directive (Proposed) (see Works Council Directive 94/45)
- Sixth Council Directive (Adopted) 82/89
- Seventh Council Directive (Adopted) 83/349
- Eighth Council Directive (Adopted) 84/253
- Ninth Council Directive (Proposed)
- Tenth Council Directive (Proposed)
- Eleventh Council Directive (Adopted) 89/666
- Twelfth Council Directive (Adopted) 89/667
- Thirteenth Council Directive (Adopted) 2004/25

---

93 Gesamtbetriebsrat der Kühne + Nagel AG + Co. KG v. Kühne + Nagel AG + Co. KG, (2004) Eur.Comm.Rep. I–787 (Case 440/00).

§ 5.10 European Companies and Partnerships

Partnerships

Innovative company law proposals include those for a European Company Statute (SE) and a European Economic Interest Grouping (EEIG). The former is intended to create a regional corporate entity, overcoming the transnational problems associated with existing methods of incorporation within member states. The EEIG, adopted by Council Regulation in 1985, is a vehicle with legal capacity formed in the manner of an international partnership of member state companies. It draws its inspiration from French "*groupement d'intérêt économique*". The EEIG is prohibited from offering proprietary interests to the public and is a nonprofit enterprise. Limited liability is not obtained. The EEIG is intended for small or medium sized research and development or marketing ventures. Utilization of EEIG has been relatively low, in part because of perceptions of uncertainty about their tax status. The EEIG should be "tax transparent," *i.e.,* the EEIG does not pay taxes. All its profits and losses pass directly to its members.

European Company (SE)

An amended proposal for a European Company was submitted by the Commission to the Council in August 1989. Nineteen years had passed since the submission of the first proposal in 1970, and 14 years since the last amended proposal in 1975. In that period, considerable harmonization had been accomplished by way of directives. Finally, late in 2001, a European Company Statute was finalized, taking effect in 2004. Forming a European Company ("Societas Europeae" or SE) is optional.

An SE operates on a European-wide basis governed by EU law. A regulation establishes its company law rules, while a directive covers worker involvement in SE. Under the Statute, an SE registered in one member state can freely move its registered office to another. SEs may be privately or publicly traded companies. SE, at least in theory, will remove the need for costly networks of subsidiaries throughout the European Union. Large legal and administrative cost savings are expected to be realized. SE must be registered in the member state where it has its administrative head office, and the Statute does not significantly alter applicable taxation.

Regarding worker participation, the issue that held up the SE proposal for over 30 years, the first duty is to try to negotiate an agreement on employee involvement. Failing that, Standard Principles attached to the directive require regular reports, consultation and information exchange between management and worker representatives. Such reports must detail business plans, production and sales, management changes, mergers, divestments, potential closures and layoffs, and the implications of all this for workers. In the case of a European Company created by merger, the Standard Principles apply when at least 25 percent of the employees have the right to participate before the merger. However, member states need *not* implement the directive on participation for SEs created by mergers, but if so, the SE can be registered only if an agreement with the employees is reached, or when no employees were covered by participation rules before the SE was created.

§ 5.11 Environmental Policy

For many years environmental law was a stepchild of the European Union. The Treaty of Rome of 1957 (now TFEU) did not expressly authorize common environmental policies. Clearly, however, differing national standards on the environment can have a substantial impact on the functioning of the Common Market. As environmental politics (remember the Green Party) and consciousness came of age in Western Europe, initial environmental efforts rested on Article 115 (harmonization) and Article 352, the Treaty's "necessary and proper" powers clause. The first Environmental Action Program commenced in 1973. The Union is now embarked on its seventh such program. Hundreds of environmental legislative acts have been adopted, including a 2003 decision to use criminal law sanctions in the environmental arena.[94] The Commission has noted at length, however, that there are serious problems with national implementation (or the lack thereof) of regional environmental law.

NAFTA/USMCA, with few exceptions, leaves environmental policy decisions to its member states.[95] In Europe, environmental law is more than cosmetic.

Policy Principles, Polluter Pays

The Single European Act of 1987 added Articles 191–193 TFEU. These articles firmly establish environmental policy as an important domain of the Union Indeed, Article 191(2) makes environmental protection requirements a mandatory component of *all* European Union policies. One of the overriding legal principles of EU

---

94 Council Framework Decision 2003/80 JHA, (2003) O.J. L29/55. The ECJ has affirmed EU law's application to environmental crimes: Commission v. Council, (2005) Eur.Comm.Rep. I–7879 (Case 176/03).

95 *See* R. Folsom and W.D. Folsom, *The USMCA, NAFTA Re-Negotiated and Its Business Impacts.*

environmental policy is that the polluter shall pay.[96] This may mean that national governments are limited in their ability to grant subsidies for environmental protection purposes.[97]

Another key principle is that member states may adopt more demanding environmental requirements, provided they are compatible with the Treaty.[98] Still another important touchstone is that environmental policy must be based on the "precautionary principle."[99]

The procedures for adoption of European Union environmental legislation and the conclusion of international environmental agreements are unusually detailed. Article 191(3) requires the Union to consider available scientific and technical data, the environmental conditions in the regions of the EU, the potential benefits and costs of regional action or inaction, the economic and social development of the EU, and balanced development of its regions when preparing environmental policy.

There are three basic thrusts to the Union's environmental policy. The first is the establishment of minimum quality standards (*e.g.*, drinking water). The second involves specific emission and waste controls (*e.g.*, the discharge of pollutants into surface and ground water). On emission controls, the Union has proceeded slowly, industry by industry, after first identifying priority problems. The first water emissions directives involve mercury and cadmium discharges. EU rules govern the biodegradability of detergents and the sulphur content of liquid fuels.[100] Among the first air pollution directives, auto emissions and lead content in gasoline have had a high priority. Since 1989, Union law requires all member states to introduce lead-free gasoline into their markets and leaded gas is reduced to a minimum content as are sulfur-free fuels.[101] Cap and trade rules for power, cement and steel industry greenhouse gases commenced in 2005, with airlines expected to follow. European emissions permits are traded in markets that suffered a major cyber-theft in 2011.

The third basic thrust of EU environmental policy is the "polluter pays" principle. Many EU directives incorporate this principle, which has proved easier to apply to private versus public

---

96 Article 191(2), TFEU. *See* Directive 2004/35.

97 *See* Commission Guidelines on State Aids for Environmental Protection, O.J. C 37/3 (Feb. 3, 2001).

98 *Id.* Article 193, TFEU. *See* Commission v. Denmark, (1988) Eur.Comm.Rep. 4607 (Danish bottle bill generally upheld).

99 *Id.* Article 191(2), TFEU.

100 Commission v. Italy, (1980) Eur.Comm.Rep. 1099 and 1115.

101 Directive 2003/17.

entities. Effective in 2007, Directive 2004/35 broadly reinforces the polluter pays principle regarding damage to water resources, national habitats, animals, land and humans.[102]

Waste Controls

Waste control directives have targeted oil, PCB and PCT discharges as priorities. Waste management issues have frequently come before the Court of Justice. For example, an Italian municipal ban on the sale and use of plastic carrying bags was upheld as consistent with Directive 75/442 on waste materials.[103] French law implementing the waste oil directive could not deny the right of oil companies to export wastes to an approved recycling center in another member state.[104] Similarly, existing Community directives meant that Belgium could not ban the disposal of hazardous waste.[105] But it could prohibit, in the name of environmental protection, importation of general waste products from neighboring countries.[106]

A strict liability directive for damages caused by commercial waste was proposed as part of the single market campaign. The producer (or transporter if negligent) would be strictly liable to individuals and public authorities for personal and property damages. If the producer of the waste cannot be found, holders or disposers will be strictly liable. When compared with the liability of companies under U.S. "superfund" legislation, however, the EU proposal may impose noticeably lower costs on industry. It is now thought unlikely that it will ever be adopted in the form of the original draft. This is the result primarily of EU cost-benefit limitations on cleanup liability and the absence of any duty to pay governments for damages to natural resources. Commentators have noted that a competitive handicap may follow for United States companies.

Labels, Audits, Impacts and Information

Questions arose as to under litigation is whether innovative German packaging laws comport with EU environmental and trade policy. These laws require acceptance for recycling of transport packaging, secondary packaging (*e.g.*, boxes), and all sales packaging including cans, plastic containers, foil, etc. The duty to take back

---

102 (2004) O.J. L143/56.

103 Enichem Base v. Commune di Cinisello Balsamo, (1989) Eur.Comm.Rep. 2491.

104 Syndicat National des Fabricants Raffineurs d'Huile de Graissage v. Groupement d'Intérêt Economique Inter-Huiles, (1983) Eur.Comm.Rep. 555. *See* also Procureur de la Republique v. Association de Defense des Bruleurs d'Huiles Usagees (ADBHU), (1995) Eur.Comm.Rep. 531 (internal French waste oil collection system upheld).

105 Commission v. Belgium, (1992) Eur.Comm.Rep. I–4431 (Case C–2/90).

106 *Id.*

sales packaging will not apply to manufacturers, distributors and retailers who participate in the "green dot" program. This program involves regular collection of sales packaging at consumers' homes or collection centers. Green dots may appear on products when a company's system meets prescribed quotas for collection and recycling.

By 1995, 80 percent of all packaging materials had to be collected and no less than 80 percent of those materials recycled or reused. Germany's early packaging laws served to stimulate a major environmental directive (No. 94/62 amended No. 2004/12). It requires recovery of at least 60 percent of all packaging by weight of which a minimum of 55 percent must be recycled.[107] Member states, like Germany, may exceed these targets assuming distortions of the regional market are avoided. The directive also requires compliance with certain packaging standards. Directive 2000/53 follows the same path on recycling end-of-life vehicles.

An *eco-labeling* system to enable consumers to identify environmentally less harmful products has been approved.[108] Using a "cradle to grave" approach, products will be evaluated for their impact on the environment throughout their lifespan. Products less damaging to the environment will receive the eco-label logo, a flower with the stars as petals enclosing the EU's Greek-style "E" symbol. Consumer trade, industry and environmental organizations are consulted on the stringency of the criteria products must meet for the award. Final decisions are taken by a regulatory committee of the member states based on Commission proposals. All products will be eligible for the labeling system except beverages, foodstuffs, pharmaceuticals and dangerous substances. National eco-labeling plans coexist with the EU system. Participation in the system will be voluntary but shifts in consumer preferences to environmentally friendly products may spur use of the logo for competitive reasons.

The Commission created an *eco-auditing* system for much of European industry in 1991. This voluntary system was adopted by the Council of Ministers in 1993 as part of a broader "eco-management" scheme.[109] Companies may participate on a site-by-site basis by adopting a company environmental policy, conducting an environmental review, introducing an environmental management system, executing an environmental audit, setting environmental performance objectives and preparing an environmental statement after the audit. All of these requirements

---

[107] *See* Commission v. Luxembourg, (2003) Eur.Comm.Rep. I–1553 (recovery includes incineration at waste plants with energy recovery).

[108] Council Regulation 880/92, revised Regulation 1980/2000.

[109] Council Regulation 1836/93.

must be verified by an independent, accredited environmental "verifier." Monitoring and reporting on subsequent environmental conditions are regularly required. The "benefits" of participation, apart from public opinion, include registration and publication of the participants by national and EU governments and by the company (but the fact of participation may not be used in advertising or on product packaging). The Commission originally sought a mandatory eco-auditing system. It is conceivable that experience with this voluntary scheme may lead ultimately to that result.

A 1985 Council Directive[110] creates an *environmental impact assessment* requirement for environmentally significant development projects. The Directive aims to "identify, describe and assess in an appropriate manner. . . the direct and indirect effects" of such projects on humans, fauna, flora, soil, water, air, climate, landscape, material assets and cultural heritage. The directive requires developers to provide national authorities with detailed information relating to the project. Such information includes: (1) a description of the project, including information on its site, design, processes and wastes; (2) an outline of the "main alternatives" considered; (3) a description of "the measures envisaged to prevent, reduce and where possible offset any significant adverse effects on the environment"; and (4) a "non-technical" summary. The EU Environmental Impact Directive does not create substantive environmental protection standards. Rather, it establishes development permission procedures to promote public review at the national level of environmental consequences.[111]

Similarly, the Directive on the Freedom of Access of Information on the Environment[112] obliges the member states to create procedures for citizens to obtain *environmental information*. Under this directive, national authorities must allow access to "any available information. . . on the state of water, air, soil, fauna, flora and natural sites and on activities. . . or measures adversely affecting, or likely so to affect these, and on activities or measures designed to protect these." However, national authorities may refuse to provide information where the request may affect foreign relations, national security, public security, commercial and industrial confidentiality, and the information, if disclosed, could increase the likelihood of environmental damage.

---

110 Council Directive 85/337. *See also* Council Directive 2001/42 (impact assessment of plans and programs).

111 *See* World Wildlife Fund v. Autonome Provinz Bozen, (1999) Eur.Comm.Rep. I–5613.

112 Council Directive 90/313 replaced by Directive 2003/4.

International Environmental Agreements

Cooperation within international organizations on the environment is shared between the Union and its member states "within their respective spheres of competence."[113] EU adoption of international environmental accords is subject to the same procedures regularly used for trade treaties.[114] One important indicator of just how sensitive the environmental field is within the Union is provided by Article 192. Under the SEA that article required a unanimous Council vote before any legislative or international action on the environment could be undertaken, specifically reserving to the Council the decision as to when qualified majority voting could be used. Most other authority added in 1987 by the Single European Act prescribed qualified majority voting.[115]

This divergence led to litigation over the proper legal basis for EU environmental legislation. The Court of Justice upheld use of Article 114 (internal market measures) with its qualified majority voting and Parliamentary cooperation rules.[116] The Maastricht European Union Treaty altered the SEA to provide regular Parliamentary cooperation on environmental legislation and general use of qualified majority voting by Council in this field.

Europe is rapidly making up for lost time and forging ahead in some areas of environmental protection. For example, regarding fluorocarbons and the ozone layer, the Commission has started using "voluntary agreements" with industry. The Commission reached such an agreement with the Federation of European Aerosol Manufacturers in 1989 committing the industry to a 90 percent reduction in the use of CFCs by 1991. This agreement was confirmed in Commission Recommendation 89/349, an act without legal force. Similar results have been achieved on the use of styrofoam in the refrigeration industry. The Commission has also proposed taxing sources of CFCs, carbon dioxide and aircraft noise. In 2008, the EU agreed to reduce carbon emissions 20% by 2020. EU member states are currently divided on the merits of "fracking" for oil and gas, an area of law not yet subject to regional rules.

The European Parliament has been a supporter of stronger environmental policies, backing up its commitment with new budgetary allocations and by promoting the creation of a European Environmental Agency. Its initial task will be to function as an

---

[113] Article 191(5), TFEU.

[114] *See* Chapter 6.

[115] *Compare* Articles 114 and 154, TFEU.

[116] Commission v. Council, (1991) Eur.Comm.Rep. I–2867 (Case C–300/89) (Titanium Dioxide). *But see* Commission v. Council, (1993) Eur.Comm.Rep. I–939 (Case C–155/91) (waste management directive properly adopted under Article 130S).

information clearinghouse. A general directive on freedom of access to information on the environment has been passed.[117] The EU has also concluded a large number of international environmental agreements, including the Basel Convention on Transboundary Movements of Hazardous Wastes, the Bonn Agreement on the Prevention of Pollution of the North Sea, the Rotterdam Convention on Hazardous Chemicals, and the Washington Convention [against] International Trade in Endangered Species of Wild Flora and Fauna.

The Council adopted a Resolution in 1993 tightening supervision and control of shipments of waste into and from the Union. This Resolution transposes the Basel Convention into EU law. One particularly innovative environmental agreement to which the Union is a party is the Barcelona Convention on the Mediterranean Sea. This Convention obligates the signatories to select from a menu of options on improvement and protection of the Mediterranean. The EU has implemented the Arhus Convention on public participation in environmental decision-making.[118]

Environmental Legislation

The following is a sampling of major European Union environmental laws:

1. **Water Pollution**

- Directive 73/404 (detergents) (replaced by Regulation 648/2004)
- Directive 75/440 (surface drinking water)
- Directive 76/160 (bathing water)
- Directive 76/464 (discharge of dangerous substances into the aquatic environment)
- Directive 78/659 (fish water)
- Directive 79/869 (measuring methods)
- Directive 79/923 (shellfish water)
- Directive 80/68 (groundwater)
- Directive 80/778 (water quality for consumption)[119]
- Directives 82/176, 84/156 (mercury discharges)
- Directive 83/513 (cadmium discharges)

---

117 Council Directive 90/313.

118 Council Directive 2003/35.

119 *See* Commission v. Germany, (1992) Eur.Comm.Rep. I–05973 (Case C–237/90) and Commission v. United Kingdom, (1992) Eur.Comm.Rep. I–06103 (Case C–337/89) for findings that Germany and U.K. failed to adequately implement Directive 80/778.

- Directive 84/491 (hexachlorocyclohexane)
- Directive 91/271 (municipal wastewater treatment)
- Directive 91/676 (agricultural nitrates)
- Directive 98/8 (biocides)
- Directive 98/83 (drinking water)

2. Air Pollution

- Directives 70/220, 88/76, 88/436, 89/458, 91/441, 93/59 (motor vehicles)
- Directive 75/516 (sulfur content in liquid fuels)
- Directives 78/1015, 89/235 (motorcycle exhaust)
- Directives 80/779, 89/427 (sulfur dioxide and particles)
- Directive 82/884 (lead in the air)
- Directive 84/360 (air pollution of industrial plants)
- Directives 84/429, 89/369 (municipal waste incineration plants)
- Directive 85/203 (nitrogen dioxide)
- Directives 85/210, 87/416 (lead content of petrol)
- Directive 87/217 (asbestos)
- Directives 88/77, 91/542 (diesel emissions)
- Directive 88/436 (diesel auto engines)
- Directives 88/609, 2001/80 (large combustion plants)
- Directive 89/369 (municipal incinerators)
- Directive 89/629 (noise emissions from civil aircraft)
- Regulation 3322/88 (CFCs)
- Regulation 594/91 (ozone depleting substances)
- Directive 92/72 (ozone air pollution)
- Directive 93/76 (carbon dioxide emissions)
- Directive 93/389 (monitor greenhouse gases)
- Directive 96/62 (air quality assessment)
- Directive 1999/30 (air pollutants)
- Regulation 2037/2000 (ozone depletion)
- Directive 2000/69 (benzene and carbon monoxide)
- Directive 2001/80 (combustion plants)

- Directive 2001/81 (air pollutants)
- Directive 2003/87 (omissions trading)

3. **Waste Pollution**

- Directive 75/439 (waste oils)
- Directives 75/442, 91/156 (framework for waste management)
- Directives 76/403, 96/59 (PCBs and PCTs)
- Directives 78/176, 82/883 (titanium dioxide)
- Directives 78/319, 91/689 (toxic wastes)
- Directive 84/631 (transborder shipment of hazardous waste)
- Directive 85/339 (beverage containers)
- Directive 86/278 (sewage sludge)
- Directives 90/245, 90/667 (veterinary waste)
- Directive 91/157 (batteries)
- Directive 91/271 (urban waste-water treatment)
- Directive 91/689 (hazardous waste)
- Regulation 259/93 (waste shipments)
- Directive 96/59 (PCBs and PCTs)
- Directive 1999/31 (landfills)
- Directive 2000/53 (end-of-life vehicles)
- Directive 2002/95 (hazardous electrical/electronics)
- Directive 2002/96 (waste electrical/electronic equipment)
- Directive 2003/11 (dangerous substances)
- Regulation 2003/2003 (fertilizers)
- Regulation 2004/12 (packaging waste)

4. **Noise Pollution**

- Directive 70/157 (motor vehicles)
- Directives 78/1015, 89/235 (motorcycles)
- Directive 80/51 (aircraft)
- Directives 84/538, 87/252, 88/180 (lawn mowers)
- Directive 86/594 (household appliances)

- Directives 86/662, 89/514 (hydraulic diggers)
- Directive 2000/14 (outdoor equipment)
- Directive 2002/49 (outdoor noise)
- Directive 2003/10 (noise at work)

5. **Conservation**

- Directive 92/43 (natural habitats, wild fauna and flora)
- Directive 2001/77 (renewable energy)

§ 5.12 Regional Policy

The TFEU is premised upon the opening of national markets to competitive trade. The Treaty, especially as amended by the Single European Act in 1987, recognizes that some areas of the Union will not succeed under these conditions. These "less developed" parts of the EU benefit from the Regional Policy. The basic provisions on Regional Policy are in Articles 174–178 under the title "economic and social cohesion."

The Regional Policy operates in conjunction with other programs, notably in agriculture, the Social Fund and coal and steel, to facilitate the growth and development of its poorer parts. The Mezzogiorno in Southern Italy was an early target for regional aid which now extends to most of Portugal, Greece and Ireland, as well as parts of the remaining member states. Some aid comes in the form of Union authorization for national subsidies. Other aid comes directly from the nonprofit European Investment Bank (EIB). The EIB is funded by the Union and the capital market. It has financed many regional development projects.

Article 174 commits the Union to the goal of reducing the disparities between its regions and the "backwardness" of its least-favored regions. A region is least favored if its per capita GDP is less than 50 percent of the EU average. A major step toward this goal accomplished by the Single European Act was formal recognition of the European Regional Development Fund. This fund has operated since 1975 in addition to, and coordinated with, those that function under the Union's Common Agricultural Policy and its Social Policy.[120]

The Regional Development Fund targets structural adjustment and conversion of declining industrial regions with aid grants. Its monies have gone a long way toward convincing the poorer regions of the Union that the campaign for a fully integrated market will bring some benefit to them. Regional development has often become the

---

120 *See* Regulation 2052/88.

grease that ensures a unanimous vote whenever needed to move the Common Market closer to a full reality.

Expanded economic aid to the least developed members of the Union was accomplished under the "cohesion funds" of the Maastricht Treaty on European Union and the European Economic Area agreement with the EFTA states (less Switzerland). Extensive and difficult negotiations over retention of such funds preceded the 2004 expansion in membership of the European Union which took in numerous states less developed than even the poorest EU member. Countries like Poland, Latvia and Slovakia (for example) receive substantial regional development funds, at the expense of Spain, Greece and Ireland (for example).

§ 5.13 Energy

Despite the specificity of the EURATOM and ECSC treaties, and the oil shocks of the 1970s, it is hard to say that the European Union has developed a viable all-encompassing energy policy. One reason is that Europe is energy poor. Those EU states with oil and gas (Britain and Holland especially) are not keen to be obliged to share these resources in a crisis with their fellow members. Neither would, one suspects, Norway. Common ground has been reached on minimum 90-day crude oil reserves,[121] funding for alternative fuels and energy efficiency, and defense of the massive Siberian natural gas pipeline project from early Reagan administration ("evil empire") attacks. The exclusive French government trading monopoly over petroleum products was finally eliminated in accordance with Article 43 TFEU.[122] And cheap energy subsidies through state enterprises to industry have frequently been condemned by the Commission and Court of Justice.[123] Directives intended to promote greater electricity and gas price competition have also been adopted.[124]

The Council has adopted Resolutions on Energy Objectives. The primary objective is to limit oil dependency to about 40 percent of the Union's total energy needs (down from 60 percent in 1973), and 15 percent of its electricity requirements. In practice, this has mostly meant more subsidies for coal and nuclear power production. However, Directives 2001/77 and 2009/28 mandate increased utilization of renewable energy sources, Directive 2003/96 harmonizes taxation of energy products, and Directive 2004/8 promotes co-generation of energy. In 1990, the Union initiated a European Energy Charter. This charter is open to all European

[121] Council Directive 72/425.

[122] Cullet v. Centre Leclerc Toulouse, (1985) Eur.Comm.Rep. 305.

[123] *See* Commission v. Netherlands, (1988) Eur.Comm.Rep. 281.

[124] *See* Council Directives 90/377, 90/547, 91/296.

nations. Its goals are security of energy supplies, energy efficiency, and safety and environmental protection. The 1993 Treaty on European Union added several provisions intended to foster the growth of trans-European networks, including energy.[125] Special emphasis is placed on inter-operability and access issues.[126]

§ 5.14 Broadcasting

The launch of the European satellite EUTELSAT in 1983 made broadcasting across borders possible. July 1994 saw the Russian Federation enlist as a full member of the EUTELSAT organization and it is likely that other Eastern Bloc nations will also join in the future. In March 1989 the Council of Europe (not an EU institution) agreed on a Transborder Television Convention. The Council's twenty-two members will permit transmission of programs by cable or satellite throughout their countries. A common set of minimum broadcasting rules govern free expression, rights of response, sponsorship, pornography, violence and incitement to racial hatred. Advertising is regulated by content (tobacco, alcohol and medicine), duration (normally not to exceed 12 minutes per hour), and impact (the program's integrity and its producer's rights must be preserved). The Convention came into effect on May 1, 1993.

Broadcasting Directive

The European Union Council of Ministers laid the basis for a statutory framework for the free movement of audiovisual programs throughout the European Union with its "Television without Frontiers" Broadcasting Directive.[127] The Broadcasting Directive has recently been extended to the EFTA countries (except for Liechtenstein and Switzerland). In short, each state must admit television broadcast from the others. The regulation of the control of the content of those broadcasts is generally left to home state control, subject to various harmonizing rules concerning rights of reply, protection of minors and advertising and sponsorship.

The Broadcasting Directive provides that "when practicable", broadcasters (many of which are government-owned) should reserve most of their time for programs of European (not just Union) origin.[128] This is more restrictive than meets the eye because broadcast time devoted to news, sports events, games, advertising, and teletext services is *excluded* when measuring compliance. Moreover, no member state may reduce the percentage of broadcast

---

125 *See* Article 170, TFEU.

126 *Id.*

127 Council Directive 89/552.

128 Article 6 of Directive 89/552.

time allotted to European works from that which existed in 1988. France imposes a 40% rule. The rules of origin for television programs focus on producer citizenship and production costs, not cultural contents. A work is "European" if it is made by producers in a member state, supervised and controlled by producers there or the contribution of EU co-producers to the cost is "preponderant". Many U.S. firms have moved quickly into co-productions intended to qualify as European under the broadcasting directive.

The Broadcasting Directive, when first proposed, contained an absolute requirement of more than 50 percent European broadcasting content. Intense lobbying by the United States, a major exporter of films and TV shows to Europe, introduced the "when practicable" limitation. Nevertheless, the long-term goal of broadcasting European television productions at least half the time is clearly stated. Many U.S. firms moved quickly into EU co-productions intended to qualify as European under the Broadcasting Directive. There is a view that the "as practicable" exception has been used (and abused) as a loophole. It is believed that plans will shortly be presented by the Audiovisual Commissioner backed by the Commission President to force European broadcasters to adhere to the majority of European programs requirement by abolishing the "when practicable" requirement. In addition, proposals will be put forward to extend the ambit of the Broadcasting Directive to interactive services such as "teleshopping".

The Broadcasting Directive is supported by decisions of the European Court of Justice that television signals constitute the provision of a "service" and thus come within the TFEU.[129] The Commission decision to waive EU competition laws to permit European broadcasters to bid collectively for the right to broadcast large sporting events illustrates the concern of the EU institutions to balance the strict application of competition laws with the wider benefit which may result in a particular case.

U.S. Reaction

The Broadcasting Directive was one of the few early single market campaign laws to attract headlines in the United States. The entertainment industry is America's second largest source of export earnings after military products and technology. The broadcasting and the banking directives caused the United States business community to wake up and become proactive in the European Union. They have been supported by Congressional resolutions denouncing

---

[129] Italy v. Saatchi, (1974) Eur.Comm.Rep. 409; Re Debauve, (1980) Eur.Comm.Rep. 833. *See* Commission v. The Netherlands, (1991) Eur.Comm.Rep. (Case C–353/89) (requirement that national broadcasting organizations commission material from Dutch companies violates Article 59 freedom to provide services).

the Broadcasting Directive, and repeated statements by the United States Trade Representative (USTR) that it is the "enemy of free trade". In 1991, the USTR put the European Union on a "priority watchlist" of nations whose intellectual property practices are suspect by U.S. standards. This was done under the "Special 301" trade sanction provisions of Section 182 of the Trade Act of 1974.

The USTR monitored national implementation of the Broadcasting Directive within the EU to determine whether, and to what degree, American programs were denied access. Since France, Italy, the United Kingdom, Spain and Portugal had already enacted broadcast quotas and the Uruguay Round of the GATT did not produce an agreement on trade in media products, the potential for unilateral Section 301 retaliation and exacerbation of the dispute between the U.S. and the EU still exists.

France refers to the United States as a "hyper-power" country whose power extends beyond economics, defense and technology to domination of attitudes, concepts, language and mode of life. More balanced observers note that the Broadcasting Directive reflects the sense of cultural and English-language invasion that many Europeans (and Canadians) resent and associate with more than just television, *e.g.*, a McDonald's on every corner. Canada, for its part, obtained a "cultural industries" exclusion from NAFTA/USMCA free trade.[130] This exclusion allows it to maintain broadcasting quotas like those of the European Union, along with magazine, film, book and other media trade restraints.

Generally, the fear of losing cultural identity within Europe had been diminishing as younger generations were educated, traveled, inter-married and took up work around the Union. The beginnings of a European "melting pot" are evident, but concern about the cultural influence of "outsiders" (including migrants) is growing and Europe will always be multilingual and multicultural. These trends affect not only American broadcasters but also Japanese and Chinese exporters, and the racial, religious and ethnic minorities of the Union.

Other EU Broadcasting Policies

The deadline for national implementation of Directive 93/83 on Satellite Broadcasting and Cable Transmission was January 1, 1995. That Directive deals with the application of copyright to cable and satellite broadcasts. The thrust of the directive is to view broadcasts as being carried out in one nation only for copyright purposes, as opposed to each receiving country. However, the test employed to

---

[130] *See* R. Folsom, and W.D. Folsom, *The USMCA, NAFTA Re-Negotiated and Its Business Implications.*

determine which country is the relevant one for copyright differs from that employed under the "television without frontiers" directive and the resulting position is that different laws may apply to broadcasters in respect of each sphere. Directive 93/83 also answers the question of where permission must be obtained for broadcasts into the EU from outside its borders, while a minimum level of protection is required throughout the EU itself.

To promote the development of audiovisual activities the European Union has created two major sources of financial support—an Action Plan to introduce advanced television services in Europe and a Media Program. An important basis for future developments arose from the publication of the Commission's Green Paper on Audiovisual Policy, which sets out the various options available and invites consultation at a wider level. Finally, the aim of promoting media pluralism in the European Union Internal Market has been recognized by its institutions for some time,[131] the underlying objective being to ensure diversity of information for the public and respect for freedom of expression.

§ 5.15 Computer Software and Databases

Two areas of technology law of particular interest to U.S. firms have been legislated amidst controversy and a blitz of American lobbying. Council Directive 91/250 requires member states to protect computer programs by copyright, something not all EU jurisdictions did. Its rules on "decompilation" (reverse engineering) for purposes of interoperability with an independently created program are liberal by U.S. standards. There is a specific right to "observe, study or test the functioning of the program in order to determine the ideas and principles that underlie any element of the program." However, decompilation may not be used for the development, production and marketing of a substantially similar computer program. The directive takes no position on the patentability of computer software. Directive 96/9 protects databases. It creates exclusive rights to databases not otherwise copyrightable but does not apply to football (soccer) fixture lists.[132]

Software Directive

Council Directive 91/250 (now 2009/24) requires member states to protect computer programs by copyright as literary works within the meaning of the Berne Convention of the Protection of Literary

---

[131] European Parliament resolution of 15th February 1990 OJ No. C68, 19/3/1990, pp. 137–138 and 16th September 1992 A3–0153/92/Corr.; Commission communication Com (90)78 and Green Paper COM (92)480 of 23rd December 1992.

[132] *See* the Fixtures Marketing Ltd cases, (2004) Eur.Comm.Rep. I–10365 (Finland), I–10497 (Sweden) and I–10549 (Greece).

and Artistic Work. "Computer programs," although not specifically defined, are deemed to include preparatory design material. Protection applies to the expression of any form of a computer program. Ideas and principles which underlie any element of a computer program, including those which underlie its interfaces, are not protected. A computer program is protected if it is original in the sense that it is the author's own intellectual creation. This test for originality accords with the approach taken in the U.S. concerning telephone directories. No other criteria (aesthetic or qualitative) are to be applied to determine its eligibility for protection.

The Software Directive was the subject of fierce industry lobbying in 1990, the two opposing camps being ECIS (the European Committee for Interoperable Systems) which had a liberal "open systems" outlook on matters such as decompilation/reverse-engineering, and SAGE (the Software Action Group for Europe) which represented the big manufacturers' interests in proprietary architectures by seeking copyright protection for interface specifications. The final form of the Directive issued in May 1991 was a victory for ECIS. The Directive was due to have been implemented by each member state by January 1, 1993: only the UK, Italy and Denmark met the deadline. Other member states (such as the Netherlands, Luxembourg, Belgium, and Portugal) were in breach of their obligations and the Commission commenced proceedings against them.

Article 4 of the Directive indicates, subject to the provisions of Articles 5 and 6, that the exclusive rights of the holder include the right to do or to authorize: (1) The permanent or temporary reproduction of a computer program by any means and in any form, in part or in whole (insofar as loading, displaying, running, transmission or storage of the computer program necessitate reproduction, such acts are subject to authorization); (2) the translation, adaptation, arrangement or other alteration of a computer program and the reproduction of the results without prejudice to the rights of the person who alters the program; and (3) any form of distribution to the public, including rental of the original computer program or copies. Following the ECJ principle of exhaustion of rights, the first commercial exploitation in the Union of a copy of a program exhausts the right to control any further distribution within the Union of that copy, except for the right to control further rental of the program or copies of it.

Article 5 of the Directive creates exceptions to the rights conveyed in Article 4 in the absence of specific contractual provisions to the contrary. To the extent reproduction is required to load, display, transmit or store the program to use it as intended, such reproduction does not require a separate authorization from the holder. The making of a back-up copy (or more than one) by a lawful user may not be prevented by contract insofar as backup(s) are necessary for use of the program by the lawful user. In general, there is a right to "observe, study, or test the functioning of the program in order to determine the ideas and principles which underlie any element of the program" provided such observation, study or test is made during permitted loading, displaying, running, transmission or storage.

Decompilation

Article 6 of the Directive deals with decompilation, also known as reverse engineering. Authorization is not required where the reproduction of the code and translation of its form are indispensable to obtaining information necessary to achieve the interoperability of an independently created computer program with other programs. However, the following conditions must be met: (1) These acts must be performed by the licensee or by another person having a right to use a copy of a program or on their behalf by a person authorized to do so; (2) the information necessary to achieve interoperability must not previously have been readily available to those persons; and (3) the acts are confined to the parts of the original program which are necessary to achieve interoperability. It remains to be seen how these tests will be applied in the courts of each member state.

Moreover, decompilation is not permitted if the information obtained through its application is to be: (1) Used for goals other than achieving the interoperability of the independently created program; (2) given to others, except when necessary for the interoperability of the independently created computer program; or (3) used for the development, production or marketing of a computer program substantially similar in its expression or for any other act that infringes copyright. Lastly, in accordance with the provisions of the Berne Convention, Article 6 may not be interpreted in such a way as to allow its application to be used in a manner which reasonably prejudices the holder's legitimate interests or conflicts with a normal exploitation of the computer program.

It has been suggested that the decompilation provisions of the EU directive change traditional software licensing clauses. The traditional clause "Licensee agrees not to cause or permit the reverse engineering, disassembly or decompilation of the Licensed Program" will have to be redrafted to something like:

> Licensee shall not decompile the Licensed Program, except to the extent necessary to achieve interoperability of the Licensed Program with an independently created program, whenever the information necessary to achieve such interoperability has not

> been made readily available by Licensor to Licensee upon Licensee's written request. Such decompilation acts shall be restricted to the parts of the Licensed Program that are necessary to achieve interoperability. In no event may Licensee subcontract such decompilation to a third party without Licensor's prior written authorization.[133]

The same practitioner suggests that a clause more adapted to the spirit of the directive would be the following:

> Licensee shall not cause or permit decompilation of the Licensed Program, except to the extent necessary to achieve interoperability of the Licensed Program with an independently created program, whenever the information necessary to achieve such interoperability has not been made readily available by Licensor to Licensee upon Licensee's written request. Such decompilation acts shall be restricted to the parts of the Licensed Program that are necessary to achieve interoperability.[134]

Remedies

The Directive provides for special measures of protection even if such acts are not "infringement" according to national copyright laws in the Union. Such measures are listed in Article 7 of the Directive. These include: (1) Any act putting into circulation or possession for commercial purposes a copy of a computer program while knowing, or having reason to believe, that it is an infringing copy; and (2) any act putting into circulation or possession for commercial purposes any means singularly intended to facilitate the unauthorized removal or circumvention of any technical device which may have been applied to protect a computer program.

§ 5.16 Telecommunications

An imposing array of European Union law is making its impact in the telecommunications field. This section summarizes on some of the leading directives and developments, including

- Telecommunications Services Directive 90/388 (now Directive 2002/77).
- Open Network Provision Directives 90/387, 98/10.
- Terminal Equipment Directives 88/301 and 91/263.

Other particularly noteworthy developments include the Commission's 1991 Guidelines on applying competition law to the

---

[133] *See* Bertone, "The EEC Directive on Computer Software," in Folsom, Lake and Nanda (eds.), *European Community Law After 1992: A Practical Guide for Lawyers Outside the Common Market* (Kluwer, 1992).

[134] *Id.*

telecommunications industry[135] and a public sector procurement directive which applies, in part, to telecommunications.[136] The 1993 Treaty on European Union added a number of provisions intended to foster the growth of trans-European networks, including telecommunications.[137] Special emphasis is placed on inter-operability and access issues.[138] A telecoms package of 2002 overhauled the regulatory framework for the industry,[139] notably leading to application of data privacy rules.[140]

Telecommunications Services

Telecommunications by phone, fax, telex and computers go to the heart of modern service-oriented economies. The European Union has recognized this and taken steps in its 1992 campaign to integrate and improve its telecommunications network. In 1990, the Council finalized the "Open Network Provision" framework directive. This legislation harmonizes the conditions of access and use of public telecommunications networks. Commission Directive 88/301 (issued under Article 110) deregulates the sale and servicing of telecommunications equipment. France failed when it challenged the authority of the Commission to issue this directive before the European Court.[141]

Council Directives 90/387 and 98/10 eliminate public monopolies over all but voice telephones and infrastructure ownership. Private sector companies may move freely into electronic mail, interactive communications, data transmission and the like. U.S. firms are particularly thought to have competitive advantages that will benefit them under the new EU telecommunications regime. In addition, there is every reason to believe from the case law of the European Court that state monopolies in the telecommunications area will be required to abandon discriminatory national practices. This case law is partly based upon the freedom to provide services across borders, and partly upon competition law.[142]

---

135 O.J.C. 233/2 (Sept. 6, 1991).

136 Directive 90/531. *See* Section 5.4.

137 *See* Article 170, TFEU.

138 *See* Directive 97/33.

139 *See* Commission IP/02/2002 (Feb. 14, 2002).

140 Directive 2002/58.

141 France v. Commission, (1991) 1 Eur.Comm.Rep. 1223.

142 *See* Procureur du Roi v. Debauve, (1980) Eur.Comm.Rep. 833 (ban on television advertising); Italy v. Commission ("British Telecom"), (1985) Eur.Comm.Rep. 873 (use of leased lines for customer service upheld); Bond van Adverteerders v. The Netherlands, (1988) Eur.Comm.Rep. 2085 (discriminatory cross-border advertising restraints); Régie des Télégraphes et des Téléphones v. SA "GB-INNO-BM" (1991) Eur.Comm.Rep. I–05981 (Case C–18/88) (public network operator's specifications for phone sets and compliance monitoring violate Treaty of Rome where operator competes with other phone suppliers); Commission v. The Netherlands,

The Commission Directive on Competition on the Markets for Telecommunications Services 90/388 (now Directive 2002/77) ("The Services Directive") permits member states to retain monopolies over "voice telephony." Voice telephony is defined as the commercial provision for the public of the "direct transport and switching of speech in real-time between public switched network termination points, enabling any user to use equipment connected to such a network termination point in order to communicate with another termination point." In contrast, the member states are obligated to "withdraw all special or exclusive rights for the supply of telecommunications services other than voice telephony and ... ensure that any operator is entitled to supply such telecommunications services ... [and] ensure that the conditions for the grant of Licenses [if any] are objective, non-discriminatory and transparent. . ."

Moreover, member states can no longer be able to prohibit the offering of leased line capacity for circuit or packet-switched data services for resale to the public. Leased lines must be made available within a reasonable period and without unjustified restrictions or charges. Technical interfaces must be published and unwarranted or discriminatory restrictions on the processing of signals before transmission or after their reception are prohibited. The Services Directive also requires member states to have an independent agency control license, specifications, frequency allocations and surveillance of usage conditions. Lastly, the Services Directive regulates the termination of telecommunications contracts. The Court of Justice upheld the issuance by the Commission of the Services Directive under Article 90/ (3).[143]

One commentator has reached the following conclusions about the Services Directive:

> Despite the pro-competition language, in some respects the Services Directives further entrenches the control of the Postal Telegraph and Telecommunications Administrations (PTTs) and as a practical matter impedes competition. For example, it relies

---

(1991) Eur.Comm.Rep. (Case C–353/89) (Dutch requirement that broadcasters receive significant part of programming from Dutch companies violates Article 59); Elliniki Radiophona Tiléorassi (ERT) AE v. Dimotiki Etairia Pliroforissis (DEP) + Anor, (1991) Eur.Comm.Rep. I–2925 Case (C–260/89) (single state broadcasting monopoly over domestic TV and retransmissions of EC programs amounts to discriminatory and excessive breach of Article 59); Commission v. Belgium, (1992) Eur.Comm.Rep. I–06757 (Case C–211/91) (language, prior authorization and culturally reserved television program rules violate Treaty of Rome); Procureur du Roi v. Lagauche & Ors, (1994) Eur.Comm.Rep. I–05267 (Cases C–46/90 and C–93/91) (radio apparatus approval rules precluded by EU directive).

[143] Spain, Belgium & Italy v. Commission, (1992) Eur.Comm.Rep. I–5833 (Cases C–271/90, 281–90).

> upon analog technology in presuming that voice telephony, which it reserves to the monopoly, is technologically distinguishable from data, which it opens to competition. In fact, digital technology does not distinguish between voice and data. Therefore, by allowing the PTTs to keep control over private lines for voice and also allowing the PTTs to define the scope of that control, the Services Directive has reinforced a significant barrier to the development of competition even in data. Likewise, the separation of regulation from operations, although recognized as a step in the right direction, cannot by itself safeguard against PTTs unwarranted control as long as the PTTs can impose tariff restrictions on the purpose for which circuits are used.[144]

ONP Directive

Council Directive 90/387 on the Establishment of the Internal Market for Telecommunications Services through the Implementation of Open Network Provision ("ONP Directive") is intended to "provide a legal framework for the medium to long-term harmonization of the conditions for telecommunications services provision." The ONP Directive concerns the harmonization of conditions for open and efficient access to and use of public telecommunications networks and services. This is to be accomplished by slowly harmonizing technical interfaces and service features under standards adopted by the European Telecommunications Standards Institute ("ETSI"). Service providers who comply with those standards fulfill the relevant essential technical and service requirements and telecommunications organizations that comply fulfill the requirements of open and efficient access. Adoption of ETSI standards will thus provide access to telecommunications networks and markets throughout the European Union.

The ONP Directive applies to leased lines, packet-and circuit-switched data services, Integrated Services Digital Network (ISDN) voice telephony service, telex services, mobile services, new types of access to the network (such as to the circuits connecting subscriber premises to the public network exchange), and access to broadband networks. It arguably reduces the opportunity for PTT to abuse their dual function status as exclusive providers of networks and services and as competing providers of nonexclusive services and equipment. However, the ONP Directive indicates that "reasons of general public interest" will restrict access when "essential requirements" are involved. Essential requirements concern noneconomic reasons which may cause a member state to restrict access to the public

[144] Beatson, "An Introduction to Telecommunications Law in the European Community," in Folsom, Lake and Nanda (eds.), *European Community Law After 1992: A Practical Guide for Lawyers Outside the Common Market* (Kluwer, 1992).

telecommunications network or public telecommunications services. These reasons include security of network operations, maintenance of network integrity, and in justified cases, interoperability of services and data protection. The ONP Directive specifies the following "framework" for its implementation by the member states:

> Open Network Provision conditions shall be drawn up in such a way as to facilitate the service providers' and users' freedom of action without unduly limiting the telecommunications organizations' responsibilities for the functions of the network and the best possible condition of communications channels.

Terminal Equipment Directive

Commission Directive 88/301 on Competition on the Markets in Telecommunications Terminal Equipment ("Terminal Equipment Directive") seeks to create a Union-wide terminal equipment market.[145] The Terminal Equipment Directive recognizes that "the last decades have seen considerable technical developments in networks, and the pace of development has been especially striking in the areas of terminal equipment." The Directive provides for a gradual elimination of PTT monopolies over terminal equipment. The Directive requires the publication of specifications and approval procedures for such equipment. The goal is to "make transparent the characteristics of the termination points of the network to which the terminal equipment is to be connected."

Council Directive 91/263 on the Approximation of Laws of the Member States Concerning Telecommunications Terminal Equipment Including the Mutual Recognition of their Conformity ("the Standards Directive") seeks to harmonize interfaces and promote "mutual recognition of type approval." Access to the network without sacrificing its integrity is the focus of this directive. The Standards Directive establishes procedures for certification, testing, marking, quality assurance and product surveillance.

§ 5.17 Research and Development

One important thrust of the Single European Act of 1987 was promotion of more research and technological development. The European Union strongly perceived itself to be falling behind the United States and Japan in these areas. The result was eleven new articles in the Treaty of Rome, now Articles 179–190 TFEU. The opening sentence of Article 179 establishes the goals of strengthening the scientific and technological bases of European industry and encouraging it to become more competitive at the international level.

---

[145] The Commission's authority to issue this directive under Article 106 TFEU has been upheld. French Republic v. Commission, (1993) Eur.Comm.Rep. I–01223 (Case 202/88).

This is to be achieved not only through coordination of national activities and a program of generous Union grants, but also via the continuing single market campaign.

When less than all the EU states participate in Union-sponsored research and development, the Council has the power to decide to what degree the resulting knowledge must be shared. To encourage commercial enterprises and research organizations across the EU to collaborate on R & D projects, without fear of challenge on the basis of competition law, the Council adopted Regulation 418/85, known as the R & D Block Exemption, which like the other block exemptions contains "whitelists" and "blacklists" of restrictions.

In 1987, the Council of Ministers adopted the Framework Program for Community Research and Development. This framework focuses on eight areas; the quality of life, information and communication, modernization of industry, exploitation and optimum use of geological resources, energy, development, marine resources and improved European science and technology cooperation. Some research is done at the Union's own Joint Research Center. Other research is sponsored through national institutes and universities. Many of the Union's research and development programs are known by acronyms such as ESPRIT (information technologies), RACE (advanced communications), DRIVE (road transport informatics and telecommunications), DELTA (learning technologies), and JET (nuclear fusion). Participation by United States companies in EU research programs has been limited.

§ 5.18 Occupational Health and Safety

The Treaty on the Functioning of the European Union is dominated by economic affairs. Nevertheless, the Union has always sought to provide for some of the concerns of the human beings who are impacted by the winds of economic change. Articles 151–164 TFEU establish the Social Policy of the European Union. These articles seek to improve working conditions and standards of living on a harmonized basis throughout the Union. The right of EU nationals to move freely to take up employment has previously been discussed in Chapter 4 in connection with the foundations of the Treaty. The Union's social policy builds upon this basic right. Article 160, for example, led to the enactment of social security legislation by the EU to ensure coverage for those who exercise their right to move freely to work.

A major impetus came in 1987 with the addition of Article 154 by the Single European Act. This article focuses on health and safety in the working environment. Acting by a qualified majority vote, the

Council in cooperation with the Parliament is empowered to issue directives establishing minimum requirements in this field. It has already done so, for example, on visual display units, heavy load handling and exposure to biological agents and carcinogens. More generally, Council directives now establish minimum safety and health requirements for most workplaces, equipment used by workers, and protective devices.[146] Article 154 specifically requires such directives to avoid imposing administrative, financial and legal constraints that would hold back the creation and development of small and medium-sized enterprises. Like the 1987 Treaty amendments creating the Environmental Policy, Article 154 allows member states to maintain or introduce more stringent legal rules on working conditions, provided these are compatible with the Treaty.

Perhaps the most prominent occupational law is the "Working Time" Directive 93/104, now 2003/96. Its controversial legal basis is discussed in Section 5.18. The directive requires rest periods, maximum 48 weeks, a minimum of four weeks of paid leave, maximum eight-hour night shifts, but contains a variety of "public sector" exceptions. It continues to generate controversy.[147]

Health and Safety Legislation

The following is a sampling of major European Union occupational health and safety laws:

- Directives 77/576, 92/58 (safety signs)
- Directives 83/477, 91/382 (asbestos)
- Directives 80/1107, 88/364 (chemical agents)
- Directive 89/391 (the workplace framework directive)
- Directive 89/654 (physical plant design)
- Directive 89/655 (equipment used by workers)
- Directive 89/656 (protective equipment)
- Directive 89/665 (use of machines, equipment and installations)
- Directives 89/686, 89/328 (personal protective equipment)
- Directives 90/219, 90/220 (biotechnology)

---

[146] *See* Council Directives 89/654, 655, 656.

[147] *See* Queen v. Secretary of State of Trade ex parte Bectu, (2001) Eur.Comm.Rep. I–04881 (June 26, 2001) (minimum employment period invalid); Sindicato de Medicos v. Conselleria de Sanidad de la Generalidad Valenciana, (2000) Eur.Comm.Rep. I–07963 (Oct. 3, 2000) (application to doctors on call).

- Directive 90/269 (heavy loads)
- Directive 90/276 (visual display units)
- Directive 90/394 (carcinogens)
- Directives 80/1107, 90/679 (biological agents)
- Directive 91/368 (machinery risks)
- Directive 92/57 (construction sites)
- Directive 92/85 (pregnant workers)
- Directive 92/91 (drilling for minerals)
- Directive 93/88 (exposure to biological agents)
- Directive 93/104 (working time)
- Directive 94/33 (children at work)
- Regulation 2062/94 (European Agency for Safety and Health at Work)
- Directive 2002/15 (working time for road transport)
- Directive 2002/44 (vibration)
- Directive 2003/10 (noise at work)

§ 5.19 Social Policy

NAFTA/USMCA is almost completely devoid of "social policy" initiatives. In contrast, Articles 162–164 TFEU created the European Social Fund. This fund comes out of the Union budget. It is used to pay up to 50 percent of the costs of the member states under their vocational retraining and worker resettlement programs.[148] EU rules have substantially harmonized these programs. Unemployment compensation is also funded when plants are converted to other production for workers who are suspended or suffer a reduction in working hours. They retain the same wage levels pending full reemployment. Commission Decision 83/516 extended the operation of the European Social Fund to promoting employment among those under age 25, women who wish to return to work, the handicapped, migrants and their families, and the long-term unemployed.

Social Charter

The 1992 campaign had a social dimension. Labor unions were especially concerned about the prospect of "social dumping," the relocation of companies to EU states with weaker unions and lower wages, a concern repeated in the NAFTA/USMCA debates about Mexico. There is no regional legislation on minimum wages, and none

[148] Article 164, TFEU.

is expected in the future. The Union's response to these concerns led to the Charter of Fundamental Social Rights for Workers, adopted in 1989 by 11 member states less Britain through the European Council. The Charter proclaims the following fundamental social rights for workers:

(1) Freedom of movement and choice of occupations.

(2) Fair remuneration (sufficient to have a decent standard of living).

(3) Improved living and working conditions (*e.g.*, paid leave).

(4) Adequate social security benefits.

(5) Free association in unions, including the right *not* to join, and the right to strike.

(6) Non-discriminatory access to vocational training.

(7) Equal treatment for women and men.

(8) Development of rights to access to information, and rights of consultation and participation.

(9) Satisfactory health and safety conditions at work.

(10) For the young, a minimum employment age of 15, substantial limitations on night work for those under 18, and start-up vocational training rights.

(11) For retirees, the right to assistance "as needed" and a decent standard of living; and

(12) For the disabled, assistance to integrate socially and professionally.[149]

The Charter was to be implemented immediately by the member states in "accordance with national practices." In addition, for each item listed above, Union legislation was anticipated by the end of 1992. Adoption of this legislation was slow chiefly because of Britain's veto power in the Council over employment matters under the Single European Act. The Commission, however, drafted several Social Action Program legislative measures. One such measure guaranteeing *minimum* maternity leave benefits of 14 weeks at statutory sick pay rates was adopted by the Council of Ministers in November of 1992.[150] A woman's employment cannot be terminated because she is pregnant. In addition, pregnant women are entitled to

---

[149] *Compare* the much less comprehensive "Labor Principles" annexed to the North American Agreement on Labor Cooperation (NAALC). *See* my Concise Hornbook on *The USMCA and Free Trade Agreements.*

[150] Council Directive 92/85.

switch from night work, exempted from work detrimental to their health, and entitled to take paid leave for pre-natal check-ups. This directive required substantial improvements to existing legislation in Ireland, Portugal and the United Kingdom. Unpaid parental leave rights are detailed in Directive 96/34.

Social Protocol

In December 1991 at the Maastricht Summit agreement was reached, save Britain, on a "social policy protocol" allowing the EU to enact laws by qualified majority vote governing many areas which bridge workers' interests and company operations. Some suggested that the "social protocol" would have been more accurately labeled a "workers' rights protocol". It focused on working environment issues including conditions of labor, health and safety, disclosure of information, sex discrimination, and worker consultation. The "social protocol" thus overlapped considerably with the Social Charter.

Despite its repeated opposition to development of a "social dimension," the United Kingdom under Conservative rule adopted or implemented over half of the measures noted in the Social Charter. What the Conservatives consistently objected to were rules relating directly to the employee-employer relationship, not worker benefits such as pregnancy leave or health or safety measures. Nevertheless, the Court of Justice repeatedly ruled against Britain in litigation challenging the adequacy of its implementation of worker-related directives (*e.g.*, on collective redundancies (mass layoffs) and transfers of enterprises).

In a major decision, the Court ruled over vehement objection that the "working time" directive (No. 93/104 now 2003/88) was properly adopted by qualified majority vote based on Article 138's authorization of worker health and safety law.[151] This ruling had the practical effect of avoiding Britain's Social Protocol opt out rights. The directive creates, inter alia, a minimum right to four weeks of paid vacation. Subsequently, the United Kingdom under the Labour Party administration of Prime Minister Blair opted into the region's Social Policy and the 1999 Amsterdam Treaty repealed the Social Protocol.

Social Policy

As amended, Articles 151–161 TFEU (the "social chapter") embrace social goals reflecting the Social Charter. There is express authority for EU legislation on worker health and safety, work conditions, information and consultation of workers, and gender equality, mostly using qualified majority voting and co-decision

---

151 United Kingdom v. Council, (1996) Eur.Comm.Rep. I–5755.

Parliamentary powers. However, there is no authorization for EU action on matters of pay, and rights of association, strike and lock-out. EU legislation can occur by unanimous vote on social security, co-determination, worker protection upon termination, and employment of third country nationals.

One business lawyer reached the following conclusions regarding the social policy of the European Community:

> From the perspective of the corporation based outside of Europe, the future of EC [EU] employment, or "social," regulation—that is, the blueprint set out in the Charter, the Social Action Program, and the Commission's 1990–1991 package of draft instruments—looks expensive. European workers already receive from their employers some of the highest pay and benefit levels in the world. Once the Social Action Program's 47 called-for instruments are in place, continental European workers' pay and benefit levels will probably rise even higher.
>
> Certain Charter rights, once implemented, will directly raise employers' marginal costs of employing workers. For example, the second right, to "fair pay," could directly raise wages—both in low-paying service industries and, via the "equitable reference wage" concept, in every other industry, as well. The third right, to "improved working conditions," could raise employers' payroll costs, if the Council implements the already-tabled proposals to extend benefits and protections to part-time and temporary workers, and to force employers to enter "indefinite" lengthy, written individual employment contracts with even non-union workers. The sixth right, to vocational training, would, if implemented, force employers (and even unions) to create and pay for career-long job training programs. And the ninth right, to expanded health and safety protections, would impose new work-procedure restrictions on certain EC employers.
>
> Other Charter rights, if implemented, could even more radically raise corporations' costs of employing Europeans; these are the rights which would affect legal liability and the structure of EC labor law. For example, the Charter's fifth right, to EC-level collective bargaining, could raise costs of employment in less economically-developed member states, as wages and benefit levels were negotiated EC-wide. The Charter's seventh right, for equal treatment between the sexes, might raise costs for corporations found to have preferred men over women in employment or pay, and, under an already-approved directive, would raise some employers' costs as regards pregnant women. If implemented, the Charter's eighth right, to worker consultation and participation, would also raise costs—to the extent that business decisions made with labor's input are less beneficial to the "bottom line" than are decisions which management makes alone.

Other Charter rights, once implemented, will most likely be EC-funded. These rights will necessarily raise employers' costs, too, if only by the incremental amount by which the EC must raise taxes to fund them. Such guarantees include the Charter's eleventh, twelfth, and thirteenth rights, to expand social programs for youth, the aged, and the disabled.

Fortunately, certain other aspects of the "social Europe" agenda will actually *benefit* employers based outside the EC. For starters, the Charter's first right, guaranteeing free movement of workers, will continue to streamline intra-European personnel transfers, thereby making personnel "immigration" matters cheaper—an important benefit for companies with trans-European operations.

Additionally, the "social Europe" program sends some positive signals to certain employers based outside the EC—particularly U.S.-based employers—through what it *omits.* The Charter and the Social Action Program are silent on several areas in which U.S. employers bear heavy domestic burdens; most notable is the virtual absence of anti-discrimination law. The EC's proposed protections for the young, the aged, and the disabled do not seem headed toward the extensive U.S. regulation of employment decisions arguably involving age or handicap, such as under the Age Discrimination in Employment Act, the Rehabilitation Act of 1973, the Americans with Disabilities Act, and analogous state laws.

Similarly, although much of the Charter and Social Action Program aims at guaranteeing increased benefits for workers, nothing in the documents raises the specter of benefit plan liability analogous to U.S. law under the Employment Retirement Income Security Act. And nothing in the Charter or Social Action Program approaches the magnitude of U.S. prohibitions, under Title VII and related state laws, against race, nationality, and religious discrimination. Thus, U.S.-based employers, at least, can take solace in that the "social Europe" program, while indisputably pro-employee, will not create for European workers causes of action on which to sue employers anything analogous to the grounds for liability which haunt companies in the 1990's U.S.[152]

§ 5.20 Employment Law

Apart from gender discrimination in employment relations,[153] the Union has undertaken relatively little by way of employment law. There are, however, some notable directives governing mass lay-offs,

---

152 Dowling, "Employment Matters and the Social Charter," in Folsom, Lake and Nanda (eds.), *European Community Law After 1992: A Practical Guide for Lawyers Outside the Common Market* (Kluwer, 1992).

153 *See* Section 5.21.

employee rights upon insolvency and business transfers, and contractual disclosure duties.

Mass Lay-Offs

Council Directive 75/129, amended in 1992 and republished as Directive 98/59 concerns mass lay-offs (collective redundancies). Any private business[154] employing more than 20 workers intending to dismiss designated numbers of employees for general economic reasons must give 30-day notice with "all relevant information" to those employees or their representatives.[155] For businesses with less than 100 workers, this duty is triggered when 10 employees are to be laid off. For businesses with 100 to 300 employees, the trigger is 10 percent of those employed. For firms with over 300 employees, the trigger is the dismissal of 30 or more employees.

Consultations on possible reductions in the lay-offs and mitigation of them follow, ordinarily with public authorities included. More demanding national rules concerning mass lay-offs are allowed, and in some countries, notably Germany, have been enacted. By 1992 amendment, this directive applies when the dismissal decision is made by parent companies of the employer located in another member state.[156]

Employee Rights in Business Transfers

Council Directive 77/187 ensures certain employee "acquired rights" when there are "transfers" of for profit and nonprofit[157] businesses or parts thereof,[158] including mergers and acquisitions but not judicial insolvency proceedings.[159] The test of whether a "transfer" occurred is the continuance of the business as a "going concern."[160] This includes lease transfers[161] but not replacement contractors.[162]

---

154 *See* Commission v. United Kingdom, (1994) Eur.Comm.Rep. I–2479 (limited applicability to businesses with trade unions invalid).

155 *See* Dansk Metalarbejderforbund v. H. Nielsen & Son, (1985) Eur.Comm.Rep. 553 (mandatory notice does not create 30-day pay rights).

156 Directive 92/56, now Directive 98/59.

157 Commission v. United Kingdom, (1994) Eur.Comm.Rep. I–2435 (nonprofits).

158 *See* Botzen v. Rotterdamsche Droogdok Maatschappij BV, (1985) Eur.Comm.Rep. 519 (partial transfer).

159 *See* D'Urso & Ors v. Ercole Marelli Elettromeccanica (EMG) & Ors, (1991) Eur.Comm.Rep. I–4105 (Case C–362/89) (employee transfer rights adhere in civil receivership proceedings when business continues to operate until transfer occurs); Abels v. Administrative Board, Case 135/83 (1985) (judicial insolvency not covered).

160 Bork Int'l A/S v. Foreningen of Arbejdsledere, (1988) Eur.Comm.Rep. 3057; Spijkers v. Benedik Abattoir CV, (1986) Eur.Comm.Rep. 119.

161 Foreningen of Arbejdsledere v. Daddy's Dance Hall A/S, (1988) Eur.Comm.Rep. 739.

162 Suzen v. Zehnacker Gebaudereinigung, (1997) Eur.Comm.Rep. I–1259.

Council Directive 77/187, amended in 1998 and republished as Directive 2001/23 requires advance notice of qualified transfers along with an analysis of the implications for workers. All employees working for businesses whose assets are transferred retain their existing terms and conditions of employment, and accrued service rights. Collective agreements are also preserved. No dismissal of employees may occur except for economic, technical or organizational reasons that change workforce needs.[163]

Any substantial change in working conditions harmful to employees is treated as a constructive dismissal and the rights of employees under Directive 77/187 cannot be waived by contract or otherwise.[164] Employee rights protected by Directive 77/187 extend to transfers of employment which amount to a contracting out for services previously managed internally.[165] But such transfers cannot force employees to remain with their new employers.[166] Pension benefits are *not* covered and they do not automatically transfer. However, more favorable national law on employee "acquired rights" is allowed. This directive often means that companies seeking to purchase shares or assets of European firms must also consult and negotiate with unions if there is any future possibility of a reduction in staff or rationalization of operations.

Pay Claims in Insolvencies

Council Directive 80/987 requires member states to guarantee certain employee back pay claims against insolvent employers.[167] Such claims do not include employer contributions due under national social security or company pension schemes. More generally, a Bankruptcy Convention has been proposed. Council Directive 91/533 requires employers to disclose in writing "essential" information applicable to employment contracts or relationships. Such information includes party identification, place and nature of work, commencement date, duration, annual leave entitlements, notice requirements, pay and method of payment, length of working day and any relevant collective agreements. Special disclosures apply when employees are sent abroad.

---

163 *See especially* Litster v. Forth Dry Dock, 1 All Eng.Rep. 1134 (1989) (House of Lords).

164 Foreningen of Arbejdsledere v. Daddy's Dance Hall A/S, (1988) Eur.Comm.Rep. 739.

165 Watson Rask & Anor v. ISS Kantineservices A/S, (1992) Eur.Comm.Rep. I–05755 (Case C–209/91).

166 Katsikas & ORS v. Konstantinidis & ORS, (1992) Eur.Comm.Rep. 06577 (Cases C–132, 138, 139/91).

167 *See* Everson & Anor v. Secretary of State for Trade, (1999) Eur.Comm.Rep. I–8903 (UK guaranty fund covers Irish branch workers).

Terms of Employment Disclosure

Directive 91/533 requires employers to provide employees with written terms of their employment, including a job description, period of employment, paid leave, remuneration and benefits, and any relevant collective agreements.[168] Directive 96/71 requires companies posting workers to other member states to generally adhere to host state rules on minimum pay, benefits (except pensions), work periods, paid leave and health and safety at work. Directive 96/34 grants unpaid parental leave rights of three months, with a right vested in employees of one year or more to return to the same job (if possible) or similar work.

§ 5.21 Equal Pay and Equal Treatment

Article 157 is probably the most prominent element in the Union's social policy. It is derived from International Labor Organization Convention No. 100 which three member states, including France, had adopted by 1957. The French were rightfully proud of this tradition of non-discrimination between the sexes on pay. They also appreciated that gender-based inequality in pay in other member states could harm the ability of their companies to compete. Article 157 thus enshrines the principle that men and women shall receive equal pay for equal work. For these purposes, "pay" is defined in Article 157 to mean wages or salary, and any other consideration in cash or kind, received directly or indirectly respecting employment. "Equal pay without discrimination based on sex" means that piece rate payment must be calculated on the same units of measurement and that time rates must be equal for the same job.

Equal Pay, Comparable Worth

Article 157 has been the subject of voluminous EU legislation and litigation. It applies, quite appropriately, to the Union as an employer.[169] Early on, the Court of Justice decided that Article 157 on equal pay for equal work is directly effective EU law.[170] This decision allowed individuals throughout the Union to challenge pay discrimination in public and private sector jobs. The ruling in *Defrenne* was applied prospectively by the Court of Justice to avoid large numbers of lawsuits for back pay. In *Defrenne,* a flight attendant for Sabena Airlines was able to allege illegal discrimination in pay and pension benefits (as a form of deferred pay)

---

[168] *See* Lange v. Georg Schunemann, (2001) Eur.Comm.Rep. I–01061 (Feb. 8, 2001) (overtime included).

[169] Sabbatini, née Bertoni v. European Parliament, (1972) Eur.Comm.Rep. 345; Razzouk v. Commission, (1984) Eur.Comm.Rep. 1509 (working conditions).

[170] Defrenne v. Sabena, (1976) Eur.Comm.Rep. 455.

to stewards and stewardesses based on EU law before a Belgian work tribunal.

Indeed, European Union law in this area enshrines the principle of "comparable worth," a most controversial issue in United States employment law. Furthermore, women who are paid less than men performing work of less worth may claim relief under Article 157.[171] The hard question is how to determine what constitutes "equal work" requiring equal pay under Article 157 or what "women's work" is worth more than that being done by men (again requiring pay adjustments). For example, does secretarial work equal custodial work? Is the work of an airline attendant worth more than that of an airline mechanic? What about speech therapists (mostly women) and pharmacists (mostly men).[172]

Council Directive 75/117 (now Directive 2006/54) complements Article 157. It makes the principle of equal pay apply to work of *equal value* (to the employer). This mandates establishment of non-discriminatory job classifications to measure the comparable worth of one job with another. The Commission successfully enforced Directive 75/117 in a prosecution before the European Court of Justice against the United Kingdom. The Sex Discrimination Act of 1975, adopted expressly to fulfill Article 157 obligations, did not meet EU standards because employers could block the introduction of job classification systems.[173]

Danish law's failure to cover nonunionized workers also breached the equal pay directive.[174] But its implementation under German law, notably by constitutional provisions, sufficed to meet Union standards.[175]

In determining equal or greater values, most states favor a job content approach. Content is determined through job evaluation systems which use factor analysis. For example, in Great Britain a job is broken down into various components such as skill, responsibility, physical requirements, mental requirements, and working conditions. Points or grades are awarded in each of these categories and totaled to determine the value of the job. Different factors may be balanced against each other. In Ireland, the demand of physical work can be balanced against the concentration required in particular skills. This is known as the "total package" approach.

---

171 Murphy v. An Bord Telecom Eireann, (1988) Eur.Comm.Rep. 673.

172 *See* Enderby v. Frenchay Health Authority, (1993) Eur.Comm.Rep. I–5535.

173 Commission v. United Kingdom, (1982) Eur.Comm.Rep. 2601.

174 Commission v. Denmark, (1986) 1 Common Mkt.L.Rep. 44.

175 Commission v. Germany, (1986) 2 Common Mkt.L.Rep. 588.

The equal job content approach relies on comparisons. This raises the question of which jobs should be deemed to be suitable for comparison. The member states have taken different approaches to this question. In Britain the comparison must be drawn from the same business establishment. In contrast, the Irish Anti-Discrimination Pay Act provides for "comparisons in the same place," and "place" includes a city, town or locality. This approach is designed to ensure that legitimate regional differences in pay are not disturbed.

Defenses

Employer defenses also vary from member state to member state. In Ireland, employers may justify a variation if they can show "grounds other than sex" for a disputed variation in pay. In Britain, employers will succeed if they can prove a "genuine material factor which is not the difference of sex." In Germany, the employer can prove that "material reasons unrelated to a particular sex" justify the differential. A further consideration in the implementation of equal pay laws has been the existence of pre-existing wage schedules set by collective agreement. In Britain and Italy, courts held that collective agreements relating to pay cannot be changed or altered except where direct discrimination can be shown.

The burden of proving "objectively justified economic grounds" to warrant pay differentials is on the employer.[176] When a woman succeeds a man in a particular position within a company (here a warehouse manager), she is entitled to equal pay absent a satisfactory explanation not based upon gender.[177] The same may be true of part-time (female) workers doing the same job as full-time (male) workers.[178] Free travel to railway employees upon retirement cannot go only to men.[179] And "pay" includes retirement benefits paid upon involuntary dismissal, which cannot be discriminatory.[180] But a protocol adopted at the 1991 Maastricht Summit makes this ruling prospective only. Pay also includes employer-paid pension benefits which cannot be for men only.[181] In this decision the Court refused to remove the retroactive effect of its judgment suggesting that *Defrenne* was adequate notice of the direct effect of Article 157 upon

---

[176] Council Directive 97/80.

[177] McCarthays Ltd. v. Smith, (1980) Eur.Comm.Rep. 1275.

[178] Jenkins v. Kingsgate (Clothing Productions) Ltd., (1981) Eur.Comm.Rep. 911.

[179] Garland v. British Rail Engineering, Ltd., (1982) Eur.Comm.Rep. 359.

[180] Barber v. The Guardian Royal Exchange Assurance Group, (1990) 1 Eur.Comm.Rep. 1889.

[181] Worringham and Humphreys v. Lloyds Bank Ltd., (1981) Eur.Comm.Rep. 767.

employers. Mobility, special training and seniority may be objectively justifiable grounds for pay discrimination.[182]

Equal Treatment

The principle of equal pay for equal work has been extended by Council Directive to *equal treatment* regarding access to employment, vocational training, promotions, and working conditions (*e.g.*, retirement deadlines).[183] This directive (now 2006/54) prohibits discrimination based upon sex, family or marital status. It extends to the self-employed.[184] Equal treatment is limited by three exceptions. Member states may distinguish between men and women if: (1) sex is a determining factor in ability to perform the work; (2) the provision protects women; or (3) the provision promotes equal opportunity for men and women. Discrimination is also permitted in "occupational activities" for which workers of only one sex are appropriate. Equal treatment must be extended to small and household businesses.[185]

Dutch Law compulsorily retiring women at age 60 and men at age 65 violated the directive.[186] Women cannot be refused employment because they are pregnant even if the employer will suffer financial losses during maternity leave.[187] Maternity and adoption leave benefits for women, however, need not be extended to men.[188] The dismissal of a woman because of repeated absences owing to sickness is lawful provided the same absences would lead to the dismissal of men.[189] General prohibitions against night work by women but not men violate equal treatment Directive 76/207. The French government failed to justify this criminal law on any special grounds.[190] Mandatory retirement of professors at 68 in Bulgaria following three years of annual contracts after 65 was upheld by the ECJ.[191]

---

182 Union of Commercial and Clerical Employees v. Danish Employers Assn. *ex parte* Danfoss, (1989) Eur.Comm.Rep. 3199.

183 Council Directive 76/207 (issued under Article 308).

184 Council Directive 86/613.

185 Commission v. United Kingdom, (1983) Eur.Comm.Rep. 3431.

186 Beets-Proper v. Van Lanschot Bankiers NV, (1986) Eur.Comm.Rep. 773. *See* Council Directive 86/378 (equal treatment regarding pensions). *Accord*, Pensionsvericherungansalt v. Kleist, (2010) Eur.Comm.Rep. I–11939 (Case 356/09) (Austria).

187 Dekker v. Stichting Vormingscentrum voor Jong Volwassenen Plus, (1990) Eur.Comm.Rep. 3941 (Case C–177–88).

188 Hoffmann v. Barmer Ersatzkasse, (1984) Eur.Comm.Rep. 3047; Commission v. Italy, (1983) Eur.Comm.Rep. 3273 (adoption leave benefits).

189 Hertz and Aldi Marked, (1990) Eur.Comm.Rep. 4047 (Case C–179/88).

190 Ministère Public v. Stoeckel, (1991) Eur.Comm.Rep. 4047 (Case C–345–89).

191 Georgiev v. Technicheski universitet, (2010) Eur.Comm.Rep. I–11869 (Cases 250/09, 268/09).

Equality also governs social security entitlements[192] such as disability or caring for the disabled pay.[193] Social security benefits cannot be based upon marital status.[194] Women police officers cannot be denied arms when men are not, even in the interest of "public safety" and "national security."[195] Women chefs can be denied entry to special combat units,[196] but general military exclusions are prohibited.[197] Equal treatment requires the elimination of preferences based upon gender in laws governing collectively bargained employment agreements.[198]

In addition, the Council adopted a declaration in December 1991 endorsing the Commission's recommended Code of Practice on sexual harassment. This Code rejects sexual harassment as contrary to EU equal treatment law. Council Directive 2002/73 codifies this approach, emphasizing the protection of employee dignity. But both the equal pay and equal treatment directives fail to cover significant categories of women workers; part-time, temporary and home workers.[199] Additional EU legislation in these areas can be expected. The equal treatment principle has been extended beyond the workplace to access and supply of goods and services.[200]

Affirmative Action

Predictably, questions of "affirmative action" have arisen in the context of Article 157 law. A controversial decision of the Court of Justice invalidated a Bremen regulation giving women of equal qualifications priority over men where women made up less than half the relevant civil service staff. While not strictly a quota, the Court

---

192 Council Directive 79/7. An important exception allows state pension schemes to retain different retirement ages for men and women. *See* Regina v. Secretary of State for Social Security, (1992) Eur.Comm.Rep. II–285 (Case C–9/91) and Article 7(1)(a) of Directive 79/7. But severe disablement allowances (SDA) and invalid care cannot be provided based on different ages. Secretary of State for Social Security v. Thomas and Ors, (1993) Eur.Comm.Rep. II–237 (Case C–328/91). *Compare* Regina Virginia Hepple v. Adjudication Officer, (2000) Eur.Comm.Rep. I–3701 (accident victims' reduced earnings allowance nondiscriminatory).

193 Drake v. Chief Adjudication Officer, (1986) Eur.Comm.Rep. 1995.

194 *Id.*

195 Johnston v. Chief Constable, (1986) Eur.Comm.Rep. 1651. *See generally* Articles 296–298, Treaty of Rome.

196 Sirdar v. The Army Board and Secretary of State for Defence, (1999) Eur.Comm.Rep. I–7043.

197 Kreil v. Federal Republic of Germany, (2000) Eur.Comm.Rep. I–69.

198 Commission v. France, (1988) Eur.Comm.Rep. 6315 (Case 312/86) (preferences for women must be removed).

199 *See* Jenkins v. Kingsgate Ltd., (1981) Eur.Comm.Rep. 911 (part-time workers paid less, and though largely female, no EC law violation). *Compare* Bilka-Kaufhaus v. Weber, (1986) Eur.Comm.Rep. 1607 (employer must show objectively justified economic grounds to pay part-timers less).

200 Directive 2004/113, (2004) O.J. L373/37.

found that Bremen had exceeded the limits of the equal treatment directive in promoting equality of opportunity.[201] Specific reservation of university professorships for women in Sweden likewise fell upon ECJ review.[202] Sweden now uses increasing targets for women in full professorships.

Article 157(4) TFEU, as amended by the Amsterdam Treaty in 1999, attempts to address such issues. It allows member states to maintain or adopt "measures for specific advantages" to make it "easier" for the "underrepresented sex" to pursue vocational activity or to prevent or compensate for "disadvantages" in professional careers.

Gender and Other Discrimination

Although Article 157 on equal pay is directly effective law binding upon public and private employers throughout the Union (*Defrenne*), it is not yet clear to what degree the equal treatment directives cited above have that effect. Clearly these directives are binding on the member states and public corporations as employers.[203] The private sector must comply after national implementing legislation is adopted, but if that legislation is deficient the only remedy may be prosecution of the member state by the Commission.[204]

There is a trend within the jurisprudence of the Court of Justice towards recognition of a broad human right of equality before the law. This is evidenced in several Article 157 cases, reliance upon the European Human Rights Convention in developing general principles of EU law,[205] and in revised Articles 8–10 TFEU. It appears that the private sector will eventually be bound by all European Union legislation on equal pay and equal treatment even in the absence of or despite national implementing law.[206] Combatting discrimination based on sex, racial or ethnic origin,

---

201 Kalanke v. Freie Hansestadt Bremen, (1995) Eur.Comm.Rep. I–3051. *Compare* permissible advantages upheld in Marschall v. Land Nordrhein Westfalen, (1997) Eur.Comm.Rep. I–6363; Badeck v. Hessischer Ministerpräsident, (2000) Eur.Comm.Rep. I–1875.

202 Abrahamsson and Anderson v. Fogelgvist, (2000) Eur.Comm.Rep. I–5539.

203 *See especially* Marshall v. Southampton and South West Hampshire Area Health Authority (Teaching), (1993) Eur.Comm.Rep. I–4367 (Case C–271/91) (discriminatory retirement ages unlawful); Foster v. British Gas, (1990) 1 Eur.Comm.Rep. 3313.

204 *See* Duke v. GEC Reliance, 1 All Eng.Rep. 626 (House of Lords, 1988) (discriminatory retirement ages lawful).

205 *See* Sections 1.01, 2.12.

206 *See* Section 3.1 (discussion of duty of national courts to interpret national law in furtherance of EU directives).

religion or belief, disability, age or sexual orientation was made a central EU policy principle by the Reform Treaty of 2009.

Transsexuals[207] and homosexuals have begun to benefit from this trend. But the Court initially refused to require equal employer travel benefits for same sex partners under Article 141 law,[208] and likewise the Court of First Instance refused to recognize homosexual partnerships as the equivalent of marriage for household allowance purposes.[209] Revisions of the 1976 equal treatment directive emphasizing an approach called "gender mainstreaming" are in progress. Directive 2000/43 broadly provides for equal treatment irrespective of racial or ethnic origin.[210] Directive 2000/78 more narrowly prohibits employment discrimination on grounds of religion or belief, disability, age or sexual orientation, effectively reversing initial ECJ decisions on sexual orientation discrimination. That Directive's limits notwithstanding, the ECJ has expanded the dynamic of age discrimination under its case law.[211]

§ 5.22 European Investment Bank

The European Investment Bank (EIB) has a separate legal personality within the Union. The task of the EIB is to contribute "to the balance and stable development of the Common Market in the interests of the Community". The bank has played a major role in funding regional development projects within the Union and external development projects under the Lomé/Cotonou Conventions and other EU trade arrangements.

The Board of Governors of the EIB consists of the Ministers of Finance of the member states. This board oversees the bank's capital resources and loan activities. In general, EIB loans are only made to private EU entities when other sources of financing are also available and the member state where the investment is located guarantees the loan. However, the EIB is not restricted to activities within the Union. Article 18 of the Protocol empowers the Board of Governors to permit the granting of loans for investment projects to be carried out outside the territories of the Member States.

---

[207] P. v. S., (1996) Eur.Comm.Rep. I–2143; K.B. v. National Health Services Pensions Agency, (2004) Eur.Comm.Rep. I–00000 (Case No. C–117/01).

[208] Grant v. South-West Trains Ltd., (1998) Eur.Comm.Rep. I–621 reversed by Maruko v. Versorgungsanstalt der Deutschen Buhnen, (2008) Eur.Comm.Rep. I–1757.

[209] *See* D. and Sweden v. Council, (2001) Eur.Comm.Rep. I–04319 (May 31, 2001).

[210] *See* Centrum voor Gelijkeid van Kansen v. Firma Feryn, (2008) Eur.Comm.Rep. I–5187.

[211] Werner Mangold v. Rüdiger Helm, (2005) Eur.Comm.Rep. I–9981 (Case C–144/04).

The EIB acts on a non-profit making basis, and may involve itself in three types of projects:

(1) Projects for development of less developed regions;

(2) Projects for the modernization or conversion of undertakings or for the development of new activities required by the progressive establishment of the common market; and

(3) Projects of common interest to several members.

In (1) and (3) above, the projects must be "of a size and nature that they cannot be entirely financed by the various means available in the individual Member States", before the EIB will consider acting. The European Investment Bank has raised substantial sums in the international money markets.

§ 5.23 Common Agricultural Policy

The TFEU establishes the basic principles governing what is perhaps the most controversial of all Union policies, the Common Agricultural Program (CAP). The inclusion of agricultural trade in the Treaty was a critical element to the politics of the Union and remains largely without precedent in other regional economic treaties throughout the world. For many reasons, including the desire for self-sufficiency in food and the protection of farmers, free trade in agricultural products is an extremely sensitive issue. When the Common Market was established in 1957, France and Italy had substantial farming communities, many of which were family based and politically powerful. Both countries envisioned that free trade in agricultural products could threaten the livelihoods of these people. The solution, as outlined in the Treaty, was to set up a "common organization of agricultural markets."

The objectives of the CAP include the increase of productivity, the maintenance of a fair standard of living for the agricultural community, the stabilization of markets, and the provision of consumer goods at reasonable prices. It has not proved possible to accommodate all these objectives. Consumer interests have generally lost out to farmers' incomes and trading company profits. Target prices for some commodities (*e.g.*, sugar, dairy products and grain) are established and supported through Union market purchases at "intervention levels".

"Variable import levies" (tariffs) are periodically changed to ensure that cheaper imports do not disrupt CAP prices. External protection of this type is also extended to meat and eggs. Fruit, vegetables and wine are subject to quality controls which limit their flow into the market. Wine and agricultural products are subject to regulated designations of origin,[212] Rioja wine from Spain[213] and Feta cheese from Greece,[214] for examples. Such regulations do not extend to generic food names, such as edam,[215] jenerver (gin)[216] and emmenthal,[217] which can be freely traded with proper labels indicating variations in product qualities.

Regulatory Controls

In recent years, perhaps the most controversial "common organization" has been for bananas. The Europeans import bananas under a complex quota system adopted in 1993 that favors former colonies and dependencies. Internally and externally, those affected have gone bananas over this regulation. Several challenges originating from Germany failed before the European Court of Justice, but in the end the United States, Mexico, Ecuador, Guatemala and Honduras prevailed in the World Trade Organization. After suffering "authorized retaliation" in the form of tariffs on EU exports, the Europeans adjusted their "common organization" for bananas by replacing its quotas with non-preferential tariffs. The European Agricultural Guidance and Guarantee Fund (better known by its French initials as FEOGA) channels the Union agricultural budget into export refunds, intervention purchases, storage, and structural adjustment. Agricultural policy regulations cannot discriminate against like or substitute products. But the bias towards producers, not consumers, in the CAP has been consistently upheld by the Court of Justice.[218]

Agricultural goods, like industrial products, can trigger free movement litigation. These issues are often raised under Articles 34–36 covered in Chapter 4. In one case, for example, the Court of Justice suggested that British animal health regulations were a disguised restraint on Union trade in poultry and eggs.[219] As with industrial goods, if the real aim is to block imports, such regulations are unlawful measures of equivalent effect to a quota. On the other hand, the United Kingdom could establish a Pear and Apple Development

---

[212] Regulation 823/87 (wine) and Regulation 2081/92 (agricultural products).

[213] *See* Belgium v. Spain, (2000) Eur.Comm.Rep. I–3123.

[214] *See* Denmark v. Commission, (1999) Eur.Comm.Rep. I–1541.

[215] Ministere Public v. Deserbais, (1988) Eur.Comm.Rep. 4907.

[216] Criminal proceedings against Miro BV, (1985) Eur.Comm.Rep. 3731.

[217] Criminal proceedings against Guimont, (2000) Eur.Comm.Rep. I–10663 (Dec. 5, 2000).

[218] Germany v. Commission, (1963) Eur.Comm.Rep. 131; Balkan-Import-Export GmbH v. Hauptzollamt Berlin-Packhof, (1973) Eur.Comm.Rep. 1091 (CAP measures valid unless "obviously unreasonable" consumer prices produced). *See* Article 34(3), Treaty of Rome.

[219] Commission v. United Kingdom, (1982) Eur.Comm.Rep. 2793 (Newcastle disease).

Council for purposes of technical advice, promotional campaigns (not intended to discourage competitive imports), and common quality standards for its members. But it could not impose a mandatory fee to finance such activities.[220]

Apart from variable tariff protection, CAP quality control regulations can serve to keep foreign agricultural products from entering the European Union market. For example, the ban on beef hormones adopted by qualified majority vote in the late 1980s stirred opposition internally.[221] In the United States, the beef hormones legislation was vehemently opposed by the White House, but accepted by the renegade Texas Department of Agriculture which offered as much hormone-free beef to the Union as it would buy. The Texas offer delighted the EU Commissioner on Agriculture who rarely has a U.S. ally and is said to have wired: "I accept."

A veritable maze of legislation and case law governs the CAP. For many years, special agricultural "monetary compensation amounts" (MCAs) have been collected at national borders, greatly contributing to the failure to achieve a Europe without internal trade frontiers. It was not until 1987 that firm arrangements were made to dismantle the MCA system. In most years, the net effect of the CAP is to raise food prices in the EU substantially above world price levels. The CAP has meant that agriculture is heavily subsidized. Indeed, it continues to consume the lion's share of the Union budget and at times seems like a spending policy that is out of control.

The Common Agricultural Policy does include a variety of "structural" programs intended to reduce the size of the farm population, increase the efficiency of its production, and hold down prices. These programs have involved retirement incentives, land reallocations, and training for other occupations. There has been a gradual reduction in the number of EU farmers over the years. In 1988, the Council adopted rules designed ultimately to reduce agricultural expenditures by linking total expenditures to the Union's rate of economic growth, establishing automatic price cuts when production ceilings are reached, and creating land set-aside and environmental protection incentives for farmers.

France and Italy in the early years of the EU, became major beneficiaries of CAP subsidies. West Germany, with a minimal agricultural sector, was the primary payor under the program. It, in turn, principally benefitted from the custom union provisions establishing free trade in industrial goods. Hence a basic tradeoff was

---

[220] The Apple and Pear Development Council v. K.J. Lewis, Ltd., (1983) Eur.Comm.Rep. 4083.

[221] United Kingdom v. Council, (1988) Eur.Comm.Rep. 855.

established in 1957 by the Treaty of Rome. France and Italy would receive substantial agricultural subsidies out of the regional budget while West Germany gained access for its industrial goods to their markets. Germany now holds a 25 percent share of internal EU trade.

Britain, like Germany, saw itself as a net payor under the CAP. It was repeatedly able to negotiate special compensatory adjustments. Greece, Spain, Portugal and Ireland, on the other hand, looked forward eagerly to membership to obtain CAP subsidies. The big cost for CAP followed enlargement of the European Union to include Hungary and Poland, among others. Each enlargement of the Union plugs more farmers into the extraordinary CAP subsidy system. The ten members admitted in 2004 obtained full payments in 2013.

The countries of Central Europe (Romania, Bulgaria, Hungary, Czech Republic, Poland) enjoy CAP subsidies with great relish. In 2019, a lengthy investigative article in the NY Times documented major corruption problems in Central EU member states where political cronies "farm" the CAP subsidies for personal and political benefit. The Commission has promised reforms.

International Ramifications

In the main like the United States, the European Union seems unable to stabilize the level of its agricultural subsidies. This results in overproduction ("butter mountains" and "wine lakes") and frequent commodity trade wars. A significant amount of fraud to obtain CAP subsidy payments has occurred. In 1989, the House of Lords Select Committee on the European Community released a scathing report on subsidy abuses entitled "Fraud against the Community." Others legitimately farm marginal land with lots of fertilizer. The excess produce is stored, used in social welfare programs and frequently "dumped" in cheap sales abroad.

Despite its incredible cost, the CAP remains one of the political and economic cornerstones of the Union. External protests from North America notwithstanding, the CAP is unlikely to disappear. The provocative question much debated in the Uruguay Round of GATT negotiations is whether a mutually satisfactory reduction in the level of North American and European Union subsidies to agriculture can be achieved. In 1992 the Council of Agricultural Ministers agreed as an internal matter to cuts in support prices of 29 percent for cereals, 15 percent for beef and 5 percent for butter. Farmers received direct payments representing the income lost from the price cuts. Further price cuts and direct payments were agreed in 1999. It was hoped that these reductions would reduce EU export subsidies on agricultural goods and international trade tensions. They also supported the argument that the extraordinary level of European subsidization of agriculture was simply not sustainable in cost or EU politics.

European Union agricultural trade restraints are of enormous consequence to North American exporters. Equally significant are EU "export refunds" on agricultural commodities, refunds that affect the opportunities of North American exporters in other parts of the world. The United States has consistently argued (at times successfully) that these refunds violate the GATT rules on subsidies, while at the same time increasing its own export subsidies on agricultural goods. The result has been an agricultural "trade war" between the U.S. and the EU. Each side has sought to outspend the other on agricultural export subsidies in a market that has been wonderful to buyers. Major attempts at a resolution or at least diminishment of the agricultural trade war was undertaken in the Uruguay Round of GATT negotiations during the late 1980s and early 1990s.

Late in 1992, both sides announced the resolution of some subsidies' disputes (notably on oilseeds) and a compromise on the contested Uruguay Round agricultural trade issues. Agreement was reached on a 20 percent mutual reduction in internal farm supports and a 21 percent mutual reduction on export subsidies measured on a volume basis over 6 years using a 1986–90 base period. After a year of French protests and further negotiations, this agreement was formally incorporated into the WTO accords. Under it, the Union has been gradually switching from production and export subsidies to direct income support for farmers and rural businesses. This decoupling of agricultural subsidies from output has steadily progressed and is crucial to the long-term viability of the CAP.

Tensions between Europe and the United States on agricultural trade have diminished (though hardly disappeared), but repeated U.S. Farm Bills threaten to reignite them. Each enlargement of the Union plugs more farmers into the extraordinary CAP subsidy system. The Amsterdam and Nice Treaties notably failed to resolve ongoing disputes over agricultural reform. A last-minute deal in 2002 capped costs at their 2006 level plus 1 percent a year starting in 2007. In theory this will force a gradual winding down of CAP subsidies. Significant efforts are being made to de-couple CAP subsidies from production levels, notably for cotton, tobacco and olive oil. Production quotas for milk were dismantled in 2015, and those for beet sugar in 2017.

Meanwhile, one wonders just how much longer European taxpayers will continue to pay for the CAP.

§ 5.24 Common Fisheries Policy

Unlike agriculture, the Union is a net importer of fish and fish products. Nevertheless, a "common organization" for the fisheries' market in the EU has also been created.[222] Following the lead of other nations, the Union extended its exclusive economic zone to 200 miles offshore in 1977. The most controversial feature of the Common Fisheries Policy (CFP) is the requirement that member states open their waters beyond six (sometimes twelve) miles to each other's fishing fleets to the limit of a "total allowable catch (TAC)" fixed by the Council. The TACs and related technical measures (*e.g.*, minimum fish net sizes) are basically conservation measures. TACs have even been zero for the evanescent herring in extreme years. It is widely perceived that EU fishing quotas are more honored in their breach than their observance.

Each TAC is divided into member state fishing quotas by the nations where the fish are found. Those states are authorized to close a fishery when a quota is exhausted. Fishery quotas are exchangeable as between the member states. Each state is required to record all landings or transfers at sea which are deducted from the country quotas. Commission review and inspection of these records and decisions is undertaken to ensure compliance with Fisheries Policy rules. Numerous cases have come before the European Court of Justice enforcing rights of entry and challenging discriminatory quotas.[223] Even the practice of "quota hopping" and "quota sharing" by registering boats under the national laws of other member states must be tolerated.[224]

The Fisheries Policy was initiated by the original six EC states in 1970 in anticipation of the enlargement to include fishery-rich nations (for whom it has become part of the price of membership). This helps explain why many people in nations like Norway and Iceland shudder at the prospect of joining the Union, and the UK after BREXIT hopes to re-capture its fisheries. The tricky part is that the UK exports most of its catch (crab, herring, salmon, langoustines) and imports most of what it enjoys consuming (haddock, cod, shrimp and tuna). See Chapter 8.

The Common Fisheries Policy also governs the marketing and price of fish in the EU. The Commission sets "official withdrawal prices" for various types of fish. These prices act as a floor to the

---

[222] Council Regulation 2796/81.

[223] Commission v. Ireland, (1978) Eur.Comm.Rep. 417; Regina v. Kirk, (1984) Eur.Comm.Rep. 2689; Commission v. United Kingdom, (1992) Eur.Comm.Rep. I–05785 (Case C–279/89).

[224] Regina v. Secretary of State for Transport, (1990) Eur.Comm.Rep. I–02433 (Case C–213/89).

market. When they are reached, fish producers can withdraw up to twenty percent of their catch and receive Union subsidies. Fish withdrawn in this manner cannot be used for human consumption. As in the agricultural area, the EU can grant export refunds to aid the sale of fish abroad, and it can protect the withdrawal price levels by limiting imports. Structural relief measures have emphasized reductions in the Union's fishing fleet and subsidies for fish farming.

The European Union has numerous international fishery agreements, including one with the United States which primarily accesses U.S. waters and "surplus fish" to EU boats while opening the Common Market to American exports.[225]

§ 5.25 Intellectual Property Rights

The European Union member states are parties to the Paris Convention on the Protection of Industrial Property (1883). The expression "industrial property" is now usually replaced by "intellectual property." This means that each of them grants national treatment rights to citizens of other member states regarding patents and trademarks. The Paris Convention also gives applicants a one year right of priority to apply in other states for patent rights and a six-month right of priority for trademark rights. These priority rights date from the initial home country application. The Paris Convention achieved limited harmonization of EU patent and trademark law.

Article 118 TFEU, added in 2009, authorizes the Council and Parliament acting via "co-decision" to create European intellectual property rights (IPR) and provide for uniform protection of IPR throughout the Union However, Article 118 specifies a unanimous Council vote on language arrangements for European IPR.

Patents and Designs

The 1973 European Patent Convention (EPC)[226] established the European Patent Office (EPO) in Munich. It allows applicants to simultaneously apply for national patent rights in any of the contracting countries. These include all the EU nations, plus a number of other European states. The applicant must meet the requirements for patentability established by the EPC. United States, Japanese and German applicants heavily use the EPC. Unlike the States, patents on business methods and software are ordinarily unavailable. For example, Amazon's "Buy now with 1-Click" patent was rejected in Europe. Challenges to patentability decisions by the EPO can be made within 9 months after granting of the patent. Thereafter, challenges must be made in national courts

225 *See* Council Decision 91/309.

226 113 Int'l Legal Mats. 268 (1974).

subject to national patent laws. The EPC basically presents a one-stop opportunity to obtain a basket of national patents in Europe. It does not foreclose the option of individual national patent applications, and it does not eliminate the expense of translation costs when EPC patents are validated by national authorities.

A long-proposed Patent Convention finally came into force in 2014 as the EU Unitary Patent (UP) regime. It is applicable in all EU member states save Spain and Italy, miffed by the omission of their languages as "official". The UP regime operates in French, German or English through its headquarters in Paris. It can issue or revoke a Common Market patent valid in any contracting state. Transfers and licenses for part of the Union are possible.

The cost-saving UP is an alternative to (but not a replacement for) national patent and European Patent Convention rights. However, the UP requires its signatories to harmonize national patent laws to conform to Unitary Patent rules on infringement, litigation procedures, exhaustion of rights and other issues. A new Unified Patent Court has been created in Luxembourg. By 2021 its centralized jurisdiction will govern infringement and validity disputes concerning national patents, European patents and Unified patents.

Biotechnology patents are mandated by Council Directive 98/44, provided industrial application is possible. The human body, its stem cells and genes are not patentable, nor are processes for cloning human beings or uses of human embryos for industrial or commercial purposes. Plant variety rights are established in Regulation 2100/94.

The protection of semiconductor topographies is regulated by Council Directive 87/54. This directive was adopted in response to U.S. requirements of reciprocity before EU nationals can obtain comparable U.S. rights under the Semiconductor Chip Protection Act of 1984. Topographies that are original ("not commonplace") are protected for ten years. This protection includes the right to prohibit reproduction of the topography and its commercial exploitation. But exclusivity is not preserved when reverse engineering occurs, or a semiconductor product is put on the market by consent. The European Union has not signed the Washington Treaty on protection of microcircuits.

After years of debate, Council Directive 98/71 harmonized national rules on design rights, an area of intellectual property rights law with diverse coverage throughout the EU. Design rights are possible for jewelry, cars, furniture, consumer electronics, machinery, tools, spare auto parts and other products. Such rights last from five to 25 years and may be used to preclude Common Market trade.[227]

Designations of Origin

Unlike the United States, designations of origin are widely protected under EU law, especially regarding wine. Spain, for example, successfully sued Belgium to stop the bottling of bulk "Rioja" wine on origin grounds.[228] Other ECJ judgments have protected "Parma" ham and "Feta" cheese.[229] EU free trade agreements, such as those with Canada, Korea and Mexico, assure protection for EU designations of origin. These agreements could create a potential barrier to U.S. exports of parma ham and feta cheese for example.

Trademarks

Late in 1993, the Council adopted a regulation creating "Community Trademarks." Businesses operating in the European Common Market may now elect to process applications for such marks through the Union's Trademark Office in Alicante, Spain using English, Italian German, French or Spanish language. This presents a streamlined alternative to seeking national trademark registration, in each member state. Any words or symbols[230] capable of distinguishing goods or services are registrable even if exclusively descriptive.[231]

Colors may also be distinctive. But the Lego brick was could not be registered since its shape was necessary to obtain a technical result.[232] Trademarks may be opposed whenever there is likelihood of confusion,[233] there are prior national registrations of the marks

---

227 *See* Consorzio Italiano v. Regie Nationale des Usines Renau H, (1988) Eur.Comm.Rep. 6039.

228 Belgium v. Spain, (2000) Eur.Comm.Rep. I–3123.

229 Prosciutto di Parma v. Asda Stores, (2003) Eur.Comm.Rep. I–5121; Denmark v. Commission, (2005) Eur.Comm.Rep. I–9115 and Germany v. Commission, (2005) Eur.Comm.Rep. I–9115 (Feta cheese).

230 *See* Proctor & Gamble v. OHIM, (2000) Eur.Comm.Rep. II–00265 (Feb. 16, 2000) (shape of soap bar not registrable); Phillips Electronics NV v. Remington Consumer Products Ltd., (2002) Eur.Comm.Rep. I–5475 (3D shapes).

231 *See* Wrigley v. OHIM, (2003) Eur.Comm.Rep. I–12447 (Case C–191/01) (Doublemint gum possibly registrable); Proctor + Gamble Co. v. OHIM, (2001) Eur.Comm.Rep. I–6251 (Baby-Dry possibly registrable). *Compare* Best Buy Concepts v. OHIM, (2003) Eur.Comm.Rep. II–02235 (Case T–220/01) (Best Buy rejected as descriptive mark); Eurcool Logistik GmbH v. OHIM, (2002) Eur.Comm.Rep. II–00683 (Case T–34/00) (Lite not registrable).

232 Libertel Groep BV v. Benelux Merkenbureau, (2003) Eur.Comm.Rep. I–03793 (Case C–104/01); Lego Juris A/S v. OHIM, (2010) Eur.Comm.Rep. (C–48/09) (Lego brick not registrable).

233 *See* Sabel v. Puma, (1997) Eur.Comm.Rep. I–6191; Lloyd v. Schuhfabrik Meyer v. Klijsen Handel, (1999) Eur.Comm.Rep. I–3819 (reasonably well informed and

that have been genuinely used, or on various disqualifying grounds (*e.g.*, generic words).[234] Community Trademarks are valid for 10 years and may be renewed. Any failure to use a mark for 5 years can cause protection to be withdrawn. Hundreds of thousands of EU marks have been issued, many to U.S. businesses. There is a Board of Appeal within the Trademark Office, followed by what have been numerous appeals to the General Court.

In addition, the Council has adopted Directive 89/104. This directive seeks to harmonize some aspects of EU trademark law, but not trademark registration procedures. A summary of its highlights follows. The directive applies to individual trademarks, service marks, collective marks, and guarantee or certification marks. It does not cover trademark rights acquired through use, which is possible in Italy, Ireland and the United Kingdom. A trademark may consist of any "sign" capable of being represented graphically. This includes words, personal names, designs, letters, numerals, and the shape of goods or their packaging, provided that such signs can distinguish the goods or services of one firm from those of others. It may therefore include such things as musical jingles or screen layouts/user interfaces for computer programs (in each case to the extent that third party rights are not infringed).

Article 3 distinguishes between absolute grounds for refusal or invalidity of marks (*e.g.*, marks devoid of distinctive character, contrary to public policy or accepted principles of morality) and relative grounds (*e.g.*, a sign of high symbolic value, particularly a religious symbol). Allowance is made for registered marks which acquire a distinctive character through use. Member states are also permitted to continue to refuse registration on grounds already in force prior to adoption of the directive. Article 4 provides that registration of a mark which is identical or confusingly like one registered nationally or as a regional trademark, or a well-known but unregistered mark, is not allowed.

A common set of infringement criteria are contemplated in Article 5 of the directive. These criteria include presentation of the use of registered trademarks on different classes of goods if detrimental to the distinctive character of the mark. Article 7 provides that the principle of the exhaustion of rights applies.[235] Licensing of marks for limited use or for limited areas is generally permissible. Article 9 states that where a proprietor for an earlier

---

reasonably observant consumer standard); Citigroup v. OHIM, (2008) Eur.Comm.Rep. II–669 (CITI registration denied as free riding on CITIBANK).

[234] *See* DVK v. OHIM, (2000) Eur.Comm.Rep. II–00001 (Jan. 12, 2000).

[235] *See* § 4.5 for a discussion of the principle of exhaustion of intellectual property rights.

trademark has acquiesced for a period of five successive years to the use of a later trademark registered in good faith in that member state while being aware of such use, he or she is no longer entitled to apply for a declaration that the trademark is invalid or to oppose the use of the later trademark. This provision resembles adverse possession. Furthermore, trademark rights can be revoked if the owner has not put the mark to genuine use for five years absent valid reasons for non-use. Use of the mark on exported goods will meet the genuine use requirement.

Copyrights

In November of 1992, the Council adopted Directive 92/100 on minimum 50-year rental and lending rights for copyrighted works. This directive requires the member states to provide authors' and producers' rights to allow or prohibit the rental or lending of original or copied copyrighted works, such as records, videos or films. The concepts of "rental" and "lending" are broadly defined to include any "direct or indirect economic or commercial advantage." Libraries that loan such works to the public at charges which do not exceed operating costs are not deemed to have an "advantage" and therefore are not caught within Directive 92/100.

The member states may override a refusal to lend for cultural promotion and other activities provided they remunerate the rights' holder but cannot override a refusal to rent. Even when there is an assignment of rental rights to record or film producers, the original holder retains an equitable right to remuneration that cannot be waived.

Performers and broadcasters obtain exclusive rights to authorize or deny the fixation of their works and their reproduction and distribution. When broadcasters use sound recordings, a mandatory remuneration scheme is triggered with the funds shared between the record producers and the performers. Exceptions to these exclusive rights may be granted, including private, reportorial, teaching, scientific and ephemeral use. In 1993, the ECJ ruled in a landmark case that Germany could not deny a British performer remedies against distribution of unauthorized CDs of a concert given in the United States. Such a denial was treated as a breach of the general principle of nondiscrimination based on nationality created in the EEC Treaty.[236]

Late in 1993, the Council adopted Directive 93/83 to harmonize copyright and related rights for satellite and cable TV transmissions. The primary goal is to ensure payment for the holders of such rights.

---

[236] Phil Collins v. Imtrat Handelsgesellschaft, (1193) Eur.Comm.Rep. (Cases C–92/92 and C–326/92).

For satellites, commencing in 1995, broadcast rights must be obtained in the country of origin not destination. Prior contracts must be adapted to this rule by the end of 1999. For cable TV, broadcast rights must be negotiated through cooperative bodies representing various categories of rights holders. Unreasonable refusals by broadcasters to retransmit programs by cable were arbitrated until 2003.

The Council also adopted Directive 93/98 to harmonize the duration of copyrights and related rights (*e.g.*, photographs and posthumous works). As from July 1, 1995, all works subject to copyright protection in the Union will last for 70 years after the death of the author. The term is 50 years for neighboring rights. For audiovisual and cinematic works, there was some dispute about who is "the author." Copyright protection for these works will extend for 70 years from the death of the last survivor of the following persons: the principal director, the author of the script, the author of the dialogue and the composer of the music. Directive 2001/84 harmonizes the law of monetary resale rights for artists ("droit de suite").

Directive 2001/29 draws upon the WIPO Copyright Treaty of 1996 and corresponds to the U.S. Digital Millennium Copyright Act of 1998. The Directive is Internet driven, and outlaws possession, making or providing all tools capable of circumventing technological measures intended to protect copyrighted material. In other words, "hackers" beware. Likewise, tampering with copyright management information (that is to say, encryption devices) is prohibited under Directive 2001/29. Remedies may vary among the member states but must be "effective." Some EU members have enacted criminal sanctions, others have limited relief to damages.

TRIPs

The European Union adheres to the WTO Agreement on Trade-Related Intellectual Property Rights (TRIPs), thereby generating substantial uniformity in intellectual property law. The TRIPs Code covers the gamut of intellectual property. On copyrights, there is protection for computer programs and databases, rental authorization controls for owners of computer software and should recordings, a 50-year motion picture and sound recording copyright term, and a general obligation to comply with the Berne Convention (except for its provisions on moral rights).

On patents, the Paris Convention (1967) prevails, product and process patents are to be available for pharmaceuticals and agricultural chemicals, limits are placed on compulsory licensing, and a general 20-year patent term from the date of application is created. United States law, which previously granted 17-year patents from the date of issuance, has been amended to conform. For trademarks, internationally prominent marks receive enhanced protection, the linking of local marks with foreign trademarks is prohibited, service marks become registrable, and compulsory licensing is banned.

In addition, trade secret protection is assisted by TRIPs rules enabling owners to prevent unauthorized use or disclosure. Integrated circuits are covered by rules intended to improve upon the Washington Treaty. Lastly, industrial designs and geographic indicators of alcoholic beverages (*e.g.*, Canadian Whiskey) are also part of the TRIPs regime.

Infringement and anti-counterfeiting remedies are included in the TRIPs, for both domestic and international trade protection. There are specific provisions governing injunctions, damages, customs seizures, and discovery of evidence. Directive 3295/94 implements the Union's remedies against counterfeit and infringing goods, but criminal sanctions are not mandatory.[237] A broad directive on enforcement of intellectual property rights was adopted in 2004.[238] It concerns evidence, injunctions, seizure, damages and related remedies.

§ 5.26 Electronic Commerce Initiative*

The European Union began considering the advent of the "Information Society," and the need to establish a Pan-European information technology infrastructure with the 1994 white paper on "Growth, Competitiveness and Employment: The Challenges and Courses for Entering into the XXIst Century" prepared by former European Commission Vice-President Martin Bangemann. The Bangemann Report led to the establishment of an Information Society Project (now Promotion) Office within the EU,[239] and a series of actions plans to promote the Information Society in Europe. These plans were intended to formulate strategies to change the existing regulatory and legal framework, technical infrastructure, and the cultural attitudes necessary to promote the Information Society. This led most recently to the e-Europe Initiative to further accelerate the development of a European Information Society.[240]

---

[237] Criminal proceedings against X, (2004) Eur.Comm.Rep. I–651 (Case C–60/02).

[238] Directive 2004/48.

* Sections 5.26 through 5.30 were prepared by Professor Andy Spanogle.

[239] *See* "Europe's Way to the Information Society—An Action Plan," COM (94) 347 final, 19.07.1994.

[240] "eEurope—An Information Society for All," COM (99) 687 final, 8.12.1999.

The EU efforts to coherently address the impact of technology on European society results in a very different approach to many of the issues raised by e-commerce than that seen in the United States for example. It is an approach which is inherently multinational and characterized by a conscious effort to harmonize or approximate legal rules throughout the different member countries in the EU. At the same time, it is an approach which also consciously seeks to identify and remove barriers to the development of e-commerce and other Information Society services. Measures related to e-commerce have been central to the various EU action plans.

These measures include the 1997 European Initiative on Electronic Commerce,[241] which focused on primarily on developing infrastructure and protecting consumers' economic and legal interests; the related 1997 Distance Selling Directive;[242] the 1999 Electronic Signature Directive;[243] and most recently the Electronic Commerce Directive in 2000.[244] There are also several other important measures aimed at particular issues, such as Privacy Directives,[245] which have a significant impact upon online transactions but which would not themselves be considered as "enabling" legislation for e-Commerce transactions.

All this said, cross-border e-commerce within the Union is plagued by nontariff trade barriers and buy/sell national proclivities that run deep. Oddly, it is a U.S. online traders like Amazon, eBay and Apple that are the most active E-commerce merchants within the European Union.

§ 5.27 Distance Selling

The Distance Selling Directive is intended to promote European consumer confidence in e-Commerce, by guaranteeing that the local consumer protection laws will apply to contracts concluded at a

---

241 "A European Initiative on Electronic Commerce," COM (97) 157 final, 16.6.1997.

242 Directive 1997/7/EC of the European Parliament and of the Council of 20 May 1997 on the Protection of Consumers in respect of Distance Contracts, *Official Journal L 144, 04/06/1997.*

243 Directive 1999/93/EC of the European Parliament and of the Council of 13 December 1999 on a Community Framework for Electronic Signatures, *Official Journal L 013, 19/01/2000.*

244 Directive 2000/31/EC of the European Parliament and of the Council of 8 June 2000 on certain legal aspects of information society services, in particular electronic commerce, in the Internal Market, *Official Journal L 178, 17/07/2000.*

245 Directive 95/46/EC of 24 October 1995 on the protection of individuals regarding the processing of personal data and on the free movement of such data, *Official Journal L 281, 23.11.1995. See* Directive 2002/58 on privacy in electronic communications.

distance.[246] By relying on the protections of local laws, presumably concerns over the nature and amount of information provided by sellers, the privacy accorded to information provided by consumers, aggressive marketing techniques, and payment fraud resulting from online transactions would be ameliorated. The Directive, however, applies to all types of contracts concluded by any means where the supplier and consumer are not in physical presence including those created by mail, telephone, videophone, radio, fax, and email, for example, and is not confined just to online transactions.[247] Each member state in the EU was required to implement the Directive's requirements in their national law, in this manner the various national laws on distance contracts through the EU "approximate" one another and achieve the same objectives.[248]

The Directive imposes several requirements. Certain types of technologies, such as automated calling machines or faxes, may not be used for unsolicited marketing without prior consent, and others may not be employed over the consumer's objection.[249] Prior to concluding the contract, consumers are to be provided with certain information in "clear and comprehensible form" covering a variety of basic details about the supplier; the cost, terms, and conditions of the transactions; and, significantly, the consumer's right to withdraw or cancel the transaction.[250]

This information must be provided either in writing or in some other "durable" media accessible to the consumer prior to delivery or completion of performance of the contract.[251] Orders placed through distance selling must ordinarily be filled within 30 days.[252] Consumers are typically given 7 business days to withdraw from a distance contract for any reason, with no penalty, and the consumer's reimbursement following withdrawal must be processed within 30 days.[253] If the supplier failed to provide the requisite information in advance of the transaction, the time period for the consumer to exercise this right of withdrawal expands to three months.[254]

---

246 Directive 1997/7/EC of the European Parliament and of the Council of 20 May 1997 on the Protection of Consumers in respect of Distance Contracts, *Official Journal L 144, 04/06/1997.* Directive 2002/65 governs distance selling of consumer financial services such as credit cards, banking, investment funds and pension plans.

247 *Id.*, Art. 2 & Annex 1.

248 *Id.*, Art. 15. EU member nations were given until the end of 2000 to implement the Directive.

249 *Id.*, Art. 10.

250 *Id.*, Art. 4.

251 *Id.*, Art. 5.

252 *Id.*, Art. 7.

253 *Id.*, Art. 6.

254 *Id.*

Not all distance selling transactions are covered, however. There are exemptions for financial services contracts, auctions, immovable property, sales of everyday consumable goods by door-to-door sales agents; accommodation, transport, catering or leisure services for specific dates, and vending machines.[255] Additionally, absent agreement, the consumer's right of withdrawal does not apply to services begun before the expiration of the withdrawal period; commodities whose price fluctuates in financial markets beyond the control of the supplier; certain custom produced/personalized goods; audio/video/software products unsealed by the consumer; periodicals; gaming or lottery services.[256]

Thus, while not exclusively aimed at e-commerce, the Distance Selling Directive imposes specific requirements on e-merchants who will be selling to consumers within the EU. These requirements will affect the nature of the transactions conducted with consumers in Europe, the way they are conducted, and even the design of the online systems by which they are accomplished.

§ 5.28 Electronic Signatures

The Electronic Signature Directive,[257] like the Distance Selling Directive, is aimed at harmonizing the national law among the various member states. The Directive was intended to create a single common legal framework for electronic signatures within the EU.[258] An electronic signature is defined as any "data in electronic form which are attached to or logically associated with other electronic data, and which serve as a method of authentication."[259] This definition is intended to be technologically neutral, and to apply to all forms of electronic signatures. However, the Directive expressly states that it is *not* intended to address national or European legal requirements as to the form or use of documents, nor the conclusion or validity of contracts.[260] It was issued in an effort simply to forestall the proliferation of different standards for electronic signatures and services related to providing such signatures at a time when several nations were considering different approaches and technologies.

The Directive establishes that a signature may not be denied legal effect of validity solely on the grounds that it is in electronic

---

[255] *Id.*, Art. 3.

[256] *Id.*, Art. 6(3).

[257] Directive 1999/93/EC of the European Parliament and of the Council of 13 December 1999 on a Community Framework for Electronic Signatures, *Official Journal L 013, 19/01/2000.*

[258] *Id.*, Art. 1.

[259] *Id.*, Art. 2.

[260] *Id.*, Art. 1.

form.[261] Additionally, member states within the EU are prohibited from imposing obligations which would restrict the free flow of electronic signature services across national borders.[262] In accord with the emphasis on consumer protection in many European measures, the Directive imposes a number of obligations upon general providers of electronic signature services, but not upon those who use electronic signature technologies within their own closed or proprietary systems.[263]

In particular, Certification Service Providers (CSPs), those who provide an "electronic attestation which links signature-verification data to a person and confirms the identity of that person," are to be supervised and regulated in the country where they are established[264] and are liable for the certifications they issue.[265] The establishment of national voluntary accreditation schemes to bolster public confidence in electronic signatures is encouraged,[266] and intended to promote the cross border acceptability of electronic signatures and their accompanying certifications.[267]

§ 5.29 Electronic Commerce

Based upon the aims and objectives stated in the 1997 Initiative,[268] the Electronic Commerce Directive[269] endeavors to establish a more certain and comprehensive legal framework to generally enable e-commerce transactions within the member states of the EU. As such, the Directive covers several issue areas beyond merely electronic contracting,[270] such as rules regarding the establishment of service providers,[271] information to be provided by service providers,[272] information to be provided in connection with commercial communications such as advertising or direct marketing,[273] liabilities of Internet intermediaries,[274] online dispute

261 *Id.*, Art. 5.

262 *Id.*, Art. 4.

263 *Id.*, Preamble (16).

264 *Id.*, Art. 3.

265 *Id.*, Art. 6.

266 *Id.*, Art. 3.

267 *Id.*, Art. 7.

268 "A European Initiative on Electronic Commerce," COM (97) 157 final, 16.6.1997.

269 Directive 2000/31/EC of the European Parliament and of the Council of 8 June 2000 on certain legal aspects of information society services, in particular electronic commerce, in the Internal Market, *Official Journal L* 178, 17/07/2000.

270 *Id.*, § 3.

271 *Id.*, § 1.

272 *Id.*

273 *Id.*, § 2.

274 *Id.*, § 4.

resolution processes,[275] and the general role of national authorities.[276]

Service Providers

There is a general "right of establishment" guaranteed by the treaties establishing the European Union. The Directive clarifies that electronic service providers are "established" where they effectively pursue an "economic activity using a fixed establishment for an indefinite period. The presence and use of the technical means and technologies required to provide the service do not, in themselves, constitute an establishment of the provider."[277] It then continues to generally prohibit member states from requiring prior authorization to establish electronic service provider operations, or from imposing other requirements which do not generally apply to the same services or operations conducted by other means.[278]

However, the use of "codes of conduct" or other voluntary measures established at the Union level with input from appropriate trade, professional, and consumer associations is encouraged.[279] Deviations from the "country or origin" and "mutual recognition" principles which underlie the Directive are permitted for public policy purposes such as crime prevention, combating hate crimes, the protection of minors, and the protection of public health. Any such measures which are imposed must be necessary, proportionate to their objective, and the European Commission has been notified.[280]

Additionally, the Electronic Commerce Directive complements the notice/disclosure provisions of the Distance Selling Directive by requiring that electronic service providers make "easily, directly, and permanently available" certain information such as its name, physical address, email address, a VAT or similar registrations, and any supervisory or professional regulatory bodies to which it might be subject—and that any pricing information which is provided must be clear and unambiguous.[281]

"Commercial communications"[282] are recognized as an integral part of any Information Society service, and subject to special

---

[275] *Id.*, Ch. IV.

[276] *Id.*

[277] *Id.*, Art. 2.

[278] *Id.*, Art. 4.

[279] *Id.*, Art. 16.

[280] *Id.*, Art. 3.

[281] *Id.*, Art. 5.

[282] The Directive generally defines "commercial communications" as "any form of communication designed to promote, directly or indirectly, the goods, services, or image of a company, organization, or person or pursuing a commercial, industrial or craft activity or exercising a regulated profession." *Id.*, Art. 2.

requirements. Advertising, direct marketing and similar communications must be clearly identified as "commercial communications" and identified as to their origin, and any conditions attached to promotional offers must be clearly identifiable and easily accessible.[283] Moreover, unsolicited email solicitations must be "identifiable clearly and unambiguously as such as soon as it is received" and service providers using unsolicited email are required to comply with opt-out registers.[284] Regulated professions, such as lawyers or accountants, are specifically authorized to use electronic commercial communications but remain subject to the rules applicable to their professions.[285]

Service providers who are merely passive conduits for Information Society services supplied by others are generally insulated from any liability, so long as they did not initiate or modify the transmission or the content of the communication, nor select the recipient of the transmission.[286] This immunity specifically extends to caching operations, or the "automatic, intermediate, and temporary storage" of information,[287] hosting operations,[288] or any obligation to engage in general monitoring of the service user's activities.[289] However, nothing in the Directive precludes member states within the EU from requiring that service providers inform the authorities of illegal activities which do come to their attention, or from acting to terminate or prevent an infringement in accordance with local judicial or administrative processes.[290] Internet marketplace providers (eBay) do not "use" or infringe trademarks when they enable unauthorized displays of trademarks by customers selling products.[291]

Means for resolving disputes arising out of the provision of Information Society services are also addressed. In addition to encouraging the formulation of EU-wide voluntary codes of conduct,[292] the member states are directed to ensure that appropriate means for alternative dispute resolution processes exist—both offline and online—particularly for consumer disputes.[293] The member states are also directed to facilitate cross-border cooperation and

---

283 *Id.*, Art. 6.

284 *Id.*, Art. 7.

285 *Id.*, Art. 8.

286 *Id.*, Art. 12.

287 *Id.*, Art. 13.

288 *Id.*, Art. 14.

289 *Id.*, Art. 15.

290 *Id.*, Art. 12(3); 13(2); 14(3); 15(2).

291 L'Oreal v. eBay Int'l, (2011) Eur.Comm.Rep. (Case 324/09).

292 *Id.*, Art. 16.

293 *Id.*, Art. 17.

promote the effective investigation and legal redress of infringements or violations throughout the EU.[294]

Electronic Contracts

At the heart of this framework, however, are the provisions enabling the formation of electronic contracts. Although brief, these provisions are significant in providing a firm basis for e-commerce and expanding upon the foundation established in the Electronic Signature Directive. In Article 9, the Electronic Commerce Directive states that the "Member States shall ensure that their legal system allows contracts to be formed by electronic means."[295] It then continues to specify that national laws should neither create obstacles to the contractual process, nor impede the effectiveness or validity of contracts formed by electronic means.[296] Only four categories are exempted from this mandate: contracts which must be registered with a public authority (*e.g.*, real estate transfers), contracts requiring the use of a notary or similar public authority, contracts governed by family law, or contracts governed by the law of succession.[297] Even within these categories, member states wishing to derogate from the general obligations of Article 9 must notify the Commission, and justify their continued exemption every five years.[298]

Additionally, when contracts are to be concluded electronically, the e-merchant must clearly and unambiguously explain—in advance—the languages in which the contract will be available, the steps involved to form the contract, precisely who will fulfill the contract, and the means for correcting any order entry errors. This information must be made available in a manner that it may be stored and reproduced. The Directive imposes these requirements on all electronic contracts, except those concluded "exclusively" by means of individual communications such as email.[299] Moreover, the Directive also requires that the receipt of orders placed electronically must be acknowledged "without undue delay and by electronic means," and specifically rejects the "mailbox rule" by stating that both orders and acknowledgments are "received" when they are accessible to the recipient.[300] These requirements ordinarily apply equally to consumers and those pursuing a trade, business, or profession—although those who are not consumers may agree to

[294] *Id.*, Arts. 18–20.

[295] *Id.*, Art. 9.

[296] *Id.*

[297] *Id.*, Art. 9(2).

[298] *Id.*, Art. 9(3).

[299] *Id.*, Art. 10.

[300] *Id.*, Art. 11.

dispense with receiving the required information or order acknowledgments.[301]

Reflecting the more comprehensive approach which comes from having a regional authority such as the European Union, the enabling legislation in the EU strives to facilitate the formation of electronic contracts—but does so in the broader context of its efforts to accelerate the formation of an Information Society. Accordingly, it attempts to integrate the issues associated with e-commerce within its plans for an e-Europe.

§ 5.30 Personal Data Protection, and Artificial Intelligence Act

General Data Protection Regulation

The European Convention on Human Rights (see Chapter 1) specifically provides that "everyone has the right to respect for his private and family life, his home and his correspondence." Article 16 TFEU recognizes that "everyone" has the right to protection of personal data. Council Directive 95/46 and its successor Regulation 2016/679 concern data privacy, the General Data Protection Regulation (GDPR).

Under these rules, any information relating to natural persons must be secure, current, relevant and not excessive in content. User location data is also protected. In most cases, personal data may be processed only with the consent of the individual involved. Processing data revealing racial or ethnic origin, political opinions, religious beliefs, philosophical or ethical persuasion, and health or sexual life is rarely permitted without written consent. Posting phone numbers, working conditions and hobbies of people on an Internet page constitutes processing of personal data within the Directive.

Directive 2002/58 concerns privacy and personal data protection in electronic communications including mobile, fixed and Internet communications. The Directive contains a Union-wide ban on sending spam to individuals as well as restraints on installing "cookies" on personal computers without consent. Social networking websites must offer privacy-friendly default settings, limit retention of data on inactive users, delete abandoned accounts, allow pseudonyms, and notify users that pictures should only be uploaded by consent.

Individual Rights

Directive 2016/79 guarantees individual access to processed information and notice of its use. Individuals may object at any time

---

301 *Id.*, Arts. 10(1), 11(1).

to the legitimacy of personal data processing. They may also demand erasure without cost of personal data before it is disclosed to or used by third parties for direct mail marketing. Data processors are required to make extensive disclosures to individuals and to governments. Such disclosure duties, for example, apply to virtually all web sites that invite registration. National authorities are empowered where appropriate to access, erase or block information held by data processors. Private civil liability and public penalty remedies are administered under member state laws, which allow electronic commerce consumers to sue in their countries of residence.

The General Data Protection Regulation mandates greater transparency on the types of data collected, designate a data protection officer, and document and notify individuals of cybersecurity breaches. Noncompliance can result in fines up to 4% of global revenue.

The GDPR details extensive rights for individuals concerning the processing of personal data, including website registrations. Individuals have broad rights to be informed of proposed usages, deny disclosure, require corrections, to disappear data (the "right to be forgotten" held by the ECJ not applicable outside the EU) and, particularly, to object to "direct marketing" use of their data. Violation of these rights can result in public prosecutions and private actions by e-commerce consumers in their country of residence.

However, personal tax data lawfully in circulation in Finland, may be released not just in newspapers but also CD-ROMs and text-messages under "journalistic" privileges. The directive prohibits the transfer of personal data to non-EU countries unless they ensure "an adequate level of protection" of EU-sourced data.

Late in 2020, French privacy regulators slapped large fines on Google and Amazon for violations of *national* e-privacy rules not subject to GDPR centralization of authority, which rests with Luxembourg for Amazon and Ireland for Google. Google's offense involved inadequately seeking individuals' consent and inadequate explanations of use of "cookies". Ireland, as lead enforcement country under the GDPR for Twitter, took two years to substantially fine that company for data privacy violations. Meta in 2023 was fined 1.2 billion Euros for GDPR violations.

Data Transfers, U.S. Safe Harbors

Directives 95/46 and 2016/79 mandate a prohibition against the transfer of personal data to non-member states (like those of North America) that fail to ensure an "adequate level of protection." Hence the adequacy of United States laws offering personal data protection is generally at issue. Exemptions from this scrutiny exist for "unambiguous" consent, when the data is necessary for contract performance between individuals and data processors (*e.g.*, billing), the transfer is legally required or serves "important public interests," the transfer is necessary to protect the individual's "vital interests," or the transfer comes from an open, public register.

Practically speaking, Directives 95/46 and 2016/79 govern most global businesses since it is very difficult to segregate European Union data from that collected elsewhere. Both online and offline data processors fall within its scope. The directive's impact has been felt, for example, in restrictive orders denying U.S. direct mail companies access to European mailing lists. More broadly, the European Commission and the U.S. Department of Commerce have sought to defuse the potentially explosive issue of the "adequacy" of U.S. law on personal data privacy. Early in 2000, agreement was reached to create a "*safe harbor*" for U.S. firms from EU data privacy litigation or prosecution.

To obtain such immunity, U.S. data processors and document storage companies could: (1) formally agree to be subject to regulatory oversight in a member EU state; (2) sign up with a U.S. self-regulating privacy group that is supervised by the U.S. Federal Trade Commission or the Department of Transportation; (3) demonstrate to European satisfaction that relevant U.S. laws were comparable to the EU; or (4) agree to refer privacy disputes to a European panel of data protection authorities. Financial services (including insurance) are not covered by these safe harbor provisions. The European Union adopted standardized financial services contracts clauses that subject U.S. data processors to European jurisdiction and ensure compliance.

Thousands of U.S. companies (Microsoft, Facebook and Google included) signed up with self-regulatory privacy groups (such as BBBOnline) to obtain shelter from EU data privacy law. Some U.S. companies (*e.g.*, Amazon.com) asserted that they were in compliance. Others (*e.g.*, DoubleClick.com) selectively curtailed their use of "cookies" to track online users. A 2009 Directive requires consent before tracking user identities and habits via cookies. Yahoo was the first net provider to allow opting out of such practices. Privacy rights "to be forgotten" by removing personal information from the Internet were added in Directive 2016/79.

Many U.S. companies found and continue to find adoption of EU GDPR rules cost effective. Other U.S. companies sometimes seem blissfully unaware of the scope and intensity of European Union data privacy law, which also impacts corporate E-data retention duties for existing and reasonably foreseeable litigation.

Alarmed after Edward Snowden's data revelations, the European Court of Justice invalidated the Safe Harbor Agreement with the United States in a 2015 judgment. This immediately put thousands of American businesses collecting personal data in Europe and transferring it to the USA under Safe Harbor protection at risk.

Negotiations generated a more rigorous sequel, known as the ***U.S.-EU Privacy Shield Framework.*** This version of a safe harbor allowed U.S. firms to self-certify compliance with EU data privacy law under the supervision of the U.S. International Trade Administration (ITA) of the Department of Commerce. Virtually all U.S. Internet search and vendor companies, and U.S. social media, sought shelter under the Framework.

But the ECJ invalidated the Privacy Shield Framework in 2020. The Court reiterated its concern that Europeans lacked "actionable rights" to challenge protected personal data transfers involving cloud services, human resources, marketing, videoconferencing, advertising, and the like. The ECJ further ruled against contracts many firms employ when sending data out of the EU, indicating such contracts are valid only if they meet the EU's stringent data privacy standards.

In 2022, the European Commission validated the ***EU-U.S. Data Privacy Framework***, *a third attempt* at creating a safe harbor. This agreement relies on the existing U.S. Data Protection Review Court for complaints regarding access to European personal data by U.S. intelligence agencies. Access by those agencies is limited to what is necessary and proportionate to protect U.S. national security. Note that this Framework agreement does not apply to the UK after BREXIT.

Companies processing EU data are required to self-certify to the EU standards via the U.S. Department of Commerce. Those standards include deletion of personal data no longer necessary for the purpose for which it was collected, and ensuring continuity of protection when data is shared with third parties. Enforcement remains with the U.S. Federal Trade Commission. In 2023, the EU Commission determined that U.S. protections under the Data Privacy Framework were "adequate" (essentially equivalent) to those of the GPDR. At this writing, challenges to this decision and the third Safe Harbor agreement are pending in Europe.

Late in 2020, French privacy regulators slapped large fines on Google and Amazon for violations of *national* e-privacy rules not subject to GDPR centralization of authority, which rests with Luxembourg for Amazon and Ireland for Google. Google's offense involved inadequately seeking individuals' consent and inadequate explanations of use of "cookies". Ireland, as lead enforcement country under the GDPR for Twitter, took two years to substantially fine that company for data privacy violations. Meta in 2023 was fined 1.2 billion Euros for GDPR violations.

The huge consumption of training data by Artificial Intelligence (AI) (discussed below) raises major legal questions under the EU's GDPR. First, if there is personal information in the AI training data sets, then AI platforms need consent from all the individuals whose data is collected. Second, can AI firms work around obtaining consent if they can prove a lawful interest to do so? U.S. based Meta is presently "engaged" with Irish Data Protection Commissioner on this issue.

GDPR sanctions are potentially severe: Up to 7% of a company's global annual revenue, or 35 million euros ($38 million). For now, Meta has delayed launching an AI assistant and is barred from doing so in Brazil. California is debating regulation of AI training.

Professor Anu Bradford has acutely observed that the EU's GDPR principles represent a "Brussels effect" under U.S.-EU Safe Harbor agreements.

U.S. State Personal Data Privacy Laws

In some U.S. states, notably California, public and private remedies for breaches of personal data privacy rules are now available. Other U.S. states have begun duplicating California's lead on personal data privacy regulation.

EU Artificial Intelligence Act

In 2024, the EU enacted a pathbreaking technology regulation . . . an Artificial Intelligence Act driven once again by U.S. developments such as ChatGPT. The Act requires revelation of the data used to train AI models and ranks levels of AI risk as prohibited, high, limited and minimal. Use of AI in the EU triggers regulatory jurisdiction with enforcement penalties based on annual worldwide turnovers. It is not clear whether the EU AI Act will have a Brussels effect in America along the lines of the EU GDPR (above).

The EU AI Act prohibits the use of AI systems that manipulate people's behavior, for example emotion-recognition systems in workplace or education settings. The Act also prohibits biometric-categorization systems that infer personal characteristics such as religious beliefs, political opinions or sexual orientation. Disclosure rules regarding AI training models apply, and AI-generated content must be identified or watermarked.

The EU Act extends to AI systems that make decisions about job or school applicants, and systems used to evaluate workers and students. Likewise, the Act covers decision-making about an individual's creditworthiness or insurance risk. Moreover, the Act applies to systems used by judicial authorities to research and interpret facts and law, and systems used in alternative dispute resolution.

Chapter 6

EU INTERNATIONAL TRADE AND FOREIGN INVESTMENT LAW

Table of Sections

This chapter makes considerable reference to World Trade Organization (WTO) agreements and procedures as the source of EU trade rules. For more coverage of the WTO's global trade regime, please see my Concise Hornbook on *International Trade Law.*

§ 6.0 EU Common Customs Law

Articles 206–207 of the Treaty on the Functioning of the European Union (TFEU) concern trade between the European Union and third countries. These articles vest in the European Union control over external commercial relations, a power completely absent from the NAFTA/USMCA agreements. This is referred to as the Union's "common commercial policy," and it covers both imports and exports. Article 207 provides some illustrative examples of the wide scope of this policy, including tariffs, quotas, trade agreements, export controls, dumping and subsidies. For example, its common rules on exports[1] generally authorize free exportation of Union products, subject to security (oil and defense) and environmental exceptions. The Common Commercial Policy can also involve the application of international boycott sanctions.[2] The 1993 Treaty on European Union added provisions intended to promote cooperation among the member states and the Union on aid to developing nations.[3]

The European Court of Justice has ruled that the member states cannot enact external commercial policy laws without "specific authorization."[4] In this field, the Union should be supreme. Operationally speaking, however, this is not always the case. This is illustrated by the following discussion of national import quotas, voluntary export restraints and "mixed" trade agreements. Surrendering national sovereignty over external commercial relations is a most sensitive area.

Customs Union

As regards customs law, which is invariably involved in any trade transaction with the Union, the relevant provisions are Articles 28–32 TFEU. The basic principle is that the EU is a customs union,[5] with a directly applicable[6] prohibition of national customs duties and measures having an equivalent effect on internal trade. The EU also has a common customs tariff. Thus, once goods have cleared customs in any member state they are released for "free circulation", moving throughout the Union without incurring any further tariffs or any other equivalent charges. Equivalent charges are understood to comprise any pecuniary charge, however small and whatever its designation and mode of application, which is imposed unilaterally on domestic or foreign goods by reason of the fact that they cross a

---

1 *See* Council Regulations 2603/69, 1934/82.

2 Article 215, TFEU. *See* Bosphorus Hava Yollari Turizim Ve Ticaret AS v. Minister for Transport, Energy and Communication, (1996) Eur.Comm.Rep. I–3953 (Serbia boycott).

3 *See* Articles 208–211, TFEU.

4 Criel and Schou v. Procureur de la République, (1976) Eur.Comm.Rep. 1921.

5 *See* Article XXIV(8)(a) GATT 1994:

"A customs union shall be understood to mean the substitution of a single customs territory for two or more customs territories, so that

(i) duties and other restrictive regulations of commerce . . . are eliminated with respect to substantially all the trade between the constituent territories of the union or at last with respect to substantially all the trade in products originating in such territories, and

(ii) substantially the same duties and other regulations of commerce are applied by each of the member of the union to the trade of territories not included in the Union".

6 Van Gend en Loos v. Nederlandse Administratie der Belastingen, (1963) Eur.Comm.Rep. 1, 13.

frontier, and which is not a customs duty in the strict sense.[7] Hence products originating in third countries enjoy the same status as goods originating in a member state for purposes of internal trade.

In addition, U.S. exporters to any of the member states will pay the same customs duties, regardless of the port of entry. This is different from NAFTA/USMCA arrangements, which establish a free trade area[8] exclusively for products originating in North America, with no common external tariff. Canada, Mexico and the U.S. have retained different tariff levels and law, and the right to pursue their own international trade agreements.

Customs Code

The customs law of the EU had been dispersed and shattered in some 25 individual directives and regulations. In a major codification effort all these texts were consolidated and further developed in a Common Customs Code which entered into force on Jan. 1, 1994.[9] This Code includes coverage of customs clearance procedures, customs warehouses and free trade zones, duty free entry for processing and re-export (inward processing arrangement), duty free entry of components of Union origin that have been processed abroad (outward processing arrangement), classification, valuation, origin, payment and customs' bonds. Judicial review of decisions of the national customs authorities must be allowed by a national court capable of referring questions of EU law to the European Court of Justice under Article 267 TFEU.[10] The EU follows the 1999 Kyoto Convention on modernized customs procedures.

§ 6.1 EU Customs Law: Tariffs, Classification, Valuation, Origin and Quotas

Tariffs

The Common Customs Tariff (CCT), now called the Combined Nomenclature (CN), has been steadily reduced over the years under the GATT/WTO tariff Rounds. After the Tokyo Round (1978), EU tariffs on manufactured goods dropped on average to about 8

---

7 Commission v. Italy, (1969) Eur.Comm.Rep. 193, 201.

8 *See* Article XXIV(8)(b) GATT 1994.

"A free-trade area shall be understood to mean a group of two or more customs territories in which the duties and other restrictive regulations of commerce... are eliminated on substantially all the trade between the constituent territories in products originating in such territories."

9 Council Regulation 2913/92, O.J. L 302/1 (October 19, 1992); implementing provisions have been promulgated by Commission Regulation 2454/93, O.J. L 253/1 (October 11, 1993) as amended last by Commission Regulation 2193/94, O.J. L 235/6 (September 9, 1994).

10 Article 243, Common Customs Code.

percent.[11] Under the Uruguay Round WTO regime[12] it dropped even further: On aggregate the weighted average Union tariff on industrial products was cut from 6.8 to 4.1 percent, a reduction of 37 percent. In some sectors (construction equipment, medical and pharmaceutical equipment, furniture, steel, agricultural equipment, paper, toys, beer and spirits) duties will disappear entirely. Even so, most imported goods enjoy more preferential tariff status under various EU trade agreements and programs. See the coverage of the GSP, Lomé/Cotonou Convention and Mediterranean Policy below.

Member states may not alter the common customs tariff by unilaterally imposing additional duties.[13] The CN is supplemented by tariff rate quotas, tariff preferences, antidumping and other special duties, all of which are reported in the "Taric." These duties are established by EU law, but it is the member states that apply the rules and collect Union tariffs. These revenues are forwarded by the national customs' services to the Commission less a 10 percent administrative charge. Litigation concerning European Union customs law therefore tends to originate in national tribunals as importers dispute classification, valuation and origin issues. These EU law issues are then typically referenced to the Court of Justice for resolution under Article 234.

The Combined Nomenclature details a tariff schedule that makes two fundamental distinctions. Goods admitted into the Common Market are subject to either "Autonomous" or "Conventional" duties. The Autonomous Duties represent the original 1968 CCT tariffs and are higher than the Conventional Duties which are the Union's current most-favored-nation (MFN) tariffs as negotiated within the GATT/WTO. For most exports to the EU, including nearly all those from the United States, the MFN rates of duty are applied. The various duty-free entry programs to which the Union subscribes[14] will almost never apply to goods originating in either Canada or the United States. Mexican exports, in contrast, benefit from EU-Mexico free trade agreements (2000, much expanded in 2020).

New members are usually phased into the EU customs union rules and tariffs over a transitional period. Portugal and Spain, for example, were only fully aligned at the end of 1992. The member

---

11 *See* Council Regulation 2658/87 (Schedule of Customs Duties).

12 Agreement establishing the World Trade Organization, Annex 1A (Multilateral Agreements on Trade in Goods) No. 1 (General Agreement on Tariffs and Trade 1994) Schedule LXXX (European Communities).

13 Sociaal Fonds voor de Diamant Arbeiders v. NG Indiamex, (1973) Eur.Comm.Rep. 1609.

14 *See* Sections 6.2, 6.9, 6.10.

states that joined the Union in 1995, however, were immediately integrated into the customs union. The ten new members joining in 2004, and Romania and Bulgaria (2007) were phased into the customs union over an extended period of years.

The common customs law of the European Union also includes regulations targeting counterfeit goods. Such goods may not be imported into the Union, nor freely circulated within it. They are subject to seizure by national customs authorities. The definition of counterfeit goods contained in this regulation refers to goods bearing marks without authorization. Thus, the regulation does not apply to trade in "gray market goods" (those produced abroad under license). The Union also operates a computerized, encoded data network known as the Customs Information System (CIS) to help combat fraud and illegal trading (especially in drugs). Customs officials at all points of entry and exit may communicate with each other, central authorities, and the Commission.

Classification

In its customs classification system,[15] the European Union follows the International Convention on the Harmonized Commodity Description and Coding System[16] created by the Customs Cooperation Council. Over 100 countries representing more than 80 percent of world trade adhere to this system. This generally corresponds to the classifications found in the Harmonized Tariff System (HTS) adopted by the United States in 1988. Starting in 1993, the Union instituted a binding tariff classification system based upon mutual recognition of classification decisions made by national customs authorities. Whenever an importer requests and obtains such a binding tariff information ("BTI"; Articles 11–12 Common Customs Code), it applies to imports of the same product in all other member states. This process reduces the number of divergent tariff classifications, particularly regarding trade sensitive textiles and electronics. That said, EU classification decisions regarding "art" versus "goods" have proven controversial and costly not only as to tariffs, but also VAT taxation.[17]

Nevertheless, there are recurrent instances where despite the general obligation to interpret the Combined Nomenclature uniformly the national authorities stick to their traditional views.[18] Products can end up being classified differently depending on the

---

[15] Council Regulations 1445/72, 2658/87.

[16] Council Decision 87/369, O.J. L 198/1 (July 20, 1987).

[17] *See* EU Regulation No. 731/2010 (light sculptures treated as fixtures increasing VAT from 5 to 20%).

[18] *See, e.g.,* Peacock AG v. Hauptzollamt Paderborn, (2000) Eur.Comm.Rep. I–08947 (Oct. 19, 2000).

member state where the release for free circulation is applied for. It is advisable, therefore, to check whether a particular product should not be imported via another member state when problems arise due to an unfavorable interpretation of the Combined Nomenclature by a national customs administration. The purpose of a binding tariff information is not just that if presented upon import the customs authorities are bound by it, but also that there may not be any post-clearance recovery of duties in case of an incorrect classification or a change of classification. The BTI, if used, offers substantial protection for an importer. It is issued upon request and is subject to judicial review by the competent judicial authorities of the member state[19].

Valuation

The valuation of goods for purpose of assessing the CN is presently done according to the GATT/WTO Customs Valuation Code.[20] This means that in most instances arms-length transaction value is the basis for tariff assessments, subject to various adjustments.[21] One notable difference between EU and U.S. implementation of the Valuation Code concerns international freight and insurance charges. Unlike the United States, the Union includes such charges in the customs value of goods subject to its common external tariff. Purchasing agents' commissions are not included in customs values for purposes of collecting the common external tariff[22] nor are export permit or quota charges[23] (irrespective of whether the quota is traded legally[24] and unless the charges concern quotas obtained from third parties[25]), weighing charges,[26] and separately invoiced intra-Union transport charges.[27] A leading case discusses

---

[19] Article 243, Common Customs Code.

[20] Articles 28–36, Common Customs Code; the Customs Valuation Code was revised during the Uruguay Round Negotiations.

[21] *See* Hauptzollamt Hamburg-Ericus v. Van Houten International GmbH, (1986) Eur.Comm.Rep. 447 (Costs of weighing imports on arrival excluded from transaction value); Hauptzollamt Schweinfurt v. Mainfrucht Obstverwertung, (1985) Eur.Comm.Rep. 3909 (Costs of internal EC transport that are separately invoiced excluded).

[22] Hauptzollamt Karlstruhe v. Gerbr Hepp & Co Kg, (1991) Eur.Comm.Rep. 4319 (Case 299/90); Hans Sommer GmbH & Co. KG v. Hauptzollamt Bremen, (2000) Eur.Comm.Rep. I–08989 (Oct. 19, 2000).

[23] Ospig Texilgesellschaft KG W. Ahlers v. Hauptzollamt Bremen-Ost, (1984) Eur.Comm.Rep. 609; Malt, (1990) Eur.Comm.Rep. 1482.

[24] Ospig Textil-Gesellschaft W. Ahlers GmbH & Co. KG v. Hauptzollamt Bremen-Freihafen, (1994) Eur.Comm.Rep. I–1963 (Case C–29/93).

[25] Klaus Thierschmidt GmbH v. Hauptzollamt Essen, (1994) I–3905 (Case C–340/93).

[26] Hauptzollamt Hamburg-Ericus v. Van Houten International GmbH, (1986) Eur.Comm.Rep. 447.

[27] Hauptzollamt Schweinfurt v. Mainfrucht Obstverwertung, (1985) Eur.Comm.Rep. 3909.

when computer software is part of the value of imported "goods" subject to the common customs tariff.[28]

Careful analysis of European Union law and an appropriate structuring of export transactions is particularly required regarding customs value questions concerning licensing fees. Article 32(1)(c) Common Customs Code provides that such fees must be added to the price paid or payable if the buyer must pay them as a condition of sale of the imported goods and to the extent that they are not yet included in the price. This means that, *e.g.*, in the case of fees paid in respect of the right to use a trademark, such fee may only be added to the price if

— The goods are resold in the same state or after minor processing,

— The goods are marketed under the trademark, and

— The buyer is not free to obtain the goods from other suppliers unrelated to the seller.[29]

In cases where the licensing fees do not have to be added to the price it is essential that the fees are invoiced separately.

Origin

As a general matter, the Union determines the origin of goods in accordance with the 1973 Kyoto Convention[30], which has not been ratified by the United States. According to the Common Customs Code a product originates either in the country where it was wholly obtained or produced[31] or—in case of a production process involving raw materials or semi-finished products from various countries—where the last, substantial, economically justified processing or working took place in an enterprise equipped for that purpose and resulting in the manufacture of a new product or representing an import stage of manufacture.[32]

This is usually the case where a change in the tariff heading occurs, *i.e.*, where the finished product is to be classified in another heading of the Combined Nomenclature as compared to the classification of the raw materials or of the semi-finished products. A process is "economically justified" if it adds value or provides

[28] *See* Brown Bover & CIE AG v. Hauptzollamt Mannheim, (1991) Eur.Comm.Rep. 1884 (Case C–79/89); *see now* Article 167, Commission Regulation 2913/92.

[29] Article 159, Commission Regulation 2913/92.

[30] Council Decision 75/199, O.J. L 100/1 (April 21, 1975) and O.J. L 166/1 (April 21, 1977).

[31] Article 23, Common Customs Code.

[32] Article 24, Common Customs Code.

commercial advantages. A process or operation is "substantial," for these purposes, only if the resulting product has its own properties and composition.[33] Cleaning, grinding, grading, and packaging a raw material do not meet this standard.[34] If the change in tariff heading approach to origin is insufficient, a "value added" analysis is pursued. This analysis focuses on the value added to the product in the claimed country of origin. Ten percent is insufficient to confer country of origin status.[35]

Specific "rules of origin" exist for semiconductors,[36] photocopiers,[37] radio and television receivers,[38] tape recorders,[39] and ball bearings[40] as well as a number of other products.[41] Most of these specific rules of origin relate to EU dumping law.[42] Rules of origin are critical to duty free or preferential entry of goods from Cotonou Convention, Mediterranean Basin or GSP developing nations as well as from EFTA countries or countries of Central and Eastern Europe.[43] Generally speaking, the rules of origin associated with these programs focus on changes in tariff headings as the determining factor. But many unique product-specific rules of origin are also created, and these often stress value added approaches. The most generous of these rules of origin apply to Cotonou exports to the EU where, for example, any Union contribution may be counted as from a Cotonou nation for purposes of value-added calculations, so-called cumulation.

Special rules of origin and EU content requirements apply to high-technology products like printed circuit boards, integrated circuits and the like. These rules often have the purpose and effect of transferring technology and production to the European Union. Processed EFTA exports originate therein and may be freely traded to the EU under rules that emphasize a change in tariff heading.

---

33 Gesellschaft für Überseehandel v. Handelskammer Hamburg, (1977) Eur.Comm.Rep. 41.

34 *Id.*

35 Brother International GmbH v. Hauptzollamt Giessen, (1989) Eur.Comm.Rep. 4253.

36 Council Regulation 288/89.

37 Council Regulation 2071/89.

38 Council Regulation 2632/70.

39 Council Regulation 861/71.

40 Council Regulation 1836/78.

41 Eggs (Council Regulation 2448/90), spare parts (Council Regulation 37/70), meat and meat products (Council Regulation 3620/90), clothing, shoes and textiles (Council Regulation 1365/91), ceramics (Council Regulation 2025/73) and grape juice (Council Regulation 2883/90).

42 *See* § 6.5.

43 *See* §§ 6.2, 6.9 and 6.10.

The many variations on the origin of goods contained in European trade agreements, including the 2021 Trade and Cooperation Agreement with Britain post BREXIT (see Chapter 8), make these rules particularly complex. A product from one country that fails to meet one of the specialized or preferential rules of origin governing entry into the Common Market will be judged under the general rule of origin discussed above.

Quotas

Until the completion of the internal market on January 1, 1993, a complicated system of import quotas for individual member states existed for various products, notably for automobiles from Japan as well as bananas. The elimination of controls at the Union's internal borders necessitated a harmonization of all European Union import and customs quotas. Regrettably this has not always resulted in liberalized access to the EU market, but in some cases the Union has introduced new regimes which make it more difficult to export to the European Union. A particularly prominent example is the Common Market Organization for bananas,[44] which although incompatible with the GATT according to the findings of GATT/WTO panels, was upheld by the European Court of Justice.[45] It resulted in discriminatory foreclosure of the Union market for Latin American bananas, which previously could be imported freely into Germany and the Benelux countries.

Since the exporters of bananas most adversely affected by the EU regime of trade restraints are U.S. multinationals, the United States was authorized by the WTO to retaliate against EU exports and did so by imposing substantial tariffs. Ecuador and other banana producers were authorized by the WTO to "cross-retaliate" by not paying intellectual property royalties to EU parties. This remarkable remedy was never utilized, but its authorization generated in 2001 a settlement of the "bananas dispute". The EU replaced its quotas with a non-preferential tariff scheme.

The EU-UK Trade and Cooperation Agreement of 2021 provides for quota-free trade, a first for the EU. See Chapter 8.

Counterfeit Goods

The common customs law of the European Union also includes Council Regulation 3842/86 targeting counterfeit goods. Such goods may not be imported or freely circulated. They are subject to seizure by national customs authorities. The definition of counterfeit goods

---

44 Council Regulation 404/93 and Commission Regulation 1442/93.

45 Germany v. Council, (1994) Eur.Comm.Rep. I–4973 (Case C–280/93).

contained in this regulation refers to goods bearing marks without authorization.

The Commission also operates a computerized, encoded data network known as the Customs Information System to help combat fraud and illegal trading (notably drugs). Customs officials at all points of entry and exit communicate with each other state authorities and the Commission. Millions of counterfeit goods have been seized, with China their major source and cigarettes the number one item.

§ 6.2 EU Customs Law: Generalized Tariff Preferences (GSP)

The European Union participates in the generalized system of tariff preferences (GSP) initiated within the GATT/WTO to give duty free access to industrial markets for selected goods coming from the developing world. This policy is implemented in the common customs tariff regulations.[46] The Central European countries were added to the Union's GSP list for the interim period between the collapse of the Communist regimes and the entry into force of the free trade and economic association agreements concluded with the EU.[47] The countries of the former USSR are GSP beneficiaries until any free-trade agreement with them comes into force, and provided they undertake to open their markets to developing-country exports.

Approximately 150 non-European developing nations now benefit from the GSP trade preferences of the EU, including China. Burma was suspended from the EU program in 1997 for human rights concerns but has since re-qualified. Since 1998, goods from South Korea, Hong Kong and Singapore no longer qualify. Similarly, the Four Dragons were "graduated" (*i.e.*, no longer treated as developing nations) out of the United States' GSP program in 1989. Brazil, Argentina and Uruguay have also been graduated.

A revised GSP regime entered into force in 1995. A solidarity mechanism was introduced and applicable in exceptional circumstances: Beneficiary countries whose exports of products covered by the GSP in a given sector exceed 25 percent of all beneficiaries' exports of those products in that sector will be excluded from GSP entitlement for that sector irrespective of their level of development.[48] In addition sector/country graduation was introduced on the basis of relative specialization (ratio of a beneficiary country's share of total Union imports in a given sector), coupled with a

---

46 *See* O.J. 1993 C–169/1.

47 GSP status has also been granted to the successor states of former Yugoslavia.

48 Commission Document COM (94) 337 final of September 19, 1994.

development weighing (development index, combining a country's per capita income and the level of its exports as compared with those of the Union). Both mechanisms were phased in gradually to keep within the framework of overall neutrality.

In 2001, the EU began phasing in complete duty-free access for the world's poorest 49 countries, a program known as "Everything But Arms". Special duty-free preferences have been granted to developing countries that combat illegal drug production. Pakistan received this status, over strenuous objections by India before the World Trade Organization. The WTO Appellate Body rejected the EU scheme in 2004 as discriminatory, and in breach of the Enabling Clause.

Subsequent EU amendments continued special duty-free tariff status for countries implementing 27 international conventions related to human and labor rights, the environment and good governance (including drug trafficking). Pakistan remains ineligible for special treatment. The WTO Appellate Body upheld the EU scheme in 2004.

The European Union system of generalized tariff preferences is selectively applied when about 130 "sensitive products" are involved. In other words, there are limitations (quotas and tariff ceilings) on duty-free access to the Common Market if the goods compete with Union manufacturers However, these GSP limitations do not apply to products already receiving duty free access under the Cotonou Convention or the Union's Mediterranean Policy.[49] Nations that are covered by the latter trade rules still obtain some margin of preference over other third world GSP beneficiaries.

§ 6.3 EU Customs Law: Safeguard Proceedings and Voluntary Trade Restraints

European Union commercial policy regulations establish common rules for imports and exports. These rules authorize "escape clause" (safeguard) measures to curb exports in the face of shortages, or to curb surging imports that threaten serious injury to similar EU products.[50] Special rules apply to escape clause proceedings when the imports are from state-trading countries.[51] European Union escape clause law on imports is derived from Article XIX of the GATT and the WTO Safeguards Agreement (1994). The counterparts in U.S. law are found in Sections 201 and 406 of the Trade Act of 1974.[52] Use of

---

49 *See* §§ 6.9, 6.10.

50 Council Regulation 3285/94.

51 *Id.*

52 319 U.S.C.A. §§ 2261, 2436.

escape clause relief triggers a duty to compensate WTO trade partners.

The protective measures authorized by the EU escape clause regulations may include tariffs, quotas, and more controversially, agreements with exporting nations to voluntarily control the flow of certain goods into the Union *or* EU nations. Such "voluntary export restraints" (VERs) have been used by the Union on consumer electronics, machine tools, food products and steel imports. The Union itself has "voluntarily" restrained the export of steel to the United States. After much effort, and adherence to the WTO escape clause agreement, Europe has greatly reduced its dependence upon VERs as a means of protection against import competition. Unlike the United States, Europe has generally refrained from frequent invocation of escape clause relief.

§ 6.4 EU Customs Law: Foreign Country Trade Barriers

Another area of the Common Commercial Policy was commenced in 1984 in response to efforts (ultimately withdrawn) by the Reagan Administration at limiting participation of European licensees of United States technology in the Siberian natural gas pipeline project. This was sometimes called the "new commercial policy" and is now embodied in the Trade Barriers Regulation No. 3286/94. It covers situations not subject to escape clause, dumping or subsidy proceedings.[53] Regulation 3286/94 concerns "obstacles to trade" by foreign *countries* and roughly approximates Section 301 of the U.S. Trade Act of 1974.[54]

When countries engage in practices that are incompatible with international agreement (*e.g.*, the GATT/WTO agreements), adversely affect a petitioner's trade and it is in the Union's interest to act, the EU may undertake international dispute settlement procedures and (possibly) retaliatory measures. The latter can include raising tariffs, suspending trade concessions or imposing quotas. Private parties can file "market access" complaints with the Commission to initiate examination of alleged obstacles to trade. Negative decisions by the Commission may be appealed to the Court of Justice.[55]

---

53 *See* §§ 6.3, 6.5 and 6.6.

54 19 U.S.C.A. § 2411.

55 FEDIOL v. Commission, (1989) Eur.Comm.Rep. 1781.

§ 6.5 EU Customs Law: Antidumping Duties

Another part of the Common Commercial Policy concerns unfair trading practices applied to goods *exported* to the Union. The two most important areas of law here concern dumping and subsidies.[56] Unlike NAFTA/USMCA, the European Union has eliminated antidumping and countervailing duties internally among its members. Similar rules apply to unfair shipping services used to bring goods to the Union.[57] In recent years, European Union use of antidumping proceedings to protect its market has risen substantially. EU companies with at least 25% of their market sector must support a dumping complaint. Nearly half of these proceedings involve goods from nonmarket economy states (NMEs).

Apart from NMEs, Chinese, Japanese and United States exports have most frequently been involved in Union antidumping proceedings. Many of these proceedings are settled by promises of the exporters to raise prices and refrain from "dumping." The standing of most exporters and complainants to challenge EU dumping decisions has been affirmed by the European Court.[58] Such persons would otherwise lack any possible judicial remedy. Importers, on the other hand, have remedies in the national courts of the member states and are therefore generally unable to challenge EU dumping decisions directly before the European Court.[59] However, importers who are end-users of the product in question and seriously affected by the antidumping duties may challenge antidumping determinations under Article 230.[60]

Dumping involves selling abroad at a price that is less than the price used to sell the same goods at home (the "normal" or "fair" value). To be unlawful, dumping must threaten or cause material injury to an industry in the export market, the market where prices are lower. Dumping is recognized by most of the trading world as an unfair practice (akin to price discrimination as an antitrust offense). Dumping is the subject of a special GATT/WTO code which establishes the basic parameters for determining when dumping exists, what constitutes material injury and the remedy of

---

56 Council Regulations 384/94 and 3284/96.

57 Council Regulation 4057/86.

58 Allied Corp. v. Commission, (1984) Eur.Comm.Rep. 1005 (named exporters may challenge imposition of dumping duties); Timex Corp. v. Council and Commission, (1985) Eur.Comm.Rep. 849 (complainant may challenge antidumping decisions).

59 Alusuisse Italia v. Council and Commission, (1982) Eur.Comm.Rep. 3463.

60 Extramet v. Council, (1991) Eur.Comm.Rep. 2527 (Case C–49/88); Nashua Corp v. Commission, (1990) 1 Eur.Comm.Rep. 719.

antidumping tariffs.[61] Such tariffs can amount to the margin of the dump, *i.e.*, the difference in the price charged at home and (say) the European Union.

Dumping Determinations

"Normal value" under Union dumping law is first defined as the comparable price actually paid or payable in the ordinary course of trade for the like product intended for consumption in the exporting country or country of origin. The Commission usually considers all sales made in the period under investigation (typically 12 months). It requires that the domestic sales exceed 5 percent of the export sales to be considered representative and this threshold has been upheld by the European Court of Justice.[62] However, only sales made in the ordinary course of business enter the calculation. Transactions between related or compensated parties may not be considered in the ordinary course of trade unless the Commission believes they are comparable to arms-length dealings. Sales below cost, for example, are regularly excluded from the Commission's determination of normal value and may trigger "constructed value" determinations if they exceed 20 percent of the sales under consideration.

If there are no sales of the like product in the ordinary course of trade on the domestic market of the exporting country or such sales are inadequate to permit a proper comparison, the Commission turns to (1) the "comparable price" of the product as exported to another surrogate country or (2) its constructed value. The constructed value methodology is often used on Chinese imports. It involves calculation of production costs plus a reasonable profit. The costs of production include materials, components and manufacturing costs, as well as sales, administrative and other general expenses. The Commission need not follow the exporter's accountings in making these calculations but must give priority to the records kept by the producers/exporters and to actual data in determining costs. In addition, the Commission adjusts for start-up operations. A profit margin of 10 percent is used.

If the goods are from nonmarket economies, a status some Central and East European countries have finally escaped, the Commission has three options for determining normal value. These are utilization of a price derived from the sale of a like product in a market country, a constructed value price based on the costs of a producer in a market country or (if needed) the price actually paid in the Union adjusted to include a reasonable profit margin. The choice

---

[61] *See* the Agreement on Implementation of Article VI of the GATT (1979) (Antidumping Code) and the Agreement on Implementation of Article VI of the General Agreement on Tariffs and Trade 1994 (WTO Antidumping Code).

[62] Goldstar v. Council, (1992) Eur.Comm.Rep. I–677.

of the "market economy third country" for purposes of normal value determination must be based on sufficient reasons and objections of parties to the investigation must be considered if they are substantiated. The failure to take them into consideration will result in the quashing of the Regulation imposing antidumping duties by the European Court of Justice[63].

Once a normal value for the goods is established by the Commission, the export price is determined. This is defined as the price actually paid or payable for the product sold for export to the Union. Relatively speaking, this calculation is less controversial except when the producer sells through its own subsidiary. In such cases the Commission practice has been to calculate the export price based on the price at which the good is first resold to an independent buyer, and deductions (adjustments) are made both for direct and indirect expenses. The normal value, however, is adjusted only for costs which are directly related to the sales. As a result, the export price is necessarily inferior to the normal value.

This asymmetrical approach has repeatedly been upheld by the European Court of Justice[64]. In addition, certain adjustments must be made to the normal value and export prices so calculated. These adjustments reflect differences in physical attributes, import charges, indirect taxes and selling expenses. The object of making these adjustments is to arrive at comparable "ex-factory" price calculations.

The EU dumping margin is the difference between the adjusted normal value and the adjusted export price. It is established by the Union institutions by comparing a weighted average normal value with individual export transactions,[65] thus excluding so called negative dumping margins, *i.e.*, the effect of export sales above the normal value upon the calculation of a weighted average export price. This dumping margin ultimately determines the maximum extra duty the EU importer must pay provided there also is material injury to an EU industry and the Commission decides that imposing the duty would be in the Union's interest. This "public interest" determination typically pits EU consumer interests against industrial interests. The manufacturers usually win out, but

---

63 Nölle v. Hauptzollamt Bremen-Freihafen, (1991) Eur.Comm.Rep. 5163.

64 Nippon Seiko v. Council, (1987) Eur.Comm.Rep. 1923; Canon and others v. Council, (1988) Eur.Comm.Rep. 5731; Matsushita Electric v. Council, (1992) Eur.Comm.Rep. I–1409; Matsushita Electric Industrial Co. Ltd., (1993) I–04981 (Case C–104/90).

65 Upheld by the European Court of Justice in NTN Tokyo, (1987) Eur.Comm.Rep. 1854.

occasionally the consumers' interest in lower-priced imports prevails.[66]

EU antidumping proceedings have of late become politicized. Actual imposition of antidumping duties requires a majority vote of the member states, for example the 13–12 vote in 2006 in favor of duties on Asian shoes, vigorously opposed by EU retailers. After much debate, a decision to remove these duties in 2010 was reversed by another bare majority in the Council of Ministers.[67] In 2013, imposition of antidumping duties on Chinese solar panels survived considerable opposition.

Dumping Duties

A *de minimis* dumping margin of 2 percent is required to establish injury. Similarly, if the volume of imports is less than 3 percent of imports of the like product the investigation must be terminated immediately—unless countries which individually account for less than 3 percent of these imports collectively account for more than 7 percent. This may entice producers in the future to direct complaints against as many countries as possible. The precise amount of the antidumping duty is supposed to represent only that which is necessary to remove the injury. European Union dumping duties are imposed prospectively, applying in most cases to all future imports during the next five years.

The EU authorities have a wide discretion to impose different forms of duty. These may be:

(a) A specific duty (*i.e.*, fixed amount per unit of product imported);

(b) An ad valorem duty; or

(c) A minimum floor price (*i.e.*, if the exporter sells below the minimum price, the difference between such a price and the minimum price is collected as duty).

In theory, the minimum price approach should be the most appropriate since the object is to eliminate the injury caused by dumping, not to punish the dumpers. In fact, ad valorem duties are the most common as they are more difficult to evade and much easier to administer, particularly when there is a range of types of the dumped product. Ad valorem duties are chosen because the payment of duties cannot be avoided simply by the exporter raising ex-factory export prices so that the imports are no longer dumped (though the importer may be able to claim a refund or seek to have the duty

66 *See* Commission Dec. May 22, 1990, O.J. L138/48 (May 31, 1990) (photo albums).

67 Re Chinese Shoes, (2010) Eur.Comm.Rep. (Case T–401/06).

reviewed in such circumstances). The Antidumping Regulation contains specific anti-absorption provisions which prevent the exporter from bearing the duty by reducing export prices so that the retail price is unaffected. If this occurs, the Union authorities may impose an additional duty, to compensate for the amount borne by the exporter.

Undertakings or commitments are commonly offered by exporters during anti-dumping investigations. Indeed, more than half of the investigations commenced by the Commission are resolved in this way. To be acceptable, the effect of the undertaking must be that either the dumping margin or the injurious effect of it is eliminated. An undertaking usually involves an upward revision of prices, though exceptionally an undertaking to limit exports may be accepted. In deciding whether to accept an undertaking, the previous violation of an enterprise may also be considered.

However, as indicated above in the section on duties, the acceptance of undertakings can also be subject to political considerations; for instance, several years ago the Council of Ministers rejected a Commission proposal that a procedure be terminated in this way in the light of the then prevailing trading relations with Japan. Although the Commission may suggest undertakings, the fact that they are not offered may not prejudice the case. But if dumping continues, the Commission may treat that as evidence that a threat of injury is more likely to lead to material injury.

Investigations

The antidumping investigation will cover a period of not less than six months immediately prior to the initiation of the proceedings and will normally be concluded either by termination or definitive action within one year. Some cases, however, take very much longer. During an investigation, the Commission may seek all necessary information from, and examine and verify the records of importers, exporters, traders, agents, producers, trade associations and organizations. Investigations in non-EU countries take place only if the firms concerned consent and their government has been notified and does not object. The member states may send officials to assist in such investigations.

Within the Union, the Commission can obtain assistance from the member states to carry out checks and inspections of importers, traders and EU producers. Although the Commission does not have the power to obtain the information it requires if an enterprise, within or outside the Union, does not wish to cooperate, findings will be made based on the facts available. Hence anti-dumping duties may be imposed on producers who refuse to cooperate based on the allegations set forth in the complaint[68] or based on the dumping found against other producers and at the highest rate imposed on those other producers[69] or even higher.[70]

As part of the investigation, the Commission will send questionnaires to producers/exporters, importers and Union producers known to it. The normal period in which to respond to the questionnaire is 37 days but an extension can be requested. The purpose of the questionnaires is to collect all the necessary information to determine normal value, export price and adjustments to enable a comparison to be made. In addition, some information relating to injury will be gleaned from the questionnaires.

Apart from the questionnaire, the most important step in an anti-dumping proceeding will be the verification visit by Commission officials to the company, which usually takes two to three days. The aim is to compare the answers to the questionnaire with the company's books to ensure that the information supplied is both correct and complete. Answers may be rejected if the officials are not satisfied that they are consistent with the business records. It is important for the company to be able to show how each figure in the questionnaire arrived at, and all materials used in the preparation of the answers should be kept.

All information obtained or received by the Commission can be used solely for the purpose for which it was requested. It cannot be passed to other Commission departments, such as the Directorate-General for Competition.[71] Confidential treatment can be requested with an indication why the information is confidential, and a non-confidential summary, or statement of reasons why the information is not susceptible to summary, should be provided. This summary is intended for supply to other parties to the proceedings. Failure to submit a summary, where summary is possible, or the unwarranted claiming of confidentiality coupled with an unwillingness to authorize disclosure in generalized or summary form, will result in the information being disregarded. Even in the absence of a request

---

[68] Video cassette recorders originating in Korea and Japan, O.J. L 57/55 (27.2.1989); Compact disk players originating in Japan and Korea; O.J. L 13/21 (16.1.1990).

[69] Large electrolytic aluminum capacitors originating in Japan, O.J. L 152/22 (June 4, 1992).

[70] Electronic weighing scales originating in Singapore and Korea, O.J. L 112/20 (May 6, 1993).

[71] *But see* for limits of confidentiality provisions the caselaw relating to the confidentiality rule in Regulation 17 on competition law infringement investigations, Dirección General de Defensa de la Competencia v. Asociación Española de Banca Privada and others, (1992) Eur.Comm.Rep. I–4785; Samenwerkende Elektriciteitsproductiebedrijven NV v. Commission, (1994) I–01911 (Case C–36/92).

for confidentiality, information will be treated as confidential if its disclosure is likely to have a significantly adverse effect on the supplier or the source of the information.

Judicial Review

Since March 1994 the Court of First Instance (CFI) (now General Court) has had jurisdiction over antidumping matters and the European Court of Justice is only competent to hear appeals against the GC judgments. The Court of Justice had restricted its control to manifest errors of appraisal and abuse of power. It had thus granted the Union institutions an extremely wide margin of discretion. The reasoning underlying this approach was that the imposition of antidumping duties involves a difficult appraisal of complex economic issues. Finally, it should be mentioned that successful litigation before the European Court in antidumping matters opens the way to a claim for damages under Article 340(2) TFEU.[72]

Critiques

Although much of the EU law on antidumping duties is consistent with the GATT/WTO code, and therefore generally conforms to United States law on the subject,[73] some interesting twists have been applied. One of the most controversial is the so-called "screwdriver plant regulation" aimed mostly at Japanese exporters.[74] These exporters, when faced with antidumping duties on top of the common customs tariff, began to assemble consumer electronics and other products inside the Union using Japanese made components plus a screwdriver. The net effect of the Union's regulatory response is to re-impose dumping duties on these products unless at least 40 percent of the components originate outside the source country (Japan).

Similar results have been achieved in certain cases when the Japanese export goods assembled in United States to the EU.[75] In the photocopiers case, the goods had qualified as American for purposes of U.S. procurement rules. This origin was rejected by the European Union. The Japanese successfully challenged the

---

72 Case T–167/94 (formerly Case C–326/93), Nölle v. EEC.

73 19 U.S.C.A. § 1673.

74 *See* Council Regulation 1761/87 and Article 13(10) of Regulation 4057/86.

75 *See* Council Regulation 3205/88 (photocopiers) (assembly does not involve a substantial operation or process to alter origin of goods). *Accord,* Brother International GmbH v. Hauptzollamt Giessen, (1989) Eur.Comm.Rep. 4253 (Case 26/88) (suggesting typewriters assembled in Taiwan originate from Japan unless assembly causes the use to which components are put to become definite and the goods to be given their specific qualities).

screwdriver regulation within the GATT.[76] The Union has indicated that its anti-circumvention rules will remain in effect.

Some have asserted that the European Union employs a double standard when calculating export prices and normal values for dumping law purposes. They claim that the EU has cloaked itself in the technical obscurity of the law to systematically inflate normal values and deflate export prices, thereby causing more dumping to be found. Use of asymmetrical methods to reach these determinations has been upheld by the European Court.[77]

Additional criticism has been levied against the Commission's refusal to disclose the information upon which it relies in making critical dumping law decisions.[78] Consumer groups have not traditionally been granted access to non-confidential files accumulated by the Commission in antidumping proceedings.[79] However, by amendment,[80] consumers and consumer organizations have been granted the right to inspect all non-confidential information made available to the Commission by any party to an investigation.

§ 6.6 EU Countervailing Duties

The internal trade problems associated with member state "aids" (subsidies) to enterprises located inside the EU have already been discussed in connection with the Union's competition policy.[81] Many of the same problems repeat in the context of the Common Commercial Policy. This time, however, the source of the subsidies is governments located *outside* the Common Market. Many subsidies, especially export subsidies, are treated as an unfair trading practice under the GATT/WTO. As with dumping, there is a separate code which creates the ground rules in this area.[82] This code (as revised after the Uruguay Round) is implemented as a matter of Common Commercial Policy by the EU and therefore parallels similar law in the United States.[83]

---

76 GATT Basic Instruments and Selected Documents (B.I.S.D.) 37S/132 (1991).

77 Miniature Bearings, Nippon Seiko v. Council, (1987) Eur.Comm.Rep. 1923.

78 *See* Al-Jubail Fertilizer Co. v. Council, (1991) Eur.Comm.Rep. 3187 (Case C–49/88).

79 BEUC v. Commission, (1991) Eur.Comm.Rep. 5709 (Case C–170/89).

80 Article 2(8) Council Regulation 521/94.

81 *See* Chapter 5.

82 *See* the Agreement on Interpretation and Application of Articles VI, XVI and XXIII of the GATT (1979) (Subsidies Code). Substantial amendments to this code under the Uruguay Round of GATT negotiations were undertaken, resulting in the 1994 WTO Subsidies Code. EU law conforms to this new Subsidies Code.

83 19 U.S.C.A. § 1671.

The types of "subsidies" subject to "countervailing duties" are in dispute internationally. European Union regulations illustrate what constitutes a countervailable subsidy.[84] Certain domestic manufacturing, production, and transportation subsidies can also be countervailed if they (like export subsidies) threaten material injury to an EU industry. The European Court of Justice has said that the concept of a countervailable subsidy presupposes the grant of an economic advantage through a charge on the public account.[85] For a domestic subsidy to be countervailable, it must have "sectoral specificity" (seek to grant an advantage only to certain firms). For an export subsidy to be countervailable, it must specifically benefit the imported product.[86] As with dumping proceedings, the Commission makes these judgments provisionally and the Council renders final judgment (issued as a customs regulation). The amount of the extra duty corresponds to the amount of the subsidy.

Relatively few external subsidy proceedings have been pursued under Union law. However, in 2020 the EU broke new legal ground by challenging PRC and Egyptian subsidies given to Chinese firms producing glass fiber fabric goods in an Egyptian Trade Cooperation Zone as part of China's Belt and Road Initiative. The EU Commission asserts these subsidies are countervailable, and that they caused material injury to EU-based producers of similar goods. CVDs of 17 to 31% were levied against them. If this ruling is replicated by the U.S. and other WTO members, it could have broad impacts on CVD law and Chinese foreign investment exports.

Commencing in 2024, the EU assessed a range of CVDs on EV exports from China.

§ 6.7 EU Trade Relations with North America, Japan and China

As a rule, trade between the United States and the Common Market is voluminous, roughly in balance and yet fractious. While the focal point in recent years has been agricultural trade, especially the problems of export subsidies and nontariff trade barriers (notably Europe's banana quotas, beef hormone bans and freeze on GMO (genetically modified organism) approvals), there are many contentious issues. For example, Airbus subsidies are said to threaten Boeing and vice versa before the WTO. These longstanding, unresolved disputes resulted in significant U.S. tariffs on EU airplanes, wine, whiskeys and more followed by EU tariffs on U.S. aircraft and goods. European digital industry taxes on Amazon,

---

84 Council Regulation 2026/97.

85 FEDIOL v. Commission, (1988) Eur.Comm.Rep. 4193.

86 *Id.*

Google and the like, and EV auto subsidies, have emerged as other flashpoints. There is continuing concern that both North America and Europe are turning inward and protective.

Trade relations between the EU and the U.S. improved in limited ways under the Transatlantic Economic Partnership Program. A 20-year dispute on wine production and labeling practices, for example, was finally resolved, and there is agreement on use of International Financial Reporting Standards, replacing U.S. Generally Accepted Accounting Principles. Common standards for electric vehicles have been agreed.

Europe, for its part, has begun imitating the United States' practice of issuing annual reports voicing *its* objections to U.S. trade barriers and unfair practices. Extraterritorial U.S. jurisdiction has been a constant complaint, including the Helms-Burton Cuban LIBERTAD and the Iran-Libya Sanctions Acts. These reports have also targeted Section 301 of the Trade Act of 1974 (see Chapter 14 in my *International Trade Law* Concise Hornbook). The Europeans perceive Section 301 as a unilateral retaliatory mechanism that runs counter to multilateral resolution of trade disputes through the GATT/WTO.

Deep underlying conflicts remain, especially regarding cultural goods (TV shows, films), agriculture, GMOs, airplane subsidies, and procurement. It is this author's view that NAFTA/USMCA, the EU and more recently China are competing with good reason for possession of the world's largest market. Larger markets bring greater leverage in intergovernmental trade negotiations, economies of scale, and improved "terms of trade" (pay less for imports, receive more for exports), as well as enhanced abilities to exercise global economic leadership. The struggle for global market power is likely to continue.

Trump, Biden and Europe

At over $1 trillion a year, the trading relationship between the United States and the European Union is one of the largest in the world, accounting for over one-third of global trade. Europe has typically had a trade in goods surplus, while the U.S. has had a trade in services surplus. Net U.S. goods and services trade with Britain has generated a slight surplus, slight deficit with France, a small deficit with Italy and a notable deficit with Germany. EU and U.S. job and technology creating investment surpasses $5 trillion in each other.

The U.S.-EU negotiations for a Transatlantic Trade and Investment Partnership (TTIP) initiated by President Obama disappeared under President Trump and were not resumed under

President Biden. After considerable delay, Canada and the EU implemented their Comprehensive Economic and Trade Partnership (CETA, below) in 2017, and Mexico substantially re-negotiated its year 2000 EU free trade deal. The EU also implemented a major FTA with Japan in 2019 (below).

The EU free trade initiatives with Canada and Mexico were in part driven by the prospect of a NAFTA re-negotiation failure. These agreements allow duty free trade in autos, avoiding an EU tariff of 10%, Canadian tariff of 6.1%, and Mexican tariff of about 7%. American car exporters, including U.S.-based European and Asian firms, may have to pay these tariffs to their competitive disadvantage.

Subjecting the European Union to U.S. national security tariffs on steel and aluminum under the Trump administration generated equivalent EU retaliation adversely impacting Harley Davidson and U.S. whiskey exports. These tariffs remain in place. President Trump's threat to impose 25% national security tariffs on all U.S. auto imports sparked increased dialogue between the EU and the United States aimed, a bit unrealistically, at negotiation of a "no subsidies, no nontariff trade barriers, and no tariffs outside industrial goods" agreement. Limited progress was made toward such an outcome. Trump raised similar threats in his 2024 Presidential campaign.

For decades, though not without disputes taken to the GATT/WTO, the United States and Europe have maintained a critically important strategic and economic partnership. NATO, for example, counts 24 of the 27 EU states as members. President Trump's rejection of the Paris accord on climate change, the Iran nuclear agreement, the short-range missile treaty with Russia, and his G7 plus Russia goals also signaled the potential for a dramatic shift in European-U.S. relations. Trump's harping on NATO defense contributions by EU member states and threats to remove troops from Germany fueled discord. U.S. national security sanctions by the Trump administration on the Nordstream and Turkstream gas pipeline projects from Russia to the EU harkened back to similar Reagan era efforts. All this suggests that America First policies and tariffs of the Trump administration placed risk on the longstanding allied relationship with Europe.

Russia's invasion of Ukraine, on the other hand, brought the U.S. and EU closer together as allies under considerably more diplomatic President Biden. For much more on Trump trade policies and disputes, and Biden impacts thereon, see my *International Trade Law* Concise Hornbook.

Canada-EU Comprehensive Economic and Trade Agreement (CETA 2017)

Given the withdrawal of the United States from the TPP, the uncertain future of TTIP negotiations between the U.S. and the EU, and the onslaught of FTAs Britain is expected to seek after BREXIT, one free trade agreement that stands out in the developed world is CETA, the Comprehensive Economic and Trade Agreement between Canada and the EU, provisionally operational since 2017. CETA had been cited by many as a model for future UK-EU trade, technology and investment relations. In the end, the EU-UK 2021 Trade and Cooperation Agreement was not as broad nor as deep as CETA. See Chapter 8.

Upon ratification, 98% of the tariffs on trade between the parties were eliminated, with tariffs on autos phasing out over seven years, subject to 50 to 55% Canadian content rules of origin except for a generous 20% content rule applicable to the first 100,000 Canadian auto exports. Considerable agreement on product standards and testing in the country of export was reached, and Canadian firms get to bid on EU contracts on the same footing as EU companies. Free trade in services is based on a "negative list", a first for the EU, and will rachet up if either party grants broader entry in any other subsequent free trade agreement. Mobility for service providers and businesspeople is extensive, and mutual recognition of professional diplomas and licensing is anticipated.

Both parties have a history of protecting their agricultural and fish/seafood markets. After various transition periods, CETA renders nearly 95% of these markets duty-free. There are exceptions for meat quotas on both sides and EU cheese export quotas. The EU obtained greater protection for geographic origin of products (Feta cheese, Parma ham), and increased pharmaceutical patent protection. Healthcare and education, along with cultural industries, are excluded under CETA, and Canada continues to control development of its natural resources.

Foreign investor rights and arbitral protections cover the entire EU, another first. Investor-state dispute settlement procedures, like those of NAFTA, were tuned up in response to numerous criticisms. Third party amicus briefs are allowed, frivolous complaints may be dismissed, biased arbitrators challenged, and there is considerably more transparency. After much debate and controversy, an Investment Dispute Court comprised of EU and Canadian members, will be created to decide investor-state disputes. Canada still gets to apply its Investment Act to EU nationals, subject to the "net benefit" to Canada test, but EU investments under $1.5 billion CDN escape review.

Japan/China-EU Trade

Europe's trade relations with Japan and China are less voluminous, less in balance and (at least superficially) less fractious than with the United States. Japan and China run growing surpluses, but the amounts are smaller than the huge surplus those countries accumulate in trading with the States.

Many Europeans speak quietly and with determination about their intent to avoid the "United States example" in their trade relations with Japan and China. Less quietly, some national governments have imposed quotas on the importation of Japanese autos and instituted demanding local content requirements for Japanese cars assembled in Europe. The Commission, for its part, has frequently invoked antidumping and countervailing duty proceedings against Japanese and especially Chinese goods. It has also demonstrated a willingness to create arcane rules of origin that promote its interests at the expense of Japan and China.

At the GATT/WTO level, however, Japan and the EU share common concerns about retaining their agricultural support systems. These concerns place them in opposition to the U.S. and others who seek to liberalize world trade in agricultural products.

The meteoric economic rise of China, combined with U.S. withdrawal from the Trans-Pacific Partnership (TPP) under President Trump, pushed Japan and the European Union into an historic free trade agreement in 2019. Each is expected to get greater (but not 100%) access to the other's markets, notably for Japanese autos to Europe and EU agricultural goods to Japan.

The Japan-EU Economic Partnership Agreement (2019)

Like CETA, the Japan-EU Economic Partnership Agreement of 2019 is a major example of free trade alternatives to America First trade policy. The agreement anticipates nearly full tariff removals on goods, notably reducing the 10% EU auto tariff to zero over 7 years. Honda, which has a large plant in the UK, announced in 2019 will close production in favor exporting from Japan under its new free trade agreement with the EU. The EU expects to export more agricultural, textile, chemicals, wood products and leather goods to Japan. Tariff rate quota limitations will protect Japan from EU wheat, dairy, pork, sugar, soft cheese and beef. Free trade will not apply to rice, Japan's "sacred" food sector, which is protected by a 777% tariff.

Many Japanese nontariff trade barriers (NTBs) will be clarified and relaxed, including those related motor vehicles, medical devices, textile labeling, and beer. In general, technical barriers to trade will be governed by international standards.

Trade in services is expanded beyond WTO commitments, notably in the following fields: Postal and courier services, telecommunications, finance, and international maritime transport. Temporary business and professional visas going beyond anything the EU had previously agreed to are adopted.

State-owned enterprises of either country will receive national treatment when buying or selling on commercial markets. Mutual procurement opportunities are expanded, especially in allowing EU firms to bid on tenders of 54 "core cities" in Japan.

There are obligations to recognize of the eight "fundamental" ILO Conventions, duty free electronic transmissions, and a bar on forced disclosure of source codes. Each side has acknowledged the "adequacy" of the other's data privacy regimes, a priority for the EU operating under its 2018 General Data Protection Regulation (see Section 5.30). Geographical indicators from Kobe beef to Feta cheese are protected.

In a first for any free trade agreement, the parties reaffirmed their commitment to the Paris Accord on Climate Change. Various provisions promote sustainable development and corporate social responsibility. There is a specific chapter on corporate governance derived from G20/OECD Principles. The EU ban on imports of whale products is retained in the face of continued Japanese whaling practices. General state-to-state dispute settlement procedures are established.

Foreign investment rules and related dispute settlement are being negotiated separately. These are particularly sensitive to Japan, which has never had to defend itself in investor-state arbitration proceedings.

§ 6.8 EU International Trade and Foreign Investment Agreements

Article 218 TFEU establishes the procedures used in the negotiation of most trade agreements with the European Union. Basically, the Commission proposes and then receives authorization from the Council to open negotiations with third countries or within an international organization. When the Commission reaches tentative agreement, conclusion or ratification must take place in the Council. If the Commission alone concludes an agreement, the European Court of Justice will declare void the act whereby the

Commission sought to conclude the agreement.[87] The Council votes by qualified majority on Common Commercial Policy agreements.[88] These include most GATT/WTO agreements.

The Council votes unanimously on association agreements[89] and on international agreements undertaken via Article 352 (*e.g.*, environmental conventions prior to 1987). The 1993 Treaty on European Union amended Article 218 to provide that the Council must also vote unanimously on international agreements covering areas where a unanimous vote is required to adopt internal EU rules.[90] Parliament's role in international agreements was expanded by the TEU and the Reform Treaty of 2009. Its assent must now be obtained for virtually all EU trade and foreign investment agreements. The Council is also authorized to take emergency measures to cut off or reduce trading with other nations for common foreign or security policy reasons.[91]

An opinion of the European Court as to the compatibility with the TFEU of the proposed agreement and the procedures used to reach it may be obtained in advance at the request of the Commission, Council or a member state. There are no public proceedings when such opinions are sought. Use of this advance ruling procedure may forestall judicial review at a later date of the compatibility of Union agreements with the Treaty.[92] This lesson was vividly made when the Court of Justice rejected the final draft of the 1991 European Economic Area Agreement between the EU and EFTA because it considered the provisions on judicial control incompatible with the authority of the Union's legal order.[93] This rejection sent the Agreement back for renegotiation and a new set of dispute settlement procedures which subsequently met with ECJ approval.[94]

Trade agreements and other international treaties of the European Union are subject to judicial review by the Court of Justice as "acts" of its institutions.[95] Moreover, such agreements are binding

---

87 France v. Commission, (1994) Eur.Comm.Rep. I–03641 (Case No. C–327/91) (Agreement between the Commission and the United States regarding the application of their competition laws).

88 Article 218(2), TFEU.

89 *See* § 6.9.

90 *See* § 2.5.

91 *See* Article 215 TFEU.

92 *See* ECJ Opinion 1/75 (1975) Eur.Comm.Rep. 1355 (Local Cost Standards).

93 ECJ Opinion 1/91 (1991) Eur.Comm.Rep. 6079.

94 ECJ Opinion 1/92 (1992) Eur.Comm.Rep. 2821.

95 *See* Articles 263, 265 and 267, TFEU, and Chapter 3. For an example of a decision voiding the act whereby the Commission sought to conclude an agreement is

on the member states which must ensure their full implementation.[96] When the European Court holds international agreements of the Union to be "directly effective" EU law, individuals may rely upon them in national litigation.[97] The direct effects doctrine has led to cases where citizens end up enforcing the trade agreements of the EU despite contrary law of their own or other member state governments.[98]

ERTA and WTO Agreements Cases

Article 220 TFEU gives the Commission the power to represent the Union within the General Agreement on Tariffs and Trade (GATT)/WTO. This representation affords EU nations much more bargaining power over tariffs and other trade issues with Canada, the United States, and Japan than they ever had individually. The exact extent and delimitation of the Union competences and the competences of the member states were disputed. With regard to the many Uruguay Round agreements, therefore, the European Commission requested the European Court of Justice to render an opinion to determine whether the Union was competent to conclude the Agreement establishing the World Trade Organization (WTO), in particular as regards the Agreement on Trade in Services (GATS), the Agreement on Trade-Related Aspects of Intellectual Property Rights, including trade in counterfeit goods (TRIPs), and with respect to products and/or services falling within the ECSC and EURATOM Treaties. This WTO Agreements opinion is discussed below.

Article 207 TFEU conveys the power to enter international commitments to the European Union. This is the case by implication even when there is no express Treaty authorization to enter into international agreements necessary to achieve internal Common Market objectives.[99] A prominent decision of the European Court holds the scope of the Union's trade agreements power to be coextensive with all *effective* surrenders of national sovereignty accomplished under the Treaty.[100] Thus, if an internal economic policy matter is governed by existing EU law, the external aspects of

---

Case C–327/91, France v. Commission, (1994) Eur.Comm.Rep. I–03641 (Case No. C–327/91).

96 Article 218(2), TFEU.

97 *See* Chapter 3.

98 Bresciani v. Amministrazione della Finanze, (1976) Eur.Comm.Rep. 129 (Yaoundé Conventions); Hauptzollamt Mainz v. Kupferberg, (1982) Eur.Comm.Rep. 3641 (EC-Portugal Free Trade Agreement); Eurim-Pharm GmbH v. Bundesgesundheitsamt, (1993) Eur.Comm.Rep. I–03723 (Case C–207/91).

99 ECJ Opinion 1/76 (1977) Eur.Comm.Rep. 741 (Inland Waterways).

100 Commission v. Council, (1971) Eur.Comm.Rep. 263 (the "*ERTA*" decision).

that policy are (either expressly or *by implication*) exclusively within the Union's competence.

More recently, the Court of Justice revisited the *ERTA* doctrine in an opinion reviewing the Uruguay Round trade agreements. The European Community had long represented the member states in the GATT and exclusively negotiated these agreements. But the General Agreement on Trade in Services (GATS) and the Agreement on Trade-Related Aspects of Intellectual Property (TRIPs) raised special concerns since the Treaty and *ERTA* were ambiguous as to whether the Union or the member states or both had the power to conclude these agreements.

The Court of Justice, in the complex *WTO Agreements* opinion, ruled that the Union had exclusive power regarding trade in goods agreements (including agriculture) based on Article 207 TFEU authorizing the Common Commercial Policy. While the cross-frontier supply of services not involving movement of persons also fell under Article 207, all other aspects of the GATS did not. Regarding TRIPs, only the provisions dealing with counterfeit goods came under the Community's exclusive Article 207 authority. Noting that the effective surrender of national sovereignty over intellectual property is not (yet) total and that internal trade in services is not "inextricably linked" to external relations, the Court ruled the competence to conclude GATS and TRIPs was jointly shared by the Community and the member states. Likewise, they share a duty to cooperate within the WTO in the administration of these agreements and disputes relating to them.[101]

Subsequently, under the Lisbon Treaty of 2009, trade in services, trade-related intellectual property rights, and notably foreign direct investment became exclusive EU competences.[102] A Court of Justice Opinion (No. 2/15 issued May 16, 2017) regarding the first of the EU's "new generation" free trade agreements between Singapore and the EU affirmed this exclusivity, excepting portfolio investment and foreign investor-state dispute settlement. The Court also held that air and maritime services, certain government procurement, non-commercial aspects of IP rights, renewable energy, and sustainable development labor and environmental standards fell within the EU's exclusive competence. Since the EU-Singapore agreement goes beyond the EU's exclusive competences, it had to be ratified by all 40 national and regional parliaments of the member states.

---

101 Opinion 1/94 (1994) Eur.Comm.Rep. I–5267 (WTO).

102 *See* Daiichi Sankyo Co v. DEMO Anonimous, (2013) Eur.Comm.Rep. (Case C–414/11) (TRIPs is now exclusive EU competence).

Member State Involvement

Article 351 TFEU indicates that most treaties the member states reached prior to joining the EU continue to be valid even if they impact on areas now governed by Union law. Many bilateral treaties of Friendship, Commerce and Navigation fall within this category despite their impact on immigration, employment and investment opportunities. For example, such a dispute between Germany and the Commission concerned the compatibility of the preference-provision in the Utilities Directive[103] for supply contracts with the German-American Treaty of Friendship and Commerce of 1953.[104] Member states are required to take all appropriate steps (*e.g.*, upon renewal) to eliminate any incompatibilities between national trade and investment agreements and the Treaty.[105] Whether prior treaties can be invoked so as to negate or fail to fulfill Treaty obligations is unclear.[106]

As a rule, member states may *not* negotiate trade treaties in EU-occupied fields. They may do so on a transitional basis in areas where the Union lacks authority or (less clearly) has not effectively implemented its authority. For example, in the early 1970s the EU had not developed an effective overall energy policy, although it clearly had competence in the coal and nuclear fields. Thus, the International Energy Agreement achieved through the Organization for Economic Cooperation and Development (OECD) in 1975 after the first oil shocks is not an EU agreement. In contrast, the Union clearly had competence in the field of export credits. OECD arrangements in this area are exclusively the province of the Union with no residual or parallel authority in the member states.[107]

Likewise, in 2002 the ECJ ruled that bilateral "open skies" aviation agreement between eight individual member states and the United States were illegal incursions into an exclusively EU domain. A United States-European Union open skies agreement followed in 2008.

The *ERTA* and to a lesser degree the *WTO* decisions of the European Court, combined with the expanding competence of the Union, leaves less and less room for national governments to enter

---

[103] Article 36, Council Directive 93/38, O.J. L 199/84 (August 9, 1993).

[104] Germany in EC row over US sanctions, Financial Times of 12/13.6.1993; EC hopes Bonn row will fade, Financial Times of 14.6.1993.

[105] *See generally* Kramer et al., (1976) Eur.Comm.Rep. 1279 (North Atlantic Fisheries); Council Decision 91/167.

[106] Compare Re Van Wesemael, (1979) Eur.Comm.Rep. 35 (International Labor Organization Convention no ground for member state failure to apply Union law) and Ministre Public & Anor v. Levy, (1993) Eur.Comm.Rep. I–04287 (Case C–158/91) (ILO Convention may take precedence over Community directive on night work by women).

[107] ECJ Opinion 1/75 (1975) Eur.Comm.Rep. 1355 (Local Cost Standards).

into trade agreements. Several ECJ decisions suggest that the Union's external authority parallels its internal powers even if it has not effectively implemented those powers.[108] However, recognizing the sensitivities involved, "mixed agreements" negotiated by the Commission (acting on a Council mandate) and representatives of the member states are frequently used. Both the Union and the member states are signatories to such accords. This has been done with the "association agreements" authorized by Article 217 TFEU, certain of the WTO Codes, the Ozone Layer Convention and the Law of the Sea Convention.

The Court of Justice has upheld the validity of mixed international agreements and procedures, but suggested that absent special circumstances their use should not occur when the Union's exclusive jurisdiction over external affairs is fully involved.[109] In other words, mixed procedures should be followed only when the competence to enter into and implement international agreements is in fact shared between the Union and its member states.[110] The Treaty of Nice (2003) makes it clear that trade agreements relating to cultural and audiovisual services, educational services, and social and human health services are shared competences. The Reform Treaty (2009) contains a lengthy list of shared competences that are found in Article 4(2) TFEU and discussed in Section 2.0 of this book.

The Reform Treaty also clarified that trade in goods and services, trade-related intellectual property rights, and foreign investment matters are an exclusive EU competence, as are the customs union, business competition rules, EURO zone monetary policy, and marine biology conservation policies. Article 3 TFEU further indicates that the Union has exclusive competence to conclude international agreements provided for by EU legislative act, necessary to enable the EU to exercise its internal powers, or where concluding an international agreement may affect common rules or alter their scope. In all these areas, therefore, trade agreements can only be concluded by the European Union and need only be approved by the European Parliament. Some have referred to this outcome as a "fast track" compared to mixed agreement ratifications by all national and regional parliaments (above).

EU Free Trade Agreements

By 2024, the EU had over 45 free trade agreements (FTA) covering some 70 trade partners, including with Algeria, Chile,

---

[108] Kramer et al., (1976) Eur.Comm.Rep. 1279 (North Atlantic Fisheries); ECJ Opinion 1/76 (1977) Eur.Comm.Rep. 741 (Inland Waterways).

[109] ECJ Opinion 1/78 (1979) Eur.Comm.Rep. 2871 (Natural Rubber Agreement).

[110] *See* Opinion 2/91 (Convention No. 170 of the ILO).

Egypt, Iceland, Israel, Jordan, Lebanon, Mexico, Morocco, Norway, Serbia, Southern Africa, Vietnam, Singapore, Japan, Canada, Tunisia, Peru, Central America (six nations), Colombia, South Korea, Singapore and Vietnam, and a customs union agreement with Turkey.

Mexico and the European Union reached a free trade agreement in 2000, much expanded and re-negotiated in 2020. Mexico, with its NAFTA membership, thus becomes a production center with duty free access to the world's two largest consumer markets.

Canada and the EU inked an historic Comprehensive Economic and Trade Agreement (CETA, below) in 2013 that, after much debate focusing primarily on investor-state dispute settlement, finally reached fruition in 2017. In 2018, Japan and the EU also reached agreement on a free trade which took effect in 2019. These two agreements are detailed in Section 6.7.

Perhaps even more remarkably, after 20 years of negotiation, the EU and MERCOSUR (Brazil, Argentina, Uruguay and Paraguay) signed a free trade deal in 2019. Overcoming protective CAP trade barriers (see Section 5.23), this FTA contains unprecedented provisions allowing expanded export of MERCOSUR agricultural and meat products to the EU. This agreement remains stalled over EU concerns regarding Brazil's environmental degradation of the Amazon.

India, ASEAN, and the Gulf Council may follow. One notable feature of EU free trade agreements is the inclusion of a Human Rights and Democracy Clause backed up by potential trade sanctions. For global coverage of FTAs, see my *USMCA and Free Trade Agreements* Concise Hornbook.

EU Foreign Investment Treaties

Foreign investment has traditionally been governed by the national laws of the member states. Hundreds of Bilateral Investment Treaties (BITs) have been negotiated between member states and other, largely developing nations. Germany, for example, has over 100 BITs, and France nearly as many. BIT "treaty shopping" inside the European Union to avoid the dubious legitimacy of national courts in Poland, Hungary, and quite a few other EU states has been undertaken by making investments in those countries via U.K., Dutch and German companies benefiting from **intra-EU** BITs.

Some 200 intra-EU member-state BIT arbitration provisions were effectively invalidated by the European Court of Justice in its landmark 2018 *Slovak Republic v. Achmea* (Case C–284/16) decision. The logic of the Court's reasoning is that such provisions interfere with the autonomy, effectiveness and primacy of the EU legal regime. As such, awards rendered thereunder are unenforceable. This decision raises questions as to whether **extra-EU** member state BIT arbitration decisions, which are numerous, may also be unenforceable.

Since the Reform Treaty of 2009, foreign investment law has become an exclusive competence of the European Union. It is expected that national BITs will in time be replaced by EU BITs. See the EU-China 2021 BIT below.

Traditionally, EU FTAs included foreign investment law rules and dispute settlement by arbitration. But recent FTAs with Vietnam, Singapore, Mexico, and the Japan-EU Economic Partnership Agreement do not. The EU's "new generation" policy for foreign investment dispute settlement anticipates using an Investment Court system instead of arbitrators.

EU Foreign Investment Controls

In 2016, Kuka, a leading German robotics company, was sold to a Chinese investor. Subsequently, an EU framework directive encourages tightening national scrutiny of foreign investment and acquisitions, especially those that are tech related. EU member states have generally done so, but in 2018 Alibaba bought Data Artisans, a Berlin specialist in managing large quantities of data, and an individual Chinese investor quietly acquired nearly 10% of Daimler, a German national champion. Chinese firms now also control Volvo, Pirelli (tires), the Greek port of Piraeus, and the Swiss agrochemical giant Syngenta. Late in 2020, the EU (much like the U.S. and China) moved to ensure closer scrutiny of national security issues concerning foreign investment.

In the absence of U.S. trade and investment leadership under President Trump, the EU has moved on. Having endured trade disruptions caused by the Trump administration and witnessing the bilateral approach of President Trump's "Phase One" truce agreement with China, the EU advanced its interests without U.S. participation. Prime examples of the EU's "strategic autonomy" policy in action include the EU free trade agreements with Canada, Japan, Mexico and MERCOSUR covered above in this Section.

Another prime example of the EU advancing its own interests is the historic China-EU bilateral investment agreement (BIT) finalized New Years' eve in 2020 *despite Biden team requests to hold off for an allied approach.*

*The EU-China 2021 Bilateral Investment Treaty (BIT)**

China and the European Union finalized very late in December 2020 a bilateral foreign investment agreement, the EU-China Comprehensive Agreement on Investment (CAI). Led by Germany, this agreement was undertaken despite requests by the incoming Biden administration to delay and organize a transatlantic U.S.-EU strategy for dealing with China. If ratified by the European Parliament, this treaty will replace 26 existing bilateral investment treaties (BITs) between China and individual EU Member States.

The CAI outlines two-way "rules of the road" for foreign investment between the EU and China. Foreign investors will obtain better access on fairer terms. The CAI opens markets with Beijing making concessions on financial services, manufacturing, real estate, construction, advertising, air transport, maritime services, telecom and, to a limited extent, cloud computing.

In turn, China secured the EU's agreement to open its renewable energy sector to Chinese investment. The CAI also prohibits forced tech transfer by EU firms that establish themselves in China and includes provisions to enhance the transparency of state subsidies for Chinese state-owned companies (which generate about 30% of the PRC's GDP). These subsidy transparency rules notably encompass services. On the human rights side, Beijing pledged to adhere to International Labor Organization's rules against forced labor. The Paris agreement on climate change is affirmed.

Commenced in 2014, the Trump trade war gave Beijing a sense of urgency to cut a deal with Brussels, particularly as U.S.-China BIT negotiations had been going nowhere. Of critical importance to Beijing is a desire to stave off any anti-China alliance. Politically symbolic, CAI represents rejection of the Trump administration's aggressive, disruptive, trade policy against both China and Europe. Indeed, a U.S.-led containment strategy for China may be the biggest loser.

The CAI demonstrates that Europe can take the lead on negotiations and stand up to China, a position that the U.S. forfeited when it abandoned U.S.-China BIT negotiations and multilateral platforms such as the TPP, TTIP and WTO. Having piled on sanctions against Chinese companies and investors in the USA, the silence on CAI from the outgoing Trump administration and incoming Biden administration on the deal was deafening.

---

* I am grateful to Attorney Jim Zimmerman for his reporting and analysis regarding CAI. For much more on international investment law and agreements, please *see* my *Foreign Investment Law and Disputes* Concise Hornbook.

All that said, the CAI has not been ratified and has not gone into effect largely because of political disputes between China and the EU Parliament.

§ 6.9 EU Association Agreements— Mediterranean Policy, Central and Eastern Europe

Association Agreements

Article 217 TFEU authorizes the Union to conclude association agreements with other nations, regional groups and international organizations. The Council must act unanimously in adopting association agreements. Since the Single European Act of 1987, association agreements also require Parliamentary assent (which it threatened to withhold from renewal of the Israeli-EU association agreement unless better treatment of Palestinian exports to the Union is achieved). The network of trade relations established by association agreements covers much of the globe. Those who are "associated" with the EU usually receive trade and aid preferences which, as a practical matter, discriminate against non-associates. Arguments about the illegality of such discrimination within the GATT/WTO and elsewhere have typically not prevailed.

Article 217 indicates that association agreements involve "*reciprocal* rights and obligations, common action and special procedures" (emphasis added). The reciprocity requirement mirrors GATT law on non-preferential trading and free trade area agreements.[111] European Union association agreements usually establish wide-ranging but hardly reciprocal trade and economic links. Greece for many years prior to membership was an EU associate. Turkey has been an associate since 1963. These two agreements illustrate the use of association agreements to convey high levels of financial, technical and commercial aid as a preliminary to membership. Turkey now has a customs union with Europe.

Another type of association agreement links the remaining EFTA nations with the European Union. These agreements originally provided for industrial free trade and symbolize an historic reconciliation of the EU (then EEC) and EFTA trading alliances in 1973. A much broader European Economic Area agreement now governs EUBEFTA trade relations.[112]

Relations between the Union and the EFTA states—except for Switzerland—were put on a new footing with the entry into force of

---

111 *See* Chapter 1.

112 *See* Chapter 1.

the Agreement on the European Economic Area[113] in 1994. The EEA establishes a free trade area larger than NAFTA/USMCA[114] and, in addition, provides that the four fundamental freedoms of the internal market of the Union (free movement of goods, persons, services and capital) as well as the competition rules and certain horizontal policies (social policy, consumer protection, environment, statistics and company law) are applied throughout the EEA area.[115] The EFTA states had to adopt the "acquis communautaire", *i.e.*, the established EU law in all these areas.

A special EFTA Surveillance Authority was set up with powers like those of the Commission, and an EFTA Court, resembling the European Court of Justice. However, the EEA Agreement did not create a customs union, thus there is no common external customs tariff. Excluded are also such sensitive subjects: agriculture, fisheries and economic and monetary policy. The lasting importance of the EEA Agreement is difficult to assess since several EFTA countries joined the EU in 1995,[116] and it now applies only to Norway, Iceland and Lichtenstein.

Mediterranean Policy

Still another type of association agreement involves pursuit of what the EU refers to as its "Mediterranean Policy." This policy acknowledges the geographic proximity and importance of Mediterranean basin nations to the Union. The Mediterranean is viewed as a European sphere of influence. Most of these association agreements grant trade preferences (including substantial duty-free EU entry) and economic aid to Mediterranean nations *without* requiring reciprocal, preferential access for Union goods. Agreements of this type have been concluded with Algeria, Morocco, Tunisia, Egypt, Jordan, Lebanon, Syria, Israel, the former Yugoslavia, Malta and Cyprus.

These agreements are not at all uniform. They may be asymmetrical free trade agreements with the final goal of a customs union (Malta, Cyprus), or without such goal (Israel, Maghreb countries) or simple cooperation agreements (*e.g.*, Egypt). In 1995, Europe and these partners agreed to create a Mediterranean industrial free trade zone. Since then, EU trade agreements in the

---

113 O.J. L 1/3 (January 3, 1994).

114 *See* R. Folsom and W.D. Folsom, *The USMCA, NAFTA Re-Negotiated and Its Business Impacts.*

115 The EEA area in 1994 comprised the EU and Austria, Finland, Iceland, Norway, Sweden and Liechtenstein.

116 Finland, Sweden and Austria have done so. This leaves only Iceland, Norway and Liechtenstein as parties to the EEA.

Mediterranean basin have moved significantly towards reciprocal trade preferences.

Central and Eastern Europe

Because the former Soviet Union and its European satellites refused for many years to even recognize the European Community (now Union), some bilateral trade and cooperation agreements between those nations and the member states continue in place. It was not until 1988 that official relations between the Union and COMECON were initiated. As more democracy has taken hold, first generation trade and aid ("Partnership and Cooperation") agreements were concluded by the EU with Hungary, Poland, the Czech and Slovak Federal Republic, Bulgaria and nearly every other Central European nation. Similar agreements were concluded with the Baltic states, Slovenia, Albania, Russia, Ukraine and other former Soviet nations.

The Union advanced to second generation "association agreements" with some of these countries. These are known as "Europe Agreements." They anticipate substantial adoption of EU law on product standards, the environment, competition, telecommunications, financial services, broadcasting, and a host of other areas. Free movement of workers is not provided. Free trading will emerge over a ten-year period with special protocols on sensitive products like steel, textiles and agricultural goods. More fundamentally, these agreements are clearly focused on the eventual incorporation of these countries into the Union, as many did in 2005 along with Romania and Bulgaria in 2007.

With respect to the former USSR, the basis of the relationship between the EU and the Commonwealth of Independent States initially was the Trade and Cooperation Agreement of 1989 concluded with the Soviet Union. This agreement has been replaced by bilateral Partnership and Cooperation Agreements. The negotiations with Ukraine were concluded in March 1994, with Kazakhstan and Kyrgyzstan in May 1994, with Russia in June 1994, and with Moldova in July 1994.

These new agreements laid down the framework for future commercial and economic cooperation and created a new legal basis for the development of trade and investment links. For example, the agreement with Russia on trade and trade-related issues removed all quotas and other quantitative restrictions on Russian exports to the European Union, excepting certain textile and steel products. In 2004, responding to the admission of 10 new EU member states, Russia and the European Union concluded a Partnership agreement. Customs duties on cargo shipments between Russia its Kaliningrad enclave on the Baltic Sea are dropped, tariffs generally lowered, Russian steel quotas increased, and EU antidumping duties relaxed. The European Union has also promised to guarantee language rights for the Russian-speaking minorities in Estonia and Latvia.

Russia has become increasingly concerned with the eastern drift of EU memberships. It is organizing its own Eurasian Economic Union to counterbalance EU expansion. Belarus, Kazakhstan and Armenia have signed on. Ukraine, Moldova and Georgia, on the other hand, though partially occupied by Russia, hope to become EU associates and eventually members.

International Agreements

In addition, the European Union has a host of other trade and cooperation agreements. These include agreements with Sri Lanka, Pakistan, Bangladesh, India, China, the ASEAN group (Thailand, Singapore, Malaysia, The Philippines, Vietnam, Cambodia, Laos, Myanmar, Brunei, and Indonesia), the Andean Pact (Bolivia, Colombia, Ecuador, Peru), Argentina, Uruguay, and Brazil.

In 1990, a Cooperation Agreement was signed with the countries of the Gulf Cooperation Council (GCC): Kuwait, Saudi Arabia, Bahrain, Qatar and the United Arab Emirates.

§ 6.10 The Lomé/Cotonou Conventions, Economic Partnership Agreements

The 1957 Treaty of Rome, in a section entitled the "association of overseas territories and countries," was intended to preserve the special trading and development preferences that came with "colonial" status. France, Belgium, Italy and The Netherlands still had a substantial number of these relationships. Article 200 TFEU completely abolished (after a transitional period) tariffs on goods coming from associated overseas territories and countries. There is no duty on the part of these regions to reciprocate with duty-free access to their markets for EU goods. Although some territories continue to exist (*e.g.*, French territories like Polynesia, New Caledonia, Guadeloupe, Martinique, etc.), most of the once associated overseas colonies are now independent nations. This is true as well for most of the former colonies of Britain, Denmark, Portugal and Spain.

As independence arrived throughout Asia, Africa and elsewhere, new conventions of association were employed by the EU as a form of developmental assistance. The first of these were the Yaoundé Conventions (1964 and 1971) with newly independent French-speaking African states. These conventions were in theory free trade agreements, but the African states could block almost any EU export and the Union in turn could protect itself from agricultural imports that threatened its Common Agricultural Policy. A healthy amount of financial and technical aid from the Union was thrown into the bargain.

Participating ACP States

When Britain joined in 1973, it naturally wished to preserve as many of the Commonwealth trade preferences as it could. The Yaoundé Conventions were already in place favoring former French colonies south of the Sahara. The compromise was the creation of a new convention, the first Lomé Convention (1975), to expand the Yaoundé principles to developing Caribbean and Pacific as well as English-speaking African nations. The fourth Lomé Convention (1990) governed trade and aid between the EU and many African, Caribbean and Pacific (ACP) states.

Lomé IV was replaced in 2000 by the Cotonou Agreement, which will operate for 20 years. The Cotonou nations presently include: Angola, Antigua & Barbuda, Bahamas, Barbados, Belize, Benin, Botswana, Burkina Faso, Burundi, Cameroon, Cape Verde, Central African Republic, Chad, Comoros, Congo, Djibouti, Dominica, Dominican Republic, Equatorial Guinea, Eritrea, Ethiopia, Fiji, Gabon, Gambia, Ghana, Grenada, Guinea, Guinea Bissau, Guyana, Haiti, Ivory Coast, Jamaica, Kenya, Kiribati, Lesotho, Liberia, Madagascar, Malawi, Mali, Mauritania, Mauritius, Mozambique, Namibia, Niger, Nigeria, Niue, Palau, Papua New Guinea, Rwanda, St. Christopher & Nevis, St. Lucia, St. Vincent & The Grenadines, Samoa, Sao Tomé & Principe, Senegal, Seychelles, Sierra Leone, Solomon Islands, Somalia, South Africa, Sudan, Suriname, Swaziland, Tanzania, Togo, Tonga, Trinidad & Tobago, Tuvalu, Uganda, Vanuatu, Zambia and Zimbabwe.

Perhaps the most important feature of this lengthy listing is the developing nations that are *not* (or no longer post BREXIT) Cotonou Convention participants. Unless they fall within the Union's Mediterranean Policy, they are apt to perceive the Lomé/Cotonou Conventions as highly discriminatory against their exports and economic interests.

Contents

Unlike the Yaoundé Conventions, the Lomé Conventions did not create (even in theory) reciprocal free trading relationships. While the Lomé states retained substantial duty-free access to the Common Market, the Union obtained no comparable benefit. The Lomé nations did promise not to discriminate in trading among EU countries and to grant each most-favored-nation (MFN) benefits. This meant, in practice, that they were free to block imports from the

EU whenever desired. This one-sided relationship was continued temporarily under the Cotonou Agreement through 2008.

Thereafter six regionally organized economic partnership agreements mutually embracing free trade were established, to be fully implemented by 2020. It is hoped that each region will internally adopt free trade principles. A variety of "development" preferences are also granted by the Union in the Cotonou Convention. These include expensive purchasing obligations on sugar, for example. There is no free movement of persons as between the ACP states and the Union. However, whenever such persons are lawfully resident and working in the other's territories, they must be given national treatment rights.

Most significantly, the Cotonou nations now participate in two innovative EU mechanisms designed to stabilize their agricultural and mineral commodity export earnings. These programs are known as STABEX and MINEX (also known as SYSMIN). STABEX covers (*inter alia*) ground nuts, cocoa, coffee, cotton, coconut, palm, rawhides, leather and wood products, and tea. MINEX deals with copper, phosphates, bauxite, alumina, manganese, iron ore, and tin. These programs are an acknowledgement of the economic dependence of many Lomé nations on commodity exports for very large portions of their hard currency earnings.

Some have argued vigorously that STABEX and MINEX perpetuate rather than relieve this dependence. Both programs provide loans and grants in aid to Lomé nations who have experienced significant declines in export earnings because of falling commodity prices, crop failures and the like. The greater the dependency and decline, the larger the EU financial transfers. These sums are not, for the most part, tied to reinvestment in the commodity sectors causing their payment, nor to the purchase of Union products or technology. In a world where most development aid is tied (*i.e.*, must usually be spent on the donor's products or projects), STABEX and MINEX represent a different approach. Many Latin American nations have lobbied the United States to create similar mechanisms for their commodities.

The Lomé IV Convention (1990) added several new features carried over under the Cotonou Agreement (2000). The European Union now financially supports structural adjustments in ACP states, including remedies for balance of payments difficulties, debt burdens, budget deficits, and public enterprises. Cultural and social cooperation, trade in services, and environmental issues are also addressed. For example, an agreement not to ship toxic and radioactive waste was reached. The Convention builds upon earlier provisions by specifying protected human rights such as equal treatment, civil and political liberty, and economic, social and cultural rights. Financial support from the EU is given to ACP nations that promote human rights and has been withheld after military coups.

The one-way nature of ACP trade benefits is inconsistent with WTO obligations. The EU has therefore undertaken to negotiate two-way "Economic Partnership Agreements (EPA)" with six groupings of ACP states. The first such EPA was finalized in 2008 with 13 Caribbean nations. Duties on nearly all European exports will be phased out by 2033, trade in services is eased, and procurement as well as investment rules are established. The second EPA was completed in 2016 with southern Africa, with other EPAs with West Africa and East Africa in the works.

§ 6.11 Duty Free Access to the EU Common Market and the USA

The end game so far as exporters are concerned is unlimited duty-free access to the world's largest market. Except for raw materials, few North American exports will qualify for such treatment. However, subsidiaries based in developing or EAA/EFTA nations may achieve this goal. This is possible because of the Union's adherence to the GSP program, its Mediterranean basin trade agreements, the Lomé/Cotonou Conventions and EU free trade agreements, including EAA/EFTA. It may also be possible to ship goods produced in Central and East European nations duty free into the Common Market under "second generation" Europe Agreements. All these topics have been previously discussed. There are, of course, exceptions and controls (quotas, NTBs) that may apply under these programs. Nevertheless, the Common Market is so lucrative that careful study of its external trade rules is warranted.

Such studies can realize unusually advantageous trade situations. For example, many developing nations are Cotonou Convention participants or GSP beneficiaries. The goods of some of these nations are also entitled to duty free access to the United States market under the U.S. version of the GSP program (currently suspended), the Caribbean Basin Economic Recovery Act (1983), or various U.S. free trade agreements. See *my USMCA and Free Trade Agreements* Concise Hornbook.

A producer strategically located in such a nation (*e.g.*, Haiti) can have the best of both worlds, *duty free access to Europe and the United States*. Since 2000, this ideal outcome is most significantly available via Mexico. Mexico is both a member of NAFTA/USMCA and has an enhanced 2020 free trade agreement with the EU. In 2017, the EU and Canada implemented a free trade deal. Likewise,

Israel, Chile, Peru, Colombia, and Morocco among others have free trade agreements with the U.S. and the EU.

Chapter 7

BUSINESS COMPETITION (ANTITRUST) LAW

Table of Sections

§ 7.0 Introduction

In the European Union, the area of law Americans call "antitrust" is referred to as "business competition" law. It is often the "first contact" with EU law that U.S. firms and their lawyers have.

The primary purpose of competition policy (called antitrust law and policy in the States) in the European Union is preservation of trade and other benefits of economic integration. The removal of governmental trade barriers without measures to ensure that businesses do not recreate those barriers would be an incomplete effort. For example, competing enterprises might agree to geographically allocate markets to each other, making the elimination of national tariffs and quotas by the Treaty on the Functioning of the European Union (TFEU) irrelevant. Similarly, a dominant enterprise in one state might tie up all important distributors or purchasers of its goods through long-term exclusive dealing contracts. The result could make entry into that market by another business exceedingly difficult.

By assisting in the formation and maintenance of an economic union, business competition law is an important component in EU competition policy. It prevents enterprise behavior from becoming a substantial nontariff trade barrier to economic integration. In contrast, coverage of competition law and policy under NAFTA/USMCA is limited and devoid of institutional force.

The secondary purpose of European Union competition policy is not unique to regional integration. This purpose is the attainment of the economic benefits generally thought to accrue in any economy organized on a competitive basis. These benefits are many. Perhaps most important of all, an economy characterized by competitive enterprise answers the questions of economic organization by maximizing the market desires of its human constituents. A genuinely competitive market is responsive to individual choice in a way that acknowledges and promotes diversity. Competition among businesses protects the public interest in having its cumulative demand for goods and services provided at the lowest possible prices and with the greatest possible degree of response to public tastes.

It is in this sense that a competitive economy is said to be guided by the principle of "consumer welfare or consumer sovereignty." When, for example, EU law prevents competing enterprises from fixing prices for their goods or prevents a dominant enterprise from charging monopoly prices at the consumers' expense, such law helps to realize the economic benefits of competition within the Euro-economy.

The Maastricht Treaty on European Union added provisions to the TFEU focused specifically on industrial competitiveness. The Union will promote a system of open and competitive markets by accelerating structural change, encouraging enterprise initiatives, fostering business cooperation, and supporting innovation, research and development. However, Article 173 indicates that this authority may not result in "any measure which could lead to a distortion of competition." The concept of non-distorted competition is developed in Section 7.2.

§ 7.1 Coal and Steel Competition Rules

The first body of business competition law was created in the Treaty of Paris establishing the European Coal and Steel Community in 1951. ECSC business competition rules were found largely in Articles 65 and 66 of the Treaty of Paris which expired in 2002 when coal and steel were merged into the Treaty of Rome (now TFEU). Their coverage in this section is primarily of historical and comparative interest.

Restraints on "Normal" Competition

Article 80 of the Treaty of Paris, which defined "enterprise" for Article 65 and 66 purposes, subjected both public and private coal and steel firms to the rules of ECSC competition law. This was important because many coal and steel businesses in the Union are state-owned. Article 65(1) prohibited and voided business agreements and concerted practices "tending directly or indirectly" to prevent, restrict or distort "normal" competition within the ECSC. Such agreements could not be relied upon before any court or tribunal in the member states. However, certain joint-buying, joint-selling and specialization agreements were, notwithstanding Article 65(1), authorized by the Commission when the conditions of Article 65(2) are met. Authorizations followed when the Commission determined that these agreements:

(1) Made a substantial improvement in the production or distribution of coal or steel;

(2) Were no more restrictive than necessary to achieve those results;

(3) Did not convey power over price, production or marketing of a substantial portion of the products concerned; and

(4) Did not shield firms against effective competition in the common coal and steel markets.

Article 65(2) authorizations were valid for limited time periods, subject to conditions and could be revoked.

As a general matter, the coal and steel business competition rules were not vigorously pursued. However, in 1961 the Commission refused to authorize a joint-selling organization for thirty-five colliery companies operating the great majority of the mines in the Ruhr valley. The organization would have supplied 73 percent of the coal consumed in West Germany and 59 percent of the Union's entire coal sales. These firms had already obtained provisional authorization for three separate joint-selling coal agencies.

The Commission, backed by the Court of Justice, found that authorization of a single agency would have conveyed the "power to determine prices" in violation of Article 65(2). The Commission noted that neither cheaper coal nor cheaper fuel oil imports in the past had caused the companies to lower their prices to competitive levels. Included in the Court's opinion is a rare and learned discussion of "pure competition" theory and the "normal" and "imperfect" competitive conditions of oligopoly in the coal sector.[1]

Mergers

Article 66 of the Treaty of Paris established extensive Commission controls over coal and steel "concentrations" (mergers). Merger authorizations were granted when the concentration did not convey the power:

> to determine prices, to control or restrict production or distribution, or to hinder effective competition in a substantial part of the market for [the] products; or to evade the rules of competition instituted under this Treaty.

No merger guidelines or regulations were issued by the Commission under its Article 66 powers.[2] Coal and steel mergers law developed on a case-by-case basis with authorizations frequently granted. Steadily increasing industrial concentration in the coal and steel sectors was given Commission approval. The Commission has

---

1 Geitling v. High Authority, (1962) Eur.Comm.Rep. 83.

2 Compare the Commission Regulation on Concentrations under the TFEU, discussed in § 7.22.

thus consistently fostered market structures for coal and steel that may be inimical to effective Common Market competition. The basis for this policy was the belief that larger and, ideally, more efficient Union enterprises were required to compete internationally with East Asian and North American firms.

Dominant Firms

Under Article 66(7) the Commission could act when it found:

> public or private undertakings which, in law or in fact, hold or acquire in the market for [coal or steel] a dominant position shielding them against effective competition in a substantial part of the common market.

The Commission was ultimately empowered to determine the prices, conditions of sale, production, or delivery schedules of a dominant firm. A dominant coal or steel enterprise need not have *abused* its market position to become subject to Commission controls.[3] The existence of the dominant position was enough, although abuse could be a reason for action by the Commission.

Relatively little use was made of Article 66(7) against dominant coal and steel businesses. In 1975, however, the Commission decreed interim measures against the publicly owned National Coal Board of Britain, requiring it to sell coal at a lower, nondiscriminatory price to a private producer of hard coke. The National Coal Board (NCB) held 88 percent of the market for domestic hard coke. The price margin between NCB's coal and hard coke sales was alleged to be insufficient to allow the private firm to operate economically and thus shielded NCB from effective competition.[4]

The Commission exercised exclusive jurisdiction over Articles 65 and 66, subject to an appeal to the European Court of Justice. After 1989, most of these appeals were lodged with the Court of First Instance (now the General Court). This exclusive jurisdiction prohibited private parties from raising ECSC business competition law issues in national courts. In other words, Articles 65 and 66 were not "directly effective" law.[5] This result contrasts sharply with the concurrent jurisdiction of national courts and authorities in many European Union competition law matters. Thus, despite its earlier birth, the facilitating "tending to" language of Article 65, and the broad coverage of Article 66, there was limited case and regulatory development of coal and steel competition law. This is the opposite of what has occurred under the TFEU (below). The utilization by the

---

[3] *Compare* Article 102, TFEU discussed in § 7.18.

[4] In re National Carbonising Co. Ltd., (1975) Common Mkt.L.Rep. D82.

[5] H.J. Banks & Co. Ltd. v. British Coal Corp., (1994) Eur.Comm.Rep. I–1209 (Case C–128/92). *See also* Chapter 3.

Commission of some market managing techniques (*e.g.*, occasional price and production controls), the exclusivity of its jurisdiction and (one suspects) the presence of so many publicly owned coal and steel enterprises accounted for this underdevelopment.

§ 7.2 Non-Distorted EU Competition Policy

One of the basic tasks of the European Union is the institution of a system ensuring that competition in the common market is "not distorted." Distorted competition is a broad English translation for the French concurrence faussée. Non-distorted competition is close to the German concept of funktionsfähiger Wettbewerb, but it is not clear to what extent this concept is a correlative of what Americans call workable or effective competition.[6] There is some suggestion that workable competition is the minimum level required in business competition law analyses.[7]

Non-distorted competition is thus a complex, evolving and distinctly European perspective on economic organization. It includes, for example, the heavy hand of agricultural price regulation and subsidies embodied in the Common Agricultural Policy.[8] Anticompetitive member state regulations, including price rules, are permissible distortions short of requiring or favoring EU competition law violations, reinforcing such violations, or delegations of state economic responsibility to private traders.[9] For example, member states may not approve or require prices fixed in violation of EU competition rules.[10]

Public and private business competition law is only one facet of non-distorted competition policy. Equally, if not at times more important, are a wide range of other Union concerns and decisions including notably state aids (subsidies).[11] Foremost of these concerns has been the implementation and maintenance of the customs union and rights of free movement, which by their very nature promote

---

6 *See* the seminal work Clark, Toward a Concept of Workable Competition, 30 Am.Econ.Rev. 241 (1940) and Hoppmann, Workable Competition (Funktionshähiger Wettbewerb) Die Entwicklung einer Idee über die Norm der Wettbewerbspolitik, 102 Zeitschrift des Bernischen Juristenvereins 249 (1966).

7 *See* Metro SB-Grossmärkte GmbH & Co. KG v. Commission, (1977) Eur.Comm.Rep. 1875.

8 *See* Chapter 5.

9 NV GB-INNO-BM v. Vereniging van de Kleinhandelaars un Tabak (INNO/ATAB), (1977) Eur.Comm.Rep. 2115. *See*, regarding state prosecutions of price discounters: *Ohra*, (1993) Eur.Comm.Rep. I–5872; *Meng*, (1993) Eur.Comm.Rep. I–5751; *Reiff*, (1993) Eur.Comm.Rep. I–5801. Regarding permissible state pricing rules for lawyers, *see* Re Manuele Arduino, (2002) Eur.Comm.Rep. I–01529 (Case C–35/99).

10 Ahmed Seed Flugreisen v. Zentrale zur Bekämpfung unlauteren Wettbewerbs, (1989) Eur.Comm.Rep. 803 (airline pricing).

11 *See* Section 5.3.

competition across borders.[12] Indeed, the whole of the single market campaign could be said to underwrite more economic competition within the Union.

Trade treaties and the Common Commercial Policy are another important element in the Union's competition regime since they heavily influence external competitive pressures.[13] Two areas of Union law with specific implications for competition policy are government subsidies and procurement.[14] In none of these fields of law, however, is there the depth and expansiveness that can be found in businesses competition law. It is very nearly impossible to avoid contact with this law in doing business with the European Union. Hence, business competition rules are often the first encounter that the North Americans have with EU law.

The coverage of competition law that follows is selective. No attempt at a comprehensive survey of this vast field has been made or is possible in a single volume. The general principles and examples chosen are illustrative of the most common types of legal problems that can be encountered.

§ 7.3 Article 101—Restraints of Trade

Article 101(1) TFEU deals with concerted business practices, business agreements and trade association decisions. Such business activities are deemed incompatible with the Common Market and are prohibited when they have the potential to affect trade between member states *and* have the object or effect of preventing, restricting or distorting competition *within* the Union. The focus of Article 101(1) is thus on cartels. By way of example, Article 101(1) lists certain prohibited activities:

(1) The fixing of prices or trading conditions;

(2) The limitation of production, markets, technical development or investment;

(3) The sharing of markets or sources of supply;

(4) The application of unequal terms to equivalent transactions, creating competitive disadvantages; and

(5) The conditioning of a contract on the acceptance of commercially unrelated additional supplies (tying arrangements).

---

12 *See* Chapter 4.

13 *See* Chapter 6.

14 *See* Chapter 5.

Article 101(1) has been used to review and challenge a wide range of anticompetitive business activities, some of which are not listed above. These activities include joint buying,[15] joint selling,[16] joint ventures and strategic alliances,[17] and data exchanges[18] among horizontal competitors. They also include an even wider range of activities between vertically related suppliers, manufacturers and franchisee/licensee/distributors.[19]

Void Agreements

Article 101(2) voids agreements and decisions prohibited by Article 101(1). The prohibitions of Article 101(1) against anticompetitive activity are absolute and immediately effective under 101(2) without prior judicial or administrative action. The open-ended text of Article 101(1) gives considerable leeway for interpretation and enforcement purposes. It has, for example, been interpreted to cover nonbinding "gentlemen's agreements."[20] Trade association "recommendations" influencing competition are caught.[21] It also generates considerable uncertainty as to the validity of many business agreements, since full market analyses of their competitive and trade impact are often required.[22]

Exemptions

Article 101(3) permits Article 101(1) to be declared inapplicable when agreements, decisions, concerted practices or classes thereof:

(1) Contribute to the improvement of the production or distribution of goods, or to the promotion of technical or economic progress; while

(2) Reserving to consumers an equitable share of the resulting benefits; and neither

---

15 *See* Intergroup (SPAR) Commission Decision 75/482, O.J. L 212/23 (Aug. 9, 1975).

16 *See* Kali & Salz AG v. Commission, (1975) Eur.Comm.Rep. 499. *Compare SAFCO,* discussed in Section 7.8.

17 *See AEG/Alcatel,* Commission Decision 90/46, O.J. L. 32/16 (Feb. 3, 1990); *Elopak,* Commission Decision 90/410, O.J. L 209/15 (Aug. 8, 1990); European Night Services v. Commission, (1998) Eur.Comm.Rep. II–3141.

18 *See* John Deere Ltd. v. Commission, (1998) Eur.Comm.Rep. I–3111.

19 *See* Sections 7.10–7.13.

20 ACF Chemiefarma v. Commission, (1970) Eur.Comm.Rep. 661.

21 Verband der Sachversicherer v. Commission, (1987) Eur.Comm.Rep. 405; Re ANSEAU-NAVEWA, (1983) Eur.Comm.Rep. 3369.

22 *See* Sections 7.15 and 7.17.

(3) Impose any restrictions not indispensable to objectives 1 and 2 (*i.e.*, least restrictive means must be used);[23] nor

(4) Make it possible for the businesses concerned to substantially eliminate competition.

The prohibitions of Article 101(1) may be tempered by "declarations of inapplicability" (exemptions) only when the circumstances of Article 101(3) are present. As befits exemptions from broad prohibitions, the terms of 101(3) are narrow and specific. Article 101(3) and Article 101(1) legal issues are often considered simultaneously in the process of analyzing the market impact of restrictive agreements, decisions and concerted practices. The overall net result resembles the "rule of reason" approach found in United States antitrust law.[24] Since May 1, 2004, Article 101(3) is directly effective law, opening the possibility of its application by national courts and authorities as well as the Commission.

§ 7.4 Commission Investigations, Attorney-Client Privilege, Prosecutorial Powers

In March of 1962 the Council of Ministers adopted Regulation 17 based on proposals from the Commission. Regulation 17 was the major piece of secondary law under Articles 81 and 82 (now 101 and 102 TFEU). Effective May 1, 2004, Regulation 17 was replaced by Regulation 1/2003. These regulations establish the scheme of enforcement for competition law. The Commission, for the most part its Competition Directorate-General, acquires a wide range of powers.

Commission Investigations

The regulations confer investigatory powers in the Commission to conduct general studies into economic sectors and to review the affairs of individual businesses and trade associations. The Commission may investigate in response to a complaint or upon its own initiative. These powers are particularly significant because (except in the case of mergers) notification of restrictive agreements, decisions and practices to the Commission, although at times beneficial, is not mandatory. The Commission may request all information *it* considers necessary and examine and make copies of record books and business documents. The Commission decides upon whether the information it obtains in competition law investigations and proceedings contains "business secrets" and whether to release

[23] Grundig, O.J. 1994 L 20/15, 21.

[24] *See* Peeters, The Rule of Reason Revisited: Prohibition on Restraints of Competition in the Sherman Act and the EEC Treaty, 37 Am.J.Comp.L. 521 (1989).

that information.[25] There is some suggestion that release may be obtained by plaintiffs before national courts in civil actions for damages caused by cartel activities.[26] However, the Court of Justice has ruled that the Commission must give the information source notice and an opportunity to challenge these decisions.[27]

In conducting its investigations, the Commission may ask for verbal explanations on the spot and have access to and seal off business premises. One author refers to these powers as "dawn raids and other nightmares." Nevertheless, the Court of Justice has affirmed this right of hostile access.[28] Effective May 1, 2004, subject to the issuance of a local court warrant, this right of access extends to private homes, motor vehicles and other personal property of corporate directors, managers and staff. In these matters the Commission acts on its own authority. It must, however, inform member states prior to taking such steps and may request their assistance.

The member states must render assistance when businesses fail to comply with competition law investigations conducted by the Commission. Although the Commission may require production of all necessary information in its competition law investigations, it may not force firms to answer questions which could lead to actual admissions of infringement.[29] Information provided to the Commission as part of an EU competition law investigation may not generally be used by member states to commence enforcement proceedings under their own competition laws.[30]

Businesses involved in the Commission's investigatory process have limited rights to notice and hearing.[31] They do not have access to the Commission's files. Any failure on the part of an enterprise to provide information requested by the Commission or to submit to its investigation can result in the imposition of considerable fines and

---

[25] *See* Samenwerkende Elektriciteitsproductiebedrijven NV v. Commission, (1994) Eur.Comm.Rep. I–01911 (Case C–36/92).

[26] Pfleiderer v. Bundeskartellamt, (2011) Eur.Comm.Rep. (Case C–360/09).

[27] AKZO Chemie BV v. Commission, (1986) Eur.Comm.Rep. 1965.

[28] Hoeschst v. Commission, (1987) Eur.Comm.Rep. 1549; Dow Chemical Nederland BV v. Commission, (1987) Eur.Comm.Rep. 4367; NV Samenwerkende lectriciteits-produktiebedrijven (SEP) v. Commission, (1991) Eur.Comm.Rep. II 649 (Case T–39/90).

[29] Orkem v. Commission, (1989) Eur.Comm.Rep. 3283. However, this principle does not necessarily apply to civil proceedings before the courts of the member states. Otto, (1993) Eur.Comm.Rep. I–05683 (Case No. C–60/92). In such cases, the right against self-incrimination depends on national law.

[30] Dirección General de Defensa de la Competencia v. Asociación Española de Banca Privada and others, (1992) Eur.Comm.Rep. I–4785.

[31] Commission Regulation 99/63. *See generally* Hoffmann-La Roche v. Commission, (1979) Eur.Comm.Rep. 461.

penalties. For example, the Belgian and French subsidiaries of the Japanese electrical and electronic group, Matsushita, were fined by the Commission for supplying it with false information about whether Matsushita recommended retail prices for its products. These sanctions are civil in nature and run against the corporation, not its directors or management.

The Commission has been increasing the use of its investigatory powers. Several procedural requirements for Commission investigations and hearings have been discussed by the Court of Justice. One notable Court decision upheld the authority of the Commission to conduct searches of corporate offices without notice or warrant when it has reason to believe that pertinent evidence may be lost.[32] Another notable decision permitted a Swiss "whistle blower" who once worked for Hoffmann-La Roche (a defendant in EU competition law proceedings) to sue the Union in tort for disclosure of his identity as an informant.[33]

Attorney-Client Privileges

Written communications with external lawyers licensed in an EU member state undertaken for defense purposes are confidential and need not be disclosed.[34] Written communications with in-house lawyers are *not* exempt from disclosure, nor are communications with external *non*-EU counsel.[35] Thus communications with North American attorneys (who are not also EU licensed attorneys) are generally discoverable. For example, shortly after the *AM & S* decision, the Commission obtained in-house counsel documents from John Deere, Inc., a Belgian subsidiary of the United States multinational. These documents were drafted as advice to management on how to avoid EU competition liability for export prohibition restraints. They were used by the Commission to justify the finding of an intentional Article 101 violation and a fine of 2 million EUROs.[36]

United States attorneys have followed these developments with amazement and trepidation. Disclaimers of possible non-confidentiality are one option to consider in dealing with clients on EU law matters. At a minimum, U.S. attorneys ought to advise their

---

[32] Re National Panasonic, (1980) Eur.Comm.Rep. 2033.

[33] Adams v. Commission, (1985) Eur.Comm.Rep. 3539.

[34] AM & S Europe Ltd. v. Commission, (1982) Eur.Comm.Rep. 1575. *Accord*, Akzo Nobel Chemicals Ltd v. Commission, (2007) Eur.Comm.Rep. II–3523 (documents) and Akzo Nobel v. Commission, (2009) Eur.Comm.Rep. I–8301 (emails received in EU subject to EU rules); Akzo Nobel Chemicals Ltd. v. Akcros, (2010) Eur.Comm.Rep. (C–48/09) (internal company communications with in-house lawyers).

[35] *Id.*

[36] John Deere O.J. 1985 L. 35/58. Accord, AKZO Nobel Chemicals v. Commission, (EC Commission) T–125/03, T–253/03.

clients that the usual rules on attorney-client privilege may not apply and always consider involving a U.S. attorney throughout.

Shared Powers

Regulation 17 and Regulation 1 envision significant cooperation between the European Union and national authorities in the field of competition law. Effective May 1, 2004, enforcement of Articles 101 and 102 is shared with the competition agencies and national courts of the member states. A new European Competition Network has been established to facilitate cooperative law enforcement and minimize divergent application of competition law principles, with the Commission to act as final arbiter on substantive matters. The principal reason for this sharing of enforcement duties is to allow the Commission to focus its energies on price fixing, cartel arrangements and other serious violations of Articles 101 and 102.

The Commission is not under an affirmative duty to carry out an investigation when a complaint is submitted to it.[37] The Court of First Instance (now the General Court) ruled that the Commission can refuse to pursue a competition law complaint if an adequate remedy is available from a national court.[38] This decision supports the Commission's customary practice of decentralized "subsidiarity" in the competition law field. Of course, subsidiarity carries with it the potential for the inconsistent application of the competition rules.[39] The ECJ has construed the power of national courts to enforce EU competition law narrowly. Since May 1, 2004, national courts may ask the Commission for support regarding Article 101 or 102, with the Commission and national authorities empowered to file opinions with the national courts.

Moreover, in all cases affecting member state trade, Regulation 1/2003 permits the Commission to issue *ex ante* binding decisions determining that a particular agreement or practice does not infringe European competition law. Such decisions would preclude different results at the national level. For an example of arguably different results in analogous situations, an example which casts doubt on Regulation 1 cooperation, see *Intrepreneur Pub Co CPC v. Crehan*.[40] The Commission has taken to regularly monitoring decisions of national competition law authorities and courts involving Articles 101 and 102.

---

[37] BEUC v. Commission, (2000) Eur.Comm.Rep. II–00101.

[38] Automec SRL v. Commission, (1992) Eur.Comm.Rep. II–367.

[39] *See* VEBIC VZW, (2010) Eur.Comm.Rep. (Case C–439/08); Prezes Urzedu v. Tele2 Polska, (2011) Eur.Comm.Rep. (Case C–375/09).

[40] 2006 U.K. House of Lords 38 (July 19, 2006) reviewed at 32 Eur. Law Rev. 260 (April 2007).

§ 7.5 Commission Prosecutions, Immunity and Sanctions

Enforcement Procedures

In addition to its investigatory powers, the Commission determines when violations of the competition law provisions of Articles 101 or 102 occur. This is the source of the Commission's power to render enforcement decisions. A regulation limits the period in which the Commission may render a decision in competition law cases to five years. All Commission decisions, including enforcement decisions and decisions to investigate, fine or penalize must be published and are subject to judicial review. Since 1989, most of these appeals have been heard by the General Court. During interim periods, the Commission has the power to order measures indispensable to its functions.[41] Interim relief should be granted when there is prima facie evidence of an Article 101 or 102 violation and an urgent need to prevent serious and irreparable private damage (or intolerable damage to the public interest).[42]

Any measures the Commission takes must, however, be temporary and conservatory in nature, restricted to what is required in the given situation and consider the legitimate interests of the enterprise which is the subject of the interim measures.[43] La Cinq, a private television service twice denied membership in the European Broadcasting Union, successfully met these criteria. The General Court rebuked the Commission's refusal to grant provisional Article 102 protection.[44] Before deciding that a competition law breach has occurred, the Commission issues a statement of "objections."[45] This statement must reveal which facts the Commission intends to rely upon in reaching a decision that a violation has occurred and be worded with sufficient clarity to enable the parties to know what conduct is being objected to.[46]

A hearing can then be requested by the alleged violator(s) or any interested person.[47] These hearings are conducted in private, with separate reviews of complainants and witnesses. The Commission must disclose only those non-confidential documents in its file upon which it intends to rely and are necessary to prepare an adequate

---

41 Camera Care v. Commission, (1980) Eur.Comm.Rep. 119.

42 Sea Containers v. Stena Sealink, O.J. L 15 (1994) 8, 15 point 56.

43 *Id.*

44 La Cinq v. Commission, (1992) Eur.Comm.Rep. II–1.

45 Regulation 99/63, Article 2(4).

46 AEG v. Commission, (1983) Eur.Comm.Rep. 3151.

47 Regulation 99/63, Article 7.

defense.[48] The parties generally receive, along with the statement of objections, a list of all the documents in the Commission's possession with an indication of the documents or parts of documents to which they may have access. Among the documents generally regarded as confidential, and therefore inaccessible, are internal Commission documents such as memoranda, drafts and other working papers.[49] After the hearing, the Commission consults with the Advisory Committee on Restrictive Practices and Monopolies, which is composed of one civil servant expert from each member state. The results of this consultation are not made public. Having consulted the Committee, the Commission is then free to render an enforcement decision.

Sanctions and Immunity

In its enforcement decision, the Commission may require businesses to "cease and desist" their infringing activities. The Commission may not, at least in an Article 101 proceeding, require a violator to contract with the complainant.[50] In practice, this power has sufficed to permit the Commission to order infringing enterprises to come up with their own remedial solutions. However, the Commission may not, at least in Article 101 proceedings, require a violator to contract with the complainant. Daily penalties may be imposed to compel adherence to the order to cease and desist. Commission decisions on violations of Articles 101 and 102 are also accompanied by a capacity to substantially fine any intentionally or negligently infringing enterprise. Fines may be based on up to 30 percent of annual sales, multiplied by the number of years of infringement. When appeals are lodged against Commission decisions imposing fines and penalties, payment is suspended but interest is charged and a bank guarantee for the amounts concerned must be provided.[51]

In the early years, fines and penalties levied by the Commission were few, relatively small in amount, and frequently reduced on appeal to the Court of Justice. As EU competition law doctrine has become clearer, these trends have all been reversed. In its more recent decisions, the Court has upheld substantial fines and penalties imposed by the Commission in competition law proceedings and recognized their deterrent value.[52] The trend towards larger

---

48 VBVB and VBBB v. Commission, (1984) Eur.Comm.Rep. 19.

49 23rd Report on Competition Policy (1994) point 353.

50 Automec SRL v. Commission, (1992) Eur.Comm.Rep. II–367. *Compare* Article 86 Case law on refusals to deal by dominant firms in Section 7.20.

51 Hasselblad v. Commission, (1982) Eur.Comm.Rep. 1555.

52 *See* Musique Diffusion Française SA v. Commission, (1983) Eur.Comm.Rep. 1825.

fines has been confirmed by the Commission in recent cases, with immunity or reduced fines granted to firms that "confess" first, or early, in EU competition law proceedings. The Commission has imposed substantial fines on cartels in the chemicals industry,[53] the carton industry[54] and the steel industry.[55] In 2001, the Commission imposed competition law fines of more than 850 million Euros on European companies for conspiring to fix prices and divide up the vitamins market. Fines against other cartels have ratcheted up since Regulation 1 took effect in 2004, hitting *inter alia* producers of industrial bags, copper fittings, fasteners, hydrogen peroxide, acrylic glass, car glass, synthetic rubber, gas insulated switches, TV/monitor tubes, auto bearings, and elevators and escalators. In 2016, a truck-makers cartel was fined 2.93 billion Euros.

Challenges to EU cartel fines based on the EU Fundamental Freedoms Charter and the European Convention on Human Rights are pending.

More recently, the Commission has granted total immunity to the first cartel participant to confess and provide material evidence. The second participant to "provide significant value" to an investigation can secure a 30 to 50 percent reduction in fines. Third and subsequent confessors may receive lesser reductions. Hence, there are strong incentives to be first in the confessional queue. U.S. chip maker Micron Technology, for example, escaped all fines by being the whistle blower on a global price-fixing chip cartel.

Any complete picture of the development of Article 101 must include the Commission's informal negotiations as well as its decisions to prosecute, exempt or clear infringing activities. Compliance with Articles 101 and 102 is often achieved short of a formal Commission decision. Word of informal file-closings is occasionally revealed. In *Re Eurofima,* for example, the Commission terminated proceedings without issuing a decision. In the process of responding to complaints from suppliers, the Commission was able to secure termination of infringing conduct from Eurofima, the most important buyer of railway rolling stock in the Union. Eurofima also undertook to continue to comply with EU competition law. The Commission announced these results in a press release.[56]

---

53 PVC, O.J. 1994 L 239/14.

54 Cartonboard, O.J. 1994 L 243/1.

55 Steel Beams, O.J. 1994 L 116/1.

56 (1973) Common Mkt.L.Rep. D217.

§ 7.6 Individual Exemptions, Negative Clearances, Comfort Letters (May 1, 2004)

Regulation 17 not only served as the basis for the investigatory and enforcement machinery of EU competition law, but also included the ways of avoiding the application of the law to business practices. Until May 1, 2004, businesses could avoid the application of Art. 101(1) if they received an exemption or negative clearance. The basic prerequisite was that the practice be properly notified to the Commission. The Commission could not grant either a negative clearance or exemption until the practice was notified.[57] Once this notification was submitted, the Commission was precluded from imposing fines regarding practices taking place after notification and before the Commission's decision.[58] On the other hand, if the practice was not notified to the Commission and it infringed Article 101(1), fines could be imposed even if the practice hypothetically fulfilled all of the requirements of 101(3).[59]

Individual Exemptions

Under Regulation 17 individual exemptions were granted by the Commission under Article 101(3) for a limited period. They were subject to review on renewal and could be conditioned upon extensive stipulations. Individual exemptions could also be revoked or altered by a subsequent Commission decision. Exempted activities could later be prohibited, when:

(1) The situation changed with respect to a factor essential in the Commission's original decision;

(2) The parties committed a breach of any obligation attached to the exemption;

(3) The original decision was based on false information or obtained fraudulently; or

(4) The parties abused the exemption.

The Commission could revoke its decision with retroactive effect in cases (2), (3) or (4).[60]

---

57 *See* ECO System/Peugeot, O.J. 1992 L 66/1, 7.

58 An application for negative clearance itself was no protection from fines, *see* John Deere, O.J. 1985 L 35/58. However, the general practice was to submit an application for negative clearance along with an application for an exemption under Art. 101(3).

59 Musique Diffusion Française SA v. Commission, (1983) Eur.Comm.Rep. 1825, 1902.

60 Art. 8(3) of Regulation 17.

Negative Clearances

Regulation 17 permitted businesses in doubt as to the applicability of Article 101(1) to their activities to request a "negative clearance" from the Commission.[61] The Commission granted negative clearances solely based on the factual and legal information then before it. A negative clearance stated that the Commission saw no grounds to intervene under Article 101(1). The Commission's decision could be because the relevant agreement, decision or concerted practice did not perceptibly affect trade between member states or did not perceptibly restrain competition within the Common Market as 101(1) requires.

There was a critical difference under Regulation 17 between a negative clearance and an individual exemption. The latter admitted an Article 101(1) infringement or potential infringement but requests a declaration of inapplicability under the special terms of Article 101(3). The former indicated that there was no infringement of 101(1) because of the terms of that Article and the nature of the activities involved. These lines of argument could be and often were pursued simultaneously before the Commission using Form A/B.[62] Only the Commission (not national authorities) could grant individual exemptions and negative clearances.

Procedures

When the Commission intended to grant a negative clearance or an Article 101(3) individual exemption, it published the "main content" of the decision after allowing for protection of legitimate business secrets. After publication, all interested third parties were invited to submit their observations to the Commission prior to its decision. Since important matters could be revealed to competitors and potential litigants, this publication requirement may have chilled business usage of the negative clearance and individual exemption procedures erected under Regulation 17.

When the Commission issued a statement of objections and before an adverse decision was made, the applicant was entitled to a hearing.[63] The Court of Justice held that the Commission had discretion whether to hear oral argument on negative clearance and individual exemption applications.[64] Third parties could have access to the hearing process on showing a legitimate interest. As with enforcement proceedings, the hearing was private, and a record was made. The Commission gave written reasons to explain whatever

---

61 Art. 2 of Regulation 17.

62 O.J. 1993 L 336/4.

63 Hoffmann-La Roche v. Commission, (1979) Eur.Comm.Rep. 461.

64 FEDETAB v. Commission, (1980) Eur.Comm.Rep. 3125.

final decision was taken, although the Court of Justice held that the Commission need not discuss every fact or law issue raised during the proceedings.[65] The issuance of an Article 101(3) exemption did not foreclose the possibility of a prosecution under Article 102 since the two provisions concern different types of distortions of competition.[66]

Comfort Letters

In addition to individual exemptions and negative clearances, the Commission increasingly relied on the use of so-called "comfort letters" to close a case. The Commission indicated that it normally dealt with notifications by issuing a comfort letter unless the case was of "particular political, economic or legal significance."[67] This type of decision, which incidentally was not addressed in Regulation 17 but developed as administrative practice, had significant practical importance since it was issued much quicker than an exemption or even a negative clearance.

A comfort letter was issued in response to an application for exemption or negative clearance and it generally stated that based on the facts presented to it the Commission saw no reason to intervene in opposition to the notified practices. Comfort letters were issued only with approval of the parties[68] but because of the time saved, the parties did not generally object. Once the parties received a comfort letter, they typically proceeded to implement their agreement. In the absence of a change in circumstances, the Commission did not alter its position and was precluded from imposing fines under Regulation 17 since the agreement remained notified.

The change of circumstances sufficient to cause the Commission to alter its position did not have to be attributable to the parties. For example, the Commission decided to intervene in a distribution system concerning ice cream for which it had previously issued comfort letters.[69] The Commission based its reasoning not on the fact that the practices of the parties had changed but rather because the circumstances in the market had changed. In this respect, the intervention by the Commission was largely due to complaints made by a competitor of the recipients of the comfort letters.

---

[65] *Id.*

[66] Tetra Pak Rausing SA v. Commission (1990) 2 Eur.Comm.Rep. 309.

[67] Notice on cooperation between national courts and the Commission in applying Articles 8[1] and 8[2] of the EEC Treaty, O.J. 1993 C 39/6, 8.

[68] 13th Report on Competition Policy (1984) p. 64.

[69] Schöller Lebensmittel GmbH & Co., KG, O.J. 1993 L 183/1; Langnese-Iglo GmbH, O.J. 1993 L 182/19.

In addition, the national courts were not bound by the comfort letter.[70] This was one of the primary disadvantages of the comfort letter since they afforded only limited legal certainty against the application of the European and national competition laws by the national courts. Nonetheless, as far as the application of the European competition law was concerned, the Commission called upon the national courts to take the comfort letter into account when deciding whether a particular practice amounts to a restraint of competition.[71]

§ 7.7 Individual Exemptions After May 1, 2004—Marine Paints Example

Effective May 1, 2004, the system of Commission notification to obtain individual exemptions, negative clearances and comfort letters outlined above was abolished. Thereafter, exemptions from Article 101 are primarily of the "group" or "block" type summarized in Section 7.9 below Member State authorities and courts, in addition to the Commission, have the power to recognize individual Article 101(3) exemptions in appropriate circumstances. See Regulation 1/2003 replacing Regulation 17, and the content of Article 101(3) discussed in Section 7.3.

Individual exemptions granted by the Commission under Article 101(3) prior to May 1, 2004, offer guidance to their issuance under Regulation 1. Such grants have stressed the projected advantages of reduced production costs, higher productivity, more effective and less costly activities, and somewhat vague notions of technical and economic progress. Exemptions denied by the Commission have stressed the likelihood of the alleged benefits occurring under competition anyway, the undesirable protection of national markets and "serious" losses of market competition. As a rule, the Commission weighs the advantages alleged in favor of the restrictive agreement, decision or practice against the resultant loss of market competition and against the likelihood that competition itself might produce similar advantages. This balancing process is well illustrated by the following example.

Re Transocean Marine Paint

In 1962 the Transocean Marine Paint Association, eighteen medium-sized marine paint manufacturers, sought to develop and market a common brand of standard quality paint. They applied for a negative clearance or, in the alternative, an individual exemption

[70] L'Oréal v. PVBA, (1980) Eur.Comm.Rep. 3775, 3789; Lancôme v. Etos, (1980) Eur.Comm.Rep. 2511, 2533.

[71] Notice on cooperation between national courts and the Commission in applying Articles 81 and 82 of the EEC Treaty, O.J.1993 C 39/6, 8.

for their agreement. Five of the manufacturers were domiciled in the Union. Sales responsibility for this brand was allocated on a territorial basis with a commission payable to offset sales in another member's territory irrespective of that member's services regarding those sales. Prices for the Association's standard paint were set individually. Members of the Association could still sell paints of either higher or lower (but not standard) quality under their own trademarks. Such nonstandard paints could not be imported into the sales territory of another member without its consent.

Since the agreement fell within all the terms of Article 101(1) and was not *de minimis,* the Commission denied the request for a negative clearance. Prior to granting a 101(3) exemption, the Commission required the association to eliminate (as incompatible with Article 101(1)) certain other territorial protection, sales allocation, collective discrimination, and price information exchange clauses. The Commission perceived that a common brand of paint would make the Association's product more marketable in the EU and world markets. The availability of standard brand paint in most of the world's shipyards was important because it is apparently desirable for technical reasons to reuse the same marine paints on ships.

Moreover, it appears that the marine paint market is quite distinct from the market for paints in general (80 percent of marine paints cannot be used for other purposes). Without citing market shares, the Commission noted that the Association manufacturers faced strong competition within the EU from other large international marine paint companies. Hence, reasoned the Commission, the loss of real or potential competition among medium-sized Association manufacturers was outweighed by the potential increase in EU competition in the standard-quality marine paint market viewed as a whole.

The exemption was subject to conditions requiring the Association to report to the Commission any alterations in its membership, any amendments or additions to their agreement, any relevant board decisions or arbitral awards, and its annual volume of sales and inter-Association deliveries. Issued in June of 1966, the Transocean Marine Paint Association exemption was effective until January of 1973.[72]

On application in 1972 for an extension of the exemption, the Association had grown to twenty in number. Five original members had withdrawn while eight new members had been admitted. Seven of the twenty were based in the enlarged Union. This time the market

---

[72] Re Transocean Marine Paint Association, (1967) Common Mkt.L.Rep. D9.

shares of the Association and its competitors were published. The Association had an expanding 5 to 10 percent of the world marine paint market, 25 percent of which was held by International Red Hand Inc., a non-associate. From 1966 to 1972 the Association members did well with their standard quality paint. Sales rose from one-third to about three-quarters of the total turnover of the membership. One Far Eastern member accounted for over 60 percent of the Association's turnover. In light of these facts, the Commission declared unjustifiable, in 1973, the Association's territorial consent on nonstandard paint sales and the territorial standard brand sales commission obligations described above. Termination of these obligations was ordered by the Commission before it granted the exemption renewal for another six years.[73]

The original 1967 conditions attached to the exemption were retained in 1973 while an additional requirement concerning concentration in the industry was attached. Any new links or changes in existing links by way of common directors or managers, or by way of financial participation between an Association member and another enterprise in the paints sector, were to be reported. The Association appealed the inclusion of this additional condition on procedural grounds. It claimed lack of notice and opportunity to present a contrary argument. The Court of Justice agreed with the Association and subsequently annulled this part of the Commission's decision.[74] In a revised monitoring requirement issued in accordance with proper procedures, shareholdings amounting to 25 percent or more of firms in the paint sector doing business in the EU had to be reported.

It is worth noting the extent to which the Commission was able to gradually filter out the most anticompetitive aspects of the Association's agreement. This process has continued over the years as the Commission has periodically renewed the exemption. In December of 1988 the Commission continued the exemption through 1998.[75] Furthermore, while the exempt practices may be illegal under competition laws elsewhere (*e.g.*, under United States antitrust law), individual exemptions do grant immunity under the *Wilhelm* case[76] from the national competition laws of member states.

---

[73] (1974) Common Mkt.L.Rep. D11.

[74] Transocean Marine Paint Association v. Commission, (1974) Eur.Comm.Rep. 1063.

[75] Re The Transocean Marine Paint Association, (1988) 4 Common Mkt.L.Rep. 674.

[76] *See* § 7.25.

§ 7.8 "Clearances" After May 1, 2004—SAFCO Example

Regulation 1 does *not* anticipate the use of negative clearances and comfort letters. However, the legal principles previously developed under those procedures are likely to operate to "clear" business practices from potential Article 101(1) liabilities. The SAFCO case detailed below highlights those principles. Negative clearance proceedings did not often involve a full examination of the market impact of a particular business practice. Instead, the Commission focused on the lack of a perceptible effect on trade between member states or on the lack of an appreciable effect on competition in the Common Market. These two legal issues were jointly considered as the SAFCO case illustrates.[77]

Re SAFCO

Seven French producers of preserved vegetables created an exclusive sales agency (SAFCO) to encourage the export of their products to West Germany. They assigned their trademarks to SAFCO for export purposes and could be expelled summarily by the SAFCO Association. Membership in the export association was limited to enterprises with less than five million French francs capital in assets and less than five hundred employees. Admissions decisions were made secretly. The SAFCO articles of association were transmitted in 1963 to the Commission along with a request for a negative clearance.

Prior to the formation of SAFCO, some of its members had been significantly involved in exports to West Germany. The export association was quite successful and obtained about 2 percent of the German market for preserved vegetables by 1972, the time of the Commission's much delayed decision on the negative clearance request. The Commission acknowledged that while export competition between the French producers was restricted by their agreement, it was not perceptibly restricted. The SAFCO enterprises remained in competition with each other in the French market and the preserved vegetable market within the EU and Germany was characterized by numerous products similar in quality and competitive in price. Producers of greatly superior size were competitors of SAFCO. An increasingly integrated and competitive common market for preserved vegetables was apparent. The Commission issued a negative clearance to SAFCO indicating, on the facts and law before it, that there was no necessity for intervention under Article 101(1).

---

77 SAFCO, (1972) Common Mkt.L.Rep. D83.

Unlike Article 101(3) exemptions, the Commission could not issue negative clearances subject to conditions, review and renewal. Although it can negotiate the removal of restrictive clauses prior to issuance, the absence of these important monitoring features made negative clearances long-term risks as regards competition policy. In SAFCO, the agreement was for ninety-nine years. What may not "perceptibly" restrict EU competition or trade in 1963 or 1972 may do so in the future. Suppose SAFCO, through competition or membership expansion, obtains 10 or 20 percent of the German market. Suppose membership denials or dismissals hasten the demise of competitors in the French market. Whether negative clearances were revocable, and if so under what terms and with what effects, were legal questions that remained largely unexplored.

§ 7.9 Group Exemptions and Notices

The Commission received an onslaught of negative clearance requests and Article 101(3) notifications in 1962 when Regulation 17 took effect. Most of the business activities involved in this deluge were in the distribution and licensing areas. As a result, the Commission sought and obtained authorization in 1965 from the Council to formulate, for limited time periods, group "declarations of inapplicability" under Article 101(3).[78] These are commonly known as "group or block exemptions." The Council granted this authorization, noting that Article 101(3) allows "classes" of exempt agreements. Group exemptions invite businesses to conform their agreements and behavior to their terms and conditions. In other words, group exemptions rely upon confidential business self-regulation.

Another important indication of permissible business practices are the various notices and guidelines which the Commission has issued. However, in contrast to the group exemptions, these notices are mere policy declarations and have no legally binding effect on the national courts or the European courts. Nonetheless, the notices provide an important indication of the Commission's policy toward certain practices and it is unlikely that the Commission will impose fines on businesses which have relied in good faith on the pronouncements of the Commission in one of its notices.[79] Competition law notices issued by the Commission have concerned agreements of "minor" importance,[80] horizontal cooperation

---

[78] Regulation 19/65.

[79] In fact, the Commission may be estopped from imposing fines in such cases. *See* Miller v. Commission, (1978) Eur.Comm.Rep. 131, 158.

[80] 1986 Official Journal C231/2, revised O.J. C 368/07 (Dec. 22, 2001).

agreements,[81] exclusive agency contracts,[82] and technology sharing agreements among small and medium-sized businesses.[83] Many business agreements are drafted with the details of these group exemption regulations and policy notices in mind.

After test enforcement decisions and definitive rulings by the Court of Justice, the Commission issued Regulation 67 in 1967. It became the first of a series of group exemptions from Article 101(1). Group exemptions now exist for vertical restraints (including distribution and franchise agreements),[84] vehicle distribution and servicing agreements,[85] production specialization agreements among small firms,[86] research and development agreements among small firms,[87] and technology transfer agreements.[88] In addition there are several group exemptions which are directed at specific sectors of the economy. These include most notably the insurance sector[89] and the transport sector.[90]

§ 7.10 Agency and Distribution Agreements, Vertical Restraints Regulation

Commercial Agents

Council Directive 86/653 coordinates member state laws regarding self-employed commercial agents. This directive was inspired by existing French and German law. In Denmark and Britain new legislation was required for its implementation. From a United States perspective, the directive is remarkably protective of the agent. It is particularly significant because many North American firms first do business in Europe through commercial agents. The directive defines a commercial agent as a "self-employed intermediary who has continuing authority to negotiate the purchase or sale of goods on behalf of another person (the principal), or to negotiate and conclude such transactions on behalf of and in the name of that principal."

Directive 86/653 establishes various rights and obligations for commercial agents and principals, *e.g.*, the agent's duty to comply with reasonable instructions and the principal's duty to act in good

[81] 2011 Official Journal C11/1.

[82] 1962 Official Journal 2921.

[83] 1979 Official Journal C1/2.

[84] Regulation 2790/99. *See* Section 19.6.

[85] Regulation 461/2010.

[86] Regulation 1218/2010.

[87] Regulation 1217/2010.

[88] Regulation 772/2004. *See* Section 19.7.

[89] Regulation 3932/92, replaced by Regulation 358/2003.

[90] Regulation 1617/93; Regulation 83/91.

faith. In the absence of an agreed compensation, customary local practices prevail (and if none, reasonable remuneration). Compensation may apparently be by commission or salary. Compensation rights before and after the effective period of the agency contract are specified. Directive 86/653 also establishes when the agent's commission becomes due and payable, as well as the conditions under which it is extinguishable. For example, the agent is entitled to compensation on all transactions in which he or she participated. Moreover, transactions that have been concluded during the term of the agreement with third parties the agent previously procured as customers for the principal fall within this rule. The agent is also entitled to compensation on transactions with customers located in his or her area of responsibility or for whom the agent is an exclusive representative.

Termination Rights

An important element concerns the notice and termination rights of the agent. Agency agreements for fixed periods of time that continue to be performed by both parties upon expiration become contracts for an indefinite period. Minimum termination notice requirements of one month per year of service up to three years, and optional notice requirements up to six months for six years are created. The member states must provide for either a right of indemnification or for damages compensation, which must be claimed within one year of termination. The agency agreement cannot waive or otherwise "derogate" these rights. The indemnity cannot exceed one year's remuneration but does not foreclose damages. The indemnity is payable if the agent has brought in new customers or increased volumes of existing customers to the substantial continuing benefit of the principal and is equitable in light of all circumstances.

The right to damages because of termination occurs when the agent is deprived of commissions which would have been earned upon proper performance to the substantial benefit of the principal. The agent may also seek damages relief when termination blocks amortization of the costs and expenses incurred on advice of the principal while performing under the agency contract. The death of the agent triggers these indemnity or compensation rights. They are also payable if the agent must terminate the contract because of age, infirmity or illness causing an inability to reasonably continue service.

If an agency agreement chooses non-EU law to govern its terms, this choice of law will not override the agent's mandatory damages remedies.[91] No indemnity or damages may be had under specified circumstances, including when the agent is in default justifying immediate termination under national law. "Restraint of trade" clauses (covenants not to compete) are permissible upon termination to the extent that they are limited to two years, the goods in question and the geographic area and/or customers of the agent. Such clauses can be made as a pre-condition to the payment of an indemnity.

Competition Law Applicability

A 1962 Commission Notice announced that agreements with "commercial agents" were outside Article 101(1) TFEU.[92] The theory behind exempting commercial agents from EU antitrust law was their "auxiliary function" on behalf of principals who were subject to the law. In *Flemish Travel Agents*,[93] however, the European Court of Justice ruled that the relationship between suppliers and independent commercial agents could present competitive implications under the Treaty. The 1962 Notice defines "commercial agents" as those who undertake for a specified territory to negotiate or conclude transactions on behalf of an enterprise either in their own name or in the name of that enterprise. The key to distinguishing agents from independent traders who are subject to Article 101 is whether the intermediary assumes any risk in the transaction, including nonpayment, title to a considerable inventory of products, liability for substantial services to customers, or control over prices or terms of sale. This definition of "commercial agents" has been somewhat narrowed by case law.[94]

In December 1990, the Commission released a draft of a new notice on commercial agency agreements. Under it, the Commission distinguishes between "integrated" agents dependent on the supplier and not generally subject to Article 101, and more independent "un-integrated" agents. An agent is "integrated" if he or she generally devotes at least one-third of the time to the principal and does not handle competing products. Certain restrictions apply even to integrated agents. For example, absolute bans on transactions with customers or suppliers outside designated territories may be prohibited. Nonintegrated agents are generally treated as independent traders subject to full review under Article 101.

---

[91] Ingmar GB v. Eaton Leonard Technologies, (2000) Eur.Comm.Rep. I–9305 (Nov. 9, 2000) (California choice of law clause).

[92] 1962 Official Journal 2921; *see* Section 7.9.

[93] 1987 Eur.Comm.Rep. 3801.

[94] *See* Cooperative Vereniging "Suiker Unie" V.A. v. Commission, (1975) Eur.Comm.Rep. 1663.

Exclusive Dealing Agreements

The Commission received an onslaught of negative clearance requests and Article 101(3) notifications in 1962 when Regulation 17 took effect. Most of the business activities involved in this deluge were in the distribution and licensing areas. As a result, the Commission sought and obtained authorization in 1965 from the Council to formulate, for limited time periods, group "declarations of inapplicability" under Article 101(3).[95] These are commonly known as "group or block exemptions." The Council granted this authorization, noting that Article 101(3) allows "classes" of exempt agreements. Group exemptions invite businesses to conform their agreements and behavior to their terms and conditions. In other words, group exemptions rely upon confidential business self-regulation.

Another important indication of permissible business practices are the various notices and guidelines which the Commission has issued. However, in contrast to the group exemptions, these notices are mere policy declarations and have no legally binding effect on the national courts or the European courts. Nonetheless, the notices provide an important indication of the Commission's policy toward certain practices and it is unlikely that the Commission will impose fines on businesses which have relied in good faith on the pronouncements of the Commission in one of its notices.[96] Competition law notices issued by the Commission have concerned agreements of "minor" importance,[97] horizontal cooperation agreements,[98] exclusive agency contracts,[99] and technology sharing agreements among small and medium-sized businesses.[100] Many business agreements are drafted with the details of these group exemption regulations and policy notices in mind.

After test enforcement decisions and definitive rulings by the Court of Justice, the Commission issued Regulation 67 in 1967. It became the first of a series of group exemptions from Article 101(1). Group exemptions now exist for vertical restraints (including distribution and franchise agreements),[101] vehicle distribution and servicing agreements,[102] production specialization agreements

---

[95] Regulation 19/65.

[96] In fact, the Commission may be estopped from imposing fines in such cases. *See* Miller v. Commission, (1978) Eur.Comm.Rep. 131, 158.

[97] 1986 Official Journal C231/2, revised O.J. C 368/07 (Dec. 22, 2001).

[98] 2011 Official Journal C11/1.

[99] 1962 Official Journal 2921.

[100] 1979 Official Journal C1/2.

[101] Regulation 2790/99. *See* Section 7.10.

[102] Regulation 461/2010.

among small firms,[103] research and development agreements among small firms,[104] and technology transfer agreements.[105] In addition there are several group exemptions which are directed at specific sectors of the economy. These include most notably the insurance sector[106] and the transport sector.[107]

Regulation 67/67 was replaced in 1983 by Regulation 1983/83 (exclusive distribution) and Regulation 1984/83 (exclusive purchasing).[108] Exclusive dealing agreements ordinarily involve restrictions on manufacturers or suppliers and independent distributors of goods. These restraints concern persons the manufacturer may supply, to whom the manufacturer or distributor may sell, and from whom the distributor may acquire the goods or similar goods. Exclusive dealing agreements should be distinguished from agency or consignment agreements where title and most risk remain with the manufacturer until the goods are sold by their retail agents to consumers. The announced EU policy position is that competition law will not require a manufacturer to compete with its agents.[109] Territorial exclusivity in genuine retail agency agreements is therefore legal.[110]

Regulation 67 and its successors may be seen as an excellent example of Commission efforts to employ and develop competition law under Article 81 (now 101 TFEU) to serve the goal of economic integration. The formation of absolute territorial trade barriers, similar in impact to national tariffs and quotas that existed prior to the creation of the Common Market, would negate some of the economic benefits of increased trade and economic integration. Yet prohibiting exclusive dealing entirely would deter Common Market sales by national manufacturers. Hence, distributive competition among goods for sale within the EU is encouraged by permitting exclusive dealing agreements between manufacturers and independent distributors *and* by ensuring that competition as between exclusive dealers in the same goods is also preserved.

---

[103] Regulation 1218/2010.

[104] Regulation 1217/2010.

[105] Regulation 772/2004. *See* Section 7.11.

[106] Regulation 3932/92, replaced by Regulation 358/2003.

[107] Regulation 1617/93; Regulation 83/91.

[108] *See* Delimitis v. Henninger Bräu, (1991) Eur.Comm.Rep. I–935 (234/89) (Regulation 1984/83 applied extensively to beer-supply agreements).

[109] Notice on exclusive agency contracts made with commercial agents, O.J.1962, 2921.

[110] *But see* Re Pittsburgh Corning Europe, (1973) Common Mkt.L.Rep. D2; Commission Announcement on Exclusive Agency Contracts Made with Commercial Agents, O.J. 1962, 2921.

It is only *absolute* territorial exclusive dealing that precludes benefit from the group exemption. It is precluded whether achieved by the exercise of national patent, copyright or trademark rights, or simply by contractual restraints between manufacturers and their exclusive dealers. For example, when territorial protection for distributors is obtained by making slight changes to a product's content, this constitutes an Article 101 violation. Manufacturers and distributors may not seek product approvals which effectively divide up the common market in this manner.[111] Pharmaceutical distribution agreements have been given somewhat wider leeway to restrict the cross-border sale of drugs given differing government price caps.[112]

According to the Commission, vertical agreements must therefore be examined on two levels:

> Firstly, the exclusive nature of a contractual relationship between a producer and a distributor is viewed as restricting competition, since it limits the parties' freedom of action on the territory covered. Secondly, the agreement may normally be exempted under Article 101(3) of the Treaty if it does not contain any provisions that create absolute territorial protection for the distributor or, at any rate, does not objectively have such an effect.[113]

Export bans applied by manufacturers to their EU distributors have attracted sizeable fines and penalties under Article 101.[114] This outcome fosters intra-brand competition in ways which have largely been abandoned under United States antitrust law.[115]

Selective Distribution

Another form of distribution which is of practical importance is selective distribution. Although, in contrast to exclusive distribution and exclusive supply agreements, the Commission has not adopted a

---

111 *See* Zera Montedison/Hinkins Staehler, O.J. 1993 L 272/28.

112 *See* Sot. Lelos v. GlaxoSmithKline, (2008) Eur.Comm.Rep. I–7139 and GlaxoSmithKline Services Ltd. v. Commission, (2006) Eur.Comm.Rep. II–02969 (Case T–168/01).

113 23rd Report on Competition Policy (1994) point 212.

114 *See, e.g.*, John Deere & Co., 28 O.J. 1985 L 35/58 (fined two million ECU for violation of Article 81(1) for imposing, accepting or practicing bans on the export of its products by dealers or distributors to other member states); Sperry New Holland, a Division of Sperry Corp., 28 O.J. 1985 L 376/21 (fined 750,000 ECU for violation of Article 101(1) for imposing, accepting or practicing a ban on export of SNH products by dealers of distributors to other member states).

115 *Compare* Continental T.V., Inc. v. GTE Sylvania Inc., 433 U.S. 36, 97 S.Ct. 2549, 53 L.Ed.2d 568 (1977); Business Electronics Corp. v. Sharp Electronics Corp., 485 U.S. 717, 108 S.Ct. 1515, 99 L.Ed.2d 808 (1988).

block exemption for selective distribution agreements,[116] there are certain rules which arise from the Commission's decisions and the case law. A selective distribution system exists where a supplier limits the number of approved distributors of its products based on criteria. Whether such a system infringes Article 101(1) depends largely on the criteria used and the justification for not supplying to certain distributors.

Generally, a selective distribution system will not infringe Article 101(1) if it is based on qualitative criteria, these criteria are objectively applied so that any qualifying distributor is admitted to the system, and it does not include any provisions which are likely to prohibit parallel imports.[117] A selective distribution system based on quantitative criteria, on the other hand, will likely infringe Article 101(1)[118] or if the nature of the products is such that a selective distribution system is not necessary.[119]

In addition, any restraints imposed on the distributors should be examined because they could individually infringe Article 101(1). For example, in the *Grundig* decision, the Commission stated that while the selective distribution system established by Grundig did not in itself infringe Article 101(1), but certain obligations imposed on the dealers did. This included the requirement that retailers carry as complete a selection of the relevant Grundig range as is necessary for the size of the specialized shop or specialized department and keep adequate stocks of a representative selection of the relevant range, and the requirement that wholesalers carry and stock as far as possible the whole Grundig range.[120]

If the selective distribution system infringes Article 101(1), it will often qualify for an exemption under Article 101(3) unless it includes absolute territorial protection, restricts parallel imports or is used to control prices. The Commission is aware that selective distribution systems can improve the distribution of the goods and that the consumer benefits from the resulting provision of specialist sales and after-sales services. Thus, the Commission is generally receptive to arguments that additional obligations such as those

---

[116] The Commission however adopted in 1985 a block exemption applicable to selective distribution systems in the automobile sector, now as amended Regulation 1400/2002.

[117] *See* Metro v. Commission, (1977) Eur.Comm.Rep. 1875; AEG v. Commission, (1983) Eur.Comm.Rep. 3151; Hasselblad v. Commission, (1984) Eur.Comm.Rep. 883; Grundig's distribution system, O.J.1994 L 20/15.

[118] Ford v. Commission, (1985) Eur.Comm.Rep. 2725; Vichy v. Commission, (1992) Eur.Comm.Rep. II–415; Omega, O.J.1970 L 242/22.

[119] Ideal Standard distribution system, O.J.1985 L 20/38; Grohe distribution system, O.J.1985 L 19/17.

[120] Grundig's distribution system, O.J.1994 L 20/15, 21 point 35.

imposed by Grundig are indispensable to the system and therefore exempt under Article 101(3).[121]

Vertical Restraints Regulations

The group exemptions for exclusive dealing, exclusive purchasing and franchise agreements were replaced in 2000 by Regulation 2790/99, known as the "Vertical Restraints Regulation." It was accompanied by lengthy vertical restraints guidelines. This regulation and its guidelines are more economic and less formalistic than their predecessors. The efficiency enhancing qualities of intra-brand vertical restraints are recognized. Supply, distribution (including selective distribution) and franchise agreements of firms with less than 30 percent market shares are generally exempt; this is known as a "safe harbor." Companies whose market shares exceed 30 percent may or may not be exempt, depending upon the results of individual competition law reviews. Since 2004, these may be undertaken by the Commission, national competition authorities and national courts.

In either case, no vertical agreements containing so-called "hard core restraints" are exempt. These restraints concern primarily resale price maintenance, territorial and customer protection leading to market allocation and in most instances exclusive dealing covenants that last more than five years.

In 2010, a new Vertical Restraints Regulation 330/10 (with accompanying Guidelines) was issued. Its content is like that of 1999. Restrictions on the use of the Internet by distributors with at least one "brick-and-mortar" store are treated as hard core restraints. For example, distributors cannot be required to reroute Internet customers outside their territories to local dealers. Nor can they be forced to pay higher prices for online sales ("dual pricing") or be limited in the amount sales made via the Internet, although a minimum number of offline sales can be stipulated.

Distributors may generally sell anywhere in the EU in response to customer demand ("passive sales"). Restraints on "actively" soliciting sales outside designated distributor territories, including by email or banner web advertising, are permissible. *Both* supplier and distributor must have less than 30% market shares to qualify for the 2010 "safe harbor."

In 2022 the Commission issued a new **Vertical Restraints Regulation** No. 2022/720 replacing that of 2010. This Regulation and its Guidelines continue much of its predecessor but adds important rules regarding coverage of commercial agents under the

[121] Grundig's distribution system, O.J.1994 L 20/15, 21.

new Regulation. Note that commercial agents are subject to an important protective 1986 Council Directive discussed immediately below.

The 2022 Vertical Restraints Guidelines distinguishes between "genuine agents" with no title to goods and no contributions to purchase or transportation costs. To escape the Vertical Restraints Regulation, genuine agents must maintain goods at their own risks and costs, take responsibility for customer non-performance, and assume responsibility to third parties for damages caused by the goods. In addition, genuine agents must invest in sales promotion, and market-specific equipment, premises, and training of personnel.

The Guidelines affirm that agency agreements may contain territorial restraints and pricing conditions. Exclusive agency provisions generally do not violate the Vertical Restraints Regulation. But single branding and post-termination non-competes with interbrand competitive impact may be subject to the Regulation.

§ 7.11 EU Patent Licensing Agreements, the Technology Transfer Regulations

In its seminal 1982 *Maize Seed* judgment, the Court of Justice addressed patent license restrictions under the Union's competition rules.[122] The Commission waited for this judgment before publishing the 1984 group exemption under Article 101(3) for patent licensing agreements. In this case, a research institute financed by the French government (INRA) bred varieties of basic seeds. In 1960, INRA assigned to Kurt Eisele plant breeder's rights for maize seed in the Federal Republic of Germany. Eisele agreed to apply for registration of these rights in accordance with German law. In 1965, a formal agreement was executed by the parties. This agreement consisted of five relevant clauses.

Clause 1 gave Eisele the exclusive rights to "organize" sales of six identified varieties of maize seed propagated from basic seeds provided by INRA. This enabled Eisele to exercise control over distribution outlets. Eisele undertook not to deal in maize varieties other than those provided by INRA. Clause 2 required Eisele to place no restriction on the supply of seed to technically suitable distributors except for rationing in conditions of shortage. The prices charged to the distributors by Eisele were fixed in consultation with INRA, according to a specified formula. Clause 3 obligated Eisele to import from France for sale in Germany at least two-thirds of that territory's requirements for the registered varieties. This restricted Eisele's own production and sale to only one-third of the German

[122] Nungesser v. Commission, (1982) Eur.Comm.Rep. 2015.

market. Clause 4 concerned the protection by Eisele of INRA's proprietary rights, including its trademark, from infringement and granted Eisele the power to take any action to that end. Clause 5 contained a promise by INRA that no exports to Germany of the relevant varieties would take place otherwise than through the agency of Eisele. This meant that INRA would ensure that its French marketing organization would prevent the relevant varieties from being exported to Germany to parallel importers.

In September 1972, it became apparent that dealers in France were selling the licensed varieties of maize seed directly to German traders who were marketing the products in breach of the breeder's rights claimed by Eisele. This resulted in an action by Eisele in the German courts against one of the traders. The parties reached a court approved settlement under which the French trader promised to refrain from offering for sale without permission any variety of maize seed within the rights held by Eisele, and to pay a fine. In February 1974, another breach took place, this time advertising in the German press by a French dealer. In response to threats of legal proceedings, this dealer lodged a complaint with the Commission alleging breach of the competition rules.

The Commission considered both the agreement and the settlement to infringe Article 101(1) because they granted an exclusive license and provided absolute territorial protection. The Court of Justice reversed the Commission with respect to exclusivity but upheld the Commission with respect to absolute territorial protection. The Court drew a distinction between "open" licenses which do not necessarily fall under Article 101(1), and "closed" licenses which do so.

Open license agreements are those which do not involve third parties. In *Maize Seed*, the obligation upon INRA or those deriving rights through INRA to refrain from producing or selling the relevant seeds in Germany was treated as an open license term. The Court held such clauses necessary to the dissemination of new technology inasmuch as potential licensees might otherwise be deterred from accepting the risk of cultivating and marketing new products. The Court defined closed licenses as those involving third parties. Thus, the obligation upon INRA or those deriving rights through INRA to prevent third parties from exporting the seeds into Germany without authorization, Eisele's concurrent use of his exclusive contractual rights, and his breeder's rights, to prevent all imports into Germany or exports to other member states were invalid under Article 101(1).

Patent Licensing Regulation

The Commission adopted in 1984 a patent licensing group exemption regulation under Article 101(3).[123] It acknowledged that patent licensing improves the production of goods and promotes technical progress by allowing licensees to operate with the latest technology. The Commission also believed that patent licensing increases both the number of production facilities and the quantity and quality of goods in the Common Market. Much of its focus concerned territorial restrictions in patent licensing agreements. Specifically, the following clauses were permitted:

(1) Restraints on licensors granting rights to other licensees or exploiting the patent in the designated territory during the life of the patent;

(2) Restraints on licensee exploitation of the invention in other EU countries to the extent the licensor has parallel patent rights;[124]

(3) Restraints on licensee manufacture, use or active selling of the product in territories licensed to others, to the extent the licensor has parallel patent rights;

(4) Restraints on licensees intended to keep them from actively or passively selling the product in territories licensed to others for five years after the product is first put on the market, to the extent the licensor has parallel patents; and

(5) Restraints on licensees mandating use of the licensor's trademark on the product.

The distinction between active and passive selling was and remains critical. "Active selling" involves sending agents to call on customers, advertising or creating an office or distribution depot in an EU country other than the licensed territory. "Passive selling" involves responding to unsolicited requests to purchase products from customers outside the licensed territory. Similar regulations governed knowhow licensing.[125]

Transfer of Technology Regulation 240/96

In 1996 the Commission enacted Regulation 240/96 on the application of Article 101(3) to transfer technology agreements. The

---

[123] Commission Regulation 2349/84 as amended by Regulation 151/93, O.J. 1993 L 21/8.

[124] Parallel patents are defined in the regulation as covering the same invention such that the licensor could bring an infringement action against unauthorized activities.

[125] Commission Regulation 2349/84 and 556/89. *See* Section 7.12.

intention of this Regulation was to combine the existing patent and knowhow block exemptions into a single regulation covering technology transfer agreements, and to simplify and harmonize the rules for patent and knowhow licensing. It contained detailed lists of permitted, permissible, and prohibited clauses.

Regulation 240/96 stated that Article 101(1) of the Treaty did not apply to "pure patent and knowhow licensing agreements and missed patent and knowhow licensing agreements," as well as to agreements with ancillary provisions relating to intellectual property other than patents, when only two undertakings are parties and when one or more of eight listed obligations were included. These were obligations of limitation, such as not to license other undertakings to exploit the technology. There were time limits (5 years for patents/10 years for knowhow) for the exemption of these eight obligations in certain situations. Article 1 was known as the Whitelist. Article 2 allowed technology transfers even when certain clauses existed (17 were listed). These clauses were considered generally not restrictive of competition. There were various obligations on the licensee, such as not divulging know-how communicated by the licensor. Article 2 was known as the Permissible List.

Article 3 of Regulation 240/96 designated that Articles 1 and 2(2) did not apply when any one of seven obligations were present, such as restricting a party in the determination of prices, competition restrictions, limitations on production quantity, licensee improvement grant-back requirements, etc. Article 3 was known as the Blacklist. Article 4 carried the scope of the exemption provided for in Articles 1 and 2 to certain other restrictive agreements which were notified to the Commission and received no Commission opposition. Article 4 was known as the Gray List. Regulation 240/96, according to Article 5, did not apply to four classes of agreements, such as most agreements within a joint venture. But under Article 5 it did apply to three forms of agreements, including where the licensor is itself a licensee of the technology and was authorized to grant sub-licenses.

The Commission retained power to withdraw benefits of the Regulation 240/96 if in a specific case the exempted agreement was incompatible with the conditions of Article 101(3). Final articles provided some definitions, a list of what were deemed patents, preservation of confidentiality of information, and the repeal of the two regulations combined in this regulation.

Transfer of Technology Regulation 772/2004

The detailed regulation of technology transfer agreement clauses contained in Regulation 240/96 was replaced by Regulation 772/2004, which applies to patent, know-how and software copyright licensing. The new Regulation distinguishes agreements between those of "competing" and "noncompeting" parties, the latter being treated less strictly than the former. Parties are deemed "competing" if they compete (without infringing each other's IP rights) in either the relevant technology or product market, determined in each instance by what buyers regard as substitutes.[126] If the competing parties have a *combined* market share of 20 percent or less, their licensing agreements are covered by group exemption under Regulation 772/2004.[127]

Noncompeting parties, on the other hand, benefit from the group exemption so long as their *individual* market shares do not exceed 30 percent.[128] Agreements initially covered by Regulation 772/2004 that subsequently exceed the "safe harbor" thresholds noted above lose their exemption subject to a two-year grace period.[129] Outside these exemptions, a "rule of reason" approach applies.

Inclusion of certain "hardcore restraints" causes license agreement to lose their group exemption. For competing parties, such restraints include price fixing,[130] output limitations on both parties,[131] limits on the licensee's ability to exploit its own technology,[132] and allocation of markets or competitors (subject to exceptions).[133] Specifically, restraints on active and passive selling by the licensee in a territory reserved for the licensor are allowed, as are active (but not passive) selling restraints by licensees in territories of other licensees.[134] Licensing agreements between noncompeting parties may not contain the "hardcore" restraint of maximum price fixing.[135] Active selling restrictions on licensees can be utilized, along with passive selling restraints in territories reserved to the licensor or (for two years) another licensee.[136] For these purposes, the

---

126 Regulation 772/2004, Article 1(1)(j).

127 *Id.*, Article 3(1).

128 *Id.*, Article 3(2).

129 *Id.*, Article 8(2).

130 *Id.*, Article 4(1)(a).

131 *Id.*, Article 4(1)(b).

132 *Id.*, Article 4(1)(d).

133 *Id.*, Article 4(1)(c).

134 *Id.*, Article 4(1)(c)(iv) and (v).

135 *Id.*, Article 4(2)(a).

136 *Id.*, Article 4(2)(b).

competitive status of the parties is decided at the outset of the agreement.[137]

Other license terms deemed "excluded restrictions" also cause a loss of exemption.[138] Such clauses include: (1) mandatory grant-backs or assignments of severable improvements by licensees, excepting nonexclusive license-backs;[139] (2) no-challenges by the licensee of the licensor's intellectual property rights, subject to the licensor's right to terminate upon challenge;[140] and (3) for noncompeting parties, restraints on the licensee's ability to exploit its own technology or either party's ability to carry out research and development (unless indispensable to prevent disclosure of the licensed Know-how).[141]

In all cases, exemption under Regulation 772/2004 may be withdrawn where an agreement has effects that are incompatible with Article 101(3).[142]

§ 7.12 EU Know-How Licensing Agreements

Prior to the 1996 technology transfer regulation (above), there were two group exemptions which applied to know-how licensing agreements. Commission Regulation 2349/84 applied to agreements combining patent and know-how licenses. However, provisions concerning know-how in such mixed agreements were only covered by the group exemption in so far as the licensed patents were necessary for achieving the objects of the licensed technology and as long as at least one of the licensed patents remained in force. In such cases, the "mixed agreement" could qualify for an exemption under Regulation 556/89.

Regulation 556/89 applied to bilateral, pure know-how licensing agreements, bilateral mixed agreements not falling under Regulation 2349/84 and bilateral, pure know-how licensing or mixed agreements containing ancillary provisions relating to trademarks and other intellectual property rights.[143] The concept of know-how was broadly conceived in this regulation to include "a body of technical information that is secret, substantial and identified in any appropriate form."[144] "Secret" meant that the know-how package as a body was not generally known or easily accessible. Each individual component of the know-how did not have to be unknown or

137 *Id.*, Article 4(3).

138 *Id.*, Article 5.

139 *Id.*, Article 5(1)(a).

140 *Id.*, Article 5(1)(b) and (c).

141 *Id.*, Article 5(2).

142 *Id.*, Article 6.

143 Art. 1(1) of Regulation 556/89.

144 Art. 1(7)(1) of Regulation 556/89.

unobtainable. "Substantial" meant that the know-how includes important information regarding a manufacturing process, a product or service, or for their development. It excluded information which is trivial.

The know-how also had to be useful. Such information was useful if it could be expected to improve the competitive position of the licensee. These approaches, along with the focus on active and passive territorial sales restraints discussed above regarding patent licenses, have largely been retained in Regulations 240/96 and 772/2004. The latter group exemption now regulates both patent licensing and know-how licensing agreements. Its content is detailed in Section 7.11.

Transfer of Technology Regulation 316/2014

Regulation 316/2014 replaced Regulation 772/2004, with a one-year transition period. It is valid until 2026 and clarifies that Regulation 316/2014 on technology transfers applies only if other EU regulations concerning research and development and/or specialization agreements are inapplicable.

The hardcore list of prohibited restraints is not changed from Regulation 772/2004, nor were the market share thresholds (see above).

Changes were made to the exemptions as follows:

(1) All *exclusive* grant-back licensee obligations require individual assessment, as do termination clauses triggered by licensee challenges to the validity of the technology.

(2) Purchase requirements from licensors of raw material or equipment are exempt only if directly related to the production or sale of products made with licensed technology.

(3) No passive sales restrictions on licensees are exempt unless objectively necessary for the licensee to penetrate a new market.

(4) Settlement agreements which lead to delayed or limited ability for licensee launch of the product in any market ("pay-for-delay" agreements) may be prohibited, as may no-challenge clauses in settlement agreements, particularly the patent was granted based on incorrect or misleading information.

(5) Technology licensing pools now enjoy a comprehensive, detailed exemption provided they adhere to Regulation 316/2014.

(6) Technology licensing pools now enjoy a comprehensive, detailed exemption provided they adhere to Regulation 316/2014.

§ 7.13 EU Franchise Agreements

The Pronuptia Case

Prior to its landmark decision in *Pronuptia,*[145] the Commission had never sought to apply Article 101 to franchise agreements. *Pronuptia* arose from the refusal of a franchisee to pay license fees to the franchisor. The distribution of the Pronuptia brand wedding attire in the Federal Republic of Germany was handled by shops operated by the German franchisor and by independent retailers through franchise agreements with that franchisor. The franchisee had obtained franchises for three areas (Hamburg, Oldenburg and Hannover). The franchisor granted exclusive rights to market and advertise under the name of "Pronuptia de Paris" in these specific territories. The franchisor promised not to open any shops or provide any goods or services to another person in those territories. The franchisor also agreed to assist the franchisee with business strategies and profitability.

The franchisee agreed to assume all the risk of opening a franchise as an independent retailer. The franchisee also agreed to the following: (1) To sell Pronuptia goods only in the store specified in the contract and to decorate and design the shop according to the franchisor's instructions; (2) to purchase 80 percent of wedding related attire and a proportion of evening dresses from the franchisor, and to purchase the rest of such merchandise only from sellers approved by the franchisor; (3) to pay a one-time entrance fee for exclusive rights to the specified territory and a yearly royalty fee of 10 percent of the total sales of Pronuptia and all other products; (4) to advertise only with the franchisor's approval in a method which would enhance the international reputation of the franchise; (5) to make the sale of bridal fashions the franchisee's main business purpose; (6) to consider the retail price recommendations of the franchisor; (7) to refrain from competing directly or indirectly during the contract period or for one year afterward with any Pronuptia store; and (8) to obtain the franchisor's prior approval before assigning the rights and obligations arising under the contract to a third party.

In due course, the case was referred to the European Court of Justice. The Court's judgment concentrates on the crucial issue of whether franchise agreements come within Article 101. The Court draws a preliminary distinction between "distribution" franchises such as Pronuptia as opposed to "service" and "production" franchises. The Court concludes that a franchising system as such

145 Pronuptia de Paris GmbH v. Pronuptia de Paris Irmgard Schillgallis, (1986) Eur.Comm.Rep. 353.

does not interfere with competition. Consequently, clauses essential to enable franchising to function are not prohibited. Thus, the franchisor can communicate know-how or assistance and help franchisees apply its methods. The franchisor can take reasonable steps to keep its know-how or assistance from becoming available to competitors. Location clauses forbidding the franchisee during the contract, or for a reasonable time thereafter, from opening a store with a similar or identical object in an area where it might compete with another member of the franchise network were necessary for distribution franchises and therefore permissible. The obligation of the franchisee not to sell a licensed store without prior consent of the franchisor was similarly allowable.

Clauses necessary to preserve the identity and reputation of the franchise network, such as decorations and trademark usage, were upheld. The reputation and identity of the network may also justify a clause requiring the franchisee to sell only products supplied by the franchisor or by approved sources, at least if it would be too expensive to monitor the quality of the stock otherwise. Nevertheless, each franchisee must be allowed to buy from other franchisees. The requirement of uniformity may also justify advertisement approvals by the franchisor, but the franchisee must be allowed to set and advertise resale prices. The Court rejected the view that clauses tending to divide the Common Market between franchisor and franchisee or between franchisees are always necessary to protect the know-how or the identity and the reputation of the network.

The location clause in *Pronuptia* was seen as potentially supporting exclusive territories. In combination, location clauses and exclusive territories may divide markets and so restrict competition within the network. Even if a potential franchisee would not take the risk of joining the network by making its own investment because it could not expect a profitable business due to the absence of protection from competition from other franchisees, that consideration (in the Court's view) could be taken into account only under an Article 101(3) individual exemption. The Commission, in fact, ultimately granted such an exemption to Pronuptia.[146]

Franchising Regulation

The Commission, following the European Court of Justice in *Pronuptia,*[147] adopted a group exemption regulation for franchise agreements under Article 101(3).[148] Regulation 4087/88 required

[146] Re Pronuptia, 30 O.J.Eur.Comm. 39 (L13/1987).

[147] Pronuptia de Paris GmbH v. Pronuptia de Paris Irmgard Schillgallis, (1986) Eur.Comm.Rep. 353.

[148] Regulation 4087/88.

each franchisee to identify itself as an independent enterprise apart from the trademark/service mark/trade name owner. This disclosure could avoid joint and several franchisor liability for the provision by franchisees of defective goods or services. Regulation 4087/88 defined a "franchise" as a package of industrial or intellectual property rights relating to trademarks, trade names, signs, utility models, designs, copyrights, know-how or patents exploited for the resale of goods or the provision of services to customers.[149] "Franchise agreements" were defined as those in which the franchisor grants the franchisee, in exchange for direct or indirect financial consideration, the right to exploit a franchise so as to market specified types of goods and/or services.[150] A "master franchise agreement" involved the right to exploit a franchise by concluding franchising agreements with third parties.[151]

Vertical Restraints Regulation

Starting with these basics, Regulation 4087/88 proceeded to detail permitted and prohibited clauses in EU franchise agreements. . . This approach remained in force until 2000, when Regulation 2790/99 (the "vertical restraints" group exemption) took over franchise agreements, along with exclusive dealing and other distribution agreements. Regulation 2790/99 is accompanied by lengthy vertical restraints guidelines. This regulation and its guidelines are more economic and less formalistic than the predecessors. Supply and distribution agreements of firms with less than 30 percent market shares are generally exempt; this is known as a "safe harbor." Companies whose market shares exceed 30 percent may or may not be exempt, depending upon the results of individual competition law reviews.

In either case, no vertical agreements containing so-called "hard core restraints" are exempt. These restraints concern primarily resale price maintenance, territorial and customer protection leading to market allocations, and in most instances exclusive dealing covenants that last more than five years. In 2010, and again in 2022, revised Vertical Restraints Regulations were issued. Their content is similar to that of 1999, except that restrictions on the use of the Internet by distributors are treated as a hard-core restraints. See Section 7.10.

---

149 *Id.*, Article 1(3)(a).

150 *Id.*, Article 1(3)(b).

151 *Id.*, Article 1(3)(c).

§ 7.14 Article 101—Undertakings and Concerted Practices

Undertakings

There can be no violation of Article 101(1) unless there is an agreement between "undertakings," a decision by an association of undertakings or a concerted practice among undertakings. In other words, unilateral behavior is not caught by Article 101(1).[152]

The term "undertaking" as used in EU competition law refers to every entity engaged in an economic activity, regardless of the legal status of the entity and the way in which it is financed.[153] Thus, partnerships, sole proprietorships and even natural persons may be "undertakings" when they engage in business or commercial activities.[154] However, employees acting in the scope of their employment[155] and public bodies serving exclusively a social function[156] are not considered undertakings. In addition, Article 101 applies to associations of undertakings such as trade and professional associations. The fact that the association itself may not be pursuing a commercial activity—in the sense that it is not profit-oriented—does not mean that it escapes the application of Article 101.[157]

Agreements and Decisions

Article 101 also requires proof of an agreement, decision of an association or a concerted practice. At first glance, one might conclude that Article 101 is much narrower in its sphere of application than Section 1 of the Sherman Act which applies to every contract, combination and conspiracy. However, the application of this requirement by the Commission and Court illustrates that this is not the case. The concept of agreement encompasses not only legally binding contracts, but also oral agreements between undertakings[158] and gentlemen's agreements.[159] According to the

---

[152] *See* Commission v. Bayer AG, (2004) Eur.Comm.Rep. I–23 (Joined Cases C–2/01P and C/3/01P) (unilateral refusal to fill large pharmaceutical orders blocks parallel trade).

[153] SAT Fluggesellschaft v. Eurocontrol, (1994) Eur.Comm.Rep. I–43 & 18; Poucet, (1993) Eur.Comm.Rep. I–637 & 17.

[154] AOIP/Beyrard, O.J.1976 L 6/8, 12; Vaessen/Moris, O.J.1979 L 19/32, 34; RAI/Unitel, O.J.1978 L 157/39, 40.

[155] Suiker Unie v. Commission, (1975) Eur.Comm.Rep. 1663, 2024 & 538. *See also* Answer of EC Commission to Question No. 2391/83, O.J.1984 C 222/21.

[156] *See e.g.,* SAT Fluggesellschaft v. Eurocontrol, (1994) Eur.Comm.Rep. I–43; Poucet, (1993) Eur.Comm.Rep. I–637.

[157] Heintz van Landewyck SARL v. Commission, (1980) Eur.Comm.Rep. 3125, 3250.

[158] Tepea v. Commission, (1978) Eur.Comm.Rep. 1391, 1412.

[159] International Chemical Cartel, O.J.1969 L 192/5.

Commission: "An agreement within the meaning of Article 101 may exist where the parties reach a common consensus on a plan which limits or is likely to limit their commercial freedom by determining the lines of their mutual action or abstention from action in the market."[160] Decisions of an association generally refer to the by-laws, internal statutes, and regulations.[161] However, even recommendations of the associations directed at its members can be considered decisions.[162]

Concerted Practices

If bilateral conduct does not fall under the definition of agreement or decision, the Commission may find that it qualifies as a concerted practice if the conduct has an appreciable restraint on competition. The meaning of concerted practice is critical to Article 101(1). It was included in Article 101 to forestall the possibility of undertakings evading the application of Article 101(1) by colluding in an anticompetitive manner falling short of definite agreement.[163]

The Commission and the Court of Justice considered the concept of a concerted practice extensively in *Imperial Chemical Industries (ICI) v. Commission.*[164] *ICI* involved nearly all the producers of aniline dyes in the EU when it had only six member states. Three industry-wide price increases between 1964 and 1967 took place over the full range of more than 6000 aniline dye products. The Commission, acting on information furnished by trade organizations using dyestuffs, found ten producers of aniline dyes in violation of Article 101(1) by concerting on these price increases. Together they held about 80 percent of the EU aniline dyes market.

Proof of the concerted practices tendered by the Commission included: (1) the near identity of the price increases in each country; (2) the uniformity of products covered by the price increases; (3) the exact timing of the increases; (4) the simultaneous dispatch to subsidiaries and representatives of price increase instructions that were nearly identical in form and content; and (5) the existence of informal contacts and occasional meetings between the enterprises concerned. The Commission decided these circumstantial facts warranted its conclusion that a concerted price fixing practice took place.[165]

---

160 PVC, O.J. 1994 L 239/14, 25 point 30.

161 Centraal Bureau voor de Rijwielhandel, O.J.1978 L 20/18 point 18; BPICA, O.J.1977 L 299/18, 23.

162 Verband der Sachversicherer v. Commission, (1987) Eur.Comm.Rep. 405, 454; Heintz van Landewyck SARL v. Commission, (1980) Eur.Comm.Rep. 3125, 3250.

163 PVC, O.J. 1994 L 239/14, 25 point 33.

164 (1972) Eur.Comm.Rep. 619.

165 (1969) Common Mkt.L.Rep. 494.

On appeal, the Court of Justice affirmed. The Court distinguished the concept of concerted practice from an agreement or decision under Article 101(1): "A form of coordination between undertakings which, without going so far as to amount to an agreement properly so called, knowingly substitutes a practical cooperation between them for the risks of competition."[166] The Court added that while independent parallel behavior by competitors did not fall within the concept of a concerted practice, the fact of such behavior could be taken as a strong indicator of a concerted practice where it produced market conditions, especially price equilibrium, different from those thought ordinarily to prevail under competition. The cartel's defense of "conscious parallelism" on prices was therefore another piece of evidence affirming the Commission's enforcement decision. The total of the evidence on which the Commission relied to find a concerted practice was explicable, in the eyes of the Court, only by convergent intentions of producers to increase prices and avoid competitive conditions in the aniline dyes market.[167]

The impact of the concept of concerted practice in competition law depends on the evidence available to prove cooperative business behavior. Parallel conduct may be relevant to the extent that it is evidence of concerted practice. Under current law, concerted conduct may be inferred if parallel behavior exists and contact between the parties is evidenced.[168] As such, whether concerted conduct exists is a question of fact rather than law and has proven useful in combatting cartels. Thus, the mere exchange of information that facilitates price conformity can be sanctioned.[169]

In the *Sugar Cartel* case, for example, the Court of Justice reaffirmed *ICI* and then laid down a general warning against competitor cooperation and contact. It held that the EU competition rules inherently require that each undertaking independently determine its activities in the Common Market.[170] Direct or indirect contact with the object or effect of influencing the market conduct of an actual or potential competitor, the disclosure of courses of market conduct of an actual or potential competitor or the disclosure of courses of market conduct intended for adoption by others, is

---

166 This has become the standard definition of concerted practiced used by the Court and the Commission. *See* Ahlström Oy & ORS v. Commission, (1993) Eur.Comm.Rep. I–1307 para. 71; Cartonboard, O.J. 1994 L 243/1, 40 point 126; PVC, O.J. 1994 L 239/14, 25 point 32.

167 ICI v. Commission, (1972) Eur.Comm.Rep. 619.

168 Società Italiano Vetro v. Commission, (1992) Eur.Comm.Rep. II–1403; Ahlström Oy & ORS v. Commission, (1993) Eur.Comm.Rep. I–1307.

169 Re Fatty Acids, O.J. 1987 L 3/17.

170 *See also* Cartonboard, O.J. 1994 L 243/1, point 126.

prohibited.[171] But quarterly price announcements, simultaneously released and identical in amount, may not constitute a concerted practice if other plausible explanations exist.[172] Expert testimony suggesting that parallel pricing can be a rational response to market forces may provide the necessary explanation. However, the Commission believes that oligopolies can be attacked using Article 102 (see Section 7.18) and a theory of collective abuse of a dominant position.[173]

§ 7.15 Article 101—Competitive Impact

Article 101(1) applies when an agreement, decision or concerted practice has as its object *or* effect the prevention, restriction or distortion of competition within the Common Market. Distinctions can be drawn as between preventing, restraining and distorting competition, but the sweep of this language basically creates a legal and conceptual net in which most activities of competing enterprises may be examined by the Commission. The way the Commission has cut official holes in this net through exemptions and policy announcements has already been discussed. Nevertheless, since there is a sense in which nearly all actions by enterprises affect their competitive position in the marketplace, the language of Article 101 grants expansive administrative power. However, the Court of Justice has imposed a "rule of reason" test when evaluating competitive impact. Only those restraints which are "sufficiently deleterious" to competition in the context in which they appear are prohibited and void.[174]

Restraints of competition by enterprises may take place at different levels of economic activity. Restraints involving competition among firms operating at the same level in the production or distribution process are known as horizontal restraints. Businesses operating at different levels may restrain competition between themselves and third parties. These are known as vertical restraints.

Consten and Grundig Case

In the prominent *Grundig* decision, the Court of Justice declined to follow the recommendations of its Advocate General and affirmed that both horizontal and vertical restraints are embraced by Article

171 Suiker Unie UA v. Commission, (1975) Eur.Comm.Rep. 1663.

172 Ahlström Oy & CRS v. Commission, (1993) Eur.Comm.Rep. I–1307 (Cases 89/85 et al.).

173 Re Flat Glass, (1990–4) Common Mkt.L.Rep. 535 (Comm. Dec. 89/93).

174 Société Technique Minière v. Maschinenbau Ulm GmbH, (1966) Eur.Comm.Rep. 235; Nungesser v. Commission, (1982) Eur.Comm.Rep. 2015; European Night Services v. Commission, (1998) Eur.Comm.Rep. II–3141.

101(1).[175] This decision involved a German manufacturer of consumer electronics that established an exclusive dealing agreement with Consten, a French distributor. In other words, *Grundig* was a vertical restraints case. The agreement was made prior to the adoption of the first group exemption, Regulation 67/67 (see Section 7.9). As part of the agreement, Grundig undertook not to deliver its products directly or indirectly to anyone else in France. Grundig also contracted to similar territorial restraints with its other Common Market dealers outside of France. Consten agreed to sell only in its French territory. The result was that no dealer or wholesaler of Grundig products in the EU could sell outside its contracted territory. To strengthen this absolute pattern of territorial distribution, Grundig assigned the French trademark "GINT" to Consten. GINT was placed on all products delivered to Consten in addition to the usual "GRUNDIG" mark.

When prices in France were 20 to 25 percent above those in Germany, a French firm began competing with Consten by importing Grundig products bearing the GINT mark from a renegade German wholesaler. Consten then sued the importer in the French courts for infringement of GINT and violation of French law on unfair competition. The importer replied that the Grundig-Consten contract and the GINT assignment were void under Articles 101(1) and 101(2). Meanwhile, Grundig notified its series of exclusive dealing agreements to the Commission and sought Article 101(3) exemptions for them.

The Cour d'Appel de Paris stayed the proceedings under French law. The Commission found the entire agreement prohibited by Article 101(1) and denied a 101(3) exemption. Although not restrictive of competition between Grundig and Consten, the agreement was restrictive of Consten and third-party sellers of Grundig products. It amounted, the Commission said, to absolute territorial protection in France from the competition of parallel imports of Grundig products. Since, in the Commission's view, the object of the agreement was to restrain competition, an extensive market analysis of its actual competitive impact was not necessary.

The Court of Justice upheld the Commission's position on coverage of vertical restraints by Article 101(1) and on the absence of need for extensive market analysis in this case. However, it partially accepted the argument that, in ascertaining whether competition was restrained under Article 101(1), the Commission ought to have considered the whole of the market for consumer electronics (where Grundig faced strong inter-brand competition). Competition within

---

175 Consten and Grundig v. Commission, (1966) Eur.Comm.Rep. 299.

the overall market, it was argued, was increased by the entry of Grundig into France through Consten's exclusive, territorially protected sales. This increase in inter-brand competition, the argument continued, outweighed the restrictions on intra-brand competition in Grundig products.

The Court responded to these arguments by holding that only certain clauses of the Grundig-Consten agreement, the absolute territorial protection clause and the GINT assignment, infringed Article 101(1). Only these clauses were automatically void under Article 101(2). The remainder of the agreement, including the exclusive dealing provisions, was severable and legally binding. Thus, Grundig could enter the French market through an exclusive retailer, but that retailer could not be sheltered from other Grundig sellers in the Common Market. These principles were subsequently incorporated in Regulation 67/67 for which *Grundig* was an important test case. A modified Grundig selective distribution system was subsequently granted an individual exemption by the Commission.[176]

§ 7.16 EU Market Division and Intellectual Property Rights

In *Grundig,* the Court of Justice affirmed the Commission's remedial order to the parties to refrain from any measure tending to obstruct or impede the acquisition of Grundig products. To reduce the negative impact of national industrial and intellectual property rights on regional trade and competition, the Commission and the Court of Justice have relied on Treaty provisions. In the *Grundig* case, the Court held that Article 101 limitations may be imposed on the exercise or use of national trademark rights. In the Court's opinion, absolute territorial distribution rights are not essential to the protection or benefit sought to be conferred by trademarks. The net result was a Court order prohibiting Consten from exercising its rights under French trademark law to use GINT as a trade and competition barrier.

When used with the object or effect of preventing, restraining or distorting Common Market competition, national industrial and intellectual property rights have generally yielded to the competition law of the European Union.[177] In *Deutsche Grammophon,* for example, results comparable to those in *Grundig* were achieved with

---

[176] Official Journal L233/1 (Aug. 30, 1985); Official Journal L20/15 (Jan. 25, 1994).

[177] In addition to the examples discussed here, *see* Herlitz v. Commission, (1994) Eur.Comm.Rep. II–00549 (Case No. T–66/92); Parker Pen v. Commission, (1994) Eur.Comm.Rep. II–00531 (Case No. T–77/92).

copyright-based territorial restraints.[178] When record imports into Germany from the French subsidiary of Deutsche Grammophon caused competition for the parent company, then enjoying lawful resale price maintenance in Germany, it sought infringement protection under German copyright law. Competition law restraints on the exercise (as opposed to the existence) of national copyright rights denied infringement protection. Deutsche Grammophon's German copyright rights were said to be "exhausted" by the sales to its French subsidiary. Dividing up the Common Market was not perceived to be essential to the financial reward and other purposes of German copyright. On the other hand, increased intra-brand Deutsche Grammophon sales and price competition was completely compatible with the Treaty of Rome.

Much of the litigation surrounding intellectual property rights in the Common Market has been undertaken in connection with Article 36 and the free movement of goods. See Chapter 4. As in the competition law area, such rights have generally given way to the TFEU.

§ 7.17 Articles 101 and 102—Trade Impact

De Minimis Trade Impact

To come within the prohibition of Article 101, an agreement, decision or concerted practice must raise a probability that it will appreciably affect trade between member states.[179] Because of this requirement, it is insufficient to consider the object of restrictive agreements under EU law without also considering their potential trade effects. While in certain cases, such as *Grundig,* it is possible to avoid an extensive market analysis of the competitive impact of restrictive agreements if an intent to restrain competition is clear, analysis of an agreement's *trade* impact is always required. This is doubly true because agreements that affect trade or competition between member states in a *de minimis* fashion are not subject to Article 101(1).

In *Völk v. Vervaecke,* a German manufacturer of washing machines contracted with a Dutch exclusive dealer, Vervaecke. The contract was like that of Consten-Grundig and provided for absolute territorial protection. Völk's share of the German washing machine market ranged between 0.20 and 0.05 percent. This time the Court of Justice, on voluntary reference from the Oberlandesgericht in Munich, emphasized the overall product market effect of the restrictive agreement. From that inter-brand perspective, the Court

[178] (1971) Eur.Comm.Rep. 487.

[179] Remia v. Commission, (1985) Eur.Comm.Rep. 2545.

advised that the agreement "affect[ed] the market insignificantly" and therefore escaped Article 101(1).[180] This *de minimis* doctrine was developed more fully in subsequent decisions and the Commission's Notice on Agreements of Minor Importance.[181]

Intrastate Trade

In theory, agreements, decisions and concerted practices of a purely national character not affecting trade between member states are outside the scope of Article 101. In practice, however, few national activities of any significance are likely to escape its reach. For example, in the *VCH* case, an entirely national cartel of cement merchants in Holland held a steadily declining two-thirds share of the Dutch retail cement market. The cartel maintained certain fixed and recommended prices and resale conditions as well as a variety of other restraints on competition among its members. Prior to 1967 the merchants' cartel had been exclusively allied with a German, Dutch and Belgian manufacturers' cartel for its supplies. The Commission noted that about one-third of the total sales of cement in Holland were of cheaper products imported from Belgium and West Germany. It held that the merchants' agreement therefore restricted competition within the Common Market and affected trade between member states. In the Commission's view, the agreement inhibited German and Belgian producers from increasing their share of the Dutch cement market. The Commission denied an Article 101(3) individual exemption and a negative clearance for the agreement.

On appeal, the Court of Justice upheld the Commission's decision in all respects.[182] It issued a broad opinion aimed at all restrictive national cartels even when imported products are not involved:

> A restrictive agreement extending to the whole territory of a member state by its very nature consolidates the national boundaries thus hindering the economic interpenetration desired by the Treaty and so protecting national production.

The expansive approach of the Court of Justice to trade impact analysis under Article 101 is also relevant to Article 102 which contains the same language.

§ 7.18 Article 102—Abuse of Dominant Positions

Article 102 TFEU prohibits abuse by one or more undertakings of a dominant position within a substantial part of the Common Market insofar as the abuse may affect trade between member states.

---

180 (1969) Eur.Comm.Rep. 295.

181 Official Journal C231/2 (1986).

182 VCH v. Commission, (1972) Eur.Comm.Rep. 977.

The existence of a dominant position is not prohibited by European law. Only its abuse is proscribed. Although both Articles 101 and 102 may be applied to the same business practices,[183] they constitute two independent legal instruments addressing different legal situations.[184] Whereas Article 101 is directed at restraints of competition through agreement or concerted practices between undertakings, Article 102 is concerned with restrictive practices arising from the position of the undertaking regardless of the existence of an agreement or concerted practice between undertakings.[185] However, fines for the same conduct under both Articles 101 and 102 will not be permitted by the ECJ.[186]

Article 102 differs fundamentally from Article 101 in other respects. There are no provisions to declare abuses automatically void, or to permit any exemptions from its prohibitions. Thus, under the administrative frameworks of Regulation 17 and Regulation 1, no individual or group exemptions can be granted by the Commission for Article 102 (see Sections 7.6–7.9). The absence of exemptions means that there has been little incentive for dominant firms to notify their abuses to the Commission. Regulations 17 and 1 grant the Commission the same powers with reference to Article 102 as it possesses under Article 101 to obtain information, investigate corporate affairs, render infringement decisions, and fine or penalize offenders.

A few Commission decisions concerning Article 102 have their origins in complaints to the Commission from competitors or those abused. Generally, however, the Commission has acted on its own initiative in Article 102 proceedings. Some of the Commission's decisions have been the subject of appeal to the Court of Justice, which occasionally has received Article 102 issues on reference from national courts under the Article 267 preliminary ruling procedure. A limited number of Article 102 cases have been resolved informally through Commission negotiations. To highlight the more important developments in the interpretation of the language and scope of Article 102, a selection of cases and issues follows.

§ 7.19 Article 102—Dominant Positions

Unless an enterprise or group of enterprises possesses a dominant position within a substantial part of the Common Market,

---

[183] Ahmed Saeed Flugreisen v. Zentrale zur Bekämpfung unlauteren Wettbewerbs, (1989) Eur.Comm.Rep. 803, 849 para. 37.

[184] Tetra Pak Rausing v. Commission, (1990) Eur.Comm.Rep. II–309, II–356 para. 22.

[185] *Id.*

[186] ACF Chemiefarma v. Commission, (1970) Eur.Comm.Rep. 661.

no questions of abuse can arise. A dominant position may exist on either the supply or demand side of the market.[187] An undertaking has a dominant position when it is able to hinder the maintenance of effective competition because it is able to behave to an appreciable extent independently of its competitors, its customers and ultimately of the consumers.[188] In determining the existence of a dominant position, the primary factor is the market share of the undertaking. According to the Court of Justice, save in exceptional circumstances, very large market shares are evidence of the existence of a dominant position.[189] This is presumptively the case, for example, where the market share is 50 percent or more.[190]

The Court has even held that a market share of 40 percent may constitute dominance under Article 102.[191] Such a percentage is well below the threshold market share associated with monopolization cases under Section 2 of the Sherman Antitrust Act. On the other end of the scale, the Court has indicated that a market share of 10 percent would ordinarily rule out the existence of dominance.[192]

Continental Can Case

A celebrated merger case involved Continental Can, a large United States corporation.[193] It is a leading case on the existence of a dominant position under Article 102 law. Evidence of Continental Can's worldwide and German national market strength in the supply of certain metal containers and tops, a concentrated market characterized by ineffective consumers and competitors, and strong technical and financial barriers to entry were sufficient for the Commission to find the existence of a dominant position in certain areas of Germany. In so doing, the Commission stressed that enterprises are in a dominant position:

> when they have the power to behave independently, which puts them in a position to act without taking into account their competitors, purchasers or suppliers. . . This power does not necessarily have to derive from an absolute domination. . . it is

---

[187] Re Eurofima, (1973) Common Mkt.L.Rep. D217 (dominant buyer).

[188] Bodson v. Pompes Funèbres, (1988) Eur.Comm.Rep. 2479, 2514; Société alsacienne et lorraine de télécommunications et d'électronique v. Novasam, (1988) Eur.Comm.Rep. 5987, 6008–9.

[189] Akzo Chemie BV v. Commission, (1991) Eur.Comm.Rep. 3359 & 60 (Case C–62–86); Hoffmann-La Roche v. Commission, (1979) Eur.Comm.Rep. 461 & 41.

[190] Akzo Chemie BV v. Commission, (1991) Eur.Comm.Rep. 3359 & 60 (Case C–62–86).

[191] United Brands Co. v. Commission, (1978) Eur.Comm.Rep. 207.

[192] Metro v. Commission, (1986) Eur.Comm.Rep. 3021.

[193] Europemballage Corporation and Continental Can Co., Inc. v. Commission, (1972) Common Mkt.L.Rep. D11 (Commission); (1973) Eur.Comm.Rep. 215 (Court of Justice).

> enough that they be strong enough as a whole to ensure to those enterprises an overall independence of behavior, even if there are differences in intensity in their influence on different partial markets.[194]

Power to behave independently of competitors, purchasers or suppliers amounting to a dominant position must be exercisable with reference to the supply or acquisition of goods or services, *i.e.,* a market. In *Continental Can* the Commission distinguished between that enterprise's powerful position around the world and in the EU with reference to the generic market for light metal containers, and its dominant position in Germany with reference to the markets for preserved meat and shellfish tins and metal caps for glass jars. Thus, initial Commission selection of the appropriate geographic and product market is the key to its analysis of whether a dominant position exists or not. It is also the key to the utility of its dominant position formula as set out in the *Continental Can* opinion.

On such selection hinges the determination of the market power of the enterprise concerned. The broader the market for goods or services is defined (light metal cans versus cans for preserved meat, etc.), the less likely there will be overall independence of behavior from competitors, purchasers or suppliers. The same is true for broader geographic markets selected by the Commission (*e.g.,* the EU versus Germany or parts thereof).

On appeal to the Court of Justice, the Commission's guiding principles for determining the existence of a dominant position under Article 102 were not seriously questioned. The Court did challenge the Commission's delineation of the relevant *product* market and its failure to explain in full how Continental Can had the power to behave independently in the preserved meat, shellfish, and metal top markets. Its German market shares were, by the Commission's calculation, 75, 85, and 55 percent respectively. Regarding the first criticism the Court said:

> The products in question have a special market only if they can be individualized not only by the mere fact that they are used for packaging certain products but also by special production characteristics which give them a specific suitability for this purpose.[195]
>
> In other words the Commission failed to make clear, for the purpose of assessing the existence of a dominant position, why the markets for preserved meat tins, preserved fish tins, and metal

---

[194] *Id.*

[195] *Id.*

> tops for glass jars should be treated separately and independently of the general market for light metal containers.

The Commission's failure here overlapped with the Court's second point:

> A dominant position in the market for light metal containers for canned meat and fish cannot be decisive insofar as it is not proved that competitors in other fields but not in the market for light metal containers cannot, by mere adaptation, enter this market with sufficient strength to form a serious counterweight.[196]
>
> The Court felt that the existence or lack of competition from substitute materials such as plastic or glass as well as potential competition from new entrants to the metal container industry or purchasers who might produce their own tins were also aspects of market power insufficiently explored by the Commission. Under the Commission's own formula for establishing a dominant position, the Court annulled the decision because it did not "sufficiently explain the facts and appraisals of which it [was] based."

The Court's emphasis in *Continental Can* on "special production characteristics," entry barriers, and potential competition amounted to instructions to the Commission to do its homework a little better in future market power analyses under Article 102. Evaluating potential competition, of course, involves hypothetical calculations with which even an expert Commission would have difficulty. Yet these factors, as well as those considered by the Commission, made up the commercial realities of the German marketplace for canned meat and fish tins and metal tops for glass jars. What is clear from the Court's *Continental Can* opinion is that dominance can be found under Article 102 in sub-product markets, provided the Commission is exhaustive in its research and analysis.

Market Analysis and Dominant Positions

Subsequent opinions of the Court have elaborated upon the product market analysis presented in *Continental Can.* The "interchangeability" of products for specific uses is a critical factor in determining the relevant product market under Article 102.[197] Thus, bananas were a proper product market since their interchangeability with other fresh fruits was limited.[198] And the replacement market for tires (as distinct from original equipment) is another sub-market capable of sustaining a dominant position.[199] In exceptional

---

196 *Id.*

197 Hoffmann-La Roche v. Commission, (1979) Eur.Comm.Rep. 461.

198 United Brands Co. v. Commission, (1978) Eur.Comm.Rep. 207.

199 Michelin NV v. Commission, (1983) Eur.Comm.Rep. 3461.

circumstances, even a brand name product may be the relevant submarket.[200]

Partial *geographic* markets can also be relevant to Article 102 market power analyses. A dominant position must exist within a "substantial" part of the Common Market. The Commission discussed geographic markets amounting to the whole of Germany in its opinion concerning tins and metal tops. Yet each of these products has different transport costs. The geographic commercial realities of competition in metal tops, given their relatively low level of transport costs, are likely to be much broader than that for tins. The same comparison can be made between small and large tins. The Court held that the Commission's geographic delineation of the markets for large and small tins in *Continental Can* was at odds with some of its own evidence on their relative transport costs. The commercial realities of potential competition in small tins appeared to go beyond the national boundaries of Germany.

The Commission's delineation of the geographic markets in *Continental Can* was insufficiently explained and appraised. Later decisions have deferred to the Commission's expertise and discretion in selecting relevant geographic markets. Belgium, Holland, and Southern Germany, for example, have been held substantial parts of the Common Market for Article 102 purposes.[201]

In 1997, the Commission issued a "Notice on the Definition of Relevant Market for Purposes of Community Competition Law."[202] This Notice covers Article 101 and 102 cases, as well as mergers and acquisitions, and considers both supply and demand-side substitutability.

When exclusive intellectual property rights are conferred by national states, the question of the existence of a dominant position remains vital. A patent, copyright or trademark for an individual product does not necessarily give an enterprise independent market power.[203] Other patented or unpatented products of a similar nature may provide effective market competition and thereby protect suppliers and purchasers from abuse. The full market power analysis required in *Continental Can* must be undertaken. Similarly, the absence of patent rights is no barrier to finding a dominant position

[200] General Motors Continental NV v. Commission, (1975) Eur.Comm.Rep. 1367 (legal monopoly over import certificates for which excessive prices were charged); Hugin Cash Registers Ltd. v. Commission, (1979) Eur.Comm.Rep. 1869 (spare parts for brand name product must be supplied to service competitor).

[201] Re European Sugar Cartel, (1975) Eur.Comm.Rep. 1663.

[202] O.J. C 372/5 (Dec. 9, 1997).

[203] Parke, Davis v. Probel and Centrafarm, (1968) Eur.Comm.Rep. 55; Sirena v. Eda GMBH, (1971) Eur.Comm.Rep. 69. *But see* Radio Telefis Eireann v. Commission (Magill TV Guide), 4 Common Mkt.L.Rep. 586 (1991).

where know-how and costly and complex technology give former patent holders complete market power.[204]

Collective Dominance

In establishing the existence of a dominant position, the Commission has tended to look at commercial realities not technical legal distinctions. Thus, a dominant position may be collectively held by several otherwise independent undertakings even if these undertakings individually do not have a dominant position. In the *European Sugar Cartel* case, the Commission concluded that two producers of sugar responsible for 85 percent of all the sugar sales in Holland held a dominant position because of the contacts between them.[205] In that case, the two producers had cooperated in the purchase of raw materials, the adoption of production quotas, the use of by-products, the pooling of research, advertising and sales promotion, and the unification of prices and terms of sale.

This theory of *collective dominance*, espoused by the Commission in subsequent cases,[206] has been accepted by the Court of Justice. The basic requirement is that the undertakings be linked in such a way that they adopt the same conduct on the market (coordinated effects).[207] In *Società Italiano Vetra SpA*,[208] for example, the Court of First Instance (now General Court) held that there is nothing to prevent two or more independent economic entities from being united by some economic links, and by virtue of that fact, together they hold a dominant position on the market. "This could be the case, for example, where two or more independent undertakings jointly have, through agreements or licenses, a technological lead affording them the power to behave to an appreciable extent independently of their competitors, their customers and ultimately of their consumers."[209]

§ 7.20 Article 102—Abuse

If the existence of a dominant position in the supply or acquisition of certain goods or services within a substantial part of the Common Market has been established, the next issue under

---

[204] Commercial Solvents Corp. v. Commission, (1973) 12 Common Mkt.L.Rev. D50 (Commission); (1974) Eur.Comm.Rep. 223 (Court of Justice).

[205] European Sugar Cartel, O.J.1973 L 140/17 on appeal Suiker Unie v. Commission, (1975) Eur.Comm.Rep. 1663.

[206] *See e.g.*, French-West African Shipowners' Committees, O.J.1992 L 134/1.

[207] Gemeente Amelo v. Energiebedrijf, (1994) Eur.Comm.Rep. I–1477 (Case No. C–393/92) at & 42. *See* Airtours v. Commission, (2002) Eur.Comm.Rep. II–2585 (Case T–342/99) (mergers); Bertelsmann v. Commission, (2008) Eur.Comm.Rep. I–4951.

[208] (1992) Eur.Comm.Rep. II–1403.

[209] *Id.* at & 358.

Article 102 is whether an abuse or exploitation of that position has occurred.

A dominant firm abuses its position when it engages in conduct that would not be possible in a competitive market.[210] According to the list of examples of abusive practices contained in Article 102, such abuse may consist of:

- Directly or indirectly imposing unfair purchase or selling prices or other unfair trading conditions;
- Limiting production, markets or technical development to the prejudice of consumers;
- Applying dissimilar conditions to equivalent transactions with other trading parties, thereby placing them at a competitive disadvantage;
- Making the conclusion of contracts subject to acceptance by the other parties of supplementary obligations which, by their nature or according to commercial usage, have no connection with the subject of such contracts ("tying arrangements").

Case Law

In *Commercial Solvents*,[211] the Commission and the Court of Justice found abuse in the activities of the only producer in the world of aminobutanol, a chemical used in the making of the drug ethambutol. Commercial Solvents, a U.S. corporation, sold the chemical in Italy to its subsidiary, Istituto Chemioterapico, which in turn sold it to Zoja, an Italian firm making the drug. After merger negotiations between Istituto and Zoja broke off, Zoja sought but failed to get supplies of the chemical from Istituto.

After receiving a complaint from Zoja, the Commission commenced Article 102 infringement proceedings. It eventually held that the *refusal to deal* of Commercial Solvents and Istituto (viewed as one enterprise) amounted to an abuse. Commercial Solvents, through its Italian subsidiary, was ordered to promptly make supplies of aminobutanol available to Zoja at a price no higher than the maximum which it normally charged.

In Re GEMA,[212] the only German authors' and composers' rights licensing society was in possession of a dominant position within a substantial part of the European Community. This dominant position was reinforced by agreements with other societies in the EU

[210] Hoffmann-La Roche v. Commission, (1979) Eur.Comm.Rep. 461, 541.

[211] *Id.*

[212] (1971) Common Mkt.L.Rep. D35; (1972) Common Mkt.L.Rep. 694.

granting exclusive rights to the various national markets. The societies were extremely advantageous and profitable to recording artists who otherwise faced formidable, if not impossible, tasks of distributing rights to their copyrighted goods on an individual basis to record manufacturers and other users. These commercial realities reinforced the Commission's conclusion that GEMA's market position was a dominant one. The Commission instituted Article 102 infringement proceedings *sua sponte*. It decided that the imposition of higher license fees on importers of records and tape recorders, compared with fees imposed on German manufacturers, was restrictive of competition between them and therefore an abuse of GEMA's dominant position relative to its purchasers.

GEMA similarly abused its dominant position by extending its members' copyrights to non-copyrighted works through a system of package license fees that failed to distinguish between copyrighted and non-copyrighted works. By *discriminating* through loyalty rebates between German users and users from different EU states, GEMA abusively helped to prevent the establishment of a single common market for the supply of recording services. In other words, it also abused its market power concerning potential Union competitors.

GEMA's discrimination against foreign members regarding management positions and a benefits scheme also constituted abuses of its dominant position. Requirements imposed on members to assign their rights to GEMA for the whole world and all marketing categories were deemed unnecessary to its operation and fell into the same category. GEMA members were also abusively excluded, by their contract terms, from recourse to the courts in the event of disputes as to distribution of GEMA funds. By requiring a six-year term, by obliging assignment of all future works during that six-year period, and by establishing a lengthy period of waiting to be eligible for certain payments, GEMA abused its dominant position through agreements with its supplier-members. By generally curtailing their mobility to join other societies in the Common Market, GEMA inhibited the process of economic integration and the creation of a single market for music publishers.

Many of the abuses found in *GEMA* do not fall under the examples provided by the Treaty terms of Article 102. From this survey of some of the abuses found, it should be apparent that once a dominant position is established the Commission feels free to roam the whole of the behavior of the dominant enterprise. Anticompetitive aspects of contractual and non-contractual relations between GEMA and its members, GEMA's constitution and by-laws, its general commercial practices, and its relations with record manufacturers and users of rights were reviewed and subjected to the Commission's regulation. Another decision in the same industry involves a French society of musical composers' rights.[213]

Hoffmann-La Roche, the large multinational Swiss firm, was fined for abusing its dominant position in seven vitamin markets in the Union. It used a network of *exclusive or preferential supply contracts*, along with loyalty rebates, to reinforce its dominance by cornering retail markets.[214] United Brands, a United States multinational, abused its dominant position in bananas through discriminatory, predatory and excessive pricing in various EU countries. Its abuses also extended to refusals to deal with important past customers and prohibiting the resale of bananas. Abuse is also a legal concept that allows the Commission to review business profits. Considering the "high profits" involved, the Commission fined United Brands 1,000,000 EUROs. In the Commission's opinion, this was a "moderate" fine under the circumstances.[215] Tying arrangements may constitute Article 102 abuses.[216]

The Court of Justice has held that *predatory pricing* can constitute an abuse of a dominant position in violation of Article 102. Predatory pricing below average total cost (as well as below average variable cost) may be abusive if undertaken to eliminate a competitor. Regarding the former, pricing below average total cost is thought to be capable of driving out competitors as efficient as the dominant firm but lacking its extensive financial resources.[217] Margin squeeze pricing by vertically integrated firms with market power may constitute abuse.[218] Other types of abuse have included refusal to supply,[219] tying,[220] and fidelity rebates,[221] and using

---

[213] *See* Greenwich Film Production, Paris v. SACEM, (1979) Eur.Comm.Rep. 3275. *See generally* regarding copyright abuses, Radio Telefis Eireann v. Commission (Magill TV Guide), 4 Common Mkt.L.Rep. 586 (1991); IMS Health GmbH & Co. OHG, (2004) Eur.Comm.Rep. I–05039 (Case C–418/01).

[214] Hoffmann-La Roche v. Commission, (1979) Eur.Comm.Rep. 461. *Accord,* Manufacture Francaise des Pneumatiques Michelin v. Commission, (Case T–203/01), (2003) Eur.Comm.Rep. II–4071.

[215] United Brands v. Commission, (1978) Eur.Comm.Rep. 207.

[216] Tetra Pak International SA v. Commission, (1994) Eur.Comm.Rep. II–7a55 *aff'd* (1996) Eur.Comm.Rep. I–5951.

[217] *Id;* Akzo Chemie BV v. Commission, (1991) Eur.Comm.Rep. I–3359 (Case C–62–86). France Telecom S.A. v. Commission, (2007) Eur.Comm.Rep. II–107 (Case T–340/03).

[218] Konkurrensverket v. TeliSonera Sverige, (2011) Eur.Comm.Rep. (Case C–52/09).

[219] Boosey & Hawkes, O.J. L 286 (1987) 36 point 19.

[220] Gemeente Amelo v. Energiebedrijf, (1994) Eur.Comm.Rep. I–1477 & 44 (Case No. C–393/92).

[221] Suiker Unie v. Commission, (1975) Eur.Comm.Rep. 1663, 2003; British Gypsum v. Commission, (1993) Eur.Comm.Rep. II–00389 (Case No. T–65/89).

dominance to move into ancillary markets.[222] It is important to note that abuse may exist without any fault of the dominant undertakings. One of the issues in *British Gypsum* was whether BPB, the British holding company of a group that controlled about half of the plasterboard production in the EU, abused its position by making promotional payments to its distributors even though the distributors themselves requested the payments.[223] With reference to the *Hoffmann-La Roche* case noted above,[224] the Court of First Instance (now general Court) held that abuse under Article 102 may occur independent of any fault.

In 2007, the General Court affirmed that Microsoft had abused its dominant Windows operating system by bundling a media player with it, and by restricting competitors' access to interoperability information. In a settlement shortly thereafter, Microsoft agreed to alter its licensing practices and royalties to favor open-source software developers such as Linux.

§ 7.21 Mergers and Acquisitions

In 1965 the Commission announced in a memorandum to the member states that regional concentration ought to be encouraged to achieve efficiency and economies of scale, and to combat competition from large United States and Japanese multinational firms. These rationales have supported a long line of merger approvals by the Commission under its coal and steel concentration controls. It was not until a European merger boom was in progress and extensive studies revealed increasing trends toward industrial concentration that the Commission acted against a merger in *Continental Can*.[225]

Continental Can Case

The Commission decided Continental Can abused its dominant positions in the manufacture of meat and fish tins and metal caps in Germany in only one fashion, by announcing an 80 percent control bid for the only Dutch meat and fish tin company. The Commission reasoned that Continental Can would strengthen its dominant German market position through this Dutch acquisition, to the detriment of consumers, and that this amounted to an abuse. The Commission emphasized that potential competition between companies located within the Union was to be eliminated. Acting quickly before the merger was a *fait accompli,* the Commission

---

[222] Sea Containers v. Stena Sealink, O.J. L 15 (1994) 8, 16; Port of Rodby, O.J. L 55 (1994) 52, 55.

[223] (1993) Eur.Comm.Rep. II–4120 (Case No. T–65/89). *See* British Airways PLC v. Commission, (2007) Eur.Comm.Rep. II–2331 (Case C–95/04) (financial incentives).

[224] (1979) Eur.Comm.Rep. 461.

[225] (1972) Common Mkt.L.Rep. D11.

underscored its inability to block proposed mergers. Continental Can was given six months to submit proposals for remedying its Article 102 infringement.

On appeal to the Court of Justice, Continental Can argued that the Commission was acting beyond its powers in attempting to control mergers under Article 102.[226] The Advocate General to the Court concurred. Nevertheless, the Court chose to go beyond the limits of the language of Articles 101 and 102 and interpret them in light of basic EU tasks and activities.

The Court reasoned that both Articles 101 and 102 were intended to assist in the maintenance of non-distorted competition. If businesses could freely merge and eliminate competition, a "breach in the whole system of competition law that could jeopardize the proper functioning of the common market" would be opened. There may therefore be abusive behavior if an enterprise in a dominant position strengthens that position so that the degree of control achieved substantially obstructs competition, *i.e.*, so that the only enterprises left in the market are those which are dependent on the dominant enterprise regarding their market behavior.[227]

One problem with relying on Article 102 for control of mergers and acquisitions was the absence of any pre-merger notification system. Once a merger is completed, it is always difficult to persuade a court or tribunal that dissolution is desirable or even possible. The key to effective mergers regulation, as the United States has learned under its Hart-Scott-Rodino pre-merger notification rules,[228] is advance warning and sufficient time to block anticompetitive mergers before they are implemented.

The possibility of using Article 101 against selected mergers was surprisingly dismissed by the Commission in an early 1966 competition policy report.[229] This is because the focus of Article 101 is on competitive behavior rather than practices which change the structure of the market. However, Article 101 may be applicable to a merger if it has the effect of influencing the competitive behavior of the companies in the relevant market. In 1984, the Commission challenged a tobacco industry acquisition as an unlawful restraint under Article 101(1). The Court of Justice held that Article 101 could be applied to the acquisition by one firm of shares in a competitor if that acquisition could influence the behavior in the marketplace of

---

[226] (1973) Eur.Comm.Rep. 215.

[227] *Id.*

[228] 15 U.S.C.A. § 18A.

[229] Commission Competition Series No. 3, *The Problem of Industrial Concentration in the Common Market* (1966).

the companies involved.[230] Likewise, Article 102 could apply if the acquisition resulted in effective control of the target company.[231]

After the ruling of the Court of Justice in *Continental Can,* the Commission submitted a comprehensive mergers' control regulation to the Council for its approval.[232] Nearly twenty years later, a regulation on mergers was finally implemented.

§ 7.22 Commission Regulation of Concentrations (Mergers)

In December of 1989, the Council of Ministers unanimously adopted Regulation 4064/89 on the Control of Concentrations between Undertakings ("Merger Control Regulation"). This regulation became effective Sept. 21, 1990, and was expanded in scope by amendment in 1997, and significantly revised in 2004. It vests in the Commission the *exclusive* power to oppose large-scale mergers and acquisitions of competitive consequence to the Common Market and the EEA.

Applicability

The Merger Control Regulation applies to concentrations with a Union dimension. The concept of concentration as used in the Merger Control Regulation is based on the notion of a change in control over another undertaking. Such a change in control may exist where two or more previously independent undertakings merge or one or more undertakings acquire, whether by purchase of securities or assets, by contract or by any other means, direct or indirect control of the whole or parts of one or more other undertakings. The most obvious example would be the outright purchase of the share capital of another undertaking.[233]

A change of control, and hence a concentration, may also exist where joint control is shared by two or more undertakings over another undertaking (*i.e.,* a joint venture). The most obvious example of joint control is where two undertakings each have a 50 percent interest in another undertaking and exercise equal control over it.[234] However, joint control may also exist in the case of a minority investment as long as the minority investor is granted rights going above and beyond its investment so that it is able to exercise control

---

[230] British American Tobacco Co. Ltd. and R.J. Reynolds Industries, Inc. v. Commission, (1987) Eur.Comm.Rep. 4487.

[231] *Id.*

[232] *See* O.J.1973 C 92/1 and 3rd Report on Competition Policy (1973) point 1.

[233] *See e.g.,* AKZO/Nobel Industrier, Comm. Decision of Jan. 10, 1994 (Case No. IV/M390).

[234] *See e.g.,* Pilkington-Techint/SIV, O.J. (1994) L 158/24, 25.

over the major commercial decisions of the joint venture.[235] Not all joint ventures fall under the Merger Control Regulation.

To qualify as a concentration, the joint venture must fulfill two additional requirements: It must perform all the functions of an autonomous economic entity on a lasting basis, and not give rise to the coordination of competitive behavior between the parents themselves or between the parents and the joint venture. Unless both conditions are fulfilled, the joint venture will be examined under Article 101 assessing its procompetitive and anticompetitive effects.[236]

To qualify as an autonomous economic entity, the joint venture must act as an independent supplier and buyer on the market. To the extent that the joint venture merely assumes specific duties assigned by its parents, this indicates that it lacks the necessary autonomy.[237] A joint venture which supplies its products or services exclusively to the parent companies will not qualify as a concentrative joint venture.[238] On the other hand, the autonomy of the joint venture will not be contested where the parents merely reserve the right to make certain decisions that are important for the development of the joint venture concerning, for example, major capital investments, increases or decreases of capital and the strategic plan of the company.

In addition, the joint venture must not lead to the coordination of the competitive behavior of the parents between themselves or between the parents and the joint venture. The risk of coordination will not generally exist where only one of the parents is active in the market of the joint venture.[239] The risk of coordination of the competitive behavior between the parents and the joint venture is similarly absent when the parents are not active in the market of the joint venture or on neighboring markets (or are active but only to a minor extent).[240]

---

[235] *See e.g.,* Hoechst/Schering, Comm. Decision of Jan. 6, 1994 (Case No. IV/M392).

[236] *See* European Night Services Ltd v. Commission, (1998) Eur.Comm.Rep. II–3141.

[237] Commission notices regarding the concentrative and cooperative operations under Council Regulation (EEC) No 4064/89 on the control of concentrations between undertakings, O.J. (1990) C 203/10 point 16.

[238] British Telecom/MCI, Comm. Decision of Sept. 13, 1993 (Case No. IV/M 353) point 6.

[239] Ericsson/Kolbe, Comm. Decision of Jan. 22, 1992 (Case No. IV/M133).

[240] Mannesmann/Vallourec/Ilva, O.J. (1994) L 102/15 point 11.

EU Dimension

Having qualified as a concentration, the issue then becomes whether it has a Union dimension. According to the Merger Control Regulation, a concentration has a Union dimension when three conditions are fulfilled (1) the combined aggregate annual worldwide turnover of all the undertakings concerned is more than 5 billion Euros, (2) the aggregate annual Union-wide turnover of each of at least two of the undertakings concerned is more than 250 million Euros, and (3) each of the undertakings involved does not achieve more than two-thirds of its aggregate Union-wide turnover within one and the same Member State. These thresholds were reviewed in 1993, when the Commission declined to lower them because "below this level concentrations would principally have a national impact and, in accordance with the subsidiarity principle, would therefore be better handled at that level."[241]

Since 1997, Union-dimension concentrations subject to notification also occur if the enterprises have a combined aggregate world-wide turnover of at least 2.5 billion Euros *and* they have a combined aggregate turnover of at least 100 million Euros in at least three member states *and* at least two of the enterprises have at least 25 million Euros turnover in the same three member states *and* at least two of them have at least 100 million Euros turnover in the European Union *unless* each of the enterprises achieves more than two-thirds of its aggregate Union-wide turnover in the same member state.

Advance Notice

Parties to a concentration with a Union dimension are under a duty to submit notification to the Commission within one week of the signing of a merger agreement, the acquisition of a controlling interest or the announcement of a takeover bid. The Commission can fine any company failing to notify it as required. The concentration is to be notified using Form CO and must be in one of the official Union languages.[242] This language becomes the language of the proceeding. Form CO is somewhat like second request Hart-Scott-Rodino pre-merger notification filings under U.S. antitrust law. However, the extensive need for detailed product and geographic market descriptions, competitive analyses, and information about the parties in Form CO suggests a more demanding submission. Form CO defines a product market as follows:

> A relevant product market comprises all those products and/or services which are regarded as interchangeable or substitutable

241 23rd Report on Competition Policy (1994) point 46.

242 O.J. 1993 L 336/63.

by the consumer, by reason of the products' characteristics, their prices and their intended use.

Meeting in advance of notification with members of the Commission on an informal basis to ascertain whether the "concentration" has a regional dimension and is compatible with the Common Market has become widely accepted. An attempt by minority shareholders to reverse the Commission's failure to review a merger allegedly affecting their interests was denied by the Court of First Instance (now General Court). The Court held that the shareholders were not directly or individually concerned by the Commission's determination that the merger fell outside the scope of EU regulation of concentrations.[243] Such meetings provide an opportunity to seek waivers from the various requests for information contained in Form CO. Since the Commission is bound by rules of professional secrecy, the substance of the discussions is confidential.

Generally, concentrations with a Union dimension cannot be put into effect and fall exclusively within the Commission's domain. The effort here is to create a "one-stop" regulatory system. However, certain exceptions apply to allow national authorities to challenge some mergers. The member states can also oppose mergers irrespective of a decision by the Commission under the Merger Control Regulation when their public security is at stake, to preserve plurality in media ownership, when financial institutions are involved or other legitimate interests are at risk.[244]

Even if the threshold criteria of the Merger Control Regulation are not met, member states can ask the Commission to investigate mergers that create or strengthen a dominant position in that state.[245] This is known as the "Dutch clause." States that lack national mergers' controls seem likely to do this.[246] Similarly, if the merger only affects a particular market sector or region in one member state, that state may request referral of the merger to it. This is known as the "German clause" reflecting Germany's insistence upon it. It has been sparingly used by the Commission.[247] Since 2004, parties to a merger that is subject to notification in three

---

[243] Zunis Holding S.A. v. Commission, (1993) Eur.Comm.Rep. II–01169 (Case T–83/92).

[244] The Commission has granted one such 21(3) authorization in IBM France/CGI, Case No. IV/M335, (19.5.93) (concentration involving French defense industry).

[245] Article 22(3), Merger Control Regulation.

[246] *See e.g.*, British Airways/Dan Air, Case No. IV/M132, (17.2.93).

[247] Steetley/Tarmac, Case No. IV/M180, (12.2.1992); McCormick/Ostmann, Case No. IV/330, (6.10.1993).

or more member states may request "one-stop" review by the Commission, which occurs provided no member state objects.

Once a concentration is notified to the Commission, it has one month to decide to investigate the merger. This can result in what are called Phase I clearance decisions, conditional or unconditional. If a formal investigation is commenced, the Commission ordinarily then has four months to challenge or approve the merger. These are known as Phase II investigations. During these months, in most cases, the concentration cannot be put into effect. The parties are precluded from proceeding with the concentration for three weeks after the notification is submitted. However, the Commission may extend the suspension period through a formal decision until it has made a final decision on the merits. The merger is on hold.

Evaluation

The Commission evaluates mergers in terms of their "compatibility" with the Common Market. Prior to May 1, 2004, using language reminiscent of *Continental Can*,[248] the Mergers Regulation stated that if the concentration creates or strengthens a dominant position such that competition is "significantly impeded," it was incompatible. This included dominance not only by a single firm but also joint dominance by more than one firm.[249] The Commission is authorized to consider in its evaluation the interests of consumers and the "development of technical and economic progress." It is uncertain whether economic efficiency arguments fall within this language. A failing company defense has been recognized by the Court of Justice and a 25 percent market share is normally the minimum for purposes of ascertaining the existence of a "dominant position." However, "collective dominance" theories involving duopoly and oligopoly markets have been recognized by the ECJ as valid bases for challenging mergers that may facilitate tacit collusion among leading firms.[250]

Effective May 1, 2004, this test was replaced by a prohibition against mergers that "significantly impede effective competition" by creating or strengthening dominant positions. The new test focuses on effects not dominance. A set of Guidelines on Horizontal Mergers issued by the Commission in 2004 elaborates upon this approach. It is thought that this change will bring EU and U.S. mergers law closer together (the U.S. test is "substantial lessening of competition").

---

248 *See* § 7.21.

249 *See* Nestlé/Perrier, O.J. 1992 L 356/1; Kali & Salz/MdK/Treuhand, O.J. 1994 L 186/38; Pilkington-Techint/SIV, O.J. 1994 L 158/24.

250 France v. Commission, (1998) Eur.Comm.Rep. I–1375 (Kali & Salz); Gencor Ltd. Commission, (1999) Eur.Comm.Rep. II–753.

In assessing the merger under the Merger Control Regulation, the Commission can obtain information and records from the parties, and request member states to help with the investigation. In conducting investigations of the undertakings, the Commission is authorized to examine the books and other business records and demand copies, ask for oral explanations on the spot and enter any premises of the undertaking. Fines and penalties back up the Commission's power to obtain records and information from the parties. This also applies if the parties give effect to the merger prior to notification or within the first three weeks after its notification. In such cases, the Commission may impose fines not exceeding 10 percent of the aggregate turnover of the undertakings concerned if the parties acted intentionally or negligently.

Approval of the merger may involve modifications of its terms or promises by the parties aimed at diminishing its anticompetitive potential. If the Commission ultimately decides to oppose the merger in a timely manner, it can order its termination by whatever means are appropriate to restore conditions of effective competition (including divestiture, fines or penalties). Such decisions can be appealed to the Court of First Instance (now General Court) since 2002 under "fast track" procedures that limit issues on appeal and promote judicial review within a year. As a practical matter, most merger proposals do not last that long. Hence, a negative Commission decision usually kills the merger.

Case Examples

The first merger blocked by the Commission on competition law grounds was the attempted acquisition of a Canadian aircraft manufacturer (DeHaviland—owned by Boeing) by two European companies (Aerospatiale SNI of France and Alenia e Selenia Spa of Italy).[251] Prior to this rejection in late 1991, the Commission had approved over 50 mergers, obtaining modifications in a few instances. The Commission, in the *DeHaviland* case, took the position that the merger would have created an unassailable dominant position in the world and EU market for turbo prop or commuter aircraft. If completed, the merged entity would have had 50 percent of the world and 67 percent of the Union market for such aircraft. In 2007, the Commission blocked the Ryanair/Aer Lingus merger.[252]

In contrast, the Commission approved (subject to certain sell-off requirements) the acquisition of Perrier by Nestlé.[253] Prior to the merger, Nestlé, Perrier and BSN controlled about 82 percent of the

---

[251] O.J. 1991 L 334/42.

[252] Case No. Comp/M.4439 (2007).

[253] O.J. 1992 L 356/1.

French bottled water market. Afterwards, Nestlé and BSN each had about 41 percent of the market. The sell-off requirements were thought sufficient by the Commission to maintain effective competition. The case also presents interesting arguments that the Commission, in granting approval, disregarded fundamental workers' social rights. This issue was unsuccessfully taken up on appeal by Perrier's trade union representative.[254]

Even though a merger may create or strengthen a dominant position, the Commission has indicated that it may be willing to approve the merger if the acquired firm would be forced out of the market but for the merger.[255] The requirements of this failing company defense are similar to those under U.S. antitrust law.[256] It must be clear that the acquired undertaking would be forced from the market in the near future but for the merger, the acquiring undertaking would take over the market share of the acquired undertaking if it were indeed forced out of the market, and there is no less anticompetitive alternative. In the *De Havilland* case, the Commission refused to apply the defense since the probability that the acquired firm would be forced out of the market but for the merger was not high enough.[257]

In 1997, the Commission dramatically demonstrated its extraterritorial jurisdiction over the *Boeing-McDonnell Douglas* merger.[258] This merger had already been cleared by the U.S. Federal Trade commission. The European Commission, however, demanded and (at the risk of a trade war) got important concessions from Boeing. These included abandonment of exclusive supply contracts with three U.S. airlines and licensing of technology derived from McDonnell Douglas' military programs at reasonable royalty rates. The Commission's success in this case was widely perceived in the United States as pro-Airbus.

The Commission blocked the MCI Worldcom/Sprint merger in 2001, as did the U.S. Dept. of Justice. Both authorities were worried about the merger's adverse effects on Internet access. For the Commission, this was the first block of a merger taking place outside the EU between two firms established outside the EU. Much more controversy arose when in 2001 the Commission blocked the GE/Honeywell merger after it had been approved by U.S. authorities.

---

254 Comité Central d'Entreprise de la Société Anonyme Vittel & Ors v. Commission, (1993) Eur.Comm.Rep. II–01247 (Case T–12/93R).

255 Kali & Salz/MdK/Treuhand, O.J.1994 L 186/38.

256 Citizens Publishing Co. v. United States, 394 U.S. 131, 89 S.Ct. 927, 22 L.Ed.2d 148 (1969); International Shoe Co. v. F.T.C., 280 U.S. 291, 50 S.Ct. 89, 74 L.Ed. 431 (1930).

257 Aérospatiale-Alenia/De Havilland, O.J. 1991 L 334/42.

258 O.J. L 336/16 (Dec. 8, 1997).

The Commission was particularly concerned about the potential for bundling engines with avionics and non-avionics to the disadvantage of rivals.[259] On appeal, the General Court rejected the Commission's legal reasoning. Nevertheless, the merger never took place. The United States and the EU, in the wake of GE/Honeywell, have agreed to follow a set of "Best Practices" on coordinated timing, evidence gathering, communication and consistency of remedies. These Best Practices facilitated the Commission's unconditional *Oracle/Sun Microsystems* merger clearance in 2011.

The General Court overturned a 1999 decision of the European Commission blocking the $1.2 billion merger of Airtours and First Choice Holidays.[260] The 2002 CFI decision was the first reversal of a merger prohibition since the 1990 inception of the review process. The GC judgment confirmed that transactions can be blocked on collective dominance grounds, but found that the Commission had failed to meet the three conditions for proving collective dominance: (1) each member of the dominant group is able to determine readily how the others are behaving, (2) there is an effective mechanism to prevent group members from departing from the agreed-upon policy, and (3) smaller competitors are unable to undercut that policy. The Commission three times blocked the merger of the London Stock Exchange and Deutsche Borse citing a "de facto monopoly" outcome in Europe, despite assertions that the merger was needed to compete with the New York Stock Exchange.

In October of 2002, acting under its new fast-track review procedures, the General Court overturned two additional mergers decisions of the Commission. In both *Schneider Electric*[261] and *Tetra Laval*[262] the Court found serious errors, omissions and inconsistencies. Credible evidence, not assumptions or "abstract and detached analysis," must be tendered to prove the strengthening or creation of a dominant position, and the likelihood that the merger will significantly impede competition. The Commission may be found liable in damages for intervening unlawfully against mergers, notably when making manifest procedural errors[263] Commission

[259] Case COMP/M.2220 (July 3, 2001).

[260] Airtours v. Commission, (2002) Eur.Comm.Rep. II–2585 (Case T–342/99).

[261] Schneider Electric v. Commission, (2002) Eur.Comm.Rep. II–04071 (Cases T–310/01 and T–77/02).

[262] Tetra Laval BV v. Commission, (2002) Eur.Comm.Rep. II–04381 (Cases T–5/02 and T–80/02).

[263] Schneider Electric v. Commission (Case T–351/03) Court of First Instance, July 11, 2007.

decisions to clear joint ventures or mergers can, in rare cases, be annulled.[264]

§ 7.22A Hostile Takeovers

In June of 2002 the European Court of Justice issued three decisions on the use by member states of so-called "golden shares." Such shares allow governments to retain veto rights with respect to acquisitions of or other significant accumulations in privatized businesses. The court outlawed a golden share decree allowing France to block a foreign takeover of a privatized oil company.[265] The golden share decree created a barrier to the free movement of capital. The court also outlawed a law giving Portugal the ability to block the acquisition of controlling stakes in privatized state companies[266], but determined as a matter of public interest that Belgium could retain its golden share in recently privatized canal and gas distribution companies.[267] In 2007, the ECJ overturned the decades-old "Volkswagen Law." This law had prevented anyone except the government of Lower Saxony from owning more than 20% of the voting rights to Volkswagen. Its invalidation allowed Porsche to complete its hostile takeover of VW.

In 2004, the EU adopted a directive on hostile takeover bids. Its two most controversial rules are optional.[268] First, boards of directors are required to obtain shareholder approval before taking defensive measures other than seeking alternative offers. Second, once a bid has been made public, restrictions on share transfers, voting restrictions, and special voting rights are unenforceable. Hence member state law on hostile takeovers is not uniform. The French, for example, allow use of any defense permitted by the home country of the bidder, and have published a list of strategic sectors that are off-limits to foreign takeovers.

§ 7.22B Employee Rights in Mergers and Acquisitions

Directive 77/187 is known as the "transfer of undertakings" or "acquired rights" directives. When European acquisitions, mergers or transfers occur, employees are entitled to keep their employment relationship and contractual rights (*e.g.*, pensions), including those originating in collective bargaining. Substantial changes in working

---

264 Independent Music Publishers and Label Assn (Impala) v. Commission, Case T–464/04, (2006) Eur.Comm.Rep. II 2289.

265 Commission v. France, (2002) Eur.Comm.Rep. I–4781.

266 Commission v. Portugal, (2002) Eur.Comm.Rep. I–473.

267 Commission v. Belgium, (2002) Eur.Comm.Rep. I–4809.

268 Directive 2004/25, (2004) O.J. L142/12.

conditions (*e.g.*, shifting employees to new locations) are deemed constructive dismissals. New employers can reduce the work force only if justified by "economic, technical or organizational reasons." Extensive pre- and post-merger employee consultation rights are provided like those applicable in cases of mass lay-offs, known as "collective redundancies," see Directive 75/129 (1975).

§ 7.23 Application to Public Enterprises

It is important to keep in mind that the provisions of Articles 101 and 102 apply to both public and private business activities. Despite a noticeable trend toward privatization, many undertakings in Europe are still in the hands of the state. Although the TFEU does not prohibit such state ownership (for example, state monopolies of gaming services have been recognized), because of the obvious advantages public undertakings have over private undertakings, it does prohibit the member states from enacting or maintaining in force any measure contrary to the competition rules concerning public undertakings or undertakings to which the member states have granted special or exclusive rights.[269]

It is noteworthy that Article 106(1) is directed at the member states and not at the undertakings themselves. These undertakings, even if public, remain subject to the direct application of the competition rules.[270] Moreover, this principle is not limited to the competition rules but applies to all Treaty provisions such as the right of establishment[271] and the free movement of goods[272] and services.[273]

When Is an Enterprise Public?

The line between public and private undertakings is often the subject of dispute. In general, an undertaking is considered public whenever a member state exerts a controlling influence over it by virtue of their ownership, financial participation or the rules which govern it.[274] The prohibition also applies to undertakings which have been granted special or exclusive rights by the state even if the state

---

269 Article 106(1), TFEU.

270 *See* Gemeente Amelo v. Energiebedrijf, (1994) Eur.Comm.Rep. I–1477 (Case No. C–393/92); Sacchi, (1974) Eur.Comm.Rep. 409.

271 Article 49 and 59, TFEU. *See* Greek Insurance, O.J. L 1985 152/25.

272 Article 34, TFEU. *See* RTT v. GB-Inno-BM, (1991) Eur.Comm.Rep. I–5941; Franzen, (1997) Eur.Comm.Rep. I–5909 (Swedish alcohol state monopoly).

273 *See* Liga Portuguesa, (2010) Eur.Comm.Rep. I–7633 (Case C–55/08) (gambling).

274 *See* Art. 2 of Directive 80/723, O.J. 1980 L 195/35 as amended by Commission Directive 93/84, O.J. 1993 L 254/16. However, the definition of public undertaking in the context of this Directive is not necessarily equivalent to that in the context of Art. 82. France v. Commission, (1982) Eur.Comm.Rep. 2545.

itself does not exercise direct control over the undertaking in the form of ownership. For example, Article 106(1) was held applicable to a corporation of navigational pilots exclusively authorized by the Italian state to provide compulsory piloting services in the port of Genoa.[275] Additional examples of undertakings which would fall under that Article would be energy companies, public transport, telecommunication companies and postal services.

The influence of government through subsidies, licensing or regulatory procedures can be important in determining the "public" versus "private" nature of an enterprise. The distinction has legal significance. An enterprise deemed private falls directly in the path of Article 102. An enterprise deemed public may also be subject to Article 106(1) or 106(2) which involves additional considerations. Article 106(2), for example, has its own exempting (and exception to the exemption) language and interpretive difficulties. The Court of Justice has indicated that companies with statutory monopolies that are unwilling or unable to fulfill market demands for their services engage in an unlawful abuse of a dominant position. Indeed, any state grant of exclusive rights that leads to an abuse of a dominant position is unlawful. Despite the uncertainties of the public versus private enterprise distinction drawn in the TFEU, the attempt at placing all businesses under the rule of competition is nothing less than fundamental.

Services of a General Economic Interest

According to Article 106(2), undertakings, regardless whether private or public, which are entrusted with the operation of services of a general economic interest are also subject to the competition rules but only in so far as the application of such rules does not obstruct the performance of the tasks assigned to them.[276] This provision can be seen as an exemption from both the prohibition placed on the member states in Article 106(1) and the competition rules of the TFEU contained in Articles 101 and 102.[277] The basic requirement is that the particular undertaking is entrusted with responsibilities of a general economic interest.

The essential issue in such cases is whether the application of the competition rules to the undertaking will undermine its ability to provide the services of a general economic interest with which it is

[275] Corsica Ferries v. Corpo dei Piloti del Porto Genova, (1994) Eur.Comm.Rep. I–596 (Case No. 18/93).

[276] *See* Albany International BV and Textile Industry Pension Funds, (1999) Eur.Comm.Rep. I–5751 (exclusive pension fund management); Deutsche Post AG v. GZS, Deutsche Post AG v. Citicorp, (2000) Eur.Comm.Rep. I–825 (postal monopolies).

[277] Gemeente Amelo v Energiebedrijf, (1994) Eur.Comm.Rep. I–1477 (Case No. C–393/92); Corbeau, (1993) Eur.Comm.Rep. I–2533 (Case No. C–320/91).

entrusted. The Court has consistently held that such undertakings may be legitimately shielded from competition in one area so that they can achieve higher profits with which to subsidize other less profitable areas.[278]

In the *Corbeau* case,[279] for example, the issue was whether a Belgian law granting the public postal services the exclusive right to collect, transport and deliver all mail in Belgium benefitted from Article 106(2) to the extent that it restricted other undertakings from competing in this market. In that case, the applicant was accused of infringing this law because he had established a service in a Belgian city consisting of collecting mail from the home of the sender and delivering it by the next day. The Court held that although the Belgian post office was an undertaking enjoying an exclusive right under Article 106(1), this provision of the Treaty must be read in connection with Article 106(2). Since the Belgian post office was an undertaking entrusted with the operation of a service of general economic interest, the question was whether the exclusive rights were necessary for it to adequately exercise this function.

The Court held that if the post office were to perform its functions in a profitable manner, it must be able to offset its losses in one sector by its profits in another sector. Otherwise, undertakings would concentrate their business in the profitable sectors and offer lower prices there since they did not have to subsidize their loss-making sectors like the undertaking entrusted with the operation of the service of a general economic interest (principle of equalization).

Another issue that has repeatedly arisen in Article 106(2) cases concerns the definition of an undertaking entrusted with the operation of services of a general economic interest. As an exception, this provision is to be interpreted narrowly.[280] Nonetheless, the Commission and Court have held that the provision of energy,[281] telephone[282] and television services[283] are of a general economic interest. In GEMA, on the other hand, the Commission decided that the only German authors' rights society did not benefit from the exemption provided for in Article 106(2).[284]

---

278 *See e.g.,* Gemeente Amelo v. Energiebedrijf, (1994) Eur.Comm.Rep. I–1477 (Case No. C–393/92); Corbeau, (1993) Eur.Comm.Rep. I–2533 (Case No. C–320/91).

279 (1993) Eur.Comm.Rep. I–2533 (Case No. C–320/91). *See* Höfner v. Macrotron GmbH, (1991) Eur.Comm.Rep. I–1979 (exclusive employment agency).

280 BRT v. SABAM, (1974) Eur.Comm.Rep. 313 & 19.

281 Gemeente Amelo v. Energiebedrijf, (1994) Eur.Comm.Rep. I–1477 (Case No. C–393/92).

282 RTT v. GB-Inno-BM, (1991) Eur.Comm.Rep. I–5941.

283 Sacchi, (1974) Eur.Comm.Rep. 409.

284 GEMA, (1971) Common Mkt.L.Rep. D35.

Commission Powers

A somewhat unique feature of Article 106(1) and (2) is that the Commission is authorized to adopt directives and decisions necessary to ensure its application.[285] This has proven an effective instrument for the Commission in those sectors which it has decided to liberalize. In 1989, for example, the Commission issued a directive requiring member states to increase competition in the market for telecommunications terminal equipment, including telephones, modems, and telex terminals at a time when these services were primarily in the hands of public monopolies.[286] The Court of Justice has repeatedly confirmed the Commission's broad authority to adopt such directives and decisions[287] despite protestations of certain member states to the contrary.[288] A controversial feature of Article 106 directives is that they bypass the normal legislative procedures, including Parliamentary prerogatives as well as Council enactment.

§ 7.24 National Litigation and Remedies for EU Competition Law Violations

Direct Effect

As primary Union law, Articles 101 and 102 are directly effective in the member states.[289] All regulations, for example, the various group exemption regulations discussed in Section 7.9, are directly applicable law in member states. Directly applicable EU provisions create the immediate right to rely on and obey Union law. This means that individuals and enterprises may raise competition law issues in private litigation before national courts and tribunals.[290] Indeed, under the supremacy doctrine, they may rely on such law to challenge contradictory national law.[291] The directly effective nature of Articles 101 and 102 and the numerous EU regulations in this area helps to explain the pervasive impact that competition law has had in European business life.

---

285 Article 106(3), TFEU.

286 Commission Directive 88/301, O.J. L 131 (1988) 73. This Directive was subsequently amended by Directive 90/388, O.J. L 192 (1990) 10 and Directive 94/46, O.J. L 268 (1994) 15.

287 *See e.g.*, Netherlands and PTT v. Commission, (1992) Eur.Comm.Rep. I–565.

288 France v. Commission, (1993) Eur.Comm.Rep. I–3283 (Case No. C–325/91); Spain v. Commission, (1992) Eur.Comm.Rep. I–5833.

289 Bosch v. deGeus, (1962) Common Mkt.L.Rep. 1; Belgische Radio en Televisie v. SABAM, (1974) Eur.Comm.Rep. 51.

290 *See* Chapter 3.

291 *See* Chapter 2.

Role of National Courts, Nullification, Damages

Article 101(2) renders agreements which infringe Article 101(1) (or parts thereof) null and void. Since this is a directly effective Treaty provision, the national courts ordinarily enjoin such agreements. This assumes of course that the agreement is not group exempted by the Commission under Article 101(3), which under the 2004 modernization rules can also be applied individually by national authorities and courts.[292] National courts and tribunals may request advice from *the Commission*.[293] Such requests may seek procedural as well as substantive advice. For example, the national courts may inquire whether a case or investigation into the same dispute is pending before the Commission, and how long the Commission will take before acting. They may also consult with the Commission on points of law, *e.g.*, whether the necessary impact on EU trade is present and whether the contested agreement is eligible for an individual exemption under Article 101(3).

National courts can also obtain statistics, market studies and economic analyses from the Commission. All this information and advice is intended to encourage national courts to efficiently and correctly apply Articles 101 and 102 to disputes coming before them. It is part of a broad policy of decentralized EU competition law enforcement designed to leave the Commission free to pursue cases of major importance.[294] National courts need not refer EU competition law questions to the Commission. They may simply rely upon their own analysis of the various group exemption regulations,[295] guidelines and policy notices issued by the Commission under Article 101(3). They may also rely on existing ECJ, GC and Commission case law.

If the agreement violates European Union competition law, it is up to the national courts to determine the consequences of the nullification of agreements by Article 101(2).[296] This could possibly include an award of damages and legal costs. The right to bring such actions in national courts has been affirmed by the European Court of Justice.[297] Article 102 does not contain a provision that is comparable to Article 101(2). The private legal remedies available

---

[292] *See* Section. 7.7.

[293] *See* Commission Press Release IP/92/1107 (Dec. 23, 1992) and Regulation 1/2003.

[294] *See* Commission Notice clarifying the application of Community competition law by national courts, 1993 O.J. C239/6.

[295] *See* § 7.9.

[296] Société de vente de Ciments Bétons v. Kerpen + Kerpen, (1983) Eur.Comm.Rep. 4173.

[297] Courage v. Crehan, (2001) Eur.Comm.Rep. I–6297 (Case C–453/99); Manfred: Joined Cases C295/04, 207–298/04.

when a dominant firm abuses its position must be determined strictly under national law. In Britain, for example, the House of Lords suggested that Article 102 creates "statutory duties," the breach of which permits the recovery of damages under torts principles.[298]

Directive 2014/104, effective late in 2016, mandates that any natural or legal person harmed by an EU competition law violation is entitled to full compensation for that harm. The directive establishes rules concerning disclosure of evidence, collateral estoppel, a five-year statute of limitations, joint and several liability, allowance of direct and indirect purchaser damages recoveries with a rebuttable presumption of indirect injury, and settlements. Implementation of this Directive at the national level is pending.

§ 7.25 Conflicts of Competition Law

Wilhelm Case

Conflicts between the European Union and national laws governing business competition occur. National competition laws are not preempted by the Treaty on the Functioning of the European Union (TFEU). In *Wilhelm v. Bundeskartellamt*, a conflict of competition laws emerged succinctly before the Court of Justice.[299] Four German producers of dyes were fined by the Bundeskartellamt authorities for price fixing activities under the German Law against Restraints of Competition. The dye producers appealed to the Kartellsenat of the Kammergericht in Berlin. The same 1967 price fixing activities of the four German firms were the subject of parallel competition law proceedings initiated by the Commission under Article 101. Before the Commission rendered its decision, defendants argued that in the light of the possibility of a conflict between EU and German competition law, the Kammergericht could not continue its proceedings. The Kammergericht stayed its proceedings and requested a preliminary ruling on that issue from the Court of Justice.

The European Court reviewed Article 103(2)(c) TFEU. This article authorizes the Council to define, by regulation or directive, the relationship between national laws and EU law on business competition. Such Council action has yet to take place, but it is worth noting that the Council could preempt national competition law entirely under this authority. While acknowledging that the EU has

---

[298] Garden Cottage Foods Ltd. v. Milk Marketing Board, (1983) 2 All Eng.Rep. 770, 1984 A.C. 130. For additional discussion *see* Hoskins, Garden Cottage Revisited: The Availability of Damages in the National Courts for Breaches of the EEC Competition Rules, 6 E.C.L.R. 257 (1992).

[299] (1969) Eur.Comm.Rep. 1.

instituted its own legal order which is integrated into that of its member states, the Court came to the following conclusions:

> In principle the national authorities in competition matters may take proceedings also with regard to situations liable to be the object of the decision of the Commission . . . conflicts between the Community rule and the national rules on competition should be resolved by the application of the principle of the primacy of the Community rule . . . the application of national law may not prejudice the full and uniform application of the Community law or the effect of acts in implementation of it.[300]

Multiple Liabilities

Insofar as EU and national laws are in harmony, their simultaneous application can result in multiple liabilities. In this case, the four German firms were fined by the Commission and ordered to cease and desist their price fixing activities. The Kammergericht in Berlin continued to hold its proceedings in abeyance and eventually, after the Commission's decision was rendered, annulled the violations and fines imposed under German competition law on constitutional and evidentiary grounds.

Supremacy

The *Wilhelm* decision reaffirms the supremacy of European Union law in the event of a conflict with national competition law. In such circumstances, litigants can ordinarily invoke EU competition law to nullify national proceedings and liability. Since EU competition law is very extensive, the *Wilhelm* rule of supremacy in the event of conflicts of competition law has wide repercussions. Regulation 1/2003 requires national courts and authorities to avoid conflicts of competition law and reaffirms the principle of supremacy. Articles 101 and 102 must be applied concurrently with national law, which cannot bar agreements and practices not prohibited by European law.

International Liability

The *Wilhelm* principles extend to United States antitrust and EU competition law conflicts. For example, one European member of an international price fixing quinine cartel was fined under Article 101.[301] Subsequently, that firm was fined for the same activities by U.S. authorities under federal antitrust law. The price fixer then requested a credit against the EU fines in the amount of the U.S.

---

300 *Id.*

301 Re Quinine Cartel, (1969) Common Mkt.L.Rep. D41.

fines. The Commission denied this request, noting that it had always been aware of the parallel United States proceedings.[302]

§ 7.26 EEA Competition Law

On January 1, 1994, the Agreement on the European Economic Area came into force between the then twelve members of the EU and five of the then seven EFTA states (Austria, Finland, Iceland, Norway, and Sweden).[303] Because Austria, Finland and Sweden joined the EU in 1995, the EEA competition law provisions outlined below now apply only to Iceland and Norway. The EEA Agreement does not introduce new substantive competition laws but rather simply adopts the competition law provisions of the TFEU. In addition, the numerous regulations which form an integral part of the EU competition law system are also adopted by the EEA Agreement. This includes, most notably, the Merger Control Regulation as well as the various group exemptions.[304] For private companies doing business in the EEA, this means essentially that the EEA Agreement does not present a new set of substantive competition law rules which must be observed, but rather geographically extends the application of the existing EU rules.

EFTA Surveillance Authority

Perhaps the most important practical aspect of the EEA Agreement is the creation of an additional competition law authority—the EFTA Surveillance Authority (ESA)—in Europe. The ESA is charged with the enforcement of the EEA competition rules and has enforcement powers equivalent to those enjoyed by the Commission.[305] For companies active in Europe, the existence of two competition law authorities presents the practical question of which authority has jurisdiction over a particular business practice. To avoid imposing additional compliance burdens on undertakings, the attribution of cases between the Commission and the ESA is based on the "one-stop-shop' principle. This means that a particular case will be attributed to either the Commission or the ESA but not both. Attribution of a particular case depends on the type of restraint at issue.

---

302 Re Boehringer Mannheim, (1972) Eur.Comm.Rep. 1281.

303 O.J. 1994 1/3. Although Switzerland signed the initial Agreement, it failed to ratify it. Because of its close economic integration with Liechtenstein, the latter also forced to postpone its membership in the EEA. Austria, Finland and Sweden subsequently joined the EU on January 1, 1995. This leaves only Iceland, Norway and potentially Liechtenstein as EEA parties.

304 Annex XIV of the EEA Agreement.

305 *See* Agreement between the EFTA States on the Establishment of a Surveillance Authority and a Court of Justice.

If the restraint is through an agreement, decision or concerted practice—the applicable provision therefore being Article 53 of the EEA Agreement—the ESA has jurisdiction in those cases where only trade between EFTA states is affected. If trade between both the EFTA States and member states of the EU is affected, the ESA has jurisdiction only if the turnover of the undertakings in the territory of the EFTA States represents 33 percent or more of their turnover in the entire EEA.[306] There is one exception to this rule: The EU Commission retains jurisdiction in all cases where trade between member states is affected.[307] If trade between EU Member States is affected but not appreciably, the ESA retains jurisdiction provided the aforementioned 33 percent threshold is met.[308]

If the challenged restraint of trade arises from the abuse of a dominant position—the applicable provision therefore being Article 54 of the EEA Agreement—the authority of the territory where the dominant position exists has jurisdiction. If the dominant position exists in EFTA as well as the European Union, then the ESA has jurisdiction only if the turnover of the undertaking in the EFTA area equals or exceeds 33 percent, and if trade between EU member states is not appreciably affected. Otherwise, the Commission has jurisdiction.

Finally, if the alleged restraint arises from a concentration—the applicable provision therefore being Article 57 of the EEA Agreement—the EU Commission has exclusive jurisdiction if the concentration has a Union dimension as defined in the Merger Control Regulation.[309] Otherwise, the ESA will be the competent authority if the relevant thresholds identical to those in the Merger Control Regulation are met in the territory of the EFTA states. In such cases, the undertakings should be aware that jurisdiction by the ESA does not preclude the national competition law authorities of the EU member states from exercising jurisdiction over the same merger.[310]

---

[306] Art. 56(1)(6) of the EAA Agreement. Articles 2 through 5 of Protocol 22 contain special rules for the determination of the turnover in the context of Art. 56. The concept of turnover corresponds basically with that defined in Art. 5 of the Merger Control Regulation. The determination of turnover in the cases of distribution and supply agreements between non-competing undertakings or the transfer of technology between such undertakings is governed by special rules contained in Art. 4(1) of Protocol 22. In effect, these rules reduce the aggregate turnover of the firms.

[307] Art. 56(1)(c), EEA Agreement.

[308] Art. 56(3), EEA Agreement.

[309] *See* § 7.22.

[310] According to Art. 57(2)(b) of the EEA Agreement, the jurisdiction of the ESA is to be exercised "without prejudice to the competence of the Member States."

When the notification or application is sent to the wrong authority, the authority must transfer the case.[311] If the notification or application is sent to the wrong authority, the effective date the notification or application is received depends on the type of restraint of trade at issue. For restraints of trade falling under Article 53(1) EEA Agreement, the effective date of notification is the date that the first authority receives it.[312] In the case of a concentration, however, it is the date on which it is received by the competent authority.[313] Although the difference may only be a matter of a day, one should keep this in mind since firms have only one week following the conclusion of the contract leading to the concentration to report to the competent authority.

Cooperation with EU Commission

According to Article 58 of the EEA Agreement, the ESA and Commission are required to cooperate in the implementation and application of the competition law provisions of the EEA Agreement. Regarding agreements in restraint of trade and the abuse of a dominant position, the duties of cooperation exist where the business practice at issue impacts trade in the territory of the other competition law authority.[314]

In the case of concentrations, the duty to cooperate exists when the combined turnover of the undertakings concerned in the territory of the EFTA states equals 25 percent or more of their total turnover within the territory covered by the EEA Agreement, or each of at least two of the undertakings concerned has a turnover exceeding 250 million EURO in the territory of the EFTA states, or the concentration is liable to create or strengthen a dominant position as a result of which effective competition would be significantly impeded in the territories of the EFTA states or a substantial part thereof.[315]

Although the required cooperation concerns primarily the relationship between the respective competition law authorities (*e.g.*, consultation, exchange of administrative letters, etc.), there are several aspects which are of particular interest for firms doing business in the EEA. Perhaps the most significant practical implication of the provisions governing the cooperation between the respective competition law authorities concerns the exchange of information. Since the duty to cooperate requires the authorities to

---

311 Art. 10(2), Protocol 23, EEA Agreement.

312 Art. 11, Protocol 23, EEA Agreement.

313 Art. 11, Protocol 24, EEA Agreement.

314 Art. 1, Protocol 23, EEA Agreement.

315 Art. 2, Protocol 24, EEA Agreement. *See e.g.*, Commission Decision of 29 July 1994, Case No.IV/M478, VoithSulzer, point 14.

exchange notifications and applications,[316] companies should be aware that in certain cases, the information submitted in conjunction with a notification or application to one of the competition law authorities may fall into the hands of the other competition law authority. Second, the ability of the respective authorities to gain access to information located in the territory of the other authority is substantial. Information requests by the competent authority can be directed to companies situated in the territory of the other authority.[317] If the information is not subsequently provided, the competent authority may request the other authority to undertake an investigation if it deems necessary.[318] Thus, even if information is located outside the territory of the competent authority, it may be still accessed through an investigation undertaken by the authority in that territory.

Finally, if a decision is reached by a competent authority that a particular agreement amounts to a restraint of trade or that a particular business practice is an abuse of a dominant position, and the infringement is not brought to an end, that authority may authorize states within the other territory or request the other authority to authorize states to take appropriate measures "needed to remedy the situation."[319] Decisions of the respective authorities which impose pecuniary obligations on undertakings as a result of a violation of the competition laws, are enforceable in the territory of the other authority.[320]

§ 7.27 The Extraterritorial Jurisdiction of Articles 101 and 102

There is a question about the extent to which the competition rules of the European Union extend to activity anywhere in the world, including activity occurring entirely or partly within the territorial limits of the United States or Canada. Decisions by the Commission and the Court of Justice suggest that the territorial reach of Articles 101 and 102 is expanding and may extend to almost any international business transaction.

For an agreement to be incompatible with the Common Market and prohibited under Article 101(1), it must be "likely to affect trade between Member States" and have the object or effect of impairing "competition within the Common Market." These requirements

---

316 Art. 2, Protocol 23, & Art. 3(1) Protocol 24, EEA Agreement.

317 Art. 8(1), Protocol 23, & Art. 8(2) Protocol 24, EEA Agreement.

318 Art. 8(3), Protocol 23, & Art. 8(4) Protocol 24, EEA Agreement.

319 Art. 55(2), EEA Agreement.

320 Art. 110, EEA Agreement.

amount to an "effects test" for extraterritorial application of Article 101, like that of the Sherman Act of the United States.

Extraterritorial Application

The Court has repeatedly held that the fact that one of the parties to an agreement is domiciled in a third country does not preclude the applicability of Article 101(1).[321] Swiss and British chemical companies, for example, argued that the Commission was not competent to impose competition law fines for acts committed in Switzerland and Britain (before joining the EU) by enterprises domiciled outside the Union even if the acts had effects within the Common Market.[322] Nevertheless, the Court held those companies in violation of Article 101 because they owned subsidiary companies within the Community and controlled their behavior.

The foreign parent and its EU subsidiaries were treated as a "single enterprise" for purposes of service of process, judgment, and collection of fines and penalties. In doing so, the Court observed that the fact that a subsidiary company has its own legal personality does not rule out the possibility that its conduct is attributable to the parent company.

The Court has extended its reasoning to the extraterritorial application of Article 102.[323] A United States parent company, for example, was held potentially liable for acquisitions by its EC subsidiary which affected market conditions within the Community.[324] In another decision, the Court held that a Maryland company's refusal to sell its product to a competitor of its affiliate company within the Union was a result of united "single enterprise" action.[325] It proceeded to state that extraterritorial conduct merely having "repercussions on competitive structures" in the Common Market fell within the parameters of Article 102. The Court ordered Commercial Solvents, through its Italian affiliate, to supply the competitor at reasonable prices.

Woodpulp Case

In 1988, the Court of Justice widened the extraterritorial reach of Article 101 in a case where wood pulp producers from the U.S., Canada, Sweden and Finland were fined for price fixing activities

---

321 Ahlström v. Commission, (1988) Eur.Comm.Rep. 5193; Zinc Producers v. Commission, (1984) Eur.Comm.Rep. 1679.

322 *See* ICI v. Commission, (1972) Eur.Comm.Rep. 619.

323 For a discussion of the extraterritorial reach of the Merger Control Regulation, *see* Montag, Common Market Merger Control of Third-Country Enterprises, Comparative Law Yearbook of International Business 47 (1991).

324 *See* Europemballage Corp. and Continental Can Co., Inc. v. Commission, (1973) Eur.Comm.Rep. 215.

325 *See* Commercial Solvents Corp. v. Commission, (1974) Eur.Comm.Rep. 223.

affecting EU trade and competition. These firms did not have substantial operations within the Union. They were primarily exporters to the Common Market. This decision's utilization of a place of implementation "effects test" is quite like that used under the Sherman Act.[326] And the reliance by the U.S. exporters upon a traditional Webb-Pomerene cartel exemption from United States antitrust law carried no weight in the European Union.

The Court has also affirmed the extraterritorial reach of Articles 101 and 102 to airfares in and out of the Union,[327] and the Mergers Regulation (see Section 7.22) clearly applies to firms located outside the Common Market.

§ 7.28 The Effects Test and Blocking Statutes

It may be a substantial jump to predict that Articles 101 and 102 bear upon a business transaction done in the United States or another non-EU country which merely inures to the competitive disadvantage of a company located within the Common Market. Yet in one of the *Dyestuffs* cases as early as 1969 the Commission took the position that:

> The rules of competition of the Treaty are therefore applicable to all restrictions on competition that produce within the Common Market effects to which Article 101, paragraph 1, applies. There is therefore no need to examine whether the enterprises that originated such restraints of competition have their head office within or outside of the Union.[328]

Although the Court's disposition of the *Dyestuffs* cases did not endorse such reasoning, the Commission has reasserted its "effects test" in subsequent arguments. The Commission's approach merits close consideration if only because the initiation of an Article 101 or 102 inquiry can generate local overhead costs for those involved in EU business transactions. That courts in the United States have also used an "effects test" in connection with the question of the extraterritoriality of American antitrust laws increases the potential for uncertainty and costs in international transactions.[329]

U.S. Extraterritorial Antitrust

United States courts have long asserted the right to apply the Sherman Antitrust Act to foreign commerce affecting the United

---

326 Woodpulp Producers v. Commission, (1988) Eur.Comm.Rep. 5193.

327 Ahmed Saeed Flugreisen v. Zentrale zur Bekämpfung unlauteren Wettbewerbs, (1989) Eur.Comm.Rep. 803.

328 Commission v. I.C.I., 8 Common Mkt.L.Rep. 494 (1969).

329 *See generally* Spencer Weber Waller, International Trade and U.S. Antitrust Law (Supp. 1994).

States market.[330] In some cases, this approach has been tempered to allow consideration of the interests of comity and foreign countries in the outcome.[331] Sherman Act amendments adopted in 1984 stress the "direct, substantial and reasonably foreseeable" nature of effects on American foreign commerce as a prerequisite to antitrust jurisdiction. Nevertheless, the potential for conflict in this field is enormous. For example, a multinational enterprise (MNE) headquartered in the U.S. but doing business in Europe could be constrained by United States antitrust law from fixing prices yet permitted by EU competition law under Article 101(3) to do exactly that.

If the price fixing in question has effects in both markets, what course of action is to be followed? There is no easy answer. When the MNE is located within a country other than one of the member states of the EU or the United States, but engages in activity having effects within those markets, the problem potential of extraterritoriality may be even more acute. Reconciling a conflict of antitrust laws applied extraterritorially by these two jurisdictions could become a flashpoint in international business transactions.

The problem becomes even more apparent when one considers the increasing influence of international trade policy on the application of antitrust laws. For example, the U.S. Department of Justice has indicated that it will take enforcement action against conduct occurring overseas that restrains exports, regardless of whether or not there is direct harm to U.S. consumers, where it is clear that the conduct has a direct, substantial and reasonably foreseeable effect on exports of goods and services from the United States, the conduct infringes U.S. antitrust laws, and the U.S. courts have jurisdiction over the foreign persons or corporations engaged in such conduct.[332] Although the application of this policy has not created any significant problems,[333] the influence of international trade policy on the application of antitrust law does carry the potential of becoming a major issue in relations with foreign countries.

---

330 *See especially* United States v. Aluminum Co. of America, 148 F.2d 416 (2d Cir. 1945) (L. Hand, J.); Hartford Fire Insurance Co. v. California, 509 U.S. 764, 113 S.Ct. 2891, 125 L.Ed.2d 612 (1993).

331 *See especially* Timberlane Lumber Co. v. Bank of America, 549 F.2d 597 (9th Cir. 1976); *Compare* Laker Airways Ltd. v. Sabena, Belgian World Airlines, 731 F.2d 909 (D.C. Cir. 1984); Hartford Fire Insurance Co. v. California, 509 U.S. 764, 113 S.Ct. 2891, 125 L.Ed.2d 612 (1993).

332 Dept. of Justice press release (3 April 1992).

333 *See* United States v. Pilkington, 7 Trade Reg.Rep. (CCH) & 50,758 (1994); United States v. MCI Communications, 7 Trade Reg.Rep. (CCH) & 50,761 (1994).

Blocking Statutes

In the case of antitrust judgments emanating from United States courts, most notably the "Uranium Cartel" treble damages litigation of the late 1970s,[334] many nations consider the flashpoint already reached. At least nine nations (Australia, Canada, France, Germany, Netherlands, New Zealand, Philippines, South Africa, and the United Kingdom) have taken retaliatory action by enacting "blocking statutes." In addition, the 41 Commonwealth nations have resolved general support for a position like that of the United Kingdom.

The United Kingdom blocking statute is the Protection of Trading Interests Act of 1980.[335] This Act (without specifying American antitrust law) makes it difficult to depose witnesses, obtain documents or enforce multiple liability judgments extraterritorially in the U.K. Violation of the 1980 Act may result in criminal penalties. Furthermore, under the "claw-back" provision of the Act, parties with outstanding multiple liabilities in foreign jurisdictions (*e.g.*, United States treble damages defendants) may recoup the punitive element of such awards in Britain against assets of the successful plaintiff. The British Act invites other nations to adopt claw-back provisions by offering claw-back reciprocity. United States attorneys confronted with a blocking statute need to understand that multiple liability judgments combined with contingency fee arrangements are virtually unknown elsewhere.

Policy Debate

The extensive array of pre-trial discovery mechanisms allowed in U.S. civil litigation rarely, if ever, have a counterpart in foreign law. Discovery subpoenas originating in American litigation often "shock" many foreign defendants. And the U.S. Supreme Court has ruled that use of letters rogatory under the Hague Convention[336] is not obligatory.[337] It is the blocking of discovery that potentially most threatens the extraterritorial application of United States laws, especially antitrust. Since United States courts may sanction parties who in bad faith fail to respond to discovery requests, foreign defendants requesting help from their home governments under blocking statutes are especially at risk. On the other hand, good faith efforts to modify or work around discovery blockades may favor

---

[334] *See* In re Uranium Antitrust Litigation (Westinghouse Electric Corp.) v. Rio Algom Limited, 617 F.2d 1248 (7th Cir. 1980).

[335] Reprinted in 21 I.L.M. 834 (1982).

[336] Hague Convention on the Taking of Evidence Abroad in Civil or Commercial Matters, 23 U.S.T. 2555, T.A.I.S. No. 7444.

[337] Société Nationale Industrielle Aérospatiale v. U.S. District Court, 482 U.S. 522, 107 S.Ct. 2542, 96 L.Ed.2d 461 (1987).

foreign defendants. Such defendants are often caught in a "no win" situation. Either way they will be penalized.

Reasons advanced to support an extraterritorial application of United States antitrust laws are founded on the idea that some extraterritorial extension is necessary to prevent their circumvention by multinational corporations which have the business sagacity to ensure that anticompetitive transactions are consummated beyond the territorial borders of the United States. An extraterritorial extension of antitrust laws can help to protect the export opportunities of domestic firms. Extraterritorial application of the antitrust laws can also help to ensure that the American consumer receives the benefit of competing imports, which in turn may spur complacent domestic industries. The effect of foreign auto imports on the car manufacturers in the United States may be cited as an example. In an increasingly internationalized world, extraterritorial antitrust may merely reflect economic reality.

On the other hand, the British argue that American extraterritoriality permits the U.S. to unjustifiably "mold the international economic and trading world to its own image." In particular, the U.S. "effects" doctrine creates legal uncertainty for international traders, and U.S. courts pay little attention to the competing policies (interests) of other concerned governments. As the House of Lords has stated: "It is axiomatic that in anti-trust matters the policy of one state may be to defend what it is the policy of another state to attack."[338]

The British also argue, not without some support, that customary international law does not permit extraterritorial application of national laws.[339] In making this argument, the British have a convenient way of forgetting about the extraterritorial scope of Articles 101 and 102, which are now part of their law. Moreover, in a curious reversal of roles illustrating the extremes of the debate, the British government applied the Protection of Trading Interests Act to block the pursuit of treble damages in *United States* courts by the liquidator of Laker Airways against British Airways and other defendants. A House of Lords decision reversed this ban but retained government restrictions on discovery related to the case.[340]

---

338 Westinghouse Electric Corp. v. Rio Tinto Zinc Corp., 2 W.L.R. 81 (1978).

339 *See* arguments presented by the British government in Hartford Fire Insurance Co. v. California discussed in Reuland, Hartford Fire Insurance Co., Comity and the Extraterritorial Reach of United States Antitrust Laws, 29 Tex.Int'l L.J. 159 (1994) and Brief of the Government of the United Kingdom of Great Britain and Northern Ireland as Amicus Curiae in Société Nationale Industrielle Aérospatiale v. U.S. District Ct., reprinted in 25 I.L.M. 1557 (1986).

340 British Airways Board v. Laker Airways, 3 W.L.R. 413 (1984).

§ 7.29 United States—European Union Cooperation on Antitrust

U.S. Antitrust Cooperation Agreements

Some evidence of international antitrust cooperation is contained in a 1967 recommendation of the OECD which provides for notification of antitrust actions, exchanges of information to the extent that the disclosure is domestically permissible, and where practical, coordination of antitrust enforcement.[341] The OECD resolution served as a model for the 1972 "Antitrust Notification and Consultation Procedure" between Canada and the United States. Following the "Uranium Cartel" litigation, Australia, and the United States reached an Agreement on Cooperation in Antitrust Matters (1982) to minimize jurisdictional conflicts.[342] Australia has taken the position that United States courts are not a proper institution to balance interests of concerned countries within the context of private antitrust litigation.

The Agreement on Cooperation provides that when the Government of Australia is concerned with private antitrust proceedings pending in a United States court, the Government of Australia may request the Government of the United States to participate in the litigation. The United States must report to the court on the substance and outcome of consultations with Australia on the matter concerned. In this way, Australia's views and interests in the litigation and its potential outcome are made known to the court. The court is not required to defer to those views, or even to openly consider them. It merely receives the "report." Australia, in turn, has indicated a willingness to be more receptive to discovery requests in U.S. antitrust litigation and to consult before invoking its blocking statute.

Similar arrangements were made in the Memorandum of Understanding between the U.S. and Canada with Respect to the Application of National Antitrust Laws (1984). No such agreement has been reached with the United Kingdom, with whom the extraterritoriality issue remains contentious, a fact which has led some to wonder whether the United States ought to have its own blocking statute against extraterritorial EU competition law. However, an antitrust cooperation agreement seems more appropriate, and late in 1991 the European Union and the United

---

[341] In 1986, the OECD issued a similar Recommendation Concerning Cooperation between Member States on Restrictive Business Practices Affecting International Trade, reprinted in 25 I.L.M. 1629 (1986).

[342] Reprinted in 21 I.L.M. 702 (1982).

States reached such an agreement.[343] Comparable agreements between the EU and Canada, and the EU and Japan have been concluded.

EU-U.S. Antitrust Cooperation

The U.S.-EU accord commits the parties to notify each other of imminent enforcement action, to share relevant information and consult on potential policy changes. An innovative feature is the inclusion of "comity" principles, each side promising to take the other's interests and requests into account when considering antitrust prosecutions. The agreement has had a significant effect on mergers of firms doing business in North America and the Union. Each side has agreed to notify and consult with the other regarding antitrust matters, including mergers and acquisitions, that "may affect important interests."

In its first six months of operation, about 45 notifications were exchanged between the Commission, the U.S. Federal Trade Commission, and the Antitrust Division of the U.S. Justice Department. A large portion of these notifications concerned international mergers and acquisitions. Since both the EU and the U.S. have premerger notification systems,[344] the exchange of such information has increased rapidly. In the first year after the cooperation agreement, U.S. antitrust enforcers sent 37 such notifications to the European Commission and received 15 in return. About 20 percent of all the mergers reviewed by the Commission under its competition law were simultaneously being reviewed by U.S. antitrust authorities, but as Section 7.22 (above) reveals, cooperative review can result in conflicting decisions.

Microsoft and U.S. Tech Companies

The agreement was prominently used to jointly negotiate a 1994 settlement on restrictive practices of the Microsoft Corporation. Since the Commission has traditionally permitted U.S. lawyers to appear before it on competition law matters, the FTC announced on the same day as the signing of the US-EU antitrust cooperation agreement that EU lawyers would be permitted to appear before it on a reciprocal basis. In the more recent round of public prosecutions of Microsoft focused on Windows as a monopoly, the United States settlement reached in 2001 is less demanding than the Commission

---

343 Because the Court of Justice held that the Cooperation Agreement with the United States was void since the Commission did not have the requisite authority to enter into such an agreement, France v. Commission, (1994) Eur.Comm.Rep. I–03641 (Case No. C–327/91), the Commission has recently asked the Council to expressly approve the Agreement.

344 *See* Section 7.22.

judgment of 2004 which also requires an unbundling of media playback capabilities.

This example reaffirms that transatlantic antitrust "cooperation" need not necessarily result in similar outcomes. In 2007, the General Court broadly confirmed the Commission's 2004 decision. Shortly thereafter, Microsoft settled the prosecution by altering its operating systems' licensing arrangements to favor "open source" software developers (*e.g.*, Linux). Prior to settlement, Microsoft had been fined, including daily noncompliance penalties of more than 2 billion Euros.

By 2008, the Commission was investigating Microsoft's bundling of its web browser with Windows, and the compatibility of its Office software with rival programs. A quick settlement "unbundled" web browsers on Windows. . . there are now a dozen or more choices. But in 2013, the Commission fined Microsoft $700 for breach of this settlement agreement.

Other U.S. technology firms have been under the EU competition law microscope: Qualcomm, Intel, IBM, Facebook, Google and Apple included. In 2009, the Commission fined Intel 1.06 billion Euros for abusing its dominant position in microprocessors for PCs. Intel's price discounts and loyalty rebates were the center of this proceeding. In 2017, Facebook paid a 110 million Euro fine for providing "misinformation" in the review of its acquisition of WhatsApp.

In the same year, Google set a record in paying a 2.42 billion Euro fine for abusing its dominance (90% market share) in internet shopping searches by favoring its own price-comparison results. Microsoft was one of the complaining parties. San Diego based chip-maker Qualcomm was fined nearly a billion Euros in 2018 for allegedly illegal payments to Apple.

§ 7.30 EU Digital Services and Digital Markets Acts

In 2023 the EU enacted major first-of-their kind laws focused on tech platforms for digital services and digital markets. These laws are concerned with abuses by dominant "gatekeeper" digital companies, often American.

The EU Digital Services Act applies to social media and search firms like X (formerly Twitter), TikTok, Meta's Facebook and Alphabet's Google. The EU Digital Markets Act covers leading market-making firms such as Amazon, E-Bay and Apple. Apple was the first U.S. firm to be charged under the Digital Markets Act for App Store restraints not allowing developers to freely direct customers to alternative ways to make purchases. Fines under the Act can be up to 10% of worldwide revenues. Apple settled another EU complaint regarding its mobile Apple Pay program by agreeing to open the program to rivals.

While not exactly traditional antitrust or business competition laws, the EU Digital Acts regulate leading tech companies in a manner designed to hopefully increase platform competition. Online content is policed, transparency required, and data reporting obligations apply. The Acts focus on systemic risks. Fines for violating EU online content rules can rise to 6% of global revenues, 20% for repeat offenders. The EU may also force the breakup of repeat tech offenders.

The first Services Act EU probe concerns Elon Musk's X. The Commission is examining X's control of illegal content and misinformation. Whether the EU Digital Acts, like the EU General Data Protection Regulation (GDPR, see Chapter 5), will migrate and serve as models for other nations or regional groups is unclear.

Chapter 8

BREXIT AND BEYOND

Table of Sections

This chapter concerns BREXIT and developments beyond the withdrawal of the United Kingdom from the European Union.

§ 8.0 COVID-19

Just as BREXIT was accomplished late in January 2020, the COVID-19 pandemic virus arrived. COVID made negotiating a UK-EU future relations agreement more difficult.

In the following months, the EU and UK responses varied considerably. Important EU rules were relaxed or overwhelmed. Government subsidies, notably regulated by EU law (see Chapter 6), proliferated as individual countries sought to rescue their economies. For example, France pumped 8 billion Euros into Renault and Germany sent 9 billion Euros into Lufthansa in return for 20% government ownership. Overall, German subsidies cannot be matched by other EU states, threatening to undermine the operation of the EU's Single Market.

Financial controls came under great pressure as Germany for the very first time acquiesced in agreement with France to *collectively backed* "coronabonds". These common EU bonds are intended to raise money for hard-hit Italy, Spain and southern member states. They are funded in part by new EU taxes on unrecycled plastic waste and digital levies. The EU Central Bank is authorized to buy coronabonds, essentially eliminating the risk of default. Resistance by "The Frugals" (Austria, Denmark, the Netherlands and Sweden) resulted in greater EU budget rebates for them, and possible "emergency brake" limits on COVID bailout funding.

In crisis mode, the ECB resumed substantial purchases of national bonds ("quantitative easing"), even Greek bonds, as the EURO Zone (see Chapter 4) struggled. Border restraints on goods, notably medical equipment and medicines, emerged. EU export controls over vaccines in 2021 served as prominent reminder to Britain that BREXIT really did alter trade relations.

Structural shifts, such as re-shoring, combined with increased supply chain protectionism, diminished economic activity. EU fiscal controls over national spending were significantly suspended. Different but major national economic contractions emerged as a European recession set in. Doom loop risks rose as shrinking economies made it harder to service national debts.

Perhaps most seriously, extensive border restraints on people essentially negated the Schengen free movement regime (see Chapter 5). Early on in 2020 EU nations adopted entry bans against each other, later relaxed selectively among "travel bubble" partners subject to mandatory COVID testing rules. In July 2020, international controls barred persons coming from COVID heavy countries like the USA, Russia and Brazil. Note that the USA had previously in the pandemic crisis barred entry to many EU residents, and in 2021 barred entry to the world absent a negative COVID test.

§ 8.1 BREXIT

Since 2009, Article 50 of the Treaty on European Union (TEU) permits member states to commence withdrawal negotiations from the European Union. Prime Minister Cameron, wanting badly to be re-elected in 2015 and seeking to appease the hard-core Euroskeptic wing of his Conservative Party, promised in his campaign to re-negotiate Britain's position in the EU and hold a referendum on remaining an EU member state. He won re-election, and after negotiating modest changes in U.K.-EU relations, put the Remain or Leave issue to a public vote.

In a hotly contested campaign, with free movement of people within the EU a prominent issue, LEAVE supporters made statements that were simply untrue, for example that Britain would save not pay money by leaving and that the National Health Service would directly benefit from these savings. Future Prime Minister Boris Johnson actively participated in promoting this idea. At no point did the leaders of the Leave movement present a clear plan for or picture of its consequences. Critics maintain that the Leave vote was secured by a campaign riddled with falsehoods that often seemed disconnected from reality. Some Brexiteers even suggested a return to nostalgic Empire glory.

Russia actively supported BREXIT, primarily via divisive Facebook accounts, much as it did in the 2016 U.S. elections in supporting Donald Trump.

After approval by 52% of its voters in a high turnout June 2016 national referendum and strong approval by the House of Commons, Britain commenced two-year withdrawal negotiations on March 29, 2017, nearly the same date as the 60th anniversary of the EU. London, Scotland and Northern Ireland voted heavily to remain, but the rest of England provided the Leave campaign with victory. Theresa May, a Minister in David Cameron's Cabinet and a quiet Remain supporter, became Prime Minister shortly after the referendum in the wake of Cameron's resignation. For a considerable period, she simply said "BREXIT means BREXIT".

Two different BREXIT negotiations occurred. The first concerned "divorce" withdrawal terms finalized in 2019. The second negotiation, commenced in 2020, concerned future relations between the UK and the EU. Absent a future relations agreement, Britain and the EU faced a "no deal" hard exit, expected by many to be very damaging. During these negotiations there was a standstill. EU law governed, with no participation by the British in its supranational development.

Rallying around a cry for sovereignty, Britain under Prime Minister May commenced over two years of withdrawal negotiations on March 29, 2017, nearly the same date as the 60th anniversary of the EU.

Prime Minister May's Divorce Agreement

Seeking to raise her bargaining power with the EU under a clear mandate from the British people, Prime Minister May held a snap election in June of 2017. Much to her surprise and that of the pollsters, the Conservative Party lost majority control of the UK Parliament. Many factors were in play during the snap election, but it appeared that at least some British voters had second thoughts about the wisdom of BREXIT, particularly the "hard" version she espoused.

The Conservatives were consequently forced to govern in coalition with a small Protestant-dominated Northern Ireland party, the DUP. This coalition was fragile. The DUP wanted agricultural subsidies post-BREXIT, continued access to EU development funds for poorer regions, and a "frictionless" border with Ireland. The DUP leaned toward remaining in the EU.

Some Brexiteers suggested pursuing the "soft exit" Norwegian or Swiss models for relations with the EU post-BREXIT. But these complicated models for the most part involved acceptance of free movement of people, the EU customs union, cash contributions to the EU budget, and deference to EU/EFTA Court decisions. To what degree would a soft exit really be an exit?

Prime Minister May indicated she would continue to pursue a "hard" exit. Prime Minister May was quoted as saying that "better no deal, than a bad deal," suggesting Britain might walk out of the negotiations. By 2019, despite repeated efforts, she was unable to secure UK Parliamentary approval for the BREXIT deal she had negotiated with the EU. The core issue was the possibility under "stopgap" provisions, if no future relations agreement was accomplished, that all the UK would remain inside the EU customs union to ensure that the border between Northern Ireland and Ireland would not become "hard". This possibility sparked fears of a return to violence and conflict like that before the Good Friday accords.

Prime Minister Johnson's Divorce Agreement

In July 2019, Prime Minister May resigned and in the ensuing elections Boris Johnson, former mayor of London and a brazen Brexiteer, became Prime Minister. In short order, he re-negotiated the BREXIT divorce deal to remove hard land border risks, essentially creating an internal UK/EU customs and immigration border in the middle of the Irish Sea cooperatively administered by British and EU authorities.

Under this Divorce Agreement, the UK firmly left the EU customs union, thus freeing up Britain to engage in trade agreement negotiations around the world. Northern Ireland remained part of the UK customs regime but obliged to collect VAT taxes and tariffs on goods (but not services) on behalf of the EU. Northern Ireland also remained in the EU's regulated "single market" for goods (see Chapter 5). It was agreed that new cooperatively run "trusted traveler" rules on goods moving between Britain and Northern Ireland be established in UK ports. These checks are meant to assure regulatory conformity (especially on agricultural goods and meat) and collect taxes/tariffs on goods "at risk" of being transported or smuggled into the EU via Northern Ireland.

Money Matters

As a mandatory prerequisite to withdrawal negotiations, early on in Prime Minister May's tenure, the EU presented Britain with an expensive "divorce bill" for what it perceived the UK would owe the Union upon departure. The demand for cash included Britain's liabilities under the generous, entirely unfunded EU pension scheme.

It also covered pre-BREXIT and post-BREXIT EU projects under the British-approved EU budget running from 2013 through 2020.

In the end, the 'divorce bill" amounted to approximately 35 billion Euros. This bill no doubt stunned many LEAVE backers, who were led to believe BREXIT would result in net savings not loss. In addition, Britain lost two well-staffed and well-paid EU agencies, one on Medicines (EMA), the other on banking (EBA).

On the flip side, the EU had to adapt to the loss of Britain as a net contributor to its budget.

Divorce Deal Done

The Johnson divorce deal (formally titled the Withdrawal Agreement) was subsequently approved by the EU and the UK Parliaments, thereby setting the formal date for BREXIT to occur on Jan. 31, 2020.

§ 8.2 The EU-UK Trade and Cooperation Agreement (TCA, 2021)

Many in the EU felt Britain should "pay a price" to leave. Put another way, to paraphrase one EU leader: "It cannot be the case that Britain ends up better off outside the EU than inside". Overall, the adverse trade consequences of BREXIT for the UK were more significant than for the EU. The UK, for example, sends nearly 50% of its exports to the EU, while less than 10% of EU exports end up in Britain. The UK depends on exports to the EU for approximately 13% of its GDP, while the EU depends on exports to the UK for only 3% of its GDP. All that said, Britain is a substantial market for EU exports (notably autos made in Germany) and the fifth biggest economy in the world, considerations which played in the UK's favor.

Bottom line: The independent UK Office for Budget Responsibility forecasted the British economy would be 4% smaller ten years after the TCA than if Britain had remained in the EU.

Nevertheless, after much negotiation and threats of failure, a complex 2,000-page UK-EU Trade and Cooperation Agreement (TCA) was finally reached on Christmas eve of 2020. It took effect Jan. 1, 2021. Fundamentally a "thin" free trade in goods (only) agreement, the TCA exits Britain from the EU customs union and the EU single market freedoms for cross-border movement of goods, services, people and capital. *Unlike most trade deals, the TCA creates more trade restraints than it removes.*

The BREXIT future relations deal needed and obtained qualified majority approval by the EU Council, which for these purposes meant 20 out of 27 member states constituting at least 65% of the EU population had to affirm the deal. The consent of the European Parliament as well as the UK Parliament was also required and obtained.

Specific Divorce and TCA provisions are noted in the topics below, followed by an outline of the TCA, which is summarized in Appendix 4.

Fishing

It may seem a bit strange, but the issue that most held up the Trade and Cooperation Agreement (TCA) was fishing. The EU created a Common Fisheries Policy (CFP) just prior to the entrance of Britain, Ireland and Denmark in 1973. It allows EU member states considerable rights to fish in traditionally national waters and regulates levels of catch. See Section 5.24.

Long a thorn in British culture and its economically insignificant fishing industry, the TCA establishes quotas that reduce by 25% over 5.5 years most EU (notably French) rights to fish in UK waters. Thereafter annual negotiations will follow. Swapping of fish quotas is no longer allowed under the TCA. The irony of this focus is that, for reasons of taste, much of the fish caught or raised in UK waters is exported to the Continent. These exports are expected to continue and are not subject to immediate EU retaliation tariffs if in breach of the TCA, a major concession by the EU that essentially closed the future relations deal.

Early signs under the TCA fishing accord suggested cod catches by British boats (the mainstay of British "Fish n' Chips") have declined. Exports of fish to the EU are tied up in new paperwork requirements. Some Scottish trawlers took to running their salmon directly to Denmark where prices were double those of the UK.

Free Movement and Residency Rights

UK students, retirees, entrepreneurs and workers and their families and pets (with pet passports!) had long enjoyed free movement residency, health care and no roaming cell phone rights throughout the Union, no work permits or visas needed. See Chapter 5. Existing residency rights (in the UK known as "settled status") were protected under the Divorce Agreement but became subject on both sides after BREXIT to substantial paperwork requirements and fees.

Many provocative questions arose. What was to happen to the nearly 1 million Poles, 350,000 Romanians, 270,000 French citizens, and the other 2 million or so EU nationals working in Britain? What was to happen to the 1.2 million British retirees and others on the continent? What about EU professionals and restaurant owners who had exercised their EU "right of establishment" to set up shop in the UK, and vice-versa?

One could argue that Britain had obtained a younger, more skilled tax-paying workforce under the EU free movement of people regime. The EU in turn received a goodly number of higher cost UK seniors.

Future "free movement" rights are eliminated. The TCA enacts visa-controlled movement of people across borders from 2021 forward. For example, the extensive EU Erasmus Program facilitating hundreds of thousands of cross-border student studies, work experiences and apprenticeships will not be available to students from England, Wales and Scotland, but (thanks to underwriting by Ireland) will be open to students from Northern Ireland. Mutual recognition of professional qualifications, such as those of doctors, nurses and architects, will be more limited than SPS under EU rules.

Apart from liberal UK-Ireland travel rules, tourist visas as between the UK and the Schengen area will only be good for 90 days of travel during any six-month period. Advance electronic authorizations were required commencing in 2022. Travel insurance with health care coverage has become standard. Mutual emergency health care generally remained available, but not automatic for kidney dialysis and the like.

Fearing the worst, some British citizens began efforts to obtain other EU passports to preserve free movement and other EU rights. Dual nationality in Ireland, Sweden and Germany ranked high on this list. A small steady flow of EU nationals out of the UK commenced early in BREXIT's evolution, but many remained.

Free Internal Trade

Agreeing to tariff free *and quota* free goods trade was relatively easy for the UK and EU in their TCA negotiations. *This was the first time the EU had ever agreed to quota free trade.* Almost immediately a notable dispute emerged concerning EU export restraints on COVID vaccines.

On both sides, hundreds of millions of customs and tax forms, fees, import licenses, security checks and certifications must now be regularly filed, a significant and costly trade barrier, especially to the UK. Facing lengthy back-ups, cross-border trucking fees are noticeably up. Cross-border online sales have been hit with hitherto absent costs and fees. Some UK and EU importers, particularly smaller firms, reduced and in some cases eliminated cross-border trade. Marks & Spencer, for example, dropped hundreds of products from its Northern Ireland stores. UK exports to the EU went down significantly under new EU customs and COVID regulations.

Complex rules of origin for goods suddenly applied. For example, gas and diesel autos must contain at least 55% UK and EU combined content to be freely traded. For electric and hybrid vehicles, the rule of origin requirement is 40%, but their batteries are limited in the amount of allowable overseas content starting with 70% and running down to 50% by 2026. More red tape is likely to proliferate, particularly as there are no common certification standards on safety, pollution and the like for autos. Dual production runs for EU and UK compliant vehicles may emerge.

For another example, Britain imports about 25% of its food from the EU while 60% of its agricultural exports head to the continent. No tariffs and quotas apply, but the absence of TCA agreement on common sanitary and phytosanitary standards (SPS) for food generates UK and in reverse EU certification and paperwork issues galore. UK exports of seafood quickly ran into EU import SPS barriers. Much the same problem and costs could emerge regarding pharmaceutical testing and safety certifications.

Britain in principle escaped the EU's voluminous "*acquis communautaire*", its vast body of internal trade legislation, regulations, and case law. But many European Union rules seem inescapable since all goods exported from Britain will need to conform to EU law, and extensive cross-border supply chains compel compliance. For example, all auto imports must under the EU End of Life Vehicles Directive be 95% reusable or recyclable.

The EU, recognizing that the two sides will inevitably become competitors, feared that the UK might become a "Singapore-upon-Thames" neighbor with low-cost product standards and taxation. It extracted significant regulatory commitments from the UK not found in its Canada or Japan free trade agreements (see Chapter 6).

The Divorce deal suggested that each side would keep the same standards on state subsidies, competition law, social and employment rules, the environment, climate change and "relevant" tax matters. In addition, the UK agreed to create an independent regulator of government subsidies along the lines of the EU competition authorities. See Chapter 5.

These "level playing field" regulations were incorporated in the TCA on a "non-regression" basis, meaning the UK promised not to dilute them, but reserved the right to do so subject to possible (but not instant) retaliatory EU trade sanctions. Arbitration procedures were established to resolve disputes in this critical area, notably avoiding the jurisdiction of the European Court of Justice (ECJ, see Chapter 4).

This author asks: When the UK retains EU standards and regulations, will not interpretations of those rules by the ECJ come along with them in dispute arbitrations?

Services and Business Passport Rights

The TCA does not retain the core EU freedom to provide services across borders (see Chapter 5). The British economy relies very heavily on its services sector, including finance, IT, legal, accounting, insurance, consultation, audio-visual, and architecture for examples.

Much of the EU services sector operates on "passport" principles under EU law. Bankers, securities firms, insurance companies and the like need only obtain a license in one EU state, which then basically qualifies them to do business in the other member states. Britain, London and The City comprise the financial center of Europe. Financial firms (including U.S. firms) used British licenses to springboard throughout the EU.

Without passport rights, and if British regulatory rules do not measure up as "equivalent" to those of the EU, British, U.S. and global finance and service companies licensed in the UK could join the BREXIT exodus. Early in the BREXIT saga this started happening, with roughly 7500 financial sector employees and $1.6 trillion in financial assets departing to the benefit of Frankfurt, Paris, Luxembourg, Dublin and even New York.

The EU has made it clear that certain financial operations traditionally done in London will be obliged to be done within its borders. Most clearing house operations, derivatives, EURO bond, carbon cap and trade, and direct client services are expected as a matter of EU law to be undertaken inside the Union. Trading of EU stocks shifted almost immediately from London to EU-based exchanges, including the London Stock Exchange's Turquoise platform in Amsterdam.

Even if some British service sector regulations are deemed "equivalent" to those of the EU, such treatment can be removed by the EU with 30 days' notice.

Foreign Investment

Many foreign, especially Asian and North American, investors have set up manufacturing and service centers in Britain. For example, Japanese car companies were notably invested in the United Kingdom. Japan was sufficiently worried about BREXIT that its government delivered a detailed memo of concern to the U.K. soon after the vote to leave in 2016.

British and foreign manufacturers based in the U.K. were especially nervous about going from zero tariff entry into the EU to paying tariffs to gain entry to what will remain the world's largest common market. Autos, for example, are subject to 10% EU import tariffs, agricultural goods subject to 30–40% tariffs. In addition, nontariff regulatory barriers could emerge if British health, safety, subsidy, and environmental standards differ from those of the EU.

British and foreign investors essentially put a hold on investment or expansion of existing operations in the U.K. after the BREXIT vote while negotiations proceeded over four years. Just before the scheduled BREXIT deadline of March 29, 2019, Honda announced it would exit production in the U.K. in favor of USA and Japanese plants. Honda anticipated free trading autos into the EU under the 2019 EU-Japan Economic Partnership Agreement. See Chapter 6.

Post BREXIT foreign and domestic investment in the UK has notably declined. Why so? The UK after BREXIT is a significantly smaller market with generally higher costs. For example, Jaguar Land Rover cut UK employment by thousands of jobs. Dyson, of vacuum cleaner fame, moved its headquarters to Singapore prior to inaugurating an electric vehicle. Nissan undertook EV auto production outside the UK. BMW pre-emptively moved its engine production back to Germany. It seems fair to say that some investors in the UK perceived that BREXIT in any form represented a clear and present danger. That perspective was not eliminated by the Trade and Cooperation Agreement of 2021.

More broadly, late in 2020 the EU completed a bilateral Cooperation Agreement on Investment (CAI, referred to as a "BIT") with China. BITs *among* EU members have been invalidated by the European Court of Justice. See Chapter 6. Britain escapes this ruling via BREXIT.

International Trade Relations

Britain pre-BREXIT derived its trade relations with the world predominantly via the EU. Absent a post-BREXIT agreement with the EU regarding future relations, it was assumed that Britain would revert to World Trade Organization rules. See my *International Trade Law* Concise Hornbook. How sound that assumption was, and what were its implications for the UK, the EU and WTO partners like the United States was unclear.

The UK had traded under WTO tariffs negotiated under the EU umbrella. Might it have been needed to start over as an independent WTO member? Would the EU have needed to compensate WTO members because its tariffs were negotiated on the premise that the

UK was included? Since 25% of American exports to the EU go to Britain, these issues mattered to the U.S. and incentivized reaching an agreement on future relations.

"Global Britain" after BREXIT hopes for lots of bilateral free trade and foreign investment deals. Initial dialogues commenced in 2020. Most of the over 70 EU free trade partners (including Korea, Canada, Mexico, Tunisia, Kenya, Southern Africa, Central America, Morocco, Egypt, Ukraine, Norway, Iceland, Japan, Vietnam, Turkey, Singapore) agreed to roll-over their EU deals to maintain "continuity" with the UK. Such free trade agreements raise critical "rules of origin" and costly documentation issues, for example regarding UK-made automobiles such as BMW's Mini-Coopers and Toyota vehicles.

Big trade deals for the UK with the likes of the United States, India, MERCOSUR and China remain to be negotiated. The EU has proposed a "New Transatlantic Agenda" with the United States focused on digital supply chain security, climate change, product standards, and dealing with COVID.

The interim year 2020 expanded the scope of UK/EU trade relation issues. Britain and France reversed policy in 2020 by removing participation by China's Huawei in their 5G network. Will the UK and the EU agree on digital revenue taxes, which would notably hit Google, Amazon, Microsoft, Facebook and other U.S. tech companies? What about data privacy concerning which the EU has been a world leader (see Chapter 5)? These issues have mostly remained contentious.

Northern Ireland and Scotland

Every political district in Scotland voted in 2016 to remain in the EU. But the Conservatives won 12 districts in the June 2017 snap election. The Scotch voted against leaving the UK several years prior to BREXIT. A second referendum could achieve Scottish independence in search of EU membership. Scotland, as an alternative to leaving the UK, might fairly ask whether special arrangements like those discussed below for Northern Ireland could be made for it.

Nearly every district in Northern Ireland voted to remain. Peace and border-free transit has been directly linked under the Good Friday Accords to Irish and UK membership in the EU. After BREXIT, the Ireland/Northern Ireland border is the only land crossing between Britain and the EU. Under the Divorce Agreement, the UK and the EU promised to cooperatively administer byzantine trade rules between Ireland and Northern Ireland to keep this border crossing free of customs and immigration controls. That said, the Windsor Framework of 2023 at least establishes Green (Northern

Island) and Red (EU) traffic lanes for "trusted trader" goods crossing the Irish Sea from the U.K.

Northern Ireland (unlike the UK) is subject to EU single market regulations (see Chapter4) and the jurisdiction of the European Court of Justice (see Chapter3). Northern Island will collect VAT and tariffs on behalf of the EU. However, its goods will enter both the EU and the UK duty-free.

These provisions were negatively received by Protestants in Northern Island, leading to a threat (ultimately not undertaken) by the UK Parliament under the Johnson administration to disavow them. The threat further undermined EU trust in Boris Johnson as a reliable trade partner. It also caused U.S. President Joe Biden to warn of his opposition against a return to a hard border.

Critics maintain that BREXIT is toxic in the long run for the future of Northern Ireland as part of the UK. Certainly, the TCA pushes the Ireland and Northern Ireland towards eventual unification. The EU-UK agreement on Northern Ireland will be reviewed every four years, opening the door for participation by the Northern Ireland Parliament if it is functioning. Britain's unilateral decision to delay a key part of the BREXIT deal regarding Northern Ireland drew quick legal action by the EU.

Ireland, a low-tax manufacturing center for many U.S. multinationals, typically ships substantial goods to the EU using Britain as an inexpensive land-bridge running from Wales to Dover to Calais. This has become a rat's nest of customs law after BREXIT. Early signs are that this now costly land-bridge can be avoided by shipping goods between Ireland and Cherbourg, France.

In addition, Ireland's food imports to and exports from the UK are significant. Irish imports from the UK dropped dramatically starting in 2021. Ireland has a big stake in BREXIT and the TCA.

Immigration and Free Movement of People

Immigration (mostly by EU nationals) was an issue central to the BREXIT vote. Since Britain does not participate in the Schengen Accord (see Chapter 5), the UK has always maintained its own external border controls for non-EU migrants. For EU and non-EU persons, Britain is establishing a new merit points-based immigration system, subject to considerable fees.

As noted above, apart from residency benefits existing as of 2021, what will change under the TCA are the extensive rights of UK and EU nationals to freely cross borders in pursuit of employment, education, retirement, or creation of a business. See Chapter 5.

Cooperation on Foreign Affairs and Security Matters

Administering the TCA will require ongoing trust and cooperation, qualities in short supply after the bruising BREXIT negotiations. The TCA provides for continued UK-EU cooperation on aviation, rail, trucking, defense, foreign affairs, climate change, energy, scientific research (Horizon), intelligence, and national security matters.

UK access to key EU databases will be by request. The UK will not be a member of Europol but will have "a presence" at its headquarters. It seems that the Euro Warrant criminal procedures may apply in or for the UK.

The Future of the EU

Britain having made its exit, whatever the price, why not others? In recent years, anti-EU parties have emerged throughout the Union. Marine Le Pen, leader of the National Rally Party in France, openly ran on a platform promising a national referendum on leaving the EU (FREXIT). She was resoundingly defeated by Emmanuel Macron, a strong pro-EU President of France under fire after Le Pen and her cohort Jordan Bardella prevailed in the 2024 EU Parliament elections. However, Macron and the French hard left coordinated their strategies and votes in the subsequent July 2024 French Parliamentary elections. But what will happen in the 2027 Presidential elections when Macron is barred from running?

Does BREXIT signal a decline or even the end of the Union? Or perhaps expansion of a "multi-speed" Union, built around a core of EURO Zone states? Remarkably, the initial BREXIT impact served to unify and harden the EU's negotiating positions on divorce and future relations. For the most part, Russia's invasion of Ukraine similarly generated EU cohesion even in the face of Hungary's close relationship to Putin.

The Future of the UK

Under an unrealistic sense of false optimism, a UK Minister for Brexit Opportunities was created. That post was scrapped two years later in 2022. Britain, in leaving the world's largest common market, becomes a middling economic power. Its trade has slowed, business investment has receded, and the UK has developed serious political turmoil . . . enough to lead to a smashing victory in the July 2024 national elections for the Labour Party.

Yes, Britain is a more independent nation, and yes it has considerable military and diplomatic resources, but it will struggle economically playing in the Big Leagues with China, the United States, and the European Union.

Even as a more nimble "Free Agent", Britain will ultimately have less power and influence in global affairs. This outcome reflects nationalistic moves toward self-sufficiency, nativist trade policies, anti-migration leadership, and heightened national security concerns around the world, in addition to China's rise to power and U.S. abandonment of the WTO under Trump and Biden. For more on these trends, see my International Trade *Law* Concise Hornbook.

Polls reveal that well over 50% of Britain's people now regret BREXIT.

Who Won?

BREXIT, in this author's opinion, harmed and will continue to harm both Britain and the European Union, more so for the former than the latter. Like the Swiss after Switzerland rejected EU membership, and given the endless joint committees and reviews provided for under the TCA, the UK should expect almost perpetual negotiations with the EU. In those negotiations, Britain (like Switzerland) is likely to generally be the supplicant.

The big BREXIT winner, in my opinion, has been Vladimir Putin.

§ 8.3 The TCA in Outline

The EU-UK Trade and Cooperation Agreement (TCA, 2021)

The TCA is expressly "based on international law, not EU law" (Article 14). Supervision and strategic guidance will be undertaken via a "Partnership Council". The TCA contains seven Parts.

Part I concerns common and institutional provisions. It creates joint cumulative rules of origin for goods (Chapter 2) and rules on technical barriers to trade building on the WTO TBT agreement (Chapter 3). Chapter 4 affirms the right of both sides to maintain their own Sanitary and Phytosanitary (SPS) measures. No mention is made of the WTO SPS Code. Chapter 5 on trade facilitation is based on WTO and WCO principles.

Part II governs trade in services and investment. It "locks in" market access in substantially all sectors along the lines of the EU and UK Free Trade Agreements with Japan. National treatment is a key principle along with temporary entry rights. Telecommunications, delivery services, international maritime, and financial services are detailed. New ground is broken for the provision of legal services by British attorneys advising clients on UK and public international law anywhere in the EU.

Title 3 liberalizes digital trade. Title 4 promotes capital movements. Title 5 focuses on IP rights, Title 6 public procurement,

Title 7 small and medium enterprises, Title 8 energy, Title 9 Transparency and Title 10 on good regulatory practices.

Perhaps the most critical controversial area, Title 11 contains extensive provisions on creation of a "level playing field" for open and fair competition and sustainable development. Subsidies, competition law, SOEs, taxation, labor and social standards, the environment and climate all fall within Title 11.

Separate headings in Part II exist for the rules on aviation, road transport, social security coordination, short-term visas and fisheries.

Part III covers law enforcement and judicial cooperation in criminal matters. Data exchanges, mutual assistance, money laundering, terrorism, and cooperation with Europol and Eurojust are anticipated.

Part IV is titled "Thematic Cooperation". Health security, cyber security and "migration security" are its focus.

Part V anticipates UK participation in EU programs upon payment of appropriate fees. EU programs such as Horizon Europe, Euratom, Copernicus, and Space Surveillance are specifically named.

Part VI creates dispute settlement procedures and safeguard remedies. The opening language provides: "This Agreement includes dispute resolution mechanisms that are appropriate for a relationship between sovereign equals. This means that there is no role for the Court of Justice of the European Union."

Consultations about asserted breaches of the Agreement precede arbitration. No specific arbitration tribunals or procedures are provided. Rectification by the Party in breach or suitable compensation may follow. If the dispute is not resolved, then the Party not in breach can suspend obligations under the Agreement. Cross-suspension may occur, subject to certain conditions and limitations.

In the event of serious economic, societal or environmental difficulties that are likely to persist, the EU or UK may unilaterally undertake strictly proportionate and time-limited remedial safeguard measures.

Part VII indicates that the Agreement is to be reviewed every five years and can be extended to new EU member states. It does not apply to Overseas Territories of the EU or UK. Either Party may terminate the Agreement with 12 months advance notice.

TCA Annexes cover nuclear cooperation and exchanges of classified information.

A Summary of the 2021 Trade and Cooperation Agreement is reproduced in Appendix 4.

Appendix 1

THE TREATY ON EUROPEAN UNION

Official Journal of the European Union C 83/13
(March 30, 2010)

TABLE OF CONTENTS

PREAMBLE

HIS MAJESTY THE KING OF THE BELGIANS, HER MAJESTY THE QUEEN OF DENMARK, THE PRESIDENT OF THE FEDERAL REPUBLIC OF GERMANY, THE PRESIDENT OF IRELAND, THE PRESIDENT OF THE HELLENIC REPUBLIC, HIS MAJESTY THE KING OF SPAIN, THE PRESIDENT OF THE FRENCH REPUBLIC, THE PRESIDENT OF THE ITALIAN REPUBLIC, HIS ROYAL HIGHNESS THE GRAND DUKE OF LUXEMBOURG, HER MAJESTY THE QUEEN OF THE

NETHERLANDS, THE PRESIDENT OF THE PORTUGUESE REPUBLIC, HER MAJESTY THE QUEEN OF THE UNITED KINGDOM OF GREAT BRITAIN AND NORTHERN IRELAND,

RESOLVED to mark a new stage in the process of European integration undertaken with the establishment of the European Communities,

DRAWING INSPIRATION from the cultural, religious and humanist inheritance of Europe, from which have developed the universal values of the inviolable and inalienable rights of the human person, freedom, democracy, equality and the rule of law,

RECALLING the historic importance of the ending of the division of the European continent and the need to create firm bases for the construction of the future Europe,

CONFIRMING their attachment to the principles of liberty, democracy and respect for human rights and fundamental freedoms and of the rule of law,

CONFIRMING their attachment to fundamental social rights as defined in the European Social Charter signed at Turin on 18 October 1961 and in the 1989 Community Charter of the Fundamental Social Rights of Workers,

DESIRING to deepen the solidarity between their peoples while respecting their history, their culture and their traditions,

DESIRING to enhance further the democratic and efficient functioning of the institutions so as to enable them better to carry out, within a single institutional framework, the tasks entrusted to them,

RESOLVED to achieve the strengthening and the convergence of their economies and to establish an economic and monetary union including, in accordance with the provisions of this Treaty and of the Treaty on the Functioning of the European Union, a single and stable currency,

DETERMINED to promote economic and social progress for their peoples, taking into account the principle of sustainable development and within the context of the accomplishment of the internal market and of reinforced cohesion and environmental protection, and to implement policies ensuring that advances in economic integration are accompanied by parallel progress in other fields,

RESOLVED to establish a citizenship common to nationals of their countries,

RESOLVED to implement a common foreign and security policy including the progressive framing of a common defence policy, which might lead to a common defence in accordance with the provisions of Article 42, thereby reinforcing the European identity and its independence in order to promote peace, security and progress in Europe and in the world,

RESOLVED to facilitate the free movement of persons, while ensuring the safety and security of their peoples, by establishing an area of freedom, security and justice, in accordance with the provisions of this Treaty and of the Treaty on the Functioning of the European Union,

RESOLVED to continue the process of creating an ever closer union among the peoples of Europe, in which decisions are taken as closely as possible to the citizen in accordance with the principle of subsidiarity,

IN VIEW of further steps to be taken in order to advance European integration,

HAVE DECIDED to establish a European Union and to this end have designated as their Plenipotentiaries: *(List of plenipotentiaries not reproduced)*

WHO, having exchanged their full powers, found in good and due form, have agreed as follows:

TITLE I
COMMON PROVISIONS

Article 1
(ex Article 1 TEU)

By this Treaty, the HIGH CONTRACTING PARTIES establish among themselves a EUROPEAN UNION, hereinafter called "the Union", on which the Member States confer competences to attain objectives they have in common.

This Treaty marks a new stage in the process of creating an ever closer union among the peoples of Europe, in which decisions are taken as openly as possible and as closely as possible to the citizen.

The Union shall be founded on the present Treaty and on the Treaty on the Functioning of the European Union (hereinafter referred to as 'the Treaties'). Those two Treaties shall have the same legal value. The Union shall replace and succeed the European Community.

Article 2

The Union is founded on the values of respect for human dignity, freedom, democracy, equality, the rule of law and respect for human rights, including the rights of persons belonging to minorities. These values are common to the Member States in a society in which pluralism, non-discrimination, tolerance, justice, solidarity and equality between women and men prevail.

Article 3
(ex Article 2 TEU)

1. The Union's aim is to promote peace, its values and the well-being of its peoples.

2. The Union shall offer its citizens an area of freedom, security and justice without internal frontiers, in which the free movement of persons is ensured in conjunction with appropriate measures with respect to external border controls, asylum, immigration and the prevention and combating of crime.

3. The Union shall establish an internal market. It shall work for the sustainable development of Europe based on balanced economic growth and price stability, a highly competitive social market economy, aiming at full employment and social progress, and a high level of protection and improvement of the quality of the environment. It shall promote scientific and technological advance.

It shall combat social exclusion and discrimination, and shall promote social justice and protection, equality between women and men, solidarity between generations and protection of the rights of the child.

It shall promote economic, social and territorial cohesion, and solidarity among Member States.

It shall respect its rich cultural and linguistic diversity, and shall ensure that Europe's cultural heritage is safeguarded and enhanced.

4. The Union shall establish an economic and monetary union whose currency is the euro.

5. In its relations with the wider world, the Union shall uphold and promote its values and interests and contribute to the protection of its citizens. It shall contribute to peace, security, the sustainable development of the Earth, solidarity and mutual respect among peoples, free and fair trade, eradication of poverty and the protection of human rights, in particular the rights of the child, as well as to the strict observance and the development of international law, including respect for the principles of the United Nations Charter.

6. The Union shall pursue its objectives by appropriate means commensurate with the competences which are conferred upon it in the Treaties.

Article 4

1. In accordance with Article 5, competences not conferred upon the Union in the Treaties remain with the Member States.

2. The Union shall respect the equality of Member States before the Treaties as well as their national identities, inherent in their fundamental structures, political and constitutional, inclusive of regional and local self-government. It shall respect their essential State functions, including ensuring the territorial integrity of the State, maintaining law and order and safeguarding national security. In particular, national security remains the sole responsibility of each Member State.

3. Pursuant to the principle of sincere cooperation, the Union and the Member States shall, in full mutual respect, assist each other in carrying out tasks which flow from the Treaties.

The Member States shall take any appropriate measure, general or particular, to ensure fulfilment of the obligations arising out of the Treaties or resulting from the acts of the institutions of the Union.

The Member States shall facilitate the achievement of the Union's tasks and refrain from any measure which could jeopardise the attainment of the Union's objectives.

Article 5
(ex Article 5 TEC)

1. The limits of Union competences are governed by the principle of conferral. The use of Union competences is governed by the principles of subsidiarity and proportionality.

2. Under the principle of conferral, the Union shall act only within the limits of the competences conferred upon it by the Member States in the Treaties to attain the objectives set out therein. Competences not conferred upon the Union in the Treaties remain with the Member States.

3. Under the principle of subsidiarity, in areas which do not fall within its exclusive competence, the Union shall act only if and in so far as the objectives of the proposed action cannot be sufficiently achieved by the Member States, either at central level or at regional and local level, but can rather, by reason of the scale or effects of the proposed action, be better achieved at Union level.

The institutions of the Union shall apply the principle of subsidiarity as laid down in the Protocol on the application of the principles of subsidiarity and proportionality. National Parliaments ensure compliance with the principle of subsidiarity in accordance with the procedure set out in that Protocol.

4. Under the principle of proportionality, the content and form of Union action shall not exceed what is necessary to achieve the objectives of the Treaties.

The institutions of the Union shall apply the principle of proportionality as laid down in the Protocol on the application of the principles of subsidiarity and proportionality.

Article 6
(ex Article 6 TEU)

1. The Union recognises the rights, freedoms and principles set out in the Charter of Fundamental Rights of the European Union of 7 December 2000, as adapted at Strasbourg, on 12 December 2007, which shall have the same legal value as the Treaties.

The provisions of the Charter shall not extend in any way the competences of the Union as defined in the Treaties.

The rights, freedoms and principles in the Charter shall be interpreted in accordance with the general provisions in Title VII of the Charter governing its interpretation and application and with due regard to the explanations referred to in the Charter, that set out the sources of those provisions.

2. The Union shall accede to the European Convention for the Protection of Human Rights and Fundamental Freedoms. Such accession shall not affect the Union's competences as defined in the Treaties.

3. Fundamental rights, as guaranteed by the European Convention for the Protection of Human Rights and Fundamental Freedoms and as they result from the constitutional traditions common to the Member States, shall constitute general principles of the Union's law.

Article 7
(ex Article 7 TEU)

1. On a reasoned proposal by one third of the Member States, by the European Parliament or by the European Commission, the Council, acting by a majority of four fifths of its members after obtaining the consent of the European Parliament, may determine that there is a clear risk of a serious breach by a Member State of the values referred to in Article 2. Before making such a determination, the Council shall hear the Member State in question and may address recommendations to it, acting in accordance with the same procedure.

The Council shall regularly verify that the grounds on which such a determination was made continue to apply.

2. The European Council, acting by unanimity on a proposal by one third of the Member States or by the Commission and after obtaining the consent of the European Parliament, may determine the existence of a serious and persistent breach by a Member State of the values referred to in Article 2, after inviting the Member State in question to submit its observations.

3. Where a determination under paragraph 2 has been made, the Council, acting by a qualified majority, may decide to suspend certain of the rights deriving from the application of the Treaties to the Member State in question, including the voting rights of the representative of the government of that Member State in the Council. In doing so, the Council shall take into account the possible consequences of such a suspension on the rights and obligations of natural and legal persons. The obligations of the Member State in question under this Treaty shall in any case continue to be binding on that State.

4. The Council, acting by a qualified majority, may decide subsequently to vary or revoke measures taken under paragraph 3 in response to changes in the situation which led to their being imposed.

5. The voting arrangements applying to the European Parliament, the European Council and the Council for the purposes of this Article are laid down in Article 354 of the Treaty on the Functioning of the European Union.

Article 8

1. The Union shall develop a special relationship with neighbouring countries, aiming to establish an area of prosperity and good neighbourliness founded on the values of the Union and characterised by close and peaceful relations based on cooperation.

2. For the purposes of paragraph 1, the Union may conclude specific agreements with the countries concerned. These agreements may contain reciprocal rights and obligations as well as the possibility of undertaking activities jointly. Their implementation shall be the subject of periodic consultation.

TITLE II
PROVISIONS ON DEMOCRATIC PRINCIPLES

Article 9

In all its activities, the Union shall observe the principle of the equality of its citizens, who shall receive equal attention from its institutions, bodies, offices and agencies. Every national of a Member State shall be a citizen of the Union. Citizenship of the Union shall be additional to and not replace national citizenship.

Article 10

1. The functioning of the Union shall be founded on representative democracy.

2. Citizens are directly represented at Union level in the European Parliament.

Member States are represented in the European Council by their Heads of State or Government and in the Council by their governments, themselves democratically accountable either to their national Parliaments, or to their citizens.

3. Every citizen shall have the right to participate in the democratic life of the Union. Decisions shall be taken as openly and as closely as possible to the citizen.

4. Political parties at European level contribute to forming European political awareness and to expressing the will of citizens of the Union.

Article 11

1. The institutions shall, by appropriate means, give citizens and representative associations the opportunity to make known and publicly exchange their views in all areas of Union action.

2. The institutions shall maintain an open, transparent and regular dialogue with representative associations and civil society.

3. The European Commission shall carry out broad consultations with parties concerned in order to ensure that the Union's actions are coherent and transparent.

4. Not less than one million citizens who are nationals of a significant number of Member States may take the initiative of inviting the European Commission, within the framework of its powers, to submit any appropriate proposal on matters where citizens consider that a legal act of the Union is required for the purpose of implementing the Treaties.

The procedures and conditions required for such a citizens' initiative shall be determined in accordance with the first paragraph of Article 24 of the Treaty on the Functioning of the European Union.

Article 12

National Parliaments contribute actively to the good functioning of the Union:

(a) through being informed by the institutions of the Union and having draft legislative acts of the Union forwarded to them in accordance with the Protocol on the role of national Parliaments in the European Union;

(b) by seeing to it that the principle of subsidiarity is respected in accordance with the procedures provided for in the Protocol on the application of the principles of subsidiarity and proportionality;

(c) by taking part, within the framework of the area of freedom, security and justice, in the evaluation mechanisms for the implementation of the Union policies in that area, in accordance with Article 70 of the Treaty on the Functioning of the European Union, and through being involved in the political monitoring of Europol and the evaluation of Eurojust's activities in accordance with Articles 88 and 85 of that Treaty;

(d) by taking part in the revision procedures of the Treaties, in accordance with Article 48 of this Treaty;

(e) by being notified of applications for accession to the Union, in accordance with Article 49 of this Treaty;

(f) by taking part in the inter-parliamentary cooperation between national Parliaments and with the European Parliament, in accordance with the Protocol on the role of national Parliaments in the European Union.

TITLE III

PROVISIONS ON THE INSTITUTIONS

Article 13

1. The Union shall have an institutional framework which shall aim to promote its values, advance its objectives, serve its interests, those of its citizens and those of the Member States, and ensure the consistency, effectiveness and continuity of its policies and actions.

The Union's institutions shall be:

— the European Parliament,

— the European Council,

— the Council,

— the European Commission (hereinafter referred to as "the Commission"),

— the Court of Justice of the European Union,

— the European Central Bank,

— the Court of Auditors.

2. Each institution shall act within the limits of the powers conferred on it in the Treaties, and in conformity with the procedures,

conditions and objectives set out in them. The institutions shall practice mutual sincere cooperation.

3. The provisions relating to the European Central Bank and the Court of Auditors and detailed provisions on the other institutions are set out in the Treaty on the Functioning of the European Union.

4. The European Parliament, the Council and the Commission shall be assisted by an Economic and Social Committee and a Committee of the Regions acting in an advisory capacity.

Article 14

1. The European Parliament shall, jointly with the Council, exercise legislative and budgetary functions. It shall exercise functions of political control and consultation as laid down in the Treaties. It shall elect the President of the Commission.

2. The European Parliament shall be composed of representatives of the Union's citizens. They shall not exceed seven hundred and fifty in number, plus the President. Representation of citizens shall be degressively proportional, with a minimum threshold of six members per Member State. No Member State shall be allocated more than ninety-six seats.

The European Council shall adopt by unanimity, on the initiative of the European Parliament and with its consent, a decision establishing the composition of the European Parliament, respecting the principles referred to in the first subparagraph.

3. The members of the European Parliament shall be elected for a term of five years by direct universal suffrage in a free and secret ballot.

4. The European Parliament shall elect its President and its officers from among its members.

Article 15

1. The European Council shall provide the Union with the necessary impetus for its development and shall define the general political directions and priorities thereof. It shall not exercise legislative functions.

2. The European Council shall consist of the Heads of State or Government of the Member States, together with its President and the President of the Commission. The High Representative of the Union for Foreign Affairs and Security Policy shall take part in its work.

3. The European Council shall meet twice every six months, convened by its President. When the agenda so requires, the members of the European Council may decide each to be assisted by a minister and, in the case of the President of the Commission, by a member of the Commission. When the situation so requires, the President shall convene a special meeting of the European Council.

4. Except where the Treaties provide otherwise, decisions of the European Council shall be taken by consensus.

5. The European Council shall elect its President, by a qualified majority, for a term of two and a half years, renewable once. In the event of an impediment or serious misconduct, the European Council can end the President's term of office in accordance with the same procedure.

6. The President of the European Council:

(a) shall chair it and drive forward its work;

(b) shall ensure the preparation and continuity of the work of the European Council in cooperation with the President of the Commission, and on the basis of the work of the General Affairs Council;

(c) shall endeavour to facilitate cohesion and consensus within the European Council;

(d) shall present a report to the European Parliament after each of the meetings of the European Council.

The President of the European Council shall, at his level and in that capacity, ensure the external representation of the Union on issues concerning its common foreign and security policy, without prejudice to the powers of the High Representative of the Union for Foreign Affairs and Security Policy.

The President of the European Council shall not hold a national office.

Article 16

1. The Council shall, jointly with the European Parliament, exercise legislative and budgetary functions. It shall carry out policy-making and coordinating functions as laid down in the Treaties.

2. The Council shall consist of a representative of each Member State at ministerial level, who may commit the government of the Member State in question and cast its vote.

3. The Council shall act by a qualified majority except where the Treaties provide otherwise.

4. As from 1 November 2014, a qualified majority shall be defined as at least 55% of the members of the Council, comprising at least fifteen of them and representing Member States comprising at least 65% of the population of the Union.

A blocking minority must include at least four Council members, failing which the qualified majority shall be deemed attained.

The other arrangements governing the qualified majority are laid down in Article 238(2) of the Treaty on the Functioning of the European Union.

5. The transitional provisions relating to the definition of the qualified majority which shall be applicable until 31 October 2014 and those which shall be applicable from 1 November 2014 to 31 March 2017 are laid down in the Protocol on transitional provisions.

6. The Council shall meet in different configurations, the list of which shall be adopted in accordance with Article 236 of the Treaty on the Functioning of the European Union.

The General Affairs Council shall ensure consistency in the work of the different Council configurations. It shall prepare and ensure the follow-up to meetings of the European Council, in liaison with the President of the European Council and the Commission.

The Foreign Affairs Council shall elaborate the Union's external action on the basis of strategic guidelines laid down by the European Council and ensure that the Union's action is consistent.

7. A Committee of Permanent Representatives of the Governments of the Member States shall be responsible for preparing the work of the Council.

8. The Council shall meet in public when it deliberates and votes on a draft legislative act. To this end, each Council meeting shall be divided into two parts, dealing respectively with deliberations on Union legislative acts and non-legislative activities.

9. The Presidency of Council configurations, other than that of Foreign Affairs, shall be held by Member State representatives in the Council on the basis of equal rotation, in accordance with the conditions established in accordance with Article 236 of the Treaty on the Functioning of the European Union.

Article 17

1. The Commission shall promote the general interest of the Union and take appropriate initiatives to that end. It shall ensure the application of the Treaties, and of measures adopted by the institutions pursuant to them. It shall oversee the application of Union law under the control of the Court of Justice of the European

Union. It shall execute the budget and manage programmes. It shall exercise coordinating, executive and management functions, as laid down in the Treaties. With the exception of the common foreign and security policy, and other cases provided for in the Treaties, it shall ensure the Union's external representation. It shall initiate the Union's annual and multiannual programming with a view to achieving interinstitutional agreements.

2. Union legislative acts may only be adopted on the basis of a Commission proposal, except where the Treaties provide otherwise. Other acts shall be adopted on the basis of a Commission proposal where the Treaties so provide.

3. The Commission's term of office shall be five years.

The members of the Commission shall be chosen on the ground of their general competence and European commitment from persons whose independence is beyond doubt.

In carrying out its responsibilities, the Commission shall be completely independent. Without prejudice to Article 18(2), the members of the Commission shall neither seek nor take instructions from any Government or other institution, body, office or entity. They shall refrain from any action incompatible with their duties or the performance of their tasks.

4. The Commission appointed between the date of entry into force of the Treaty of Lisbon and 31 October 2014, shall consist of one national of each Member State, including its President and the High Representative of the Union for Foreign Affairs and Security Policy who shall be one of its Vice-Presidents.

5. As from 1 November 2014, the Commission shall consist of a number of members, including its President and the High Representative of the Union for Foreign Affairs and Security Policy, corresponding to two thirds of the number of Member States, unless the European Council, acting unanimously, decides to alter this number.

The members of the Commission shall be chosen from among the nationals of the Member States on the basis of a system of strictly equal rotation between the Member States, reflecting the demographic and geographical range of all the Member States. This system shall be established unanimously by the European Council in accordance with Article 244 of the Treaty on the Functioning of the European Union.

6. The President of the Commission shall:

(a) lay down guidelines within which the Commission is to work;

(b) decide on the internal organisation of the Commission, ensuring that it acts consistently, efficiently and as a collegiate body;

(c) appoint Vice-Presidents, other than the High Representative of the Union for Foreign Affairs and Security Policy, from among the members of the Commission.

A member of the Commission shall resign if the President so requests. The High Representative of the Union for Foreign Affairs and Security Policy shall resign, in accordance with the procedure set out in Article 18(1), if the President so requests.

7. Taking into account the elections to the European Parliament and after having held the appropriate consultations, the European Council, acting by a qualified majority, shall propose to the European Parliament a candidate for President of the Commission. This candidate shall be elected by the European Parliament by a majority of its component members. If he does not obtain the required majority, the European Council, acting by a qualified majority, shall within one month propose a new candidate who shall be elected by the European Parliament following the same procedure.

The Council, by common accord with the President-elect, shall adopt the list of the other persons whom it proposes for appointment as members of the Commission. They shall be selected, on the basis of the suggestions made by Member States, in accordance with the criteria set out in paragraph 3, second subparagraph, and paragraph 5, second subparagraph.

The President, the High Representative of the Union for Foreign Affairs and Security Policy and the other members of the Commission shall be subject as a body to a vote of consent by the European Parliament. On the basis of this consent the Commission shall be appointed by the European Council, acting by a qualified majority.

8. The Commission, as a body, shall be responsible to the European Parliament. In accordance with Article 234 of the Treaty on the Functioning of the European Union, the European Parliament may vote on a motion of censure of the Commission. If such a motion is carried, the members of the Commission shall resign as a body and the High Representative of the Union for Foreign Affairs and Security Policy shall resign from the duties that he carries out in the Commission.

Article 18

1. The European Council, acting by a qualified majority, with the agreement of the President of the Commission, shall appoint the High Representative of the Union for Foreign Affairs and Security

Policy. The European Council may end his term of office by the same procedure.

2. The High Representative shall conduct the Union's common foreign and security policy. He shall contribute by his proposals to the development of that policy, which he shall carry out as mandated by the Council. The same shall apply to the common security and defence policy.

3. The High Representative shall preside over the Foreign Affairs Council.

4. The High Representative shall be one of the Vice-Presidents of the Commission. He shall ensure the consistency of the Union's external action. He shall be responsible within the Commission for responsibilities incumbent on it in external relations and for coordinating other aspects of the Union's external action. In exercising these responsibilities within the Commission, and only for these responsibilities the High Representative shall be bound by Commission procedures to the extent that this is consistent with paragraphs 2 and 3.

Article 19

1. The Court of Justice of the European Union shall include the Court of Justice, the General Court and specialised courts. It shall ensure that in the interpretation and application of the Treaties the law is observed.

Member States shall provide remedies sufficient to ensure effective legal protection in the fields covered by Union law.

2. The Court of Justice shall consist of one judge from each Member State. It shall be assisted by Advocates-General.

The General Court shall include at least one judge per Member State.

The Judges and the Advocates-General of the Court of Justice and the Judges of the General Court shall be chosen from persons whose independence is beyond doubt and who satisfy the conditions set out in Articles 253 and 254 of the Treaty on the Functioning of the European Union. They shall be appointed by common accord of the governments of the Member States for six years. Retiring Judges and Advocates-General may be reappointed.

3. The Court of Justice of the European Union shall, in accordance with the Treaties:

(a) rule on actions brought by a Member State, an institution or a natural or legal person;

(b) give preliminary rulings, at the request of courts or tribunals of the Member States, on the interpretation of Union law or the validity of acts adopted by the institutions;

(c) rule in other cases provided for in the Treaties.

TITLE IV
PROVISIONS ON ENHANCED COOPERATION

Article 20
(ex Articles 27*a* to 27*e*, 40 to 40*b* and 43 to 45 TEU and ex Articles 11 and 11*a* TEC)

1. Member States which wish to establish enhanced cooperation between themselves within the framework of the Union's non-exclusive competences may make use of its institutions and exercise those competences by applying the relevant provisions of the Treaties, subject to the limits and in accordance with the detailed arrangements laid down in this Article and in Articles 326 to 334 of the Treaty on the Functioning of the European Union.

Enhanced cooperation shall aim to further the objectives of the Union, protect its interests and reinforce its integration process. Such cooperation shall be open at any time to all Member States, in accordance with Article 328 of the Treaty on the Functioning of the European Union.

2. The decision authorising enhanced cooperation shall be adopted by the Council as a last resort, when it has established that the objectives of such cooperation cannot be attained within a reasonable period by the Union as a whole, and provided that at least nine Member States participate in it. The Council shall act in accordance with the procedure laid down in Article 329 of the Treaty on the Functioning of the European Union.

3. All members of the Council may participate in its deliberations, but only members of the Council representing the Member States participating in enhanced cooperation shall take part in the vote. The voting rules are set out in Article 330 of the Treaty on the Functioning of the European Union.

4. Acts adopted in the framework of enhanced cooperation shall bind only participating Member States. They shall not be regarded as part of the *acquis* which has to be accepted by candidate States for accession to the Union.

TITLE V
GENERAL PROVISIONS ON THE UNION'S EXTERNAL ACTION AND SPECIFIC PROVISIONS ON THE COMMON FOREIGN AND SECURITY POLICY

CHAPTER 1
GENERAL PROVISIONS ON THE UNION'S EXTERNAL ACTION

Article 21

1. The Union's action on the international scene shall be guided by the principles which have inspired its own creation, development and enlargement, and which it seeks to advance in the wider world: democracy, the rule of law, the universality and indivisibility of human rights and fundamental freedoms, respect for human dignity, the principles of equality and solidarity, and respect for the principles of the United Nations Charter and international law.

The Union shall seek to develop relations and build partnerships with third countries, and international, regional or global organisations which share the principles referred to in the first subparagraph. It shall promote multilateral solutions to common problems, in particular in the framework of the United Nations.

2. The Union shall define and pursue common policies and actions, and shall work for a high degree of cooperation in all fields of international relations, in order to:

(a) safeguard its values, fundamental interests, security, independence and integrity;

(b) consolidate and support democracy, the rule of law, human rights and the principles of international law;

(c) preserve peace, prevent conflicts and strengthen international security, in accordance with the purposes and principles of the United Nations Charter, with the principles of the Helsinki Final Act and with the aims of the Charter of Paris, including those relating to external borders;

(d) foster the sustainable economic, social and environmental development of developing countries, with the primary aim of eradicating poverty;

(e) encourage the integration of all countries into the world economy, including through the progressive abolition of restrictions on international trade;

(f) help develop international measures to preserve and improve the quality of the environment and the sustainable management of global natural resources, in order to ensure sustainable development;

(g) assist populations, countries and regions confronting natural or man-made disasters; and

(h) promote an international system based on stronger multilateral cooperation and good global governance.

3. The Union shall respect the principles and pursue the objectives set out in paragraphs 1 and 2 in the development and implementation of the different areas of the Union's external action covered by this Title and by Part Five of the Treaty on the Functioning of the European Union, and of the external aspects of its other policies.

The Union shall ensure consistency between the different areas of its external action and between these and its other policies. The Council and the Commission, assisted by the High Representative of the Union for Foreign Affairs and Security Policy, shall ensure that consistency and shall cooperate to that effect.

Article 22

1. On the basis of the principles and objectives set out in Article 21, the European Council shall identify the strategic interests and objectives of the Union.

Decisions of the European Council on the strategic interests and objectives of the Union shall relate to the common foreign and security policy and to other areas of the external action of the Union. Such decisions may concern the relations of the Union with a specific country or region or may be thematic in approach. They shall define their duration, and the means to be made available by the Union and the Member States.

The European Council shall act unanimously on a recommendation from the Council, adopted by the latter under the arrangements laid down for each area. Decisions of the European Council shall be implemented in accordance with the procedures provided for in the Treaties.

2. The High Representative of the Union for Foreign Affairs and Security Policy, for the area of common foreign and security policy, and the Commission, for other areas of external action, may submit joint proposals to the Council.

CHAPTER 2
SPECIFIC PROVISIONS ON THE COMMON FOREIGN AND SECURITY POLICY

SECTION 1
COMMON PROVISIONS

Article 23

The Union's action on the international scene, pursuant to this Chapter, shall be guided by the principles, shall pursue the objectives of, and be conducted in accordance with, the general provisions laid down in Chapter 1.

Article 24
(ex Article 11 TEU)

1. The Union's competence in matters of common foreign and security policy shall cover all areas of foreign policy and all questions relating to the Union's security, including the progressive framing of a common defence policy that might lead to a common defence.

The common foreign and security policy is subject to specific rules and procedures It shall be defined and implemented by the European Council and the Council acting unanimously, except where the Treaties provide otherwise. The adoption of legislative acts shall be excluded. The common foreign and security policy shall be put into effect by the High Representative of the Union for Foreign Affairs and Security Policy and by Member States, in accordance with the Treaties. The specific role of the European Parliament and of the Commission in this area is defined by the Treaties. The Court of Justice of the European Union shall not have jurisdiction with respect to these provisions, with the exception of its jurisdiction to monitor compliance with Article 40 of this Treaty and to review the legality of certain decisions as provided for by the second paragraph of Article 275 of the Treaty on the Functioning of the European Union.

2. Within the framework of the principles and objectives of its external action, the Union shall conduct, define and implement a common foreign and security policy, based on the development of mutual political solidarity among Member States, the identification of questions of general interest and the achievement of an ever-increasing degree of convergence of Member States' actions.

3. The Member States shall support the Union's external and security policy actively and unreservedly in a spirit of loyalty and mutual solidarity and shall comply with the Union's action in this area.

The Member States shall work together to enhance and develop their mutual political solidarity. They shall refrain from any action which is contrary to the interests of the Union or likely to impair its effectiveness as a cohesive force in international relations.

The Council and the High Representative shall ensure compliance with these principles.

Article 25
(ex Article 12 TEU)

The Union shall conduct the common foreign and security policy by:

(a) defining the general guidelines;

(b) adopting decisions defining:

(i) actions to be undertaken by the Union;

(ii) positions to be taken by the Union;

(iii) arrangements for the implementation of the decisions referred to in points (i) and (ii); and by

(c) strengthening systematic cooperation between Member States in the conduct of policy.

Article 26
(ex Article 13 TEU)

1. The European Council shall identify the Union's strategic interests, determine the objectives of and define general guidelines for the common foreign and security policy, including for matters with defence implications. It shall adopt the necessary decisions.

If international developments so require, the President of the European Council shall convene an extraordinary meeting of the European Council in order to define the strategic lines of the Union's policy in the face of such developments.

2. The Council shall frame the common foreign and security policy and take the decisions necessary for defining and implementing it on the basis of the general guidelines and strategic lines defined by the European Council.

The Council and the High Representative of the Union for Foreign Affairs and Security Policy shall ensure the unity, consistency and effectiveness of action by the Union.

3. The common foreign and security policy shall be put into effect by the High Representative and by the Member States, using national and Union resources.

Article 27

1. The High Representative of the Union for Foreign Affairs and Security Policy, who shall chair the Foreign Affairs Council, shall contribute through his proposals to the development of the common foreign and security policy and shall ensure implementation of the decisions adopted by the European Council and the Council.

2. The High Representative shall represent the Union for matters relating to the common foreign and security policy. He shall conduct political dialogue with third parties on the Union's behalf and shall express the Union's position in international organisations and at international conferences.

3. In fulfilling his mandate, the High Representative shall be assisted by a European External Action Service. This service shall work in cooperation with the diplomatic services of the Member States and shall comprise officials from relevant departments of the General Secretariat of the Council and of the Commission as well as staff seconded from national diplomatic services of the Member States. The organisation and functioning of the European External Action Service shall be established by a decision of the Council. The Council shall act on a proposal from the High Representative after consulting the European Parliament and after obtaining the consent of the Commission.

Article 28
(ex Article 14 TEU)

1. Where the international situation requires operational action by the Union, the Council shall adopt the necessary decisions. They shall lay down their objectives, scope, the means to be made available to the Union, if necessary their duration, and the conditions for their implementation.

If there is a change in circumstances having a substantial effect on a question subject to such a decision, the Council shall review the principles and objectives of that decision and take the necessary decisions.

2. Decisions referred to in paragraph 1 shall commit the Member States in the positions they adopt and in the conduct of their activity.

3. Whenever there is any plan to adopt a national position or take national action pursuant to a decision as referred to in paragraph 1, information shall be provided by the Member State concerned in time to allow, if necessary, for prior consultations within the Council. The obligation to provide prior information shall not

apply to measures which are merely a national transposition of Council decisions.

4. In cases of imperative need arising from changes in the situation and failing a review of the Council decision as referred to in paragraph 1, Member States may take the necessary measures as a matter of urgency having regard to the general objectives of that decision. The Member State concerned shall inform the Council immediately of any such measures.

5. Should there be any major difficulties in implementing a decision as referred to in this Article, a Member State shall refer them to the Council which shall discuss them and seek appropriate solutions. Such solutions shall not run counter to the objectives of the decision referred to in paragraph 1 or impair its effectiveness.

Article 29
(ex Article 15 TEU)

The Council shall adopt decisions which shall define the approach of the Union to a particular matter of a geographical or thematic nature. Member States shall ensure that their national policies conform to the Union positions.

Article 30
(ex Article 22 TEU)

1. Any Member State, the High Representative of the Union for Foreign Affairs and Security Policy, or the High Representative with the Commission's support, may refer any question relating to the common foreign and security policy to the Council and may submit to it, respectively, initiatives or proposals.

2. In cases requiring a rapid decision, the High Representative, of his own motion, or at the request of a Member State, shall convene an extraordinary Council meeting within 48 hours or, in an emergency, within a shorter period.

Article 31
(ex Article 23 TEU)

1. Decisions under this Chapter shall be taken by the European Council and the Council acting unanimously, except where this Chapter provides otherwise. The adoption of legislative acts shall be excluded.

When abstaining in a vote, any member of the Council may qualify its abstention by making a formal declaration under the present subparagraph. In that case, it shall not be obliged to apply the decision, but shall accept that the decision commits the Union. In a spirit of mutual solidarity, the Member State concerned shall refrain from any action likely to conflict with or impede Union action based on that decision and the other Member States shall respect its position. If the members of the Council qualifying their abstention in this way represent at least one third of the Member States comprising at least one third of the population of the Union, the decision shall not be adopted.

2. By derogation from the provisions of paragraph 1, the Council shall act by qualified majority:

— when adopting a decision defining a Union action or position on the basis of a decision of the European Council relating to the Union's strategic interests and objectives, as referred to in Article 22(1),

— when adopting a decision defining a Union action or position, on a proposal which the High Representative of the Union for Foreign Affairs and Security Policy has presented following a specific request from the European Council, made on its own initiative or that of the High Representative,

— when adopting any decision implementing a decision defining a Union action or position,

— when appointing a special representative in accordance with Article 33.

If a member of the Council declares that, for vital and stated reasons of national policy, it intends to oppose the adoption of a decision to be taken by qualified majority, a vote shall not be taken. The High Representative will, in close consultation with the Member State involved, search for a solution acceptable to it. If he does not succeed, the Council may, acting by a qualified majority, request that the matter be referred to the European Council for a decision by unanimity.

3. The European Council may unanimously adopt a decision stipulating that the Council shall act by a qualified majority in cases other than those referred to in paragraph 2.

4. Paragraphs 2 and 3 shall not apply to decisions having military or defence implications.

5. For procedural questions, the Council shall act by a majority of its members.

Article 32
(ex Article 16 TEU)

Member States shall consult one another within the European Council and the Council on any matter of foreign and security policy of general interest in order to determine a common approach. Before undertaking any action on the international scene or entering into any commitment which could affect the Union's interests, each Member State shall consult the others within the European Council or the Council. Member States shall ensure, through the convergence of their actions, that the Union is able to assert its interests and values on the international scene. Member States shall show mutual solidarity.

When the European Council or the Council has defined a common approach of the Union within the meaning of the first paragraph, the High Representative of the Union for Foreign Affairs and Security Policy and the Ministers for Foreign Affairs of the Member States shall coordinate their activities within the Council.

The diplomatic missions of the Member States and the Union delegations in third countries and at international organisations shall cooperate and shall contribute to formulating and implementing the common approach.

Article 33
(ex Article 18 TEU)

The Council may, on a proposal from the High Representative of the Union for Foreign Affairs and Security Policy, appoint a special representative with a mandate in relation to particular policy issues. The special representative shall carry out his mandate under the authority of the High Representative.

Article 34
(ex Article 19 TEU)

1. Member States shall coordinate their action in international organisations and at international conferences. They shall uphold the Union's positions in such forums. The High Representative of the Union for Foreign Affairs and Security Policy shall organise this coordination.

In international organisations and at international conferences where not all the Member States participate, those which do take part shall uphold the Union's positions.

2. In accordance with Article 24(3), Member States represented in international organisations or international conferences where not all the Member States participate shall keep the other Member States and the High Representative informed of any matter of common interest.

Member States which are also members of the United Nations Security Council will concert and keep the other Member States and the High Representative fully informed. Member States which are members of the Security Council will, in the execution of their functions, defend the positions and the interests of the Union, without prejudice to their responsibilities under the provisions of the United Nations Charter.

When the Union has defined a position on a subject which is on the United Nations Security Council agenda, those Member States which sit on the Security Council shall request that the High Representative be invited to present the Union's position.

Article 35
(ex Article 20 TEU)

The diplomatic and consular missions of the Member States and the Union delegations in third countries and international conferences, and their representations to international organisations, shall cooperate in ensuring that decisions defining Union positions and actions adopted pursuant to this Chapter are complied with and implemented.

They shall step up cooperation by exchanging information and carrying out joint assessments.

They shall contribute to the implementation of the right of citizens of the Union to protection in the territory of third countries as referred to in Article 20(2)(c) of the Treaty on the Functioning of the European Union and of the measures adopted pursuant to Article 23 of that Treaty.

Article 36
(ex Article 21 TEU)

The High Representative of the Union for Foreign Affairs and Security Policy shall regularly consult the European Parliament on the main aspects and the basic choices of the common foreign and security policy and the common security and defence policy and inform it of how those policies evolve. He shall ensure that the views of the European Parliament are duly taken into consideration. Special representatives may be involved in briefing the European Parliament.

The European Parliament may address questions or make recommendations to the Council or the High Representative. Twice a year it shall hold a debate on progress in implementing the common foreign and security policy, including the common security and defence policy.

Article 37
(ex Article 24 TEU)

The Union may conclude agreements with one or more States or international organisations in areas covered by this Chapter.

Article 38
(ex Article 25 TEU)

Without prejudice to Article 240 of the Treaty on the Functioning of the European Union, a Political and Security Committee shall monitor the international situation in the areas covered by the common foreign and security policy and contribute to the definition of policies by delivering opinions to the Council at the request of the Council or of the High Representative of the Union for Foreign Affairs and Security Policy or on its own initiative. It shall also monitor the implementation of agreed policies, without prejudice to the powers of the High Representative.

Within the scope of this Chapter, the Political and Security Committee shall exercise, under the responsibility of the Council and of the High Representative, the political control and strategic direction of the crisis management operations referred to in Article 43.

The Council may authorise the Committee, for the purpose and for the duration of a crisis management operation, as determined by the Council, to take the relevant decisions concerning the political control and strategic direction of the operation.

Article 39

In accordance with Article 16 of the Treaty on the Functioning of the European Union and by way of derogation from paragraph 2 thereof, the Council shall adopt a decision laying down the rules relating to the protection of individuals with regard to the processing of personal data by the Member States when carrying out activities which fall within the scope of this Chapter, and the rules relating to the free movement of such data. Compliance with these rules shall be subject to the control of independent authorities.

Article 40
(ex Article 47 TEU)

The implementation of the common foreign and security policy shall not affect the application of the procedures and the extent of the powers of the institutions laid down by the Treaties for the exercise of the Union competences referred to in Articles 3 to 6 of the Treaty on the Functioning of the European Union.

Similarly, the implementation of the policies listed in those Articles shall not affect the application of the procedures and the extent of the powers of the institutions laid down by the Treaties for the exercise of the Union competences under this Chapter.

Article 41
(ex Article 28 TEU)

1. Administrative expenditure to which the implementation of this Chapter gives rise for the institutions shall be charged to the Union budget.

2. Operating expenditure to which the implementation of this Chapter gives rise shall also be charged to the Union budget, except for such expenditure arising from operations having military or defence implications and cases where the Council acting unanimously decides otherwise.

In cases where expenditure is not charged to the Union budget, it shall be charged to the Member States in accordance with the gross national product scale, unless the Council acting unanimously decides otherwise. As for expenditure arising from operations having military or defence implications, Member States whose representatives in the Council have made a formal declaration under Article 31(1), second subparagraph, shall not be obliged to contribute to the financing thereof.

3. The Council shall adopt a decision establishing the specific procedures for guaranteeing rapid access to appropriations in the Union budget for urgent financing of initiatives in the framework of the common foreign and security policy, and in particular for preparatory activities for the tasks referred to in Article 42(1) and Article 43. It shall act after consulting the European Parliament.

Preparatory activities for the tasks referred to in Article 42(1) and Article 43 which are not charged to the Union budget shall be financed by a start-up fund made up of Member States' contributions.

The Council shall adopt by a qualified majority, on a proposal from the High Representative of the Union for Foreign Affairs and Security Policy, decisions establishing:

(a) the procedures for setting up and financing the start-up fund, in particular the amounts allocated to the fund;

(b) the procedures for administering the start-up fund;

(c) the financial control procedures.

When the task planned in accordance with Article 42(1) and Article 43 cannot be charged to the Union budget, the Council shall authorise the High Representative to use the fund. The High Representative shall report to the Council on the implementation of this remit.

SECTION 2
PROVISIONS ON THE COMMON SECURITY AND DEFENCE POLICY

Article 42
(ex Article 17 TEU)

1. The common security and defence policy shall be an integral part of the common foreign and security policy. It shall provide the Union with an operational capacity drawing on civilian and military assets. The Union may use them on missions outside the Union for peace-keeping, conflict prevention and strengthening international security in accordance with the principles of the United Nations Charter. The performance of these tasks shall be undertaken using capabilities provided by the Member States.

2. The common security and defence policy shall include the progressive framing of a common Union defence policy. This will lead to a common defence, when the European Council, acting unanimously, so decides. It shall in that case recommend to the Member States the adoption of such a decision in accordance with their respective constitutional requirements.

The policy of the Union in accordance with this Section shall not prejudice the specific character of the security and defence policy of certain Member States and shall respect the obligations of certain Member States, which see their common defence realised in the North Atlantic Treaty Organisation (NATO), under the North Atlantic Treaty and be compatible with the common security and defence policy established within that framework.

3. Member States shall make civilian and military capabilities available to the Union for the implementation of the common security and defence policy, to contribute to the objectives defined by the Council. Those Member States which together establish multinational forces may also make them available to the common security and defence policy.

Member States shall undertake progressively to improve their military capabilities. The Agency in the field of defence capabilities development, research, acquisition and armaments (hereinafter referred to as "the European Defence Agency") shall identify operational requirements, shall promote measures to satisfy those requirements, shall contribute to identifying and, where appropriate, implementing any measure needed to strengthen the industrial and technological base of the defence sector, shall participate in defining a European capabilities and armaments policy, and shall assist the Council in evaluating the improvement of military capabilities.

4. Decisions relating to the common security and defence policy, including those initiating a mission as referred to in this Article, shall be adopted by the Council acting unanimously on a proposal from the High Representative of the Union for Foreign Affairs and Security Policy or an initiative from a Member State. The High Representative may propose the use of both national resources and Union instruments, together with the Commission where appropriate.

5. The Council may entrust the execution of a task, within the Union framework, to a group of Member States in order to protect the Union's values and serve its interests. The execution of such a task shall be governed by Article 44.

6. Those Member States whose military capabilities fulfil higher criteria and which have made more binding commitments to one another in this area with a view to the most demanding missions shall establish permanent structured cooperation within the Union framework. Such cooperation shall be governed by Article 46. It shall not affect the provisions of Article 43.

7. If a Member State is the victim of armed aggression on its territory, the other Member States shall have towards it an obligation of aid and assistance by all the means in their power, in accordance with Article 51 of the United Nations Charter. This shall not prejudice the specific character of the security and defence policy of certain Member States.

Commitments and cooperation in this area shall be consistent with commitments under the North Atlantic Treaty Organisation, which, for those States which are members of it, remains the foundation of their collective defence and the forum for its implementation.

Article 43

1. The tasks referred to in Article 42(1), in the course of which the Union may use civilian and military means, shall include joint disarmament operations, humanitarian and rescue tasks, military advice and assistance tasks, conflict prevention and peace-keeping tasks, tasks of combat forces in crisis management, including peace-making and post-conflict stabilisation. All these tasks may contribute to the fight against terrorism, including by supporting third countries in combating terrorism in their territories.

2. The Council shall adopt decisions relating to the tasks referred to in paragraph 1, defining their objectives and scope and the general conditions for their implementation. The High Representative of the Union for Foreign Affairs and Security Policy,

acting under the authority of the Council and in close and constant contact with the Political and Security Committee, shall ensure coordination of the civilian and military aspects of such tasks.

Article 44

1. Within the framework of the decisions adopted in accordance with Article 43, the Council may entrust the implementation of a task to a group of Member States which are willing and have the necessary capability for such a task. Those Member States, in association with the High Representative of the Union for Foreign Affairs and Security Policy, shall agree among themselves on the management of the task.

2. Member States participating in the task shall keep the Council regularly informed of its progress on their own initiative or at the request of another Member State. Those States shall inform the Council immediately should the completion of the task entail major consequences or require amendment of the objective, scope and conditions determined for the task in the decisions referred to in paragraph 1. In such cases, the Council shall adopt the necessary decisions.

Article 45

1. The European Defence Agency referred to in Article 42(3), subject to the authority of the Council, shall have as its task to:

(a) contribute to identifying the Member States' military capability objectives and evaluating observance of the capability commitments given by the Member States;

(b) promote harmonisation of operational needs and adoption of effective, compatible procurement methods;

(c) propose multilateral projects to fulfil the objectives in terms of military capabilities, ensure coordination of the programmes implemented by the Member States and management of specific cooperation programmes;

(d) support defence technology research, and coordinate and plan joint research activities and the study of technical solutions meeting future operational needs;

(e) contribute to identifying and, if necessary, implementing any useful measure for strengthening the industrial and technological base of the defence sector and for improving the effectiveness of military expenditure.

2. The European Defence Agency shall be open to all Member States wishing to be part of it. The Council, acting by a qualified majority, shall adopt a decision defining the Agency's statute, seat

and operational rules. That decision should take account of the level of effective participation in the Agency's activities. Specific groups shall be set up within the Agency bringing together Member States engaged in joint projects. The Agency shall carry out its tasks in liaison with the Commission where necessary.

Article 46

1. Those Member States which wish to participate in the permanent structured cooperation referred to in Article 42(6), which fulfil the criteria and have made the commitments on military capabilities set out in the Protocol on permanent structured cooperation, shall notify their intention to the Council and to the High Representative of the Union for Foreign Affairs and Security Policy.

2. Within three months following the notification referred to in paragraph 1 the Council shall adopt a decision establishing permanent structured cooperation and determining the list of participating Member States. The Council shall act by a qualified majority after consulting the High Representative.

3. Any Member State which, at a later stage, wishes to participate in the permanent structured cooperation shall notify its intention to the Council and to the High Representative.

The Council shall adopt a decision confirming the participation of the Member State concerned which fulfils the criteria and makes the commitments referred to in Articles 1 and 2 of the Protocol on permanent structured cooperation. The Council shall act by a qualified majority after consulting the High Representative. Only members of the Council representing the participating Member States shall take part in the vote.

A qualified majority shall be defined in accordance with Article 238(3)(a) of the Treaty on the Functioning of the European Union.

4. If a participating Member State no longer fulfils the criteria or is no longer able to meet the commitments referred to in Articles 1 and 2 of the Protocol on permanent structured cooperation, the Council may adopt a decision suspending the participation of the Member State concerned.

The Council shall act by a qualified majority. Only members of the Council representing the participating Member States, with the exception of the Member State in question, shall take part in the vote.

A qualified majority shall be defined in accordance with Article 238(3)(a) of the Treaty on the Functioning of the European Union.

5. Any participating Member State which wishes to withdraw from permanent structured cooperation shall notify its intention to the Council, which shall take note that the Member State in question has ceased to participate.

6. The decisions and recommendations of the Council within the framework of permanent structured cooperation, other than those provided for in paragraphs 2 to 5, shall be adopted by unanimity. For the purposes of this paragraph, unanimity shall be constituted by the votes of the representatives of the participating Member States only.

TITLE VI
FINAL PROVISIONS

Article 47

The Union shall have legal personality.

Article 48
(ex Article 48 TEU)

1. The Treaties may be amended in accordance with an ordinary revision procedure. They may also be amended in accordance with simplified revision procedures.

Ordinary revision procedure

2. The Government of any Member State, the European Parliament or the Commission may submit to the Council proposals for the amendment of the Treaties. These proposals may, *inter alia*, serve either to increase or to reduce the competences conferred on the Union in the Treaties. These proposals shall be submitted to the European Council by the Council and the national Parliaments shall be notified.

3. If the European Council, after consulting the European Parliament and the Commission, adopts by a simple majority a decision in favour of examining the proposed amendments, the President of the European Council shall convene a Convention composed of representatives of the national Parliaments, of the Heads of State or Government of the Member States, of the European Parliament and of the Commission. The European Central Bank shall also be consulted in the case of institutional changes in the monetary area. The Convention shall examine the proposals for amendments and shall adopt by consensus a recommendation to a conference of representatives of the governments of the Member States as provided for in paragraph 4.

The European Council may decide by a simple majority, after obtaining the consent of the European Parliament, not to convene a

Convention should this not be justified by the extent of the proposed amendments. In the latter case, the European Council shall define the terms of reference for a conference of representatives of the governments of the Member States.

4. A conference of representatives of the governments of the Member States shall be convened by the President of the Council for the purpose of determining by common accord the amendments to be made to the Treaties.

The amendments shall enter into force after being ratified by all the Member States in accordance with their respective constitutional requirements.

5. If, two years after the signature of a treaty amending the Treaties, four fifths of the Member States have ratified it and one or more Member States have encountered difficulties in proceeding with ratification, the matter shall be referred to the European Council.

Simplified revision procedures

6. The Government of any Member State, the European Parliament or the Commission may submit to the European Council proposals for revising all or part of the provisions of Part Three of the Treaty on the Functioning of the European Union relating to the internal policies and action of the Union.

The European Council may adopt a decision amending all or part of the provisions of Part Three of the Treaty on the Functioning of the European Union. The European Council shall act by unanimity after consulting the European Parliament and the Commission, and the European Central Bank in the case of institutional changes in the monetary area. That decision shall not enter into force until it is approved by the Member States in accordance with their respective constitutional requirements.

The decision referred to in the second subparagraph shall not increase the competences conferred on the Union in the Treaties.

7. Where the Treaty on the Functioning of the European Union or Title V of this Treaty provides for the Council to act by unanimity in a given area or case, the European Council may adopt a decision authorising the Council to act by a qualified majority in that area or in that case. This subparagraph shall not apply to decisions with military implications or those in the area of defence.

Where the Treaty on the Functioning of the European Union provides for legislative acts to be adopted by the Council in accordance with a special legislative procedure, the European Council may adopt a decision allowing for the adoption of such acts in accordance with the ordinary legislative procedure.

Any initiative taken by the European Council on the basis of the first or the second subparagraph shall be notified to the national Parliaments. If a national Parliament makes known its opposition within six months of the date of such notification, the decision referred to in the first or the second subparagraph shall not be adopted. In the absence of opposition, the European Council may adopt the decision.

For the adoption of the decisions referred to in the first and second subparagraphs, the European Council shall act by unanimity after obtaining the consent of the European Parliament, which shall be given by a majority of its component members.

Article 49
(ex Article 49 TEU)

Any European State which respects the values referred to in Article 2 and is committed to promoting them may apply to become a member of the Union. The European Parliament and national Parliaments shall be notified of this application. The applicant State shall address its application to the Council, which shall act unanimously after consulting the Commission and after receiving the consent of the European Parliament, which shall act by a majority of its component members. The conditions of eligibility agreed upon by the European Council shall be taken into account.

The conditions of admission and the adjustments to the Treaties on which the Union is founded, which such admission entails, shall be the subject of an agreement between the Member States and the applicant State. This agreement shall be submitted for ratification by all the contracting States in accordance with their respective constitutional requirements.

Article 50

1. Any Member State may decide to withdraw from the Union in accordance with its own constitutional requirements.

2. A Member State which decides to withdraw shall notify the European Council of its intention. In the light of the guidelines provided by the European Council, the Union shall negotiate and conclude an agreement with that State, setting out the arrangements for its withdrawal, taking account of the framework for its future relationship with the Union. That agreement shall be negotiated in accordance with Article 218(3) of the Treaty on the Functioning of the European Union. It shall be concluded on behalf of the Union by the Council, acting by a qualified majority, after obtaining the consent of the European Parliament.

3. The Treaties shall cease to apply to the State in question from the date of entry into force of the withdrawal agreement or, failing that, two years after the notification referred to in paragraph 2, unless the European Council, in agreement with the Member State concerned, unanimously decides to extend this period.

4. For the purposes of paragraphs 2 and 3, the member of the European Council or of the Council representing the withdrawing Member State shall not participate in the discussions of the European Council or Council or in decisions concerning it.

A qualified majority shall be defined in accordance with Article 238(3)(b) of the Treaty on the Functioning of the European Union.

5. If a State which has withdrawn from the Union asks to rejoin, its request shall be subject to the procedure referred to in Article 49.

Article 51

The Protocols and Annexes to the Treaties shall form an integral part thereof.

Article 52

1. The Treaties shall apply to the Kingdom of Belgium, the Republic of Bulgaria the Czech Republic, the Kingdom of Denmark, the Federal Republic of Germany, the Republic of Estonia, Ireland, the Hellenic Republic, the Kingdom of Spain, the French Republic, the Italian Republic, the Republic of Cyprus, the Republic of Latvia, the Republic of Lithuania, the Grand Duchy of Luxembourg, the Republic of Hungary, the Republic of Malta, the Kingdom of the Netherlands, the Republic of Austria, the Republic of Poland, the Portuguese Republic, Romania, the Republic of Slovenia, the Slovak Republic, the Republic of Finland, the Kingdom of Sweden and the United Kingdom of Great Britain and Northern Ireland.

2. The territorial scope of the Treaties is specified in Article 355 of the Treaty on the Functioning of the European Union.

Article 53
(ex Article 51 TEU)

This Treaty is concluded for an unlimited period.

Article 54
(ex Article 52 TEU)

1. This Treaty shall be ratified by the High Contracting Parties in accordance with their respective constitutional requirements. The instruments of ratification shall be deposited with the Government of the Italian Republic.

2. This Treaty shall enter into force on 1 January 1993, provided that all the Instruments of ratification have been deposited, or, failing that, on the first day of the month following the deposit of the Instrument of ratification by the last signatory State to take this step.

Article 55
(ex Article 53 TEU)

1. This Treaty, drawn up in a single original in the Bulgarian, Czech, Danish, Dutch, English, Estonian, Finnish, French, German, Greek, Hungarian, Irish, Italian, Latvian, Lithuanian, Maltese, Polish, Portuguese, Romanian, Slovak, Slovenian, Spanish and Swedish languages, the texts in each of these languages being equally authentic, shall be deposited in the archives of the Government of the Italian Republic, which will transmit a certified copy to each of the governments of the other signatory States.

2. This Treaty may also be translated into any other languages as determined by Member States among those which, in accordance with their constitutional order, enjoy official status in all or part of their territory. A certified copy of such translations shall be provided by the Member States concerned to be deposited in the archives of the Council.

Appendix 2

THE TREATY ON THE FUNCTIONING OF THE EUROPEAN UNION

Official Journal of the European Union C 83/51
(March 30, 2010)

TABLE OF CONTENTS

PREAMBLE

HIS MAJESTY THE KING OF THE BELGIANS, THE PRESIDENT OF THE FEDERAL REPUBLIC OF GERMANY, THE PRESIDENT OF THE FRENCH REPUBLIC, THE PRESIDENT OF THE ITALIAN REPUBLIC, HER ROYAL HIGHNESS THE GRAND DUCHESS OF LUXEMBOURG, HER MAJESTY THE QUEEN OF THE NETHERLANDS

DETERMINED to lay the foundations of an ever closer union among the peoples of Europe,

RESOLVED to ensure the economic and social progress of their States by common action to eliminate the barriers which divide Europe,

AFFIRMING as the essential objective of their efforts the constant improvements of the living and working conditions of their peoples,

RECOGNISING that the removal of existing obstacles calls for concerted action in order to guarantee steady expansion, balanced trade and fair competition,

ANXIOUS to strengthen the unity of their economies and to ensure their harmonious development by reducing the differences existing between the various regions and the backwardness of the less favoured regions,

DESIRING to contribute, by means of a common commercial policy, to the progressive abolition of restrictions on international trade,

INTENDING to confirm the solidarity which binds Europe and the overseas countries and desiring to ensure the development of their prosperity, in accordance with the principles of the Charter of the United Nations,

RESOLVED by thus pooling their resources to preserve and strengthen peace and liberty, and calling upon the other peoples of Europe who share their ideal to join in their efforts,

DETERMINED to promote the development of the highest possible level of knowledge for their peoples through a wide access to education and through its continuous updating,

and to this end HAVE DESIGNATED as their Plenipotentiaries *(List of plenipotentiaries not reproduced)*

WHO, having exchanged their full powers, found in good and due form, have agreed as follows.

PART ONE
PRINCIPLES

Article 1

1. This Treaty organises the functioning of the Union and determines the areas of, delimitation of, and arrangements for exercising its competences.

2. This Treaty and the Treaty on European Union constitute the Treaties on which the Union is founded. These two Treaties, which have the same legal value, shall be referred to as "the Treaties".

TITLE I
CATEGORIES AND AREAS OF UNION COMPETENCE

Article 2

1. When the Treaties confer on the Union exclusive competence in a specific area, only the Union may legislate and adopt legally binding acts, the Member States being able to do so themselves only if so empowered by the Union or for the implementation of Union acts.

2. When the Treaties confer on the Union a competence shared with the Member States in a specific area, the Union and the Member States may legislate and adopt legally binding acts in that area. The Member States shall exercise their competence to the extent that the Union has not exercised its competence. The Member States shall

again exercise their competence to the extent that the Union has decided to cease exercising its competence.

3. The Member States shall coordinate their economic and employment policies within arrangements as determined by this Treaty, which the Union shall have competence to provide.

4. The Union shall have competence, in accordance with the provisions of the Treaty on European Union, to define and implement a common foreign and security policy, including the progressive framing of a common defence policy.

5. In certain areas and under the conditions laid down in the Treaties, the Union shall have competence to carry out actions to support, coordinate or supplement the actions of the Member States, without thereby superseding their competence in these areas.

Legally binding acts of the Union adopted on the basis of the provisions of the Treaties relating to these areas shall not entail harmonisation of Member States' laws or regulations.

6. The scope of and arrangements for exercising the Union's competences shall be determined by the provisions of the Treaties relating to each area.

Article 3

1. The Union shall have exclusive competence in the following areas:

(a) customs union;

(b) the establishing of the competition rules necessary for the functioning of the internal market;

(c) monetary policy for the Member States whose currency is the euro;

(d) the conservation of marine biological resources under the common fisheries policy;

(e) common commercial policy.

2. The Union shall also have exclusive competence for the conclusion of an international agreement when its conclusion is provided for in a legislative act of the Union or is necessary to enable the Union to exercise its internal competence, or in so far as its conclusion may affect common rules or alter their scope.

Article 4

1. The Union shall share competence with the Member States where the Treaties confer on it a competence which does not relate to the areas referred to in Articles 3 and 6.

2. Shared competence between the Union and the Member States applies in the following principal areas:

(a) internal market;

(b) social policy, for the aspects defined in this Treaty;

(c) economic, social and territorial cohesion;

(d) agriculture and fisheries, excluding the conservation of marine biological resources;

(e) environment;

(f) consumer protection;

(g) transport;

(h) trans-European networks;

(i) energy;

(j) area of freedom, security and justice;

(k) common safety concerns in public health matters, for the aspects defined in this Treaty.

3. In the areas of research, technological development and space, the Union shall have competence to carry out activities, in particular to define and implement programmes; however, the exercise of that competence shall not result in Member States being prevented from exercising theirs.

4. In the areas of development cooperation and humanitarian aid, the Union shall have competence to carry out activities and conduct a common policy; however, the exercise of that competence shall not result in Member States being prevented from exercising theirs.

Article 5

1. The Member States shall coordinate their economic policies within the Union. To this end, the Council shall adopt measures, in particular broad guidelines for these policies.

Specific provisions shall apply to those Member States whose currency is the euro.

2. The Union shall take measures to ensure coordination of the employment policies of the Member States, in particular by defining guidelines for these policies.

3. The Union may take initiatives to ensure coordination of Member States' social policies.

Article 6

The Union shall have competence to carry out actions to support, coordinate or supplement the actions of the Member States. The areas of such action shall, at European level, be:

(a) protection and improvement of human health;

(b) industry;

(c) culture;

(d) tourism;

(e) education, vocational training, youth and sport;

(f) civil protection;

(g) administrative cooperation.

TITLE II
PROVISIONS HAVING GENERAL APPLICATION

Article 7

The Union shall ensure consistency between its policies and activities, taking all of its objectives into account and in accordance with the principle of conferral of powers.

Article 8
(ex Article 3(2) TEC)

In all its activities, the Union shall aim to eliminate inequalities, and to promote equality, between men and women.

Article 9

In defining and implementing its policies and activities, the Union shall take into account requirements linked to the promotion of a high level of employment, the guarantee of adequate social protection, the fight against social exclusion, and a high level of education, training and protection of human health.

Article 10

In defining and implementing its policies and activities, the Union shall aim to combat discrimination based on sex, racial or ethnic origin, religion or belief, disability, age or sexual orientation.

Article 11
(ex Article 6 TEC)

Environmental protection requirements must be integrated into the definition and implementation of the Union's policies and activities, in particular with a view to promoting sustainable development.

Article 12
(ex Article 153(2) TEC)

Consumer protection requirements shall be taken into account in defining and implementing other Union policies and activities.

Article 13

In formulating and implementing the Union's agriculture, fisheries, transport, internal market, research and technological development and space policies, the Union and the Member States shall, since animals are sentient beings, pay full regard to the welfare requirements of animals, while respecting the legislative or administrative provisions and customs of the Member States relating in particular to religious rites, cultural traditions and regional heritage.

Article 14
(ex Article 16 TEC)

Without prejudice to Article 4 of the Treaty on European Union or to Articles 93, 106 and 107 of this Treaty, and given the place occupied by services of general economic interest in the shared values of the Union as well as their role in promoting social and territorial cohesion, the Union and the Member States, each within their respective powers and within the scope of application of the Treaties, shall take care that such services operate on the basis of principles and conditions, particularly economic and financial conditions, which enable them to fulfil their missions. The European Parliament and the Council, acting by means of regulations in accordance with the ordinary legislative procedure, shall establish these principles and set these conditions without prejudice to the competence of Member States, in compliance with the Treaties, to provide, to commission and to fund such services.

Article 15
(ex Article 255 TEC)

1. In order to promote good governance and ensure the participation of civil society, the Union's institutions, bodies, offices and agencies shall conduct their work as openly as possible.

2. The European Parliament shall meet in public, as shall the Council when considering and voting on a draft legislative act.

3. Any citizen of the Union, and any natural or legal person residing or having its registered office in a Member State, shall have a right of access to documents of the Union's institutions, bodies, offices and agencies, whatever their medium, subject to the principles and the conditions to be defined in accordance with this paragraph.

General principles and limits on grounds of public or private interest governing this right of access to documents shall be determined by the European Parliament and the Council, by means of regulations, acting in accordance with the ordinary legislative procedure.

Each institution, body, office or agency shall ensure that its proceedings are transparent and shall elaborate in its own Rules of Procedure specific provisions regarding access to its documents, in accordance with the regulations referred to in the second subparagraph.

The Court of Justice of the European Union, the European Central Bank and the European Investment Bank shall be subject to this paragraph only when exercising their administrative tasks.

The European Parliament and the Council shall ensure publication of the documents relating to the legislative procedures under the terms laid down by the regulations referred to in the second subparagraph.

Article 16
(ex Article 286 TEC)

1. Everyone has the right to the protection of personal data concerning them.

2. The European Parliament and the Council, acting in accordance with the ordinary legislative procedure, shall lay down the rules relating to the protection of individuals with regard to the processing of personal data by Union institutions, bodies, offices and agencies, and by the Member States when carrying out activities which fall within the scope of Union law, and the rules relating to the free movement of such data. Compliance with these rules shall be subject to the control of independent authorities.

The rules adopted on the basis of this Article shall be without prejudice to the specific rules laid down in Article 39 of the Treaty on European Union.

Article 17

1. The Union respects and does not prejudice the status under national law of churches and religious associations or communities in the Member States.

2. The Union equally respects the status under national law of philosophical and non-confessional organisations.

3. Recognising their identity and their specific contribution, the Union shall maintain an open, transparent and regular dialogue with these churches and organisations.

PART TWO
NON-DISCRIMINATION AND CITIZENSHIP OF THE UNION

Article 18
(ex Article 12 TEC)

Within the scope of application of the Treaties, and without prejudice to any special provisions contained therein, any discrimination on grounds of nationality shall be prohibited.

The European Parliament and the Council, acting in accordance with the ordinary legislative procedure, may adopt rules designed to prohibit such discrimination.

Article 19
(ex Article 13 TEC)

1. Without prejudice to the other provisions of the Treaties and within the limits of the powers conferred by them upon the Union, the Council, acting unanimously in accordance with a special legislative procedure and after obtaining the consent of the European Parliament, may take appropriate action to combat discrimination based on sex, racial or ethnic origin, religion or belief, disability, age or sexual orientation.

2. By way of derogation from paragraph 1, the European Parliament and the Council, acting in accordance with the ordinary legislative procedure, may adopt the basic principles of Union incentive measures, excluding any harmonisation of the laws and regulations of the Member States, to support action taken by the Member States in order to contribute to the achievement of the objectives referred to in paragraph 1.

Article 20
(ex Article 17 TEC)

1. Citizenship of the Union is hereby established. Every person holding the nationality of a Member State shall be a citizen of the Union. Citizenship of the Union shall be additional to and not replace national citizenship.

2. Citizens of the Union shall enjoy the rights and be subject to the duties provided for in the Treaties. They shall have, inter alia:

(a) the right to move and reside freely within the territory of the Member States;

(b) the right to vote and to stand as candidates in elections to the European Parliament and in municipal elections in their Member State of residence, under the same conditions as nationals of that State;

(c) the right to enjoy, in the territory of a third country in which the Member State of which they are nationals is not represented, the protection of the diplomatic and consular authorities of any Member State on the same conditions as the nationals of that State;

(d) the right to petition the European Parliament, to apply to the European Ombudsman, and to address the institutions and advisory bodies of the Union in any of the Treaty languages and to obtain a reply in the same language.

These rights shall be exercised in accordance with the conditions and limits defined by the Treaties and by the measures adopted thereunder.

Article 21
(ex Article 18 TEC)

1. Every citizen of the Union shall have the right to move and reside freely within the territory of the Member States, subject to the limitations and conditions laid down in the Treaties and by the measures adopted to give them effect.

2. If action by the Union should prove necessary to attain this objective and the Treaties have not provided the necessary powers, the European Parliament and the Council, acting in accordance with the ordinary legislative procedure, may adopt provisions with a view to facilitating the exercise of the rights referred to in paragraph 1.

3. For the same purposes as those referred to in paragraph 1 and if the Treaties have not provided the necessary powers, the Council, acting in accordance with a special legislative procedure, may adopt measures concerning social security or social protection. The Council shall act unanimously after consulting the European Parliament.

Article 22
(ex Article 19 TEC)

1. Every citizen of the Union residing in a Member State of which he is not a national shall have the right to vote and to stand as a candidate at municipal elections in the Member State in which he resides, under the same conditions as nationals of that State. This right shall be exercised subject to detailed arrangements adopted by the Council, acting unanimously in accordance with a special legislative procedure and after consulting the European Parliament; these arrangements may provide for derogations where warranted by problems specific to a Member State.

2. Without prejudice to Article 223(1) and to the provisions adopted for its implementation, every citizen of the Union residing in

a Member State of which he is not a national shall have the right to vote and to stand as a candidate in elections to the European Parliament in the Member State in which he resides, under the same conditions as nationals of that State. This right shall be exercised subject to detailed arrangements adopted by the Council, acting unanimously in accordance with a special legislative procedure and after consulting the European Parliament; these arrangements may provide for derogations where warranted by problems specific to a Member State.

Article 23
(ex Article 20 TEC)

Every citizen of the Union shall, in the territory of a third country in which the Member State of which he is a national is not represented, be entitled to protection by the diplomatic or consular authorities of any Member State, on the same conditions as the nationals of that State. Member States shall adopt the necessary provisions and start the international negotiations required to secure this protection.

The Council, acting in accordance with a special legislative procedure and after consulting the European Parliament, may adopt directives establishing the coordination and cooperation measures necessary to facilitate such protection.

Article 24
(ex Article 21 TEC)

The European Parliament and the Council, acting by means of regulations in accordance with the ordinary legislative procedure, shall adopt the provisions for the procedures and conditions required for a citizens' initiative within the meaning of Article 11 of the Treaty on European Union, including the minimum number of Member States from which such citizens must come.

Every citizen of the Union shall have the right to petition the European Parliament in accordance with Article 227.

Every citizen of the Union may apply to the Ombudsman established in accordance with Article 228.

Every citizen of the Union may write to any of the institutions or bodies referred to in this Article or in Article 13 of the Treaty on European Union in one of the languages mentioned in Article 55(1) of the Treaty on European Union and have an answer in the same language.

Article 25
(ex Article 22 TEC)

The Commission shall report to the European Parliament, to the Council and to the Economic and Social Committee every three years on the application of the provisions of this Part. This report shall take account of the development of the Union.

On this basis, and without prejudice to the other provisions of the Treaties, the Council, acting unanimously in accordance with a special legislative procedure and after obtaining the consent of the European Parliament, may adopt provisions to strengthen or to add to the rights listed in Article 20(2). These provisions shall enter into force after their approval by the Member States in accordance with their respective constitutional requirements.

PART THREE
UNION POLICIES AND INTERNAL ACTIONS

TITLE I
THE INTERNAL MARKET

Article 26
(ex Article 14 TEC)

1. The Union shall adopt measures with the aim of establishing or ensuring the functioning of the internal market, in accordance with the relevant provisions of the Treaties.

2. The internal market shall comprise an area without internal frontiers in which the free movement of goods, persons, services and capital is ensured in accordance with the provisions of the Treaties.

3. The Council, on a proposal from the Commission, shall determine the guidelines and conditions necessary to ensure balanced progress in all the sectors concerned.

Article 27
(ex Article 15 TEC)

When drawing up its proposals with a view to achieving the objectives set out in Article 26, the Commission shall take into account the extent of the effort that certain economies showing differences in development will have to sustain for the establishment of the internal market and it may propose appropriate provisions.

If these provisions take the form of derogations, they must be of a temporary nature and must cause the least possible disturbance to the functioning of the internal market.

TITLE II
FREE MOVEMENT OF GOODS

Article 28
(ex Article 23 TEC)

1. The Union shall comprise a customs union which shall cover all trade in goods and which shall involve the prohibition between Member States of customs duties on imports and exports and of all charges having equivalent effect, and the adoption of a common customs tariff in their relations with third countries.

2. The provisions of Article 30 and of Chapter 2 of this Title shall apply to products originating in Member States and to products coming from third countries which are in free circulation in Member States.

Article 29
(ex Article 24 TEC)

Products coming from a third country shall be considered to be in free circulation in a Member State if the import formalities have been complied with and any customs duties or charges having equivalent effect which are payable have been levied in that Member State, and if they have not benefited from a total or partial drawback of such duties or charges.

CHAPTER 1
THE CUSTOMS UNION

Article 30
(ex Article 25 TEC)

Customs duties on imports and exports and charges having equivalent effect shall be prohibited between Member States. This prohibition shall also apply to customs duties of a fiscal nature.

Article 31
(ex Article 26 TEC)

Common Customs Tariff duties shall be fixed by the Council on a proposal from the Commission.

Article 32
(ex Article 27 TEC)

In carrying out the tasks entrusted to it under this Chapter the Commission shall be guided by:

(a) the need to promote trade between Member States and third countries;

(b) developments in conditions of competition within the Union in so far as they lead to an improvement in the competitive capacity of undertakings;

(c) the requirements of the Union as regards the supply of raw materials and semi-finished goods; in this connection the Commission shall take care to avoid distorting conditions of competition between Member States in respect of finished goods;

(d) the need to avoid serious disturbances in the economies of Member States and to ensure rational development of production and an expansion of consumption within the Union.

CHAPTER 2
CUSTOMS COOPERATION

Article 33
(ex Article 135 TEC)

Within the scope of application of the Treaties, the European Parliament and the Council, acting in accordance with the ordinary legislative procedure, shall take measures in order to strengthen customs cooperation between Member States and between the latter and the Commission.

CHAPTER 3
PROHIBITION OF QUANTITATIVE RESTRICTIONS BETWEEN MEMBER STATES

Article 34
(ex Article 28 TEC)

Quantitative restrictions on imports and all measures having equivalent effect shall be prohibited between Member States.

Article 35
(ex Article 29 TEC)

Quantitative restrictions on exports, and all measures having equivalent effect, shall be prohibited between Member States.

Article 36
(ex Article 30 TEC)

The provisions of Articles 34 and 35 shall not preclude prohibitions or restrictions on imports, exports or goods in transit justified on grounds of public morality, public policy or public security; the protection of health and life of humans, animals or plants; the protection of national treasures possessing artistic, historic or archaeological value; or the protection of industrial and commercial property. Such prohibitions or restrictions shall not, however, constitute a means of arbitrary discrimination or a disguised restriction on trade between Member States.

Article 37
(ex Article 31 TEC)

1. Member States shall adjust any State monopolies of a commercial character so as to ensure that no discrimination regarding the conditions under which goods are procured and marketed exists between nationals of Member States.

The provisions of this Article shall apply to any body through which a Member State, in law or in fact, either directly or indirectly supervises, determines or appreciably influences imports or exports between Member States. These provisions shall likewise apply to monopolies delegated by the State to others.

2. Member States shall refrain from introducing any new measure which is contrary to the principles laid down in paragraph 1 or which restricts the scope of the articles dealing with the prohibition of customs duties and quantitative restrictions between Member States.

3. If a State monopoly of a commercial character has rules which are designed to make it easier to dispose of agricultural products or obtain for them the best return, steps should be taken in applying the rules contained in this Article to ensure equivalent safeguards for the employment and standard of living of the producers concerned.

TITLE III
AGRICULTURE AND FISHERIES

Article 38
(ex Article 32 TEC)

1. The Union shall define and implement a common agriculture and fisheries policy.

The internal market shall extend to agriculture, fisheries and trade in agricultural products. "Agricultural products" means the products of the soil, of stockfarming and of fisheries and products of first-stage processing directly related to these products. References to the common agricultural policy or to agriculture, and the use of the term "agricultural", shall be understood as also referring to fisheries, having regard to the specific characteristics of this sector.

2. Save as otherwise provided in Articles 39 to 44, the rules laid down for the establishment and functioning of the internal market shall apply to agricultural products.

3. The products subject to the provisions of Articles 39 to 44 are listed in Annex I.

4. The operation and development of the internal market for agricultural products must be accompanied by the establishment of a common agricultural policy.

Article 39
(ex Article 33 TEC)

1. The objectives of the common agricultural policy shall be:

(a) to increase agricultural productivity by promoting technical progress and by ensuring the rational development of agricultural production and the optimum utilisation of the factors of production, in particular labour;

(b) thus to ensure a fair standard of living for the agricultural community, in particular by increasing the individual earnings of persons engaged in agriculture;

(c) to stabilise markets;

(d) to assure the availability of supplies;

(e) to ensure that supplies reach consumers at reasonable prices.

2. In working out the common agricultural policy and the special methods for its application, account shall be taken of:

(a) the particular nature of agricultural activity, which results from the social structure of agriculture and from structural and natural disparities between the various agricultural regions;

(b) the need to effect the appropriate adjustments by degrees;

(c) the fact that in the Member States agriculture constitutes a sector closely linked with the economy as a whole.

Article 40
(ex Article 34 TEC)

1. In order to attain the objectives set out in Article 39, a common organisation of agricultural markets shall be established.

This organisation shall take one of the following forms, depending on the product concerned:

(a) common rules on competition;

(b) compulsory coordination of the various national market organisations;

(c) a European market organisation.

2. The common organisation established in accordance with paragraph 1 may include all measures required to attain the objectives set out in Article 39, in particular regulation of prices, aids for the production and marketing of the various products, storage and carryover arrangements and common machinery for stabilising imports or exports.

The common organisation shall be limited to pursuit of the objectives set out in Article 39 and shall exclude any discrimination between producers or consumers within the Union.

Any common price policy shall be based on common criteria and uniform methods of calculation.

3. In order to enable the common organisation referred to in paragraph 1 to attain its objectives, one or more agricultural guidance and guarantee funds may be set up.

Article 41
(ex Article 35 TEC)

To enable the objectives set out in Article 39 to be attained, provision may be made within the framework of the common agricultural policy for measures such as:

(a) an effective coordination of efforts in the spheres of vocational training, of research and of the dissemination of agricultural knowledge; this may include joint financing of projects or institutions;

(b) joint measures to promote consumption of certain products.

Article 42
(ex Article 36 TEC)

The provisions of the Chapter relating to rules on competition shall apply to production of and trade in agricultural products only to the extent determined by the European Parliament and the Council within the framework of Article 43(2) and in accordance with the procedure laid down therein, account being taken of the objectives set out in Article 39.

The Council, on a proposal from the Commission, may authorise the granting of aid:

(a) for the protection of enterprises handicapped by structural or natural conditions;

(b) within the framework of economic development programmes.

Article 43
(ex Article 37 TEC)

1. The Commission shall submit proposals for working out and implementing the common agricultural policy, including the replacement of the national organisations by one of the forms of common organisation provided for in Article 40(1), and for implementing the measures specified in this Title.

These proposals shall take account of the interdependence of the agricultural matters mentioned in this Title.

2. The European Parliament and the Council, acting in accordance with the ordinary legislative procedure and after consulting the Economic and Social Committee, shall establish the common organisation of agricultural markets provided for in Article 40(1) and the other provisions necessary for the pursuit of the objectives of the common agricultural policy and the common fisheries policy.

3. The Council, on a proposal from the Commission, shall adopt measures on fixing prices, levies, aid and quantitative limitations and on the fixing and allocation of fishing opportunities.

4. In accordance with paragraph 2, the national market organisations may be replaced by the common organisation provided for in Article 40(1) if:

(a) the common organisation offers Member States which are opposed to this measure and which have an organisation of their own for the production in question equivalent safeguards for the employment and standard of living of the producers concerned, account being taken of the adjustments that will be possible and the specialisation that will be needed with the passage of time;

(b) such an organisation ensures conditions for trade within the Union similar to those existing in a national market.

5. If a common organisation for certain raw materials is established before a common organisation exists for the corresponding processed products, such raw materials as are used for processed products intended for export to third countries may be imported from outside the Union.

Article 44
(ex Article 38 TEC)

Where in a Member State a product is subject to a national market organisation or to internal rules having equivalent effect which affect the competitive position of similar production in another

Member State, a countervailing charge shall be applied by Member States to imports of this product coming from the Member State where such organisation or rules exist, unless that State applies a countervailing charge on export.

The Commission shall fix the amount of these charges at the level required to redress the balance; it may also authorise other measures, the conditions and details of which it shall determine.

TITLE IV
FREE MOVEMENT OF PERSONS, SERVICES AND CAPITAL

CHAPTER 1
WORKERS

Article 45
(ex Article 39 TEC)

1. Freedom of movement for workers shall be secured within the Union.

2. Such freedom of movement shall entail the abolition of any discrimination based on nationality between workers of the Member States as regards employment, remuneration and other conditions of work and employment.

3. It shall entail the right, subject to limitations justified on grounds of public policy, public security or public health:

(a) to accept offers of employment actually made;

(b) to move freely within the territory of Member States for this purpose;

(c) to stay in a Member State for the purpose of employment in accordance with the provisions governing the employment of nationals of that State laid down by law, regulation or administrative action;

(d) to remain in the territory of a Member State after having been employed in that State, subject to conditions which shall be embodied in regulations to be drawn up by the Commission.

4. The provisions of this Article shall not apply to employment in the public service.

Article 46
(ex Article 40 TEC)

The European Parliament and the Council shall, acting in accordance with the ordinary legislative procedure and after consulting the Economic and Social Committee, issue directives or make regulations setting out the measures required to bring about freedom of movement for workers, as defined in Article 45, in particular:

(a) by ensuring close cooperation between national employment services;

(b) by abolishing those administrative procedures and practices and those qualifying periods in respect of eligibility for available employment, whether resulting from national legislation or from agreements previously concluded between Member States, the maintenance of which would form an obstacle to liberalisation of the movement of workers;

(c) by abolishing all such qualifying periods and other restrictions provided for either under national legislation or under agreements previously concluded between Member States as imposed on workers of other Member States conditions regarding the free choice of employment other than those imposed on workers of the State concerned;

(d) by setting up appropriate machinery to bring offers of employment into touch with applications for employment and to facilitate the achievement of a balance between supply and demand in the employment market in such a way as to avoid serious threats to the standard of living and level of employment in the various regions and industries.

Article 47
(ex Article 41 TEC)

Member States shall, within the framework of a joint programme, encourage the exchange of young workers.

Article 48
(ex Article 42 TEC)

The European Parliament and the Council shall, acting in accordance with the ordinary legislative procedure, adopt such measures in the field of social security as are necessary to provide freedom of movement for workers; to this end, they shall make arrangements to secure for employed and self-employed migrant workers and their dependants:

(a) aggregation, for the purpose of acquiring and retaining the right to benefit and of calculating the amount of benefit, of all periods taken into account under the laws of the several countries;

(b) payment of benefits to persons resident in the territories of Member States.

Where a member of the Council declares that a draft legislative act referred to in the first subparagraph would affect important aspects of its social security system, including its scope, cost or financial structure, or would affect the financial balance of that system, it may request that the matter be referred to the European Council. In that case, the ordinary legislative procedure shall be suspended. After discussion, the European Council shall, within four months of this suspension, either:

(a) refer the draft back to the Council, which shall terminate the suspension of the ordinary legislative procedure; or

(b) take no action or request the Commission to submit a new proposal; in that case, the act originally proposed shall be deemed not to have been adopted.

CHAPTER 2
RIGHT OF ESTABLISHMENT

Article 49
(ex Article 43 TEC)

Within the framework of the provisions set out below, restrictions on the freedom of establishment of nationals of a Member State in the territory of another Member State shall be prohibited. Such prohibition shall also apply to restrictions on the setting-up of agencies, branches or subsidiaries by nationals of any Member State established in the territory of any Member State.

Freedom of establishment shall include the right to take up and pursue activities as self-employed persons and to set up and manage undertakings, in particular companies or firms within the meaning of the second paragraph of Article 54, under the conditions laid down for its own nationals by the law of the country where such establishment is effected, subject to the provisions of the Chapter relating to capital.

Article 50
(ex Article 44 TEC)

1. In order to attain freedom of establishment as regards a particular activity, the European Parliament and the Council, acting in accordance with the ordinary legislative procedure and after consulting the Economic and Social Committee, shall act by means of directives.

2. The European Parliament, the Council and the Commission shall carry out the duties devolving upon them under the preceding provisions, in particular:

(a) by according, as a general rule, priority treatment to activities where freedom of establishment makes a particularly valuable contribution to the development of production and trade;

(b) by ensuring close cooperation between the competent authorities in the Member States in order to ascertain the particular situation within the Union of the various activities concerned;

(c) by abolishing those administrative procedures and practices, whether resulting from national legislation or from agreements previously concluded between Member States, the maintenance of which would form an obstacle to freedom of establishment;

(d) by ensuring that workers of one Member State employed in the territory of another Member State may remain in that territory for the purpose of taking up activities therein as self-employed persons, where they satisfy the conditions which they would be required to satisfy if they were entering that State at the time when they intended to take up such activities;

(e) by enabling a national of one Member State to acquire and use land and buildings situated in the territory of another Member State, in so far as this does not conflict with the principles laid down in Article 39(2);

(f) by effecting the progressive abolition of restrictions on freedom of establishment in every branch of activity under consideration, both as regards the conditions for setting up agencies, branches or subsidiaries in the territory of a Member State and as regards the subsidiaries in the territory of a Member State and as regards the conditions governing the entry of personnel belonging to the main establishment into managerial or supervisory posts in such agencies, branches or subsidiaries;

(g) by coordinating to the necessary extent the safeguards which, for the protection of the interests of members and others, are required by Member States of companies or firms within the meaning of the second paragraph of Article 54 with a view to making such safeguards equivalent throughout the Union;

(h) by satisfying themselves that the conditions of establishment are not distorted by aids granted by Member States.

Article 51
(ex Article 45 TEC)

The provisions of this Chapter shall not apply, so far as any given Member State is concerned, to activities which in that State are connected, even occasionally, with the exercise of official authority.

The European Parliament and the Council, acting in accordance with the ordinary legislative procedure, may rule that the provisions of this Chapter shall not apply to certain activities.

Article 52
(ex Article 46 TEC)

1. The provisions of this Chapter and measures taken in pursuance thereof shall not prejudice the applicability of provisions laid down by law, regulation or administrative action providing for special treatment for foreign nationals on grounds of public policy, public security or public health.

2. The European Parliament and the Council shall, acting in accordance with the ordinary legislative procedure, issue directives for the coordination of the abovementioned provisions.

Article 53
(ex Article 47 TEC)

1. In order to make it easier for persons to take up and pursue activities as self-employed persons, the European Parliament and the Council shall, acting in accordance with the ordinary legislative procedure, issue directives for the mutual recognition of diplomas, certificates and other evidence of formal qualifications and for the coordination of the provisions laid down by law, regulation or administrative action in Member States concerning the taking-up and pursuit of activities as self-employed persons.

2. In the case of the medical and allied and pharmaceutical professions, the progressive abolition of restrictions shall be dependent upon coordination of the conditions for their exercise in the various Member States.

Article 54
(ex Article 48 TEC)

Companies or firms formed in accordance with the law of a Member State and having their registered office, central administration or principal place of business within the Union shall, for the purposes of this Chapter, be treated in the same way as natural persons who are nationals of Member States.

"Companies or firms" means companies or firms constituted under civil or commercial law, including cooperative societies, and other legal persons governed by public or private law, save for those which are non-profit-making.

Article 55
(ex Article 294 TEC)

Member States shall accord nationals of the other Member States the same treatment as their own nationals as regards participation in the capital of companies or firms within the meaning of Article 54, without prejudice to the application of the other provisions of the Treaties.

CHAPTER 3
SERVICES

Article 56
(ex Article 49 TEC)

Within the framework of the provisions set out below, restrictions on freedom to provide services within the Union shall be prohibited in respect of nationals of Member States who are established in a Member State other than that of the person for whom the services are intended.

The European Parliament and the Council, acting in accordance with the ordinary legislative procedure, may extend the provisions of the Chapter to nationals of a third country who provide services and who are established within the Union.

Article 57
(ex Article 50 TEC)

Services shall be considered to be "services" within the meaning of the Treaties where they are normally provided for remuneration, in so far as they are not governed by the provisions relating to freedom of movement for goods, capital and persons.

"Services" shall in particular include:

(a) activities of an industrial character;

(b) activities of a commercial character;

(c) activities of craftsmen;

(d) activities of the professions.

Without prejudice to the provisions of the Chapter relating to the right of establishment, the person providing a service may, in order to do so, temporarily pursue his activity in the Member State where the service is provided, under the same conditions as are imposed by that State on its own nationals.

Article 58
(ex Article 51 TEC)

1. Freedom to provide services in the field of transport shall be governed by the provisions of the Title relating to transport.

2. The liberalisation of banking and insurance services connected with movements of capital shall be effected in step with the liberalisation of movement of capital.

Article 59
(ex Article 52 TEC)

1. In order to achieve the liberalisation of a specific service, the European Parliament and the Council, acting in accordance with the ordinary legislative procedure and after consulting the Economic and Social Committee, shall issue directives.

2. As regards the directives referred to in paragraph 1, priority shall as a general rule be given to those services which directly affect production costs or the liberalisation of which helps to promote trade in goods.

Article 60
(ex Article 53 TEC)

The Member States shall endeavour to undertake the liberalisation of services beyond the extent required by the directives issued pursuant to Article 59(1), if their general economic situation and the situation of the economic sector concerned so permit.

To this end, the Commission shall make recommendations to the Member States concerned.

Article 61
(ex Article 54 TEC)

As long as restrictions on freedom to provide services have not been abolished, each Member State shall apply such restrictions without distinction on grounds of nationality or residence to all persons providing services within the meaning of the first paragraph of Article 56.

Article 62
(ex Article 55 TEC)

The provisions of Articles 51 to 54 shall apply to the matters covered by this Chapter.

CHAPTER 4
CAPITAL AND PAYMENTS

Article 63
(ex Article 56 TEC)

1. Within the framework of the provisions set out in this Chapter, all restrictions on the movement of capital between Member States and between Member States and third countries shall be prohibited.

2. Within the framework of the provisions set out in this Chapter, all restrictions on payments between Member States and between Member States and third countries shall be prohibited.

Article 64
(ex Article 57 TEC)

1. The provisions of Article 63 shall be without prejudice to the application to third countries of any restrictions which exist on 31 December 1993 under national or Union law adopted in respect of the movement of capital to or from third countries involving direct investment—including in real estate—establishment, the provision of financial services or the admission of securities to capital markets. In respect of restrictions existing under national law in Bulgaria, Estonia and Hungary, the relevant date shall be 31 December 1999.

2. Whilst endeavouring to achieve the objective of free movement of capital between Member States and third countries to the greatest extent possible and without prejudice to the other Chapters of the Treaties, the European Parliament and the Council, acting in accordance with the ordinary legislative procedure, shall adopt the measures on the movement of capital to or from third countries involving direct investment—including investment in real estate—establishment, the provision of financial services or the admission of securities to capital markets.

3. Notwithstanding paragraph 2, only the Council, acting in accordance with a special legislative procedure, may unanimously, and after consulting the European Parliament, adopt measures which constitute a step backwards in Union law as regards the liberalisation of the movement of capital to or from third countries.

Article 65
(ex Article 58 TEC)

1. The provisions of Article 63 shall be without prejudice to the right of Member States:

(a) to apply the relevant provisions of their tax law which distinguish between taxpayers who are not in the same situation with regard to their place of residence or with regard to the place where their capital is invested;

(b) to take all requisite measures to prevent infringements of national law and regulations, in particular in the field of taxation and the prudential supervision of financial institutions, or to lay down procedures for the declaration of capital movements for purposes of administrative or statistical information, or to take measures which are justified on grounds of public policy or public security.

2. The provisions of this Chapter shall be without prejudice to the applicability of restrictions on the right of establishment which are compatible with the Treaties.

3. The measures and procedures referred to in paragraphs 1 and 2 shall not constitute a means of arbitrary discrimination or a disguised restriction on the free movement of capital and payments as defined in Article 63.

4. In the absence of measures pursuant to Article 64(3), the Commission or, in the absence of a Commission decision within three months from the request of the Member State concerned, the Council, may adopt a decision stating that restrictive tax measures adopted by a Member State concerning one or more third countries are to be considered compatible with the Treaties in so far as they are justified by one of the objectives of the Union and compatible with the proper functioning of the internal market. The Council shall act unanimously on application by a Member State.

Article 66
(ex Article 59 TEC)

Where, in exceptional circumstances, movements of capital to or from third countries cause, or threaten to cause, serious difficulties for the operation of economic and monetary union, the Council, on a proposal from the Commission and after consulting the European Central Bank, may take safeguard measures with regard to third countries for a period not exceeding six months if such measures are strictly necessary.

TITLE V
AREA OF FREEDOM, SECURITY AND JUSTICE

CHAPTER 1
GENERAL PROVISIONS

Article 67
(ex Article 61 TEC and ex Article 29 TEU)

1. The Union shall constitute an area of freedom, security and justice with respect for fundamental rights and the different legal systems and traditions of the Member States.

2. It shall ensure the absence of internal border controls for persons and shall frame a common policy on asylum, immigration and external border control, based on solidarity between Member States, which is fair towards third-country nationals. For the purpose of this Title, stateless persons shall be treated as third-country nationals.

3. The Union shall endeavour to ensure a high level of security through measures to prevent and combat crime, racism and xenophobia, and through measures for coordination and cooperation between police and judicial authorities and other competent authorities, as well as through the mutual recognition of judgments in criminal matters and, if necessary, through the approximation of criminal laws.

4. The Union shall facilitate access to justice, in particular through the principle of mutual recognition of judicial and extrajudicial decisions in civil matters.

Article 68

The European Council shall define the strategic guidelines for legislative and operational planning within the area of freedom, security and justice.

Article 69

National Parliaments ensure that the proposals and legislative initiatives submitted under Chapters 4 and 5 comply with the principle of subsidiarity, in accordance with the arrangements laid down by the Protocol on the application of the principles of subsidiarity and proportionality.

Article 70

Without prejudice to Articles 258, 259 and 260, the Council may, on a proposal from the Commission, adopt measures laying down the arrangements whereby Member States, in collaboration with the Commission, conduct objective and impartial evaluation of the implementation of the Union policies referred to in this Title by Member States' authorities, in particular in order to facilitate full application of the principle of mutual recognition. The European Parliament and national Parliaments shall be informed of the content and results of the evaluation.

Article 71
(ex Article 36 TEU)

A standing committee shall be set up within the Council in order to ensure that operational cooperation on internal security is promoted and strengthened within the Union. Without prejudice to Article 240, it shall facilitate coordination of the action of Member States' competent authorities. Representatives of the Union bodies, offices and agencies concerned may be involved in the proceedings of this committee. The European Parliament and national Parliaments shall be kept informed of the proceedings.

Article 72
(ex Article 64(1) TEC and ex Article 33 TEU)

This Title shall not affect the exercise of the responsibilities incumbent upon Member States with regard to the maintenance of law and order and the safeguarding of internal security.

Article 73

It shall be open to Member States to organise between themselves and under their responsibility such forms of cooperation and coordination as they deem appropriate between the competent departments of their administrations responsible for safeguarding national security.

Article 74
(ex Article 66 TEC)

The Council shall adopt measures to ensure administrative cooperation between the relevant departments of the Member States in the areas covered by this Title, as well as between those departments and the Commission. It shall act on a Commission proposal, subject to Article 76, and after consulting the European Parliament.

Article 75
(ex Article 60 TEC)

Where necessary to achieve the objectives set out in Article 67, as regards preventing and combating terrorism and related activities, the European Parliament and the Council, acting by means of regulations in accordance with the ordinary legislative procedure, shall define a framework for administrative measures with regard to capital movements and payments, such as the freezing of funds, financial assets or economic gains belonging to, or owned or held by, natural or legal persons, groups or non-State entities.

The Council, on a proposal from the Commission, shall adopt measures to implement the framework referred to in the first paragraph.

The acts referred to in this Article shall include necessary provisions on legal safeguards.

Article 76

The acts referred to in Chapters 4 and 5, together with the measures referred to in Article 74 which ensure administrative cooperation in the areas covered by these Chapters, shall be adopted:

(a) on a proposal from the Commission, or

(b) on the initiative of a quarter of the Member States.

CHAPTER 2
POLICIES ON BORDER CHECKS, ASYLUM AND IMMIGRATION

Article 77
(ex Article 62 TEC)

1. The Union shall develop a policy with a view to:

(a) ensuring the absence of any controls on persons, whatever their nationality, when crossing internal borders;

(b) carrying out checks on persons and efficient monitoring of the crossing of external borders;

(c) the gradual introduction of an integrated management system for external borders.

2. For the purposes of paragraph 1, the European Parliament and the Council, acting in accordance with the ordinary legislative procedure, shall adopt measures concerning:

(a) the common policy on visas and other short-stay residence permits;

(b) the checks to which persons crossing external borders are subject;

(c) the conditions under which nationals of third countries shall have the freedom to travel within the Union for a short period;

(d) any measure necessary for the gradual establishment of an integrated management system for external borders;

(e) the absence of any controls on persons, whatever their nationality, when crossing internal borders.

3. If action by the Union should prove necessary to facilitate the exercise of the right referred to in Article 20(2)(a), and if the Treaties have not provided the necessary powers, the Council, acting in accordance with a special legislative procedure, may adopt provisions concerning passports, identity cards, residence permits or any other such document. The Council shall act unanimously after consulting the European Parliament.

4. This Article shall not affect the competence of the Member States concerning the geographical demarcation of their borders, in accordance with international law.

Article 78

(ex Articles 63, points 1 and 2, and 64(2) TEC)

1. The Union shall develop a common policy on asylum, subsidiary protection and temporary protection with a view to offering appropriate status to any third-country national requiring international protection and ensuring compliance with the principle of *non-refoulement*. This policy must be in accordance with the Geneva Convention of 28 July 1951 and the Protocol of 31 January 1967 relating to the status of refugees, and other relevant treaties.

2. For the purposes of paragraph 1, the European Parliament and the Council, acting in accordance with the ordinary legislative procedure, shall adopt measures for a common European asylum system comprising:

(a) a uniform status of asylum for nationals of third countries, valid throughout the Union;

(b) a uniform status of subsidiary protection for nationals of third countries who, without obtaining European asylum, are in need of international protection;

(c) a common system of temporary protection for displaced persons in the event of a massive inflow;

(d) common procedures for the granting and withdrawing of uniform asylum or subsidiary protection status;

(e) criteria and mechanisms for determining which Member State is responsible for considering an application for asylum or subsidiary protection;

(f) standards concerning the conditions for the reception of applicants for asylum or subsidiary protection;

(g) partnership and cooperation with third countries for the purpose of managing inflows of people applying for asylum or subsidiary or temporary protection.

3. In the event of one or more Member States being confronted by an emergency situation characterised by a sudden inflow of nationals of third countries, the Council, on a proposal from the Commission, may adopt provisional measures for the benefit of the Member State(s) concerned. It shall act after consulting the European Parliament.

Article 79

(ex Article 63, points 3 and 4, TEC)

1. The Union shall develop a common immigration policy aimed at ensuring, at all stages, the efficient management of migration flows, fair treatment of third-country nationals residing legally in Member States, and the prevention of, and enhanced measures to combat, illegal immigration and trafficking in human beings.

2. For the purposes of paragraph 1, the European Parliament and the Council, acting in accordance with the ordinary legislative procedure, shall adopt measures in the following areas:

(a) the conditions of entry and residence, and standards on the issue by Member States of long-term visas and residence permits, including those for the purpose of family reunification;

(b) the definition of the rights of third-country nationals residing legally in a Member State, including the conditions governing freedom of movement and of residence in other Member States;

(c) illegal immigration and unauthorised residence, including removal and repatriation of persons residing without authorisation;

(d) combating trafficking in persons, in particular women and children.

3. The Union may conclude agreements with third countries for the readmission to their countries of origin or provenance of third-country nationals who do not or who no longer fulfil the conditions for entry, presence or residence in the territory of one of the Member States.

4. The European Parliament and the Council, acting in accordance with the ordinary legislative procedure, may establish measures to provide incentives and support for the action of Member States with a view to promoting the integration of third-country

nationals residing legally in their territories, excluding any harmonisation of the laws and regulations of the Member States.

5. This Article shall not affect the right of Member States to determine volumes of admission of third-country nationals coming from third countries to their territory in order to seek work, whether employed or self-employed.

Article 80

The policies of the Union set out in this Chapter and their implementation shall be governed by the principle of solidarity and fair sharing of responsibility, including its financial implications, between the Member States. Whenever necessary, the Union acts adopted pursuant to this Chapter shall contain appropriate measures to give effect to this principle.

CHAPTER 3
JUDICIAL COOPERATION IN CIVIL MATTERS

Article 81
(ex Article 65 TEC)

1. The Union shall develop judicial cooperation in civil matters having cross-border implications, based on the principle of mutual recognition of judgments and of decisions in extrajudicial cases. Such cooperation may include the adoption of measures for the approximation of the laws and regulations of the Member States.

2. For the purposes of paragraph 1, the European Parliament and the Council, acting in accordance with the ordinary legislative procedure, shall adopt measures, particularly when necessary for the proper functioning of the internal market, aimed at ensuring:

(a) the mutual recognition and enforcement between Member States of judgments and of decisions in extrajudicial cases;

(b) the cross-border service of judicial and extrajudicial documents;

(c) the compatibility of the rules applicable in the Member States concerning conflict of laws and of jurisdiction;

(d) cooperation in the taking of evidence;

(e) effective access to justice;

(f) the elimination of obstacles to the proper functioning of civil proceedings, if necessary by promoting the compatibility of the rules on civil procedure applicable in the Member States;

(g) the development of alternative methods of dispute settlement;

(h) support for the training of the judiciary and judicial staff.

3. Notwithstanding paragraph 2, measures concerning family law with cross-border implications shall be established by the Council, acting in accordance with a special legislative procedure. The Council shall act unanimously after consulting the European Parliament.

The Council, on a proposal from the Commission, may adopt a decision determining those aspects of family law with cross-border implications which may be the subject of acts adopted by the ordinary legislative procedure. The Council shall act unanimously after consulting the European Parliament.

The proposal referred to in the second subparagraph shall be notified to the national Parliaments. If a national Parliament makes known its opposition within six months of the date of such notification, the decision shall not be adopted. In the absence of opposition, the Council may adopt the decision.

CHAPTER 4
JUDICIAL COOPERATION IN CRIMINAL MATTERS

Article 82
(ex Article 31 TEU)

1. Judicial cooperation in criminal matters in the Union shall be based on the principle of mutual recognition of judgments and judicial decisions and shall include the approximation of the laws and regulations of the Member States in the areas referred to in paragraph 2 and in Article 83.

The European Parliament and the Council, acting in accordance with the ordinary legislative procedure, shall adopt measures to:

(a) lay down rules and procedures for ensuring recognition throughout the Union of all forms of judgments and judicial decisions;

(b) prevent and settle conflicts of jurisdiction between Member States;

(c) support the training of the judiciary and judicial staff;

(d) facilitate cooperation between judicial or equivalent authorities of the Member States in relation to proceedings in criminal matters and the enforcement of decisions.

2. To the extent necessary to facilitate mutual recognition of judgments and judicial decisions and police and judicial cooperation in criminal matters having a cross-border dimension, the European

Parliament and the Council may, by means of directives adopted in accordance with the ordinary legislative procedure, establish minimum rules. Such rules shall take into account the differences between the legal traditions and systems of the Member States.

They shall concern:

(a) mutual admissibility of evidence between Member States;

(b) the rights of individuals in criminal procedure;

(c) the rights of victims of crime;

(d) any other specific aspects of criminal procedure which the Council has identified in advance by a decision; for the adoption of such a decision, the Council shall act unanimously after obtaining the consent of the European Parliament.

Adoption of the minimum rules referred to in this paragraph shall not prevent Member States from maintaining or introducing a higher level of protection for individuals.

3. Where a member of the Council considers that a draft directive as referred to in paragraph 2 would affect fundamental aspects of its criminal justice system, it may request that the draft directive be referred to the European Council. In that case, the ordinary legislative procedure shall be suspended. After discussion, and in case of a consensus, the European Council shall, within four months of this suspension, refer the draft back to the Council, which shall terminate the suspension of the ordinary legislative procedure.

Within the same timeframe, in case of disagreement, and if at least nine Member States wish to establish enhanced cooperation on the basis of the draft directive concerned, they shall notify the European Parliament, the Council and the Commission accordingly. In such a case, the authorisation to proceed with enhanced cooperation referred to in Article 20(2) of the Treaty on European Union and Article 329(1) of this Treaty shall be deemed to be granted and the provisions on enhanced cooperation shall apply.

Article 83
(ex Article 31 TEU)

1. The European Parliament and the Council may, by means of directives adopted in accordance with the ordinary legislative procedure, establish minimum rules concerning the definition of criminal offences and sanctions in the areas of particularly serious crime with a cross-border dimension resulting from the nature or impact of such offences or from a special need to combat them on a common basis.

These areas of crime are the following: terrorism, trafficking in human beings and sexual exploitation of women and children, illicit drug trafficking, illicit arms trafficking, money laundering, corruption, counterfeiting of means of payment, computer crime and organised crime.

On the basis of developments in crime, the Council may adopt a decision identifying other areas of crime that meet the criteria specified in this paragraph. It shall act unanimously after obtaining the consent of the European Parliament.

2. If the approximation of criminal laws and regulations of the Member States proves essential to ensure the effective implementation of a Union policy in an area which has been subject to harmonisation measures, directives may establish minimum rules with regard to the definition of criminal offences and sanctions in the area concerned. Such directives shall be adopted by the same ordinary or special legislative procedure as was followed for the adoption of the harmonisation measures in question, without prejudice to Article 76.

3. Where a member of the Council considers that a draft directive as referred to in paragraph 1 or 2 would affect fundamental aspects of its criminal justice system, it may request that the draft directive be referred to the European Council. In that case, the ordinary legislative procedure shall be suspended. After discussion, and in case of a consensus, the European Council shall, within four months of this suspension, refer the draft back to the Council, which shall terminate the suspension of the ordinary legislative procedure.

Within the same timeframe, in case of disagreement, and if at least nine Member States wish to establish enhanced cooperation on the basis of the draft directive concerned, they shall notify the European Parliament, the Council and the Commission accordingly. In such a case, the authorisation to proceed with enhanced cooperation referred to in Article 20(2) of the Treaty on European Union and Article 329(1) of this Treaty shall be deemed to be granted and the provisions on enhanced cooperation shall apply.

Article 84

The European Parliament and the Council, acting in accordance with the ordinary legislative procedure, may establish measures to promote and support the action of Member States in the field of crime prevention, excluding any harmonisation of the laws and regulations of the Member States.

Article 85
(ex Article 31 TEU)

1. Eurojust's mission shall be to support and strengthen coordination and cooperation between national investigating and prosecuting authorities in relation to serious crime affecting two or more Member States or requiring a prosecution on common bases, on the basis of operations conducted and information supplied by the Member States' authorities and by Europol.

In this context, the European Parliament and the Council, by means of regulations adopted in accordance with the ordinary legislative procedure, shall determine Eurojust's structure, operation, field of action and tasks. These tasks may include:

(a) the initiation of criminal investigations, as well as proposing the initiation of prosecutions conducted by competent national authorities, particularly those relating to offences against the financial interests of the Union;

(b) the coordination of investigations and prosecutions referred to in point (a);

(c) the strengthening of judicial cooperation, including by resolution of conflicts of jurisdiction and by close cooperation with the European Judicial Network.

These regulations shall also determine arrangements for involving the European Parliament and national Parliaments in the evaluation of Eurojust's activities.

2. In the prosecutions referred to in paragraph 1, and without prejudice to Article 86, formal acts of judicial procedure shall be carried out by the competent national officials.

Article 86

1. In order to combat crimes affecting the financial interests of the Union, the Council, by means of regulations adopted in accordance with a special legislative procedure, may establish a European Public Prosecutor's Office from Eurojust. The Council shall act unanimously after obtaining the consent of the European Parliament.

In the absence of unanimity in the Council, a group of at least nine Member States may request that the draft regulation be referred to the European Council. In that case, the procedure in the Council shall be suspended. After discussion, and in case of a consensus, the European Council shall, within four months of this suspension, refer the draft back to the Council for adoption.

Within the same timeframe, in case of disagreement, and if at least nine Member States wish to establish enhanced cooperation on the basis of the draft regulation concerned, they shall notify the European Parliament, the Council and the Commission accordingly. In such a case, the authorisation to proceed with enhanced cooperation referred to in Article 20(2) of the Treaty on European Union and Article 329(1) of this Treaty shall be deemed to be granted and the provisions on enhanced cooperation shall apply.

2. The European Public Prosecutor's Office shall be responsible for investigating, prosecuting and bringing to judgment, where appropriate in liaison with Europol, the perpetrators of, and accomplices in, offences against the Union's financial interests, as determined by the regulation provided for in paragraph 1. It shall exercise the functions of prosecutor in the competent courts of the Member States in relation to such offences.

3. The regulations referred to in paragraph 1 shall determine the general rules applicable to the European Public Prosecutor's Office, the conditions governing the performance of its functions, the rules of procedure applicable to its activities, as well as those governing the admissibility of evidence, and the rules applicable to the judicial review of procedural measures taken by it in the performance of its functions.

4. The European Council may, at the same time or subsequently, adopt a decision amending paragraph 1 in order to extend the powers of the European Public Prosecutor's Office to include serious crime having a cross-border dimension and amending accordingly paragraph 2 as regards the perpetrators of, and accomplices in, serious crimes affecting more than one Member State. The European Council shall act unanimously after obtaining the consent of the European Parliament and after consulting the Commission.

CHAPTER 5
POLICE COOPERATION

Article 87
(ex Article 30 TEU)

1. The Union shall establish police cooperation involving all the Member States' competent authorities, including police, customs and other specialised law enforcement services in relation to the prevention, detection and investigation of criminal offences.

2. For the purposes of paragraph 1, the European Parliament and the Council, acting in accordance with the ordinary legislative procedure, may establish measures concerning:

(a) the collection, storage, processing, analysis and exchange of relevant information;

(b) support for the training of staff, and cooperation on the exchange of staff, on equipment and on research into crime-detection;

(c) common investigative techniques in relation to the detection of serious forms of organised crime.

3. The Council, acting in accordance with a special legislative procedure, may establish measures concerning operational cooperation between the authorities referred to in this Article. The Council shall act unanimously after consulting the European Parliament.

In case of the absence of unanimity in the Council, a group of at least nine Member States may request that the draft measures be referred to the European Council. In that case, the procedure in the Council shall be suspended. After discussion, and in case of a consensus, the European Council shall, within four months of this suspension, refer the draft back to the Council for adoption.

Within the same timeframe, in case of disagreement, and if at least nine Member States wish to establish enhanced cooperation on the basis of the draft measures concerned, they shall notify the European Parliament, the Council and the Commission accordingly. In such a case, the authorisation to proceed with enhanced cooperation referred to in Article 20(2) of the Treaty on European Union and Article 329(1) of this Treaty shall be deemed to be granted and the provisions on enhanced cooperation shall apply.

The specific procedure provided for in the second and third subparagraphs shall not apply to acts which constitute a development of the Schengen *acquis*.

Article 88

(ex Article 30 TEU)

1. Europol's mission shall be to support and strengthen action by the Member States' police authorities and other law enforcement services and their mutual cooperation in preventing and combating serious crime affecting two or more Member States, terrorism and forms of crime which affect a common interest covered by a Union policy.

2. The European Parliament and the Council, by means of regulations adopted in accordance with the ordinary legislative procedure, shall determine Europol's structure, operation, field of action and tasks. These tasks may include:

(a) the collection, storage, processing, analysis and exchange of information, in particular that forwarded by the authorities of the Member States or third countries or bodies;

(b) the coordination, organisation and implementation of investigative and operational action carried out jointly with the Member States' competent authorities or in the context of joint investigative teams, where appropriate in liaison with Eurojust.

These regulations shall also lay down the procedures for scrutiny of Europol's activities by the European Parliament, together with national Parliaments.

3. Any operational action by Europol must be carried out in liaison and in agreement with the authorities of the Member State or States whose territory is concerned. The application of coercive measures shall be the exclusive responsibility of the competent national authorities.

Article 89
(ex Article 32 TEU)

The Council, acting in accordance with a special legislative procedure, shall lay down the conditions and limitations under which the competent authorities of the Member States referred to in Articles 82 and 87 may operate in the territory of another Member State in liaison and in agreement with the authorities of that State. The Council shall act unanimously after consulting the European Parliament.

TITLE VI
TRANSPORT

Article 90
(ex Article 70 TEC)

The objectives of the Treaties shall, in matters governed by this Title, be pursued within the framework of a common transport policy.

Article 91
(ex Article 71 TEC)

1. For the purpose of implementing Article 90, and taking into account the distinctive features of transport, the European Parliament and the Council shall, acting in accordance with the ordinary legislative procedure and after consulting the Economic and Social Committee and the Committee of the Regions, lay down:

(a) common rules applicable to international transport to or from the territory of a Member State or passing across the territory of one or more Member States;

(b) the conditions under which non-resident carriers may operate transport services within a Member State;

(c) measures to improve transport safety;

(d) any other appropriate provisions.

2. When the measures referred to in paragraph 1 are adopted, account shall be taken of cases where their application might seriously affect the standard of living and level of employment in certain regions, and the operation of transport facilities.

Article 92
(ex Article 72 TEC)

Until the provisions referred to in Article 91(1) have been laid down, no Member State may, unless the Council has unanimously adopted a measure granting a derogation, make the various provisions governing the subject on 1 January 1958 or, for acceding States, the date of their accession less favourable in their direct or indirect effect on carriers of other Member States as compared with carriers who are nationals of that State.

Article 93
(ex Article 73 TEC)

Aids shall be compatible with the Treaties if they meet the needs of coordination of transport or if they represent reimbursement for the discharge of certain obligations inherent in the concept of a public service.

Article 94
(ex Article 74 TEC)

Any measures taken within the framework of the Treaties in respect of transport rates and conditions shall take account of the economic circumstances of carriers.

Article 95
(ex Article 75 TEC)

1. In the case of transport within the Union, discrimination which takes the form of carriers charging different rates and imposing different conditions for the carriage of the same goods over the same transport links on grounds of the country of origin or of destination of the goods in question shall be prohibited.

2. Paragraph 1 shall not prevent the European Parliament and the Council from adopting other measures pursuant to Article 91(1).

3. The Council shall, on a proposal from the Commission and after consulting the European Parliament and the Economic and

Social Committee, lay down rules for implementing the provisions of paragraph 1.

The Council may in particular lay down the provisions needed to enable the institutions of the Union to secure compliance with the rule laid down in paragraph 1 and to ensure that users benefit from it to the full.

4. The Commission shall, acting on its own initiative or on application by a Member State, investigate any cases of discrimination falling within paragraph 1 and, after consulting any Member State concerned, shall take the necessary decisions within the framework of the rules laid down in accordance with the provisions of paragraph 3.

Article 96
(ex Article 76 TEC)

1. The imposition by a Member State, in respect of transport operations carried out within the Union, of rates and conditions involving any element of support or protection in the interest of one or more particular undertakings or industries shall be prohibited, unless authorised by the Commission.

2. The Commission shall, acting on its own initiative or on application by a Member State, examine the rates and conditions referred to in paragraph 1, taking account in particular of the requirements of an appropriate regional economic policy, the needs of underdeveloped areas and the problems of areas seriously affected by political circumstances on the one hand, and of the effects of such rates and conditions on competition between the different modes of transport on the other.

After consulting each Member State concerned, the Commission shall take the necessary decisions.

3. The prohibition provided for in paragraph 1 shall not apply to tariffs fixed to meet competition.

Article 97
(ex Article 77 TEC)

Charges or dues in respect of the crossing of frontiers which are charged by a carrier in addition to the transport rates shall not exceed a reasonable level after taking the costs actually incurred thereby into account.

Member States shall endeavour to reduce these costs progressively.

The Commission may make recommendations to Member States for the application of this Article.

Article 98
(ex Article 78 TEC)

The provisions of this Title shall not form an obstacle to the application of measures taken in the Federal Republic of Germany to the extent that such measures are required in order to compensate for the economic disadvantages caused by the division of Germany to the economy of certain areas of the Federal Republic affected by that division. Five years after the entry into force of the Treaty of Lisbon, the Council, acting on a proposal from the Commission, may adopt a decision repealing this Article.

Article 99
(ex Article 79 TEC)

An Advisory Committee consisting of experts designated by the governments of Member States shall be attached to the Commission. The Commission, whenever it considers it desirable, shall consult the Committee on transport matters.

Article 100
(ex Article 80 TEC)

1. The provisions of this Title shall apply to transport by rail, road and inland waterway.

2. The European Parliament and the Council, acting in accordance with the ordinary legislative procedure, may lay down appropriate provisions for sea and air transport. They shall act after consulting the Economic and Social Committee and the Committee of the Regions.

TITLE VII
COMMON RULES ON COMPETITION, TAXATION AND APPROXIMATION OF LAWS

CHAPTER 1
RULES ON COMPETITION

SECTION 1
RULES APPLYING TO UNDERTAKINGS

Article 101
(ex Article 81 TEC)

1. The following shall be prohibited as incompatible with the internal market: all agreements between undertakings, decisions by associations of undertakings and concerted practices which may affect trade between Member States and which have as their object or effect the prevention, restriction or distortion of competition within the internal market, and in particular those which:

(a) directly or indirectly fix purchase or selling prices or any other trading conditions;

(b) limit or control production, markets, technical development, or investment;

(c) share markets or sources of supply;

(d) apply dissimilar conditions to equivalent transactions with other trading parties, thereby placing them at a competitive disadvantage;

(e) make the conclusion of contracts subject to acceptance by the other parties of supplementary obligations which, by their nature or according to commercial usage, have no connection with the subject of such contracts.

2. Any agreements or decisions prohibited pursuant to this Article shall be automatically void.

3. The provisions of paragraph 1 may, however, be declared inapplicable in the case of:

— any agreement or category of agreements between undertakings,

— any decision or category of decisions by associations of undertakings,

— any concerted practice or category of concerted practices,

which contributes to improving the production or distribution of goods or to promoting technical or economic progress, while allowing consumers a fair share of the resulting benefit, and which does not:

(a) impose on the undertakings concerned restrictions which are not indispensable to the attainment of these objectives;

(b) afford such undertakings the possibility of eliminating competition in respect of a substantial part of the products in question.

Article 102
(ex Article 82 TEC)

Any abuse by one or more undertakings of a dominant position within the internal market or in a substantial part of it shall be prohibited as incompatible with the internal market in so far as it may affect trade between Member States.

Such abuse may, in particular, consist in:

(a) directly or indirectly imposing unfair purchase or selling prices or other unfair trading conditions;

(b) limiting production, markets or technical development to the prejudice of consumers;

(c) applying dissimilar conditions to equivalent transactions with other trading parties, thereby placing them at a competitive disadvantage;

(d) making the conclusion of contracts subject to acceptance by the other parties of supplementary obligations which, by their nature or according to commercial usage, have no connection with the subject of such contracts.

Article 103
(ex Article 83 TEC)

1. The appropriate regulations or directives to give effect to the principles set out in Articles 101 and 102 shall be laid down by the Council, on a proposal from the Commission and after consulting the European Parliament.

2. The regulations or directives referred to in paragraph 1 shall be designed in particular:

(a) to ensure compliance with the prohibitions laid down in Article 101(1) and in Article 102 by making provision for fines and periodic penalty payments;

(b) to lay down detailed rules for the application of Article 101(3), taking into account the need to ensure effective supervision on the one hand, and to simplify administration to the greatest possible extent on the other;

(c) to define, if need be, in the various branches of the economy, the scope of the provisions of Articles 101 and 102;

(d) to define the respective functions of the Commission and of the Court of Justice of the European Union in applying the provisions laid down in this paragraph;

(e) to determine the relationship between national laws and the provisions contained in this Section or adopted pursuant to this Article.

Article 104
(ex Article 84 TEC)

Until the entry into force of the provisions adopted in pursuance of Article 103, the authorities in Member States shall rule on the admissibility of agreements, decisions and concerted practices and on abuse of a dominant position in the internal market in accordance with the law of their country and with the provisions of Article 101, in particular paragraph 3, and of Article 102.

Article 105
(ex Article 85 TEC)

1. Without prejudice to Article 104, the Commission shall ensure the application of the principles laid down in Articles 101 and 102. On application by a Member State or on its own initiative, and in cooperation with the competent authorities in the Member States, which shall give it their assistance, the Commission shall investigate cases of suspected infringement of these principles. If it finds that there has been an infringement, it shall propose appropriate measures to bring it to an end.

2. If the infringement is not brought to an end, the Commission shall record such infringement of the principles in a reasoned decision. The Commission may publish its decision and authorise Member States to take the measures, the conditions and details of which it shall determine, needed to remedy the situation.

3. The Commission may adopt regulations relating to the categories of agreement in respect of which the Council has adopted a regulation or a directive pursuant to Article 103(2)(b).

Article 106
(ex Article 86 TEC)

1. In the case of public undertakings and undertakings to which Member States grant special or exclusive rights, Member States shall neither enact nor maintain in force any measure contrary to the rules contained in the Treaties, in particular to those rules provided for in Article 18 and Articles 101 to 109.

2. Undertakings entrusted with the operation of services of general economic interest or having the character of a revenue-producing monopoly shall be subject to the rules contained in the Treaties, in particular to the rules on competition, in so far as the application of such rules does not obstruct the performance, in law or in fact, of the particular tasks assigned to them. The development of trade must not be affected to such an extent as would be contrary to the interests of the Union.

3. The Commission shall ensure the application of the provisions of this Article and shall, where necessary, address appropriate directives or decisions to Member States.

SECTION 2
AIDS GRANTED BY STATES

Article 107
(ex Article 87 TEC)

1. Save as otherwise provided in the Treaties, any aid granted by a Member State or through State resources in any form whatsoever which distorts or threatens to distort competition by favouring certain undertakings or the production of certain goods shall, in so far as it affects trade between Member States, be incompatible with the internal market.

2. The following shall be compatible with the internal market:

(a) aid having a social character, granted to individual consumers, provided that such aid is granted without discrimination related to the origin of the products concerned;

(b) aid to make good the damage caused by natural disasters or exceptional occurrences;

(c) aid granted to the economy of certain areas of the Federal Republic of Germany affected by the division of Germany, in so far as such aid is required in order to compensate for the economic disadvantages caused by that division. Five years after the entry into force of the Treaty of Lisbon, the Council, acting on a proposal from the Commission, may adopt a decision repealing this point.

3. The following may be considered to be compatible with the internal market:

(a) aid to promote the economic development of areas where the standard of living is abnormally low or where there is serious underemployment, and of the regions referred to in Article 349, in view of their structural, economic and social situation;

(b) aid to promote the execution of an important project of common European interest or to remedy a serious disturbance in the economy of a Member State;

(c) aid to facilitate the development of certain economic activities or of certain economic areas, where such aid does not adversely affect trading conditions to an extent contrary to the common interest

(d) aid to promote culture and heritage conservation where such aid does not affect trading conditions and competition in the Union to an extent that is contrary to the common interest;

(e) such other categories of aid as may be specified by decision of the Council on a proposal from the Commission.

Article 108
(ex Article 88 TEC)

1. The Commission shall, in cooperation with Member States, keep under constant review all systems of aid existing in those States. It shall propose to the latter any appropriate measures required by the progressive development or by the functioning of the internal market.

2. If, after giving notice to the parties concerned to submit their comments, the Commission finds that aid granted by a State or through State resources is not compatible with the internal market having regard to Article 107, or that such aid is being misused, it shall decide that the State concerned shall abolish or alter such aid within a period of time to be determined by the Commission.

If the State concerned does not comply with this decision within the prescribed time, the Commission or any other interested State may, in derogation from the provisions of Articles 258 and 259, refer the matter to the Court of Justice of the European Union direct.

On application by a Member State, the Council may, acting unanimously, decide that aid which that State is granting or intends to grant shall be considered to be compatible with the internal market, in derogation from the provisions of Article 107 or from the regulations provided for in Article 109, if such a decision is justified by exceptional circumstances. If, as regards the aid in question, the Commission has already initiated the procedure provided for in the first subparagraph of this paragraph, the fact that the State concerned has made its application to the Council shall have the effect of suspending that procedure until the Council has made its attitude known.

If, however, the Council has not made its attitude known within three months of the said application being made, the Commission shall give its decision on the case.

3. The Commission shall be informed, in sufficient time to enable it to submit its comments, of any plans to grant or alter aid. If it considers that any such plan is not compatible with the internal market having regard to Article 107, it shall without delay initiate the procedure provided for in paragraph 2. The Member State concerned shall not put its proposed measures into effect until this procedure has resulted in a final decision.

4. The Commission may adopt regulations relating to the categories of State aid that the Council has, pursuant to Article 109,

determined may be exempted from the procedure provided for by paragraph 3 of this Article.

Article 109
(ex Article 89 TEC)

The Council, on a proposal from the Commission and after consulting the European Parliament, may make any appropriate regulations for the application of Articles 107 and 108 and may in particular determine the conditions in which Article 108(3) shall apply and the categories of aid exempted from this procedure.

CHAPTER 2
TAX PROVISIONS

Article 110
(ex Article 90 TEC)

No Member State shall impose, directly or indirectly, on the products of other Member States any internal taxation of any kind in excess of that imposed directly or indirectly on similar domestic products.

Furthermore, no Member State shall impose on the products of other Member States any internal taxation of such a nature as to afford indirect protection to other products.

Article 111
(ex Article 91 TEC)

Where products are exported to the territory of any Member State, any repayment of internal taxation shall not exceed the internal taxation imposed on them whether directly or indirectly.

Article 112
(ex Article 92 TEC)

In the case of charges other than turnover taxes, excise duties and other forms of indirect taxation, remissions and repayments in respect of exports to other Member States may not be granted and countervailing charges in respect of imports from Member States may not be imposed unless the measures contemplated have been previously approved for a limited period by the Council on a proposal from the Commission

Article 113
(ex Article 93 TEC)

The Council shall, acting unanimously in accordance with a special legislative procedure and after consulting the European Parliament and the Economic and Social Committee, adopt provisions for the harmonisation of legislation concerning turnover taxes, excise duties and other forms of indirect taxation to the extent that such harmonisation is necessary to ensure the establishment and the functioning of the internal market and to avoid distortion of competition.

CHAPTER 3
APPROXIMATION OF LAWS

Article 114
(ex Article 95 TEC)

1. Save where otherwise provided in the Treaties, the following provisions shall apply for the achievement of the objectives set out in Article 26. The European Parliament and the Council shall, acting in accordance with the ordinary legislative procedure and after consulting the Economic and Social Committee, adopt the measures for the approximation of the provisions laid down by law, regulation or administrative action in Member States which have as their object the establishment and functioning of the internal market.

2. Paragraph 1 shall not apply to fiscal provisions, to those relating to the free movement of persons nor to those relating to the rights and interests of employed persons.

3. The Commission, in its proposals envisaged in paragraph 1 concerning health, safety, environmental protection and consumer protection, will take as a base a high level of protection, taking account in particular of any new development based on scientific facts. Within their respective powers, the European Parliament and the Council will also seek to achieve this objective.

4. If, after the adoption of a harmonisation measure by the European Parliament and the Council, by the Council or by the Commission, a Member State deems it necessary to maintain national provisions on grounds of major needs referred to in Article 36, or relating to the protection of the environment or the working environment, it shall notify the Commission of these provisions as well as the grounds for maintaining them.

5. Moreover, without prejudice to paragraph 4, if, after the adoption of a harmonisation measure by the European Parliament and the Council, by the Council or by the Commission, a Member State deems it necessary to introduce national provisions based on new scientific evidence relating to the protection of the environment or the working environment on grounds of a problem specific to that Member State arising after the adoption of the harmonisation measure, it shall notify the Commission of the envisaged provisions as well as the grounds for introducing them.

6. The Commission shall, within six months of the notifications as referred to in paragraphs 4 and 5, approve or reject the national provisions involved after having verified whether or not they are a means of arbitrary discrimination or a disguised restriction on trade between Member States and whether or not they shall constitute an obstacle to the functioning of the internal market.

In the absence of a decision by the Commission within this period the national provisions referred to in paragraphs 4 and 5 shall be deemed to have been approved.

When justified by the complexity of the matter and in the absence of danger for human health, the Commission may notify the Member State concerned that the period referred to in this paragraph may be extended for a further period of up to six months.

7. When, pursuant to paragraph 6, a Member State is authorised to maintain or introduce national provisions derogating from a harmonisation measure, the Commission shall immediately examine whether to propose an adaptation to that measure.

8. When a Member State raises a specific problem on public health in a field which has been the subject of prior harmonisation measures, it shall bring it to the attention of the Commission which shall immediately examine whether to propose appropriate measures to the Council.

9. By way of derogation from the procedure laid down in Articles 258 and 259, the Commission and any Member State may bring the matter directly before the Court of Justice of the European Union if it considers that another Member State is making improper use of the powers provided for in this Article.

10. The harmonisation measures referred to above shall, in appropriate cases, include a safeguard clause authorising the Member States to take, for one or more of the non-economic reasons referred to in Article 36, provisional measures subject to a Union control procedure.

Article 115
(ex Article 94 TEC)

Without prejudice to Article 114, the Council shall, acting unanimously in accordance with a special legislative procedure and after consulting the European Parliament and the Economic and Social Committee, issue directives for the approximation of such laws, regulations or administrative provisions of the Member States as directly affect the establishment or functioning of the internal market.

Article 116
(ex Article 96 TEC)

Where the Commission finds that a difference between the provisions laid down by law, regulation or administrative action in Member States is distorting the conditions of competition in the internal market and that the resultant distortion needs to be eliminated, it shall consult the Member States concerned.

If such consultation does not result in an agreement eliminating the distortion in question, the European, Parliament and the Council, acting in accordance with the ordinary legislative procedure, shall issue the necessary directives. Any other appropriate measures provided for in the Treaties may be adopted.

Article 117
(ex Article 97 TEC)

1. Where there is a reason to fear that the adoption or amendment of a provision laid down by law, regulation or administrative action may cause distortion within the meaning of Article 116, a Member State desiring to proceed therewith shall consult the Commission. After consulting the Member States, the Commission shall recommend to the States concerned such measures as may be appropriate to avoid the distortion in question.

2. If a State desiring to introduce or amend its own provisions does not comply with the recommendation addressed to it by the Commission, other Member States shall not be required, pursuant to Article 116, to amend their own provisions in order to eliminate such distortion. If the Member State which has ignored the recommendation of the Commission causes distortion detrimental only to itself, the provisions of Article 116 shall not apply.

Article 118

In the context of the establishment and functioning of the internal market, the European Parliament and the Council, acting in accordance with the ordinary legislative procedure, shall establish measures for the creation of European intellectual property rights to provide uniform protection of intellectual property rights throughout the Union and for the setting up of centralised Union-wide authorisation, coordination and supervision arrangements.

The Council, acting in accordance with a special legislative procedure, shall by means of regulations establish language arrangements for the European intellectual property rights. The Council shall act unanimously after consulting the European Parliament.

TITLE VIII
ECONOMIC AND MONETARY POLICY

Article 119
(ex Article 4 TEC)

1. For the purposes set out in Article 3 of the Treaty on European Union, the activities of the Member States and the Union shall include, as provided in the Treaties, the adoption of an economic policy which is based on the close coordination of Member States' economic policies, on the internal market and on the definition of common objectives, and conducted in accordance with the principle of an open market economy with free competition.

2. Concurrently with the foregoing, and as provided in the Treaties and in accordance with the procedures set out therein, these activities shall include a single currency, the euro, and the definition and conduct of a single monetary policy and exchange-rate policy the primary objective of both of which shall be to maintain price stability and, without prejudice to this objective, to support the general economic policies in the Union, in accordance with the principle of an open market economy with free competition.

3. These activities of the Member States and the Union shall entail compliance with the following guiding principles: stable prices, sound public finances and monetary conditions and a sustainable balance of payments.

CHAPTER 1
ECONOMIC POLICY

Article 120
(ex Article 98 TEC)

Member States shall conduct their economic policies with a view to contributing to the achievement of the objectives of the Union, as defined in Article 3 of the Treaty on European Union, and in the context of the broad guidelines referred to in Article 121(2). The Member States and the Union shall act in accordance with the principle of an open market economy with free competition, favouring an efficient allocation of resources, and in compliance with the principles set out in Article 119.

Article 121
(ex Article 99 TEC)

1. Member States shall regard their economic policies as a matter of common concern and shall coordinate them within the Council, in accordance with the provisions of Article 120.

2. The Council shall, on a recommendation from the Commission, formulate a draft for the broad guidelines of the economic policies of the Member States and of the Union, and shall report its findings to the European Council.

The European Council shall, acting on the basis of the report from the Council, discuss a conclusion on the broad guidelines of the economic policies of the Member States and of the Union.

On the basis of this conclusion, the Council shall adopt a recommendation setting out these broad guidelines. The Council shall inform the European Parliament of its recommendation.

3. In order to ensure closer coordination of economic policies and sustained convergence of the economic performances of the Member States, the Council shall, on the basis of reports submitted by the Commission, monitor economic developments in each of the Member States and in the Union as well as the consistency of economic policies with the broad guidelines referred to in paragraph 2, and regularly carry out an overall assessment.

For the purpose of this multilateral surveillance, Member States shall forward information to the Commission about important measures taken by them in the field of their economic policy and such other information as they deem necessary.

4. Where it is established, under the procedure referred to in paragraph 3, that the economic policies of a Member State are not consistent with the broad guidelines referred to in paragraph 2 or that they risk jeopardising the proper functioning of economic and monetary union, the Commission may address a warning to the Member State concerned. The Council, on a recommendation from the Commission, may address the necessary recommendations to the Member State concerned. The Council may, on a proposal from the Commission, decide to make its recommendations public.

Within the scope of this paragraph, the Council shall act without taking into account the vote of the member of the Council representing the Member State concerned.

A qualified majority of the other members of the Council shall be defined in accordance with Article 238(3)(a).

5. The President of the Council and the Commission shall report to the European Parliament on the results of multilateral surveillance. The President of the Council may be invited to appear before the competent committee of the European Parliament if the Council has made its recommendations public.

6. The European Parliament and the Council, acting by means of regulations in accordance with the ordinary legislative procedure,

may adopt detailed rules for the multilateral surveillance procedure referred to in paragraphs 3 and 4.

Article 122
(ex Article 100 TEC)

1. Without prejudice to any other procedures provided for in the Treaties, the Council, on a proposal from the Commission, may decide, in a spirit of solidarity between Member States, upon the measures appropriate to the economic situation, in particular if severe difficulties arise in the supply of certain products, notably in the area of energy.

2. Where a Member State is in difficulties or is seriously threatened with severe difficulties caused by natural disasters or exceptional occurrences beyond its control, the Council, on a proposal from the Commission may grant, under certain conditions, Union financial assistance to the Member State concerned. The President of the Council shall inform the European Parliament of the decision taken.

Article 123
(ex Article 101 TEC)

1. Overdraft facilities or any other type of credit facility with the European Central Bank or with the central banks of the Member States (hereinafter referred to as "national central banks") in favour of Union institutions, bodies, offices or agencies, central governments, regional, local or other public authorities, other bodies governed by public law, or public undertakings of Member States shall be prohibited, as shall the purchase directly from them by the European Central Bank or national central banks of debt instruments.

2. Paragraph 1 shall not apply to publicly owned credit institutions which, in the context of the supply of reserves by central banks, shall be given the same treatment by national central banks and the European Central Bank as private credit institutions.

Article 124
(ex Article 102 TEC)

Any measure, not based on prudential considerations, establishing privileged access by Union institutions, bodies, offices or agencies, central governments, regional, local or other public authorities, other bodies governed by public law, or public undertakings of Member States to financial institutions, shall be prohibited.

Article 125
(ex Article 103 TEC)

1. The Union shall not be liable for or assume the commitments of central governments, regional, local or other public authorities, other bodies governed by public law, or public undertakings of any Member State, without prejudice to mutual financial guarantees for the joint execution of a specific project. A Member State shall not be liable for or assume the commitments of central governments, regional, local or other public authorities, other bodies governed by public law, or public undertakings of another Member State, without prejudice to mutual financial guarantees for the joint execution of a specific project.

2. The Council, on a proposal from the Commission and after consulting the European Parliament, may, as required, specify definitions for the application of the prohibitions referred to in Articles 123 and 124 and in this Article.

Article 126
(ex Article 104 TEC)

1. Member States shall avoid excessive government deficits.

2. The Commission shall monitor the development of the budgetary situation and of the stock of government debt in the Member States with a view to identifying gross errors. In particular it shall examine compliance with budgetary discipline on the basis of the following two criteria:

(a) whether the ratio of the planned or actual government deficit to gross domestic product exceeds a reference value, unless:

— either the ratio has declined substantially and continuously and reached a level that comes close to the reference value,

— or, alternatively, the excess over the reference value is only exceptional and temporary and the ratio remains close to the reference value;

(b) whether the ratio of government debt to gross domestic product exceeds a reference value, unless the ratio is sufficiently diminishing and approaching the reference value at a satisfactory pace.

The reference values are specified in the Protocol on the excessive deficit procedure annexed to the Treaties.

3. If a Member State does not fulfil the requirements under one or both of these criteria, the Commission shall prepare a report.

The report of the Commission shall also take into account whether the government deficit exceeds government investment expenditure and take into account all other relevant factors, including the medium-term economic and budgetary position of the Member State.

The Commission may also prepare a report if, notwithstanding the fulfilment of the requirements under the criteria, it is of the opinion that there is a risk of an excessive deficit in a Member State.

4. The Economic and Financial Committee shall formulate an opinion on the report of the Commission.

5. If the Commission considers that an excessive deficit in a Member State exists or may occur, it shall address an opinion to the Member State concerned and shall inform the Council accordingly.

6. The Council shall, on a proposal from the Commission, and having considered any observations which the Member State concerned may wish to make, decide after an overall assessment whether an excessive deficit exists.

7. Where the Council decides, in accordance with paragraph 6, that an excessive deficit exists, it shall adopt, without undue delay, on a recommendation from the Commission, recommendations addressed to the Member State concerned with a view to bringing that situation to an end within a given period. Subject to the provisions of paragraph 8, these recommendations shall not be made public.

8. Where it establishes that there has been no effective action in response to its recommendations within the period laid down, the Council may make its recommendations public.

9. If a Member State persists in failing to put into practice the recommendations of the Council, the Council may decide to give notice to the Member State to take, within a specified time limit, measures for the deficit reduction which is judged necessary by the Council in order to remedy the situation.

In such a case, the Council may request the Member State concerned to submit reports in accordance with a specific timetable in order to examine the adjustment efforts of that Member State.

10. The rights to bring actions provided for in Articles 258 and 259 may not be exercised within the framework of paragraphs 1 to 9 of this Article.

11. As long as a Member State fails to comply with a decision taken in accordance with paragraph 9, the Council may decide to apply or, as the case may be, intensify one or more of the following measures:

— to require the Member State concerned to publish additional information, to be specified by the Council, before issuing bonds and securities,

— to invite the European Investment Bank to reconsider its lending policy towards the Member State concerned,

— to require the Member State concerned to make a non-interest-bearing deposit of an appropriate size with the Union until the excessive deficit has, in the view of the Council, been corrected,

— to impose fines of an appropriate size.

The President of the Council shall inform the European Parliament of the decisions taken.

12. The Council shall abrogate some or all of its decisions or recommendations referred to in paragraphs 6 to 9 and 11 to the extent that the excessive deficit in the Member State concerned has, in the view of the Council, been corrected. If the Council has previously made public recommendations, it shall, as soon as the decision under paragraph 8 has been abrogated, make a public statement that an excessive deficit in the Member State concerned no longer exists.

13. When taking the decisions or recommendations referred to in paragraphs 8, 9, 11 and 12, the Council shall act on a recommendation from the Commission.

When the Council adopts the measures referred to in paragraphs 6 to 9, 11 and 12, it shall act without taking into account the vote of the member of the Council representing the Member State concerned.

A qualified majority of the other members of the Council shall be defined in accordance with Article 238(3)(a).

14. Further provisions relating to the implementation of the procedure described in this Article are set out in the Protocol on the excessive deficit procedure annexed to the Treaties.

The Council shall, acting unanimously in accordance with a special legislative procedure and after consulting the European Parliament and the European Central Bank, adopt the appropriate provisions which shall then replace the said Protocol.

Subject to the other provisions of this paragraph, the Council shall, on a proposal from the Commission and after consulting the European Parliament, lay down detailed rules and definitions for the application of the provisions of the said Protocol.

CHAPTER 2
MONETARY POLICY

Article 127

(ex Article 105 TEC)

1. The primary objective of the European System of Central Banks (hereinafter referred to as "the ESCB") shall be to maintain price stability. Without prejudice to the objective of price stability, the ESCB shall support the general economic policies in the Union with a view to contributing to the achievement of the objectives of the Union as laid down in Article 3 of the Treaty on European Union. The ESCB shall act in accordance with the principle of an open market economy with free competition, favouring an efficient allocation of resources, and in compliance with the principles set out in Article 119.

2. The basic tasks to be carried out through the ESCB shall be:

— to define and implement the monetary policy of the Union,

— to conduct foreign-exchange operations consistent with the provisions of Article 219,

— to hold and manage the official foreign reserves of the Member States,

— to promote the smooth operation of payment systems.

3. The third indent of paragraph 2 shall be without prejudice to the holding and management by the governments of Member States of foreign-exchange working balances.

4. The European Central Bank shall be consulted:

— on any proposed Union act in its fields of competence,

— by national authorities regarding any draft legislative provision in its fields of competence, but within the limits and under the conditions set out by the Council in accordance with the procedure laid down in Article 129(4).

The European Central Bank may submit opinions to the appropriate Union institutions, bodies, offices or agencies or to national authorities on matters in its fields of competence.

5. The ESCB shall contribute to the smooth conduct of policies pursued by the competent authorities relating to the prudential supervision of credit institutions and the stability of the financial system.

6. The Council, acting by means of regulations in accordance with a special legislative procedure, may unanimously, and after consulting the European Parliament and the European Central Bank, confer specific tasks upon the European Central Bank concerning policies relating to the prudential supervision of credit institutions and other financial institutions with the exception of insurance undertakings.

Article 128
(ex Article 106 TEC)

1. The European Central Bank shall have the exclusive right to authorise the issue of euro banknotes within the Union. The European Central Bank and the national central banks may issue such notes. The banknotes issued by the European Central Bank and the national central banks shall be the only such notes to have the status of legal tender within the Union.

2. Member States may issue euro coins subject to approval by the European Central Bank of the volume of the issue. The Council, on a proposal from the Commission and after consulting the European Parliament and the European Central Bank, may adopt measures to harmonise the denominations and technical specifications of all coins intended for circulation to the extent necessary to permit their smooth circulation within the Union.

Article 129
(ex Article 107 TEC)

1. The ESCB shall be governed by the decision-making bodies of the European Central Bank which shall be the Governing Council and the Executive Board.

2. The Statute of the European System of Central Banks and of the European Central Bank (hereinafter referred to as "the Statute of the ESCB and of the ECB") is laid down in a Protocol annexed to the Treaties.

3. Articles 5.1, 5.2, 5.3, 17, 18, 19.1, 22, 23, 24, 26, 32.2, 32.3, 32.4, 32.6, 33.1(a) and 36 of the Statute of the ESCB and of the ECB may be amended by the European Parliament and the Council, acting in accordance with the ordinary legislative procedure. They shall act either on a recommendation from the European Central Bank and after consulting the Commission or on a proposal from the Commission and after consulting the European Central Bank.

4. The Council, either on a proposal from the Commission and after consulting the European Parliament and the European Central Bank or on a recommendation from the European Central Bank and after consulting the European Parliament and the Commission, shall

adopt the provisions referred to in Articles 4, 5.4, 19.2, 20, 28.1, 29.2, 30.4 and 34.3 of the Statute of the ESCB and of the ECB.

Article 130
(ex Article 108 TEC)

When exercising the powers and carrying out the tasks and duties conferred upon them by the Treaties and the Statute of the ESCB and of the ECB, neither the European Central Bank, nor a national central bank, nor any member of their decision-making bodies shall seek or take instructions from Union institutions, bodies, offices or agencies, from any government of a Member State or from any other body. The Union institutions, bodies, offices or agencies and the governments of the Member States undertake to respect this principle and not to seek to influence the members of the decision-making bodies of the European Central Bank or of the national central banks in the performance of their tasks.

Article 131
(ex Article 109 TEC)

Each Member State shall ensure that its national legislation including the statutes of its national central bank is compatible with the Treaties and the Statute of the ESCB and of the ECB.

Article 132
(ex Article 110 TEC)

1. In order to carry out the tasks entrusted to the ESCB, the European Central Bank shall, in accordance with the provisions of the Treaties and under the conditions laid down in the Statute of the ESCB and of the ECB:

— make regulations to the extent necessary to implement the tasks defined in Article 3.1, first indent, Articles 19.1, 22 and 25.2 of the Statute of the ESCB and of the ECB in cases which shall be laid down in the acts of the Council referred to in Article 129(4),

— take decisions necessary for carrying out the tasks entrusted to the ESCB under the Treaties and the Statute of the ESCB and of the ECB,

— make recommendations and deliver opinions.

2. The European Central Bank may decide to publish its decisions, recommendations and opinions.

3. Within the limits and under the conditions adopted by the Council under the procedure laid down in Article 129(4), the European Central Bank shall be entitled to impose fines or periodic

penalty payments on undertakings for failure to comply with obligations under its regulations and decisions.

Article 133

Without prejudice to the powers of the European Central Bank, the European Parliament and the Council, acting in accordance with the ordinary legislative procedure, shall lay down the measures necessary for the use of the euro as the single currency. Such measures shall be adopted after consultation of the European Central Bank.

CHAPTER 3
INSTITUTIONAL PROVISIONS

Article 134
(ex Article 114 TEC)

1. In order to promote coordination of the policies of Member States to the full extent needed for the functioning of the internal market, an Economic and Financial Committee is hereby set up.

2. The Economic and Financial Committee shall have the following tasks:

— to deliver opinions at the request of the Council or of the Commission, or on its own initiative for submission to those institutions,

— to keep under review the economic and financial situation of the Member States and of the Union and to report regularly thereon to the Council and to the Commission, in particular on financial relations with third countries and international institutions,

— without prejudice to Article 240, to contribute to the preparation of the work of the Council referred to in Articles 66, 75, 121(2), (3), (4) and (6), 122, 124, 125, 126, 127(6), 128(2), 129(3) and (4), 138, 140(2) and (3), 143, 144(2) and (3), and in Article 219, and to carry out other advisory and preparatory tasks assigned to it by the Council,

— to examine, at least once a year, the situation regarding the movement of capital and the freedom of payments, as they result from the application of the Treaties and of measures adopted by the Council; the examination shall cover all measures relating to capital movements and payments; the Committee shall report to the Commission and to the Council on the outcome of this examination.

The Member States, the Commission and the European Central Bank shall each appoint no more than two members of the Committee.

3. The Council shall, on a proposal from the Commission and after consulting the European Central Bank and the Committee referred to in this Article, lay down detailed provisions concerning the composition of the Economic and Financial Committee. The President of the Council shall inform the European Parliament of such a decision.

4. In addition to the tasks set out in paragraph 2, if and as long as there are Member States with a derogation as referred to in Article 139, the Committee shall keep under review the monetary and financial situation and the general payments system of those Member States and report regularly thereon to the Council and to the Commission.

Article 135
(ex Article 115 TEC)

For matters within the scope of Articles 121(4), 126 with the exception of paragraph 14, 138, 140(1), 140(2), first subparagraph, 140(3) and 219, the Council or a Member State may request the Commission to make a recommendation or a proposal, as appropriate. The Commission shall examine this request and submit its conclusions to the Council without delay.

CHAPTER 4
PROVISIONS SPECIFIC TO MEMBER STATES WHOSE CURRENCY IS THE EURO

Article 136

1. In order to ensure the proper functioning of economic and monetary union, and in accordance with the relevant provisions of the Treaties, the Council shall, in accordance with the relevant procedure from among those referred to in Articles 121 and 126, with the exception of the procedure set out in Article 126(14), adopt measures specific to those Member States whose currency is the euro:

(a) to strengthen the coordination and surveillance of their budgetary discipline;

(b) to set out economic policy guidelines for them, while ensuring that they are compatible with those adopted for the whole of the Union and are kept under surveillance.

2. For those measures set out in paragraph 1, only members of the Council representing Member States whose currency is the euro shall take part in the vote.

A qualified majority of the said members shall be defined in accordance with Article 238(3)(a).

Article 137

Arrangements for meetings between ministers of those Member States whose currency is the euro are laid down by the Protocol on the Euro Group.

Article 138
(ex Article 111(4), TEC)

1. In order to secure the euro's place in the international monetary system, the Council, on a proposal from the Commission, shall adopt a decision establishing common positions on matters of particular interest for economic and monetary union within the competent international financial institutions and conferences. The Council shall act after consulting the European Central Bank.

2. The Council, on a proposal from the Commission, may adopt appropriate measures to ensure unified representation within the international financial institutions and conferences. The Council shall act after consulting the European Central Bank.

3. For the measures referred to in paragraphs 1 and 2, only members of the Council representing Member States whose currency is the euro shall take part in the vote.

A qualified majority of the said members shall be defined in accordance with Article 238(3)(a).

CHAPTER 5
TRANSITIONAL PROVISIONS

Article 139

1. Member States in respect of which the Council has not decided that they fulfil the necessary conditions for the adoption of the euro shall hereinafter be referred to as "Member States with a derogation".

2. The following provisions of the Treaties shall not apply to Member States with a derogation:

(a) adoption of the parts of the broad economic policy guidelines which concern the euro area generally (Article 121(2));

(b) coercive means of remedying excessive deficits (Article 126(9) and (11));

(c) the objectives and tasks of the ESCB (Article 127(1) to (3) and (5));

(d) issue of the euro (Article 128);

(e) acts of the European Central Bank (Article 132);

(f) measures governing the use of the euro (Article 133);

(g) monetary agreements and other measures relating to exchange-rate policy (Article 219);

(h) appointment of members of the Executive Board of the European Central Bank (Article 283(2));

(i) decisions establishing common positions on issues of particular relevance for economic and monetary union within the competent international financial institutions and conferences (Article 138(1));

(j) measures to ensure unified representation within the international financial institutions and conferences (Article 138(2)).

In the Articles referred to in points (a) to (j), "Member States" shall therefore mean Member States whose currency is the euro.

3. Under Chapter IX of the Statute of the ESCB and of the ECB, Member States with a derogation and their national central banks are excluded from rights and obligations within the ESCB.

4. The voting rights of members of the Council representing Member States with a derogation shall be suspended for the adoption by the Council of the measures referred to in the Articles listed in paragraph 2, and in the following instances:

(a) recommendations made to those Member States whose currency is the euro in the framework of multilateral surveillance, including on stability programmes and warnings (Article 121(4));

(b) measures relating to excessive deficits concerning those Member States whose currency is the euro (Article 126(6), (7), (8), (12) and (13)).

A qualified majority of the other members of the Council shall be defined in accordance with Article 238(3)(a).

Article 140

(ex Articles 121(1), 122(2), second sentence, and 123(5) TEC)

1. At least once every two years, or at the request of a Member State with a derogation, the Commission and the European Central Bank shall report to the Council on the progress made by the Member States with a derogation in fulfilling their obligations regarding the achievement of economic and monetary union. These reports shall include an examination of the compatibility between the national

legislation of each of these Member States, including the statutes of its national central bank, and Articles 130 and 131 and the Statute of the ESCB and of the ECB. The reports shall also examine the achievement of a high degree of sustainable convergence by reference to the fulfilment by each Member State of the following criteria:

— the achievement of a high degree of price stability; this will be apparent from a rate of inflation which is close to that of, at most, the three best performing Member States in terms of price stability,

— the sustainability of the government financial position; this will be apparent from having achieved a government budgetary position without a deficit that is excessive as determined in accordance with Article 126(6),

— the observance of the normal fluctuation margins provided for by the exchange-rate mechanism of the European Monetary System, for at least two years, without devaluing against the euro,

— the durability of convergence achieved by the Member State with a derogation and of its participation in the exchange-rate mechanism being reflected in the long-term interest-rate levels.

The four criteria mentioned in this paragraph and the relevant periods over which they are to be respected are developed further in a Protocol annexed to the Treaties. The reports of the Commission and the European Central Bank shall also take account of the results of the integration of markets, the situation and development of the balances of payments on current account and an examination of the development of unit labour costs and other price indices.

2. After consulting the European Parliament and after discussion in the European Council, the Council shall, on a proposal from the Commission, decide which Member States with a derogation fulfil the necessary conditions on the basis of the criteria set out in paragraph 1, and abrogate the derogations of the Member States concerned.

The Council shall act having received a recommendation of a qualified majority of those among its members representing Member States whose currency is the euro. These members shall act within six months of the Council receiving the Commission's proposal. The qualified majority of the said members, as referred to in the second subparagraph, shall be defined in accordance with Article 238(3)(a).

3. If it is decided, in accordance with the procedure set out in paragraph 2, to abrogate a derogation, the Council shall, acting with

the unanimity of the Member States whose currency is the euro and the Member State concerned, on a proposal from the Commission and after consulting the European Central Bank, irrevocably fix the rate at which the euro shall be substituted for the currency of the Member State concerned, and take the other measures necessary for the introduction of the euro as the single currency in the Member State concerned.

Article 141

(ex Articles 123(3) and 117(2) first five indents, TEC)

1. If and as long as there are Member States with a derogation, and without prejudice to Article 129(1), the General Council of the European Central Bank referred to in Article 44 of the Statute of the ESCB and of the ECB shall be constituted as a third decision-making body of the European Central Bank.

2. If and as long as there are Member States with a derogation, the European Central Bank shall, as regards those Member States:

— strengthen cooperation between the national central banks,

— strengthen the coordination of the monetary policies of the Member States, with the aim of ensuring price stability,

— monitor the functioning of the exchange-rate mechanism,

— hold consultations concerning issues falling within the competence of the national central banks and affecting the stability of financial institutions and markets,

— carry out the former tasks of the European Monetary Cooperation Fund which had subsequently been taken over by the European Monetary Institute.

Article 142

(ex Article 124(1) TEC)

Each Member State with a derogation shall treat its exchange-rate policy as a matter of common interest. In so doing, Member States shall take account of the experience acquired in cooperation within the framework of the exchange-rate mechanism.

Article 143

(ex Article 119 TEC)

1. Where a Member State with a derogation is in difficulties or is seriously threatened with difficulties as regards its balance of payments either as a result of an overall disequilibrium in its balance

of payments, or as a result of the type of currency at its disposal, and where such difficulties are liable in particular to jeopardise the functioning of the internal market or the implementation of the common commercial policy, the Commission shall immediately investigate the position of the State in question and the action which, making use of all the means at its disposal, that State has taken or may take in accordance with the provisions of the Treaties. The Commission shall state what measures it recommends the State concerned to take.

If the action taken by a Member State with a derogation and the measures suggested by the Commission do not prove sufficient to overcome the difficulties which have arisen or which threaten, the Commission shall, after consulting the Economic and Financial Committee, recommend to the Council the granting of mutual assistance and appropriate methods therefor.

The Commission shall keep the Council regularly informed of the situation and of how it is developing.

2. The Council shall grant such mutual assistance; it shall adopt directives or decisions laying down the conditions and details of such assistance, which may take such forms as:

(a) a concerted approach to or within any other international organisations to which Member States with a derogation may have recourse;

(b) measures needed to avoid deflection of trade where the Member State with a derogation which is in difficulties maintains or reintroduces quantitative restrictions against third countries;

(c) the granting of limited credits by other Member States, subject to their agreement.

3. If the mutual assistance recommended by the Commission is not granted by the Council or if the mutual assistance granted and the measures taken are insufficient, the Commission shall authorise the Member State with a derogation which is in difficulties to take protective measures, the conditions and details of which the Commission shall determine.

Such authorisation may be revoked and such conditions and details may be changed by the Council.

Article 144
(ex Article 120 TEC)

1. Where a sudden crisis in the balance of payments occurs and a decision within the meaning of Article 143(2) is not

immediately taken, a Member State with a derogation may, as a precaution, take the necessary protective measures. Such measures must cause the least possible disturbance in the functioning of the internal market and must not be wider in scope than is strictly necessary to remedy the sudden difficulties which have arisen.

2. The Commission and the other Member States shall be informed of such protective measures not later than when they enter into force. The Commission may recommend to the Council the granting of mutual assistance under Article 143.

3. After the Commission has delivered a recommendation and the Economic and Financial Committee has been consulted, the Council may decide that the Member State concerned shall amend, suspend or abolish the protective measures referred to above.

TITLE IX
EMPLOYMENT

Article 145
(ex Article 125 TEC)

Member States and the Union shall, in accordance with this Title, work towards developing a coordinated strategy for employment and particularly for promoting a skilled, trained and adaptable workforce and labour markets responsive to economic change with a view to achieving the objectives defined in Article 3 of the Treaty on European Union.

Article 146
(ex Article 126 TEC)

1. Member States, through their employment policies, shall contribute to the achievement of the objectives referred to in Article 145 in a way consistent with the broad guidelines of the economic policies of the Member States and of the Union adopted pursuant to Article 121(2).

2. Member States, having regard to national practices related to the responsibilities of management and labour, shall regard promoting employment as a matter of common concern and shall coordinate their action in this respect within the Council, in accordance with the provisions of Article 148.

Article 147
(ex Article 127 TEC)

1. The Union shall contribute to a high level of employment by encouraging cooperation between Member States and by supporting and, if necessary, complementing their action. In doing so, the competences of the Member States shall be respected.

2. The objective of a high level of employment shall be taken into consideration in the formulation and implementation of Union policies and activities.

Article 148
(ex Article 128 TEC)

1. The European Council shall each year consider the employment situation in the Union and adopt conclusions thereon, on the basis of a joint annual report by the Council and the Commission.

2. On the basis of the conclusions of the European Council, the Council, on a proposal from the Commission and after consulting the European Parliament, the Economic and Social Committee, the Committee of the Regions and the Employment Committee referred to in Article 150, shall each year draw up guidelines which the Member States shall take into account in their employment policies. These guidelines shall be consistent with the broad guidelines adopted pursuant to Article 121(2).

3. Each Member State shall provide the Council and the Commission with an annual report on the principal measures taken to implement its employment policy in the light of the guidelines for employment as referred to in paragraph 2.

4. The Council, on the basis of the reports referred to in paragraph 3 and having received the views of the Employment Committee, shall each year carry out an examination of the implementation of the employment policies of the Member States in the light of the guidelines for employment. The Council, on a recommendation from the Commission, may, if it considers it appropriate in the light of that examination, make recommendations to Member States.

5. On the basis of the results of that examination, the Council and the Commission shall make a joint annual report to the European Council on the employment situation in the Union and on the implementation of the guidelines for employment.

Article 149
(ex Article 129 TEC)

The European Parliament and the Council, acting in accordance with the ordinary legislative procedure and after consulting the Economic and Social Committee and the Committee of the Regions, may adopt incentive measures designed to encourage cooperation between Member States and to support their action in the field of employment through initiatives aimed at developing exchanges of information and best practices, providing comparative analysis and advice as well as promoting innovative approaches and evaluating experiences, in particular by recourse to pilot projects.

Those measures shall not include harmonisation of the laws and regulations of the Member States.

Article 150
(ex Article 130 TEC)

The Council, acting by a simple majority after consulting the European Parliament, shall establish an Employment Committee with advisory status to promote coordination between Member States on employment and labour market policies. The tasks of the Committee shall be:

— to monitor the employment situation and employment policies in the Member States and the Union,

— without prejudice to Article 240, to formulate opinions at the request of either the Council or the Commission or on its own initiative, and to contribute to the preparation of the Council proceedings referred to in Article 148.

In fulfilling its mandate, the Committee shall consult management and labour.

Each Member State and the Commission shall appoint two members of the Committee.

TITLE X
SOCIAL POLICY

Article 151
(ex Article 136 TEC)

The Union and the Member States, having in mind fundamental social rights such as those set out in the European Social Charter signed at Turin on 18 October 1961 and in the 1989 Community Charter of the Fundamental Social Rights of Workers, shall have as their objectives the promotion of employment, improved living and working conditions, so as to make possible their harmonisation while the improvement is being maintained, proper social protection, dialogue between management and labour, the development of human resources with a view to lasting high employment and the combating of exclusion.

To this end the Union and the Member States shall implement measures which take account of the diverse forms of national practices, in particular in the field of contractual relations, and the need to maintain the competitiveness of the Union's economy.

They believe that such a development will ensue not only from the functioning of the internal market, which will favour the harmonisation of social systems, but also from the procedures provided for in the Treaties and from the approximation of provisions laid down by law, regulation or administrative action.

Article 152

The Union recognises and promotes the role of the social partners at its level, taking into account the diversity of national systems. It shall facilitate dialogue between the social partners, respecting their autonomy.

The Tripartite Social Summit for Growth and Employment shall contribute to social dialogue.

Article 153
(ex Article 137 TEC)

1. With a view to achieving the objectives of Article 151, the Union shall support and complement the activities of the Member States in the following fields:

(a) improvement in particular of the working environment to protect workers' health and safety;

(b) working conditions;

(c) social security and social protection of workers;

(d) protection of workers where their employment contract is terminated;

(e) the information and consultation of workers;

(f) representation and collective defence of the interests of workers and employers, including co-determination, subject to paragraph 5;

(g) conditions of employment for third-country nationals legally residing in Union territory;

(h) the integration of persons excluded from the labour market, without prejudice to Article 166;

(i) equality between men and women with regard to labour market opportunities and treatment at work;

(j) the combating of social exclusion;

(k) the modernisation of social protection systems without prejudice to point (c).

2. To this end, the European Parliament and the Council:

(a) may adopt measures designed to encourage cooperation between Member States through initiatives aimed at improving knowledge, developing exchanges of information and best practices, promoting innovative approaches and evaluating experiences, excluding any harmonisation of the laws and regulations of the Member States;

(b) may adopt, in the fields referred to in paragraph 1(a) to (i), by means of directives, minimum requirements for gradual implementation, having regard to the conditions and technical rules obtaining in each of the Member States. Such directives shall avoid imposing administrative, financial and legal constraints in a way which would hold back the creation and development of small and medium-sized undertakings.

The European Parliament and the Council shall act in accordance with the ordinary legislative procedure after consulting the Economic and Social Committee and the Committee of the Regions.

In the fields referred to in paragraph 1(c), (d), (f) and (g), the Council shall act unanimously, in accordance with a special legislative procedure, after consulting the European Parliament and the said Committees.

The Council, acting unanimously on a proposal from the Commission, after consulting the European Parliament, may decide to render the ordinary legislative procedure applicable to paragraph 1(d), (f) and (g).

3. A Member State may entrust management and labour, at their joint request, with the implementation of directives adopted pursuant to paragraph 2, or, where appropriate, with the implementation of a Council decision adopted in accordance with Article 155.

In this case, it shall ensure that, no later than the date on which a directive or a decision must be transposed or implemented, management and labour have introduced the necessary measures by agreement, the Member State concerned being required to take any necessary measure enabling it at any time to be in a position to guarantee the results imposed by that directive or that decision.

4. The provisions adopted pursuant to this Article:

— shall not affect the right of Member States to define the fundamental principles of their social security systems and must not significantly affect the financial equilibrium thereof,

— shall not prevent any Member State from maintaining or introducing more stringent protective measures compatible with the Treaties.

5. The provisions of this Article shall not apply to pay, the right of association, the right to strike or the right to impose lock-outs.

Article 154
(ex Article 138 TEC)

1. The Commission shall have the task of promoting the consultation of management and labour at Union level and shall take any relevant measure to facilitate their dialogue by ensuring balanced support for the parties.

2. To this end, before submitting proposals in the social policy field, the Commission shall consult management and labour on the possible direction of Union action.

3. If, after such consultation, the Commission considers Union action advisable, it shall consult management and labour on the content of the envisaged proposal. Management and labour shall forward to the Commission an opinion or, where appropriate, a recommendation.

4. On the occasion of the consultation referred to in paragraphs 2 and 3, management and labour may inform the Commission of their wish to initiate the process provided for in Article 155. The duration of this process shall not exceed nine months, unless the management and labour concerned and the Commission decide jointly to extend it.

Article 155
(ex Article 139 TEC)

1. Should management and labour so desire, the dialogue between them at Union level may lead to contractual relations, including agreements.

2. Agreements concluded at Union level shall be implemented either in accordance with the procedures and practices specific to management and labour and the Member States or, in matters covered by Article 153, at the joint request of the signatory parties, by a Council decision on a proposal from the Commission. The European Parliament shall be informed.

The Council shall act unanimously where the agreement in question contains one or more provisions relating to one of the areas for which unanimity is required pursuant to Article 153(2).

Article 156
(ex Article 140 TEC)

With a view to achieving the objectives of Article 151 and without prejudice to the other provisions of the Treaties, the Commission shall encourage cooperation between the Member States and facilitate the coordination of their action in all social policy fields under this Chapter, particularly in matters relating to:

— employment,

— labour law and working conditions,

— basic and advanced vocational training,

— social security,

— prevention of occupational accidents and diseases,

— occupational hygiene,

— the right of association and collective bargaining between employers and workers.

To this end, the Commission shall act in close contact with Member States by making studies, delivering opinions and arranging consultations both on problems arising at national level and on those of concern to international organisations, in particular initiatives aiming at the establishment of guidelines and indicators, the organisation of exchange of best practice, and the preparation of the necessary elements for periodic monitoring and evaluation. The European Parliament shall be kept fully informed.

Before delivering the opinions provided for in this Article, the Commission shall consult the Economic and Social Committee.

Article 157
(ex Article 141 TEC)

1. Each Member State shall ensure that the principle of equal pay for male and female workers for equal work or work of equal value is applied.

2. For the purpose of this Article, "pay" means the ordinary basic or minimum wage or salary and any other consideration, whether in cash or in kind, which the worker receives directly or indirectly, in respect of his employment, from his employer.

Equal pay without discrimination based on sex means:

(a) that pay for the same work at piece rates shall be calculated on the basis of the same unit of measurement;

(b) that pay for work at time rates shall be the same for the same job.

3. The European Parliament and the Council, acting in accordance with the ordinary legislative procedure, and after consulting the Economic and Social Committee, shall adopt measures to ensure the application of the principle of equal opportunities and equal treatment of men and women in matters of employment and occupation, including the principle of equal pay for equal work or work of equal value.

4. With a view to ensuring full equality in practice between men and women in working life, the principle of equal treatment shall not prevent any Member State from maintaining or adopting measures providing for specific advantages in order to make it easier for the underrepresented sex to pursue a vocational activity or to prevent or compensate for disadvantages in professional careers.

Article 158
(ex Article 142 TEC)

Member States shall endeavour to maintain the existing equivalence between paid holiday schemes.

Article 159
(ex Article 143 TEC)

The Commission shall draw up a report each year on progress in achieving the objectives of Article 151, including the demographic situation in the Union. It shall forward the report to the European Parliament, the Council and the Economic and Social Committee.

Article 160
(ex Article 144 TEC)

The Council, acting by a simple majority after consulting the European Parliament, shall establish a Social Protection Committee with advisory status to promote cooperation on social protection policies between Member States and with the Commission. The tasks of the Committee shall be:

— to monitor the social situation and the development of social protection policies in the Member States and the Union,

— to promote exchanges of information, experience and good practice between Member States and with the Commission,

— without prejudice to Article 240, to prepare reports, formulate opinions or undertake other work within its fields of competence, at the request of either the Council or the Commission or on its own initiative.

In fulfilling its mandate, the Committee shall establish appropriate contacts with management and labour.

Each Member State and the Commission shall appoint two members of the Committee.

Article 161
(ex Article 145 TEC)

The Commission shall include a separate chapter on social developments within the Union in its annual report to the European Parliament.

The European Parliament may invite the Commission to draw up reports on any particular problems concerning social conditions.

TITLE XI
THE EUROPEAN SOCIAL FUND

Article 162
(ex Article 146 TEC)

In order to improve employment opportunities for workers in the internal market and to contribute thereby to raising the standard of living, a European Social Fund is hereby established in accordance with the provisions set out below; it shall aim to render the employment of workers easier and to increase their geographical and occupational mobility within the Union, and to facilitate their adaptation to industrial changes and to changes in production systems, in particular through vocational training and retraining.

Article 163
(ex Article 147 TEC)

The Fund shall be administered by the Commission.

The Commission shall be assisted in this task by a Committee presided over by a Member of the Commission and composed of representatives of governments, trade unions and employers' organisations.

Article 164
(ex Article 148 TEC)

The European Parliament and the Council, acting in accordance with the ordinary legislative procedure and after consulting the Economic and Social Committee and the Committee of the Regions, shall adopt implementing regulations relating to the European Social Fund.

TITLE XII
EDUCATION, VOCATIONAL TRAINING, YOUTH AND SPORT

Article 165
(ex Article 149 TEC)

1. The Union shall contribute to the development of quality education by encouraging cooperation between Member States and, if necessary, by supporting and supplementing their action, while fully respecting the responsibility of the Member States for the content of teaching and the organisation of education systems and their cultural and linguistic diversity.

The Union shall contribute to the promotion of European sporting issues, while taking account of the specific nature of sport, its structures based on voluntary activity and its social and educational function.

2. Union action shall be aimed at:

— developing the European dimension in education, particularly through the teaching and dissemination of the languages of the Member States,

— encouraging mobility of students and teachers, by encouraging inter alia, the academic recognition of diplomas and periods of study,

— promoting cooperation between educational establishments,

— developing exchanges of information and experience on issues common to the education systems of the Member States,

— encouraging the development of youth exchanges and of exchanges of socio-educational instructors, and encouraging the participation of young people in democratic life in Europe,

— encouraging the development of distance education,

— developing the European dimension in sport, by promoting fairness and openness in sporting competitions and cooperation between bodies responsible for sports, and by protecting the physical and moral integrity of sportsmen and sportswomen, especially the youngest sportsmen and sportswomen.

3. The Union and the Member States shall foster cooperation with third countries and the competent international organisations in the field of education and sport, in particular the Council of Europe.

4. In order to contribute to the achievement of the objectives referred to in this Article:

— the European Parliament and the Council, acting in accordance with the ordinary legislative procedure, after consulting the Economic and Social Committee and the Committee of the Regions, shall adopt incentive measures, excluding any harmonisation of the laws and regulations of the Member States,

— the Council, on a proposal from the Commission, shall adopt recommendations.

Article 166

(ex Article 150 TEC)

1. The Union shall implement a vocational training policy which shall support and supplement the action of the Member States, while fully respecting the responsibility of the Member States for the content and organisation of vocational training.

2. Union action shall aim to:

— facilitate adaptation to industrial changes, in particular through vocational training and retraining,

— improve initial and continuing vocational training in order to facilitate vocational integration and reintegration into the labour market,

— facilitate access to vocational training and encourage mobility of instructors and trainees and particularly young people,

— stimulate cooperation on training between educational or training establishments and firms,

— develop exchanges of information and experience on issues common to the training systems of the Member States.

3. The Union and the Member States shall foster cooperation with third countries and the competent international organisations in the sphere of vocational training.

4. The European Parliament and the Council, acting in accordance with the ordinary legislative procedure and after consulting the Economic and Social Committee and the Committee of the Regions, shall adopt measures to contribute to the achievement of the objectives referred to in this Article, excluding any harmonisation of the laws and regulations of the Member States, and the Council, on a proposal from the Commission, shall adopt recommendations.

TITLE XIII
CULTURE

Article 167
(ex Article 151 TEC)

1. The Union shall contribute to the flowering of the cultures of the Member States, while respecting their national and regional diversity and at the same time bringing the common cultural heritage to the fore.

2. Action by the Union shall be aimed at encouraging cooperation between Member States and, if necessary, supporting and supplementing their action in the following areas:

— improvement of the knowledge and dissemination of the culture and history of the European peoples,

— conservation and safeguarding of cultural heritage of European significance,

— non-commercial cultural exchanges,

— artistic and literary creation, including in the audiovisual sector.

3. The Union and the Member States shall foster cooperation with third countries and the competent international organisations in the sphere of culture, in particular the Council of Europe.

4. The Union shall take cultural aspects into account in its action under other provisions of the Treaties, in particular in order to respect and to promote the diversity of its cultures.

5. In order to contribute to the achievement of the objectives referred to in this Article:

— the European Parliament and the Council acting in accordance with the ordinary legislative procedure and after consulting the Committee of the Regions, shall adopt incentive measures, excluding any harmonisation of the laws and regulations of the Member States,

— the Council, on a proposal from the Commission, shall adopt recommendations.

TITLE XIV
PUBLIC HEALTH

Article 168
(ex Article 152 TEC)

1. A high level of human health protection shall be ensured in the definition and implementation of all Union policies and activities.

Union action, which shall complement national policies, shall be directed towards improving public health, preventing physical and mental illness and diseases, and obviating sources of danger to physical and mental health. Such action shall cover the fight against the major health scourges, by promoting research into their causes, their transmission and their prevention, as well as health information and education, and monitoring, early warning of and combating serious cross-border threats to health.

The Union shall complement the Member States' action in reducing drugs-related health damage, including information and prevention.

2. The Union shall encourage cooperation between the Member States in the areas referred to in this Article and, if necessary, lend support to their action. It shall in particular encourage cooperation between the Member States to improve the complementarity of their health services in cross-border areas.

Member States shall, in liaison with the Commission, coordinate among themselves their policies and programmes in the areas referred to in paragraph 1. The Commission may, in close contact with the Member States, take any useful initiative to promote such coordination, in particular initiatives aiming at the establishment of guidelines and indicators, the organisation of exchange of best practice, and the preparation of the necessary elements for periodic monitoring and evaluation. The European Parliament shall be kept fully informed.

3. The Union and the Member States shall foster cooperation with third countries and the competent international organisations in the sphere of public health.

4. By way of derogation from Article 2(5) and Article 6(a) and in accordance with Article 4(2)(k) the European Parliament and the Council, acting in accordance with the ordinary legislative procedure and after consulting the Economic and Social Committee and the Committee of the Regions, shall contribute to the achievement of the objectives referred to in this Article through adopting in order to meet common safety concerns:

(a) measures setting high standards of quality and safety of organs and substances of human origin, blood and blood derivatives; these measures shall not prevent any Member State from maintaining or introducing more stringent protective measures;

(b) measures in the veterinary and phytosanitary fields which have as their direct objective the protection of public health;

(c) measures setting high standards of quality and safety for medicinal products and devices for medical use.

5. The European Parliament and the Council, acting in accordance with the ordinary legislative procedure and after consulting the Economic and Social Committee and the Committee of the Regions, may also adopt incentive measures designed to protect and improve human health and in particular to combat the major cross-border health scourges, measures concerning monitoring, early warning of and combating serious cross-border threats to health, and measures which have as their direct objective the protection of public health regarding tobacco and the abuse of alcohol, excluding any harmonisation of the laws and regulations of the Member States.

6. The Council, on a proposal from the Commission, may also adopt recommendations for the purposes set out in this Article.

7. Union action shall respect the responsibilities of the Member States for the definition of their health policy and for the organisation and delivery of health services and medical care. The responsibilities of the Member States shall include the management of health services and medical care and the allocation of the resources assigned to them. The measures referred to in paragraph 4(a) shall not affect national provisions on the donation or medical use of organs and blood.

TITLE XV
CONSUMER PROTECTION

Article 169
(ex Article 153 TEC)

1. In order to promote the interests of consumers and to ensure a high level of consumer protection, the Union shall contribute to protecting the health, safety and economic interests of consumers, as well as to promoting their right to information, education and to organise themselves in order to safeguard their interests.

2. The Union shall contribute to the attainment of the objectives referred to in paragraph 1 through:

(a) measures adopted pursuant to Article 114 in the context of the completion of the internal market;

(b) measures which support, supplement and monitor the policy pursued by the Member States.

3. The European Parliament and the Council, acting in accordance with the ordinary legislative procedure and after consulting the Economic and Social Committee, shall adopt the measures referred to in paragraph 2(b).

4. Measures adopted pursuant to paragraph 3 shall not prevent any Member State from maintaining or introducing more stringent protective measures. Such measures must be compatible with the Treaties. The Commission shall be notified of them.

TITLE XVI
TRANS-EUROPEAN NETWORKS

Article 170
(ex Article 154 TEC)

1. To help achieve the objectives referred to in Articles 26 and 174 and to enable citizens of the Union, economic operators and regional and local communities to derive full benefit from the setting-up of an area without internal frontiers, the Union shall contribute to the establishment and development of trans-European networks in the areas of transport, telecommunications and energy infrastructures.

2. Within the framework of a system of open and competitive markets, action by the Union shall aim at promoting the interconnection and interoperability of national networks as well as access to such networks. It shall take account in particular of the need to link island, landlocked and peripheral regions with the central regions of the Union.

Article 171
(ex Article 155 TEC)

1. In order to achieve the objectives referred to in Article 170, the Union:

— shall establish a series of guidelines covering the objectives, priorities and broad lines of measures envisaged in the sphere of trans-European networks; these guidelines shall identify projects of common interest,

— shall implement any measures that may prove necessary to ensure the interoperability of the networks, in particular in the field of technical standardisation,

— may support projects of common interest supported by Member States, which are identified in the framework of the guidelines referred to in the first indent, particularly through feasibility studies, loan guarantees or interest-rate subsidies; the Union may also contribute, through the Cohesion Fund set up pursuant to Article 177, to the financing of specific projects in Member States in the area of transport infrastructure.

The Union's activities shall take into account the potential economic viability of the projects.

2. Member States shall, in liaison with the Commission, coordinate among themselves the policies pursued at national level which may have a significant impact on the achievement of the objectives referred to in Article 170. The Commission may, in close cooperation with the Member State, take any useful initiative to promote such coordination.

3. The Union may decide to cooperate with third countries to promote projects of mutual interest and to ensure the interoperability of networks.

Article 172
(ex Article 156 TEC)

The guidelines and other measures referred to in Article 171(1) shall be adopted by the European Parliament and the Council, acting in accordance with the ordinary legislative procedure and after consulting the Economic and Social Committee and the Committee of the Regions.

Guidelines and projects of common interest which relate to the territory of a Member State shall require the approval of the Member State concerned.

TITLE XVII
INDUSTRY

Article 173
(ex Article 157 TEC)

1. The Union and the Member States shall ensure that the conditions necessary for the competitiveness of the Union's industry exist.

For that purpose, in accordance with a system of open and competitive markets, their action shall be aimed at:

— speeding up the adjustment of industry to structural changes,

— encouraging an environment favourable to initiative and to the development of undertakings throughout the Union, particularly small and medium-sized undertakings,

— encouraging an environment favourable to cooperation between undertakings,

— fostering better exploitation of the industrial potential of policies of innovation, research and technological development.

2. The Member States shall consult each other in liaison with the Commission and, where necessary, shall coordinate their action. The Commission may take any useful initiative to promote such coordination, in particular initiatives aiming at the establishment of guidelines and indicators, the organisation of exchange of best practice, and the preparation of the necessary elements for periodic monitoring and evaluation. The European Parliament shall be kept fully informed.

3. The Union shall contribute to the achievement of the objectives set out in paragraph 1 through the policies and activities it pursues under other provisions of the Treaties. The European Parliament and the Council, acting in accordance with the ordinary legislative procedure and after consulting the Economic and Social Committee, may decide on specific measures in support of action taken in the Member States to achieve the objectives set out in paragraph 1, excluding any harmonisation of the laws and regulations of the Member States.

This Title shall not provide a basis for the introduction by the Union of any measure which could lead to a distortion of competition or contains tax provisions or provisions relating to the rights and interests of employed persons.

TITLE XVIII
ECONOMIC, SOCIAL AND TERRITORIAL COHESION

Article 174
(ex Article 158 TEC)

In order to promote its overall harmonious development, the Union shall develop and pursue its actions leading to the strengthening of its economic, social and territorial cohesion.

In particular, the Union shall aim at reducing disparities between the levels of development of the various regions and the backwardness of the least favoured regions.

Among the regions concerned, particular attention shall be paid to rural areas, areas affected by industrial transition, and regions which suffer from severe and permanent natural or demographic handicaps such as the northernmost regions with very low population density and island, cross-border and mountain regions.

Article 175
(ex Article 159 TEC)

Member States shall conduct their economic policies and shall coordinate them in such a way as, in addition, to attain the objectives set out in Article 174. The formulation and implementation of the Union's policies and actions and the implementation of the internal market shall take into account the objectives set out in Article 174 and shall contribute to their achievement. The Union shall also support the achievement of these objectives by the action it takes through the Structural Funds (European Agricultural Guidance and Guarantee Fund, Guidance Section; European Social Fund; European Regional Development Fund), the European Investment Bank and the other existing Financial Instruments.

The Commission shall submit a report to the European Parliament, the Council, the Economic and Social Committee and the Committee of the Regions every three years on the progress made towards achieving economic, social and territorial cohesion and on the manner in which the various means provided for in this Article have contributed to it. This report shall, if necessary, be accompanied by appropriate proposals.

If specific actions prove necessary outside the Funds and without prejudice to the measures decided upon within the framework of the other Union policies, such actions may be adopted by the Council acting in accordance with the ordinary legislative procedure and after consulting the Economic and Social Committee and the Committee of the Regions.

Article 176
(ex Article 160 TEC)

The European Regional Development Fund is intended to help to redress the main regional imbalances in the Union through participation in the development and structural adjustment of regions whose development is lagging behind and in the conversion of declining industrial regions.

Article 177
(ex Article 161 TEC)

Without prejudice to Article 178, the European Parliament and the Council, acting by means of regulations in accordance with the ordinary legislative procedure and consulting the Economic and Social Committee and the Committee of the Regions, shall define the tasks, priority objectives and the organisation of the Structural Funds, which may involve grouping the Funds. The general rules applicable to them and the provisions necessary to ensure their effectiveness and the coordination of the Funds with one another and with the other existing Financial Instruments shall also be defined by the same procedure.

A Cohesion Fund set up in accordance with the same procedure shall provide a financial contribution to projects in the fields of environment and trans-European networks in the area of transport infrastructure.

Article 178
(ex Article 162 TEC)

Implementing regulations relating to the European Regional Development Fund shall be taken by the European Parliament and the Council, acting in accordance with the ordinary legislative procedure and after consulting the Economic and Social Committee and the Committee of the Regions.

With regard to the European Agricultural Guidance and Guarantee Fund, Guidance Section, and the European Social Fund, Articles 43 and 164 respectively shall continue to apply.

TITLE XIX
RESEARCH AND TECHNOLOGICAL DEVELOPMENT AND SPACE

Article 179
(ex Article 163 TEC)

1. The Union shall have the objective of strengthening its scientific and technological bases by achieving a European research area in which researchers, scientific knowledge and technology circulate freely, and encouraging it to become more competitive, including in its industry, while promoting all the research activities deemed necessary by virtue of other Chapters of the Treaties.

2. For this purpose the Union shall, throughout the Union, encourage undertakings, including small and medium-sized undertakings, research centres and universities in their research and technological development activities of high quality; it shall support their efforts to cooperate with one another, aiming, notably, at permitting researchers to cooperate freely across borders and at enabling undertakings to exploit the internal market potential to the full, in particular through the opening-up of national public contracts, the definition of common standards and the removal of legal and fiscal obstacles to that cooperation.

3. All Union activities under the Treaties in the area of research and technological development, including demonstration projects, shall be decided on and implemented in accordance with the provisions of this Title.

Article 180
(ex Article 164 TEC)

In pursuing these objectives, the Union shall carry out the following activities, complementing the activities carried out in the Member States:

(a) implementation of research, technological development and demonstration programmes, by promoting cooperation with and between undertakings, research centres and universities;

(b) promotion of cooperation in the field of Union research, technological development and demonstration with third countries and international organisations;

(c) dissemination and optimisation of the results of activities in Union research, technological development and demonstration;

(d) stimulation of the training and mobility of researchers in the Union.

Article 181
(ex Article 165 TEC)

1. The Union and the Member States shall coordinate their research and technological development activities so as to ensure that national policies and Union policy are mutually consistent.

2. In close cooperation with the Member State, the Commission may take any useful initiative to promote the coordination referred to in paragraph 1, in particular initiatives aiming at the establishment of guidelines and indicators, the organisation of exchange of best practice, and the preparation of the necessary elements for periodic monitoring and evaluation. The European Parliament shall be kept fully informed.

Article 182
(ex Article 166 TEC)

1. A multiannual framework programme, setting out all the activities of the Union, shall be adopted by the European Parliament and the Council, acting in accordance with the ordinary legislative procedure after consulting the Economic and Social Committee.

The framework programme shall:

— establish the scientific and technological objectives to be achieved by the activities provided for in Article 180 and fix the relevant priorities,

— indicate the broad lines of such activities,

— fix the maximum overall amount and the detailed rules for Union financial participation in the framework programme and the respective shares in each of the activities provided for.

2. The framework programme shall be adapted or supplemented as the situation changes.

3. The framework programme shall be implemented through specific programmes developed within each activity. Each specific programme shall define the detailed rules for implementing it, fix its duration and provide for the means deemed necessary. The sum of the amounts deemed necessary, fixed in the specific programmes, may not exceed the overall maximum amount fixed for the framework programme and each activity.

4. The Council, acting in accordance with a special legislative procedure and after consulting the European Parliament and the Economic and Social Committee, shall adopt the specific programmes.

5. As a complement to the activities planned in the multiannual framework programme, the European Parliament and the Council, acting in accordance with the ordinary legislative procedure and after consulting the Economic and Social Committee, shall establish the measures necessary for the implementation of the European research area.

Article 183
(ex Article 167 TEC)

For the implementation of the multiannual framework programme the Union shall:

— determine the rules for the participation of undertakings, research centres and universities,

— lay down the rules governing the dissemination of research results.

Article 184
(ex Article 168 TEC)

In implementing the multiannual framework programme, supplementary programmes may be decided on involving the participation of certain Member States only, which shall finance them subject to possible Union participation.

The Union shall adopt the rules applicable to supplementary programmes, particularly as regards the dissemination of knowledge and access by other Member States.

Article 185
(ex Article 169 TEC)

In implementing the multiannual framework programme, the Union may make provision, in agreement with the Member States concerned, for participation in research and development programmes undertaken by several Member States, including participation in the structures created for the execution of those programmes.

Article 186
(ex Article 170 TEC)

In implementing the multiannual framework programme the Union may make provision for cooperation in Union research, technological development and demonstration with third countries or international organisations.

The detailed arrangements for such cooperation may be the subject of agreements between the Union and the third parties concerned.

Article 187
(ex Article 171 TEC)

The Union may set up joint undertakings or any other structure necessary for the efficient execution of Union research, technological development and demonstration programmes.

Article 188
(ex Article 172 TEC)

The Council, on a proposal from the Commission and after consulting the European Parliament and the Economic and Social Committee, shall adopt the provisions referred to in Article 187.

The European Parliament and the Council, acting in accordance with the ordinary legislative procedure and after consulting the Economic and Social Committee, shall adopt the provisions referred to in Articles 183, 184 and 185. Adoption of the supplementary programmes shall require the agreement of the Member States concerned.

Article 189

1. To promote scientific and technical progress, industrial competitiveness and the implementation of its policies, the Union shall draw up a European space policy. To this end, it may promote joint initiatives, support research and technological development and coordinate the efforts needed for the exploration and exploitation of space.

2. To contribute to attaining the objectives referred to in paragraph 1, the European Parliament and the Council, acting in accordance with the ordinary legislative procedure, shall establish the necessary measures, which may take the form of a European space programme, excluding any harmonisation of the laws and regulations of the Member States.

3. The Union shall establish any appropriate relations with the European Space Agency.

4. This Article shall be without prejudice to the other provisions of this Title

Article 190
(ex Article 173 TEC)

At the beginning of each year the Commission shall send a report to the European Parliament and to the Council. The report shall include information on research and technological development activities and the dissemination of results during the previous year, and the work programme for the current year.

TITLE XX
ENVIRONMENT

Article 191
(ex Article 174 TEC)

1. Union policy on the environment shall contribute to pursuit of the following objectives:

— preserving, protecting and improving the quality of the environment,

— protecting human health,

— prudent and rational utilisation of natural resources,

— promoting measures at international level to deal with regional or worldwide environmental problems, and in particular combating climate change.

2. Union policy on the environment shall aim at a high level of protection taking into account the diversity of situations in the various regions of the Union. It shall be based on the precautionary principle and on the principles that preventive action should be taken, that environmental damage should as a priority be rectified at source and that the polluter should pay.

In this context, harmonisation measures answering environmental protection requirements shall include, where appropriate, a safeguard clause allowing Member States to take provisional measures, for non-economic environmental reasons, subject to a procedure of inspection by the Union.

3. In preparing its policy on the environment, the Union shall take account of:

— available scientific and technical data,

— environmental conditions in the various regions of the Union,

— the potential benefits and costs of action or lack of action,

— the economic and social development of the Union as a whole and the balanced development of its regions.

4. Within their respective spheres of competence, the Union and the Member States shall cooperate with third countries and with the competent international organisations. The arrangements for Union cooperation may be the subject of agreements between the Union and the third parties concerned.

The previous subparagraph shall be without prejudice to Member States' competence to negotiate in international bodies and to conclude international agreements.

Article 192
(ex Article 175 TEC)

1. The European Parliament and the Council, acting in accordance with the ordinary legislative procedure and after consulting the Economic and Social Committee and the Committee of the Regions, shall decide what action is to be taken by the Union in order to achieve the objectives referred to in Article 191.

2. By way of derogation from the decision-making procedure provided for in paragraph 1 and without prejudice to Article 114, the Council acting unanimously in accordance with a special legislative procedure and after consulting the European Parliament, the Economic and Social Committee and the Committee of the Regions, shall adopt:

(a) provisions primarily of a fiscal nature;

(b) measures affecting:

— town and country planning,

— quantitative management of water resources or affecting, directly or indirectly, the availability of those resources,

— land use, with the exception of waste management;

(c) measures significantly affecting a Member State's choice between different energy sources and the general structure of its energy supply.

The Council, acting unanimously on a proposal from the Commission and after consulting the European Parliament, the Economic and Social Committee and the Committee of the Regions, may make the ordinary legislative procedure applicable to the matters referred to in the first subparagraph.

3. General action programmes setting out priority objectives to be attained shall be adopted by the European Parliament and the Council, acting in accordance with the ordinary legislative procedure and after consulting the Economic and Social Committee and the Committee of the Regions.

The measures necessary for the implementation of these programmes shall be adopted under the terms of paragraph 1 or 2, as the case may be.

4. Without prejudice to certain measures adopted by the Union, the Member States shall finance and implement the environment policy.

5. Without prejudice to the principle that the polluter should pay, if a measure based on the provisions of paragraph 1 involves costs deemed disproportionate for the public authorities of a Member State, such measure shall lay down appropriate provisions in the form of:

— temporary derogations, and/or

— financial support from the Cohesion Fund set up pursuant to Article 177.

Article 193
(ex Article 176 TEC)

The protective measures adopted pursuant to Article 192 shall not prevent any Member State from maintaining or introducing more stringent protective measures. Such measures must be compatible with the Treaties. They shall be notified to the Commission.

TITLE XXI
ENERGY

Article 194

1. In the context of the establishment and functioning of the internal market and with regard for the need to preserve and improve the environment, Union policy on energy shall aim, in a spirit of solidarity between Member States, to:

(a) ensure the functioning of the energy market;

(b) ensure security of energy supply in the Union;

(c) promote energy efficiency and energy saving and the development of new and renewable forms of energy; and

(d) promote the interconnection of energy networks.

2. Without prejudice to the application of other provisions of the Treaties, the European Parliament and the Council, acting in accordance with the ordinary legislative procedure, shall establish the measures necessary to achieve the objectives in paragraph 1. Such measures shall be adopted after consultation of the Economic and Social Committee and the Committee of the Regions.

Such measures shall not affect a Member State's right to determine the conditions for exploiting its energy resources, its choice between different energy sources and the general structure of its energy supply, without prejudice to Article 192(2)(c).

3. By way of derogation from paragraph 2, the Council, acting in accordance with a special legislative procedure, shall unanimously and after consulting the European Parliament, establish the measures referred to therein when they are primarily of a fiscal nature.

TITLE XXII
TOURISM

Article 195

1. The Union shall complement the action of the Member States in the tourism sector, in particular by promoting the competitiveness of Union undertakings in that sector.

To that end, Union action shall be aimed at:

(a) encouraging the creation of a favourable environment for the development of undertakings in this sector;

(b) promoting cooperation between the Member States, particularly by the exchange of good practice.

2. The European Parliament and the Council, acting in accordance with the ordinary legislative procedure, shall establish specific measures to complement actions within the Member States to achieve the objectives referred to in this Article, excluding any harmonisation of the laws and regulations of the Member States.

TITLE XXIII

CIVIL PROTECTION

Article 196

1. The Union shall encourage cooperation between Member States in order to improve the effectiveness of systems for preventing and protecting against natural or man-made disasters.

Union action shall aim to:

(a) support and complement Member States' action at national, regional and local level in risk prevention, in preparing their civil-protection personnel and in responding to natural or man-made disasters within the Union;

(b) promote swift, effective operational cooperation within the Union between national civil-protection services;

(c) promote consistency in international civil-protection work.

2. The European Parliament and the Council, acting in accordance with the ordinary legislative procedure shall establish the measures necessary to help achieve the objectives referred to in paragraph 1, excluding any harmonisation of the laws and regulations of the Member States.

TITLE XXIV
ADMINISTRATIVE COOPERATION

Article 197

1. Effective implementation of Union law by the Member States, which is essential for the proper functioning of the Union, shall be regarded as a matter of common interest.

2. The Union may support the efforts of Member States to improve their administrative capacity to implement Union law. Such action may include facilitating the exchange of information and of civil servants as well as supporting training schemes. No Member State shall be obliged to avail itself of such support. The European Parliament and the Council, acting by means of regulations in accordance with the ordinary legislative procedure, shall establish the necessary measures to this end, excluding any harmonisation of the laws and regulations of the Member States.

3. This Article shall be without prejudice to the obligations of the Member States to implement Union law or to the prerogatives and duties of the Commission. It shall also be without prejudice to other provisions of the Treaties providing for administrative

cooperation among the Member States and between them and the Union.

PART FOUR
ASSOCIATION OF THE OVERSEAS COUNTRIES AND TERRITORIES

Article 198
(ex Article 182 TEC)

The Member States agree to associate with the Union the non-European countries and territories which have special relations with Denmark, France, the Netherlands and the United Kingdom. These countries and territories (hereinafter called the "countries and territories") are listed in Annex II.

The purpose of association shall be to promote the economic and social development of the countries and territories and to establish close economic relations between them and the Union as a whole.

In accordance with the principles set out in the preamble to this Treaty, association shall serve primarily to further the interests and prosperity of the inhabitants of these countries and territories in order to lead them to the economic, social and cultural development to which they aspire.

Article 199
(ex Article 183 TEC)

Association shall have the following objectives:

1. Member States shall apply to their trade with the countries and territories the same treatment as they accord each other pursuant to the Treaties.

2. Each country or territory shall apply to its trade with Member States and with the other countries and territories the same treatment as that which it applies to the European State with which it has special relations.

3. The Member States shall contribute to the investments required for the progressive development of these countries and territories.

4. For investments financed by the Union, participation in tenders and supplies shall be open on equal terms to all natural and legal persons who are nationals of a Member State or of one of the countries and territories.

5. In relations between Member States and the countries and territories the right of establishment of nationals and companies or firms shall be regulated in accordance with the

provisions and procedures laid down in the Chapter relating to the right of establishment and on a non-discriminatory basis, subject to any special provisions laid down pursuant to Article 203.

Article 200
(ex Article 184 TEC)

1. Customs duties on imports into the Member States of goods originating in the countries and territories shall be prohibited in conformity with the prohibition of customs duties between Member States in accordance with the provisions of the Treaties.

2. Customs duties on imports into each country or territory from Member States or from the other countries or territories shall be prohibited in accordance with the provisions of Article 30.

3. The countries and territories may, however, levy customs duties which meet the needs of their development and industrialisation or produce revenue for their budgets.

The duties referred to in the preceding subparagraph may not exceed the level of those imposed on imports of products from the Member State with which each country or territory has special relations.

4. Paragraph 2 shall not apply to countries and territories which, by reason of the particular international obligations by which they are bound, already apply a non-discriminatory customs tariff.

5. The introduction of or any change in customs duties imposed on goods imported into the countries and territories shall not, either in law or in fact, give rise to any direct or indirect discrimination between imports from the various Member States.

Article 201
(ex Article 185 TEC)

If the level of the duties applicable to goods from a third country on entry into a country or territory is liable, when the provisions of Article 200(1) have been applied, to cause deflections of trade to the detriment of any Member State, the latter may request the Commission to propose to the other Member States the measures needed to remedy the situation.

Article 202
(ex Article 186 TEC)

Subject to the provisions relating to public health, public security or public policy, freedom of movement within Member States for workers from the countries and territories, and within the countries and territories for workers from Member States, shall be regulated by acts adopted in accordance with Article 203.

Article 203
(ex Article 187 TEC)

The Council, acting unanimously on a proposal from the Commission, shall, on the basis of the experience acquired under the association of the countries and territories with the Union and of the principles set out in the Treaties, lay down provisions as regards the detailed rules and the procedure for the association of the countries and territories with the Union. Where the provisions in question are adopted by the Council in accordance with a special legislative procedure, it shall act unanimously on a proposal from the Commission and after consulting the European Parliament.

Article 204
(ex Article 188 TEC)

The provisions of Articles 198 to 203 shall apply to Greenland, subject to the specific provisions for Greenland set out in the Protocol on special arrangements for Greenland, annexed to the Treaties.

PART FIVE
THE UNION'S EXTERNAL ACTION

TITLE I
GENERAL PROVISIONS ON THE UNION'S EXTERNAL ACTION

Article 205

The Union's action on the international scene, pursuant to this Part, shall be guided by the principles, pursue the objectives and be conducted in accordance with the general provisions laid down in Chapter 1 of Title V of the Treaty on European Union.

TITLE II
COMMON COMMERCIAL POLICY

Article 206
(ex Article 131 TEC)

By establishing a customs union in accordance with Articles 28 to 32, the Union shall contribute, in the common interest, to the harmonious development of world trade, the progressive abolition of restrictions on international trade and on foreign direct investment, and the lowering of customs and other barriers.

Article 207
(ex Article 133 TEC)

1. The common commercial policy shall be based on uniform principles, particularly with regard to changes in tariff rates, the conclusion of tariff and trade agreements relating to trade in goods and services, and the commercial aspects of intellectual property, foreign direct investment, the achievement of uniformity in measures of liberalisation, export policy and measures to protect trade such as those to be taken in the event of dumping or subsidies. The common commercial policy shall be conducted in the context of the principles and objectives of the Union's external action.

2. The European Parliament and the Council, acting by means of regulations in accordance with the ordinary legislative procedure, shall adopt the measures defining the framework for implementing the common commercial policy.

3. Where agreements with one or more third countries or international organisations need to be negotiated and concluded, Article 218 shall apply, subject to the special provisions of this Article.

The Commission shall make recommendations to the Council, which shall authorise it to open the necessary negotiations. The Council and the Commission shall be responsible for ensuring that the agreements negotiated are compatible with internal Union policies and rules.

The Commission shall conduct these negotiations in consultation with a special committee appointed by the Council to assist the Commission in this task and within the framework of such directives as the Council may issue to it. The Commission shall report regularly to the special committee and to the European Parliament on the progress of negotiations.

4. For the negotiation and conclusion of the agreements referred to in paragraph 3, the Council shall act by a qualified majority.

For the negotiation and conclusion of agreements in the fields of trade in services and the commercial aspects of intellectual property, as well as foreign direct investment, the Council shall act unanimously where such agreements include provisions for which unanimity is required for the adoption of internal rules.

The Council shall also act unanimously for the negotiation and conclusion of agreements:

(a) in the field of trade in cultural and audiovisual services, where these agreements risk prejudicing the Union's cultural and linguistic diversity;

(b) in the field of trade in social, education and health services, where these agreements risk seriously disturbing the national organisation of such services and prejudicing the responsibility of Member States to deliver them.

5. The negotiation and conclusion of international agreements in the field of transport shall be subject to Title VI of Part Three and to Article 218.

6. The exercise of the competences conferred by this Article in the field of the common commercial policy shall not affect the delimitation of competences between the Union and the Member States, and shall not lead to harmonisation of legislative or regulatory provisions of the Member States in so far as the Treaties exclude such harmonisation.

TITLE III
COOPERATION WITH THIRD COUNTRIES AND HUMANITARIAN AID

CHAPTER 1
DEVELOPMENT COOPERATION

Article 208
(ex Article 177 TEC)

1. Union policy in the field of development cooperation shall be conducted within the framework of the principles and objectives of the Union's external action. The Union's development cooperation policy and that of the Member States complement and reinforce each other.

Union development cooperation policy shall have as its primary objective the reduction and, in the long term, the eradication of poverty. The Union shall take account of the objectives of development cooperation in the policies that it implements which are likely to affect developing countries.

2. The Union and the Member States shall comply with the commitments and take account of the objectives they have approved in the context of the United Nations and other competent international organisations.

Article 209
(ex Article 179 TEC)

1. The European Parliament and the Council, acting in accordance with the ordinary legislative procedure, shall adopt the

measures necessary for the implementation of development cooperation policy, which may relate to multiannual cooperation programmes with developing countries or programmes with a thematic approach.

2. The Union may conclude with third countries and competent international organisations any agreement helping to achieve the objectives referred to in Article 21 of the Treaty on European Union and in Article 208 of this Treaty.

The first subparagraph shall be without prejudice to Member States' competence to negotiate in international bodies and to conclude agreements.

3. The European Investment Bank shall contribute, under the terms laid down in its Statute, to the implementation of the measures referred to in paragraph 1.

Article 210
(ex Article 180 TEC)

1. In order to promote the complementarity and efficiency of their action, the Union and the Member States shall coordinate their policies on development cooperation and shall consult each other on their aid programmes, including in international organisations and during international conferences. They may undertake joint action. Member States shall contribute if necessary to the implementation of Union aid programmes.

2. The Commission may take any useful initiative to promote the coordination referred to in paragraph 1.

Article 211
(ex Article 181 TEC)

Within their respective spheres of competence, the Union and the Member States shall cooperate with third countries and with the competent international organisations.

CHAPTER 2
ECONOMIC, FINANCIAL AND TECHNICAL COOPERATION WITH THIRD COUNTRIES

Article 212
(ex Article 181*a* TEC)

1. Without prejudice to the other provisions of the Treaties, and in particular Articles 208 to 211, the Union shall carry out economic, financial and technical cooperation measures, including assistance, in particular financial assistance, with third countries other than developing countries. Such measures shall be consistent with the development policy of the Union and shall be carried out

within the framework of the principles and objectives of its external action. The Union's operations and those of the Member States shall complement and reinforce each other.

2. The European Parliament and the Council, acting in accordance with the ordinary legislative procedure, shall adopt the measures necessary for the implementation of paragraph 1.

3. Within their respective spheres of competence, the Union and the Member States shall cooperate with third countries and the competent international organisations. The arrangements for Union cooperation may be the subject of agreements between the Union and the third parties concerned.

The first subparagraph shall be without prejudice to the Member States' competence to negotiate in international bodies and to conclude international agreements.

Article 213

When the situation in a third country requires urgent financial assistance from the Union, the Council shall adopt the necessary decisions on a proposal from the Commission.

CHAPTER 3
HUMANITARIAN AID

Article 214

1. The Union's operations in the field of humanitarian aid shall be conducted within the framework of the principles and objectives of the external action of the Union. Such operations shall be intended to provide ad hoc assistance and relief and protection for people in third countries who are victims of natural or man-made disasters, in order to meet the humanitarian needs resulting from these different situations. The Union's measures and those of the Member States shall complement and reinforce each other.

2. Humanitarian aid operations shall be conducted in compliance with the principles of international law and with the principles of impartiality, neutrality and non-discrimination.

3. The European Parliament and the Council, acting in accordance with the ordinary legislative procedure, shall establish the measures defining the framework within which the Union's humanitarian aid operations shall be implemented.

4. The Union may conclude with third countries and competent international organisations any agreement helping to achieve the objectives referred to in paragraph 1 and in Article 21 of the Treaty on European Union.

The first subparagraph shall be without prejudice to Member States' competence to negotiate in international bodies and to conclude agreements.

5. In order to establish a framework for joint contributions from young Europeans to the humanitarian aid operations of the Union, a European Voluntary Humanitarian Aid Corps shall be set up. The European Parliament and the Council, acting by means of regulations in accordance with the ordinary legislative procedure, shall determine the rules and procedures for the operation of the Corps.

6. The Commission may take any useful initiative to promote coordination between actions of the Union and those of the Member States, in order to enhance the efficiency and complementarity of Union and national humanitarian aid measures.

7. The Union shall ensure that its humanitarian aid operations are coordinated and consistent with those of international organisations and bodies, in particular those forming part of the United Nations system.

TITLE IV
RESTRICTIVE MEASURES

Article 215

(ex Article 301 TEC)

1. Where a decision, adopted in accordance with Chapter 2 of Title V of the Treaty on European Union, provides for the interruption or reduction, in part or completely, of economic and financial relations with one or more third countries, the Council, acting by a qualified majority on a joint proposal from the High Representative of the Union for Foreign Affairs and Security Policy and the Commission, shall adopt the necessary measures. It shall inform the European Parliament thereof.

2. Where a decision adopted in accordance with Chapter 2 of Title V of the Treaty on European Union so provides, the Council may adopt restrictive measures under the procedure referred to in paragraph 1 against natural or legal persons and groups or non-State entities.

3. The acts referred to in this Article shall include necessary provisions on legal safeguards.

TITLE V
INTERNATIONAL AGREEMENTS

Article 216

1. The Union may conclude an agreement with one or more third countries or international organisations where the Treaties so provide or where the conclusion of an agreement is necessary in order to achieve, within the framework of the Union's policies, one of the objectives referred to in the Treaties, or is provided for in a legally binding Union act or is likely to affect common rules or alter their scope.

2. Agreements concluded by the Union are binding upon the institutions of the Union and on its Member States.

Article 217
(ex Article 310 TEC)

The Union may conclude with one or more third countries or international organisations agreements establishing an association involving reciprocal rights and obligations, common action and special procedure.

Article 218
(ex Article 300 TEC)

1. Without prejudice to the specific provisions laid down in Article 207, agreements between the Union and third countries or international organisations shall be negotiated and concluded in accordance with the following procedure.

2. The Council shall authorise the opening of negotiations, adopt negotiating directives, authorise the signing of agreements and conclude them.

3. The Commission, or the High Representative of the Union for Foreign Affairs and Security Policy where the agreement envisaged relates exclusively or principally to the common foreign and security policy, shall submit recommendations to the Council, which shall adopt a decision authorising the opening of negotiations and, depending on the subject of the agreement envisaged, nominating the Union negotiator or the head of the Union's negotiating team.

4. The Council may address directives to the negotiator and designate a special committee in consultation with which the negotiations must be conducted.

5. The Council, on a proposal by the negotiator, shall adopt a decision authorising the signing of the agreement and, if necessary, its provisional application before entry into force.

6. The Council, on a proposal by the negotiator, shall adopt a decision concluding the agreement.

Except where agreements relate exclusively to the common foreign and security policy, the Council shall adopt the decision concluding the agreement:

(a) after obtaining the consent of the European Parliament in the following cases:

(i) association agreements;

(ii) agreement on Union accession to the European Convention for the Protection of Human Rights and Fundamental Freedoms;

(iii) agreements establishing a specific institutional framework by organising cooperation procedures;

(iv) agreements with important budgetary implications for the Union;

(v) agreements covering fields to which either the ordinary legislative procedure applies, or the special legislative procedure where consent by the European Parliament is required.

The European Parliament and the Council may, in an urgent situation, agree upon a time-limit for consent.

(b) after consulting the European Parliament in other cases. The European Parliament shall deliver its opinion within a time-limit which the Council may set depending on the urgency of the matter. In the absence of an opinion within that time-limit, the Council may act.

7. When concluding an agreement, the Council may, by way of derogation from paragraphs 5, 6 and 9, authorise the negotiator to approve on the Union's behalf modifications to the agreement where it provides for them to be adopted by a simplified procedure or by a body set up by the agreement. The Council may attach specific conditions to such authorisation.

8. The Council shall act by a qualified majority throughout the procedure.

However, it shall act unanimously when the agreement covers a field for which unanimity is required for the adoption of a Union act as well as for association agreements and the agreements referred to in Article 212 with the States which are candidates for accession. The Council shall also act unanimously for the agreement on accession of the Union to the European Convention for the Protection of Human

Rights and Fundamental Freedoms; the decision concluding this agreement shall enter into force after it has been approved by the Member States in accordance with their respective constitutional requirements.

9. The Council, on a proposal from the Commission or the High Representative of the Union for Foreign Affairs and Security Policy, shall adopt a decision suspending application of an agreement and establishing the positions to be adopted on the Union's behalf in a body set up by an agreement, when that body is called upon to adopt acts having legal effects, with the exception of acts supplementing or amending the institutional framework of the agreement.

10. The European Parliament shall be immediately and fully informed at all stages of the procedure.

11. A Member State, the European Parliament, the Council or the Commission may obtain the opinion of the Court of Justice as to whether an agreement envisaged is compatible with the Treaties. Where the opinion of the Court is adverse, the agreement envisaged may not enter into force unless it is amended or the Treaties are revised.

Article 219

(ex Article 111(1) to (3) and (5) TEC)

1. By way of derogation from Article 218, the Council, either on a recommendation from the European Central Bank or on a recommendation from the Commission and after consulting the European Central Bank, in an endeavour to reach a consensus consistent with the objective of price stability, may conclude formal agreements on an exchange-rate system for the euro in relation to the currencies of third States. The Council shall act unanimously after consulting the European Parliament and in accordance with the procedure provided for in paragraph 3.

The Council may, either on a recommendation from the European Central Bank or on a recommendation from the Commission, and after consulting the European Central Bank, in an endeavour to reach a consensus consistent with the objective of price stability, adopt, adjust or abandon the central rates of the euro within the exchange-rate system. The President of the Council shall inform the European Parliament of the adoption, adjustment or abandonment of the euro central rates.

2. In the absence of an exchange-rate system in relation to one or more currencies of third States as referred to in paragraph 1, the Council, either on a recommendation from the Commission and after consulting the European Central Bank or on a recommendation from

the European Central Bank, may formulate general orientations for exchange-rate policy in relation to these currencies. These general orientations shall be without prejudice to the primary objective of the ESCB to maintain price stability.

3. By way of derogation from Article 218, where agreements concerning monetary or foreign exchange regime matters need to be negotiated by the Union with one or more third States or international organisations, the Council, on a recommendation from the Commission and after consulting the European Central Bank, shall decide the arrangements for the negotiation and for the conclusion of such agreements. These arrangements shall ensure that the Union expresses a single position. The Commission shall be fully associated with the negotiations.

4. Without prejudice to Union competence and Union agreements as regards economic and monetary union, Member States may negotiate in international bodies and conclude international agreements.

TITLE VI
THE UNION'S RELATIONS WITH INTERNATIONAL ORGANISATIONS AND THIRD COUNTRIES AND UNION DELEGATIONS

Article 220
(ex Articles 302 to 304 TEC)

1. The Union shall establish all appropriate forms of cooperation with the organs of the United Nations and its specialised agencies, the Council of Europe, the Organisation for Security and Cooperation in Europe and the Organisation for Economic Cooperation and Development.

The Union shall also maintain such relations as are appropriate with other international organisations.

2. The High Representative of the Union for Foreign Affairs and Security Policy and the Commission shall implement this Article.

Article 221

1. Union delegations in third countries and at international organisations shall represent the Union.

2. Union delegations shall be placed under the authority of the High Representative of the Union for Foreign Affairs and Security Policy. They shall act in close cooperation with Member States' diplomatic and consular missions.

TITLE VII
SOLIDARITY CLAUSE

Article 222

1. The Union and its Member States shall act jointly in a spirit of solidarity if a Member State is the object of a terrorist attack or the victim of a natural or man-made disaster. The Union shall mobilise all the instruments at its disposal, including the military resources made available by the Member States, to:

(a) — prevent the terrorist threat in the territory of the Member States;

— protect democratic institutions and the civilian population from any terrorist attack;

— assist a Member State in its territory, at the request of its political authorities, in the event of a terrorist attack;

(b) assist a Member State in its territory, at the request of its political authorities, in the event of a natural or man-made disaster.

2. Should a Member State be the object of a terrorist attack or the victim of a natural or man-made disaster, the other Member States shall assist it at the request of its political authorities. To that end, the Member States shall coordinate between themselves in the Council.

3. The arrangements for the implementation by the Union of the solidarity clause shall be defined by a decision adopted by the Council acting on a joint proposal by the Commission and the High Representative of the Union for Foreign Affairs and Security Policy. The Council shall act in accordance with Article 31(1) of the Treaty on European Union where this decision has defence implications. The European Parliament shall be informed.

For the purposes of this paragraph and without prejudice to Article 240, the Council shall be assisted by the Political and Security Committee with the support of the structures developed in the context of the common security and defence policy and by the Committee referred to in Article 71; the two committees shall, if necessary, submit joint opinions.

4. The European Council shall regularly assess the threats facing the Union in order to enable the Union and its Member States to take effective action.

PART SIX
INSTITUTIONAL AND FINANCIAL PROVISIONS

TITLE I
INSTITUTIONAL PROVISIONS

CHAPTER 1
THE INSTITUTIONS

SECTION 1
THE EUROPEAN PARLIAMENT

Article 223

(ex Article 190(4) and (5) TEC)

1. The European Parliament shall draw up a proposal to lay down the provisions necessary for the election of its Members by direct universal suffrage in accordance with a uniform procedure in all Member States or in accordance with principles common to all Member States.

The Council, acting unanimously in accordance with a special legislative procedure and after obtaining the consent of the European Parliament, which shall act by a majority of its component Members, shall lay down the necessary provisions. These provisions shall enter into force following their approval by the Member States in accordance with their respective constitutional requirements.

2. The European Parliament, acting by means of regulations on its own initiative in accordance with a special legislative procedure after seeking an opinion from the Commission and with the consent of the Council, shall lay down the regulations and general conditions governing the performance of the duties of its Members. All rules or conditions relating to the taxation of Members or former Members shall require unanimity within the Council.

Article 224

(ex Article 191, second subparagraph, TEC)

The European Parliament and the Council, acting in accordance with the ordinary legislative procedure, by means of regulations, shall lay down the regulations governing political parties at European level referred to in Article 10(4) of the Treaty on European Union and in particular the rules regarding their funding.

Article 225

(ex Article 192, second subparagraph, TEC)

The European Parliament may, acting by a majority of its component Members request the Commission to submit any appropriate proposal on matters on which it considers that a Union act is required for the purpose of implementing the Treaties. If the

Commission does not submit a proposal, it shall inform the European Parliament of the reasons.

Article 226
(ex Article 193 TEC)

In the course of its duties, the European Parliament may, at the request of a quarter of its component Members, set up a temporary Committee of Inquiry to investigate, without prejudice to the powers conferred by the Treaties on other institutions or bodies, alleged contraventions or maladministration in the implementation of Union law, except where the alleged facts are being examined before a court and

The temporary Committee of Inquiry shall cease to exist on the submission of its report.

The detailed provisions governing the exercise of the right of inquiry shall be determined by the European Parliament, acting by means of regulations on its own initiative in accordance with a special legislative procedure, after obtaining the consent of the Council and the Commission.

Article 227
(ex Article 194 TEC)

Any citizen of the Union, and any natural or legal person residing or having its registered office in a Member State, shall have the right to address, individually or in association with other citizens or persons, a petition to the European Parliament on a matter which comes within the Union's fields of activity and which affects him, her or it directly.

Article 228
(ex Article 195 TEC)

1. A European Ombudsman, elected by the European Parliament, shall be empowered to receive complaints from any citizen of the Union or any natural or legal person residing or having its registered office in a Member State concerning instances of maladministration in the activities of the Union institutions, bodies, offices or agencies, with the exception of the Court of Justice of the European Union acting in its judicial role. He or she shall examine such complaints and report on them.

In accordance with his duties, the Ombudsman shall conduct inquiries for which he finds grounds, either on his own initiative or on the basis of complaints submitted to him direct or through a Member of the European Parliament, except where the alleged facts are or have been the subject of legal proceedings. Where the Ombudsman establishes an instance of maladministration, he shall refer the matter to the institution, body, office or agency concerned, which shall have a period of three months in which to inform him of its views. The Ombudsman shall then forward a report to the European Parliament and the institution, body, office or agency concerned. The person lodging the complaint shall be informed of the outcome of such inquiries.

The Ombudsman shall submit an annual report to the European Parliament on the outcome of his inquiries.

2. The Ombudsman shall be elected after each election of the European Parliament for the duration of its term of office. The Ombudsman shall be eligible for reappointment.

The Ombudsman may be dismissed by the Court of Justice at the request of the European Parliament if he no longer fulfils the conditions required for the performance of his duties or if he is guilty of serious misconduct

3. The Ombudsman shall be completely independent in the performance of his duties. In the performance of those duties he shall neither seek nor take instructions from any Government, institution, body, office or entity. The Ombudsman may not, during his term of office, engage in any other occupation, whether gainful or not.

4. The European Parliament acting by means of regulations on its own initiative in accordance with a special legislative procedure shall, after seeking an opinion from the Commission and with the consent of the Council, lay down the regulations and general conditions governing the performance of the Ombudsman's duties.

Article 229

(ex Article 196 TEC)

The European Parliament shall hold an annual session. It shall meet, without requiring to be convened, on the second Tuesday in March.

The European Parliament may meet in extraordinary part-session at the request of a majority of its component Members or at the request of the Council or of the Commission.

Article 230

(ex Article 197, second, third and fourth paragraph, TEC)

The Commission may attend all the meetings and shall, at its request, be heard.

The Commission shall reply orally or in writing to questions put to it by the European Parliament or by its Members.

The European Council and the Council shall be heard by the European Parliament in accordance with the conditions laid down in the Rules of Procedure of the European Council and those of the Council.

Article 231
(ex Article 198 TEC)

Save as otherwise provided in the Treaties, the European Parliament shall act by a majority of the votes cast.

The Rules of Procedure shall determine the quorum.

Article 232
(ex Article 199 TEC)

The European Parliament shall adopt its Rules of Procedure, acting by a majority of its Members.

The proceedings of the European Parliament shall be published in the manner laid down in the Treaties and in its Rules of Procedure.

Article 233
(ex Article 200 TEC)

The European Parliament shall discuss in open session the annual general report submitted to it by the Commission.

Article 234
(ex Article 201 TEC)

If a motion of censure on the activities of the Commission is tabled before it, the European Parliament shall not vote thereon until at least three days after the motion has been tabled and only by open vote.

If the motion of censure is carried by a two-thirds majority of the votes cast, representing a majority of the component Members of the European Parliament, the members of the Commission shall resign as a body and the High Representative of the Union for Foreign Affairs and Security Policy shall resign from duties that he or she carries out in the Commission. They shall remain in office and continue to deal with current business until they are replaced in accordance with Article 17 of the Treaty on European Union. In this case, the term of office of the members of the Commission appointed to replace them shall expire on the date on which the term of office of the members of the Commission obliged to resign as a body would have expired.

SECTION 2
THE EUROPEAN COUNCIL

Article 235

1. Where a vote is taken, any member of the European Council may also act on behalf of not more than one other member.

Article 16(4) of the Treaty on European Union and Article 238(2) of this Treaty shall apply to the European Council when it is acting by a qualified majority. Where the European Council decides by vote, its President and the President of the Commission shall not take part in the vote.

Abstentions by members present in person or represented shall not prevent the adoption by the European Council of acts which require unanimity.

2. The President of the European Parliament may be invited to be heard by the European Council.

3. The European Council shall act by a simple majority for procedural questions and for the adoption of its Rules of Procedure.

4. The European Council shall be assisted by the General Secretariat of the Council.

Article 236

The European Council shall adopt by a qualified majority:

(a) a decision establishing the list of Council configurations, other than those of the General Affairs Council and of the Foreign Affairs Council, in accordance with Article 16(6) of the Treaty on European Union;

(b) a decision on the Presidency of Council configurations, other than that of Foreign Affairs, in accordance with Article 16(9) of the Treaty on European Union.

SECTION 3
THE COUNCIL

Article 237
(ex Article 204 TEC)

The Council shall meet when convened by its President on his own initiative or at the request of one of its Members or of the Commission.

Article 238
(ex Article 205(1) and (2), TEC)

1. Where it is required to act by a simple majority, the Council shall act by a majority of its component members.

2. By way of derogation from Article 16(4) of the Treaty on European Union, as from 1 November 2014 and subject to the provisions laid down in the Protocol on transitional provisions, where the Council does not act on a proposal from the Commission or from the High Representative of the Union for Foreign Affairs and Security Policy, the qualified majority shall be defined as at least 72% of the members of the Council, representing Member States comprising at least 65% of the population of the Union.

3. As from 1 November 2014 and subject to the provisions laid down in the Protocol on transitional provisions, in cases where, under the Treaties, not all the members of the Council participate in voting, a qualified majority shall be defined as follows:

(a) A qualified majority shall be defined as at least 55% of the members of the Council representing the participating Member States, comprising at least 65% of the population of these States.

A blocking minority must include at least the minimum number of Council members representing more than 35% of the population of the participating Member States, plus one member, failing which the qualified majority shall be deemed attained;

(b) By way of derogation from point (a), where the Council does not act on a proposal from the Commission or from the High Representative of the Union for Foreign Affairs and Security Policy, the qualified majority shall be defined as at least 72% of the members of the Council representing the participating Member States, comprising at least 65% of the population of these States.

4. Abstentions by Members present in person or represented shall not prevent the adoption by the Council of acts which require unanimity.

Article 239
(ex Article 206 TEC)

Where a vote is taken, any Member of the Council may also act on behalf of not more than one other member.

Article 240
(ex Article 207 TEC)

1. A committee consisting of the Permanent Representatives of the Governments of the Member States shall be responsible for preparing the work of the Council and for carrying out the tasks assigned to it by the latter. The Committee may adopt procedural decisions in cases provided for in the Council's Rules of Procedure.

2. The Council shall be assisted by a General Secretariat, under the responsibility of a Secretary-General appointed by the Council.

The Council shall decide on the organisation of the General Secretariat by a simple majority.

3. The Council shall act by a simple majority regarding procedural matters and for the adoption of its Rules of Procedure.

Article 241

(ex Article 208 TEC)

The Council, acting by a simple majority, may request the Commission to undertake any studies the Council considers desirable for the attainment of the common objectives, and to submit to it any appropriate proposals. If the Commission does not submit a proposal, it shall inform the Council of the reasons.

Article 242

(ex Article 209 TEC)

The Council, acting by a simple majority shall, after consulting the Commission, determine the rules governing the committees provided for in the Treaties.

Article 243

(ex Article 210 TEC)

The Council shall determine the salaries, allowances and pensions of the President of the European Council, the President of the Commission, the High Representative of the Union for Foreign Affairs and Security Policy, the Members of the Commission, the Presidents, Members and Registrars of the Court of Justice of the European Union, and the Secretary-General of the Council. It shall also determine any payment to be made instead of remuneration.

SECTION 4

THE COMMISSION

Article 244

In accordance with Article 17(5) of the Treaty on European Union, the Members of the Commission shall be chosen on the basis of a system of rotation established unanimously by the European Council and on the basis of the following principles:

(a) Member States shall be treated on a strictly equal footing as regards determination of the sequence of, and the time spent by, their nationals as members of the Commission; consequently, the difference between the total number of terms of office held by nationals of any given pair of Member States may never be more than one;

(b) subject to point (a), each successive Commission shall be so composed as to reflect satisfactorily the demographic and geographical range of all the Member States.

Article 245
(ex Article 213 TEC)

The Members of the Commission shall refrain from any action incompatible with their duties. Member States shall respect their independence and shall not seek to influence them in the performance of their tasks.

The Members of the Commission may not, during their term of office, engage in any other occupation, whether gainful or not. When entering upon their duties they shall give a solemn undertaking that, both during and after their term of office, they will respect the obligations arising therefrom and in particular their duty to behave with integrity and discretion as regards the acceptance, after they have ceased to hold office, of certain appointments or benefits. In the event of any breach of these obligations, the Court of Justice may, on application by the Council acting by a simple majority or the Commission, rule that the Member concerned be, according to the circumstances, either compulsorily retired in accordance with Article 247 or deprived of his right to a pension or other benefits in its stead.

Article 246
(ex Article 215 TEC)

Apart from normal replacement, or death, the duties of a Member of the Commission shall end when he resigns or is compulsorily retired.

A vacancy caused by resignation, compulsory retirement or death shall be filled for the remainder of the Member's term of office by a new Member of the same nationality appointed by the Council, by common accord with the President of the Commission, after consulting the European Parliament and in accordance with the criteria set out in the second subparagraph of Article 17(3) of the Treaty on European Union.

The Council may, acting unanimously on a proposal from the President of the Commission, decide that such a vacancy need not be filled, in particular when the remainder of the Member's term of office is short.

In the event of resignation, compulsory retirement or death, the President shall be replaced for the remainder of his term of office. The procedure laid down in the first subparagraph of Article 17(7) of the Treaty on European Union shall be applicable for the replacement of the President.

In the event of resignation, compulsory retirement or death, the High Representative of the Union for Foreign Affairs and Security Policy shall be replaced, for the remainder of his or her term of office, in accordance with Article 18(1) of the Treaty on European Union.

In the case of the resignation of all the Members of the Commission, they shall remain in office and continue to deal with current business until they have been replaced, for the remainder of their term of office, in accordance with Article 17 of the Treaty on European Union.

Article 247

(ex Article 216 TEC)

If any Member of the Commission no longer fulfils the conditions required for the performance of his duties or if he has been guilty of serious misconduct, the Court of Justice may, on application by the Council acting by a simple majority or the Commission, compulsorily retire him.

Article 248

(ex Article 217(2) TEC)

Without prejudice to Article 18(4) of the Treaty on European Union, the responsibilities incumbent upon the Commission shall be structured and allocated among its members by its President, in accordance with Article 17(6) of that Treaty. The President may reshuffle the allocation of those responsibilities during the Commission's term of office. The Members of the Commission shall carry out the duties devolved upon them by the President under his authority.

Article 249

(ex Articles 218(2) and 212 TEC)

1. The Commission shall adopt its Rules of Procedure so as to ensure that both it and its departments operate. It shall ensure that these Rules are published.

2. The Commission shall publish annually, not later than one month before the opening of the session of the European Parliament, a general report on the activities of the Union.

Article 250

(ex Article 219 TEC)

The Commission shall act by a majority of its Members.

Its Rules of Procedure shall determine the quorum.

SECTION 5
THE COURT OF JUSTICE OF THE EUROPEAN UNION

Article 251
(ex Article 221 TEC)

The Court of Justice shall sit in chambers or in a Grand Chamber, in accordance with the rules laid down for that purpose in the Statute of the Court of Justice of the European Union.

When provided for in the Statute, the Court of Justice may also sit as a full Court.

Article 252
(ex Article 222 TEC)

The Court of Justice shall be assisted by eight Advocates-General. Should the Court of Justice so request, the Council, acting unanimously, may increase the number of Advocates-General.

It shall be the duty of the Advocate-General, acting with complete impartiality and independence, to make, in open court, reasoned submissions on cases which, in accordance with the Statute of the Court of Justice of the European Union, require his involvement.

Article 253
(ex Article 223 TEC)

The Judges and Advocates-General of the Court of Justice shall be chosen from persons whose independence is beyond doubt and who possess the qualifications required for appointment to the highest judicial offices in their respective countries or who are jurisconsults of recognised competence; they shall be appointed by common accord of the governments of the Member States for a term of six years, after consultation of the panel provided for in Article 255.

Every three years there shall be a partial replacement of the Judges and Advocates-General, in accordance with the conditions laid down in the Statute of the Court of Justice of the European Union.

The Judges shall elect the President of the Court of Justice from among their number for a term of three years. He may be re-elected.

Retiring Judges and Advocates-General may be reappointed.

The Court of Justice shall appoint its Registrar and lay down the rules governing his service.

The Court of Justice shall establish its Rules of Procedure. Those Rules shall require the approval of the Council.

Article 254
(ex Article 224 TEC)

The number of Judges of the General Court shall be determined by the Statute of the Court of Justice of the European Union. The Statute may provide for the General Court to be assisted by Advocates-General.

The members of the General Court shall be chosen from persons whose independence is beyond doubt and who possess the ability required for appointment to high judicial office. They shall be appointed by common accord of the governments of the Member States for a term of six years, after consultation of the panel provided for in Article 255. The membership shall be partially renewed every three years. Retiring members shall be eligible for reappointment.

The Judges shall elect the President of the General Court from among their number for a term of three years. He may be re-elected.

The General Court shall appoint its Registrar and lay down the rules governing his service.

The General Court shall establish its Rules of Procedure in agreement with the Court of Justice. Those Rules shall require the approval of the Council.

Unless the Statute of the Court of Justice of the European Union provides otherwise, the provisions of the Treaties relating to the Court of Justice shall apply to the General Court.

Article 255

A panel shall be set up in order to give an opinion on candidates' suitability to perform the duties of Judge and Advocate-General of the Court of Justice and the General Court before the governments of the Member States make the appointments referred to in Articles 253 and 254.

The panel shall comprise seven persons chosen from among former members of the Court of Justice and the General Court, members of national supreme courts and lawyers of recognised competence, one of whom shall be proposed by the European Parliament. The Council shall adopt a decision establishing the panel's operating rules and a decision appointing its members. It shall act on the initiative of the President of the Court of Justice.

Article 256
(ex Article 225 TEC)

1. The General Court shall have jurisdiction to hear and determine at first instance actions or proceedings referred to in Articles 263, 265, 268, 270 and 272, with the exception of those

assigned to a specialised court set up under Article 257 and those reserved in the Statute for the Court of Justice. The Statute may provide for the General Court to have jurisdiction for other classes of action or proceeding.

Decisions given by the General Court under this paragraph may be subject to a right of appeal to the Court of Justice on points of law only, under the conditions and within the limits laid down by the Statute.

2. The General Court shall have jurisdiction to hear and determine actions or proceedings brought against decisions of the specialised courts.

Decisions given by the General Court under this paragraph may exceptionally be subject to review by the Court of Justice, under the conditions and within the limits laid down by the Statute, where there is a serious risk of the unity or consistency of Union law being affected.

3. The General Court shall have jurisdiction to hear and determine questions referred for a preliminary ruling under Article 267, in specific areas laid down by the Statute.

Where the General Court considers that the case requires a decision of principle likely to affect the unity or consistency of Union law, it may refer the case to the Court of Justice for a ruling.

Decisions given by the General Court on questions referred for a preliminary ruling may exceptionally be subject to review by the Court of Justice, under the conditions and within the limits laid down by the Statute, where there is a serious risk of the unity or consistency of Union law being affected.

Article 257
(ex Article 225*a* TEC)

The European Parliament and the Council, acting in accordance with the ordinary legislative procedure, may establish specialised courts attached to the General Court to hear and determine at first instance certain classes of action or proceeding brought in specific areas. The European Parliament and the Council shall act by means of regulations either on a proposal from the Commission after consultation of the Court of Justice or at the request of the Court of Justice after consultation of the Commission.

The regulation establishing a specialised court shall lay down the rules on the organisation of the court and the extent of the jurisdiction conferred upon it.

Decisions given by specialised courts may be subject to a right of appeal on points of law only or, when provided for in the regulation establishing the specialised court, a right of appeal also on matters of fact, before the General Court.

The members of the specialised courts shall be chosen from persons whose independence is beyond doubt and who possess the ability required for appointment to judicial office. They shall be appointed by the Council, acting unanimously.

The specialised courts shall establish their Rules of Procedure in agreement with the Court of Justice. Those Rules shall require the approval of the Council.

Unless the regulation establishing the specialised court provides otherwise, the provisions of the Treaties relating to the Court of Justice of the European Union and the provisions of the Statute of the Court of Justice of the European Union shall apply to the specialised courts. Title I of the Statute and Article 64 thereof shall in any case apply to the specialised courts.

Article 258
(ex Article 226 TEC)

If the Commission considers that a Member State has failed to fulfil an obligation under the Treaties, it shall deliver a reasoned opinion on the matter after giving the State concerned the opportunity to submit its observations.

If the State concerned does not comply with the opinion within the period laid down by the Commission, the latter may bring the matter before the Court of Justice of the European Union.

Article 259
(ex Article 227 TEC)

A Member State which considers that another Member State has failed to fulfil an obligation under the Treaties may bring the matter before the Court of Justice of the European Union.

Before a Member State brings an action against another Member State for an alleged infringement of an obligation under the Treaties, it shall bring the matter before the Commission.

The Commission shall deliver a reasoned opinion after each of the States concerned has been given the opportunity to submit its own case and its observations on the other party's case both orally and in writing.

If the Commission has not delivered an opinion within three months of the date on which the matter was brought before it, the absence of such opinion shall not prevent the matter from being brought before the Court.

Article 260
(ex Article 228 TEC)

1. If the Court of Justice of the European Union finds that a Member State has failed to fulfil an obligation under the Treaties, the State shall be required to take the necessary measures to comply with the judgment of the Court.

2. If the Commission considers that the Member State concerned has not taken the necessary measures to comply with the judgment of the Court, it may bring the case before the Court after giving that State the opportunity to submit its observations. It shall specify the amount of the lump sum or penalty payment to be paid by the Member State concerned which it considers appropriate in the circumstances.

If the Court finds that the Member State concerned has not complied with its judgment it may impose a lump sum or penalty payment on it.

This procedure shall be without prejudice to Article 259.

3. When the Commission brings a case before the Court pursuant to Article 258 on the grounds that the Member State concerned has failed to fulfil its obligation to notify measures transposing a directive adopted under a legislative procedure, it may, when it deems appropriate, specify the amount of the lump sum or penalty payment to be paid by the Member State concerned which it considers appropriate in the circumstances.

If the Court finds that there is an infringement it may impose a lump sum or penalty payment on the Member State concerned not exceeding the amount specified by the Commission. The payment obligation shall take effect on the date set by the Court in its judgment.

Article 261
(ex Article 229 TEC)

Regulations adopted jointly by the European Parliament and the Council, and by the Council, pursuant to the provisions of the Treaties, may give the Court of Justice of the European Union unlimited jurisdiction with regard to the penalties provided for in such regulations.

Article 262
(ex Article 229*a* TEC)

Without prejudice to the other provisions of the Treaties, the Council, acting unanimously in accordance with a special legislative procedure and after consulting the European Parliament, may adopt provisions to confer jurisdiction, to the extent that it shall determine, on the Court of Justice of the European Union in disputes relating to the application of acts adopted on the basis of the Treaties which create European intellectual property rights. These provisions shall enter into force after their approval by the Member States in accordance with their respective constitutional requirements.

Article 263
(ex Article 230 TEC)

The Court of Justice of the European Union shall review the legality of legislative acts, of acts of the Council, of the Commission and of the European Central Bank, other than recommendations and opinions, and of acts of the European Parliament and of the European Council intended to produce legal effects *vis-à-vis* third parties. It shall also review the legality of acts of bodies, offices or agencies of the Union intended to produce legal effects *vis-à-vis* third parties.

It shall for this purpose have jurisdiction in actions brought by a Member State, the European Parliament, the Council or the Commission on grounds of lack of competence, infringement of an essential procedural requirement, infringement of the Treaties or of any rule of law relating to their application, or misuse of powers.

The Court shall have jurisdiction under the same conditions in actions brought by the Court of Auditors, by the European Central Bank and by the Committee of the Regions for the purpose of protecting their prerogatives.

Any natural or legal person may, under the conditions laid down in the first and second paragraphs, institute proceedings against an act addressed to that person or which is of direct and individual concern to them, and against a regulatory act which is of direct concern to them and does not entail implementing measures.

Acts setting up bodies, offices and agencies of the Union may lay down specific conditions and arrangements concerning actions brought by natural or legal persons against acts of these bodies, offices or agencies intended to produce legal effects in relation to them.

The proceedings provided for in this Article shall be instituted within two months of the publication of the measure, or of its notification to the plaintiff, or, in the absence thereof, of the day on which it came to the knowledge of the latter, as the case may be.

Article 264
(ex Article 231 TEC)

If the action is well founded, the Court of Justice of the European Union shall declare the act concerned to be void.

However, the Court shall, if it considers this necessary, state which of the effects of the act which it has declared void shall be considered as definitive.

Article 265
(ex Article 232 TEC)

Should the European Parliament, the European Council, the Council, the Commission or the European Central Bank, in infringement of the Treaties, fail to act, the Member States and the other institutions of the Union may bring an action before the Court of Justice of the European Union to have the infringement established. This Article shall apply, under the same conditions, to bodies, offices and agencies of the Union which fail to act.

The action shall be admissible only if the institution, body, office or agency concerned has first been called upon to act. If, within two months of being so called upon, the institution, body, office or agency concerned has not defined its position, the action may be brought within a further period of two months.

Any natural or legal person may, under the conditions laid down in the preceding paragraphs, complain to the Court that an institution, body, office or agency of the Union has failed to address to that person any act other than a recommendation or an opinion.

Article 266
(ex Article 233 TEC)

The institution whose act has been declared void or whose failure to act has been declared contrary to the Treaties shall be required to take the necessary measures to comply with the judgment of the Court of Justice of the European Union.

This obligation shall not affect any obligation which may result from the application of the second paragraph of Article 340.

Article 267
(ex Article 234 TEC)

The Court of Justice of the European Union shall have jurisdiction to give preliminary rulings concerning:

(a) the interpretation of the Treaties;

(b) the validity and interpretation of acts of the institutions, bodies, offices or agencies of the Union;

Where such a question is raised before any court or tribunal of a Member State, that court or tribunal may, if it considers that a decision on the question is necessary to enable it to give judgment, request the Court to give a ruling thereon.

Where any such question is raised in a case pending before a court or tribunal of a Member State against whose decisions there is no judicial remedy under national law, that court or tribunal shall bring the matter before the Court.

If such a question is raised in a case pending before a court or tribunal of a Member State with regard to a person in custody, the Court of Justice of the European Union shall act with the minimum of delay.

Article 268
(ex Article 235 TEC)

The Court of Justice of the European Union shall have jurisdiction in disputes relating to compensation for damage provided for in the second and third paragraphs of Article 340.

Article 269

The Court of Justice shall have jurisdiction to decide on the legality of an act adopted by the European Council or by the Council pursuant to Article 7 of the Treaty on European Union solely at the request of the Member State concerned by a determination of the European Council or of the Council and in respect solely of the procedural stipulations contained in that Article.

Such a request must be made within one month from the date of such determination. The Court shall rule within one month from the date of the request.

Article 270
(ex Article 236 TEC)

The Court of Justice of the European Union shall have jurisdiction in any dispute between the Union and its servants within the limits and under the conditions laid down in the Staff Regulations of Officials and the Conditions of Employment of other servants of the Union.

Article 271
(ex Article 237 TEC)

The Court of Justice of the European Union shall, within the limits hereinafter laid down, have jurisdiction in disputes concerning:

(a) the fulfilment by Member States of obligations under the Statute of the European Investment Bank. In this connection, the Board of Directors of the Bank shall enjoy the powers conferred upon the Commission by Article 258;

(b) measures adopted by the Board of Governors of the European Investment Bank. In this connection, any Member State, the Commission or the Board of Directors of the Bank may institute proceedings under the conditions laid down in Article 263;

(c) measures adopted by the Board of Directors of the European Investment Bank. Proceedings against such measures may be instituted only by Member States or by the Commission, under the conditions laid down in Article 263, and solely on the grounds of non-compliance with the procedure provided for in Article 19(2), (5), (6) and (7) of the Statute of the Bank;

(d) the fulfilment by national central banks of obligations under the Treaties and the Statute of the ESCB and of the ECB. In this connection the powers of the Governing Council of the European Central Bank in respect of national central banks shall be the same as those conferred upon the Commission in respect of Member States by Article 258. If the Court finds that a national central bank has failed to fulfil an obligation under the Treaties, that bank shall be required to take the necessary measures to comply with the judgment of the Court.

Article 272
(ex Article 238 TEC)

The Court of Justice of the European Union shall have jurisdiction to give judgment pursuant to any arbitration clause contained in a contract concluded by or on behalf of the Union, whether that contract be governed by public or private law.

Article 273
(ex Article 239 TEC)

The Court of Justice shall have jurisdiction in any dispute between Member States which relates to the subject matter of the Treaties if the dispute is submitted to it under a special agreement between the parties.

Article 274
(ex Article 240 TEC)

Save where jurisdiction is conferred on the Court of Justice of the European Union by the Treaties, disputes to which the Union is a party shall not on that ground be excluded from the jurisdiction of the courts or tribunals of the Member States.

Article 275

The Court of Justice of the European Union shall not have jurisdiction with respect to the provisions relating to the common foreign and security policy nor with respect to acts adopted on the basis of those provisions.

However, the Court shall have jurisdiction to monitor compliance with Article 40 of the Treaty on European Union and to rule on proceedings, brought in accordance with the conditions laid down in the fourth paragraph of Article 263 of this Treaty, reviewing the legality of decisions providing for restrictive measures against natural or legal persons adopted by the Council on the basis of Chapter 2 of Title V of the Treaty on European Union.

Article 276

In exercising its powers regarding the provisions of Chapters 4 and 5 of Title V of Part Three relating to the area of freedom, security and justice, the Court of Justice of the European Union shall have no jurisdiction to review the validity or proportionality of operations carried out by the police or other law-enforcement services of a Member State or the exercise of the responsibilities incumbent upon Member States with regard to the maintenance of law and order and the safeguarding of internal security.

Article 277
(ex Article 241 TEC)

Notwithstanding the expiry of the period laid down in Article 263, sixth paragraph, any party may, in proceedings in which an act of general application adopted by an institution, body, office or agency of the Union is at issue, plead the grounds specified in Article 263, second paragraph, in order to invoke before the Court of Justice of the European Union the inapplicability of that act.

Article 278
(ex Article 242 TEC)

Actions brought before the Court of Justice of the European Union shall not have suspensory effect. The Court may, however, if it considers that circumstances so require, order that application of the contested act be suspended.

Article 279
(ex Article 243 TEC)

The Court of Justice of the European Union may in any cases before it prescribe any necessary interim measures.

Article 280
(ex Article 244 TEC)

The judgments of the Court of Justice of the European Union shall be enforceable under the conditions laid down in Article 299.

Article 281
(ex Article 245 TEC)

The Statute of the Court of Justice of the European Union shall be laid down in a separate Protocol.

The European Parliament and the Council, acting in accordance with the ordinary legislative procedure, may amend the provisions of the Statute, with the exception of Title I and Article 64. The European Parliament and the Council shall act either at the request of the Court of Justice and after consultation of the Commission, or on a proposal from the Commission and after consultation of the Court of Justice.

SECTION 6
THE EUROPEAN CENTRAL BANK

Article 282

1. The European Central Bank, together with the national central banks, shall constitute the European System of Central Banks (ESCB). The European Central Bank, together with the national central banks of the Member States whose currency is the euro, which constitute the Eurosystem, shall conduct the monetary policy of the Union.

2. The ESCB shall be governed by the decision-making bodies of the European Central Bank. The primary objective of the ESCB shall be to maintain price stability. Without prejudice to that objective, it shall support the general economic policies in the Union in order to contribute to the achievement of the latter's objectives.

3. The European Central Bank shall have legal personality. It alone may authorise the issue of the euro. It shall be independent in the exercise of its powers and in the management of its finances. Union institutions, bodies, offices and agencies and the governments of the Member States shall respect that independence.

4. The European Central Bank shall adopt such measures as are necessary to carry out its tasks in accordance with Articles 127

to 133, with Article 138, and with the conditions laid down in the Statute of the ESCB and of the ECB. In accordance with these same Articles, those Member States whose currency is not the euro, and their central banks, shall retain their powers in monetary matters.

5. Within the areas falling within its responsibilities, the European Central Bank shall be consulted on all proposed Union acts, and all proposals for regulation at national level, and may give an opinion.

Article 283
(ex Article 112 TEC)

1. The Governing Council of the European Central Bank shall comprise the members of the Executive Board of the European Central Bank and the Governors of the national central banks of the Member States whose currency is the euro.

2. The Executive Board shall comprise the President, the Vice-President and four other members.

The President, the Vice-President and the other members of the Executive Board shall be appointed by the European Council, acting by a qualified majority, from among persons of recognised standing and professional experience in monetary or banking matters, on a recommendation from the Council, after it has consulted the European Parliament and the Governing Council of the European Central Bank.

Their term of office shall be eight years and shall not be renewable.

Only nationals of Member States may be members of the Executive Board.

Article 284
(ex Article 113 TEC)

1. The President of the Council and a Member of the Commission may participate, without having the right to vote, in meetings of the Governing Council of the European Central Bank.

The President of the Council may submit a motion for deliberation to the Governing Council of the European Central Bank.

2. The President of the European Central Bank shall be invited to participate in Council meetings when the Council is discussing matters relating to the objectives and tasks of the ESCB.

3. The European Central Bank shall address an annual report on the activities of the ESCB and on the monetary policy of both the previous and current year to the European Parliament, the Council

and the Commission, and also to the European Council. The President of the European Central Bank shall present this report to the Council and to the European Parliament, which may hold a general debate on that basis.

The President of the European Central Bank and the other members of the Executive Board may, at the request of the European Parliament or on their own initiative, be heard by the competent committees of the European Parliament.

SECTION 7
THE COURT OF AUDITORS

Article 285
(ex Article 246 TEC)

The Court of Auditors shall carry out the Union's audit.

It shall consist of one national of each Member State. Its Members shall be completely independent in the performance of their duties, in the Union's general interest.

Article 286
(ex Article 247 TEC)

1. The Members of the Court of Auditors shall be chosen from among persons who belong or have belonged in their respective States to external audit bodies or who are especially qualified for this office. Their independence must be beyond doubt.

2. The Members of the Court of Auditors shall be appointed for a term of six years. The Council, after consulting the European Parliament, shall adopt the list of Members drawn up in accordance with the proposals made by each Member State. The term of office of the Members of the Court of Auditors shall be renewable.

They shall elect the President of the Court of Auditors from among their number for a term of three years. The President may be re-elected.

3. In the performance of these duties, the Members of the Court of Auditors shall neither seek nor take instructions from any government or from any other body. The Members of the Court of Auditors shall refrain from any action incompatible with their duties.

4. The Members of the Court of Auditors may not, during their term of office, engage in any other occupation, whether gainful or not. When entering upon their duties they shall give a solemn undertaking that, both during and after their term of office, they will respect the obligations arising therefrom and in particular their duty to behave with integrity and discretion as regards the acceptance,

after they have ceased to hold office, of certain appointments or benefits.

5. Apart from normal replacement, or death, the duties of a Member of the Court of Auditors shall end when he resigns, or is compulsorily retired by a ruling of the Court of Justice pursuant to paragraph 6.

The vacancy thus caused shall be filled for the remainder of the Member's term of office.

Save in the case of compulsory retirement, Members of the Court of Auditors shall remain in office until they have been replaced.

6. A Member of the Court of Auditors may be deprived of his office or of his right to a pension or other benefits in its stead only if the Court of Justice, at the request of the Court of Auditors, finds that he no longer fulfils the requisite conditions or meets the obligations arising from his office.

7. The Council shall determine the conditions of employment of the President and the Members of the Court of Auditors and in particular their salaries, allowances and pensions. It shall also determine any payment to be made instead of remuneration.

8. The provisions of the Protocol on the privileges and immunities of the European Union applicable to the Judges of the Court of Justice of the European Union shall also apply to the Members of the Court of Auditors.

Article 287
(ex Article 248 TEC)

1. The Court of Auditors shall examine the accounts of all revenue and expenditure of the Union. It shall also examine the accounts of all revenue and expenditure of all bodies, offices or agencies set up by the Union in so far as the relevant constituent instrument does not preclude such examination.

The Court of Auditors shall provide the European Parliament and the Council with a statement of assurance as to the reliability of the accounts and the legality and regularity of the underlying transactions which shall be published in the *Official Journal of the European Union*. This statement may be supplemented by specific assessments for each major area of Union activity.

2. The Court of Auditors shall examine whether all revenue has been received and all expenditure incurred in a lawful and regular manner and whether the financial management has been sound. In doing so, it shall report in particular on any cases of irregularity.

The audit of revenue shall be carried out on the basis both of the amounts established as due and the amounts actually paid to the Union.

The audit of expenditure shall be carried out on the basis both of commitments undertaken and payments made.

These audits may be carried out before the closure of accounts for the financial year in question.

3. The audit shall be based on records and, if necessary, performed on the spot in the other institutions of the Union, on the premises of any body, office or agency which manages revenue or expenditure on behalf of the Union and in the Member States, including on the premises of any natural or legal person in receipt of payments from the budget. In the Member States the audit shall be carried out in liaison with national audit bodies or, if these do not have the necessary powers, with the competent national departments. The Court of Auditors and the national audit bodies of the Member States shall cooperate in a spirit of trust while maintaining their independence. These bodies or departments shall inform the Court of Auditors whether they intend to take part in the audit.

The other institutions of the Union, any bodies, offices or agencies managing revenue or expenditure on behalf of the Union, any natural or legal person in receipt of payments from the budget, and the national audit bodies or, if these do not have the necessary powers, the competent national departments, shall forward to the Court of Auditors, at its request, any document or information necessary to carry out its task.

In respect of the European Investment Bank's activity in managing Union expenditure and revenue, the Court's rights of access to information held by the Bank shall be governed by an agreement between the Court, the Bank and the Commission. In the absence of an agreement, the Court shall nevertheless have access to information necessary for the audit of Union expenditure and revenue managed by the Bank.

4. The Court of Auditors shall draw up an annual report after the close of each financial year. It shall be forwarded to the other institutions of the Union and shall be published, together with the replies of these institutions to the observations of the Court of Auditors, in the *Official Journal of the European Union*.

The Court of Auditors may also, at any time, submit observations, particularly in the form of special reports, on specific questions and deliver opinions at the request of one of the other institutions of the Union.

It shall adopt its annual reports, special reports or opinions by a majority of its Members. However, it may establish internal chambers in order to adopt certain categories of reports or opinions under the conditions laid down by its Rules of Procedure.

It shall assist the European Parliament and the Council in exercising their powers of control over the implementation of the budget.

The Court of Auditors shall draw up its Rules of Procedure. Those rules shall require the approval of the Council.

CHAPTER 2
LEGAL ACTS OF THE UNION, ADOPTION PROCEDURES AND OTHER PROVISIONS

SECTION 1
THE LEGAL ACTS OF THE UNION

Article 288
(ex Article 249 TEC)

To exercise the Union's competences, the institutions shall adopt regulations, directives, decisions, recommendations and opinions.

A regulation shall have general application. It shall be binding in its entirety and directly applicable in all Member States.

A directive shall be binding, as to the result to be achieved, upon each Member State to which it is addressed, but shall leave to the national authorities the choice of form and methods.

A decision shall be binding in its entirety. A decision which specifies those to whom it is addressed shall be binding only on them.

Recommendations and opinions shall have no binding force.

Article 289

1. The ordinary legislative procedure shall consist in the joint adoption by the European Parliament and the Council of a regulation, directive or decision on a proposal from the Commission. This procedure is defined in Article 294.

2. In the specific cases provided for by the Treaties, the adoption of a regulation, directive or decision by the European Parliament with the participation of the Council, or by the latter with the participation of the European Parliament, shall constitute a special legislative procedure.

3. Legal acts adopted by legislative procedure shall constitute legislative acts.

4. In the specific cases provided for by the Treaties, legislative acts may be adopted on the initiative of a group of Member States or of the European Parliament, on a recommendation from the European Central Bank or at the request of the Court of Justice or the European Investment Bank.

Article 290

1. A legislative act may delegate to the Commission the power to adopt non-legislative acts of general application to supplement or amend certain non-essential elements of the legislative act.

The objectives, content, scope and duration of the delegation of power shall be explicitly defined in the legislative acts. The essential elements of an area shall be reserved for the legislative act and accordingly shall not be the subject of a delegation of power.

2. Legislative acts shall explicitly lay down the conditions to which the delegation is subject; these conditions may be as follows:

(a) the European Parliament or the Council may decide to revoke the delegation;

(b) the delegated act may enter into force only if no objection has been expressed by the European Parliament or the Council within a period set by the legislative act.

For the purposes of (a) and (b), the European Parliament shall act by a majority of its component members, and the Council by a qualified majority.

3. The adjective "delegated" shall be inserted in the title of delegated acts.

Article 291

1. Member States shall adopt all measures of national law necessary to implement legally binding Union acts.

2. Where uniform conditions for implementing legally binding Union acts are needed, those acts shall confer implementing powers on the Commission, or, in duly justified specific cases and in the cases provided for in Articles 24 and 26 of the Treaty on European Union, on the Council.

3. For the purposes of paragraph 2, the European Parliament and the Council, acting by means of regulations in accordance with the ordinary legislative procedure, shall lay down in advance the rules and general principles concerning mechanisms for control by

Member States of the Commission's exercise of implementing powers.

4. The word "implementing" shall be inserted in the title of implementing acts.

Article 292

The Council shall adopt recommendations. It shall act on a proposal from the Commission in all cases where the Treaties provide that it shall adopt acts on a proposal from the Commission. It shall act unanimously in those areas in which unanimity is required for the adoption of a Union act. The Commission, and the European Central Bank in the specific cases provided for in the Treaties, shall adopt recommendations.

SECTION 2

PROCEDURES FOR THE ADOPTION OF ACTS AND OTHER PROVISIONS

Article 293

(ex Article 250 TEC)

1. Where, pursuant to the Treaties, the Council acts on a proposal from the Commission, it may amend that proposal only by acting unanimously, except in the cases referred to in paragraphs 10 and 13 of Article 294, in Articles 310, 312 and 314 and in the second paragraph of Article 315.

2. As long as the Council has not acted, the Commission may alter its proposal at any time during the procedures leading to the adoption of a Union act.

Article 294

(ex Article 251 TEC)

1. Where reference is made in the Treaties to the ordinary legislative procedure for the adoption of an act, the following procedure shall apply.

2. The Commission shall submit a proposal to the European Parliament and the Council.

First reading

3. The European Parliament shall adopt its position at first reading and communicate it to the Council.

4. If the Council approves the European Parliament's position, the act concerned shall be adopted in the wording which corresponds to the position of the European Parliament.

5. If the Council does not approve the European Parliament's position, it shall adopt its position at first reading and communicate it to the European Parliament.

6. The Council shall inform the European Parliament fully of the reasons which led it to adopt its position at first reading. The Commission shall inform the European Parliament fully of its position.

Second reading

7. If, within three months of such communication, the European Parliament:

(a) approves the Council's position at first reading or has not taken a decision, the act concerned shall be deemed to have been adopted in the wording which corresponds to the position of the Council;

(b) rejects, by a majority of its component members, the Council's position at first reading, the proposed act shall be deemed not to have been adopted;

(c) proposes, by a majority of its component members, amendments to the Council's position at first reading, the text thus amended shall be forwarded to the Council and to the Commission, which shall deliver an opinion on those amendments.

8. If, within three months of receiving the European Parliament's amendments, the Council, acting by a qualified majority:

(a) approves all those amendments, the act in question shall be deemed to have been adopted;

(b) does not approve all the amendments, the President of the Council, in agreement with the President of the European Parliament, shall within six weeks convene a meeting of the Conciliation Committee.

9. The Council shall act unanimously on the amendments on which the Commission has delivered a negative opinion.

Conciliation

10. The Conciliation Committee, which shall be composed of the members of the Council or their representatives and an equal number of members representing the European Parliament, shall have the task of reaching agreement on a joint text, by a qualified majority of the members of the Council or their representatives and by a majority of the members representing the European Parliament

within six weeks of its being convened, on the basis of the positions of the European Parliament and the Council at second reading.

11. The Commission shall take part in the Conciliation Committee's proceedings and shall take all necessary initiatives with a view to reconciling the positions of the European Parliament and the Council.

12. If, within six weeks of its being convened, the Conciliation Committee does not approve the joint text, the proposed act shall be deemed not to have been adopted.

Third reading

13. If, within that period, the Conciliation Committee approves a joint text, the European Parliament, acting by a majority of the votes cast, and the Council, acting by a qualified majority, shall each have a period of six weeks from that approval in which to adopt the act in question in accordance with the joint text. If they fail to do so, the proposed act shall be deemed not to have been adopted.

14. The periods of three months and six weeks referred to in this Article shall be extended by a maximum of one month and two weeks respectively at the initiative of the European Parliament or the Council.

Special provisions

15. Where, in the cases provided for in the Treaties, a legislative act is submitted to the ordinary legislative procedure on the initiative of a group of Member States, on a recommendation by the European Central Bank, or at the request of the Court of Justice, paragraph 2, the second sentence of paragraph 6, and paragraph 9 shall not apply.

In such cases, the European Parliament and the Council shall communicate the proposed act to the Commission with their positions at first and second readings. The European Parliament or the Council may request the opinion of the Commission throughout the procedure, which the Commission may also deliver on its own initiative. It may also, if it deems it necessary, take part in the Conciliation Committee in accordance with paragraph 11.

Article 295

The European Parliament, the Council and the Commission shall consult each other and by common agreement make arrangements for their cooperation. To that end, they may, in compliance with the Treaties, conclude interinstitutional agreements which may be of a binding nature.

Article 296
(ex Article 253 TEC)

Where the Treaties do not specify the type of act to be adopted, the institutions shall select it on a case-by-case basis, in compliance with the applicable procedures and with the principle of proportionality.

Legal acts shall state the reasons on which they are based and shall refer to any proposals, initiatives, recommendations, requests or opinions required by the Treaties.

When considering draft legislative acts, the European Parliament and the Council shall refrain from adopting acts not provided for by the relevant legislative procedure in the area in question.

Article 297
(ex Article 254 TEC)

1. Legislative acts adopted under the ordinary legislative procedure shall be signed by the President of the European Parliament and by the President of the Council.

Legislative acts adopted under a special legislative procedure shall be signed by the President of the institution which adopted them.

Legislative acts shall be published in the *Official Journal of the European Union*. They shall enter into force on the date specified in them or, in the absence thereof, on the twentieth day following that of their publication.

2. Non-legislative acts adopted in the form of regulations, directives or decisions, when the latter do not specify to whom they are addressed, shall be signed by the President of the institution which adopted them.

Regulations and directives which are addressed to all Member States, as well as decisions which do not specify to whom they are addressed, shall be published in the *Official Journal of the European Union*. They shall enter into force on the date specified in them or, in the absence thereof, on the twentieth day following that of their publication.

Other directives, and decisions which specify to whom they are addressed, shall be notified to those to whom they are addressed and shall take effect upon such notification.

Article 298

1. In carrying out their missions, the institutions, bodies, offices and agencies of the Union shall have the support of an open, efficient and independent European administration.

2. In compliance with the Staff Regulations and the Conditions of Employment adopted on the basis of Article 336, the European Parliament and the Council, acting by means of regulations in accordance with the ordinary legislative procedure, shall establish provisions to that end.

Article 299
(ex Article 256 TEC)

Acts of the Council, the Commission or the European Central Bank which impose a pecuniary obligation on persons other than States, shall be enforceable.

Enforcement shall be governed by the rules of civil procedure in force in the State in the territory of which it is carried out. The order for its enforcement shall be appended to the decision, without other formality than verification of the authenticity of the decision, by the national authority which the government of each Member State shall designate for this purpose and shall make known to the Commission and to the Court of Justice of the European Union.

When these formalities have been completed on application by the party concerned, the latter may proceed to enforcement in accordance with the national law, by bringing the matter directly before the competent authority.

Enforcement may be suspended only by a decision of the Court. However, the courts of the country concerned shall have jurisdiction over complaints that enforcement is being carried out in an irregular manner.

CHAPTER 3
THE UNION'S ADVISORY BODIES

Article 300

1. The European Parliament, the Council and the Commission shall be assisted by an Economic and Social Committee and a Committee of the Regions, exercising advisory functions.

2. The Economic and Social Committee shall consist of representatives of organisations of employers, of the employed, and of other parties representative of civil society, notably in socio-economic, civic, professional and cultural areas.

3. The Committee of the Regions shall consist of representatives of regional and local bodies who either hold a regional or local authority electoral mandate or are politically accountable to an elected assembly.

4. The members of the Economic and Social Committee and of the Committee of the Regions shall not be bound by any mandatory instructions. They shall be completely independent in the performance of their duties, in the Union's general interest.

5. The rules referred to in paragraphs 2 and 3 governing the nature of the composition of the Committees shall be reviewed at regular intervals by the Council to take account of economic, social and demographic developments within the Union. The Council, on a proposal from the Commission, shall adopt decisions to that end.

SECTION 1
THE ECONOMIC AND SOCIAL COMMITTEE

Article 301
(ex Article 258 TEC)

The number of members of the Economic and Social Committee shall not exceed 350.

The Council, acting unanimously on a proposal from the Commission, shall adopt a decision determining the Committee's composition.

The Council shall determine the allowances of members of the Committee.

Article 302

1. The members of the Committee shall be appointed for five years The Council shall adopt the list of members drawn up in accordance with the proposals made by each Member State. The term of office of the members of the Committee shall be renewable.

2. The Council shall act after consulting the Commission. It may obtain the opinion of European bodies which are representative of the various economic and social sectors and of civil society to which the Union's activities are of concern.

Article 303
(ex Article 260 TEC)

The Committee shall elect its chairman and officers from among its members for a term of two and a half years.

It shall adopt its Rules of Procedure.

The Committee shall be convened by its chairman at the request of the European Parliament, the Council or of the Commission. It may also meet on its own initiative.

Article 304
(ex Article 262 TEC)

The Committee shall be consulted by the European Parliament, by the Council or by the Commission where the Treaties so provide. The Committee may be consulted by these institutions in all cases in which they consider it appropriate. It may issue an opinion on its own initiative in cases in which it considers such action appropriate.

The European Parliament, the Council or the Commission shall, if it considers it necessary, set the Committee, for the submission of its opinion, a time limit which may not be less than one month from the date on which the chairman receives notification to this effect. Upon expiry of the time limit, the absence of an opinion shall not prevent further action.

The opinion of the Committee, together with a record of the proceedings, shall be forwarded to the European Parliament, to the Council and to the Commission.

SECTION 2
THE COMMITTEE OF THE REGIONS

Article 305
(ex Article 263, second, third and fourth paragraphs, TEC)

The number of members of the Committee of the Regions shall not exceed 350.

The Council, acting unanimously on a proposal from the Commission, shall adopt a decision determining the Committee's composition.

The members of the Committee and an equal number of alternate members shall be appointed for five years. Their term of office shall be renewable. The Council shall adopt the list of members and alternate members drawn up in accordance with the proposals made by each Member State. When the mandate referred to in Article 300(3) on the basis of which they were proposed comes to an end, the term of office of members of the Committee shall terminate automatically and they shall then be replaced for the remainder of the said term of office in accordance with the same procedure. No member of the Committee shall at the same time be a Member of the European Parliament.

Article 306
(ex Article 264 TEC)

The Committee of the Regions shall elect its chairman and officers from among its members for a term of two and a half years.

It shall adopt its Rules of Procedure.

The Committee shall be convened by its chairman at the request of the European Parliament, the Council or of the Commission. It may also meet on its own initiative.

Article 307
(ex Article 265 TEC)

The Committee of the Regions shall be consulted by the European Parliament, by the Council or by the Commission where the Treaties so provide and in all other cases, in particular those which concern cross-border cooperation, in which one of these institutions considers it appropriate.

The European Parliament, the Council or the Commission shall, if it considers it necessary, set the Committee, for the submission of its opinion, a time limit which may not be less than one month from the date on which the chairman receives notification to this effect. Upon expiry of the time limit, the absence of an opinion shall not prevent further action.

Where the Economic and Social Committee is consulted pursuant to Article 304, the Committee of the Regions shall be informed by the European Parliament, the Council or the Commission of the request for an opinion. Where it considers that specific regional interests are involved, the Committee of the Regions may issue an opinion on the matter.

It may issue an opinion on its own initiative in cases in which it considers such action appropriate.

The opinion of the Committee, together with a record of the proceedings, shall be forwarded to the European Parliament, to the Council and to the Commission.

CHAPTER 4
THE EUROPEAN INVESTMENT BANK

Article 308
(ex Article 266 TEC)

The European Investment Bank shall have legal personality.

The members of the European Investment Bank shall be the Member States.

The Statute of the European Investment Bank is laid down in a Protocol annexed to the Treaties. The Council acting unanimously in accordance with a special legislative procedure, at the request of the European Investment Bank and after consulting the European Parliament and the Commission, or on a proposal from the Commission and after consulting the European Parliament and the European Investment Bank, may amend the Statute of the Bank.

Article 309

(ex Article 267 TEC)

The task of the European Investment Bank shall be to contribute, by having recourse to the capital market and utilising its own resources, to the balanced and steady development of the internal market in the interest of the Union. For this purpose the Bank shall, operating on a non-profit-making basis, grant loans and give guarantees which facilitate the financing of the following projects in all sectors of the economy:

(a) projects for developing less-developed regions;

(b) projects for modernising or converting undertakings or for developing fresh activities called for by the establishment or functioning of the internal market, where these projects are of such a size or nature that they cannot be entirely financed by the various means available in the individual Member States;

(c) projects of common interest to several Member States which are of such a size or nature that they cannot be entirely financed by the various means available in the individual Member States.

In carrying out its task, the Bank shall facilitate the financing of investment programmes in conjunction with assistance from the Structural Funds and other Union Financial Instruments.

TITLE II
FINANCIAL PROVISIONS

Article 310

(ex Article 268 TEC)

1. All items of revenue and expenditure of the Union shall be included in estimates to be drawn up for each financial year and shall be shown in the budget.

The Union's annual budget shall be established by the European Parliament and the Council in accordance with Article 314.

The revenue and expenditure shown in the budget shall be in balance.

2. The expenditure shown in the budget shall be authorised for the annual budgetary period in accordance with the regulation referred to in Article 322.

3. The implementation of expenditure shown in the budget shall require the prior adoption of a legally binding Union act providing a legal basis for its action and for the implementation of the corresponding expenditure in accordance with the regulation referred to in Article 322, except in cases for which that law provides.

4. With a view to maintaining budgetary discipline, the Union shall not adopt any act which is likely to have appreciable implications for the budget without providing an assurance that the expenditure arising from such an act is capable of being financed within the limit of the Union's own resources and in compliance with the multiannual financial framework referred to in Article 312.

5. The budget shall be implemented in accordance with the principle of sound financial management. Member States shall cooperate with the Union to ensure that the appropriations entered in the budget are used in accordance with this principle.

6. The Union and the Member States, in accordance with Article 325, shall counter fraud and any other illegal activities affecting the financial interests of the Union.

CHAPTER 1
THE UNION'S OWN RESOURCES

Article 311
(ex Article 269 TEC)

The Union shall provide itself with the means necessary to attain its objectives and carry through its policies.

Without prejudice to other revenue, the budget shall be financed wholly from own resources.

The Council, acting in accordance with a special legislative procedure, shall unanimously and after consulting the European Parliament adopt a decision laying down the provisions relating to the system of own resources of the Union. In this context it may establish new categories of own resources or abolish an existing category. That decision shall not enter into force until it is approved by the Member States in accordance with their respective constitutional requirements.

The Council, acting by means of regulations in accordance with a special legislative procedure, shall lay down implementing measures for the Union's own resources system in so far as this is provided for in the decision adopted on the basis of the third paragraph. The Council shall act after obtaining the consent of the European Parliament.

CHAPTER 2
THE MULTIANNUAL FINANCIAL FRAMEWORK

Article 312

1. The multiannual financial framework shall ensure that Union expenditure develops in an orderly manner and within the limits of its own resources.

It shall be established for a period of at least five years.

The annual budget of the Union shall comply with the multiannual financial framework.

2. The Council, acting in accordance with a special legislative procedure, shall adopt a regulation laying down the multiannual financial framework. The Council shall act unanimously after obtaining the consent of the European Parliament, which shall be given by a majority of its component members.

The European Council may, unanimously, adopt a decision authorising the Council to act by a qualified majority when adopting the regulation referred to in the first subparagraph.

3. The financial framework shall determine the amounts of the annual ceilings on commitment appropriations by category of expenditure and of the annual ceiling on payment appropriations. The categories of expenditure, limited in number, shall correspond to the Union's major sectors of activity.

The financial framework shall lay down any other provisions required for the annual budgetary procedure to run smoothly.

4. Where no Council regulation determining a new financial framework has been adopted by the end of the previous financial framework, the ceilings and other provisions corresponding to the last year of that framework shall be extended until such time as that act is adopted.

5. Throughout the procedure leading to the adoption of the financial framework, the European Parliament, the Council and the Commission shall take any measure necessary to facilitate its adoption.

CHAPTER 3
THE UNION'S ANNUAL BUDGET

Article 313

(ex Article 272(1), TEC)

The financial year shall run from 1 January to 31 December.

Article 314
(ex Article 272(2) to (10), TEC)

The European Parliament and the Council, acting in accordance with a special legislative procedure, shall establish the Union's annual budget in accordance with the following provisions.

1. With the exception of the European Central Bank, each institution shall, before 1 July, draw up estimates of its expenditure for the following financial year. The Commission shall consolidate these estimates in a draft budget. which may contain different estimates.

The draft budget shall contain an estimate of revenue and an estimate of expenditure.

2. The Commission shall submit a proposal containing the draft budget to the European Parliament and to the Council not later than 1 September of the year preceding that in which the budget is to be implemented.

The Commission may amend the draft budget during the procedure until such time as the Conciliation Committee, referred to in paragraph 5, is convened.

3. The Council shall adopt its position on the draft budget and forward it to the European Parliament not later than 1 October of the year preceding that in which the budget is to be implemented. The Council shall inform the European Parliament in full of the reasons which led it to adopt its position.

4. If, within forty-two days of such communication, the European Parliament:

(a) approves the position of the Council, the budget shall be adopted;

(b) has not taken a decision, the budget shall be deemed to have been adopted;

(c) adopts amendments by a majority of its component members, the amended draft shall be forwarded to the Council and to the Commission. The President of the European Parliament, in agreement with the President of the Council, shall immediately convene a meeting of the Conciliation Committee. However, if within ten days of the draft being forwarded the Council informs the European Parliament that it has approved all its amendments, the Conciliation Committee shall not meet.

5. The Conciliation Committee, which shall be composed of the members of the Council or their representatives and an equal

number of members representing the European Parliament, shall have the task of reaching agreement on a joint text, by a qualified majority of the members of the Council or their representatives and by a majority of the representatives of the European Parliament within twenty-one days of its being convened, on the basis of the positions of the European Parliament and the Council.

The Commission shall take part in the Conciliation Committee's proceedings and shall take all the necessary initiatives with a view to reconciling the positions of the European Parliament and the Council.

6. If, within the twenty-one days referred to in paragraph 5, the Conciliation Committee agrees on a joint text, the European Parliament and the Council shall each have a period of fourteen days from the date of that agreement in which to approve the joint text.

7. If, within the period of fourteen days referred to in paragraph 6:

(a) the European Parliament and the Council both approve the joint text or fail to take a decision, or if one of these institutions approves the joint text while the other one fails to take a decision, the budget shall be deemed to be definitively adopted in accordance with the joint text; or

(b) the European Parliament, acting by a majority of its component members, and the Council both reject the joint text, or if one of these institutions rejects the joint text while the other one fails to take a decision, a new draft budget shall be submitted by the Commission; or

(c) the European Parliament, acting by a majority of its component members, rejects the joint text while the Council approves it, a new draft budget shall be submitted by the Commission; or

(d) the European Parliament approves the joint text whilst the Council rejects it, the European Parliament may, within fourteen days from the date of the rejection by the Council and acting by a majority of its component members and three-fifths of the votes cast, decide to confirm all or some of the amendments referred to in paragraph 4(c). Where a European Parliament amendment is not confirmed, the position agreed in the Conciliation Committee on the budget heading which is the subject of the amendment shall be retained. The budget shall be deemed to be definitively adopted on this basis.

8. If, within the twenty-one days referred to in paragraph 5, the Conciliation Committee does not agree on a joint text, a new draft budget shall be submitted by the Commission.

9. When the procedure provided for in this Article has been completed, the President of the European Parliament shall declare that the budget has been definitively adopted.

10. Each institution shall exercise the powers conferred upon it under this Article in compliance with the Treaties and the acts adopted thereunder, with particular regard to the Union's own resources and the balance between revenue and expenditure.

Article 315
(ex Article 273 TEC)

If, at the beginning of a financial year, the budget has not yet been definitively adopted, a sum equivalent to not more than one twelfth of the budget appropriations for the preceding financial year may be spent each month in respect of any chapter of the budget in accordance with the provisions of the Regulations made pursuant to Article 322; that sum shall not, however, exceed one twelfth of the appropriations provided for in the same chapter of the draft budget.

The Council on a proposal by the Commission, may, provided that the other conditions laid down in the first paragraph are observed, authorise expenditure in excess of one twelfth in accordance with the regulations made pursuant to Article 322. The Council shall forward the decision immediately to the European Parliament.

The decision referred to in the second paragraph shall lay down the necessary measures relating to resources to ensure application of this Article, in accordance with the acts referred to in Article 311.

It shall enter into force thirty days following its adoption if the European Parliament, acting by a majority of its component Members, has not decided to reduce this expenditure within that time-limit.

Article 316
(ex Article 271 TEC)

In accordance with conditions to be laid down pursuant to Article 322, any appropriations, other than those relating to staff expenditure, that are unexpended at the end of the financial year may be carried forward to the next financial year only.

Appropriations shall be classified under different chapters grouping items of expenditure according to their nature or purpose and subdivided in accordance with the regulations made pursuant to Article 322.

The expenditure of the European Parliament, the European Council and the Council, the Commission and the Court of Justice of the European Union shall be set out in separate parts of the budget, without prejudice to special arrangements for certain common items of expenditure.

CHAPTER 4
IMPLEMENTATION OF THE BUDGET AND DISCHARGE

Article 317
(ex Article 274 TEC)

The Commission shall implement the budget in cooperation with the Member States, in accordance with the provisions of the regulations made pursuant to Article 322, on its own responsibility and within the limits of the appropriations, having regard to the principles of sound financial management. Member States shall cooperate with the Commission to ensure that the appropriations are used in accordance with the principles of sound financial management.

The regulations shall lay down the control and audit obligations of the Member States in the implementation of the budget and the resulting responsibilities. They shall also lay down the responsibilities and detailed rules for each institution concerning its part in effecting its own expenditure.

Within the budget, the Commission may, subject to the limits and conditions laid down in the regulations made pursuant to Article 322, transfer appropriations from one chapter to another or from one subdivision to another.

Article 318
(ex Article 275 TEC)

The Commission shall submit annually to the European Parliament and to the Council the accounts of the preceding financial year relating to the implementation of the budget. The Commission shall also forward to them a financial statement of the assets and liabilities of the Union.

The Commission shall also submit to the European Parliament and to the Council an evaluation report on the Union's finances based on the results achieved, in particular in relation to the indications given by the European Parliament and the Council pursuant to Article 319.

Article 319
(ex Article 276 TEC)

1. The European Parliament, acting on a recommendation from the Council, shall give a discharge to the Commission in respect of the implementation of the budget. To this end, the Council and the European Parliament in turn shall examine the accounts, the financial statement and the evaluation report referred to in Article 318, the annual report by the Court of Auditors together with the replies of the institutions under audit to the observations of the Court of Auditors, the statement of assurance referred to in Article 287(1), second subparagraph and any relevant special reports by the Court of Auditors.

2. Before giving a discharge to the Commission, or for any other purpose in connection with the exercise of its powers over the implementation of the budget, the European Parliament may ask to hear the Commission give evidence with regard to the execution of expenditure or the operation of financial control systems. The Commission shall submit any necessary information to the European Parliament at the latter's request.

3. The Commission shall take all appropriate steps to act on the observations in the decisions giving discharge and on other observations by the European Parliament relating to the execution of expenditure, as well as on comments accompanying the recommendations on discharge adopted by the Council.

At the request of the European Parliament or the Council, the Commission shall report on the measures taken in the light of these observations and comments and in particular on the instructions given to the departments which are responsible for the implementation of the budget. These reports shall also be forwarded to the Court of Auditors.

CHAPTER 5
COMMON PROVISIONS

Article 320
(ex Article 277 TEC)

The multiannual financial framework and the annual budget shall be drawn up in euro.

Article 321
(ex Article 278 TEC)

The Commission may, provided it notifies the competent authorities of the Member States concerned, transfer into the currency of one of the Member States its holdings in the currency of another Member State, to the extent necessary to enable them to be used for purposes which come within the scope of the Treaties. The Commission shall as far as possible avoid making such transfers if it possesses cash or liquid assets in the currencies which it needs.

The Commission shall deal with each Member State through the authority designated by the State concerned. In carrying out financial operations the Commission shall employ the services of the bank of issue of the Member State concerned or of any other financial institution approved by that State.

Article 322

(ex Article 279 TEC)

1. The European Parliament and the Council, acting in accordance with the ordinary legislative procedure, and after consulting the Court of Auditors, shall adopt by means of regulations:

(a) the financial rules which determine in particular the procedure to be adopted for establishing and implementing the budget and for presenting and auditing accounts;

(b) rules providing for checks on the responsibility of financial actors, in particular authorising officers and accounting officers.

2. The Council, acting on a proposal from the Commission and after consulting the European Parliament and the Court of Auditors, shall determine the methods and procedure whereby the budget revenue provided under the arrangements relating to the Union's own resources shall be made available to the Commission, and determine the measures to be applied, if need be, to meet cash requirements.

Article 323

The European Parliament, the Council and the Commission shall ensure that the financial means are made available to allow the Union to fulfil its legal obligations in respect of third parties.

Article 324

Regular meetings between the Presidents of the European Parliament, the Council and the Commission shall be convened, on the initiative of the Commission, under the budgetary procedures referred to in this Title. The Presidents shall take all the necessary steps to promote consultation and the reconciliation of the positions of the institutions over which they preside in order to facilitate the implementation of this Title.

CHAPTER 6
COMBATTING FRAUD

Article 325
(ex Article 280 TEC)

1. The Union and the Member States shall counter fraud and any other illegal activities affecting the financial interests of the Union through measures to be taken in accordance with this Article, which shall act as a deterrent and be such as to afford effective protection in the Member States, and in all the Union's institutions, bodies, offices and agencies.

2. Member States shall take the same measures to counter fraud affecting the financial interests of the Union as they take to counter fraud affecting their own financial interests.

3. Without prejudice to other provisions of the Treaties, the Member States shall coordinate their action aimed at protecting the financial interests of the Union against fraud. To this end they shall organise, together with the Commission, close and regular cooperation between the competent authorities.

4. The European Parliament and the Council, acting in accordance with the ordinary legislative procedure, after consulting the Court of Auditors, shall adopt the necessary measures in the fields of the prevention of and fight against fraud affecting the financial interests of the Union with a view to affording effective and equivalent protection in the Member States and in all the Union's institutions, bodies, offices and agencies.

5. The Commission, in cooperation with Member States, shall each year submit to the European Parliament and to the Council a report on the measures taken for the implementation of this Article.

TITLE III
ENHANCED COOPERATION

Article 326
(ex Articles 27*a* to 27*e*, 40 to 40*b* and 43 to 45 TEU and ex Articles 11 and 11*a* TEC)

Any enhanced cooperation shall comply with the Treaties and Union law.

Such cooperation shall not undermine the internal market or economic, social and territorial cohesion. It shall not constitute a barrier to or discrimination in trade between Member States, nor shall it distort competition between them.

Article 327
(ex Articles 27*a* to 27*e*, 40 to 40*b* and 43 to 45 TEU
and ex Articles 11 and 11*a* TEC)

Any enhanced cooperation shall respect the competences, rights and obligations of those Member States which do not participate in it. Those Member States shall not impede its implementation by the participating Member States.

Article 328
(ex Articles 27*a* to 27*e*, 40 to 40*b* and 43 to 45 TEU
and ex Articles 11 and 11*a* TEC)

1. When enhanced cooperation is being established, it shall be open to all Member States, subject to compliance with any conditions of participation laid down by the authorising decision. It shall also be open to them at any other time, subject to compliance with the acts already adopted within that framework, in addition to those conditions.

The Commission and the Member States participating in enhanced cooperation shall ensure that they promote participation by as many Member States as possible.

2. The Commission and, where appropriate, the High Representative of the Union for Foreign Affairs and Security Policy shall keep the European Parliament and the Council regularly informed regarding developments in enhanced cooperation.

Article 329
(ex Articles 27*a* to 27*e*, 40 to 40*b* and 43 to 45 TEU
and ex Articles 11 and 11*a* TEC)

1. Member States which wish to establish enhanced cooperation between themselves in one of the areas covered by the Treaties, with the exception of fields of exclusive competence and the common foreign and security policy, shall address a request to the Commission, specifying the scope and objectives of the enhanced cooperation proposed. The Commission may submit a proposal to the Council to that effect. In the event of the Commission not submitting a proposal, it shall inform the Member States concerned of the reasons for not doing so.

Authorisation to proceed with the enhanced cooperation referred to in the first subparagraph shall be granted by the Council, on a proposal from the Commission and after obtaining the consent of the European Parliament.

2. The request of the Member States which wish to establish enhanced cooperation between themselves within the framework of the common foreign and security policy shall be addressed to the

Council. It shall be forwarded to the High Representative of the Union for Foreign Affairs and Security Policy, who shall give an opinion on whether the enhanced cooperation proposed is consistent with the Union's common foreign and security policy, and to the Commission, which shall give its opinion in particular on whether the enhanced cooperation proposed is consistent with other Union policies. It shall also be forwarded to the European Parliament for information.

Authorisation to proceed with enhanced cooperation shall be granted by a decision of the Council acting unanimously.

Article 330
(ex Articles 27*a* to 27*e*, 40 to 40*b* and 43 to 45 TEU and ex Articles 11 and 11*a* TEC)

All members of the Council may participate in its deliberations, but only members of the Council representing the Member States participating in enhanced cooperation shall take part in the vote.

Unanimity shall be constituted by the votes of the representatives of the participating Member States only.

A qualified majority shall be defined in accordance with Article 238(3).

Article 331
(ex Articles 27*a* to 27*e*, 40 to 40*b* and 43 to 45 TEU and ex Articles 11 and 11*a* TEC)

1. Any Member State which wishes to participate in enhanced cooperation in progress in one of the areas referred to in Article 329(1) shall notify its intention to the Council and the Commission.

The Commission shall, within four months of the date of receipt of the notification, confirm the participation of the Member State concerned. It shall note where necessary that the conditions of participation have been fulfilled and shall adopt any transitional measures necessary with regard to the application of the acts already adopted within the framework of enhanced cooperation.

However, if the Commission considers that the conditions of participation have not been fulfilled, it shall indicate the arrangements to be adopted to fulfil those conditions and shall set a deadline for re-examining the request. On the expiry of that deadline, it shall re-examine the request, in accordance with the procedure set out in the second subparagraph. If the Commission considers that the conditions of participation have still not been met, the Member State concerned may refer the matter to the Council, which shall decide on the request. The Council shall act in accordance with Article 330. It may also adopt the transitional measures referred to in the second subparagraph on a proposal from the Commission.

2. Any Member State which wishes to participate in enhanced cooperation in progress in the framework of the common foreign and security policy shall notify its intention to the Council, the High Representative of the Union for Foreign Affairs and Security Policy and the Commission.

The Council shall confirm the participation of the Member State concerned, after consulting the High Representative of the Union for Foreign Affairs and Security Policy and after noting, where necessary, that the conditions of participation have been fulfilled. The Council, on a proposal from the High Representative, may also adopt any transitional measures necessary with regard to the application of the acts already adopted within the framework of enhanced cooperation. However, if the Council considers that the conditions of participation have not been fulfilled, it shall indicate the arrangements to be adopted to fulfil those conditions and shall set a deadline for re-examining the request for participation.

For the purposes of this paragraph, the Council shall act unanimously and in accordance with Article 330.

Article 332

(ex Articles 27*a* to 27*e*, 40 to 40*b* and 43 to 45 TEU and ex Articles 11 and 11*a* TEC)

Expenditure resulting from implementation of enhanced cooperation, other than administrative costs entailed for the institutions, shall be borne by the participating Member States, unless all members of the Council, acting unanimously after consulting the European Parliament, decide otherwise.

Article 333

(ex Articles 27*a* to 27*e*, 40 to 40*b* and 43 to 45 TEU and ex Articles 11 and 11*a* TEC)

1. Where a provision of the Treaties which may be applied in the context of enhanced cooperation stipulates that the Council shall act unanimously, the Council, acting unanimously in accordance with the arrangements laid down in Article 330, may adopt a decision stipulating that it will act by a qualified majority.

2. Where a provision of the Treaties which may be applied in the context of enhanced cooperation stipulates that the Council shall adopt acts under a special legislative procedure, the Council, acting unanimously in accordance with the arrangements laid down in Article 330, may adopt a decision stipulating that it will act under

the ordinary legislative procedure. The Council shall act after consulting the European Parliament.

3. Paragraphs 1 and 2 shall not apply to decisions having military or defence implications.

Article 334
(ex Articles 27*a* to 27*e*, 40 to 40*b* and 43 to 45 TEU and ex Articles 11 and 11*a* TEC)

The Council and the Commission shall ensure the consistency of activities undertaken in the context of enhanced cooperation and the consistency of such activities with the policies of the Union, and shall cooperate to that end.

PART SEVEN
GENERAL AND FINAL PROVISIONS

Article 335
(ex Article 282 TEC)

In each of the Member States, the Union shall enjoy the most extensive legal capacity accorded to legal persons under their laws; it may, in particular, acquire or dispose of movable and immovable property and may be a party to legal proceedings. To this end, the Union shall be represented by the Commission. However, the Union shall be represented by each of the institutions, by virtue of their administrative autonomy, in matters relating to their respective operation.

Article 336
(ex Article 283 TEC)

The European Parliament and the Council shall, acting by means of regulations in accordance with the ordinary legislative procedure and after consulting the other institutions concerned, lay down the Staff Regulations of Officials of the European Union and the Conditions of Employment of other servants of the Union.

Article 337
(ex Article 284 TEC)

The Commission may, within the limits and under conditions laid down by the Council acting by a simple majority in accordance with the provisions of the Treaties, collect any information and carry out any checks required for the performance of the tasks entrusted to it.

Article 338
(ex Article 285 TEC)

1. Without prejudice to Article 5 of the Protocol on the Statute of the European System of Central Banks and of the European Central Bank, the European Parliament and the Council, acting in accordance with the ordinary legislative procedure, shall adopt measures for the production of statistics where necessary for the performance of the activities of the Union.

2. The production of Union statistics shall conform to impartiality, reliability, objectivity, scientific independence, cost-effectiveness and statistical confidentiality; it shall not entail excessive burdens on economic operators.

Article 339
(ex Article 287 TEC)

The members of the institutions of the Union, the members of committees, and the officials and other servants of the Union shall be required, even after their duties have ceased, not to disclose information of the kind covered by the obligation of professional secrecy, in particular information about undertakings, their business relations or their cost components.

Article 340
(ex Article 288 TEC)

The contractual liability of the Union shall be governed by the law applicable to the contract in question.

In the case of non-contractual liability, the Union shall, in accordance with the general principles common to the laws of the Member States, make good any damage caused by its institutions or by its servants in the performance of their duties.

Notwithstanding the second paragraph, the European Central Bank shall, in accordance with the general principles common to the laws of the Member States, make good any damage caused by it or by its servants in the performance of their duties.

The personal liability of its servants towards the Union shall be governed by the provisions laid down in their Staff Regulations or in the Conditions of Employment applicable to them.

Article 341
(ex Article 289 TEC)

The seat of the institutions of the Union shall be determined by common accord of the governments of the Member States.

Article 342
(ex Article 290 TEC)

The rules governing the languages of the institutions of the Union shall, without prejudice to the provisions contained in the Statute of the Court of Justice of the European Union, be determined by the Council, acting unanimously by means of regulations.

Article 343
(ex Article 291 TEC)

The Union shall enjoy in the territories of the Member States such privileges and immunities as are necessary for the performance of its tasks, under the conditions laid down in the Protocol of 8 April 1965 on the privileges and immunities of the European Union. The same shall apply to the European Central Bank and the European Investment Bank.

Article 344
(ex Article 292 TEC)

Member States undertake not to submit a dispute concerning the interpretation or application of the Treaties to any method of settlement other than those provided for therein.

Article 345
(ex Article 295 TEC)

The Treaties shall in no way prejudice the rules in Member States governing the system of property ownership.

Article 346
(ex Article 296 TEC)

1. The provisions of the Treaties shall not preclude the application of the following rules:

(a) no Member State shall be obliged to supply information the disclosure of which it considers contrary to the essential interests of its security;

(b) any Member State may take such measures as it considers necessary for the protection of the essential interests of its security which are connected with the production of or trade in arms, munitions and war material; such measures shall not adversely affect the conditions of competition in the internal market regarding products which are not intended for specifically military purposes.

2. The Council may, acting unanimously on a proposal from the Commission, make changes to the list, which it drew up on 15

April 1958, of the products to which the provisions of paragraph 1(b) apply.

Article 347
(ex Article 297 TEC)

Member States shall consult each other with a view to taking together the steps needed to prevent the functioning of the internal market being affected by measures which a Member State may be called upon to take in the event of serious internal disturbances affecting the maintenance of law and order, in the event of war, serious international tension constituting a threat of war, or in order to carry out obligations it has accepted for the purpose of maintaining peace and international security.

Article 348
(ex Article 298 TEC)

If measures taken in the circumstances referred to in Articles 346 and 347 have the effect of distorting the conditions of competition in the internal market, the Commission shall, together with the State concerned, examine how these measures can be adjusted to the rules laid down in the Treaties.

By way of derogation from the procedure laid down in Articles 258 and 259, the Commission or any Member State may bring the matter directly before the Court of Justice if it considers that another Member State is making improper use of the powers provided for in Articles 346 and 347. The Court of Justice shall give its ruling in camera.

Article 349
(ex Article 299(2), second, third and fourth subparagraphs, TEC)

Taking account of the structural social and economic situation of Guadeloupe, French Guiana, Martinique, Réunion, Saint-Barthélemy, Saint-Martin, the Azores, Madeira and the Canary Islands, which is compounded by their remoteness, insularity, small size, difficult topography and climate, economic dependence on a few products, the permanence and combination of which severely restrain their development, the Council, on a proposal from the Commission and after consulting the European Parliament, shall adopt specific measures aimed, in particular, at laying down the conditions of application of the Treaties to those regions, including common policies. Where the specific measures in question are adopted by the Council in accordance with a special legislative procedure, it shall also act on a proposal from the Commission and after consulting the European Parliament.

The measures referred to in the first paragraph concern in particular areas such as customs and trade policies, fiscal policy, free zones, agriculture and fisheries policies, conditions for supply of raw materials and essential consumer goods, State aids and conditions of access to structural funds and to horizontal Union programmes.

The Council shall adopt the measures referred to in the first paragraph taking into account the special characteristics and constraints of the outermost regions without undermining the integrity and the coherence of the Union legal order, including the internal market and common policies.

Article 350
(ex Article 306 TEC)

The provisions of the Treaties shall not preclude the existence or completion of regional unions between Belgium and Luxembourg, or between Belgium, Luxembourg and the Netherlands, to the extent that the objectives of these regional unions are not attained by application of the Treaties.

Article 351
(ex Article 307 TEC)

The rights and obligations arising from agreements concluded before 1 January 1958 or, for acceding States, before the date of their accession, between one or more Member States on the one hand, and one or more third countries on the other, shall not be affected by the provisions of the Treaties.

To the extent that such agreements are not compatible with the Treaties, the Member State or States concerned shall take all appropriate steps to eliminate the incompatibilities established. Member States shall, where necessary, assist each other to this end and shall, where appropriate, adopt a common attitude.

In applying the agreements referred to in the first paragraph, Member States shall take into account the fact that the advantages accorded under the Treaties by each Member State form an integral part of the establishment of the Union and are thereby inseparably linked with the creation of common institutions, the conferring of powers upon them and the granting of the same advantages by all the other Member States.

Article 352
(ex Article 308 TEC)

1. If action by the Union should prove necessary, within the framework of the policies defined in the Treaties, to attain one of the objectives set out in the Treaties, and the Treaties have not provided the necessary powers, the Council, acting unanimously on a proposal

from the Commission and after obtaining the consent of the European Parliament, shall adopt the appropriate measures. Where the measures in question are adopted by the Council in accordance with a special legislative procedure, it shall also act unanimously on a proposal from the Commission and after obtaining the consent of the European Parliament.

2. Using the procedure for monitoring the subsidiarity principle referred to in Article 5(3) of the Treaty on European Union, the Commission shall draw national Parliaments' attention to proposals based on this Article.

3. Measures based on this Article shall not entail harmonisation of Member States' laws or regulations in cases where the Treaties exclude such harmonisation.

4. This Article cannot serve as a basis for attaining objectives pertaining to the common foreign and security policy and any acts adopted pursuant to this Article shall respect the limits set out in Article 40, second paragraph, of the Treaty on European Union.

Article 353

Article 48(7) of the Treaty on European Union shall not apply to the following Articles:

— Article 311, third and fourth paragraphs,

— Article 312(2), first subparagraph,

— Article 352, and

— Article 354.

Article 354

(ex Article 309 TEC)

For the purposes of Article 7 of the Treaty on European Union on the suspension of certain rights resulting from Union membership, the member of the European Council or of the Council representing the Member State in question shall not take part in the vote and the Member State in question shall not be counted in the calculation of the one third or four fifths of Member States referred to in paragraphs 1 and 2 of that Article. Abstentions by members present in person or represented shall not prevent the adoption of decisions referred to in paragraph 2 of that Article.

For the adoption of the decisions referred to in paragraphs 3 and 4 of Article 7 of the Treaty on European Union, a qualified majority shall be defined in accordance with Article 238(3)(b) of this Treaty.

Where, following a decision to suspend voting rights adopted pursuant to paragraph 3 of Article 7 of the Treaty on European

Union, the Council acts by a qualified majority on the basis of a provision of the Treaties, that qualified majority shall be defined in accordance with Article 238(3)(b) of this Treaty, or, where the Council acts on a proposal from the Commission or from the High Representative of the Union for Foreign Affairs and Security Policy, in accordance with Article 238(3)(a).

For the purposes of Article 7 of the Treaty on European Union, the European Parliament shall act by a two-thirds majority of the votes cast, representing the majority of its component Members.

Article 355
(ex Article 299(2), first subparagraph,
and Article 299(3) to (6) TEC)

In addition to the provisions of Article 52 of the Treaty on European Union relating to the territorial scope of the Treaties, the following provisions shall apply:

1. The provisions of the Treaties shall apply to Guadeloupe, French Guiana, Martinique, Réunion, Saint-Barthélemy, Saint-Martin, the Azores, Madeira and the Canary Islands in accordance with Article 349.

2. The special arrangements for association set out in Part Four shall apply to the overseas countries and territories listed in Annex II.

The Treaties shall not apply to those overseas countries and territories having special relations with the United Kingdom of Great Britain and Northern Ireland which are not included in the aforementioned list.

3. The provisions of the Treaties shall apply to the European territories for whose external relations a Member State is responsible.

4. The provisions of the Treaties shall apply to the land Islands in accordance with the provisions set out in Protocol 2 to the Act concerning the conditions of accession of the Republic of Austria, the Republic of Finland and the Kingdom of Sweden.

5. Notwithstanding Article 52 of the Treaty on European Union and paragraphs 1 to 4 of this Article:

(a) the Treaties shall not apply to the Faeroe Islands;

(b) the Treaties shall not apply to the United Kingdom Sovereign Base Areas of Akrotiri and Dhekelia in Cyprus except to the extent necessary to ensure the implementation of the arrangements set out in the Protocol on the Sovereign Base Areas of the United Kingdom of Great Britain and Northern

Ireland in Cyprus annexed to the Act concerning the conditions of accession of the Czech Republic, the Republic of Estonia, the Republic of Cyprus, the Republic of Latvia, the Republic of Lithuania, the Republic of Hungary, the Republic of Malta, the Republic of Poland, the Republic of Slovenia and the Slovak Republic to the European Union and in accordance with the terms of that Protocol;

(c) the Treaties shall apply to the Channel Islands and the Isle of Man only to the extent necessary to ensure the implementation of the arrangements for those islands set out in the Treaty concerning the accession of new Member States to the European Economic Community and to the European Atomic Energy Community signed on 22 January 1972.

6. The European Council may, on the initiative of the Member State concerned, adopt a decision amending the status, with regard to the Union, of a Danish, French or Netherlands country or territory referred to in paragraphs 1 and 2. The European Council shall act unanimously after consulting the Commission.

Article 356
(ex Article 312 TEC)

This Treaty is concluded for an unlimited period.

Article 357
(ex Article 313 TEC)

This Treaty shall be ratified by the High Contracting Parties in accordance with their respective constitutional requirements. The Instruments of ratification shall be deposited with the Government of the Italian Republic.

This Treaty shall enter into force on the first day of the month following the deposit of the Instrument of ratification by the last signatory State to take this step. If, however, such deposit is made less than 15 days before the beginning of the following month, this Treaty shall not enter into force until the first day of the second month after the date of such deposit.

Article 358

The provisions of Article 55 of the Treaty on European Union shall apply to this Treaty.

Appendix 3

CHARTER OF FUNDAMENTAL RIGHTS OF THE EUROPEAN UNION

Official Journal of the European Union C 364/01 (2000)
(2010/C 83/02)

Official Journal of the European Union C 83/389 (Mar. 30, 2010)

The European Parliament, the Council and the Commission solemnly proclaim the following text as the Charter of Fundamental Rights of the European Union:

Preamble

The peoples of Europe, in creating an ever closer union among them, are resolved to share a peaceful future based on common values.

Conscious of its spiritual and moral heritage, the Union is founded on the indivisible, universal values of human dignity, freedom, equality and solidarity; it is based on the principles of democracy and the rule of law. It places the individual at the heart of its activities, by establishing the citizenship of the Union and by creating an area of freedom, security and justice.

The Union contributes to the preservation and to the development of these common values while respecting the diversity of the cultures and traditions of the peoples of Europe as well as the national identities of the Member States and the organisation of their public authorities at national, regional and local levels; it seeks to promote balanced and sustainable development and ensures free movement of persons, services, goods and capital, and the freedom of establishment.

To this end, it is necessary to strengthen the protection of fundamental rights in the light of changes in society, social progress and scientific and technological developments by making those rights more visible in a Charter.

This Charter reaffirms, with due regard for the powers and tasks of the Union and for the principle of subsidiarity, the rights as they result, in particular, from the constitutional traditions and international obligations common to the Member States, the European Convention for the Protection of Human Rights and Fundamental Freedoms, the Social Charters adopted by the Union and by the Council of Europe and the case-law of the Court of Justice of the European Union and of the European Court of Human Rights. In this context the Charter will be interpreted by the courts of the Union and the Member States with due regard to the explanations prepared under the authority of the Praesidium of the Convention which drafted the Charter and updated under the responsibility of the Praesidium of the European Convention.

Enjoyment of these rights entails responsibilities and duties with regard to other persons, to the human community and to future generations.

The Union therefore recognises the rights, freedoms and principles set out hereafter.

TITLE I
DIGNITY

Article 1
Human dignity

Human dignity is inviolable. It must be respected and protected.

Article 2
Right to life

1. Everyone has the right to life.

2. No one shall be condemned to the death penalty, or executed.

Article 3
Right to the integrity of the person

1. Everyone has the right to respect for his or her physical and mental integrity.

2. In the fields of medicine and biology, the following must be respected in particular:

(a) the free and informed consent of the person concerned, according to the procedures laid down by law;

(b) the prohibition of eugenic practices, in particular those aiming at the selection of persons;

(c) the prohibition on making the human body and its parts as such a source of financial gain;

(d) the prohibition of the reproductive cloning of human beings.

Article 4

Prohibition of torture and inhuman or degrading treatment or punishment

No one shall be subjected to torture or to inhuman or degrading treatment or punishment.

Article 5

Prohibition of slavery and forced labour

1. No one shall be held in slavery or servitude.

2. No one shall be required to perform forced or compulsory labour.

3. Trafficking in human beings is prohibited.

TITLE II
FREEDOMS

Article 6

Right to liberty and security

Everyone has the right to liberty and security of person.

Article 7

Respect for private and family life

Everyone has the right to respect for his or her private and family life, home and communications.

Article 8

Protection of personal data

1. Everyone has the right to the protection of personal data concerning him or her.

2. Such data must be processed fairly for specified purposes and on the basis of the consent of the person concerned or some other legitimate basis laid down by law. Everyone has the right of access to data which has been collected concerning him or her, and the right to have it rectified.

3. Compliance with these rules shall be subject to control by an independent authority.

Article 9

Right to marry and right to found a family

The right to marry and the right to found a family shall be guaranteed in accordance with the national laws governing the exercise of these rights.

Article 10

Freedom of thought, conscience and religion

1. Everyone has the right to freedom of thought, conscience and religion. This right includes freedom to change religion or belief and freedom, either alone or in community with others and in public or in private, to manifest religion or belief, in worship, teaching, practice and observance.

2. The right to conscientious objection is recognised, in accordance with the national laws governing the exercise of this right.

Article 11

Freedom of expression and information

1. Everyone has the right to freedom of expression. This right shall include freedom to hold opinions and to receive and impart information and ideas without interference by public authority and regardless of frontiers.

2. The freedom and pluralism of the media shall be respected.

Article 12

Freedom of assembly and of association

1. Everyone has the right to freedom of peaceful assembly and to freedom of association at all levels, in particular in political, trade union and civic matters, which implies the right of everyone to form and to join trade unions for the protection of his or her interests.

2. Political parties at Union level contribute to expressing the political will of the citizens of the Union.

Article 13

Freedom of the arts and sciences

The arts and scientific research shall be free of constraint. Academic freedom shall be respected.

Article 14

Right to education

1. Everyone has the right to education and to have access to vocational and continuing training.

2. This right includes the possibility to receive free compulsory education.

3. The freedom to found educational establishments with due respect for democratic principles and the right of parents to ensure the education and teaching of their children in conformity with their religious, philosophical and pedagogical convictions shall be

respected, in accordance with the national laws governing the exercise of such freedom and right.

Article 15

Freedom to choose an occupation and right to engage in work

1. Everyone has the right to engage in work and to pursue a freely chosen or accepted occupation.

2. Every citizen of the Union has the freedom to seek employment, to work, to exercise the right of establishment and to provide services in any Member State.

3. Nationals of third countries who are authorised to work in the territories of the Member States are entitled to working conditions equivalent to those of citizens of the Union.

Article 16

Freedom to conduct a business

The freedom to conduct a business in accordance with Union law and national laws and practices is recognised.

Article 17

Right to property

1. Everyone has the right to own, use, dispose of and bequeath his or her lawfully acquired possessions. No one may be deprived of his or her possessions, except in the public interest and in the cases and under the conditions provided for by law, subject to fair compensation being paid in good time for their loss. The use of property may be regulated by law in so far as is necessary for the general interest.

2. Intellectual property shall be protected.

Article 18

Right to asylum

The right to asylum shall be guaranteed with due respect for the rules of the Geneva Convention of 28 July 1951 and the Protocol of 31 January 1967 relating to the status of refugees and in accordance with the Treaty on European Union and the Treaty on the Functioning of the European Union (hereinafter referred to as "the Treaties").

Article 19

Protection in the event of removal, expulsion or extradition

1. Collective expulsions are prohibited.

2. No one may be removed, expelled or extradited to a State where there is a serious risk that he or she would be subjected to the death penalty, torture or other inhuman or degrading treatment or punishment.

TITLE III
EQUALITY

Article 20

Equality before the law

Everyone is equal before the law.

Article 21

Non-discrimination

1. Any discrimination based on any ground such as sex, race, colour, ethnic or social origin, genetic features, language, religion or belief, political or any other opinion, membership of a national minority, property, birth, disability, age or sexual orientation shall be prohibited.

2. Within the scope of application of the Treaties and without prejudice to any of their specific provisions, any discrimination on grounds of nationality shall be prohibited.

Article 22

Cultural, religious and linguistic diversity

The Union shall respect cultural, religious and linguistic diversity.

Article 23

Equality between women and men

Equality between women and men must be ensured in all areas, including employment, work and pay.

The principle of equality shall not prevent the maintenance or adoption of measures providing for specific advantages in favour of the under-represented sex.

Article 24

The rights of the child

1. Children shall have the right to such protection and care as is necessary for their well-being. They may express their views freely.

Such views shall be taken into consideration on matters which concern them in accordance with their age and maturity.

2. In all actions relating to children, whether taken by public authorities or private institutions, the child's best interests must be a primary consideration.

3. Every child shall have the right to maintain on a regular basis a personal relationship and direct contact with both his or her parents, unless that is contrary to his or her interests.

Article 25

The rights of the elderly

The Union recognises and respects the rights of the elderly to lead a life of dignity and independence and to participate in social and cultural life.

Article 26

Integration of persons with disabilities

The Union recognises and respects the right of persons with disabilities to benefit from measures designed to ensure their independence, social and occupational integration and participation in the life of the community.

TITLE IV
SOLIDARITY

Article 27

Workers' right to information and consultation within the undertaking

Workers or their representatives must, at the appropriate levels, be guaranteed information and consultation in good time in the cases and under the conditions provided for by Union law and national laws and practices.

Article 28

Right of collective bargaining and action

Workers and employers, or their respective organisations, have, in accordance with Union law and national laws and practices, the right to negotiate and conclude collective agreements at the appropriate levels and, in cases of conflicts of interest, to take collective action to defend their interests, including strike action.

Article 29

Right of access to placement services

Everyone has the right of access to a free placement service.

Article 30

Protection in the event of unjustified dismissal

Every worker has the right to protection against unjustified dismissal, in accordance with Union law and national laws and practices.

Article 31

Fair and just working conditions

1. Every worker has the right to working conditions which respect his or her health, safety and dignity.

2. Every worker has the right to limitation of maximum working hours, to daily and weekly rest periods and to an annual period of paid leave.

Article 32

Prohibition of child labour and protection of young people at work

The employment of children is prohibited. The minimum age of admission to employment may not be lower than the minimum school-leaving age, without prejudice to such rules as may be more favourable to young people and except for limited derogations.

Young people admitted to work must have working conditions appropriate to their age and be protected against economic exploitation and any work likely to harm their safety, health or physical, mental, moral or social development or to interfere with their education.

Article 33

Family and professional life

1. The family shall enjoy legal, economic and social protection.

2. To reconcile family and professional life, everyone shall have the right to protection from dismissal for a reason connected with maternity and the right to paid maternity leave and to parental leave following the birth or adoption of a child.

Article 34

Social security and social assistance

1. The Union recognises and respects the entitlement to social security benefits and social services providing protection in cases such as maternity, illness, industrial accidents, dependency or old age, and in the case of loss of employment, in accordance with the rules laid down by Union law and national laws and practices.

2. Everyone residing and moving legally within the European Union is entitled to social security benefits and social advantages in accordance with Union law and national laws and practices.

3. In order to combat social exclusion and poverty, the Union recognises and respects the right to social and housing assistance so as to ensure a decent existence for all those who lack sufficient resources, in accordance with the rules laid down by Union law and national laws and practices.

Article 35

Health care

Everyone has the right of access to preventive health care and the right to benefit from medical treatment under the conditions established by national laws and practices. A high level of human health protection shall be ensured in the definition and implementation of all the Union's policies and activities.

Article 36

Access to services of general economic interest

The Union recognises and respects access to services of general economic interest as provided for in national laws and practices, in accordance with the Treaties, in order to promote the social and territorial cohesion of the Union.

Article 37

Environmental protection

A high level of environmental protection and the improvement of the quality of the environment must be integrated into the policies of the Union and ensured in accordance with the principle of sustainable development.

Article 38

Consumer protection

Union policies shall ensure a high level of consumer protection.

TITLE V

CITIZENS' RIGHTS

Article 39

Right to vote and to stand as a candidate at elections to the European Parliament

1. Every citizen of the Union has the right to vote and to stand as a candidate at elections to the European Parliament in the Member State in which he or she resides, under the same conditions as nationals of that State.

2. Members of the European Parliament shall be elected by direct universal suffrage in a free and secret ballot.

Article 40

Right to vote and to stand as a candidate at municipal elections

Every citizen of the Union has the right to vote and to stand as a candidate at municipal elections in the Member State in which he or she resides under the same conditions as nationals of that State.

Article 41

Right to good administration

1. Every person has the right to have his or her affairs handled impartially, fairly and within a reasonable time by the institutions, bodies, offices and agencies of the Union.

2. This right includes:

(a) the right of every person to be heard, before any individual measure which would affect him or her adversely is taken;

(b) the right of every person to have access to his or her file, while respecting the legitimate interests of confidentiality and of professional and business secrecy;

(c) the obligation of the administration to give reasons for its decisions.

3. Every person has the right to have the Union make good any damage caused by its institutions or by its servants in the performance of their duties, in accordance with the general principles common to the laws of the Member States.

4. Every person may write to the institutions of the Union in one of the languages of the Treaties and must have an answer in the same language.

Article 42

Right of access to documents

Any citizen of the Union, and any natural or legal person residing or having its registered office in a Member State, has a right of access to documents of the institutions, bodies, offices and agencies of the Union, whatever their medium.

Article 43

European Ombudsman

Any citizen of the Union and any natural or legal person residing or having its registered office in a Member State has the right to refer to the European Ombudsman cases of maladministration in the activities of the institutions, bodies, offices or agencies of the Union, with the exception of the Court of Justice of the European Union acting in its judicial role.

Article 44
Right to petition

Any citizen of the Union and any natural or legal person residing or having its registered office in a Member State has the right to petition the European Parliament.

Article 45
Freedom of movement and of residence

1. Every citizen of the Union has the right to move and reside freely within the territory of the Member States.

2. Freedom of movement and residence may be granted, in accordance with the Treaties, to nationals of third countries legally resident in the territory of a Member State.

Article 46
Diplomatic and consular protection

Every citizen of the Union shall, in the territory of a third country in which the Member State of which he or she is a national is not represented, be entitled to protection by the diplomatic or consular authorities of any Member State, on the same conditions as the nationals of that Member State.

TITLE VI
JUSTICE

Article 47
Right to an effective remedy and to a fair trial

Everyone whose rights and freedoms guaranteed by the law of the Union are violated has the right to an effective remedy before a tribunal in compliance with the conditions laid down in this Article.

Everyone is entitled to a fair and public hearing within a reasonable time by an independent and impartial tribunal previously established by law. Everyone shall have the possibility of being advised, defended and represented.

Legal aid shall be made available to those who lack sufficient resources in so far as such aid is necessary to ensure effective access to justice.

Article 48
Presumption of innocence and right of defence

1. Everyone who has been charged shall be presumed innocent until proved guilty according to law.

2. Respect for the rights of the defence of anyone who has been charged shall be guaranteed.

Article 49

Principles of legality and proportionality of criminal offences and penalties

1. No one shall be held guilty of any criminal offence on account of any act or omission which did not constitute a criminal offence under national law or international law at the time when it was committed. Nor shall a heavier penalty be imposed than the one that was applicable at the time the criminal offence was committed. If, subsequent to the commission of a criminal offence, the law provides for a lighter penalty, that penalty shall be applicable.

2. This Article shall not prejudice the trial and punishment of any person for any act or omission which, at the time when it was committed, was criminal according to the general principles recognised by the community of nations.

3. The severity of penalties must not be disproportionate to the criminal offence.

Article 50

Right not to be tried or punished twice in criminal proceedings for the same criminal offence

No one shall be liable to be tried or punished again in criminal proceedings for an offence for which he or she has already been finally acquitted or convicted within the Union in accordance with the law.

TITLE VII
GENERAL PROVISIONS GOVERNING THE INTERPRETATION AND APPLICATION OF THE CHARTER

Article 51

Field of application

1. The provisions of this Charter are addressed to the institutions, bodies, offices and agencies of the Union with due regard for the principle of subsidiarity and to the Member States only when they are implementing Union law. They shall therefore respect the rights, observe the principles and promote the application thereof in accordance with their respective powers and respecting the limits of the powers of the Union as conferred on it in the Treaties.

2. The Charter does not extend the field of application of Union law beyond the powers of the Union or establish any new power or task for the Union, or modify powers and tasks as defined in the Treaties.

Article 52

Scope and interpretation of rights and principles

1. Any limitation on the exercise of the rights and freedoms recognised by this Charter must be provided for by law and respect the essence of those rights and freedoms. Subject to the principle of proportionality, limitations may be made only if they are necessary and genuinely meet objectives of general interest recognised by the Union or the need to protect the rights and freedoms of others.

2. Rights recognised by this Charter for which provision is made in the Treaties shall be exercised under the conditions and within the limits defined by those Treaties.

3. In so far as this Charter contains rights which correspond to rights guaranteed by the Convention for the Protection of Human Rights and Fundamental Freedoms, the meaning and scope of those rights shall be the same as those laid down by the said Convention. This provision shall not prevent Union law providing more extensive protection.

4. In so far as this Charter recognises fundamental rights as they result from the constitutional traditions common to the Member States, those rights shall be interpreted in harmony with those traditions.

5. The provisions of this Charter which contain principles may be implemented by legislative and executive acts taken by institutions, bodies, offices and agencies of the Union, and by acts of Member States when they are implementing Union law, in the exercise of their respective powers. They shall be judicially cognisable only in the interpretation of such acts and in the ruling on their legality.

6. Full account shall be taken of national laws and practices as specified in this Charter.

7. The explanations drawn up as a way of providing guidance in the interpretation of this Charter shall be given due regard by the courts of the Union and of the Member States.

Article 53

Level of protection

Nothing in this Charter shall be interpreted as restricting or adversely affecting human rights and fundamental freedoms as recognised, in their respective fields of application, by Union law and international law and by international agreements to which the Union or all the Member States are party, including the European Convention for the Protection of Human Rights and Fundamental Freedoms, and by the Member States' constitutions.

Article 54

Prohibition of abuse of rights

Nothing in this Charter shall be interpreted as implying any right to engage in any activity or to perform any act aimed at the destruction of any of the rights and freedoms recognised in this Charter or at their limitation to a greater extent than is provided for herein.

Appendix 4

SUMMARY OF EU-UK TRADE AND COOPERATION AGREEMENT (2021)*

Introduction

1. This document sets out the core provisions of the Agreement and how they apply to businesses and citizens.

TRADE AND COOPERATION AGREEMENT: OVERVIEW

2. The United Kingdom and the European Union have agreed to unprecedented 100% tariff liberalisation. This means there will be no tariffs or quotas on the movement of goods we produce between the UK and the EU. This is the first time the EU has agreed a zero tariff zero quota deal with any other trading partner.

3. The Agreement also includes provisions to support trade in services (including financial services and legal services). This will provide many UK service suppliers with legal guarantees that they will not face barriers to trade when selling into the EU and will support the mobility of UK professionals who will continue to do business across the EU.

4. The Agreement firmly and explicitly recognises UK sovereignty over our fishing waters and puts us in a position to rebuild our fishing fleet and increase quotas in the next few years, finally overturning the inequity that British fishermen have faced for over four decades. Beyond this Agreement, we will also invest in our fishing communities and restore the UK's fishing fleet across the whole UK, including supporting our Scottish fishermen.

5. The Agreement ensures streamlined co-operation on law enforcement to ensure we continue to effectively tackle serious organised crime and counter terrorism—protecting the public and bringing criminals to justice.

---

* Adapted from https://assets.publishing.service.gov.uk/government/uploads/system/uploads/attachment_data/file/957694/TCA_SUMMARY_PDF_V1.pdf (publishing.service.gov.uk).

6. The Agreement is based on international law, not EU law. There is no role for the European Court of Justice and no requirements for the UK to continue following EU law.

7. The Government has embedded into this Agreement our manifesto commitment to high labour environment and climate standards without giving the EU any say over our rules.

8. This Agreement ends the EU State Aid regime in Great Britain and allows us to introduce our own modern subsidy system so that we can better support businesses to grow and thrive in a way that best suits the interests of British industries.

9. The Agreement also includes arrangements for airlines and hauliers that provides them with certainty and gives people the ability to travel to and from the EU easily. It also includes a social security agreement that has practical benefits for UK citizens including accessing healthcare when travelling in the EU; agreements on energy provision which will benefit consumers; and collaboration on scientific research, fulfilling the Government's manifesto commitment to make the UK a science and research superpower.

10. The Agreement is structured into 7 Parts:

- Part 1 covers the common and institutional provisions in the Agreement;
- Part 2 covers trade and other economic aspects of the relationship, such as aviation, energy, road transport, and social security;
- Part 3 covers cooperation on law enforcement and criminal justice;
- Part 4 covers so-called "thematic" issues, notably health collaboration;
- Part 5 covers participation in EU Programmes, principally scientific collaboration through Horizon;
- Part 6 covers dispute settlement;
- Part 7 sets out final provisions.

11. Our original approach was that some of these policy aspects should form separate agreements rather than be incorporated into one overall one. We have nevertheless agreed robust provisions that, when necessary, treat the different parts separately, for example as regards the (very limited) scope for cross-suspension following disputes, or the separate and distinct termination clauses in most areas.

12. In parallel, we have agreed a separate Nuclear Cooperation Agreement and an agreement on Security Procedures for Exchanging and Protecting Classified Information.

Common and Institutional Provisions

13. These provisions provide for a range of matters across the Agreement including setting the object and purpose of the Agreement. These provisions also reaffirm the independence of the two Parties and remove any ambiguity about the UK's status as a sovereign nation.

Principles of interpretation and definitions

14. These provisions deliver on the Government's commitment to ensure that the relationship between the UK and the EU is based on international law, not EU law.

Institutional framework

15. These arrangements establish the necessary fora for both political and technical discussion. A Partnership Council will supervise the operation of the Agreement at a political level, providing strategic direction. Any decisions made will be by mutual consent. The UK must agree to anything for it to be binding. The Partnership Council will be supported by a network of other committees, including on trade. These will provide necessary opportunities for technical discussion to ensure the smooth implementation of the Agreement and its stable operation.

TRADE IN GOODS

Chapter 1—National treatment and market access for goods (including trade remedies)

16. The Agreement establishes zero tariffs or quotas on trade between the UK and the EU, where goods meet the relevant rules of origin. The Chapter includes provisions which reaffirm, incorporate and build upon WTO commitments and principles, facilitate trade, and address non-tariff barriers (such as import and export licensing restrictions). It also ensures that trade remedy measures are investigated and applied in a proportionate and transparent manner.

Chapter 2—Rules of origin

17. The UK and EU have agreed a rules of origin Chapter which contains modern and appropriate rules of origin ensuring that only 'originating' goods are able to benefit from the liberalised market access arrangements agreed in the TCA, while reflecting the requirements of UK and EU industry. For example, the RoO we have agreed for batteries and electric vehicles will ensure that UK-made

electric vehicles are eligible for preferential tariff rates, supporting our move towards Net Zero.

18. The Chapter also provides for full bilateral cumulation (cumulation of both materials and processing) between the UK and the EU, allowing EU inputs and processing to be counted as UK input in UK products exported to the EU and vice versa. The ambitious arrangements include facilitations on average pricing, accounting segregation for certain products, as well as all materials, and tolerance by value. The rules are also supported by predictable and low-cost administrative arrangements for proving origin.

Chapter 3—Technical Barriers to Trade (TBT)

19. This Agreement includes a TBT Chapter which addresses regulatory barriers to trade between the UK and EU, while allowing both Parties the freedom to regulate goods in the way most appropriate for their own market. This Chapter builds on the WTO TBT agreement and includes provisions on technical regulation, conformity assessment, standardisation, accreditation, market surveillance and marking and labelling.

20. The Agreement also envisages arrangements to share information on dangerous and non-compliant products on the UK and EU markets. Combined with operational cooperation between UK and EU market surveillance authorities, this exchange of information will help both Parties better protect their consumers.

21. In line with common FTA practice, the TBT Chapter also includes a number of sector-specific Annexes which seek to promote cooperation and tackle barriers to trade in the automotive, chemical, pharmaceutical, organic products and wine sectors.

Annex on medicinal products

22. This Annex aims to facilitate availability of medicines, promote public health and protect high levels of consumer and environmental protection in respect of medicinal products. It provides for mutual recognition of Good Manufacturing Practice (GMP) inspections and certificates, meaning that manufacturing facilities do not need to undergo separate UK and EU inspections, as well as ongoing co-operation.

Annex on motor vehicles and equipment and parts thereof

23. The objective of the Annex is to eliminate and prevent unnecessary barriers to trade in motor vehicles and parts. It confirms that the Parties will mutually recognise approvals based on UN regulations. It establishes dedicated cooperation mechanisms to address regulatory barriers, and provides for information exchange to support activities including market surveillance.

Annex on organic products

24. The Annex will provide for an equivalence agreement between the UK and EU. This means products that are certified as organic in one market will be recognised as organic in the other. There are also wider benefits, including provisions for effective regulatory cooperation to combat fraud, upholding the integrity of our organics production and control systems, and collaboration on the future development of organic standards.

Annex on trade in wine

25. The Annex provides for simplified certification, documentation, labelling and packaging requirements for the imports of wine produced in the other Party, reducing costs for exporters and consumers. It also sets out requirements to share information and to jointly review the agreement in future with a view to further facilitating trade in wine.

Annex on chemicals

26. The Annex seeks to facilitate trade in chemicals, ensure high levels of environmental and health protection and provides for cooperation between authorities. It includes joint commitments to comprehensive implementation of international classification and labelling rules as well as commitments to ongoing cooperation and information exchange.

Chapter 4—Sanitary and Phytosanitary (SPS) Measures

27. This Agreement includes an SPS Chapter which ensures that the UK and the EU can maintain fully independent SPS rules to protect human, animal and plant life and health, preserving each Party's right to independently regulate, while not creating unjustified barriers to trade. This is standard practice in free trade agreements.

28. The Chapter includes commitments on regionalisation, which enables UK and EU trade to continue from disease or pest-free areas. Together with provisions on rapid notification and emergency measures, this will help both Parties to move quickly to protect their consumers, animals and plants during disease and pest outbreaks and food and feed safety incidents, while minimising the impacts on trade.

29. The Chapter also establishes a framework for cooperation on the fight against antimicrobial resistance, protecting animal welfare and sustainable food systems. All of these are areas where the UK and the EU are global leaders.

30. The Chapter includes bespoke arrangements for the UK and the EU to hold regular, joint reviews of their respective SPS border controls. The aim of these reviews is to see if each Party can further facilitate trade without compromising biosecurity.

Chapter 5—Customs and Trade Facilitation (CTF)

31. The Agreement is based on the WTO Trade Facilitation Agreement and the World Customs Organisation (WCO) Revised Kyoto Convention and provides for efficient customs arrangements covering all trade in goods. As well as facilitating trade, the Agreement ensures that the customs authorities of both Parties remain able to protect their respective regulatory, security and financial interests.

32. The CTF Chapter includes measures to facilitate legitimate trade by addressing administrative barriers for traders, including through mutual recognition of 'trusted trader' (AEO) schemes. This includes provisions to support the efficiency of documentary clearance, transparency, advance rulings and non-discrimination. We have agreed measures that are bespoke to the UK-EU trading relationship, such as cooperation at 'roll-on roll-off' ports like Dover and Holyhead and also on exploring the possibility of sharing import and export declaration data, including by setting up pilot programmes where appropriate. This aims at reducing administrative burdens on business in the longer term.

33. The core provisions on CTF are accompanied by additional Protocols and an Annex to provide for specific forms of cooperation and trade facilitation.

Protocol on mutual administrative assistance on customs matters

34. This Protocol enables the Parties to work together while upholding their respective customs regimes, to safeguard revenue and prevent fraud through efficient and reciprocal exchange of information and mutual assistance across customs matters.

Annex on Authorised Economic Operators (AEOs)

35. This Annex provides for the mutual recognition of the Parties' respective Authorised Economic Operator security and safety schemes. As a result, AEOs assessed and recognised under either the UK or EU scheme will face fewer controls relating to safety and security when moving their goods between the UK and the EU, facilitating trade and flow at the border.

Protocol on administrative cooperation and combating fraud in the field of Value Added Tax and on mutual assistance for the recovery of claims relating to taxes and duties

36. This Protocol builds on existing international agreements, including the OECD Convention on Mutual Administrative Assistance in Tax Matters. It will enable UK and EU authorities to cooperate and exchange information relating to VAT, including for the purpose of combating VAT fraud. The Protocol will also allow for either Party to make a request of the other to recover unpaid customs duties, excise or VAT on its behalf.

TRADE IN SERVICES AND INVESTMENT

37. The Agreement establishes the treatment and level of access the UK and EU have agreed to grant each other's service suppliers and investors. These provisions will offer businesses and individuals the certainty and support they need to continue trading profitably with the EU, while maintaining the UK's right to regulate as an independent nation.

38. The Agreement significantly builds on the Parties' commitments under WTO rules and locks in market access across substantially all sectors. The level of ambition reflects the UK and EU's respective Free Trade Agreements with Japan, although in a few areas—most notably legal services—the agreement breaks new ground.

Chapter 1—General provisions

39. This Chapter establishes the scope and definitions for the Agreement on Services and Investment and sets out provisions that apply to the whole title. It also includes a commitment for the Parties to review the services and investment provisions, with a view to introducing future improvements.

Chapters 2 and 3—Cross-border trade in services and investment

40. The Agreement includes well-established provisions on cross-border trade in services and investment that will secure continued market access across a broad range of sectors, including professional and business services, financial services and transport services, and will support new and continued foreign direct investment. These chapters include obligations on: a. Market Access, to ensure service suppliers and investors do not face limitations such as economic needs tests, restrictions on corporate form and foreign equity caps; b. National Treatment, to provide for non-discriminatory treatment between UK and EU service suppliers and investors; c. Local Presence, to ensure that cross-border trade is not inhibited by establishment requirements. This is only the second time the EU has

agreed a separate obligation on Local Presence; d. Prohibition of performance requirements, to ensure investments are not subject to conditions such as domestic content requirements or export restrictions; e. Senior management and boards of directors, to prevent nationality restrictions on senior personnel; and f. Most Favoured Nation, to ensure that the Agreement keeps pace with the Parties' future FTAs.

41. For all sectors covered by these chapters, the provisions on cross-border trade in services and investment liberalisation apply unless otherwise stated. Exceptions to these obligations are set out in Annexes to the Agreement.

42. These Annexes builds on existing agreements including: a. The EU and UK have scheduled new commitments on home title legal services; b. The Parties have improved their level of commitment on combined transport services and telecommunications services; and c. The UK has secured new protections for its competition regime and provided a clear statement of our policy space with respect to investment in the UK's fishing industry.

Chapter 4—Temporary entry and stay of natural persons for business purposes

43. The Agreement sets out the commitments taken by the UK and EU on business mobility. These provisions will give the UK's firms and individuals the legal certainty and administrative clarity they need to continue engaging in business activity and delivering services in the EU when the transition period ends.

44. The Agreement includes well established commitments on short-term business visitors; business visitors for establishment purposes; intra-corporate transferees; contractual service suppliers; and independent professionals. The Parties have agreed not to impose market access restrictions (such as economic needs tests) or discriminatory barriers on businesspersons falling into these categories.

45. The Parties have also agreed commitments on length of stay that broadly reflect the outcome reached in the EU-Japan Economic Partnership Agreement. This includes the ability for UK short-term business visitors to travel to the EU for 90 days in any 180-day month period. The Parties have also agreed not to impose work permits on business visitors for establishment purposes.

46. Exceptions to the Parties' commitments on business mobility are set out in the Agreement's Annexes.

47. The Agreement also includes comprehensive measures on transparency and procedural facilitations, easing the burden on

future visa and work permit applicants. It guarantees that intra-corporate transferees can be accompanied by their partners and dependents when placed abroad, with minimal administrative burdens.

48. All of this supports the government's new immigration policy, ensuring that the brightest and best global talent can come to the UK for business purposes.

Chapter 5—Regulatory framework

Section 1—Domestic Regulation

49. While preserving the regulatory autonomy of both Parties, the Domestic Regulation provisions will limit 'behind the border' barriers, such as lengthy and opaque authorisation processes. These provisions build on the Joint Initiative on Services Domestic Regulation under negotiation at the WTO and will enable service providers and investors in both the UK and the EU to conduct their business effectively.

Section 2—Mutual recognition of professional qualifications

50. The UK and the EU have agreed a framework for the recognition of qualifications between the Parties which is based on the EU's recent FTA agreements. It makes improvements on those agreements, which are designed to make the system more flexible and easier for regulatory authorities to use.

51. This approach will allow the UK and its regulators to maintain standards of professional competence. From early 2021, the government will provide help and guidance to UK regulatory authorities and professional bodies to help them benefit from these provisions as well as other recognition paths.

52. The Agreement clarifies that the provisions on professional qualifications are without prejudice to alternative arrangements that the UK may agree with the EU, allowing for improved mechanisms to be agreed in future. Agreements will be negotiated on a profession-by-profession basis.

Section 3—Telecommunications Services

53. The provisions on telecommunications regulation lock in existing levels of liberalisation in UK and EU markets, confirming both sides' leadership in this area and our commitment to openness. The Agreement includes standard provisions on authorisations, access to and use of telecoms networks, interconnection, fair and transparent regulation and the allocation of scarce resources. The provision on authorisation is the most liberalised authorisation regime agreed in any FTA. It ensures that businesses from either

Party will not have to wait for prior authorisation before they begin to deliver services, giving our operators access to EU telecoms markets which is without precedent in an FTA.

54. The Agreement contains measures to encourage cooperation on the promotion of fair and transparent rates for international mobile roaming. It also covers obligations on net neutrality, which fulfils the UK's dual aims of securing commitments towards an open internet and protecting the safety of users online.

Section 4—Delivery Services

55. The Agreement confirms the Parties' commitment to open and fair markets in delivery services. It promotes trade in postal and delivery services, while protecting the UK and EU's right to define national standards and regulatory requirements. Both Parties must maintain an independent regulatory body and prevent designated national suppliers from engaging in market distortive practices.

Section 5—International Maritime Transport Services

56. The International Maritime Transport Services provisions include commitments on non-discriminatory access to ports; the use of port infrastructure; the use of maritime auxiliary services such as storage and warehousing; customs facilities and the assignment of berths and facilities for loading and unloading. The Agreement also includes important provisions which allow UK shipping companies to move empty containers and provide feeder services between ports in an EU Member State, subject to authorisation.

Section 6—Financial Services

57. The Agreement includes provisions on cross-border trade in financial services and investment that will secure continued market access. The Agreement provides protections that will ensure that our regulatory and supervisory authorities will be able to act to ensure financial stability, market integrity and protect investors and consumers.

58. The Parties have agreed a joint declaration setting out their commitment to these shared objectives and have agreed to enhanced cooperation as well as information sharing and bilateral dialogue in order to establish a durable and stable relationship.

59. The declaration reaffirms the integrity of our respective, autonomous equivalence frameworks. The Parties will discuss how we move forward on specific equivalence determinations. The Parties will codify the framework for regulatory cooperation in a Memorandum of Understanding.

Section 7—Legal Services

60. The Agreement includes ground-breaking provisions on legal services that go beyond what the EU has included in any other FTA to date. These measures will improve the clarity and certainty of market access for UK lawyers. The Agreement will give UK solicitors, barristers and advocates the right to advise their clients across the EU on UK and public international law using their home professional titles, except where EU Member States have placed specific limits on this activity.

61. Where EU Member States require UK lawyers to register in order to provide advice on UK and public international law, the Agreement makes clear this cannot mean requalification or admission to the local legal profession.

DIGITAL TRADE

62. The Agreement contains some of the most liberalising and modern digital trade provisions in the world. These provisions will promote trade in digital services and facilitate new forms of trade in goods and services. The Agreement also ensures that the UK and the EU will cooperate on digital trade issues in future, including emerging technologies. This is the first time the EU has agreed provisions on data in a free trade agreement. The provision helps to facilitate the cross-border flow of data by prohibiting requirements to store or process data in a certain location. This prevents the imposition of costly requirements for British businesses. The Agreement confirms strong data protection commitments by both the UK and the EU, protecting consumers and helping to promote trust in the digital economy.

63. The Agreement includes a guarantee that neither the UK nor the EU will discriminate against electronic signatures or electronic documents on the basis that they are in digital form. The Agreement also ensures that contracts can be completed digitally, with a small number of exceptions.

64. The Agreement includes online consumer protection and anti-spam provisions giving consumers strong protections when buying from businesses in either the UK or the EU. The Agreement contains specially tailored exceptions to preserve policy space for the UK or the EU to protect users online. In parallel it ensures companies are protected by a guarantee against the forced transfer of source code, protecting valuable intellectual property.

65. The Agreement also includes a novel provision on open government data, inspired by recent discussions at the WTO. When governments choose to make non-personal or anonymised public

sector data available, this provision will encourage them to make that data easily accessible and in machine readable formats.

CAPITAL MOVEMENTS, PAYMENTS, TRANSFERS AND TEMPORARY SAFEGUARD MEASURES

66. The UK and EU have agreed commitments on the free flow of capital and payments for goods and services in order to facilitate trade and investment. The provisions ensure that the UK and EU can still pursue public policy objectives in their respective jurisdictions. We have also agreed specific exceptions allowing the Parties to impose appropriate temporary reservations—for example, in the event of a balance of payments crisis.

INTELLECTUAL PROPERTY

67. The Agreement includes precedented commitments on Intellectual Property (IP) that provide high standards of protection for, and enforcement of, IP rights. These include registered IP rights such as patents, trade marks and designs, and unregistered rights such as copyright, trade secrets and unregistered designs. These provisions refer to, and in many areas exceed, the standards set out in international agreements such as the WTO Agreement on Trade-Related Aspects of Intellectual Property (TRIPS) and World Intellectual Property Organization (WIPO) treaties.

68. The Agreement includes mechanisms for cooperation and exchange of information on IP issues of mutual interest. The Agreement also retains regulatory flexibility for each Party, enabling the UK to develop an IP system in line with our domestic priorities.

69. With respect to Geographical Indications (GIs), the Agreement enables both Parties to set their own rules and the future directions of their respective schemes. The UK and EU have agreed a review clause on GIs, which provides that the UK and EU may, if both Parties agree it is in their interests, use reasonable endeavours to agree rules for the protection and domestic enforcement of their GIs.

PUBLIC PROCUREMENT

70. The Agreement ensures that the UK can maintain a separate and independent procurement regime and will enable the Government to enact reform of our system. The Agreement provides for a transparent and nondiscriminatory framework of rules for trade in public procurement. These rules are based on the WTO Government Procurement Agreement (GPA), with some precedented additions for covered procurement, including the use of electronic means in procurement, electronic publication of notices, environmental, social and labour considerations, and domestic review procedures.

71. The UK and EU have also agreed an extension of market access coverage beyond the GPA, which includes: the gas and heat distribution sector; private utilities that act as a monopoly; and a range of additional services in the hospitality, telecoms, real estate, education and other business sectors. This will provide businesses with additional opportunities and will benefit contracting authorities through increased competition, creating better value for money for the taxpayer.

SMALL AND MEDIUM-SIZED ENTERPRISES (SMES)

72. The Agreement includes typical commitments to provide SMEs with clear and accessible online information about the Agreement, helping them to trade and do business in each Party's jurisdiction. This covers customs procedures, intellectual property rights, and public procurement. The Agreement commits each Party to provide for a searchable online database, on measures such as customs duties, taxes and rules of origin.

73. The Agreement also establishes a framework that will allow the Parties to work together to increase opportunities for SMEs and to report on their activities.

ENERGY

74. The energy provisions support and strengthen the UK and the EU's respective energy and climate ambitions. This includes the way in which the parties trade electricity and gas over interconnectors, work together on security of supply, integrate renewables into our respective markets and cooperate to develop opportunities in the North Sea.

75. The Agreement commits both Parties to develop and implement new, efficient trading arrangements by April 2022. These will ensure that capacity on the interconnectors is maximised and that there is implicit trading in how this capacity is allocated (i.e. capacity and electricity are sold together). This will benefit UK consumers and help integrate renewables and other clean technologies onto the grid in line with our domestic commitment to net zero emissions. Whilst this system is being implemented, alternative trading arrangements will be in place for electricity. We have also agreed arrangements that will ensure we continue to trade gas efficiently via the PRISMA platform.

76. The UK and EU have agreed to enhance our cooperation on renewable energy, including in the North Sea. This will facilitate the development of hybrid projects that combine interconnectors and offshore windfarms, and opens up the potential for a North Sea grid.

This will help realise the region's huge potential, enabling renewable energy to continue to power our homes and businesses in the future.

77. The Agreement provides for a new set of arrangements for extensive technical cooperation between the respective regulators and system operators, particularly with regard to security of supply, market abuse and network development.

78. The Agreement supports trade and investment in energy goods and raw materials between the UK and EU. These will help facilitate open and competitive markets, removing unnecessary barriers to trade.

TRANSPARENCY

79. This Chapter recognises the benefits of a transparent and predictable regulatory environment. Reflecting existing UK practice, it provides for the publication of laws and regulations, procedures and administrative rulings to the public and business; a mechanism for enquiries from the public; and the possibility for review and appeal of administrative decisions. It applies only to the trade part of the Agreement.

GOOD REGULATORY PRACTICES AND REGULATORY COOPERATION

80. This Chapter provides principles of good regulatory practice, which reflect existing UK practice, as well as providing the basis for voluntary regulatory cooperation between the UK and the EU.

LEVEL PLAYING FIELD FOR OPEN AND FAIR COMPETITION AND SUSTAINABLE DEVELOPMENT

81. The Agreement's provisions in this area, implementing commitments made in the 2019 Political Declaration, were the subject of considerable controversy during the negotiations. The EU was forced to drop its ambitious demands for dynamic alignment and for the UK to be legally required to maintain equivalent legislative systems to the EU's in some areas. The system that has been agreed upon does not compromise the UK's sovereignty in any area, does not involve the European Court of Justice in any way, and is reciprocal. Both sides have the right to set their own laws, subject to the broad constraints of this Agreement in this area as in any other. And both sides have the right, in certain constrained ways, and subject to arbitration, to take countermeasures if they believe they are being damaged by measures taken by the other Party in subsidy policy, labour and social policy, or climate and environment policy. If such measures are used too frequently either side can trigger a review of these provisions and the trade aspects of the Treaty more broadly, aiming to end with a different balance of rights and obligations.

Chapter 1: General Provisions

82. The Chapter sets out some principles and objectives for this title. It recognises the right of each Party to set its own policies and priorities and determine the levels of protection it deems appropriate in its laws.

Chapter 2: Competition

83. The Agreement commits both Parties to maintain their high standards of competition law, including enforcing these laws, maintaining their independent competition authorities, and applying competition law on a procedurally fair, transparent and non-discriminatory basis. The Chapter enables further cooperation between the UK and EU competition authorities.

Chapter 3: Subsidies

84. The Agreement ensures that each Party will have in place its own independent system of subsidy control and that neither Party is bound to follow the rules of the other. It includes some broad principles which shape the design of both sides' systems, aiming to ensure that the granting of subsidy does not have detrimental effects on trade between the Parties. It also includes some specific principles on subsidies that are particularly distortive, such as those prohibited by the WTO. The Agreement makes clear that it is for each Party to determine how these principles will be implemented in its domestic law. There is a separate joint declaration that provides nonbinding guidance on additional sectors which either side may take into consideration in their respective systems of subsidy control.

85. The Agreement requires both sides to be transparent about the subsidies they grant and to establish or maintain an independent body with an appropriate role in their respective subsidy systems, while retaining full discretion over any functions that body may have. The Agreement includes provisions on the role of domestic courts in reviewing domestic subsidy decisions. For the UK, this 19 reflects existing practice under the UK's system of judicial review. The UK and EU have also agreed that, in certain circumstances, domestic courts should have the power to order recovery of subsidies that have been granted illegally under domestic law.

86. Finally, the UK and the EU have agreed a reciprocal mechanism that allows either side to take rapid action where a subsidy granted by the other Party is causing or is at serious risk of causing significant harm to its industries. These measures can be challenged using an accelerated arbitration procedure and there is the possibility of compensation if a Party has used these measures in an unnecessary or disproportionate manner.

Chapter 4: State owned enterprises, enterprises granted special rights or privileges and designated monopolies

87. The Chapter commits both parties to additional disciplines on their Stateowned enterprises, designated monopolies and enterprises granted special rights or privileges and to make best use of international standards when regulating them, in line with provisions in other FTAs.

Chapter 5: Taxation

88. The Agreement commits both Parties to uphold global standards on tax transparency and fighting tax avoidance (which the UK has played a leading role in developing and implementing through the G20 and OECD). It contains commitments to specific tax standards as they stand at the end of the transition period, including the international standards on exchange of information, anti-tax avoidance, as well as relevant standards in legislation on public country by country reporting by credit-institutions and investment firms.

89. The commitments on tax between the UK and the EU are also captured in a stand-alone Joint Political Declaration on Countering Harmful Tax Regimes. This is a political commitment to the principles of countering harmful tax regimes, and reflects the work done by the OECD in this area.

90. There are no provisions constraining our domestic tax regime or tax rates.

Chapter 6: Labour and social standards

91. The Agreement includes reciprocal commitments not to reduce the level of protection for workers or fail to enforce employment rights in a manner that has an effect on trade. This is very much in line with similar "non-regression" clauses in other FTAs and with international norms. The provisions are clear that both Parties have the freedom and ability to make their own decisions on how they regulate—meaning that retained EU law will not have a special place on the UK's statute books. This Chapter is not subject to the Agreement's main dispute resolution mechanism but will instead be governed by a bespoke Panel of Experts procedure.

Chapter 7: Environment and climate

92. In a similar way, the Agreement includes reciprocal commitments not to reduce the level of environmental or climate protection or fail to enforce its 20 laws in a manner that has an effect on trade. This includes reciprocal commitments to cross-economy greenhouse gas emission reduction targets. The Agreement gives both Parties the freedom to set their own climate and environmental

policies in the way most appropriate to achieve our world leading domestic aims. The domestic supervisory bodies of the UK and EU will cooperate to ensure effective enforcement of their respective environmental and climate laws. Once again, this chapter is not subject to the Agreement's main dispute resolution mechanism but will instead be governed by a bespoke Panel of Experts procedure.

93. The Agreement makes clear both parties will have their own effective systems of carbon pricing in place to help fulfil our respective climate goals. The Parties have agreed to cooperate on carbon pricing in future and consider linking their respective systems, although they are not under any obligation to do so.

Chapter 8: Other instruments for trade and sustainable development

94. The Agreement affirms the Parties' existing commitments to a range of international conventions and other commitments in the area of labour, environment, and climate, in a way that is standard in FTAs. This includes committing the Parties to the effective implementation of the Paris Agreement.

Chapter 9: Institutional provisions

95. The Agreement sets out tailored provisions for dispute settlement for Chapters 6–8 involving a Panel of Experts. Any recommendations made by the Panel of Experts are not binding on the Parties.

96. The Agreement provides for a rebalancing mechanism which allows the Parties to formally review the balance of the Agreement over time and enter into a negotiation on amendments to the economic provisions of the Agreement at the request of one Party. It also provides for Parties to take strictly limited and proportionate rebalancing measures on a more short-term basis, subject to the approval of an independent arbitration panel.

Exceptions

97. This Title provides for a number of exceptions to ensure that a range of legitimate UK domestic policy aims are not affected by this Agreement. It applies to the trade part of the agreement. The exceptions provide that existing national security practices are not affected by the terms of the trade agreement. There is also an exception which protects legitimate domestic taxation policy. Finally, there is a general exception which allows for UK action in a list of areas, such as the protection of public security or public morals to maintain public order, or measures necessary to protect human, animal or plant life or health.

98. The Chapter also provides for the treatment of confidential information and WTO waivers.

AIR TRANSPORT

99. The Agreement builds on existing precedent and sets out the arrangements for the operation of air transport services between the UK and the EU. UK airlines that are majority owned and controlled by UK and/or EU/EEA/EFTA nationals at the end of December 2020 may continue to operate air transport services between the UK and the EU. EU airlines that are majority owned and controlled by EU/EEA/EFTA nationals may also continue to operate air transport services between the UK and the EU.

100. The Agreement provides operational flexibilities for UK and EU airlines. For example, UK airlines may lease aircraft and crew from UK or EU airlines and other providers to operate air transport services between the UK and the EU. UK airlines will also have extensive opportunities to cooperate with other airlines to offer a wide range of tickets to consumers.

101. The Agreement reflects the shared ambition of both the UK and the EU to cooperate in future, including commitments for continued cooperation and consultation on air traffic management, aviation security and consumer protection.

102. The Agreement also sets out the conditions under which the operation of air transport services between the UK and EU would not be permitted. Grounds for such action include reasons of aviation safety and security.

AVIATION SAFETY

103. The Agreement is largely in line with precedent and sets out a framework for cooperation on aviation safety, and a process for agreeing Annexes to the agreement that will facilitate recognition of UK and EU certificates, approvals and licences. Areas where the UK and EU could agree Annexes in future include: monitoring of maintenance organisations; personnel licences and training; operation of aircraft; and air traffic management.

104. The airworthiness Annex to the Agreement sets out the conditions for the UK and EU to recognise each other's aeronautical products and designs. For example, minor changes and repairs to aeronautical products and designs that are approved in the UK will be automatically accepted by the EU. In addition, the Annex foresees the possibility of the EU extending their scope of automatic recognition of UK aeronautical products and designs once it gains confidence in the UK's capability for overseeing design certification.

105. The Annex also provides for the recognition of production certificates and regulatory oversight. For example, UK production certificates and oversight will be automatically recognised by the EU providing that the relevant aeronautical products were subject to UK oversight before the end of December 2020.

TRANSPORT OF GOODS BY ROAD

106. The Agreement ensures continued market access rights for UK and EU road haulage operators. Operators will continue to be able to move goods to, from and through each other's territories with no permit requirements, and make additional movements within each other's territories, with limits on the number of permitted movements.

107. The Agreement also sets out the standards to which operators must adhere when undertaking international journeys between the UK and the EU. These standards only apply to international journeys and do not affect the UK's ability to regulate the domestic market. These standards for the international carriage of goods broadly reflect the standards to which UK operators are already subject when operating internationally, with some bespoke standards aimed at ensuring greater road safety and effective regulation. These standards include restrictions on driver hours, requirements about professional qualifications and tachographs and vehicle weight and dimension limits. There is a tailored mechanism to manage differences in national regulations in these areas in the unlikely event that they emerge. The ultimate safeguard in the case of real difficulties is that either side may terminate this Heading.

108. The Agreement also provides for a Specialised Committee process through which the Parties can agree, for example, to adopt additional measures to safeguard the proper functioning of the Agreement, including by amending the Annexes in the Agreement.

109. The Agreement includes a declaration reiterating the importance of the good and efficient management of visa and border arrangements for road hauliers, in particular across the United Kingdom-Union border. This declaration confirms the UK and EU's agreement to appropriately facilitate the entry and stay of hauliers.

PASSENGER TRANSPORT

110. The Agreement provides additional market access rights for UK and EU passenger transport operators, above and beyond what is provided by the multilateral Interbus Agreement. Operators will be able to continue running occasional services to, from and through each other's territories. The Agreement also provides a temporary bridging arrangement for regular and special regular services to

continue, until the Interbus Agreement is expanded to cover these services.

111. Services on the island of Ireland will also be able to pick up and set down passengers in both Ireland and Northern Ireland, enabling cross-border services to continue with no restrictions.

112. The Agreement also provides for a Specialised Committee process through which the Parties can agree to adopt measures to implement the Chapter and to amend the Annexes in the Agreement to reflect regulatory developments.

SOCIAL SECURITY COORDINATION AND VISAS FOR SHORT-TERM

113. The provisions in the Protocol on Social Security Coordination will ensure that individuals who move between the UK and the EU in the future will have their social security position in respect of certain important benefits protected. Individuals will be able to have access to a range of social security benefits, including reciprocal healthcare cover and an uprated state pension.

114. This Protocol supports business and trade by ensuring that crossborder workers and their employers are only liable to pay social security contributions in one state at a time. Generally, this will be in the country where work is undertaken, irrespective of whether the worker resides within the EU or the UK, or indeed whether the employer is based in the EU or the UK.

115. UK workers who are sent by their employer to work temporarily in an EU Member State which has agreed to apply the "detached worker" rules will remain liable to only pay social security contributions in the UK for the period of work in that EU Member State. Similarly, if an EU worker is sent by their employer to work temporarily in the UK from a Member State which has agreed to apply the "detached worker" rules, they will remain liable to only pay contributions in that EU Member State.

116. Under the Protocol, the UK and EU Member States will be able to take into account relevant contributions paid into each other's social security systems, or relevant periods of work or residence, by individuals for determining entitlement to a state pension and to a range of benefits. This will provide a good level of protection for people working in the UK and EU Member States. The Protocol also provides for the uprating of the UK State Pension paid to pensioners who retire to the EU.

117. On healthcare, where the UK or an EU Member State is responsible for the healthcare of an individual, they will be entitled to reciprocal healthcare cover. This includes certain categories of

cross-border workers and state pensioners who retire to the UK or to the EU.

118. In addition, the Protocol will ensure necessary healthcare provisions—akin to those provided by the European Health Insurance Card (EHIC) scheme—continue. This means individuals who are temporarily staying in another country, for example a UK national who is in an EU Member State for a holiday, will have their necessary healthcare needs met for the period of their stay.

119. The Protocol also protects the ability of individuals to seek authorisation to receive planned medical treatment in the UK or the EU, funded by their responsible State.

VISAS FOR SHORT-TERM VISITS

120. The Agreement confirms that the UK will treat the EU as a bloc for short-term visit visas. This provision will not apply to future Member States unless the UK agrees to do so.

121. This provision allows the UK to determine whether short-term visits from the EU should be subject to visa requirements. At present the United Kingdom provides for visa-free travel for short-term visits in respect of nationals of all Member States.

FISHERIES

122. The Agreement provides a framework for our future relationship on matters relating to fisheries.

123. The Agreement reflects the UK's departure from the EU's Common Fisheries Policy and new identity as a sovereign independent coastal State with the right to manage the resources in its waters. The UK is now free to create its own laws and fisheries management practices to the benefit of fishers and coastal communities across the whole UK.

124. The Agreement sets out the objectives and principles for fisheries management which the UK and EU share. It enshrines our joint commitment to sustainable fisheries management alongside shared principles of promoting long-term environmental, social and economic sustainability; protecting juveniles and spawning fish; protecting marine ecosystems; and timely cooperation, including sharing data to manage conservation and combat illegal fishing.

125. The Agreement provides for a significant uplift in quota for UK fishers, equal to 25% of the value the EU catch in UK waters. This is worth £146m for the UK fleet phased in over five years. It ends the dependence of the UK fleet on the unfair 'relative stability' mechanism enshrined in the EU's Common Fisheries Policy, and

increases the share of the total catch taken in UK waters taken by UK vessels to circa two thirds.

126. New quota arrangements will be phased in over five years to allow the respective fleets time to adapt to the changed opportunities. There will be also be an adjustment period for access to waters which provide stable access for 5 ½ years. For the adjustment period, the Agreement also provides access to a limited part of the UK territorial waters for vessels which have traditionally fished in those areas.

127. Under the framework provided for in this Agreement, the UK will conduct annual fisheries negotiations with the EU alongside negotiations with other coastal States and international organisations regarding Total Allowable Catches for shared stock. These negotiations will also cover access arrangements.

128. The agreement includes arrangements for compensation if a Party decides not to grant access to its waters and dispute settlement, in the event that a Party breaches the obligations. All such measures must be commensurate to the economic and social impact caused by the actions of the other party and are subject to arbitration.

129. The Agreement includes an obligation on each Party to share relevant data and information necessary for implementing the Agreement, as well as ensuring compliance with fisheries management measures to deter and eliminate illegal, unreported and unregulated fishing.

130. The Agreement establishes a Specialised Committee on Fisheries which will provide a forum for the UK and the EU to discuss and cooperate on a range of fisheries matters. These include, but are not limited to: cooperation ahead of annual fisheries consultations, multi-year strategies, data-sharing and monitoring and compliance.

131. The Agreement can be terminated at any point with nine months notice. If the Agreement is terminated, any obligations of the Parties will continue until the end of the year.

132. The Agreement also contains provisions on the Crown Dependencies, which providing those jurisdictions so decide, would allow EU vessels to fish in Crown Dependency waters to levels consistent with historic patterns of fishing while ensuring they can benefit from the goods provisions in the Agreement.

Other Provisions

133. This Chapter provides for a number of technical matters relating to the trade part of the agreement. This includes definitions, relationship to the WTO agreement, how WTO case law is to be

considered in arbitration proceedings, and how amendments to any international agreements referred to are to be treated.

LAW ENFORCEMENT AND JUDICIAL COOPERATION IN CRIMINAL MATTERS

134. The safety and security of our citizens is the Government's top priority. The Agreement provides a comprehensive package of operational capabilities that will help protect the public and bring criminals to justice.

GENERAL PROVISIONS

135. The scope of this Part, as set out in the General Provisions, is to provide for law enforcement and judicial cooperation between the UK, the EU and its Member States in relation to the prevention, investigation, detection and prosecution of criminal offences and the prevention of and fight against money laundering and financing of terrorism.

136. The Agreement is based on a shared and longstanding respect for democracy, the rule of law and protection of fundamental rights. Any cooperation that takes place under this Part must be done in compliance with human rights.

EXCHANGES OF DNA, FINGERPRINTS AND VEHICLE REGISTRATION DATA

137. The Agreement provides for the fast and effective exchange of national DNA, fingerprint and vehicle registration data between the UK and individual EU Member States to aid law enforcement agencies in investigating crime and terrorism.

138. DNA and fingerprint data will continue to be exchanged through the Prüm system and the Agreement enables the exchange of vehicle registration data in the future, in line with precedents between the EU and Norway, Iceland, Liechtenstein and Switzerland. This will enable us to build on the current operational benefits derived from our Prüm connections on DNA, which have been live since July 2019 and expand our fingerprints connections which commenced in October 2020.

TRANSFER AND PROCESSING OF PASSENGER NAME RECORD DATA

139. The Agreement provides for transfers of PNR data from the EU to the UK to be used to protect the public from terrorism and serious crime.

140. The Agreement is based on precedents for PNR agreements between the EU and third countries such as Australia and the US. It provides for more frequent transfers of PNR data from airlines to the

UK prior to flights taking off between the EU and the UK than current arrangements. The agreement also provides for specific data protection safeguards, for a period of implementation during which the UK will make necessary technical adjustments to its systems to effectively operate those safeguards, and for cooperation between the UK and EU authorities that use PNR data.

COOPERATION ON OPERATIONAL INFORMATION

141. The Agreement provides an additional basis for bilateral law enforcement cooperation to continue between the UK and EU Member States at the end of the transition period.

142. This includes information sharing in response to requests, as well as the spontaneous provision of information, including that which relates to wanted and missing persons and objects.

COOPERATION WITH EUROPOL

143. The Agreement supports effective multilateral cooperation between the UK and EU Member States through Europol on serious and organised crime and terrorism. In line with third country precedent, it does not provide for membership of Europol.

144. The Agreement is broadly in line with those that Europol has with third countries such as the US but takes account of the scale and nature of the UK's contribution to the Agency. It enables the presence of UK liaison officers in Europol headquarters alongside their EU counterparts to facilitate crossborder cooperation, UK access to the SIENA secure messaging system and the fast and effective exchange of data, including personal data. This Agreement will be supplemented by more detailed administrative and working arrangements between the UK and the Agency.

COOPERATION WITH EUROJUST

145. The Agreement supports effective multilateral cooperation between the UK and EU Member States through Eurojust on the investigation and prosecution of serious cross-border criminal cases. In line with third country precedent, it does not provide for membership of Eurojust.

146. The Agreement is broadly in line with those that Eurojust has with third countries such as the US but takes account of the scale and nature of the UK's contribution to the Agency. It enables the UK to second a Liaison Prosecutor and their Assistants to Eurojust headquarters alongside their EU counterparts, and for the UK to exchange personal data and information with Eurojust. The Agreement will be supplemented by a more detailed working arrangement between the UK and the Agency.

SURRENDER

147. The Agreement provides for streamlined extradition arrangements, akin to the EU's Surrender Agreement with Norway and Iceland, but with appropriate further safeguards for individuals beyond those in the European Arrest Warrant.

148. To streamline cooperation, the Agreement provides for direct transmission between judicial authorities, limited grounds for refusal and time-limited processes. It also includes additional provisions which make clear that a person's surrender can be refused if their fundamental rights are at risk, extradition would be disproportionate, or they are likely to face long periods of pre-trial detention. Where extradition of own nationals from certain EU Member States is not possible due to their constitutional principles, we have ensured there is nevertheless a path to justice in every case, for example, by obliging EU Member States to refer cases to their own prosecution authorities.

MUTUAL ASSISTANCE

149. The Agreement supports effective cooperation on mutual legal assistance in criminal matters supplementing the relevant Council of Europe Conventions by providing for streamlined processes, including standard formats for making requests and specific timescales for action.

150. The Agreement provides for direct transmission allowing UK prosecutors to send requests directly to competent authorities in EU Member States. This will ensure action can be taken quickly and effectively.

EXCHANGE OF CRIMINAL RECORD INFORMATION

151. The Agreement provides for the fast and effective exchange of criminal records data between the UK and individual EU Member States, recognising that this is important for investigations, prosecutions and sentencing, as well as for wider community safety.

152. The arrangements include streamlined and time-limited processes for exchanging criminal records information and specify that information can be exchanged for crime prevention and safeguarding purposes. The Agreement provides that criminal records will continue to be exchanged between the UK and EU Member States through shared technical infrastructure.

ANTI-MONEY LAUNDERING AND COUNTER-TERRORIST FINANCING

153. The Agreement commits the UK and EU to support international efforts to prevent and fight against money laundering

and terrorist financing, exchange relevant information, and maintain comprehensive anti-money laundering and counter-terrorist financing regimes.

154. The Agreement commits the UK and EU to maintain high standards of beneficial ownership transparency. It goes beyond the international Financial Action Task Force Standards (FATF) in requiring registers of beneficial ownership of corporate entities and includes provisions on beneficial ownership of legal arrangements that are in line with the FATF Standards.

FREEZING AND CONFISCATION

155. The Agreement supports effective cooperation on asset freezing and confiscation, supplementing the relevant Council of Europe Conventions by providing for streamlined processes, including standard formats for making requests and specific timescales for action.

156. The Agreement provides for more limited grounds for refusal of a request allowing for the broadest cooperation possible.

Other Provisions

157. The Agreement sets out the specific circumstances in which either Party can suspend or terminate this area of cooperation, reflecting the different nature of this Part. For example, in addition to being able to terminate the law enforcement Part for any reason, either Party may suspend cooperation where it considers there are serious and systemic deficiencies in the way the other Party is protecting fundamental rights, the rule of law or data protection.

Dispute Settlement

158. The dispute settlement mechanism for the Law Enforcement Part is political in nature and only involves the Parties, with no arbitration or role for the CJEU. In the event of a dispute the parties can avail themselves of a time limited, consultations procedure in order to reach a mutually agreed solution.

THEMATIC COOPERATION

159. The agreement provides for future cooperation between the UK and EU on emerging challenges, including health and cyber security. The UK and EU have also agreed a joint declaration noting the importance of effectively managing migratory flows, and the UK's intention to engage in bilateral discussion with key EU Member States to discuss suitable practical arrangements on asylum, returns, family reunion for unaccompanied minors and illegal migration.

HEALTH SECURITY

160. The Agreement supports effective arrangements and information sharing between the UK and the EU in the event of a serious cross border threat to health, which is particularly important in the context of Covid-19. The agreement enables the UK to request access to the EU's Early Warning and Response System in respect of a serious cross-border health threat so that the UK, the EU institutions and EU Member States can exchange information and coordinate measures to protect public health.

161. The Agreement provides that the EU may invite the UK to participate in the EU Health Security Committee to support the exchange of information and facilitate coordination in relation to specific serious cross-border threats to health. It also makes provision for cooperation on scientific and technical matters between the UK and the European Centre for Disease Prevention and Control (ECDC), including by concluding a MoU similar to those ECDC has with other third countries such as Canada.

CYBER SECURITY

162. The Agreement provides a framework for UK-EU cooperation in the field of cyber security, an area where cooperation is mutually beneficial given the cross-border nature of cyber threats and challenges.

163. The Agreement includes arrangements to support the exchange of information and cooperation in international bodies and fora to strengthen global cyber resilience where we believe it is in our mutual interest to do so. It also facilitates the UK's voluntary participation in the activities of expert bodies including the European Union Agency for Cybersecurity (ENISA) and the Network and Information Systems (NIS) Cooperation Group as well as voluntary cooperation with the EU's Computer Emergency Response Team (CERT-EU).

PARTICIPATION IN UNION PROGRAMMES

164. This Part sets out the arrangements for the UK's participation in Union programmes and access to programme services. These terms provide for a fair and appropriate financial contribution towards the programmes, fair treatment of UK participants, balanced provisions to ensure the sound financial management of programme funds, and appropriate governance arrangements.

165. The additional detail on the individual programmes the UK is intending to participate in—Horizon Europe, Euratom Research and Training, and Copernicus—will be included in a protocol to the main Agreement, once the regulations establishing the programmes are

settled, a draft of which has been published alongside the main Agreement.

General conditions for participation in Union programmes

166. This Chapter covers the general terms of participation in programmes, including the treatment of UK entities and UK involvement in the governance of the programmes such as committees and working groups. It also sets out how the UK's financial contribution will be calculated and how the UK will be reimbursed if its participants are excluded from a part of the programme. It also sets out the grounds on which the UK and EU may review, suspend or terminate the UK's participation.

Sound Financial Management

167. This Chapter sets out how the UK and EU ensure programme funds are properly managed and includes provisions on communication and exchange of information to implement EU programmes, and statistical cooperation between the respective UK and EU bodies.

Access of the United Kingdom to services under Union programmes

168. This Chapter sets out the terms for the UK to access programme services without participating in programmes. A protocol to the Agreement will set out the UK's access to services from the EU Space Surveillance and Tracking programme on these terms and will be adopted by the Specialised Committee when the relevant Union regulations are finalised, a draft of which has also been published alongside this Agreement.

Reviews

169. This Chapter states that there will be a review of the UK's participation in EU programmes and that either Party may request that changes affecting the terms of participation be considered following the outcome of the review.

Participation fee in the years 2021–2026

170. The UK will pay a participation fee towards the administration costs of the Programmes, which will be introduced gradually.

DISPUTE SETTLEMENT AND HORIZONTAL PROVISIONS

Dispute settlement

171. This Agreement includes dispute resolution mechanisms that are appropriate for a relationship between sovereign equals. This means that there is no role for the Court of Justice of the European

Union. All these mechanisms are fully reciprocal and equally available to both Parties.

172. For certain areas of cooperation there is a process of consultations between the Parties, followed by independent arbitration if there is still disagreement. If the arbitration panel finds that there has been a breach, the Party at fault must either rectify the breach, or agree to provide suitable compensation. If it does not do either, then the other Party can suspend obligations in response to any imbalance identified. Conditions and limitations apply to cross-suspension in some areas.

173. Disputes relating to participation in Union programmes can also be subject to independent arbitration. There are also a series of specific conditions whereby the UK or EU can suspend or terminate participation in Union programmes.

174. For SSC, only disputes related to the way in which the EU or UK have enabled individuals to enforce their rights may be arbitrated. Individual's cases may not. In health security and cyber security, both sides can use the consultation process to resolve any problems that might arise. Given these areas concern the sharing of information and cooperation where it is in the Parties' mutual interest to do so, this governance mechanism is appropriate.

Basis for cooperation

175. To underpin cooperation under this Agreement, the UK and EU have restated existing commitments to human rights, the rule of law, the fight against climate change and countering the proliferation of weapons of mass destruction. The UK and EU have also restated commitments in other areas—including small arms and light weapons, serious crimes of concern to the international community, counter-terrorism, and issues of shared economic, environmental and social interest.

176. The UK and EU have restated their commitment to high personal data protection standards, which contribute to trust in the digital economy and to the development of trade, and are key enabler for effective law enforcement cooperation.

Fulfilment of obligations and safeguard measures

177. In the event a serious economic, societal or environmental difficulty arises and is likely to persist, the UK or the EU unilaterally may take strictly proportionate and time-limited measures to remedy the situation.

FINAL PROVISIONS

178. This Part provides for a range of provisions that apply across the agreement, such as when and how the Agreement enters into force, and the authentic languages of the agreement.

179. It provides for a review of the agreement between the EU and the UK every five years. It also provides for the procedure to be followed if a new country accedes to the EU.

180. This agreement applies without prejudice to any previous bilateral agreement between the UK and the EU. Both parties reaffirm their obligations to implement any such agreement.

181. Either the UK or EU may decide to terminate the Agreement with 12 months' notice. This overall termination clause is without prejudice to other termination clauses in the Agreement; certain areas of cooperation have bespoke termination clauses, meaning that either Party can decide to cease cooperation in these areas without the whole agreement being terminated.

182. This Part also includes a provision to provide for the continued free flow of personal data from the EU and EEA EFTA States to the UK until adequacy decisions are adopted, and for no longer than 6 months. The UK has, on a transitional basis, deemed the EU and EEA EFTA States to be adequate to allow for data flows from the UK.

Territorial Scope

183. This Chapter specifies that the Agreement applies to the United Kingdom and, in some respects, to the Crown Dependencies (see below). Given the EU's clear position that it did not have the competence to negotiate on them, this Agreement does not apply to the overseas countries and territories of the EU and nor does it apply to the UK's Overseas Territories.

184. The UK, Gibraltar and Spain will continue to negotiate arrangements to seek the best possible outcome for the people of Gibraltar and the surrounding region. The Commission have confirmed that a separate UK-EU agreement on Gibraltar is possible and that they stand ready to examine any request from Spain and the UK to take this forward.

185. The Agreement between the UK and the EU includes arrangements relating to the trade in goods between the Crown Dependencies and the EU and sets out provisions for mutual fisheries access.

Table of Cases

Index

References are to Sections